HISTORY OF THEOLOGY

II
The Middle Ages

HISTORY OF THEOLOGY

II
The Middle Ages

Giulio D'Onofrio

Translated by
Matthew J. O'Connell

A Michael Glazier Book

LITURGICAL PRESS
Collegeville, Minnesota

www.litpress.org

A Michael Glazier Book published by Liturgical Press

Cover design by David Manahan, OSB.

This book was originally published in Italian under the title *Storia della teologia II, eta' medievale* © Edizioni Piemme Spa (Via del Carmine 5, 15033 Casale Monferrato [AL], Italy). All rights reserved.

ISBN 978-0-8146-5915-1 (vol. I)
ISBN 978-0-8146-5916-8 (vol. II)
ISBN 978-0-8146-5917-5 (vol. III)

1   2   3   4   5   6   7   8

Library of Congress Cataloging-in-Publication Data

Storia della teologia.   English.
    History of theology / edited by Angelo Di Berardino and Basil Studer ; translated by Matthew J. O'Connell.
        p.   cm.
    Includes bibliographical references and index.
    Contents: I. The patristic period.
    ISBN 0-8146-5915-2
        1. Theology, Doctrinal—History.   2. Catholic Church—Doctrines—History.
    I. Di Berardino, Angelo.   II. Studer, Basil, 1925–   III. Title.

    BT21.2.S7613   1996
    230'.09—DC20   96-42160
                                                                        CIP

Contents

Preface

The fall of 1996 saw the publication of three volumes of a *History of Theology in the Middle Ages* (titled respectively I. *Principles*, II. *The Great Flowering*, and III. *The Theology of the Schools*), which I edited for Edizioni Piemme. That work had its origin in the setting of a planned *History of Theology* that was to comprise several volumes. The idea for this *History* came from His Excellency Msgr. Luciano Pacomio, at that time Rector of the Collegio Capranica in Rome and now bishop of Mondovi. Volume II of the series was to cover the medieval period, but the length of the many contributions requested of specialists in the various phases and problem areas of medieval theology suggested it would be better to publish the resulting three volumes separately from the planned *History* and as an independent project. That three-volume history represented the first time that the study of medieval theological thought was presented in a form both analytical and exhaustive, and accompanied by an up-to-date and comprehensive bibliography of the entire historical development in all its parts. The unforeseen length of the work was justified by the need to adequately fill a very large scholarly gap in our modern intellectual panorama.

Now, again at the request of Msgr. Pacomio, to whom I am grateful for having several times involved me, to my delight, in his earlier project, I have been asked to contribute to the completion of the *History of Theology* by writing the second volume, *The Middle Ages*.

In producing a synthetic presentation of the history of Christian theology in the Middle Ages, I have chosen to give the work a popular form; that is, one without learned notes, bibliographies, and chronological tables. My intention in choosing this kind of presentation is to make possible an unbroken and organized reading of the history of medieval theological thought even by those readers who stand outside the restricted circle of experts and frequenters of specialized libraries.

In accepting this propitious opportunity to provide a tool aimed rather at a synthesis for the ordinary reader, I conceived the present volume not as a compendium of the three large volumes, but as a new and original exposition of the history of medieval theology. The exposition is based, as far as possible, on a direct study of the sources: it is an *editio minor* (or an *ars brevis*, to use the language of the Scholastics) of an introductory kind. It can, I hope, be used also as a means of studying and making basic preparation (by individuals or in a university setting) for acquiring a knowledge of the broad realm of medieval theological studies. The reader who wants more advanced studies of the subjects or desires bibliographical information, either on the works of the authors with whom I deal or on the secondary literature, can go to the three volumes of the *History of Theology in the Middle Ages*. The present volume is not intended as a substitute for these, but rather as a preparation for them.

Giulio d'Onofrio
Rome, June 30, 2003

Introduction

The Principles of Medieval Theology

1. The True Philosophy: A Synthesis of Faith and Reason

> Peter is offered to us as a model of action and faith. John the Theologian, on the other hand, is a symbol of contemplation and knowledge. . . . Both, however, run to the tomb. The tomb of Christ is divine Scripture, in which the mysteries of his divinity and his humanity are covered over by the weight of the letter as by a stone over a tomb. But John runs more quickly than Peter and arrives before him. In fact, the power of contemplation, which is already purified, is able to penetrate the inner secrets of the words written by God and to do so with greater acuteness and rapidity than action can, which still needs purification. Yet Peter was the first to enter the tomb; only then did John follow him. Thus both ran and both entered. They entered in that order because Peter symbolizes faith and John understanding. Therefore, since it is written: "Unless you first believe, you cannot understand" (Isa 7:9), faith must enter first into the monument of Scripture; then, following it, the intellect may likewise enter, its access being made possible precisely by faith.

This charming allegorical reading of the race of the two apostles to the tomb of Christ after the announcement of the resurrection was introduced by a Carolingian, John Scotus Eriugena, into his *Homily* on the Prologue of the Fourth Gospel. It illustrates in an especially effective way the relationship Christians ought to be able to establish for themselves between faith and understanding. John the Evangelist, who rested his head on the breast of Christ at the Last Supper, is a symbol of the human ability to draw near to the truth solely by natural inquiry. Peter, who sometimes wavers in the face of the mystery, is a symbol of faith, which ensures a complete possession of truth, but one based on the acceptance of what claims, without other confirmation or arguments, to come from God himself.

Both apostles run toward the fundamental mystery of faith, which the words of Scripture enclose as would a sacred funeral monument. That is, faith and reason run together toward the sacred page with the purpose of penetrating its literal meaning and drawing near to the union of the divine and the human in Christ. Theoretical knowledge reaches its completion through the exercise of reason, which immunizes it against the deceitful obscurities of corporeal reality. It also runs more quickly as it moves with assurance toward what is intelligible. However, it is compelled to halt on the threshold of the truth, which remains incomprehensible to it because the age-old inquiries of the philosophers, as they look for answers to their questions on the origin and meaning of life, are destined to reach only incomplete results that cannot be verified unless the intellect is willing to advance with the slower but surer footsteps of faith.

"Unless you believe, you will not understand." This variant, which Augustine preferred, came from the (Greek) Septuagint and differed from both the Hebrew and the Vulgate (which have "Unless you believe you will not be strengthened"). Here the text of Isaiah becomes a prophecy putting the seal of approval on the synthesis of Christian faith and philosophical reason by which the whole of medieval theological thought is linked to the speculative quest of the Fathers of the church. The well-chosen allegory of John Scotus sums up the teaching of the *Letter to Consentius*, which Augustine wrote in 410, the year in which the brutal sack of Rome by the Visigoths symbolized the irreversible decline of the imperial civilization of antiquity. According to the *Letter*, natural reason must be brought into play by the believer both before the act of faith, in order to justify it, and after it, in order better to establish its contents. It is for this reason that, again according to Augustine, a Christian cannot but love understanding: "Have a great love of understanding!"

The linking of "believe" and "understand" is thus taken to be a *habitudo* or "state of being," a natural connection of the two sources from which human beings can derive truth. Faith risks remaining inauthentic unless it is accompanied by an understanding of the words of revelation and, consequently, trusts the intervention of a moderate rationality, which is capable of putting itself in the service of revelation. It does so in order to provide clarity about what faith believes, but without claiming to pass any judgment on the truthfulness of that belief.

At the same time, a limited complementarity of faith and understanding was regarded by many, beginning in the very first centuries of Christianity, as an essential condition for the survival of philosophy itself. In fact, pagan intellectuals had for some time already noted with concern the chronic weakness of their philosophical researches. Seeing the contradictions among all the philosophical schools, which were a sign of the insufficiency and falsity of their teachings, Cicero himself, the common teacher of Latin-language thinkers, had realized the necessity of adopting the probabilist or moderately skeptical position of the Academics. According to the latter, who were the final heirs of the Platonic school, truth will remain forever beyond the reach of humanity, and the wise will renounce the claim to know it; they will, instead, limit themselves to accepting as probable the best teachings of the practitioners of philosophy and will devote themselves simply to devising pragmatic norms for finding their places in nature and society.

But a philosophy reduced to a simple methodological support for practical activity betrays the very longings for objective truth that philosophy was intended to satisfy. For Augustine, therefore, "the true philosophy" or "the correct teaching" can only be that of the Christians, who have realized from whom the truth must first be sought, without fear of being deceived, in order then to study it, confirm it, and penetrate it more fully with the rational tools discovered by the sages of old.

Once again it was John Scotus, in his first piece of writing, the little book *Predestination*, who was inspired this time by a remark of Augustine in the pages of his *The True Religion* to coin a formula that summed up in a sentence the medieval program of theological research based on the rational understanding of the faith. Once we realize, Scotus says, that God is truth, there can be no contradiction between the truth of religion and the truth of philosophy; therefore, "the true philosophy is the true religion and, conversely, the true religion is the true philosophy." With the same clarity of vision, Anselm of Aosta addresses God in his *Monologion* as the one who "gives understanding of the faith." Then, at the beginning of the twelfth century and in response to the accusation of logical rationalism, Peter Abelard declares in his *Logic* that true knowledge, which brings human beings close to the truth, can never, when correctly used, contradict the true faith. For "truth is never opposed to truth," and two correct acquisitions of truth cannot contradict one another, even if they differ in their origin and manner of application.

The true philosophy and true religion of medieval Christians sprang from the conquest of doubt, not with the help of external, logical, or experimental evidence, but through acknowledging the authenticity of truth that is communicated by an authority beyond dispute, that of God himself. The true philosophy and the true religion give rise in the believing subject to an "idea": that is, a sure knowledge that is more reliable than any scientific construct and, at the same time, more credible than any other religious creed whatsoever. In the all-inclusive overturning of the ordinary processes of human speculation that results from this turning to God, the act that founds medieval Christian theology in its entirety comes down to the antecedent decision to give the mind's assent to a "word" whose reliability can be proved solely on the basis of what that word itself claims, and then to move on to a search for further possible ways of knowing. Like a traveler who knows her destination but not the roads she must travel to reach it, or like a student who is told in advance the solution of a mathematical problem but must then figure out on his own the right procedure for reaching it, so the medieval theological mind knew in advance its own goal, which was identical with revelation and with the early interpretations of it given by the Fathers, but then had the task of seeking to demonstrate it, to go more deeply into its meaning and bring out its possible consequences.

2. Sound Doctrine: The Gold of the Egyptians and the Coinage of the King

Luke tells us (Acts 17:16-34) that when Paul met on the Areopagus with representatives of the ancient philosophical schools he followed the rules of rhetoric and took as the starting point of his discourse the possible convergences between the new thesis he intended to present and the positions already held by his hearers. According to his line of argument, the subject of Christian preaching was the "unknown god" whose existence the human mind had managed to intuit, along with this god's fundamental attributes: oneness, efficacious causality, and providence. On the basis of this initial agreement the apostle exhorts the philosophers to accept the teaching of Christ, in whose life, death, and resurrection they can contemplate the fulfillment of all human hopes.

When Paul's invitation was thus spelled out it elicited mirth in the majority of the hearers, who went away with the mocking remark, "We shall listen to you on this matter at another time." And yet Luke ends by saying that some of those present were converted, one of them worth mentioning: the philosopher Dionysius, a member of the Areopagus. Thus, despite Paul's apparent failure, Scripture records that thanks to his words in the place that was the heart of Hellenistic-Roman philosophical civilization, revelation was for the first time grafted onto the unsuccessful quest of human knowledge.

The philosophical reasoning of antiquity had shown its inability to understand a truth it had only been able to glimpse over the centuries. Yet converts to Christianity, who believed that they possessed this truth through God's unmerited gift, regarded themselves as allowed to see in the best, even if limited, scientific conquests of the philosophers of the past a useful, though unnecessary, help in organizing their understanding of the revealed data into a structured discipline. Paul himself confirms this outlook when he urges the unification of the faith in the form of "sound doctrine" (Titus 1:9), a solid intellectual organization of doctrine that is able to stand up to the doubts of unbelievers and the deceits of heretics.

The people of the Middle Ages started with the presupposition that the Fathers of the church (Augustine chief among them) had already completed that task and had made them the heirs of "sound doctrine," the truth of which was guaranteed by two proofs: its revealed origin and the permanence given to it by reason. They even saw the first fruit of this Christian appropriation of the classical philosophical patrimony in the celebration of the *logos* that opens the Prologue of the Fourth Gospel. Here a concept of philosophical origin, but raised to a higher level by prophetic inspiration, becomes a key factor in explaining to believers that both the work of the world's creation and the work of redemption were due to a causality exercised by the second divine Person.

This core concept was then refined by the preachers of the early centuries, who had made the language of philosophy their own in order to enter into dialogue with the representatives of the pagan schools and to rebut their accusations of ignorance and superstition. The same refinement was carried further, from the third to the fifth centuries, by the leaders in the speculative stage of patristic thought and by the first ecumenical councils. These men rectified every heretical attempt at an excessive rationalization of the mysteries while showing the logical coherence of the divine attributes attested in the Scriptures and thereby establishing the foundational elements of subsequent trinitarian and christological dogmatic terminology.

But the need to keep theological reason alert to heresies did not cease with the early centuries. In fact, the critical period into which the Roman empire entered only intensified the need to make a common understanding of dogma the basis of the unity of the Christian civilization that was being born out of the successive conversions of the barbarian peoples who were being incorporated into the old political system. As a result, the insistent plea of the Fathers remained relevant: to draw upon the ancient schools, selecting their best teachings and the tools most useful in ensuring a clear formulation of the faith. At the same time, Christians had to follow the criteria set down by the faith itself in accepting, as occasion suggested, the most trustworthy results of pagan thought, but without feeling an obligation to accept that thought in its entirety. In this way they would be successful in avoiding the contradictions that had weakened that thought.

The need, then, was to take from among the teachings of Socrates, Plato, or Aristotle those most in harmony with the foundations of the Christian religion. Similarly, it was necessary to accept, but only to a limited extent, the ethics of the Stoics and the physics of the Peripatetics and to be persuaded that Seneca had carried on a correspondence with St. Paul and that Virgil had been able to sense the coming of Christ, although without understanding it.

A lengthy tradition in theological studies would justify this instrumental use of pagan knowledge by means of some effective allegories, drawn for the most part from the writings of the Fathers, in order to show the correct approach to the relationship between reason and religion. Thus, for example, wise Christians can look to the part played by Hagar, the handmaiden who became wife to Abraham the patriarch but nonetheless remained always subject to her mistress, Sarah, mother of Isaac (Gen 16:1-16). From this they will see that they must not set an excessive value on the secular sciences, but rather make use of them in order to ascend to true theological wisdom, which is founded on the word of God and is both the mistress of these sciences and the ultimate goal of their true precepts.

There was also the Mosaic principle that required the sons of Israel to shave the heads, pare the nails, and destroy the garments of female slaves taken in war before uniting with them and making them their wives (Deut 21:10-13). This mandate demanded that those desirous of using human knowledge to strengthen their own belief must remove from that knowledge anything that is superfluous and cannot be ordered to the service of the faith; only then can they take over that knowledge in order to make it fruitful for themselves.

Again, the gold of which Israelites robbed the Egyptians before leaving for the Promised Land (Exod 12:35-36) becomes a reference to the right of Christ's followers to take possession of the pagan arts. Thus those using these riches to satisfy the illicit cognitive aspirations of the rational mind will only make for themselves an idolatrous image of a golden calf. In contrast, those who purify that knowledge and make it part of true wisdom for the understanding of revelation are obeying the divine law and can use the melted-down gold of the ancients to adorn the ark of the covenant in which the tablets of the Law are kept.

Thus, throughout the medieval centuries, respect for the relationship God has established between revealed truth and the results of the philosophers' natural skills guaranteed the consistency and correctness of theological research. In contrast, the reversal of that order by yielding to the temptation to give human questions priority over total assent to the mystery of faith could only beget false teachings.

The principal motive for esteeming the new teaching that resulted from this measured, syncretistic approach to the best fruits of human science was the renewed opportunity for the mind to gain access once again to a systematic wisdom that had seemed beyond reach. The very organization of contents that can be seen in the first dogmatic formulations (from the Apostolic Creed to the canons of the major ecumenical councils) is evidence of the felt need of translating into the language of complete explanation the systematic tension inherent in the historical character of the divine plan revealed in Scripture and running from creation to the end of time. This idea of systematization had been brought to maturity in the speculative area by some of the major theological works of the Fathers from Origen to Augustine. It now became the common mark of Christian thought: "doctrine" that is "sound" is such insofar as it is absolutely one and unquestionable; in turn, and because of its divine origin, this oneness is due to its being complete in all the parts that make it up, without any gaps or imperfections. Thus the fact that "sound doctrine" differs from the incompleteness of human teachings is a sign showing the superiority, even intellectual, of the divine message when the latter is correctly spelled out by the argumentative method of the theologians.

A careful diagnosis of this situation came down to the Middle Ages in a model passage of the *corpus dionysianum* or *areopagiticum*, a collection of extremely dense theological texts. Under the false paternity of the Dionysius mentioned earlier, who had become a convert after Paul's address on the Areopagus, this collection introduced into the Christian world subtle but structurally solid elements of Neoplatonic theology that were taken from the teaching of the pagan philosopher Proclus of Constantinople (d. 485). At the beginning of his seventh Letter the Areopagite says that he has never engaged in barren controversies with the Greek philosophers since they, too, are sincerely seeking the truth just as Christians do. On the other hand, the philosophers must not presume to impose their own theses, which are always imperfect, as though something completely true and irrefutable were embodied in each thesis. Otherwise it will be utterly useless even to discuss any matter with them. "Each says that his own bit of money is the real thing when in fact what he has may be a counterfeit copy of some part of the truth."[1]

A short time after the Pseudo-Dionysian writings were composed, a similar image was proposed in the Latin world by Severinus Boethius. The latter, however, though a Christian and the author of short works on theological subjects, took the important step of linking his image to the legitimacy of developing a true philosophy that is purely rational and independent of religion. After being condemned to death by Theodoric, king of the Ostrogoths, Boethius tells us in the introduction to his well-known *Consolation of Philosophy* that while in prison he met Philosophy personified as a noble, imposing woman whose head touched the heavens, while the hem of her spotless robe bore the mark of violent tearing. She explained that those responsible for the tears were petty, untrustworthy pagan philosophers. These had tried in vain to win her over to them; then, having managed to tear away a few little pieces of her robe, they went about the world displaying these as though they had mastered the entire truth.

In the ensuing pages of the *Consolation* Boethius makes no reference to the promises of redemption that the religion of Christ had introduced into human history. The explanation of his search for a purely philosophical reply to his own fundamental questions about human life and the uses of suffering is probably to be found in the idea that, in addition to accepting the decisive proclamation of redemption brought by the Gospel, human beings ought also to seek a rational justification of what seemingly eludes their understanding. Boethius claims to find this justification in the speculative content of the same teaching that, now viewed by him within a Christian hermeneutic of the faith, also nourished the thinking of the author of the *corpus dionysianum*, namely, the Neoplatonism of late antiquity.

The Neoplatonic school came into existence precisely in order to resist the new and successful Christian religious outlook. Beginning with the *Enneads* of Plotinus (d. 270 C.E.), the school sought to ensure the recovery of the autonomy and stability of natural thought, basing that recovery on a forcibly harmonized, or concordist, synthesis of the best teachings developed by the major philosophical currents of the past. The core of the synthesis was the metaphysical teaching of Plato and, in particular, the Platonic principle of the intelligibility and immutability of what is true. In Platonic speculation, then, human reason attempted to produce a stringently formulated, unified philosophical system that could surmount the contradictions of the schools and render an account of both the visible and the invisible, the material world and the intelligible world.

The attainment of this goal relied, above all in Proclus, on the introduction of a novel gnoseological approach that was closely connected with the thought of Plato. According to this analysis, many forms representing one and the same object are produced in the human soul; these are seemingly contradictory but can all be acknowledged as true, provided they are not presumed to have any validity outside the effective scope of the corresponding cognitive organ. According to the best-attested interpretation of them, these various forms of knowledge are related to at least three faculties: the senses, which translate data from the external world into notions; dialectical reason, which works out intelligible concepts through a series of mediations and distinctions; and the intellect, which is able to grasp the truth in a direct and complete intuition.

This teaching made possible a simple, consoling justification of philosophy, liberating it from its seeming fate of producing only doctrinal disagreement. The opinions of the philosophers had been contradictory because, although these opinions were due to the incompleteness of each one's dianoetic thought, they had claimed validity as though they were conveying a perfect vision of reality, a vision possible only to the noetic intellect for which no contradiction is possible. In order to correct this error, reason must submit to the unifying teaching of noetic intuition, while recognizing that knowledge can be objective only if the limits of the faculty producing it are acknowledged and looking to a higher order of truth for a new harmonization.

When faced with this approach to the unification and consolidation of knowledge under the guidance of a higher intelligence, the "new" Christian philosophers expressed doubts about the possibility that human beings could sufficiently grasp noetic truth in itself, uncontaminated by the partial and mediated processes of discursive reason. On the other hand, they accepted and made their own the Platonic hierarchy of the forms of knowledge. In their turn, however, they proposed that by a free yet radical choice the human quest for knowledge should be subordinated to the divine Intellect itself, which is utterly true and always the same and has made itself accessible to all by embodying itself in the words of scriptural revelation.

In dealing with the Neoplatonists, Christians had valid arguments justifying this choice. To begin with, once dianoetic reason has accepted the invitation to let itself be guided by revealed truth it will no longer be oriented toward a longing for a superior intuition that is by its nature not expressible or conceptualizable, nor will it be exposed any longer to the danger of contaminating this intuition by tailoring it to reason's possibilities of expression. Rather, thanks to the words of Scripture, reason will share in a complete and utterly gratuitous manifestation of truth, which it can then readily explain in definable and communicable ways.

Second, while Neoplatonism explained the ascent of the wise man as a purely mental and intuitive encounter with God, Christianity guarantees every believer the possibility of sharing in the historical event of a real encounter between the human and the divine, an encounter that, according to the faith, took place in time in the incarnation of Christ and is promised for the end of time in the universal resurrection (again as a matter of faith). This linking of the creator with creatures allows Christians, in a way far exceeding what the pagan philosophers could hope for, to see the entire history of creation as directed toward the certainty of the eschatological return of all particular truths to the Truth in itself from which they sprang, of all imperfect goods to the supreme Good that produced them, and of all forms of evanescent, mutable temporal things to the stability of the Eternal.

Christian "sound doctrine" thus claims to be a summary revaluation of all reality, both corporeal and intelligible. It also derives from the unqualified and all-embracing truthfulness of revelation the same systematic character which the Neoplatonic sages could achieve only at the cost of an irreparable devaluation of the sensible world, the multiple, and the accidental. Moreover, Christian philosophy brings with it the possibility of retrieving the whole of reality in a global justification of being, both visible and invisible, that is based on the words of him who truly is, and is the being of everything (Exod 3:14: "I am who am"). As a result, this philosophy can successfully aspire to offer itself as a completely systematic teaching that comprehends the entire truth of the reality flowing from God's creative act, from the beginning of time to its end.

3. Sacred Utterances: The Word of God and Human Language

In the course of the first centuries, in order to provide a solid resistance to the interpretive deviations of heretics and to strengthen believers in their acceptance of the faith, the ecclesiastical magisterium established a norm for the recognition of theological truth. This norm was the principle of tradition, which said that all interpretations and further explanations of the scriptural basis of the Christian religion were trustworthy provided they were in agreement with the entire intellectual patrimony developed by teachers universally recognized as authoritative and set down in formulas approved by conciliar assemblies. In the first half of the fifth century this principle was summed up by Vincent of Lérins in his *Notebooks* in a strikingly apt formula that was destined to pervade the entire history of medieval theology. The formula: "Everything, and nothing else, that has been believed everywhere, at all times, and by all" is true and must be acknowledged as such, without unjustified changes or additions. Only such teaching as possesses these characteristics can have a universal value, that is, be "catholic."

The understanding of this commonly accepted truth can certainly be the subject of further intellectual investigation, both in its form and in its content, but always while respecting the uniformity of the patrimony of tradition. This is to say that in order for any theological progress to be accepted it must be shown to be in harmony with the unanimous teaching of all the Fathers (the principle of the "unanimous consensus of the Fathers") and with the teaching of the universal ecclesiastical tradition (the principle of the "teaching/teaching office of the church").

The unanimity of the Christian world must be based, then, on Scripture and on tradition. Medieval theology had its origin in a prolonged response to the need for strengthening this spiritual unity on the basis of revelation, to which were added commentaries and deeper understandings derived from the works of the Fathers. For this reason it is characteristic of medieval literature that it is marked throughout not only by very frequent and recurring verses of Scripture but also by a remarkable harvest of citations—some short, but more often real extracts on the subject—from the works of the Latin and Greek Christian writers of the early centuries. The writings of the Fathers and the texts of conciliar canons (the latter regarded as being in their entirety documents that transmit the "authentic," that is, authoritative teaching of the Christian theological magisterium) are at times used by medieval authors as confirmations, but more often as the argumentative basis on which their own doctrinal positions are developed. The wisdom of the Fathers is thus accepted, in practice, as a prolongation of revelation and as offering, with the help of a sound use of reason, the first trustworthy explanatory clarification of that revelation.

In order to ensure an appropriate acknowledgment of the authority of the Fathers, there emerged rather quickly the need to establish a patristic canon. This explains the success of the document known as the decree on *Books to be Accepted or Not to be Accepted*, which was attributed to Pope Gelasius I (492–96) but was in fact drawn up some decades later by an anonymous cleric in southern Gaul. It offers an authoritative list of the patristic texts believers should accept as the material supporting the understanding of revelation.

This expansion of the number of fundamental texts that can be used in interpreting religious truth had, however, a further effect. It brought home the urgent need for theologians to formulate a careful judgment on the expressive power of the human words used in revelation itself and by its interpreters in communicating the faith to believers. Even if we prescind from the superimposition of the different linguistic webs brought into play by translations, first Greek and then Latin, of the Bible, there is the natural imperfection of the human language in which the word of God is expressed; this imperfection places limitations on the inexhaustible expressive power of a perfect truth the world cannot contain. The profound meaning of the human discourse God uses in revealing himself, and therefore of every human discourse about God, belongs to a higher order as compared with all the tools used in natural knowledge. This fact intensifies the power of the call to replace theological discourse with a meaningful silence, even though this seems to be a rejection of the human access to revelation that is sought in theological study.

The great medieval success of the body of writings wrongly attributed to Dionysius the Areopagite was promoted first and foremost by the urgent and powerful exhortation that is found on every page of his writings, but especially in his treatise on *The Divine Names*, namely, always to combine the positive language of doctrine with the deep riches of a theology of silence. The latter looks beyond the particular meaning of the words in which the faith is expressed to a limitless semantic potentiality that is peculiar to revelation.

Throughout the whole of medieval Latin civilization, the authority of Pseudo-Dionysius gave direction to all human desires to speak of God and to speak with God by confronting them with the distinction and yet complementarity between a *positive* or *kataphatic* theology that applies to the divine all the terms that can be derived from biblical language and from tradition, and a *negative* or *apophatic* theology that immediately denies the possibility of such an application and brings any attempt at an understanding of the faith up against the ultimate impenetrability of that which is truth in itself. The dynamics of the two theologies, which constantly refute one another to the point of making nonunderstanding the most effective possible representation of the being of God, lead therefore, in the short but closely argued treatise on *The Mystical Theology*, to the final introduction of the believer into the blinding light of the supreme and most authentic manifestation of the divine. Here only a mystical abandonment allows the soul to lose itself in the best possible acquisition of the truth.

It is important to observe that this combination of positive and negative discourses in the movement to establish a mystical theology reintroduces, in religious terms, the Proclian multiplication of levels of knowledge. From several points of view, then, medieval "sound doctrine" is nourished mainly by an ascensional tension that raises the various powers of the theologian's soul toward the ineffable sublimity of knowledge of the true. The soul can then turn back from these heights, enriched now with information and truth, descend to the dianoetic level of meaningful and descriptive rationality, and achieve organization in expressive forms that are governed by the laws of thought. By means of these forms the theologian can then communicate with the community of believers and teach them what he has learned at a higher and more perfect level.

This theological communication is the foundation on which the construction of Christendom was based. In 827, during the Carolingian period, after political unification had recently laid the foundations for the civic and religious renewal of medieval Christian civilization, Michael II, the Byzantine ruler, sent the gift of a sumptuous codex containing the works of Dionysius to Louis the Pious, the Frankish emperor; the Latins regarded this gift as an act of special sacral value. Hilduin, a monk and abbot of St. Denis, was charged with the first Latin translation; it was now that he invented the legendary identification of the Areopagite convert with "Dionysius," bishop of Paris (d. during the persecution of Decius around the middle of the third century), who gave his name to Hilduin's monastery, in whose library the precious codex was kept.

In this invention, which combined in one individual the philosophical wisdom of the Areopagite intellectual, the theological authority of the body of writings attributed to him, and the merit of having spread Christianity in the several Gauls, we may think we are seeing the first manifestation of the historical self-consciousness of a Christian people who had recently risen out of the destruction caused by the barbarian invasions. As Virgil had celebrated the divine status of Augustus by singing of his descent from Aeneas, so Hilduin's legend established for the following centuries the bond between the new Carolingian Christendom and the apostolic roots of the universal religion. In so doing it ensured the authenticity and salvific mission of this new Christianity and authorized the work of the intellectuals within it who undertook, in their theological studies, to explain and go more deeply into the contents of revealed truth.

4. The Divine Ordering: The Order of Creation—Essences, Ideas, Numbers, Intelligences

Two other works in the Pseudo-Dionysian corpus, *The Celestial Hierarchy* and *The Ecclesiastical Hierarchy*, influenced the theological outlook of the entire Middle Ages by describing the created universe as an orderly, descending distribution by the Creator of degrees of being. Nine hosts of angels transmit to humanity the inexhaustible truths of the divine secrets; these are received first of all by the bishops, the heads of the earthly hierarchy, and then spread by them, but with an ever increasing scatteredness, to the lower rungs of the priestly ladder. Three "hierarchical operations," entrusted to each intelligence (angelic and then human) in the thus reconstructed cosmic order, control the twofold process of the distribution and then the sacred restoration of being to its divine source. The three are: *purification* (deliverance from polluting contacts with the materiality of the multiple), *illumination* (the activity of cognitive attraction that leads lower degrees toward the beauty of the higher degrees and their greater resemblance to the divine), and *perfection* (the actualization of all creaturely potentialities in the direction of a universal assimilation to and union with God).

Here again the success of the theological thought of Pseudo-Dionysius introduced into the world of Christian thought another Neoplatonic theme: the theory of the hierarchical descent of the multiple from the One, who is the source of the harmonious perfection of the entire created universe. But here, too, Christianity added a new element, borrowed from the faith, to the Neoplatonic conception: the idea of a *creation from nothing*, which was inconceivable to pagan philosophers because of their logical principle that nothing can spring from nothing. This new element opened up for the metaphysics of Christians an unexpected and extremely rich speculative realm that had decisive results for the entire conception of finite reality and its history. In fact, the idea of creation from nothing became for intellectual believers an effective theoretical completion of the derivation of all things from the One, inasmuch as it ensured the unchangeable perfection of the Source in the process of giving rise to the multiple; it did so because the creative act was conceived of as freely posited in a nontemporal instant.

The dependence of the created world on a free divine choice also implied that its derivative existence is neither eternal nor necessary, and allowed thinkers to regard it as always possible that at a determined moment of history the derivation of effects from the Source could change into a universal return. Christian eschatology thus reinterpreted and brought to perfection the Neoplatonic dialectic of the two phases of descent and conversion as phases of a universal process; that is, not only as phases in the ethico-cognitive order and reserved to the wise, but as really applicable to all the effects of the First Cause. Finally, all this made it possible to surmount dualist temptations and explain the presence of evil in creation as something not really subsisting but rather as a diminution of the divine perfection down through all the levels of derivative being. In other words, everything created from nothing by a good God is really something good, even if imperfectly so.

This optimistic view of the cosmos, which is set forth by Dionysius in the fourth chapter of his *The Divine Names* (where he is drawing on Proclus' *The Existence of Evils*), thus reached the West together with its Plotinian presuppositions, which were disseminated in the work of Augustine. The result was that this same optimism directed the entire history of medieval religious thought.

Thanks, then, to a harmonious convergence of the thought of Augustine and the Areopagite, the relationship between God and his creation yielded a complete *metaphysics of order* that was directly linked to the theological image of the *logos* introduced by the Prologue of the Fourth Gospel. In this metaphysics the existence of all creatures is made to depend first on an atemporal act of knowledge in which the Word, the source of creative intelligence, shows them forth eternally in his ideas, which are the eternal models of everything that has been, is, or shall be, and, second, on the act of voluntary love with which the Holy Spirit effectively makes them exist. It is to the formal perfection of this work, which vaguely resembles that of human mathematical knowledge, that reference is made in the words often cited by the medieval theologians and spoken by divine Wisdom, that is, the Word, about himself: "You have ordered all things with measure and number and weight" (Wis 11:21).

On the basis of God's twofold revelation through the prophetic communication of his word (Scripture) and the sapiential ordering of creation (nature), medieval theology would include not only reflection on the sacred texts but also descriptions of the divine ordering of the universe in which the Platonic-intellectualist conception of order and of the eternal ideal exemplars is combined with motifs typical of the eastern religious outlook, such as justice, predestination, providence, divine law, and divine government. The Christian doctrine of *exemplarism* would thus become one of the cornerstones of the western theological thought that would be passed on from the Fathers to the Middle Ages, while gathering contributions down the years from many philosophical and sapiential sources and from the most diverse quarters: from late pagan Platonism to the Byzantine world and to Islamic and Hebrew thought.

In Seneca's fifty-eighth letter to Lucilius the author presents the Platonic doctrine of the ideas to the Latin cultural world; he describes their hierarchical descent from the most universal substance, through an organized succession of genera and species (that is, extensions of reality that are immutable but also increasingly circumscribed and limited), to the production of multiple individuals that are subject to chance and change. Porphyry of Tyre, a direct disciple of Plotinus, then schematized the doctrine in a slender little work of introduction of Aristotelean logic, appropriately titled *Isagoge* ("Introduction"). This work, which was spread far and wide in the Middle Ages as a preface to the *Organon*, outlined the formal structure of this metaphysical descent of the real, describing its ramification into genera and species not only in the area of substance but in each of the ten categories. Modern authors describe this pattern as "Porphyry's tree"; it helped to impress on the western theological mind the idea of a double ladder, ascending and descending, to be seen in the derivation of being from God.

In the fourth century Chalcidius, a Spanish philosopher and probably a convert to Christianity, translated the first part of the *Timaeus* into Latin and commented on it, following the Porphyrian outline. Thanks to his commentary this dialogue of Plato, the only one widely known in a Latin translation in the Middle Ages, ensured the Christian world the possession of a complete cosmological vision that could serve as a suitable support for the metaphysical doctrine of order. The three Platonic principles—the demiurge, the exemplars, and matter—became the three familiar foundations of Christian metaphysics: God the Father, the *logos*, and creatures. The divine government ensured by Plato's universal lifegiving soul became the universal lifegiving presence of the Holy Spirit.

From the divine ideas spring the lower forms (species or innate forms), which combine with matter to give rise to individuals. The mechanism of the four primordial elements (water, air, earth, and fire) and of the combinations of their respective qualities (hot, cold, humid, dry), which in Plato explain the organization of visible changes, is inserted into the tissue of creation as woven by divine providence. The natural knowableness of the cosmic order invites intelligent beings to traverse the pyramidal structure of reality in the reverse direction, to the point of recovering through true knowledge (which rises above the lower forms) a direct understanding of the divine ideas.

A few years later Macrobius, a pagan scholar, composed his *Commentary on the Dream of Scipio*, another work destined to become widely known in the Middle Ages as a vehicle of the theological idea of order. This was a commentary on the concluding section of Cicero's *On the State*, which reported a metaphysical dream of the young Scipio on universal metempsychosis. Macrobius saw the course of this dream as a paradigm of the lot of the individual soul, which loses an original perfection of knowledge and then rises to the contemplation of the universal source of the cosmos and its laws, this through an asceticism that purifies the intellect as it knows and studies the organization of nature.

At a later date Arabic Neoplatonism (and, in particular, the cosmological-metaphysical teaching of Avicenna) and the Jewish Platonism of Avicebron helped to enrich in various ways this complex, systematic description of the cosmic order. Within the shared Christian theology of history they strengthened the synthesis of those doctrines that have been described, in an especially penetrating phrase, as the "connected Platonisms" of medieval thought. Thus on the common foundation of the doctrine of the divine ordering all the successive proposals for constructing a Christian ontology, physics, metaphysics, psychology, and gnoseology developed the various forms of a single synthesis of Revelation and knowledge. In this synthesis the story of the six days of creation (the *Hexaemeron*) was reconciled and fused with the organization of reality as told in the *Timaeus*.

5. Christian Instruction: The Two Libraries: Human Literature and Divine Literature

The new philosophico-theological program that marked Christian wisdom from the post-Constantinian period onward was based, then, on the parallel development of understanding of the revealed data, on the one hand, and of the study of natural phenomena, on the other. Both activities were aimed at human knowledge of God: in the first instance on the basis of the self-revelation of the mystery and, in the second, through understanding of the order imposed on the universe by divine Providence. These two lines of study, which correspond to the concepts of Scripture and nature, obviously had to be supported down the centuries by an appropriate set of cognitive tools that were adapted to the differing specific needs of each study but were also not exempt from reciprocal interactions.

The understanding of the content of Scripture was subordinated, before all else, to the canon of biblical books accepted as inspired, and then to the interpretations of the Fathers that were authorized by the ecclesiastical magisterium. In contrast, the reading of nature depended on the exercise of scientific skills which over time human reason had organized into a series of principles, respect for which made it possible, in the various fields, to reconstruct the creaturely order established by the divine intelligence. But the complementarity of reason and faith also established necessary interconnections between these two types of study; that is, a correct biblical exegesis could not but observe the rules of the sciences of nature, while the natural disciplines could not but subordinate the results of their researches to a final control by faith, the ultimate rule or standard of their truthfulness.

According to a charming image used by Virgilius Grammaticus, Christian intellectuals should therefore assign the documentation for their wisdom to two libraries, consisting of the texts of the masters of ancient science and philosophy and those of the "Christian philosophers" (that is, the Bible and the Fathers). They will then have available a complete set of the documents needed for their study of the truth. ("Virgilius Grammaticus" was an anonymous scholar who lived in a Romano-barbarian region in the seventh-eighth centuries and was falsely identified with the author of the *Aeneid*.) Cassiodorus was obeying the same ideal principle when at the beginning of the sixth century he organized his *Institutes*, a handbook explaining the essentials of Christian wisdom, into two parallel series of short systematic treatises, devoted respectively to the science of revelation (*Institutes of Divine Literature*) and the science of nature (*Institutes of Human or Secular Literature*).

Relying on the solid support of these two libraries, medieval theological study would have the character of a structured investigation into the specific realm of knowledge provided by the Scriptures, but an investigation supported by the recognized authorities in the various fields of research and rendered orderly by respect for the procedural standards carefully defined in the works of those authorities. This made it possible to compile the knowledge gained in the form of an *institutio* or "established practice" (a term derived from late Latin juridical language); this was done first, even before Cassiodorus, by Lactantius (author of a collection of *Divine Institutes*). What was meant was a summary *handbook* or *manual* (*promptuarium*) of theological wisdom that had a formal organization and was complete in its contents as a result of combining the reading of Scripture with the results of investigation carried on over the centuries by scientific and philosophical reason.

The curriculum of secular studies generally followed in the late imperial period and inherited by the Christian Middle Ages had long since been divided, for ease in teaching and to ensure the completeness of the educational program, into a set number of arts or disciplines. The first systematization of this program probably went back to the lost *Books on the Disciplines* of Varro. Augustine, who planned a never-completed set of manuals of his own, is the first witness to the future agreement on seven different areas of study: the seven arts known as *liberal* (reserved to persons "free" of material necessities). These were arranged in an ascending order that made it possible to move from the understanding of visible realities to an understanding of invisible realities; at the summit, therefore, was the definitive acquisition of philosophy.

The seven were soon divided into two general areas of knowledge: the first, consisting of three disciplines, had for its purpose the regulating of human language and its ability to express the truth; the second, consisting of four disciplines, was aimed at a strictly quantitative (more exactly, qualitative) description of the inner structure of the visible world. Both sectors, the linguistic and the mathematical, ensured so accurate an identification of formal principles that they could be accepted by the human mind as a satisfactory explanation of the divine law that sustains the universal orderly arrangement of creatures. Beginning in the early Middle Ages and on the basis of a suggestion by Boethius it became customary to give the name *quadrivium* to the educational process conducted by the four mathematical disciplines; only later was the name *trivium* given to the first three disciplines.

The first of the "arts of speaking" was *grammar*, which not only described the principles of Latin morphology but also brought out the linguistic bases that assured the completeness of meaningful utterances. To *logic* or *dialectic* (to use the term widely employed in late antiquity and accepted by the Middle Ages) was reserved a fundamental role in the scientific formation of the wise person: as a true "wellspring of knowledge," this discipline made it possible to distinguish the true from the false, to describe all the conceptual contents of the mind, and to make thought flow from idea through argumentation. Logic merited being called the "art governing all the arts" (*ars artium*) and the "discipline governing all the disciplines" because its rightful task was to set down the rules that had to be respected by any science claiming to be true. The task of *rhetoric*, finally, was to teach how to induce a hearer (or reader) to accept or reject the contents of a teaching; it did so through the study of the formal elements that make human utterances more persuasive and therefore capable also of influencing people's ethical choices and the practice of virtue.

As sciences of quantities and of the numbers that describe them, the arts of the *quadrivium* acquired in the Middle Ages the function that physics had in ancient wisdom, namely, to describe the elements of the cosmic order and their harmony as actuations of the divine model from which they derived. *Arithmetic* studied numbers as such, with their possible combinations; *geometry* studied number as extended in space and also went on to the measurement of the terrestrial sphere and to geography; *music*, understood as a theoretical study of the successive relationships among sounds, studied number in relation to time; finally, *astronomy* considered numbers as arranged in space and time, that is, in motion, but with reference exclusively to the only moved reality that is eternally identical with itself and therefore scientifically exact, namely, the perfectly circular movement of the heavenly bodies.

The explanation of the contents proper to each liberal discipline was based on the teaching of one or two classical authors who were the first students of the discipline or even its founders. These were Donatus and Priscian for grammar, Aristotle for dialectic, Cicero for rhetoric, Euclid for geometry, and so on. The need, however, to summarize their works in a form more useful for teaching brought about the insertion into liberal studies of many syntheses, sometimes devoted to a single discipline, sometimes conceived as a series of compendia that brought all the essential principles together in a complete encyclopedia.

This second category included the succinct explanations of the liberal arts by Cassiodorus in his *Institutes* and later, in imitation of Cassiodorus, by Isidore of Seville in his *Etymologies* and by Alcuin in his handbooks. Especially, however, it was this approach that ensured the success of Martianus Capella (a not further identifiable African writer of the fifth century) and his work *The Marriage of Philology and Mercury*. Without exaggeration, this can be called one of the ancient texts most widely circulated and read by every educated person in the early medieval centuries. It is a complete manual in nine books, modeled on

Varro, that summarizes in full the scope of each of the seven disciplines; the latter are personified here and invited, one at a time, to be present at a meeting of the Olympian gods as bridesmaids at the marriage of the god Mercury and a human virgin, Philology.

This introductory setting, described in the first two books of the work, has a complex symbolism alluding to the union between the divine Intellect, which is responsible for the order of the cosmos, and the human mind, which studies this order. This fact allowed Christian writers to accept the external pagan guise, especially because the assumption of Philology among the deities (at the end of the explanation of the seven disciplines, books three to nine) reflected perfectly the Christian conception of the propaedeutic function of the human arts in relation to theological wisdom.

These foundational texts served as the basis for the development of the gloss, which characterized the entire medieval period. A gloss was an annotated commentary that made the texts more accessible to the reader; it took the form either of more or less extensive marginal notes or of a continuous commentary guiding the reader. Text thus sprang from text, and commentary sometimes accompanied the work to which it referred; sometimes, however, it replaced the work as a means of teaching and became itself the subject of teaching and commentary. Thus the scientific methodology of the Middle Ages acquired an ever more fruitful ability to systematize a unified body of knowledge that brought the seven arts together using one and same methodology and that in the end came to be identified with philosophy as a whole. The arts thus supported and even produced philosophy, and, since philosophy was subordinated to theological knowledge, they nourished the true philosophy that was born of the synthesis of faith and reason.

The rules governing the arts were essential for theological knowledge because, first and foremost, they made it possible to understand the language of the biblical text, which is made up of human words, consists of logical and rhetorical discourses, and makes continual references to numbers and to the order of the visible world. In addition, these rules enabled the created intellect to ascend from the organization of the natural world to the world of changelessness and thus to the divine and to the primordial logical and numerical essences, that is, to the very forms and ideas in divine Wisdom that preside over creation. According to an idea found in the second book of Augustine's *Teaching Christianity* and often cited by medieval writers, the sages of the past who "invented" the arts did not base these on one or another convention and thus imprison them in the formal interlocking categories of the mind; rather, in keeping with the authentic meaning of *invenire*, that is, to "find" or "discover," those sages recognized the rules at work in nature, where they existed as traces of the higher, divine ordering mind.

There is a fine example of this integration of philosophy and faith in the fact that, beginning with Cassiodorus, countless medieval writers made an allegorical identification of the arts with the seven pillars supporting Solomon's temple of Wisdom (Prov 9:1). In this perspective the human intellect anticipates and supports divine truth but must not presume that it can replace it. Augustine never tires of warning his readers that even when natural science disposes the human mind for the attainment of necessary items of knowledge, all of its certainties always spring from its participation in the divine Intellect, a participation that comes, either directly within the soul or in some mediated fashion, through contemplation of the perfection of the created world.

In Augustine's view, then, whenever the soul draws near to immutable truth, this is to be explained as a result of an *illumination*, which occurs every time the soul discovers within itself the perfection of the inherently intelligible, of that which is separated from everything sensible and is free of any accidental change whatsoever. This happy Augustinian metaphor of the divine light that shows itself in knowledge came to be combined with the Pseudo-Dionysian theory of illumination as a hierarchic operation. The result was to introduce into Christian speculation the Platonic doctrine of remembrance, even while rejecting the need to accept a preexistence of the soul before the body. Moreover, since alongside a supernatural illumination produced by a special intervention of grace there is always possible a natural illumination brought about by mental operations working with a correct development of empirical data, it is clear that this second form of true knowledge is precisely what is achieved through the study and application of the liberal arts.

Theological knowledge, then, based as it is on a synthesis of rational and revealed knowledge, springs from the convergence of intellectual light and the light of grace. This explains why the people of the Middle Ages thought it indispensable to submit even the textual inheritance that produced the knowledge of things divine (the patrimony, that is, of Scripture and the works of the Church Fathers) to the same kind of systematization and analysis that was applied to the classical and late antique writers who supplied the teachings contained in the liberal arts.

Furthermore, even the teaching of the Fathers, especially in their role as interpreters of revelation, came to be anthologized and then abridged in summarizing treatises. Here again the extensive production of annotated commentaries, both on Scripture and on its commentators, multiplied and made more complex the several levels of reading. Thus the analysis of the sacred text was always accompanied by a selective reworking of readings from the Fathers; the latter, in turn, were artificially linked among themselves to the point of producing a continuous reading of all the biblical books, from Genesis to Revelation.

In addition, over the centuries there developed alongside the liberal arts, though with a lesser degree of systematization, treatises on the "theological" arts (sacred rhetoric, symbolic arithmetic, and numerology), handbooks on exegetical methods, and lists of liturgical symbols. Finally, with the progressive development of medieval epistemology (that is, from the twelfth century on) we see the emergence of a true methodology of the knowledge of faith; that is, a normative meditation on the methods and procedures of theological reflection. Only at this point, as it spread throughout the medieval schools, did this reflection acquire the name of *theology*.

Christian theological wisdom had come into being during the patristic period as a result of an initial grafting onto the trunk of philosophical rationality. Now, slowly but steadily advancing through the medieval centuries, this wisdom became a distinct reality and took on the forms proper to an autonomous area of study, one endowed not only with a specific subject matter ("subject" was the term the Scholastics would use) but also with its own scientific status and method.

This growth would follow diverse and sometimes opposite courses depending on the many levels on which meditation on sacred Scripture would develop: the logico-descriptive, argumentative level with its definitions and deductions; the level of interior affective and meditative spirituality that was supported by the individual's life of prayer, by the representational power of language, and by the almost litanic repetitions of the truths of the faith; the level of artistic and poetic, verbal, and visual expression that addressed the psychological self by means of technical virtuosities and by stirring the emotions; the symbolic level, at which the images emerging from the biblical text were studied, intensified, and enriched with further meanings that constantly referred to one another. These and other possible courses, and the various structures that developed within them, were not strictly distinct among themselves. They could coexist and be simultaneously present even in exponents of one and the same current of thought, in the works of one and the same author, and even within a single text. The reason: all the writers were aiming, even in different ways, at a common development of a complex cognitive system that, because of its higher origin, was inexhaustible and could not be rigidified into a single formal schema.

It seems, then, that the parallelism of the two libraries, viewed specifically from the theoretico-cultural point of view, is one of the many forms of recurring dualism (this, too, originally Platonic) that were typical of medieval Christianity. There were the dualisms of the spiritual and the physical, soul and body, being (immutable, formal, universal, and eternal) and matter, the city of God and the city of humanity. The orientation of Christianity to goals not of this world (an orientation that from the beginning had annoyed paganism, as can be seen from Celsus's critique addressed to Origen) did not exclude a productive confrontation with the political and intellectual past of the civilization that had accepted and allowed the spread of Christianity. But in this confrontation Christianity demanded that this past be retrieved and justified within a perspective directed to an eschatological future: in other words, a perspective that looked ahead, within history, both to the establishment of a better society based on participation in a supernatural truth and to the assertion of the superiority of theological truth over the scientific truth that supported theology, as well as of faith over reason, the inwardness of the spirit over the outward garb of the letter, and the soul over the flesh.

6. The Ages of the World: The Temporal Boundaries of the Theological Middle Ages: Problems of Periodization and Methodology

The invented story of Pseudo-Dionysius as first a pagan philosopher and then a theologian, missionary, bishop, and martyr was only one of the many tesserae in a mosaic of narratives that runs through the history of the medieval world. The purpose of all these stories was to show the continuity between, on the one hand, the ancient roots that fed Christian civilization at its birth, along with the institutional structure that supported it, and, on the other, its animating intellectual life. The universality and uniformity marking the common acceptance of one and the same faith were in practice a distinguishing sign and identifying criterion of the society that arose in Europe from the ashes of the Roman empire. It is therefore legitimate to set specific temporal boundaries for the entire period in which those characteristics remained dominant in the area that saw the spread of Christianity.

Whether or not it is appropriate to continue giving this period the name "Middle Ages" is a purely secondary issue. It does not call into question either the substantial unity of a set of civic, social, economic, and cultural conditions or the suitability of summing these up, for easier study, as a single historiographical period and under a single name. On the other hand, it is obvious that (while prescinding from the name given) the retention of this historical category, which implies a strong reference to the politico-religious unity of the western civilization that continued without important breaks for about ten centuries, is especially successful and fruitful from the specific perspective of the history of theological thought, this at the levels of both research and teaching.

After being formulated for the first time by a Christian, Melito of Sardis, in his *Apologia* to Marcus Aurelius, the ideal identification of religious unity and civil society runs through the whole of medieval civilization. Even after the lengthy crisis of the Avignon Captivity of the papacy and the Western Schism, the ideal lost its unifying power only with the eruption of the Protestant Reform and the irremediable loss of universal agreement. From Constantine to Charles V of Habsburg, from the Council of Nicaea to that of Trent, from the agreement (or edict) of Milan (313 C.E.), which paved the way for the Christian pacification of the ancient Roman empire by guaranteeing freedom of worship to Christians, to the Peace of Augsburg (1555), which marked the definitive end of religious harmony or agreement by granting confessional autonomy to the Protestant countries—throughout this entire period the whole of "medieval" theological thought was always subordinated to a single fundamental principle. That principle was the universal acceptance by the entire Christian body politic of the divine truth that exists (as St. Paul puts it) in the changeless reality of the "ages of eternity" and manifests itself in the course of the temporal vicissitudes of the earthly city, or of the "ages of the world," with their fortuitousness, their rises and falls, their uncertainties and dependence on conditions.

The history of medieval theological civilization lasted as long as the spiritual and intellectual activities that constituted it were directed by this mental paradigm. Consequently, the traditional, conventional dates accepted by historians for the beginning and end of the Middle Ages do not take sufficient account of the development described. Rather than in 476, the year in which Odoacer, the barbarian, returned the insignia of the western empire to Zeno, emperor of the East, the process creating Christian civilization began with the writing of Paul's letters and of the Fourth Gospel and can be considered to have been completed at the beginning of Constantine's Christian empire, that is, in the year of the Edict of Milan or else the year of the Council of Nicaea (325).

In like manner, it is not so much the discovery of the Americas in 1492 as it is the conciliar canons of Constance (1414–1418) and Basel (1431–1439), or even the convocation of the Council of Trent (1545) that should be taken as marking the coming of a new consciousness in the Christian world. In other words, the end of the Middle Ages came when account had to be taken of the irremediable politico-religious ruptures that caused the collapse of the very idea of an identification of human civilization and the kingdom of God.

On the other hand, it seems necessary to distinguish phases and periods within this single protracted unfolding of "medieval" theological history under the influence of a generally accepted and constantly used fundamental speculative paradigm. The distinction is required in particular when we consider the revolutionary results of the introduction of Greco-Arabic thought into the West in the final decades of the twelfth century and the first decades of the thirteenth. In medieval intellectual history this phenomenon can be regarded as the dividing point between the *early* and the *late Middle Ages*. In addition, however, within each of these two major phases it is possible to discern a sequence of periods corresponding to the various forms of growth and development.

In the early Middle Ages several periods may be distinguished. After the collapse of the western empire there is the period of slow cultural revival in the Romano-barbarian kingdoms from the sixth century to the halt of Islamic penetration into Europe at the battle of Poitiers (732). Then there is the intellectual flowering of the Carolingian world in the eighth and ninth centuries, followed by a new decline that reflected the crisis in the socio-political system in the tenth and eleventh centuries and continued down to the rise of the national kingdoms and the strengthening of the imperial system in the Germanic world. Finally, there is the age of ecclesiastical reform and the investiture struggle leading to the Concordat of Worms (1122), with that age's revival of dedication to theological clarification and spiritual pacification, culminating in the great effort at restoring the Christian self-consciousness that lay behind the undertaking of the first Crusade (1096).

In the middle, between the early and the late Middle Ages, there is the so-called "renaissance of the twelfth century," with its revival of urbanization and the emergence of the episcopal schools at the major cathedrals. There follows an intermediate phase (coextensive, more or less, with the reign of Philip II Augustus in France, 1165–1223), which saw an important development of theological methodology and the discovery of Greco-Arabic and Hebraic wisdom.

At this point there began the development of the "scholastic" Middle Ages in the strict sense: the rise of the universities (Paris in particular, with the approval of its first statutes in 1215) and the first stage in the teaching of the masters of theology and the systematization of their thought. This continued until the convocation of the second ecumenical Council of Lyons (1274). The latter event was marked by the disappearance from the scene of the two leading figures in the theological flowering of the Mendicant Orders: Thomas and Bonaventure. There followed a lively thirty-year period of settling down, marked by discussions, changes of opinion, and new systematic proposals; this period ran from the controversies over official censures passed on theological Aristoteleanism (1277) to the confirmation of the doctrine of the soul as form of the body in the canons of the ecumenical Council of Vienne (1311–1312).

Finally, there was the period of the Avignon papacy and the ensuing Western Schism, leading to the Councils of Constance and Basel. This period saw a slowly developing crisis in university methods, the first proposals for a reform of studies, and a deepening of individual religious experience. The leading figures in the implementation of this last would be the scholars active in the period of the humanistic rebirth of theology down to the Council of Trent.

This division of periods and historical settings, which takes into account parallel (but not always coextensive) periodizations used by historians of politics, society, and economics, is evidently a pragmatic one. With some historiographical objectivity, the division reflects the development of the typical cultural factors that had the strongest influence on intellectual life. In any case, the location of the birth and development of theological doctrines within a single frame of reference allows us to see the theoretical importance of this framework inasmuch as it places thought in a closer real relationship with the actual demands and competencies that direct the thinking of a given author.

A further factor of importance for the historiographical assessment of medieval thought is language. The common use of Latin in the schools of the West and the influence of the Vulgate version of the Bible on the language and thinking of all western authors evidently determined the shape of the philosophical and theological literature of these centuries. Failure to take account of this conditioning factor would bring the risk of adulterating and often even falsifying the authentic meaning of a text (or even simply of an argument or a formula).

The history of theology in the medieval centuries must therefore be pursued with constant attention to its context, that is, to its historico-cultural coordinates and the temporal conditions that guided the approach to and content of the various speculative proposals set forth in theology. Throughout the development of this history it will thus be possible to see how different modes and worlds of thought spring from a shared speculative paradigm, namely, the constant correlation of reason and faith, which exercised a determining influence on all the speculation of the medieval centuries.

Endnote

1. *Pseudo-Dionysius: The Complete Works*, trans. Colm Luibheid (New York and Mahwah, NJ: Paulist Press, 1987) 266.

Chapter 1

From the Roman World to the Christian World: The Collapse and Rebirth of the Christian Empire of the West

I. The Theology of the "Founders"

In the second half of the fifth century, a few decades before the final dissolution of the western Roman empire, Salvian of Marseilles, a Spanish scholar and enthusiastic reader of Augustine, wrote a treatise on *The Government of God*. His purpose was to prove that, despite the dramatic signs of the crisis overwhelming human society, no one could deny that the whole of creation is subject to the immutable order decreed by Providence. Indeed, if the decay of social and political structures is a consequence of the immorality of the human beings who established them, this is in any case a confirmation of God's government and justice. In addition, if the providential perfection of the cosmos were denied, what motivation would be left for the irrepressible human aspiration for happiness?

The beginnings of medieval theological reflection are marked by similar exhortations not to abandon the ultimate spiritual certainties in an uncertain world lit by apocalyptic lightnings. The settlement of the barbarian populations in lands that had once been flourishing provinces of the empire and the artificial rise of feeble kingdoms controlled by their mercenary leaders were the final outcome of the political decay that had for centuries been eating away at the institutional unity of Roman civilization. But even though the maximum degree of civilizational disintegration had been reached, due to the unifying impulses still springing from its cultural and religious roots this fragmented world was still traversed by a tenacious ideological aspiration to preserve social cohesion and spiritual unity. In fact, the new barbarian rulers themselves did not take over the ancient institutions in order to replace them; rather, they even asked that they be given room to settle within the solid embrace of the existing order so that they too might be nourished by the life-giving sap that had for centuries sustained it.

When Odoacer deposed Romulus Augustus in 476 he did not have himself crowned emperor, but symbolically restored the trappings of the western empire to Zeno, the eastern emperor, whom even the barbarians, despite their remoteness, acknowledged as legitimate heir and continuer of the ancient tradition. In addition, although the conquerors were chiefly Arians, once the respective kingdoms had been firmly established their rulers slowly led the various ethnic groups toward conversion to Roman Christianity; this would confirm their acquired integration into the tradition of "Romanness," to which, decade after decade, all sought to gain entry.

King Clovis and the Salian Franks, who occupied northern Gaul, were converted as early as 496. The Christianization of the Visigoths, who ruled in Spain, would be slower but would be sanctioned by Recared at the third Council of Toledo in 589. Theodoric, who deposed Odoacer and settled the Arian Ostrogoths in Italy, was not himself converted but, as early as 493, did initiate a policy of rebuilding his own kingdom on the basis of a religious peace with the Latins and the eastern empire. He also fostered a mutual institutional acceptance among the new kingdoms by pursuing a policy of dynastic marriages. On the same lines, with the support of a submissive senatorial aristocracy, he began the cultural Romanization of the new world he had built; he made Ravenna a center of Romano-Greek culture and art, and at his court he fostered a flowering of literary and philosophical studies in Latin.

The Romano-barbarian world thus arose from a fusion, solid even if artificial, of religion, culture, and political power that laid the foundations of a new and at the same time ancient idea of civilization. The new reality possessed an internal power of growth and continuity that enabled it, two centuries later, to stand up to the advance of the new Islamic conquerors and win an unlikely victory at Poitiers in 732 under the Frankish leader, Charles Martel. Throughout this slow and laborious process of reconstruction an obvious unifying role was played both by the desire to become heirs of the juridical and cultural Roman tradition and by the sharing of a common religion. The rulers of the Romano-barbarian kingdoms tried in various ways to find legitimacy for their role by claiming fanciful historical roots and even descent from Greek or Trojan heroes. Meanwhile, the Latins continued to shoulder the task of supporting and unifying this new framework by a renewed literary, religious, and philosophical production.

There was indeed a succession of new wars connected with settlement, the most ferocious of which, the Greco-Gothic conflict following the death of Theodoric in 526, was neither the first nor the last. There were also new invasions, among which that of the Lombards into Italy beginning in 568 was marked by special cruelty. But during these same decades there was no lack of active thinkers belonging to both the church and the Roman nobility; against that very turbulent background these men began and continued, by means of translations and manuals, the first concrete efforts to preserve or recover the ancient cultural and religious patrimony.

It has been suggested that all of those authors, or at least the most important among them, be given the collective title of "founders of the Middle Ages." It is true, of course, that in addition to Boethius not only Cassiodorus, Isidore, and Gregory the Great but perhaps even other "lesser" writers might aspire to share with the author of the *Consolation* the title "last of the Romans and first of the Scholastics" (which a multitude of historians have agreed to reserve to Boethius) or other showy descriptions suitable for distinguishing them as leading figures at a decisive moment of passage between two eras. Nevertheless, the historical effectiveness of their work can be correctly understood only when that work is closely connected with the historical conditions in which the authors lived. Only this accurate perspective makes it possible to judge satisfactorily the degree to which they anticipated a not easily foreseeable future.

These leading figures who mediated the Latin cultural tradition from antiquity to the Middle Ages were all connected, directly or indirectly, with religious life or ecclesiastical institutions. They may have been priests or bishops who for catechetical or pastoral reasons planned an education of the Christian people. But they may also have been laypersons who, as in the case of Boethius, were closely involved in the political and theoretical strengthening of institutions, including religious ones. Or again, and with increasing frequency, they may have been monks who directed their use and preservation of documents of the past toward a deepened spirituality. In view of all this we should not be surprised by the predominantly religious character of the greater part of their original works; the aims, methods, and perspectives adopted were obviously influenced to a perceptible degree by the still-recent model of the Fathers of the church.

Initially, inspired by their devotion as followers, these writers often saw their task as one simply of compiling the opinions of the great teachers. This was true especially with reference to Augustine, as can be seen in the case of Prosper of Aquitaine, a layman (d. after 455), who collected in summary form a series of *Theses Gleaned from the Works of Augustine.*

Others, for their part, began attempts at a summary systematization of the thought of the Fathers. One such was John Cassian, a monk at Marseilles in the first half of the fifth century, whose *Conferences on the Fathers* presented moral examples and ethical teachings from the greatest masters of eastern and western monasticism. Likewise at Marseilles and in the still lively intellectual environment of southern Gaul there was Gennadius, a priest (d. between 492 and 505), who wrote a continuation of Jerome's *Famous Men*, adding the names and works of fifth-century writers. He also composed a lengthy *Answer to All the Heresies* in eight books, but only the final section has survived, a succinct summary of dogmas.

In contrast to these writers, Claudian Mamertus of Vienne (d. 474) directed his attention to Christian anthropology and in his *Condition of the Soul* provided a synthesis of Platonic-Pythagorean psychology, but one Christianized in the light of Augustine. In the early centuries of the Middle Ages this work helped spread the idea of the soul as an invisible, individual substance that is joined to the body but is free of matter and not subject to accidental changes.

The Italian area saw the emergence of new summaries of patristic theology, inspired by catechetico-pastoral concerns, in the collected *Homilies* of Peter Chrysologus, archbishop of Ravenna (d. 450), and Maximus, bishop of Turin (d. after 465). The order of the sermons suggests that they were intended as a continuous commentary on the official list of principal liturgical feasts.

In the time of Theodoric, Magnus Felix Ennodius, bishop of Pavia (d. 521), compiled a manual titled *Exhortation to Instruction* as a guide for religious in their acquisition of the rhetorical and scientific knowledge needed by any highly educated person. In fact, during this period it was the bishops who were the most determined, through effective action in the religious sphere, to keep alive the sense of belonging to a common civilization, which, given their Christian hope, they refused to admit had disappeared. Evidence of this is the lofty inspiration (always dependent on patristic sources) to be found in the sermons and theological treatises of Caesarius of Arles (d. 542). Further evidence is the ability shown in the work of Fulgentius of Ruspe (d. ca. 533) to compress the catechetical tradition of the past into effective compendia (such as the *Rule of Faith*) in order to hold back the spread of Arianism in Vandal-controlled Africa.

Toward the end of the sixth century, in the *History of the Franks* of Gregory, bishop of Tours, there appears, perhaps for the first time, the idea that the handover of power from the Romans to the barbarians was legitimate because willed by divine Providence.

System and organic development marked these first attempts to find in the recovery of the patristic tradition the basis for the rebirth of historical consciousness in a people still united and called upon to build on earth a kingdom guided by principles of a higher order. These same characteristics increased considerably in the work of the few Latin writers of the sixth and seventh centuries and did so in inverse proportion to the worsening of social and political conditions in the Christian West. Moreover, it is properly to these isolated exceptional personalities who, because of their intellectual stature and their abilities as compilers, stood out in the desolate cultural landscape of the time, that the image of *founders* seems to apply best. And it is perhaps correct so to apply it, even if in fact, with the exception of Boethius, their task seems to have been primarily that of preparing for and foreshadowing future developments in medieval Christian religious thought and leading up to them. In an image drawn from classical archaeology and not unsuited to this landscape of excavations among the ruins, we might describe these men as "vestibules" whose isolated but already imposing majesty leads the visitor on to the monuments on the acropolis, monuments that were now beginning to be planned and built.

1. Boethius and Wisdom

The program of work that only a premature death (execution under Theodoric in ca. 524/25) prevented Roman nobleman Manlius Anicius Severinus Boethius from completing was certainly an ambitious one. His aim was to recover and organize the entire philosophical patrimony of antiquity and to set forth its contents in Latin in a systematic fashion, beginning with the principles of logic and arithmetic and moving on to the highest metaphysical and theological truths. In his second commentary on Aristotle's *Hermeneutics* he spoke of how he intended to implement this program: he would translate, and provide with an analytical commentary, all the works of Plato and Aristotle, in order to demonstrate by a correct interpretation of them that, contrary to what most people believed, the thought of these two founders of classical philosophy was marked by a basic and undeniable agreement.

It is a well-known fact that on the subject of reconciling Plato and Aristotle, Boethius had illustrious predecessors in Platonic circles in Alexandria and Rome (Cicero tells us this) and then, and especially, among the Neoplatonists and Christians influenced by Neoplatonism (down to and including Augustine). But we are given the impression that when Boethius took up the subject once again as both a pledge and, at the same time, a supporting framework of an entire plan for recovering and systematizing human philosophy, he was justifying the deeper meaning of this cultural undertaking. That is, he was ensuring that the ancient world, mortally stricken by historical circumstances, would be guaranteed the inalienable possession of a unified and certain body of knowledge that places human beings in a position of undeniable privilege in relation to all other created beings because it allows them to enter into dialogue with the divine Intelligence itself.

This wisdom is precisely what is incarnated in the feminine figure who, in the poetic story told in *The Consolation of Philosophy*, appeared to Boethius in a prison, perhaps not far from Pavia. There he was spending his final days as a victim of the bloody crackdown on the Roman senate that defiled the end of Theodoric's reign in Italy.

As Boethius approached death he was disappointed by the failure of all his plans, embittered by unjust accusations, and depressed by the realization of the unbroken victory of the wicked over the good; all human aspirations and desires now seemed unattainable and empty. A prisoner and ill in mind more than in body, he abandoned himself to the melancholic laments of the Muses, who were present with him, but these could not console him. For it was not the lifeless plaints of poetry but only the solid formation of a sufficient knowledge of truth that could enable the human mind to grasp the real meaning of the invisible order that supports and justifies every event.

For this reason, when Philosophy herself comes in turn into Boethius' cell, her first act is a vigorous dismissal of those false consolers. Then she sits down beside her former pupil and begins with him a lengthy dialogue whose sole purpose is to help him regain an authentic understanding of truth. If this task was to be fulfilled it was necessary that the wisdom that approaches the seeker of truth in order to lead him to the goal of his quest should be not *a* philosophy among others, that of one master as opposed to that of others, but only the one *true* Philosophy. This was precisely the philosophy of Socrates and the sages before him, such as Parmenides and Anaxagoras, who prepared for his coming, and then of his disciples, Plato and Aristotle, who agreed among themselves.

The diversified written works that preceded the composition of the *Consolation* were mature works, laudable in their literary density, and following the classical model of the *prosimetrum* with its regular succession of poetry and prose. They document the author's lengthy journey as he pursued his plan of a complete and organized exposition of human knowledge. There were two youthful works on the disciplines of the quadrivium: *The Teaching of Arithmetic* and *The Teaching of Music*. These are in fact paraphrases of similar treatises by Nicomachus of Gerasa, a Neopythagorean (1st–2nd century C.E.). But, despite their evident lack of any great originality, they show how the attainment of truth must be first of all the result, in the various areas of knowledge, of diverse routes followed with methodological rigor by each scientific discipline worthy of the name.

More specifically, as is explicitly stated in the introduction to the work on arithmetic, true wisdom consists in the knowledge of immutable realities that alone deserve to be said to "exist" in the full sense of the word. The individual sciences or disciplines describe the various courses that enable the mind to draw near to these invisible truths by leading it from the world of accidental and corporeal change to the world of eternal forms or prime essences. In particular, the four disciplines of the quadrivium describe the ways in which those essences make themselves known in accordance with the various manifestations of quantity (discrete or continuous, regarded in itself or in something else).

But the same approach marks the works Boethius devoted to logic: the translation of the works in Aristotle's *Organon*, the commentaries on these (sometimes in two versions: a more literal and a more penetrating), and then some original monographs on the syllogism and on argumentation. At this point we should recall how these texts—even though they were the only completed part of Boethius' plan to mediate the whole of ancient Aristoteleanism and Platonism—were to have an incalculable influence in the history of logic and therefore in the history also of the philosophy and theology of the entire Middle Ages.

The importance, moreover, of Boethius' works on logic can be seen not only in their extent but also, on the strictly epistemological level, in the fact that they furnish a synthesis of teachings coming not only from the *Organon* but also from both Stoic and Neoplatonic logic. As a result, the entire systematic discipline Boethius passed on to subsequent centuries can be seen as a unified structure in which are interwoven and thoroughly harmonized all the formal instruments developed by the various ancient schools and currents of thought for the purpose of enabling reason to organize and control the possible reflections of the prime essences in human discourse and thought.

The idea of true knowledge as an ascent from sensible appearances to immutable eternal principles also led Boethius to face the question of the reality of those forms or essences. He thereby also introduced into medieval culture basic philosophical ideas on the nature of what would later on, in the twelfth century, be called "universals." When dealing with the universals in the writings on logic he did indeed take the Aristotelean doctrinal position (the universals are present in individual things, determining their mode of existing and their knowableness); in these works he was, after all, expounding the doctrine of logical predicables according to the teaching of Aristotle. But from Boethian texts on mathematics there emerges a much more essentialist and exemplarist view of the prime essences, one that is Platonic-Pythagorean in kind.

All this, however, amounts to saying that in the final analysis a true understanding of reality in itself is always, for Boethius, an eminently theological act of knowing. For insofar as the word "divine" means eternal and immutable, it describes the nature of the essences sought in all of human sapiential investigation and in all the areas of their manifestation to the human mind (areas that correspond to the division of the philosophical sciences). As a result, the problem inescapably arises here of assessing the relationship that exists, in Boethius' view, between rationality and faith. For once it is granted that science always seeks the truth of the divine, it must at some point come to grips with the self-revelation of God (who is, in himself, that truth) as made known in the Sacred Scriptures and in the religious traditions Christians regard as true.

The doubts raised about Boethius' assent to Christianity, in rare cases by some medieval readers but above all by many historians and interpreters of the recent past, arise mainly from the already mentioned absence of explicit references to the faith and the Bible in the *Consolation* and in the logical and scientific works. But Boethius also wrote five *Short Sacred Works*, brief theological treatises, four of which deal explicitly with the interpretation of Christian dogma; no one can any longer suggest reasonable doubts about their authenticity. In fact, there is no real reason for questioning that Boethius sincerely intended to be a mathematician when writing mathematical works, a logician when speaking of logic, and a philosopher when, facing death, he carries on a dialogue with Philosophy, the comforter. The issue here is not relativism but the understanding and coordination of the different degrees of the human approach to the truth. At the summit of these degrees can be placed both natural theology and, specifically distinct from it, theology as reflection on the dogmas of Christianity.

It is not by accident, then, that in the collection of *Short Sacred Works* there is one, the third, in which Boethius raises a problem of a theological kind and resolves it using only rational demonstration, without any reference to the faith. This short text takes as its starting point an initial reference to a fuller, now lost treatise on parallel themes entitled *Weeks*; as a result, the little work would likewise be known throughout the Middle Ages as *On Weeks*.

The question taken up in this short text has to do with the way in which finite substances can be good, given the fact that they are not good in themselves, since then they would be God. The development of the treatise takes the form of a theological application of the axiomatic method, which is typical of geometry but not exclusive to it. That is, the writer lists a short series of self-evident principles (among them is the happy ontological distinction between being as a predicate, or *esse*, and being as the existence of a thing or an *id quod est*). Next there is a strictly deductive explicitation of what follows from these premises in relation to the problem to be solved. The conclusion can then be drawn (one that matches the content of the Christian faith, but is independent of it) that if all finite things are good, this is due not to an intrinsic goodness of their substance or to an extrinsic participation in the divine substance but to a determinative and necessitating act of the will of God, who is the productive cause that brings them into being.

Boethius then distinguishes, without opposing, natural theology, that is, the metaphysics of Aristotle, from the faith; the two are different levels, distinct but not contradictory, of the unified wisdom that leads human beings to the truth. The first of these two he calls "theology," and he considers it to be a science, one of those into which philosophy is divided; it too, then, like the others that precede it, is a constitutive element of true wisdom. Like every science, theology has a special method that allows it to grasp in the most appropriate way the objects proper to it.

Thus in the first of the *Short Sacred Works*, titled *The Trinity*, in which Boethius intends to set forth the nature of the method specific to natural theological knowledge, he harks back to Neoplatonic teaching on the threefold hierarchic division, mentioned earlier, of the faculties or powers of human knowledge: the senses, discursive reason, and noetic and intuitive intelligence. He says that in theology the correct method corresponds to the third and highest faculty, and he therefore uses the adverb "intellectually" in referring to it. In order to grasp its divine object, which is incommensurably superior to its natural capacities, the human mind endeavors to raise itself to the supreme level attainable by its cognitive powers. It attempts, that is, to penetrate to being in itself by means of an intuitive and comprehensive vision that brings it closer to the way in which things are known to the divinity than to the way in which they appear in the world of finitude and particularity.

This, then, is the supreme goal of true philosophy, the goal pursued throughout their lives by the most trustworthy of its followers, such as Socrates, Plato, and Aristotle, above all others. These men endeavored to raise their minds to the point of bringing into play the pure intuitiveness of the intellect and then to return to the level of discursive rationality and communicate the content of their intuition of the truth to human minds still immersed in time and space. It was at those heights that Socrates and Plato contemplated the Supreme Good; it was there that Aristotle discovered that God is pure thought and that Pythagoras grasped the mathematical perfection of the ordering source of the cosmos.

In the main part of the *Consolation*, Philosophy herself teaches that between reason and intelligence there is a relationship like that between being and becoming, or the center of a circle and its circumference, or eternity and time. And she explains that since "every object of knowledge is known not according to the nature of the object but according to the nature of the knowing subject," the elevation of the mind to the intuitive gaze of the intellect amounts to an attempt to assimilate itself, as far as possible, to the cognitive condition proper to God and therefore to the knowledge with which God knows things. It is precisely at that point that the process of cognitive improvement leads to and brings about the consolation promised to human beings by Philosophy (that is, by its highest natural form, theology, which moves toward its object "intellectually").

In the second book of the *Consolation*, Boethius shows the unreliableness and relative character of the blessings bestowed fortuitously by Fortune, and in the third book the unlimited goodness of the rule exercised throughout the cosmos by its divine source. In the fourth and fifth books Philosophy then applies its strongest curative powers in order to heal Boethius of his sufferings. She shows him that these sufferings spring from his own inability to rise to the heights of the gaze with which God himself looks upon and governs his works. As soon as Boethius succeeds in this effort and reaches by means of the intellect the vision of the harmonization of the many and the differentiated in the unity of truth he will see how the limited perspective of human beings as well as their individual destiny are not irreconcilable with the divine goodness and justice; how their freedom is not contradicted by the foreknowledge of God; and how the inevitable, mechanical succession of natural causes and effects is not opposed to that foreknowledge, but results from a view of truth that is different from the higher and more authentic view of it taken by divine Providence. All of these philosophical antinomies are in fact only consequences of the one original disharmony between conceptual-discursive knowledge on the one hand, and intuitive-immediate knowledge on the other. But the oneness of truth, which is one and the same in both perspectives, urges the follower of Philosophy to make the final, courageous effort whose reward is the attainment of the only true happiness, that which the divine mind in its simplicity enjoys eternally.

It is true, however, that God alone possesses truth fully, directly, and eternally, at a level beyond the reach of this final philosophical effort, which leads indeed to happiness in eternal life, but in this life remains always a movement that cannot reach its goal. It follows that wisdom can ascend to a still higher degree of cognitive perfection, which resides at the top of the ladder of the sciences: it does so by accepting by faith the contents of Christian revelation. Scripture indeed uses words belonging to the order of rational discourse in order to express and communicate to finite intelligences truths that are perfect and by their nature known only to God. Nevertheless, without any merit on humanity's part, Scripture places reason in a position to acquire from the very source of truth elements of knowledge it would never be able to gain by its own powers alone and that in the realm of the true transcend even the highest intellectual intuitions.

The science of faith, therefore, consists in ensuring the assent of reason to divine mysteries that in themselves are unknowable, and it does so by means of tools and procedures borrowed from logic and natural philosophy. As Boethius writes at the end of *The Trinity*, this science thereby liberates reason from all "mental representations linked to the conditions of the sensible world" and, in contrast, brings it close to everything that "can most fitly be received as an object of understanding" among the things believed by faith.

In summary, in these short theological works Boethius is able to interpret the fundamental dogmas of the Christian faith by means of a convergence of intelligence and revelation in a procedure that leads, in a form guaranteed by the most reliable of all authorities, the divine, to the highest forms of understanding of truth that are possible for the human intellect. Thus in *The Trinity*, for the purpose of protecting believers from heretical errors, the understanding of the true meaning of the orthodox formula of the trinitarian faith is subordinated to a check on whether the terms corresponding to the divine attributes have a place in the semantic grid furnished by Aristotle's ten categories.

Boethius' analysis shows that while all the theological terms expressing a divine property seem to have their place in the categories of quantity (such as "great"), quality ("good," "just"), action ("creator"), time ("eternal"), and so on, they always and solely signify the divine substance. But this last is not a substance like others that are the subject of accidents, but is rather a "supersubstance," in the supernatural reality of which the other theological determinants likewise express a maximal substantial meaning. In particular, the category of relation, which theologians agree is the one to which the predication of the trinitarian names belongs ("father," "son," and "spirit" understood as "gift" of God), introduces into God predications that always and only refer to God's single and identically shared "supersubstantiality." Dianoetic reason is thus enabled to ascertain the fact, which it cannot understand, that trinitarian predications made of God signify relations, but relations that do not imply any multiplicity of substantial subjects.

Boethius' method is applied in the same manner to the mystery of the Incarnation in the fifth of the *Short Sacred Works*, known as *Answer to Eutyches and Nestorius*. The conjoining of the human and the divine in a single subject, something unintelligible and impossible to rational logic, is here illumined by a strict definition of the terms used in its formulation: "nature" and "person." Since nature is correctly understood in this context as "the difference that allows one reality to be distinguished from another that has a different specific form," all believers will agree (against the Monophysitism of Eutyches) that there are two different natures in Christ. And since philosophers understand person as "an individual substance endowed with its own intellect and its own particular will," the use of this term in the christological formula (aimed at Nestorius) will ensure the unity of the natures in the really existing single individual who is at once human and divine.

The fourth of the theological works is titled *Faith* (here again the last doubts about its authenticity seem vanquished today), and it differs from the others. It gives a paraphrase of the Nicene Creed in the form of a discursive but systematic explanation of the dogmatic foundations on which the entire truth of the Christian religion rests. It is as if, recalling the list of philosophical axioms that preside over the cosmic optimism of the third short work, Boethius wanted to formulate a parallel series of formal principles that are agreed upon by all believers based on the assent of faith. These can then stand as the foundations of the lines of argument proper to the theological science of revelation, such as those put into practice in the first and the fifth of the *Short Theological Works*.

2. Truth and the Reorganization of Knowledge:
   Cassiodorus and Isidore of Seville

Flavius Magnus Aurelius Cassiodorus, a Latin nobleman born between 488 and 490, survived the violent ending of the age of Theodoric and remained at the court of Ravenna as tutor and secretary of the young king, Atalaric, until the final catastrophe. This came when the Greeks invaded and laid waste to the Italian peninsula and deported the conquered to Constantinople. After difficult and painful years Cassiodorus returned to an Italy devastated by wars and ravaged by famine and shortages. Following the example of other thinkers of that period, he decided to withdraw to a place apart where, far from the uproar of an unsafe world, he devoted himself to the education of young monks and the preservation of the relics of the past.

Vivarium, the clearly symbolic name of the monastic center Cassiodorus established at an undetermined location in the South (in Campagna or Calabria), came into existence as a place of study and prayer. There the residents meditated on revelation and practiced the liberal disciplines, which were essential for understanding and interiorizing the truths of Scripture. Cassiodorus pulled together the main lines of this program of work in a slender handbook in which he gave a summary account of the knowledge he regarded as indispensable for his monks. He gave it the by-then-classic title of *Institutes* and, as mentioned earlier, divided it into two sections. The first was an introduction to sacred studies: *Institutes of Divine Literature*, a summary presentation of the succession of biblical books and of the principal commentators on them. The second was an introduction to secular studies, that is, the liberal arts: *Institutes of Human Literature*, the teachings of which he summarized in short compendia while also naming the more authoritative writers in each area.

This short "study guide" was indeed an original production, but it was also little more than a list, with brief notes, of the basic books a monastic library ought to have and of their respective contents. Yet the short *Institutes* soon took on the role of a practical aid in teaching, rich in content although very sparing in its comments and illustrations; it also proved practical for use outside the walls of Vivarium. In periods when books were difficult to find and interest in deeper personal study was weak, an instructional aid of this kind easily became a tool that replaced the study of the original texts on which the author had drawn. Even in the following centuries the work enjoyed a certain popularity among all thinkers because it mediated the complete and organized remembrance of an intellectual, religious, and scientifico-philosophical activity that could be revived, as soon as this became possible, on the basis of the bibliographical information and the programmatic ideas it contained.

If Cassiodorus thought possible the combination of parallel sacred and secular studies he produced in his handbook, it was because he was convinced by his Augustinian model that both kinds of study derived from a single source, divine Wisdom, which had inspired the prophets and given order to the universe. The stages in the two parallel courses of instruction supported the believing intellect as it mounted the rungs of a ladder of knowledge that rose from the sensible world to the pure intelligibility of the divine. Using the same approach, Cassiodorus also wrote a short treatise on *The Soul*, in which, following a path already marked out by Claudian Mamertus, he combined philosophical arguments and scriptural testimonies to prove the purely immaterial and spiritual nature of the human soul. But the best example of how his program of dynamically combining the rules of the arts and meditation on the faith took a concrete form is to be seen in his spacious and profound *Explanation of the Psalms*, which he intended as an effective model of such a program and as reading matter for his monks.

Of special interest is the explanation, in the preface to the work, of the idea of the circularity of truth, namely, that the explanation of the truth of the faith is supported by the truth of the arts, while at the same time the former grounds and validates the latter. Since the Scripture is truth, it was natural for the inspired writers to make ample use of the tools developed by the rational minds of the ancient philosophers in order to support and confirm the truth of their discourses. On the other hand, the faith reveals to us that if the rules of the arts are true, it is because in ordering the universe God applied the laws of his perfect wisdom, which the teachers of the past understood, codified, and explained in a unified doctrinal exposition. For this reason the Christian sage must likewise know the rules of the arts in order to draw near by means of them to the depths of the divine mind, whether by investigating nature or reading Scripture, in both of which these depths are present like the wine in the grapes and the harvests in the seeds of grain. Cassiodorus' monumental explanation of the Psalms, which unfolds on the basis of this preface, is completely built on an analytical application of these initial precepts.

Less clearly, perhaps, but no less effectively, the same principle is behind the composition of other impressive theologico-cultural syntheses written during the difficult years when the Romano-barbarian kingdoms were prematurely aging. In particular, certainty about the reciprocal support and reinforcement given each other by natural knowledge and the truths of faith is at the basis of the *Etymologies* of Isidore, bishop of Seville in the kingdom of the Visigoths (d. 636). This wide-ranging encyclopedic collection, with its twenty books of learned facts of every kind, was widely known and used in the early Middle Ages because of its practicality and wealth of information. The title conveys the program of the work: to assemble and catalogue all useful ideas from very diverse sources, starting with an explanation of the origin and meaning of the terms involved: liberal arts, medicine, law, biblical exegesis, ecclesiastical tradition, the literatures and languages of antiquity, botany and zoology, mineralogy, counting and the sciences of measurement, naval and military skills, theatrical art, agriculture and gardening, building, utensils, clothing, culinary recipes and the consumption of food, and so on.

Like Cassiodorus' handbook, but dealing with a much broader and more subdivided range of contents, Isidore's collection sought to bring together in a unified and orderly educational plan all the areas of competence needed by civilized believers. This was so that they might be able to know and organize the world of visible things and then move beyond the limits of this world in a constant desire to lead the intellect from the scatteredness of multiplicity to the greatest possible likeness to the single gaze of God as he contemplates his creation.

The ultimate intention of the work is therefore not simply to tell stories and inform, as its external form, that of a dispassionate inventory of data, might suggest. Something more radical and deeper emerges from the work as a whole, from its complex, varied, and only seemingly disorganized nature. In fact, the intention of the *Etymologies* is to supply believers with a heritage of knowledge by which they might understand themselves and on which they could base their own membership in Roman and Christian civilization. For the survival of this civilization amid the juridical, social, and economic fragmentation that marked everyday life depended on preserving an awareness of unity and uniformity, which are the fundamental traits of truth itself.

Other texts flowing from the many-sided fruitfulness of Isidore the writer give evidence of the extent to which the desire for spiritual unity guided him in coping with his awareness of belonging to an impoverished world whose very memories were in danger of disappearing. Isidore's *Distinctions* offers another learned list of words that appear similar ("wisdom" and "science," "intellect" and "mind," and so on) but whose differentiations and definitions make it possible to advance both one's understanding of the order of nature and one's accompanying mastery of the language in which that order is expressed. The *Authoritative Statements*, in three books, are modeled on Prosper of Aquitaine: on the basis of an anthological stitching together of passages from the works of Augustine and from the *Morals* of Isidore's contemporary, Gregory the Great, the work offers a unified and annotated exposition of the principal themes and problems of the Christian faith.

Next, and even more interesting, is the attempt at a theological rhetoric, titled *Synonyms*. In this short treatise in two books an interior monologue between the soul and the rational mind (halfway between a solemn prayer and a confession of sins) is developed, broadened, and refined by means of a constant rapprochement of three, four, or even more words that have a very similar but never identical meaning (the writer is here reversing the method of the *Distinctions*). But the resultant paradoxical amplification of theological language is neither ostentation nor word play. Rather, as Isidore dilutes his discourse by an inexhaustible repetition of theological terms he seems to be making a tormented effort to intensify the expressive power of creaturely language in response to the difficulty of putting the highest and truest realities into words.

A few decades later, Isidore's *Synonyms* provided Ildefonsus, archbishop of Toledo (d. 667), with the linguistic methods he needed in composing his *Short Book on the Perpetual Virginity of Blessed Mary*, one of the first examples of medieval Mariology devoted to the defense of the perpetual virginity of the Mother of Christ (a teaching confirmed a few years later, in 693, by the sixteenth Council of Toledo).

It is especially interesting to see how, at the very moment when this author enfolds the reader in the terminological labyrinth created by the rhetorical repetition of theological terms, he links Mariology and Christology. That is, he links the virginity of Mary and the divinity of Christ in a single rigorous line of argument in which each supports the other, as he makes explicit the logical connection of all the truths of faith. (If Mary is a virgin it is because she gives birth, contrary to the laws of nature, to one who is true man and true God, while if Christ is true God, he can only be born of a virgin.) In addition, the Isidoran method of multiplying synonyms also helps in unfolding the perfect circularity of theological truth (which we saw above in Cassiodorus), because the very repetition of the truth is enough to clarify it. As the Prologue says, truth alone demonstrates and confirms truth, because truth is God, and everything that is true comes from God:

> Truth lasts eternally; whatever is true, lives; whatever springs from truth does not pass away. Truth is not subject to falsehood; deceit does not overcome truth; falsehoods do not change things that are true. Even if truth is hidden by the shadow of deceit, the truth, though hidden, will in the end reveal what is true. Indeed, what is false will not abide; what is true will never be lacking; what is alien to truth will be vain; what is distant from truth will prove to be empty. The reason: truth is God; whatever is of God is true; and whatever comes from God is truly real, in virtue of its truth alone.

3. Gregory the Great

Because of the wounds opened by the Byzantine wars of reconquest and the progressive decadence of the Romano-barbaric kingdoms, the representatives of the Christian ecclesiastical hierarchy were increasingly compelled to take over the task of maintaining or recovering the spiritual unity of what remained of the already transformed Latin civilization of the West. Even the gradually growing distance (which was ideological and cultural before being political) from the eastern empire and the Greek church helped push the church of Rome to undertake the increasingly more demanding task of spiritual consolidation of Christianity; this work was directed first to the religious aspect of life and was then extended to the cultural and social spheres.

These policies clearly characterized, in particular, the pontificate of Gregory, known as the Great (590–604), a Roman, the first of the popes who bore that name. He promoted the religious consolidation of the Christian world in two ways. The first was the establishment of a vast network of diplomatic agreements and a careful plan of ecclesiastical control in the territories of the Romano-Germanic kingdoms. The second was the dispatch of courageous missionary expeditions to the regions of northern Europe, which had remained outside or had been barely touched by Roman civilization; of special importance was the mission sent to the British Isles under the leadership of the monk Augustine, who later became the first archbishop of Canterbury.

Italy, meanwhile, had for several decades been invaded by new conquerors, the Lombards, who had profited by the weakness of the Byzantine governors to settle unopposed in the northern part of the peninsula and in the central duchies of Spoleto and Benevento. The peacemaking work of Gregory succeeded in moderating the harsh attitude of the occupiers, bringing about a gradual recovery of autonomy for property owners and for the administrative responsibilities of the clergy, and thereby promoting an admittedly unstable coexistence. This coexistence was later formally sealed by the baptism, celebrated by Gregory himself, of the son of the Lombard king Agilulf and Theodolinda, a Catholic.

Gregory devoted himself to consolidating the autonomy of ecclesiastical institutions against Lombard and Byzantine interferences and to pursuing an increasingly rigid policy of requiring the subordination of all the bishops to Roman authority. At the same time he took steps to improve their scientific and cultural education, urging them to an organized study of the ancient disciplines, a study that was evidently subordinated to, and had as its goal a better knowledge and understanding of the truths of the faith. For this reason both his very extensive correspondence and his *Pastoral Rule*, which was intended as a *vademecum* for the complete bishop, abounded in exhortations not to neglect the study of the liberal arts and the practice of the classical writers. The reason: knowledge is a gift of the Holy Spirit, and it is not possible for believers to have a suitable faith in the religious mysteries if their shepherd is not capable of teaching them, humbly but competently, to read revelation correctly.

It is true, on the other hand, that the secular arts are not to be studied for the sake of ostentation or vainglory or even simply for the pleasure to be derived from the contents of human literature. In a pastoral letter Gregory harshly rebukes Bishop Decentius of Vienne, who studied grammar and read the poets solely out of a stubborn love of things classical as an end in themselves. In contrast, Gregory praises Bishop Anastasius of Antioch for his polished rhetoric that was devoutly placed at the service of Christian pastoral activity and Christian ethics.

Worldly knowledge, Gregory says, is not itself the truth, but is a useful tool for fostering a manifestation of truth to weak human minds. Separated from faith, the words of knowledge are only a shadow of the truth; for that reason the pagan sages of the past, who thought they could entrust their lives and happiness to philosophical teachings alone, were like blind men who wander in a darkness they mistake for reality. But those who believe in the word of Christ and accept him as their mediator between the shadows and the light, ignorance and truth, are able by his merits to free themselves from the prison of worldly wisdom and discover the true source of wisdom, the only source that can be regarded as truthful. Christian shepherds are therefore enjoined to bring this mission to completion by urging the faithful who still wander in the darkness of the world to let themselves be enlightened by the words of the Gospel.

In an interesting page of his *Dialogues* Gregory seems to provide a basis for this program by harking back, but as a theologian, to the Platonic myth of the cave (which he probably knew from Cicero). Gregory writes that a child born of a woman imprisoned in a dark jail who has never seen anything outside the prison has no other evidence than his mother's nostalgic stories for the existence of an outside world full of lights and wonders; so too human beings can only believe the loving witness of Christ and the voice of the successors of the apostles if they are to know the happiness and truth of the divine and aspire to reach these.

This fundamental idea pervades and supports the major works of Gregory the Great, all of them of an exegetical character: his collections of *Homilies* on the prophecies of Ezekiel and on the gospels, the allegorical commentaries on the first book of Kings and the Song of Songs, and above all the majestic meditation on ethico-existential religion that is set forth in a searching commentary on the story of Job (the *Morals* or *Moral Teachings Drawn from Job*).

This last work, with Boethius' *Consolation*, stands at the beginning of the Middle Ages as an exemplary model of lofty moral meditation and justification of human life. From the *Morals*, in particular, there emerges most fully the real focus of Gregory's theological thought, which springs from the contemplation (occasionally underscored by events of the time) of the tragic and inexplicable character of the human condition within the plan of universal history and the interweaving of particular events.

The ancient philosophers had engaged in their reflections on visible nature in order to develop satisfactory answers to the questions all human beings ask about their own origin and their own destined end. So too, faith in Christ claims to be the only true philosophy on which the soul can draw to satisfy its thirst for knowledge when confronted with the most inexplicable problems, those of sickness, suffering, and death (these are the only natural certitudes, being based on direct experience). And while ancient wisdom saw in virtue and self-possession the key to overcoming suffering, Christians want something more radical and profound, conscious as they are that simply convincing oneself of the nonexistence of suffering cannot be a way of truly overcoming it. The interior dissatisfaction of Job as he asks whether it was right to accept everything God allowed to befall him is for Gregory a dissatisfaction proper to all human beings, It is only by believing in Christ that they can verify the truth that present suffering is a consequence of sin and can search out the right ways of remedying it and recovering the authentic creaturely dignity God has willed all to have.

Only meditation on Scripture, then, can help human beings to an understanding of how suffering is foreseen by God as an element in a universal harmony and given to them as a useful tool for drawing them away from love of the world and urging them to aspire to the acquisition of everlasting happiness. This discovery is not possible, however, unless, when answering the questions of philosophy and setting forth the solutions of faith, the human intellect voluntarily renounces its own arrogant claim to understand and justify. Humility, then, or the Christian attitude of readiness to be guided by Christ, who is the only one to have a complete experience of truth, is a further fundamental key giving the believer access to true wisdom. Humility is the principle that makes it possible to restrain oneself in the use of the liberal arts and to open oneself to the knowledge of revelation. It is also the primary virtue that makes known to each human being the irreplaceable and essential role that, during the short space of earthly life, he or she is called to play in relation to the universal order.

Humility, understood as an existential characteristic of human beings when confronted with truth, also underlies the formulation (in one of the *Homilies* on the gospels) of the well-known, seemingly paradoxical principle of "meritorious faith." According to this principle "a faith is not truly meritorious that is supported by reason." It is not possible to find or licit to seek reasons external to revelation itself that would justify believing in its truth. Thus Gregory subordinates even the inestimable value of the Christian faith to the ethical perfection of the voluntary free choice that leads to it. That is, the faith that saves is a disinterested faith that is accepted not in order to satisfy the theoretical or aesthetic aspirations of the mind but solely because of a passionate desire to welcome within oneself the voice of truth, which is the voice of God. And if this acceptance already brings happiness to the individual in the present life and even before the future life, this is only because faith, if authentic, is able to satisfy its own every desire and expectation without any merit on its part.

Just as truth proves truth, so faith is its own sole support. The trustworthiness of Scripture and of the interpretation given of it by the most authoritative witnesses to it, the correctness of the trinitarian and christological formulas, the Roman primacy of ecclesial jurisdiction, the authenticity of the decrees of the major ecumenical councils, the indissolubility of the sacraments: all these are objects of faith. In many passages of his works and his correspondence Gregory the Great was anxious to ensure the unqualified openness of believers to these truths of faith, without basing this openness on external considerations not already implicit in the very statement of the truths.

This fact allows us to identify, between the lines of Gregory's writings, a gradual clarification of the idea of dogma as the unconditional object of a faith whose validity is based on the harmony of this object with all the other truths that are equally deserving of belief. Dogma is thus clearly distinguished from other doctrinal opinions or theses that are put forth by the interpreters of Scripture solely on the basis of their intellectual competence, and therefore as suggestions intended as practical complements to the understanding of the faith. Examples of such theses are the ideas that the angels were created at the same time as the visible world or that they are arranged in nine choirs or other such conceptual systematizations that are useful in catechesis, such as the list of the seven vices or the four virtues.

4. A "Monastic" Civilization

A. BENEDICT OF NURSIA AND BENEDICTINE MONASTICISM

In Pope Gregory's work for the religious and cultural restoration of the church, as well as in his plan for the missionary spread of the Catholic faith, the Benedictine monks played an especially important part. The close connection between the pontiff and the most widespread monastic movement of his time is documented by Gregory himself in his *Dialogues*, in which, in conversation with Peter, a deacon, he narrates the lives of a great many Italian saints. The stories are rich in models of virtue and edifying episodes, all of them inspired by a passionately held ideal of sanctification to be attained through removal from the world and a life of asceticism and prayer. The *Dialogues* appear to be, in both style and content, rather different from the themes taken up in his exegetico-theological writings, but they were widely read in the monastic centers of later centuries as displaying a model of perfection.

The entire second book of Gregory's *Dialogues* is devoted to the life of Benedict of Nursia (d. ca. 547). In 529 Benedict founded Montecassino, which became the heart of the monastic movement whose rapid spread in the early centuries of the Middle Ages gave rise to a closely connected network of communities throughout Christian Europe. A special merit of Benedict was that he was able to tone down the original eremitical approach typical of late antique monastic asceticism in the East, in which the controlling idea was the mortification of the flesh and the repression of temptations. In its stead he gave western monasticism a decisive orientation to the cenobitical life and, at the same time, called for special attention to the perfection of the individual monk.

The Benedictine style of religious life was valued by many bishops and popes, who promoted its spread beyond the Italian peninsula. It provided an immediate and satisfactory response to the situation of social diaspora and the crisis of cultural identity that afflicted the Romano-barbarian kingdoms. Subsequently it became the chief instrument for the spread throughout Europe of the religious and intellectual restoration begun by the Carolingians. In addition to a wise encouragement of manual work and the trades needed for the very survival of the monastic community, the *Rule* of Benedict provided for the biblico-liturgical education that was an indispensable means for the spiritual improvement of the individual.

The monk was urged to commit himself daily, but especially during some particular periods of the year, to the reading of (*lectio*) and interior reflection on (*meditatio*) the pages of revelation until he worked through the entire collection of canonical books. He did so with the help of patristic commentaries that offered further ideas on the interpretation of these writings. In preparation for this work the monk was obliged to have at least an essential knowledge of grammar and then also of such rhetorico-dialectical and numerological skills as were indispensable for an adequate grasp of what he was reading. The Benedictine community soon acquired the structure needed for achieving these goals: a school or place of studies for the training of the young and then a place for copying manuscripts (a scriptorium) and a library for the editing and preservation of the necessary manuscript codices.

These cultural aspects were indeed initially only marginal or at most complementary to the spiritual activity of the Benedictines and were not meant to take priority over the intense religious, catechetical, and evangelizing work that provided the context for them. At the same time, however, we may not underestimate the effectiveness with which that initial step gave direction in later centuries to the development of early medieval civilization. For, at least from the viewpoint of religious and intellectual life, this civilization can suitably be described as "monastic," being based on a desire for spiritual perfection that regarded a literary education as one of its constitutive elements.

B. ENGLISH MONASTICISM AND BEDE THE VENERABLE

The emphasis on the importance of a literary culture—always directed, initially, to liturgical and religious goals—also marked, to a considerable degree, another parallel monastic movement that at first had its own specific traits but then was increasingly faced with and finally merged with the Benedictine Rule. This movement began in the second half of the fifth century in Ireland and spread first to Britain and then to the continent. We must not overestimate the value of this pre-Carolingian Irish culture or the influence of the phenomenon known as the "peregrination of the Irish" (*peregrinatio Scottorum*), that is, the migration of individual monks from Ireland (which the Romans called *Scotia maior*) to the regions of northern Europe. But it cannot be denied that some of those individuals displayed especially noteworthy scientific, classical, biblical, and patristic abilities.

Whether or not it was due in part to the influence of the cultural contribution made by these *Scoti*, it is certain that, as early as the end of the seventh century and then with even more notable successes during the eighth, there occurred a religious and cultural awakening that was still limited to the monastic world. It began in Scotland and the northern regions of England, where it combined with the flourishing ecclesiastical reorganization promoted by Augustine of Canterbury. It was seen next in the Germanic territories beyond the Rhine, where Irish and English monastic missions contributed greatly to the introduction of Christianity, a movement then completed by the military conquest of Charlemagne.

The most important and most representative witnesses to the intellectual awakening in the English world are the varied works of Bede the Venerable (d. 735), who was one of the major transmitters of ancient culture during these centuries. Bede wrote many short works and more or less extensive exegetical, homiletic, hagiographical, didactic, computational, and historical treatises, but his reputation is linked mainly to an encyclopedic summary of scientific information inherited from the world of late antiquity; it bears the expressive title *The Nature of Things*. It is a learned book, but it does not depart from the basic biblical approach that marks Bede's entire body of work, for it is conceived as a description of the order of the cosmos that, following the model of the principal patristic commentaries, is set within the framework of the story of the six days of creation.

Supported by his awareness of the purpose of his own scientific competence, Bede felt authorized to introduce into the Christian mental universe a mechanistic conception of cosmic physiology that was based on the combination of the four elements and the development of the seminal principles scattered throughout the entire creation. His thought was that these results of secular scientific investigation into natural events were a permanently valid contribution to a better knowledge of the hidden but universally present plan of divine providence. In this manner philosophy once again made its entrance into the monastic world as a comprehensive explanation of the knowledge of truth that is based on faith in revelation. According to the inspired allegorical exegesis Bede gives of the biblical description of Solomon's temple, Christian sages are comparable to the large slanting windows that admitted into the heart of the building the rays of the sun as these made their way in through the higher fissures. Such men mediate the divine illumination, knowing as they do how to make use of the liberal arts and their earthly skills in transmitting this light to the people gathered in assembly.

c. Virgilius Grammaticus and Ethicus Ister

The works of Bede likewise became part of the limited but orderly didactic baggage that constituted the basic learning of educated monks in the early Middle Ages. This supplemented the efforts of the pre-Carolingian monastic world to search out its own religious and sapiential roots. This it did by looking, slowly but fruitfully, into now deteriorated and inactive libraries and civil and episcopal archives for the ancient monuments, both patristic and classical, on which to base its recognition of its own cultural identity. In the process it saw to the copying, study, and conservation of these monuments in its scriptoria. Precisely in order to hasten the attainment of the goal, these models were preserved and frequently anthologized in feeble collections of excerpts. In addition, odd ways of reinventing the foundations of the Romano-barbarian cultural universe made their appearance, their purpose being to make these more useful in supporting the reconstruction going on in the politico-religious world.

For example, the name of the author of the *Aeneid* hides the already mentioned counterfeiter who called himself Virgilius Maro Grammaticus and was the author of two learned collections. One was a collection of *Epitomes* (that is, doctrinal summaries). The other was a collection of *Letters* in which problems of a philosophico-grammatical kind were treated in an artificial style and with the frequent introduction of passages from authors and teachers who were likewise invented or at least hidden behind pseudonyms imitative of the classics. These works were perhaps compiled in the second half of the seventh century or the first half of the eighth and in a learned setting scholars have located in southern France, or in an environment not alien to Irish influence, or in the environment of the rabbinical communities scattered throughout western Europe.

The writings of Virgilius Grammaticus frequently display interesting meditations on the effectiveness of the liberal arts in raising the human intellect toward the acquisition of truth. In this approach, which was symbolically expressed, as we noted earlier, in the happy image of the two libraries, pagan and Christian, we can already see, in a preliminary form, the essential methodological structure of a great deal of future medieval theological speculation. The human sciences, each in its own sphere and all of them together in a common educational curriculum, were organized in a hierarchical series of increasingly expansive acquisitions of knowledge. The aim was to effect a progressive sharpening of the soul's cognitive powers, which themselves were arranged in Platonic fashion as an ascending hierarchy of perfections. All of these reach their completion in the illumination of the theological intelligence, which is based on revelation and ordered to the investigation of the mysteries of the divine thought.

The author doubly disguises himself in an anonymous work titled *Cosmography*. This, too, was composed at some unidentifiable point in the seventh century, very probably on the periphery of the Carolingian politico-cultural renaissance, whose ideas of cosmopolitanism and of religious and intellectual uniformity it seems to anticipate. The text claims, indeed, to be a Christianized reworking of a treatise composed by a pagan Greek philosopher named Ethicus Ister (that is, from Istria); the writer who did the reworking says he is a presbyter named Jerome; both personages are evidently fictitious. By means of this artificial doubling of authors and therefore of authorial responsibilities the anonymous inventor of the entire cultural operation is able to stitch together the two different approaches, philosophical and religious. The teachings and philosophical ideas of the fictitious pagan author can be corrected and nuanced by the continual interventions of the equally fictitious Christian translator and commentator.

In its content, which reflects a taste for encyclopedic learning shared by the writer with Isidore and Bede, the work offers a kind of variegated geographical and physiological description of the structure and shape of the visible cosmos. The description is supplemented by numerous philosophical teachings that are certainly derived from late antique models such as Chalcidius and Macrobius. These teachings have to do with the four elements, the hylomorphic composition of the corporeal order, the creation of paradise using the better parts of matter (similar to the way in which, in the *Timaeus*, the demiurge works in giving existence to the world-soul), the nature of invisible beings (angels and demons), and the ideal preexistence of all created things in the divine wisdom. The criticisms, complements, and observations of presbyter Jerome seek constantly to bring the teachings of Ethicus and his masters into conformity with biblical cosmology as interpreted in line with the Fathers. Thus the fundamental point of the work proves once again to be a concern to recover whatever of value and usefulness for human knowledge of truth had been acquired by ancient seekers, and to do so while purifying it of the inevitable errors caused by an ignorance of revelation.

The writings of Virgilius Grammaticus and the *Cosmography* of Ethicus Ister cannot be traced back directly to authors writing in the monastic world. Even if, however, we leave aside their documented circulation in pre-Carolingian Benedictine centers, it is certain that the cultural enterprise that inspired them was the same as that which, decade after decade and with ever-increasing effectiveness, guided both the curiosity with which monks probed the texts of classical paganism in search of material that would improve their understanding of Scripture, and their scrupulous adherence to the religious teachings of the Fathers. On the other hand, the better representatives of monastic spirituality were aware of and concerned about the fact that the ignorance of churchmen was a defect that could become a dangerous source of even doctrinal errors and that this ignorance could be checked only by increasing their liberal knowledge.

Witness to this consciousness of the essential role of education in the formation of monks can be seen in an unusual episode in the life of Wynfrith (d. 754). The latter was an English monk who, after taking the Latin name of Boniface, oversaw a widespread evangelizing activity, under the control of the papal see, in halfheartedly Christian or still-pagan areas of eastern France and Saxony. When Boniface saw the signs of a serious cultural backwardness in the clergy of Austrasia, he wrote to Pope Zacharias (d. 752) for ideas on what to do to stem the plague of baptisms administered with the scandalous formula: "In the name of the Father, the *Daughter*, and the Holy Spirit." We know the pope's answer: It was not necessary to repeat these baptisms, nor should Boniface fear the spread of a new dreadful heresy; it was, however, absolutely necessary to compel the ignorant prelates responsible for such errors to study grammar.

D. BEATUS OF LIÉBANA AND AMBROSE AUTPERT

There was, then, almost at the dawn of the Carolingian renaissance an as yet unachieved balance between the most authentic spiritual motivations of monastic life and the monks' quest for a fundamental but indispensable literary preparation. This prompted some isolated learned monks to urge on the Christian people a decisive return to the model of cultural experience provided by the Fathers of the Church. In Asturia, one of the few parts of the Iberian Peninsula that had remained free of the rapid Islamic occupation at the beginning of the seventh century, this goal inspired a monk, Beatus of Liébana (d. 798), who derived from it a strong impulse toward his own theological development.

Beatus possessed a high degree of exegetical skill as well as refined powers of rhetorical expression. He conducted an impassioned campaign against Felix, bishop of Urgel, and Elipandus, archbishop of Toledo, both of them representatives of the Mozarabic clergy (that is, of the Christian community that was struggling in the regions controlled by Arabic overlords). He attacked them because they were spreading an adoptionist christological doctrine, which claimed that the man Jesus could not be regarded as the true Son of the Father (an attribute proper to the divine nature of the Word) but only as an adoptive son.

Beatus' explicit aim was to avoid any weakening of the faith taught by the Fathers, a faith that was true precisely insofar as it was one in the organic structure of its dogmas and was shared by the entire people of Christ. In fact, for people separated by borders and difficult conditions or isolated in hermitages (the only possible refuges from the storms of history), only the sharing of a common faith could in fact be the way to the true salvation ensured by Christ. Just as multiplicity and division had entered the world with the sin of Adam, so too redemption was possible only if human beings returned to the moral and spiritual unity offered by a common participation in the same understanding of the mysteries of the faith. In response, then, to "novelty" and "diversity," which according to the unanimous agreement of the Fathers lead to heresy and are heresy's marks, it was necessary to put at the service of the faith the liberal education the Fathers themselves had already used against heretics in order to ensure the unity and cohesion of the authentic religious and cultic tradition.

The same exhortation to uniformity in the understanding of the faith pervades Beatus of Liébana's best-known work, his monumental commentary on the Apocalypse, which is marked by powerful images aimed at producing an emotional involvement of its readers. This work was destined to have great success and become widely read during the ensuing centuries. Its success was due not only to the power of its allegorical interpretations, which were enhanced by solid rhetorical skills, but also to the beauty and effectiveness of the painted images that often accompanied the work in sumptuous codexes. These miniatures gave the early Middle Ages a valuable tool for the preaching of theological truth, namely, a visual element and symbolic language.

Ambrose Autpert (d. 784), a monk of San Vincenzo al Volturno in south central Italy, likewise bore witness, again in a commentary on the Apocalypse, to a similar aspiration for the development of a spiritual philosophy. This was a philosophy springing not from a denial but from an anagogical transcending of the natural limits of a mind that, though meant to contemplate the highest truths, must labor here to detach itself from the easy but fruitless consideration of this world's outward appearances. Justification of the need to provide monasteries with authentic centers for the intellectual training and moral strengthening of monks was to be found in the fact that an intensive and progressive intellectual preparation of monks had as its role to accompany them on their necessary cognitive ascent to spiritual realities.

In his short moral work *The Struggle between the Vices and the Virtues* Autpert issues a strong call for such preparation. He also takes the occasion here to condemn the custom of itinerant monasticism. This, he says, robs the development of individuals vowed to interior meditation of the stability and continuity that only life in a monastery ensures as the foundation both of spiritual growth and of the desired solid culture. Only here, in the spiritual training ground of a monastic community with its convergence of sacred and secular education, will soldiers of Christ find themselves called to a constant quest for truth that will never be completed in the present life. Yet this quest is the only authentic "pilgrimage" (*peregrinatio*), one that is entirely interior and leads the human person to the happiness of paradise.

According to Ambrose Autpert, the model of such an unceasing human longing to search unwearyingly for an authentic knowledge of the faith is the Virgin Mary, in homage to whom he preached two well-received sermons. After having experienced in her own body the fullness of the deepest mystery of the faith, namely, the Incarnation, Mary continued to contemplate it with a complete openness of mind but also with the absolute certainty that she could not comprehend it. At this time the birth of a new, closely-knit cultural world was at hand, a world about to issue from the successful restoration of the empire under Charlemagne. Autpert's open proclamation of the irrepressibility and, at the same time, the inevitable incompleteness of human knowledge in face of the fullness of truth believed by faith seems to have been meant as a clear and effective bulwark against excesses. But it was aimed also at dull-witted abridgements of the dynamic compenetration of absolute faith and the rigorous use of reason, a compenetration fully documented in the wisdom of the Church Fathers.

5. The Greek East from Justinian to the Second Council of Nicaea

A. THE SIXTH CENTURY AND JOHN PHILOPONUS

In the Latin West learned individuals were committed to the defense and recovery of the classical and patristic roots on which the rebirth of a past spiritual world depended. In the Greek regions of the Mediterranean, on the other hand, the institutions of imperial Rome continued to rule public life in a relatively stable manner. Within the borders of the empire cultural life, too, could be described as a continuation of the late antique Roman tradition that was still fed, as it had been in the time of Constantine the Great, by the dynamic collaboration of Roman jurisprudence, the Christian religion, and classical Greek philosophy. These several components tended to be combined in a unified outlook in the works of the authors most representative of the sixth century. On the other hand, the balance of the theologico-speculative synthesis they tried to bring about on that basis was unstable and always threatened by the twists and turns of internal discussions and controversies.

The representatives of the ecclesiastical hierarchy acquired increasingly extensive power. The final claims of the teachers of philosophy and jurisprudence to an intellectual autonomy vanished due to the harsh legislation promulgated by Justinian (emperor from 527 to 565). In 529 he issued edicts restricting the freedom of pagans to teach; these led as a matter of course to the closing of the Neoplatonic school in Athens. In contrast, the rival school of Alexandria enjoyed greater freedom from politico-religious limitations, due in part to its position in an area of strategic importance for the reconquest of Vandal Africa. As a result, the conservatism of the pagan philosophers there was also less radical.

In addition, once the tensions of preceding centuries had been assuaged (these culminated in 415 with the murder of Hypatia, the learned daughter of Theon the mathematician, by fanatical supporters of patriarch Cyril), Alexandria gradually became a tolerant center of studies that was marked by the coexistence and contrast between pagan and Christian theology. In fact, numerous Christian intellectuals studied at the school of Hierocles, a pagan. Among these was Aeneas (d. 594), founder of a school of rhetoric and philosophy in Gaza. In a treatise titled *Theophrastus or the Immortality of the Soul* he defended some fundamental Christian positions on the basis of a strange syncretistic combination of Hellenic philosophies: the soul is immortal because, as Plato taught, it is an autonomously subsisting substance, but it is also, with Aristotle, the formal principle of the body, the resurrection of which it ensures by retaining after death the ability to put the various parts back together. On the other hand, the same writer refuted the idea of the eternity of the world by using the Stoic argument that the world is composed of heterogeneous parts that are subject to becoming and destined to break up.

At Alexandria, again, John the Grammarian (d. 574), the greatest Christian thinker of the sixth century, studied at the school of Neoplatonist Ammonius of

Hermia; John was nicknamed Philoponus ("lover of fatigue"), probably because of his extensive production. He did in fact write many commentaries on Aristotle's works on physics and logic, two philosophical treatises on *The Eternity of the World* (one against Proclus in 529 and one against Aristotle), a work on *The Making of the World*, mathematical writings, and theological treatises.

The special mark of Philoponus' speculative synthesis is his constant concern to give a correct Christian interpretation of the teaching of the great philosophers of the past, and of Aristotle in particular. He achieves this interpretation by means of rational tests of their teachings, tests inspired by their own thought. For example, the idea of creation, which is revealed by Scripture but at which the philosophers could not arrive because it is not deducible from experience, can be introduced with complete logical coherence into Aristotelean physics and even makes it possible to avoid some insoluble aporias connected with the eternity of matter.

The thesis on the eternity of the world can likewise be refuted on the basis of Aristotelean principles: if the world is spatially finite inasmuch as spatiality springs from extension, then it is also temporally finite because temporality is its very life. In the same perspective, and anticipating to some extent the late medieval theory of *impetus* (the energy by which a body moves), Philoponus suggests correcting the mechanicism of Aristotelean physics by explaining the movement of projectiles as a causal relationship between mover and moved; this makes it possible to trace every movement back to the efficient causality of God, whose provident motor energy presides over the entire life of the created world.

But in this initial phase of the Byzantine effort to synthesize philosophy and theology, the limits beyond which it was not permissible to push, the rational interpretation of the mysteries of faith were not yet well defined, and logical rigor applied to the reading of dogmas could lead to solutions irreconcilable with the orthodox tradition. Thus the identification of *ousia* (essence, substance) with *physis* (nature) led John Philoponus to regard "nature" as a universal (a genus) and, since each individual can participate in only one nature, to come close to the Monophysite position. At least, this was what he was accused of by Leontius of Byzantium (d. ca. 543), a theologian inspired by Neoplatonism and a supporter of Justinian's religious policy. It is worth noting how these crisscrossing discussions led to recourse to the logical definition of the meaning of the theological terms involved; this process shows some unusual similarities to the method followed by Boethius in his short works a few decades earlier in the West.

B. THE SEVENTH CENTURY AND MAXIMUS THE CONFESSOR

This philosophically based search for terminological accuracy was further emphasized in the following centuries, due in part to the spread of the writings of Pseudo-Dionysius (whose appearance in Byzantine religious history goes back to the early decades of the sixth century). For, as we said earlier, these writings were marked throughout by the search for an effective speculative synthesis between the dogmas of the faith and the most solid doctrinal positions reached by the thinkers of antiquity. A first successful implementation of this program can be seen in the theological works of Maximus the Confessor (d. 662/663).

Maximus was representative of the aristocrats of Constantinople who withdrew into monastic life in northern Africa. He was among the most indefatigable opponents of Monotheletism, the doctrine that claimed that in Christ there was but a single personal will. This teaching was favored by Emperor Heraclius because it was useful in reaching a compromise with Monophysitism, but it was condemned as heretical by Pope Martin I at a Lateran synod in 649 because it implied that the human nature of the Redeemer was less than complete.

Maximus supported the condemnation and was imprisoned by Constans II, nephew and successor of Heraclius; he was then exiled to Transcaucasia and suffered the mutilation of his tongue and right hand (whence his title as a "confessor," that is, of the faith). His most mature works date from his African period and were devoted to the complicated exposition of a theological system of a christocentric kind. He wrote various exegetical and ascetical treatises; also worth mentioning are the *Ambigua* or *Disputed Points* addressed to John and the *Questions* addressed to Thalassius, works that offer a coherent clarification of theological problems arising, respectively, from Scripture and from the writings of Gregory of Nazianzus (the "theologian" par excellence in the Byzantine world); the *Mystagogy*, an explanation of the liturgical symbols and mysteries of the church; and an explanation of the Our Father.

In Maximus' thought the perfect synthesis of divine and human natures in the Incarnation is the center of the history of the cosmos. This began with the creation of multiplicity by God, who is perfect Monad and perfect Triad, and is destined to end in the return to Unity of every division and every imperfection, a return that will at the same time bring the actuation of all creaturely potentialities. On the basis of a prudent synthesis of Platonism and Aristoteleanism Maximus gives an optimistic description of the movement of everything created toward the eschatological completion of the redemption wrought by Christ; this completion at the end of time will not exclude any element in the entire reality of the cosmos and, in particular, any element of the human being.

As Maximus sees it, all the elements, both material and spiritual, of the created world are present in the natural makeup of the human being, who is composed of a body and a soul that is at once an autonomously existing substance and the formative principle and mover of the body. Without losing its own substantial simplicity, the soul works to produce activity and knowledge throughout the hierarchy of vital and spiritual functions (vegetative and nutritive, sensible, imaginative, rational, intellectual). By taking flesh in a complete human nature, the Word began a historical process whereby the whole of creation is reunited with the divine. This process takes place in a series of steps: from the liberation of individual persons from the passions and the perfecting of their virtues and all their higher capacities to the universal reabsorption of matter by pure spirit, and on to the final reunification of creatures, through the Word, with the ineffable perfection of the trinitarian mystery.

C. THE EIGHTH CENTURY:
THE QUESTION OF IMAGES AND JOHN DAMASCENE

A new crisis affecting the delicate balance of Byzantine theology and the relations of Byzantium with the Roman church arose out of the attack on the veneration of sacred images, triggered in 726 by an edict of Leo III the Isaurian prohibiting the practice. The hardening of the imperial position in a series of forceful steps for the destruction of images (iconoclasm) was due to political considerations but also to the desire to suppress excesses in popular devotion to icons (*iconodulia*), since these increased the power and independence of the monastic world. The synod of Hieria, held in 754 with the support of Constantine V Copronymus, son of Leo III, gave a first victory to iconoclasm and unleashed a real persecution of recalcitrant monks.

Patriarch Germanus of Constantinople seems to have made himself the spokesman of moderate theologians, whose most natural reaction was an attempt to follow the lead of philosophy and introduce a clear definition of the meaning of the objects involved in the controversy, such as *image* and *prototype* (that is, the sacred reality represented by the image), as well as of the kinds of veneration shown to such objects. Thus there was *latreia* (worship), which is reserved to God alone, but also *proskynesis* (obeisance, act of reverence, veneration), which the defenders of *iconodulia* maintained could be paid to images.

The iconoclastic crisis had a first conclusion after the death of Leo IV in 780 when the emperor's mother, Irene, adopted a policy of tolerance toward the advocates of veneration of images in order to broaden acceptance of her assumption of power as regent in the name of her second son, Constantine VI. In this action she had the support of the monks, Patriarch Tarasius, and the Roman see. This was the situation until the convocation in 787 of the second Council of Nicaea (which was regarded as ecumenical because of the participation of the legates of Pope Hadrian I); this council proclaimed the legitimacy of *iconodulia*, which was always to be distinguished from adoration, this being reserved to God alone.

The spacious and coherent theological works of John of Damascus, or John Damascene (d. ca. 750), were produced during the most violent years of the controversy. To the latter he made his own contribution in the form of three treatises in defense of *iconodulia*, his primary concern being to show that the cult of images was part of the earliest Christian tradition. In fact, the whole of

Damascene's theological reflection, published in a large number of wide-ranging writings, is permeated by a constant concern to see religious controversies in the perspective of a uniform religious wisdom that is backed by continuous references to the scriptural foundations and the teachings of the Fathers. This attitude and approach were justified chiefly by the fact that John lived his life in Greek-speaking regions that had been for several decades under Islamic rule—first in Damascus, capital (from 656) of the Umayyad Dynasty, and then in the monastery of St. Sabas near Jerusalem. His plan to reinforce traditional theological wisdom with the help of a critical competence in philosophy was consciously aimed at rooting more deeply in himself and in his readers a sense of belonging to the universal Christian community and avoiding the impending danger of religious dispersion and cultural breakdown.

This ideal also inspired John's major work, *The Fountain of Knowledge*, which was written after 743 and is divided into three parts corresponding to the ascending hierarchy of knowledges that lead to God. The first part is a *Dialectic* (also cited as "Philosophical Chapters"), which explains the rules developed by the philosophers for avoiding equivocations and giving deductive coherence to the natural sciences; this meant essentially the teachings of Aristotelean logic, explained in the order established by the Neoplatonic commentators on the *Organon*.

The second part is a treatise on *Heresies*, that is, a catalogue of one hundred chapters (to a large extent taken verbatim from Epiphanius of Salamis) explaining the errors that can arise from an uncontrolled application of rational norms to the interpretation of dogmas. It is noteworthy that the final heresy treated was also the most recent, namely the religion of Islam.

The third and final section is devoted to an *Explanation of the Faith*, which Burgundione of Pisa translated into Latin in 1115 under the title of *The Orthodox Faith*. This section is again divided into one hundred chapters and offers a synthesis of the thought of the Fathers. The synthesis is organized into a series of themes, beginning with the unity and trinity of God, passing then to the nature of the cosmos, with an extensive section on cosmology (invisible world and angels, then the visible world) and anthropology (with a good deal of space given to psychological doctrines), and moving on to the theory of redemption, which is explained by following the fundamental passages of the Creed.

While not possessing any originality or any real speculative depth, the work of John Damascene has a more than secondary importance in the history of theological thought because of the formal comprehensiveness and accuracy in compilation that mark his systematic approach. From the viewpoint of methodology, John's certainty about the ancillary role of philosophical proficiency in relation to faith (as ensured by the concordant testimony of the Fathers) allows him to draw freely on the patristic sources and at times even to produce on his own a series of rational arguments that prepare the way for the explanation of dogmas. Some examples: notes on anthropology and psychology, valuable for explaining some important but unclear aspects of the doctrine of the Incarnation; rational postulates, presented as universally accepted by the wise, such as the government of the cosmos by the Supreme Good, which is indispensable in asserting against the Manichees the universal goodness of the created world despite the seeming existence of evil.

II. Carolingian Unanimity

> Charles had recently begun to reign over the territories of the West and to concentrate all power in his own hands. Meanwhile, the study of letters had almost everywhere been completely forgotten, with the result that the worship of the true godhead was languishing. Then, one day, there landed on the shores of Gaul, along with a group of Breton merchants, two *Scoti* from Ireland, individuals whose knowledge of letters, both secular and sacred, was unparalleled. Having no visible merchandise to display, their custom was to address the crowds that hastened to them in the hope of acquiring something. "If anyone wants wisdom, come to us to acquire it, for in fact it is from us that you can buy it." The news of this spread so quickly and with such an outcry that people who were either amazed or convinced that the two were madmen brought it to the attention of Charles, who had always been an ardent lover of wisdom. He then received the men and kept them with him for a while. Then, when he was obliged to go off on his wars of conquest, he ordered one of the two to remain in Gaul and devote himself to the education of young boys, some from the nobility, others of less high rank, and still others of lowly birth. The other he sent to Italy and put him in charge of an important monastery near Pavia, where he might welcome all those desirous of learning.

We owe this first version of the story about the beginnings of the renaissance to Notker Balbo, a monk of St. Gall, who recorded it in his *The Deeds of Charles* toward the end of the ninth century. By that time the imperial civilization established by Charlemagne and the great period of cultural growth that accompanied it had already shown signs of a first, untimely exhaustion. In later times this story was to be fused with another cultural legend connected with the epic of Charlemagne. The later story, showing little respect for real historical lapses of time, made the founding of the University of Paris the work of some eminent representatives of the community of scholars involved in Charles' political activity: Alcuin, Rhabanus Maurus, Claude of Turin, and John Scotus. All four (still according to the legend) were disciples of Bede, sent by the latter to the continent in order to complete the "transfer of studies" (*translatio studiorum*) that had started in Athens, then passed to Rome, and now reached France by way of the British Isles.

These mythical stories make clear the close connection between the "transfer of studies" and the "transfer of imperial power" (*translatio imperii*), their purpose being to provide the best ideological justification of the latter. That is, Charles had the right to call himself "emperor" of the Romans because he had created a new political and religious unification of the western peoples and was approved by his solemn coronation in Rome on Christmas night, 800. But this authority was never dissociated either in his mind or in historical fact from his plan to promote a solid cultural education, especially of churchmen (that they might then become his agents in dealing with the other sectors of the population) and thereby to promote also the acceptance by his subjects of a unifying consciousness of being participants in the ongoing political renewal.

Spiritual unity had been the foundation and source of juridical unity in the political thinking of the Carolingian military leaders ever since the first exploits of Charles Martel, victor over the Arabs at Poitiers (732) as head of a military and religious coalition of Christian fighters, and of Pepin the Short, crowned king of the Franks (in 754) by Pope Stephen II in exchange for his support of the church against the territorial usurpations of the Lombards.

Finally, in the case of Charlemagne, the official reestablishment of the Christian empire, based on the model given by Constantine, was explicitly connected with the intention of bringing about a uniformity in morals and ideas among his subjects, this being ensured by faith in revealed truth more than by any other means of persuasion. But if this "unanimity" (the term often used by Alcuin of York, Charles' cultural adviser, teacher, and personal friend) were to be translated into a real and sincere subordination of minds to the structures erected by a common set of beliefs, it had to be first and foremost a unanimity of the spiritual order and therefore had to spring from a spontaneous and positive voluntary acceptance. Such an acceptance could never be ensured solely by military might and political coercion. In other words, the force leading to such an acceptance would certainly have to be a cultural and religious education.

1. Institutional Reform and Cultural and Religious Rebirth

A telling episode during the successful military campaigns by which Charles rebuilt the empire shows that the intellectuals who worked with him had a keen awareness of their own irreplaceable task as builders and defenders of spiritual unity. In 786, after an exhausting war, Charles succeeded in subduing pagan Saxony and carrying the banners of Christianity into territories never reached by Roman civilization. He also imposed baptism on the entire population, threatening the unwilling with death.

At that point Alcuin wrote the king a courageous letter of reproach in which he criticized the harsh reign of terror thus established in those distant regions. It was neither ethical nor evangelical (he said), and moreover it was useless, to try to force the name of Christ on the barbarians by means of the sword and bloodshed; conversion gained solely by fear would never last. Instead, Charles ought to build schools in the Germanic countries and send scholars there to teach pagans the arts and philosophy as a means of explaining to them the words of Scripture. Only by educating and persuading the rational faculty that all human beings possess and urging them to recognize the truth communicated by the Gospel, to learn it and find in it the complete fulfillment of all their expectations, would it be possible to bring to life a truly Christian earthly kingdom that would last through the centuries.

The deep humanism that inspired these ideas is the real ideological foundation of the organizational solidity of Carolingian civilization. By means of successive documents and edicts (capitularies) Charles played an active part, from the very beginning of his reign, in promoting and regulating scholastic institutions and advancing the education of monks and churchmen, but also of laypersons possessing jurisdictional responsibilities (it is enough to mention, among the best known of his edicts, the *General Admonition* of 789 and the *Letter on the Cultivation of Letters*).

These documents maintain that a liberal education is a necessary, though not sufficient, foundation for the participation of humanity in the redemption of Christ and, therefore, an indispensable help in consolidating the new political system, which is expressly seen in the context of an essentially religious mission. The restoration of the empire is thereby closely bound up with a rebirth of culture and religion, this being initially based chiefly on the recovery of the literary, scientifico-philosophical, and theological tradition of the past, to the extent that traces and evidence of this tradition could be found on the shelves of impoverished civic archives and the still-small monastic libraries.

It is easy to see how this search for ancient evidences, continuing as it were the effort of thinkers of the Romano-barbaric period to recover their classical roots, was initially directed chiefly toward concise encyclopedic abbreviations of knowledge (Cassiodorus, Isidore, Bede, etc.). The latter, moreover, continued to be used as models of the new handbooks devoted to the liberal arts by the early Carolingian teachers.

Then, little by little, the information found in the late antique manuals and collections became the starting point for more comprehensive readings and led to a search for and retrieval of the ancient or late antique texts from which the manuals were derived. From brief notes on the teaching of grammar scholars went back to the works of Donatus and Priscian; a deepening interest in logic brought into circulation once more Boethius' translations of the initial works of the *Organon*; interest in rhetoric sent readers back to the direct study of the works of Cicero and Quintilian; scattered bits of numerology and cosmology led to the renewed reading of Boethius' monographs on the quadrivium and the cosmologico-physiological treatises of Macrobius and Chalcidius. Literary taste became more refined and imitation of the classical models was practiced once again: Virgil and Ovid, Martial and Terence became popular once more, as did the moral contribution of Seneca and, to a lesser degree, the physiological work of Lucretius.

However, given the conscious premise that these readings always had as their ultimate goal the knowledge and understanding of the Bible, an even greater, indeed essential importance was given to the recovery and spread of the works of the Fathers of the Church. These were carefully read and studied, copied and often anthologized, whether in florilegia ("collections of flowers") organized by subject, or in new continuous commentaries on the sacred books that began with the erudite stitching together of extracts from Augustine, Ambrose, Jerome, Gregory the Great, and Bede.

Beginning in the early years of the ninth century an impressive number of sacred and secular manuscripts filled the libraries of the larger abbeys, bearing witness to the quantitative but also qualitative increase in intellectual activity in the empire. Charles' exhortation to open and organize study centers was immediately answered, especially by the Benedictine monasteries. But schools for advanced juridical and literary studies also came quickly into existence at the cathedrals in cities, though the population there was relatively small. Moreover, a "palace school" or "court school" was established at the itinerant court (or residence) of Charles, who liked to surround himself with masters who taught and carried on dialogues, including with him and his friends and relatives, on literature, the liberal arts, philosophy, and religion.

These same scholars then formed an "academy" of intellectuals with the ruler as its center; they were partly serious, partly jesting, and hid themselves behind the names of ancient poets and men of letters. This cultural world was naturally inclined to dialogue and cultural interchange, which was a source of growth in knowledge. Extensive learned correspondences attest to the exchange of scientific information, moral advice, and religious ideas between teachers and students. In addition, dialogue was often the literary genre preferred in composing new compendia of liberal wisdom, as Alcuin in particular did for explicitly pedagogical purposes. Thus the monotonous handbooks of late antiquity were revised in the form of lively series of rapid questions and lapidary answers; this form was more effective for the direct transmission of information and was better suited for learning by memory. Charlemagne himself, the first student of the empire, is often depicted in these dialogues in the guise of a diligent though educated learner who questions the teacher and in turn reacts satisfactorily to the latter's queries.

With this real consolidation of basic knowledge in place, the political program of integrating races and customs, no matter how varied, into the imperial unity could be introduced and bear fruit. As in the legend of the "merchants of wisdom," the men of letters who came to Charlemagne's court had been trained in the most distant regions of Europe; they came from the islands of the north, like Alcuin; from the Iberian Peninsula, like Theodulf of Orleans; from Bavaria, like Leidrad of Lyons; from Italy, like Peter of Pisa and Paulinus of Aquileia; and from the Lombard south, like historian Paul the Deacon.

The well-educated Carolingian world thus had its origin in the confluence of many traditions. But this fact brought with it the necessity of planning energetic ways of intervening in order to ensure cohesiveness and solidity in the new system: linguistic unification through the improvement and spread of ecclesiastical Latin; uniformity in writing and spelling, achieved through the spread of a common form of writing that was clear, legible, and elegant; the philological revision and spread of a common text of the Bible; uniformity in liturgical practices; the imposition of a single method of liturgical computation in order to establish a single calendar. In addition—and this was of more than secondary importance—a careful moral and organizational reform of the secular clergy and a compulsory adoption of the *Rule* of Benedict in all monastic communities were successfully carried out.

In summary, a classicizing culture, the unity of the faith, and a moral and institutional reform were the closely interwoven load-bearing elements of the renewal of western Christianity. It is obvious, therefore, that the idea of "unanimity," on which the entire construction of the new Christian kingdom was based, had a fundamental theological dimension. The task of the emperor was to form and consolidate a community of believers in which, under the harmonious leadership of the episcopate and the military aristocracy, there might come to pass, through a conscious agreement on common goals, a unity of kingdom and church, or, in other words, of the Romano-Carolingian political entity and the mystical body of the apostolic tradition. The attainment of these common goals was subordinated to the active achievement by the Christian people of a complete convergence of faith and reason, of truth revealed and believed and truth naturally grasped by the humanity that, as with each rational individual, is the primary characteristic and distinctive mark of every subject who respects laws and common moral standards.

Boethius in his *Consolation* looked back with longing to the philosopher-king of the ancient Platonic tradition, while Alcuin, following Boethius, expressly called that ideal to mind ("Happy those kingdoms in which philosophers reign and in which kings study philosophy!"). But in this new context the philosopher-king was also to be a priest-king (precedents: the David of the Bible and the historical Constantine), who would foster the knowledge of truth in his subjects by spreading the revealed word throughout his kingdom and seeing that it was heard there.

2. The Theological Wisdom of Charlemagne's Liegemen

A. TRADITION AND METHOD IN ALCUIN'S THEOLOGICAL WRITINGS

Alcuin of York (d. 804), who often used the pen name "Albinus," occasionally wrote, in some of his many *Letters*, about the intellectual understanding of the contents of revelation, although only in general terms. But never in his writings does he use the word "theology." At most we hear him speak of "wisdom" or "the true philosophy"; in this he resembled almost all of his contemporaries who, like himself, were more or less influenced by the example of Augustine.

True, at the beginning of his *Dialectic* or *Logic*, a compendium of late antique logic, where he is copying verbatim the division of philosophy given by Isidore in his *Etymologies*, he writes "theology" instead of "theoretical" (philosophy) (but that may have been the reading in the manuscript of Isidore he had before him). But this did not clash completely with his overall conception of knowledge, because in his view the purest philosophical knowledge is always ordered to "the contemplation of heavenly realities."

An example is given in a short work in dialogue form that bears the expressive title *The True Philosophy* and is intended as an introduction to his slender manuals on the seven arts (one of which is the *Dialectic*). Alcuin here describes human wisdom as an incarnation of immutable and eternal truth in this temporal and transient world; like Christ the Word, of which this wisdom is an image, it participates in both natures, the human and the divine. As such, wisdom is the ultimate goal of human knowledge and action. In addition, as Alcuin reminds Charles in a fine letter of consolation on the occasion of the death of his wife, Liutgard, it is the source of consolation and happiness for all human beings because it assures the soul that it will possess the pleasure proper to the angels and saints, which springs from their union through knowledge with the supreme Good. But Alcuin's wisdom, which owes a heavy debt to Boethius' depiction of Philosophy, is also human because it has slowly taken form through the ages due to the laborious studies of the founders of the arts as they endeavored to organize their systems of rules and their classifications of the kinds of knowledge.

Divine Wisdom is the Logos himself, the eternal source of the perfect rationality that marks all of creation. As Alcuin says in another letter to Charles, in which he takes up an Augustinian idea to which we referred earlier, it is therefore evident that "the philosophers were not the creators, but the discoverers of the arts." In creating, God determined the laws proper to the natural world, and the sages of antiquity "discovered them in nature" and codified the truth thus grasped, though limited and partial, in the teachings of the seven disciplines.

After Boethius, this was perhaps the first explicit revival in medieval thought of the Platonic-Augustinian idea that there is a cosmic order governed by the perfect rationality of the Word, which is reflected in the rules of thought and of the language expressing it, in numbers, proportions, and the harmony of sounds and the celestial bodies. To be philosophers meant, then, to know and understand the divine laws at work in creation and therefore to know the Word; in other words, it meant to be true theologians. Thus in Alcuin's manual, *Rhetoric and the Virtues*, when Charlemagne, wearing the robe of a disciple, asks what the difference is between the ancient philosophers and Christians, the author replies with the pithy remark: "Only baptism and faith."

The foundation that is Scripture gives human reason certainty about a knowledge that is then regulated by the classifications and argumentative formulations of the arts. This convergence guarantees the soul the possession of a true body of knowledge that in turn is the presupposition and means of its participation in the knowledge God has of himself and his work. To this essential cooperation between faith and the rational arts Alcuin himself bears witness in his own writings on theological subjects.

This is true in particular of works Alcuin published to support and carry further the attack of Beatus of Liébana on the Iberian adoptionists. In his capacity as spokesman for both the kingdom of Charlemagne and the church of Christ he makes the condemnation official in several works: a short *Answer to the Heresy of Felix*, a longer treatise in seven books, *Answer to Felix of Urgel*, and one in four books, *Answer to Elipandus of Toledo*. In all these works Alcuin cites a wide range of scriptural and patristic texts to show the "novelty" of the adoptionist doctrine in relation to the orthodox tradition and by that very fact its complete alienation from Christian truth. He then offers a series of rational arguments in order to show the absurd and erroneous consequences flowing from the supposedly doctrinal formulas Felix and Elipandus have introduced, thereby corrupting the true faith.

It is thus possible to discern, in the argumentative procedures adopted by Alcuin in support of orthodoxy, the emergence of the essential norms of a still-embryonic yet already clearcut theologico-speculative method. There is, to begin with, the invocation of Scripture, which has been entrusted to humanity just as a ruler sends out a delegation among his subjects in order to make his wishes known to them. Then there is the recourse to the Fathers, who combined their intense faith with a fully developed rational approach and on this twofold basis provided perfect examples of correct scriptural exegesis. Then, too, there is the comparison of results with the orthodox tradition, which was developed on the basis of patristic teaching and consolidated and defended down the centuries by the authority of the Roman church, with the support of the political authorities. Finally, there is the rational approach of the modern interpreter; this means the application first of the rules of logic and then of those of all the liberal arts, which make possible the stringent testing of orthodoxy in the case of new controversies caused by heretics or unbelievers.

Alcuin's last work was composed during the years of his withdrawal from public life (801–804), while he served as abbot of the monastery of Tours, and it is the most successful example of his theological method. The work is *Belief in the Holy Trinity* in three books. Here a paraphrastic explanation of the Christian creed, supported by a judicious but careful application of the rules of logic, leads the author on to sketch a summary and systematic picture of the overall contents of the orthodox faith and its principal parts (from Trinitarian doctrine to christology, and from redemption to eschatology). But Alcuin's method aims only at a first approach to orthodoxy and not at the penetration of the human soul into the mysterious depths of the faith, which can never be made the subject of fully intelligible and exhaustive definitions.

Consequently Alcuin says, with explicit reference to the cultural precedent given by the *Trinity* of Augustine (and, implicitly, that given by Boethius), that one thing must be made clear about all the forms used in the logical organization of a discourse (categories, distinctions between substance and accident or act and potency, the conversion of a proposition, or syllogistic deduction, and so on). This one thing is that whenever these are used in theological discourse as a help in interpretation (and not as positing conditions for the truth of dogma), they must to some extent surrender something of their demonstrative force and lose as least some measure of their formal rigor.

Human beings have learned the rules of science by studying the traces of the Creator in nature in order then to guide their rational procedures for searching out the truth in visible things. But these rules are altered and suffer changes in their stringency and in the conditions of their use when they are applied to searching out in Scripture the truth of those invisible and supernatural realities from which they are descended. From this twofold process of the descent of the truth of the arts from the truth of the Word and then of the return and transformation of their relative necessity into the absolute necessity of God is born a new knowledge that is theological truth, the loftiest form of knowledge, which allows the human being to draw near the perfect divine rationality, though without comprehending it.

B. Fridugisus of Tours and Alcuin's "Circle"

The charismatic personality of Alcuin the teacher made him the center of a group of disciples whose work as thinkers is only partially attested by direct documentation. These men put into practice, sometimes more boldly than did their teacher, the method of argumentation he endorsed in the area of theological discussion and demonstration.

The most notable of these disciples was Fridugisus (or Fredegisus) (d. 834), who succeeded Alcuin as head of the abbey of Tours. He wrote a short work titled *The Substance of Nothing and Darkness*, in which he sets out to impose on human language in all its applications, and therefore on Scripture, which uses human language, a strict dependence on the logical principle that to every substantive conveying a meaning there always corresponds a substantial reality.

Thus even the word "nothing" (*nihil*), which points to that out of which (*ex quo*) God brought all creatures into being, and the word "darkness" (*tenebrae*), which describes that which (*quid*) filled the universe prior to the creation of light, necessarily denote something real and existing. And if the words used to express these realities are negative in form (because "nothing" = non-being and "darkness" = non-light, that is, something real but different from the usual substantial being of creatures), the reason is that they certainly hide "something very important and meaningful," and therefore something not directly perceptible by natural human knowledge. If "nothing" has a meaning, as logic assures us it does, it must necessarily signify something that is, or, in other words, a "what is not" that *is* precisely "what is not." It would therefore be unreasonable to claim that "that-which-is-something is not something-that-is."

Because of this very lack of direct perceptibility Fridugisus does not further explain the nature of such a nothing-that-certainly-is-something. By doing so he leaves modern readers with the question of whether or not he is speaking of a preexistent matter such as that of which the classical philosophers had spoken. In any case, it remains true that the embryonic philosophy of language that inspires Fridugisus' line of argument is expressly supported by methodological principles, that is, by a balanced combination of the various kinds of information provided by the true authority and procedures practiced by true reason. The fundamental conviction guiding the writer's thinking is that the relationship between reason and faith, both of which are sources of truth, is so strong and reciprocal as to be circular. First reason and then faith are asked about this "nothing": the former says this "nothing" is something, and the latter teaches that everything has been created by God "from nothing," that is, that the "something" that "nothing" is precedes everything else not only chronologically but in importance and dignity.

When dealing with "darkness" Fridugisus proceeds in the opposite direction. He starts with the faith, that is, with Genesis, which says that the darkness preceded the light and that God differentiated the light from the darkness. He then confronts reason with this fact, and reason remarks that if the "darkness" is perceptible and as such can be given a name, then it must have a real existence.

A letter Charlemagne wrote to Dungal, abbot of Saint-Denis, asking about the correctness of Fridugisus' method bears witness to the puzzlement to which his short work must have given rise in some contemporary readers, especially because it excluded any possibility of submitting the words of Scripture to the allegorical interpretation that had been widely used and recommended by patristic exegetes. It is clear, however, that the question raised by *The Substance of Nothing and Darkness* was not simply a problem of exegesis, because in fact it raises for discussion the very delimitation of the right of logico-deductive reason to intervene in the area of knowledge covered by the authority of the faith.

Alongside this problem of the limits to be placed on rational method as applied to the faith there immediately arises a different problem: that of the possibility of using rational methods in dealing with theological subjects, but doing so *independently* of (that is, while prescinding from) the truth of the faith, although, of course, not in opposition to it.

That this further aspect of the matter was explicitly discussed by the first generation of Carolingian thinkers is shown by a collection of short texts that clearly depend directly on the teaching and personality of Alcuin. The texts are fragmentary, explicitly philosophical from the viewpoint of method, and brought together under the title *Statements*. They are anonymous except for two, the seventh and eighth, which are attributed respectively to Alcuin himself and to his immediate disciple Wizo, nicknamed Candidus. Historians on the whole agree that these unhomogeneous and fragmentary texts are evidence of the intellectual work that went on in "Alcuin's circle," so called. In practical terms the circle was a group of friends and disciples of the abbot of Tours who were testing the possibility of applying the autonomous demonstrative powers of reason to knowledge of the divine, but without reference to the Scriptures.

Among other shorter reflections on trinitarian doctrine and on the soul, all of them manifestly dependent on models found in Alcuin, a degree of interest attaches to two methods of demonstration that are to be seen in the third and fourth fragments. The aim here is to prove by purely rational arguments the necessity of acknowledging the existence of God, thereby confirming by logic and philosophy what is already made certain, at the level of simple faith, by the authority of revelation. These two early medieval examples of arguments demonstrating with necessity the existence of God are both inspired by the basic Pauline principle that the invisible reality of the divine can be known from visible creatures (Rom 1:20). The arguments are stringently based on logical skills available at the time, the same ones that are brought together in Alcuin's *Dialectic*. They make use, in particular, of the discursive and syllogistic development of an axiomatic and intuitive principle; in logical terms, they use an argument whose evidential character is directly and immediately present to the human intellect.

In the first case (the procedure attested in the third fragment), the starting point is certainty about the hierarchic organization of reality as a whole, following the model of the Porphyrian tree, according to which the higher levels include and govern the lower levels by bringing all the partial perfections of the latter to their completion. Thus simple being is perfected in the living being, and life, in turn, is perfected in intellectual knowledge. It is therefore legitimate to prolong this ascent by admitting a level of existence higher than that of the knowing soul (which is in itself imperfect); this will be the existence of a truly supreme and eternal being who does not depend on other still-higher perfections but governs the entire created cosmos and gives the soul the ability to govern the body.

Taking its cue from the type of dialogue Alcuin preferred, the fourth fragment is structured as a set of questions and answers. In an impressive anticipation of the procedure hallowed about two centuries later in the *Proslogion* of Anselm of Aosta, the argument is based this time on the indubitable self-evidential character of the true definition of God as "a good than which no other is better and a power than which no other is more powerful." The reasoning starts with the premise that if it is possible to find among existing realities one that corresponds to that definition, it will be proven that God exists. At this point (and paralleling what was done in the preceding text), the interlocutor is led by way of a hierarchized consideration of creation to accept that above and beyond the human intellect, which is the highest good and the highest power given us to know, there exists still another, which is the cause of all lesser things. This good being will necessarily be the best of all, or the supreme Good, and its power will be the greatest of all, or omnipotence, for otherwise we would have to admit that it depends on a still higher cause. But if such a perfect power can truly be thought of, then this being, which is God, must necessarily exist; for "if it did not exist, it would not be truly powerful."

C. THEOLOGICAL METHOD IN THE *LIBRI CAROLINI*

Also linked to the intellectual personality of Alcuin (we prescind from the problem of the author's identity) is another important instance of theological reflection in the first stage of the Carolingian period: namely, *The Capitulary on Images* or *Work against the Synod*, traditionally known as the *Carolingian Books*. Though the text is in fact a real theological treatise of an apologetic-polemical kind, written in a bombastic and redundant style and divided into four books, it presents itself formally, as indicated by the term *capitulare* (used in Frankish legislation), in the garb of a decree issued by the sovereign around 790 and having the force of law in all the territories of the empire.

The document represents an intervention in religious matters, having for its purpose to claim for the king and soon-to-be-emperor of the West the right to demand that his unchallengeable approval be required for the ratification of all episcopal, papal, and conciliar decrees about the true faith. On the basis of this principle Charlemagne issued the *Capitulary*, which repudiated the decrees, mentioned earlier, of the second Council of Nicaea in 787. His reason: in proclaiming the legitimacy of the veneration of images the Council relied on an agreement reached by Empress Irene and Pope Hadrian I without any consultation of the Frankish monarchy and its representatives. In view of the urgent need for official confirmation of Charlemagne's right to make himself arbiter and guarantor on matters of faith, the Frankish scholars were given the task of developing a text that would serve as a formal condemnation of both iconoclasm and iconodulism and propose a middle way between these two heresies. This middle way meant in practice a respectful esteem of images, not as objects of veneration but as a suitable means of raising the mind of the believer to supra-sensible reality through a sensible representation of it that is purely symbolic.

A still-not-completely settled historiographical debate has yielded various suggestions for the identification of the drafter of this text. Some have opted for Alcuin himself, because it is possible to find many stylistic and, above all, methodological parallels in his writings. Others prefer Theodulf of Orleans, who was in charge of a philological revision of the Bible on which numerous citations in the text seem to depend. In fact, it is probable that the text resulted from the collaborative efforts of a team of specialists; Alcuin and Theodulf may have been members of this team along with others among the more important representatives of the scholars at the court, who had been commissioned to compose a solid refutation of the teaching favorable to the veneration of images that the Council imposed.

The Frankish attack was shot through with the proud claim of a supposed cultural superiority of the West over the materialistic and figurative mentality of the Byzantines. Central to the attack was the idea, remotely Platonic in origin, of the incurable division between corporeity, which is deceitful, disordered, and fortuitous, and suprasensible reality, which is true and immutable. The uneducated oriental theologians maintained that they could attribute to sacred images, made though they were of ugly, corporeal matter, the absurd ability to mediate between the visible and the invisible. In fact, all material images are nothing but shadows of the truth, formed of corporeal elements in order to be used solely as imitations of the changeless. Only when understood in this way can they be offered for the attention of the simple faithful, and then only after careful religious instruction.

The repeated urging of the text to activate the "inner eye," the eye of the mind that does not let itself be deceived by corporeal appearances, is in fact inspired by the Platonic principle that like knows like. That is, only the intellectual soul that is created in the image of God (and certainly not bodily sensation, which limits itself to the exterior aspect of images) is able to draw near, even if imperfectly, to the suprasensible reality.

The *Carolingian Books* constantly apply these doctrinal principles in the course of a kind of analytical commentary on the canons of Nicaea, which are more or less faithfully translated into Latin. The commentary is supported by a complicated tangle of arguments directed by the rules of the liberal arts and especially logic; there is a continual contrapuntal appeal to the "authority of Scripture" and the "rational investigation of the truth." The doctrine of the predicables and categories, the square of opposed propositions, topical arguments and various kinds of syllogisms, as well as procedures of a grammatical, rhetorical, arithmological, and mathematical kind—all these are interwoven without letup. Their purpose, however, is not to demonstrate, but only to point to the truth, which, by prejudgment and without any uncertainty, is taken to be identical with the assertions of the true faith, that is, what has always been taught by the western tradition and the Roman church.

3. Systematization and Speculative Advances in the Age of Louis the Pious

As early as the first decade following the proclamation of the empire in the West, a generational change brought to the footlights of the educated Latin world the names of new thinkers who were ready not only to accept the wisdom inherited from their teachers but also to adjust it through verification and experiment. This development of the skills and methodologies of scholars, men of letters, and religious men profited also from a greater degree of distance and autonomy from the centers of political power. With this was combined a cultural decentralization that increasingly began to involve both the great abbeys and the major episcopal sees. A development of this kind also led inevitably to the rise of increasingly sharper kinds of ideological debates; not infrequently, however, controversies on religious and philosophical subjects concealed reasons for personal dissent and conflicts of a political or administrative kind. Above all, therefore, the reign of Charlemagne's son, Louis the Pious (814–840), during which administrative division became progressively more extensive due to the rise of a tendency to political disaggregation among the regions making up the empire, also saw an increasingly hostile confrontation between the various tendencies and approaches in theological thought.

A. AGOBARD OF LYONS AND THE EARLY THEOLOGICAL DEBATES WITHIN THE CAROLINGIAN WORLD

One of the most productive controversialists of this period was Agobard (d. 840), a Spaniard called to Lyons by bishop Leidrad, whose pupil and then successor he became. He wrote numerous works on a variety of theological subjects; these often corresponded to actions he undertook in an official capacity. He made himself the spokesman for a balanced conception of rational reflection on dogma and was sincerely opposed both to an exaggerated raising of intellectual problems concerning the faith and to the excesses of naïve devotion found among less educated believers, devotion that came perilously close to barbarian superstition.

The book with the explicit title *Answer to the Objections of Fridugisus* belongs to the first of these areas. In it the author openly attacks the methods of Abbot Fridugisus of Tours by answering some of the criticisms the latter had made of him during a controversy that had evidently been going on for some time, but of whose early stages we are not directly informed. Still, what we read in this text is enough to help us understand the importance and significance of the conflict between the two men. Without making any direct reference to the question of the substantial character of nothing and darkness, the bishop of Lyons expressly criticizes the presumptuousness shown by Fridugisus when he subjects the language of Scripture to insistent and useless justifications of a logico-grammatical kind.

Of interest, too, is that Agobard did not scorn to enter directly into the heart of the controversy with a temperate but shrewd rational criticism aimed at showing the inconsistencies in his adversary's overly rigid and subtle arguments. In this way Agobard made clear his own certainty that error does not spring from the meeting of faith and reason as such, but rather from the lack of moderation in conducting the encounter.

For example, the abbot of Tours says that "God" is something different from "truth," because the sense of the nouns is differently defined. Agobard, however, appealing to the authority of Augustine who maintains the identity of truth and God, replies that the meaning of words is never rigidly fixed by some divine law and that it can even vary according to the use made of it, provided the use is correct. The meaning of the word "truth," therefore, can be narrowed or broadened and, because there can be many truths, one can use the word in its broadest sense and say that "God, too, is truth."

In like manner Fridugisus maintains that it is erroneous to say that there could have been "Christians" before the coming of Christ; his reason for this claim is that the name of a class of beings can be true and therefore predicable only once the founder of the class is in existence. Agobard urges him, here again, to recognize that the requirements of the faith are more truthful than the rules set down by the arts and that, since the name of Christ is eternally true, the holiness of the Old Testament patriarchs and prophets can suitably be described as "Christian." In short, precisely because the application of the logico-grammatical method to theological truth can be useful for the growth of the faith, it is expedient always to use the method under the guidance of the light of revelation and to do so case by case. It is truth that makes the rules of the arts acceptable, and not the other way around.

Agobard thus claims to be the true heir of Alcuin's method, which was based on moderation and balance, as compared with the excessive concern of Fridugisus for technical procedures. In making this claim Agobard also associates himself with the rational humanism of the common teacher of all the Carolingians. Thus, in his work *The Baptism of Converted Jews*, he maintains that a wise Jew who has been baptized can be honored as a teacher even by Christians.

At the same time he regards it as suitable to fall back on his moderate rationalism only when this is indispensable. For example, when in 818, after the death of Felix of Urgel, he wrote to confirm the erroneousness of the adoptionist teaching, he did not think it necessary to have recourse to arguments of a rational kind that had already been used extensively by Blessed Alcuin and other conquerors of the heresy. He was satisfied, instead, to cram his own work with patristic citations that confirmed the conclusions of those earlier writers. In contrast, when he turned his anxious attention to the survival among the Christian faithful of foolish barbarian beliefs, such as recourse to magicians to bring rain or to the practice of the ordeal and the "judgment of God," he willingly lingered on simple but direct and well-founded uses of argumentative reason in support of good sense, explaining that anything not created by God did not exist and was therefore pure falsehood.

This principle of an intellectual moderation that was neither a rejection of reason nor an excessive use of it was especially useful to Agobard when he had to tackle the complicated problem set by the liturgical reform associated with Amalarius of Metz; he was deeply involved in this for reasons connected with his task as bishop. Agobard had fallen into disfavor with Louis the Pious because during the first phase of the struggles accompanying the division of the Frankish kingdom he had supported the king's rebellious firstborn son Lothar. For this reason he was temporarily suspended from his duties and replaced by Amalarius, who served as a "chorbishop" (that is, an auxiliary bishop assigned to be administrator).

Amalarius, for his part, was a fervent supporter of the appropriateness of introducing into the Christian Latin liturgy a strongly symbolic interpretation of the formulas and the sacred objects and furnishings and of every gesture of the priest at the altar. In his view this allegorical interpretation of the liturgical action had value as an easy way of bringing the faithful closer, by anagogy, to the deeper meanings of the mysteries. During his stay in Lyons, which lasted about four years, Amalarius worked diligently to impose his program of liturgical reform on the province.

Once Agobard was restored to favor and placed again on the episcopal chair of Lyons he took strong steps to annul what Amalarius had done and even to refute it on the theoretical level. The controversy burned fiercely and involved other important thinkers in the religious world of Lyons; prominent among them was Florus, a monk and a fervent supporter of Agobard. The bishop wrote some intense and angry pages in connection with this controversy. Here again, however, his predominant concern was to cut down to size any unjustified intrusion of philosophical and reductively anthropomorphic and creaturely mental formularies such as were used, in vain, by incompetent interpreters of the faith in their attempt to imprison within them the supernatural meaning of divine realities.

The controversies of which Agobard tells us were obviously not always a matter simply of conflict between individual theses, but often involved different individuals in a broad and variously nuanced debate. This was true in particular of an umpteenth revival of discussion about the veneration of images. Claudius, a Spaniard and bishop of Turin (d. 827) and another longtime representative of Carolingian theology, was led by the text of the *Carolingian Books* to adopt for his own diocese the hardline position of forbidding any representation whatsoever of the divine, whether realistic or symbolic. His intention was to exclude every danger of an excessive materialism of the imagination in the weak minds of the simple faithful. But the political situation had by now changed decisively as compared with the end of the eighth century, and Carolingian interests led in the direction of a comfortable reconciliation with the Byzantines and, above all, with the papacy. In 824 Louis the Pious convoked a synod in Paris in order officially to sanction a moderate attitude of the Frankish episcopate toward iconodulia.

In the following years Louis pressed Dungal of Saint-Denis to intervene and find fault with Claudius. As a result, disagreement over the liceity of veneration of sacred images once again inflamed minds. Dungal urged Claudius to have methodical recourse to the rules of the liberal arts in order thereby to acquire a greater awareness of the value of sacred symbols and a reasonable use of them to the advantage of the faith. But his arguments gave the impulse to a new intervention by the now-elderly Agobard: in a *Book on Paintings and Images* he raised his voice once again to condemn not so much Dungal's position as the presumptuousness the latter showed in appealing to earthly knowledge in order to justify an abusive extension of the act of worship to something that was only a pale shadow of the divine.

B. RHABANUS MAURUS AND THE ORGANIZATION OF KNOWLEDGE

Even though the debates thus far described were marked by factiousness and the adoption of strong individual positions, they were always guided, in the minds of those involved, by a lively concern to preserve the unity of Christian wisdom. In each of these men this goal, even if in different and opposing ways, fed the conviction that they were working in complete continuity with the firm ideals of those who first led the theological and cultural rebirth of the empire. These same years of the reign of Louis the Pious saw, therefore, the appearance of many balanced writers who chose to remain apart from the controversies and devote themselves to safeguarding the systematic character of the original plan of spiritual cohesion and unification that the rulers were entrusting to Carolingian scholars.

Such was the perspective, for example, of Benedict, abbot of Aniane, who led and provided the theoretical basis for the restoration of the authentic Benedictine Rule, a restoration aimed at giving new vitality to the spiritual and cultural task of monasticism. In a short dogmatic work titled *The Protective Walls of the Faith*, Benedict gave new currency to the traditional theological method of collecting patristic authorities, among which he included extensive extracts from the early Carolingian teachers (in particular from the *Statements* of Alcuin's circle), since these had by now become universally recognized models of religious wisdom. Such an approach amounted to manifesting a clear awareness of belonging to an integrated and cohesive theological civilization that could renew itself, constructively and without violent tremors, in constant continuity with its own past.

Other writers, each in a particular area of intellectual activity and working in regional centers scattered throughout the empire, likewise contributed to strengthening the same continuity between old and new. They did so through various efforts to update systematically the learned syntheses of late antiquity. In this connection we may mention the contribution of Christian of Stavelot and Angelomus of Luxeuil in the realm of biblical exegesis and that of Sedulius Scotus and Smaragdus of Saint-Mihiel, who wrote new grammatical handbooks in which they took note of new "modern" phenomena in Christian Latin due to the influence of the Bible and the liturgy. In addition there was the collection of *Decretals*, attributed to a not more closely identified Isidore Mercator, who offered a first, orderly, and rationalized *summa* of the official documents dealing with canonical jurisdiction.

There were also not a few, though still-embryonic syntheses of ideas for the training of an aristocrat, such as the *Education of a King* by Jonas of Orleans, the *Royal Way* of Smaragdus, and the well-known *Handbook*, which combined elements of theology with moral advice and was written by Dhuoda, an educated aristocratic lady, for the education of her son.

All these limited contributions were, however, transcended by the monumental literary and religious output of Rhabanus Maurus, the foremost writer and Carolingian scholar of the Germanic world; his great importance was due to his outstanding completeness and depth as an expositor. In his youth Rhabanus was a pupil of Alcuin; he became a teacher, then abbot of the monastery of Fulda, and finally archbishop of Mainz from 847 to 856, the year of his death. He was certainly the best interpreter and implementer of the effort, widespread during these years, to achieve a critical reorganization of knowledge.

His first noteworthy piece of writing, a real masterpiece of theological thinking and, at the same time, of unprecedented rhetorical and poetic ability, gives explicit and important witness to his constant interior desire to present the contents of the Christian faith in an organized, analytical, and unified way. The work is known as *In Praise* (or *The Praises*) *of the Holy Cross*. It consists of a cycle of twenty-eight "figured" poems; that is (following a model that had appeared in the Constantinian era), poetic compositions whose verses use the letters of the words in them to form a number of lattice-like rectangles; within these are graceful sacred, geometrical, or representational illustrations provided by miniaturists working under the author's guidance. Or else the verses form numerous frameworks or vertical, diagonal, or circular lines that make known the presence of other verses hidden in the intricate web of each image.

Each poem is devoted to bringing out an aspect of the rich symbolism of the cross, the fundamental religious sign that in its dense composition of deep mysteries sums up the truth of the dogmas by connecting all of them with the central theme of the Passion of Christ. Paraphrases and comments in prose explain the theoretical aspects of the compositions, the scriptural and numerological symbols used, and the allegories and eschatological allusions in the poems. Thanks to the complicated overlapping of these numerous semantic levels, *The Praises* become a theological treatise of great depth and density, the carrier of a complex but compact doctrinal system by means of which the author elevates the understanding and devotion of the reader with the help of the arts and very subtle poetic and evocative procedures.

After becoming a teacher at Fulda, Rhabanus wrote *The Training of Clerics*, that is, a manual on the instruction of the monks in which the same ideal, the ascending completion of the understanding of the Christian faith, is now developed into a theological and religious pedagogy. This pedagogy has an organic unity that is secured by using a strict parallelism with the structure of the philosophical sciences. Thus the physics of monastic spirituality is provided by the scriptural *lectio*, which contains the world, that is, the "nature" to which the believer's search for knowledge is directed. Ethics derives from the practice of the evangelical, theological, and cardinal virtues. Logic, finally, emerges from the totality of the doctrines and methodologies taught by secular scholarship, which formally supports the doctrinal certainties marking Christian knowledge and morality.

In his mature years, first as abbot of Fulda and then as bishop, Rhabanus set out to prepare a systematic presentation of a complete reading of Scripture that was not only to be theoretical but could also be consulted for concrete and practical purposes; this was to be realized through the compilation of an (almost) complete commentary on the entire scriptural canon. The commentary served as an explanatory aid, built up out of numerous extracts, stitched together here and there by the compiler's original remarks, that were carefully selected from the works of the most reliable commentators of the patristic age and identified by the book to which they referred. The work derived further clarity through careful indications of the origin of the various excerpts, this by means of easily decipherable sigla. In the following centuries this ingenious compilation of the best and most authoritative interpretations of the Bible would be available to monastic readers, among whom it was widely used and appreciated as a very valuable exegetical help. Owing to its anthological nature, it was characterized by a completeness of information and an instructional precision that made it superior to any other available commentary.

There is a fundamental idea that marks Rhabanus' exegetical work but is also in practice the inspiring principle of all his theological writings and the best key for reading them. It is expressed in his commentary on the book of Wisdom in connection with his exegesis of the verse "You have arranged all things by measure, number, and weight" (Wis 11:21). The quantitative and qualitative order of the universe is a sign (he says) of the harmonious arrangement established at the moment of creation by the perfect planning of the divine Intellect. This order is therefore the common reality sought in all the cognitive investigations of the human mind, which by means of these investigations seeks to identify and study the laws governing nature and to compare these with the internal norms of created thought as codified and taught by the liberal arts. In thus discovering the parallelism between the order of creation and the order of thought, human beings learn to know also the organizing perfection of the thought of the Creator, that is, of divine Wisdom, which is the cause of both orders. They can also hope to ascend toward this Wisdom through knowledge and faith, to the point of becoming completely assimilated to its truth.

Rhabanus' final, likewise very ambitious work, was an encyclopedic *The Natures of Things*, an attempt to give an intellectual description of the created world in order better to draw near to the Creator's own understanding of it. The attempt yields a concrete, organized collection of erudite information that is drawn from the extensive heritage of learning accumulated by the Carolingians during the first fifty years of the intellectual renaissance. The original, purely antiquarian and conservational aims of late antique and Romano-barbarian encyclopedic collections are here carried to a new level by Rhabanus in a plan to place knowledge on a new religious foundation. This new foundation promotes and accompanies the ascensional movement of the soul by setting it free of the bonds of the corporeal world, purifying it through the practice of virtue, and leading it to the most perfect contemplation of the truth.

This deeply theological dimension of the work is here again brought out by a direct reference to the ternary presence, recognizable in every creature, of the principles of universal order established by God in the image of his own Trinity. The being of every thing is determined by the supreme Wisdom which arranges things according to "measure" or quality, "number" or quantity, and "weight," that is, the proportion or harmonious character of the qualitative and quantitative components, all this in the context of a universal arrangement that is at once rigorously logical, organically esthetic, and ethically perfect.

4. Theological Debate in Carolingian Europe after Verdun

The theological influence of Rhabanus Maurus, a man already greatly respected and unanimously esteemed during his lifetime, became widespread after his death, especially in the Germanic area. In particular, his encyclopedic and systematic outlook became the dominant characteristic of his more direct disciples. One example is Walafrid Strabo (d. 849), who carefully revised Rhabanus' commentaries on the Pentateuch and himself wrote a handbook, *Matters Ecclesiastical*, on the essential proficiencies of a churchman.

The same effort at compilation can also be seen in the lengthy *Letter* that Ermenrich of Ellwagen (d. 874), a pupil of Walafrid, sent to Grimoald, abbot of the Swiss monastery of Sankt-Gallen, though the letter shows a lesser degree of methodological consistency. In it the writer explains and paraphrases the twofold evangelical commandment of divine and human love, producing a variegated mosaic of learned variations on the theme; the mosaic feeds a rhapsodic religious meditation with a large number of excerpts, ideas, definitions, models, and precepts attested in the first century of Carolingian literature.

In contrast, the model provided by Rhabanus also stimulated new efforts at methodological development and conceptual accuracy in the use of traditional theological terminology. Eginard, an already elderly man (d. 840), was one of the last survivors of Alcuin's generation and was known primarily for a famous biography of Charlemagne. He was a close friend of Rhabanus, having been a fellow student at Fulda; with a sure touch he gave voice to the influence of this friendship in his work *The Adoration of the Cross*, which he composed in 836.

In this final echo of the Carolingian debate on images, Eginard set out to explain the legitimate kind of veneration to be reserved for the cross of Christ. He found his answer to the problem in a careful terminological distinction between *oratio* (prayer) and *adoratio* (adoration, worship, veneration). The former is spiritual and interior and is reserved for God alone; the latter, which implies a bodily gesture, is permitted even in relation to sacred objects, the angels, and holy human beings and is therefore most appropriate in relation to the cross as the fundamental sign of the redemption that leads the soul toward the invisible truth of the divine. Eginard's contribution is valuable chiefly as a testimony to the felt need, widespread in the territories of the empire, of defining the semantic heritage of traditional theological language and safeguarding it against ambiguities and challenges.

Once again, however, efforts such as these at uniformity and the preclusion of possible variations of custom in theology were an indirect sign of the growing tension that was shaking the Carolingian intellectual world. The tension was due to the acceleration of civil conflicts and political divisions caused by the far-from-peaceful parceling out of the territorial inheritance of Louis the Pious among his sons. When the treaty of Verdun in 843 put a temporary end to the civil wars by dividing the empire into three distinct kingdoms, the unifying and centralizing political plan of Charlemagne was henceforth transformed in practice into a complex machinery of divided and polarized authorities that took turns controlling one another. The writers of political treatises during these years showed a clear awareness of the change that had occurred. Sedulius Scotus, for example, in his *Christian Rulers*, which he dedicated to the sons of Louis the Pious, continued to assert the emperor's original role as "vicar of Christ in the government of the church," but he expressly subordinated the activity of earthly rulers to the advice and judgment of the bishops, who are the sole means of control and sole guarantors of continuity for the very exercise of political power.

One of the most effective witnesses to the increased moral and administrative responsibilities of the clergy in the government of the "Christian State" during the decades after the treaty of Verdun was undoubtedly Hincmar, archbishop of Rheims from 845 to 882, the year of his death. From the very beginning of his own governmental activities he was concerned to defend the autonomy of the church against any abuse or interference by the feudal nobility and even by the kings themselves. He never ceased to maintain the directly divine origin of political authority and therefore the obligation of kings and emperors to subordinate their activity to the ministry of the bishops. This doctrine is very clearly expressed in, for example, the treatise *The Divorce of Lothar and Theutberga*, written to condemn Lothar II's intention of repudiating Queen Theutberga in order to marry his concubine.

The control of orthodoxy was evidently another area in which the interventions of Hincmar and other bishops having the same conception of ecclesiastical authority were an indispensable and even symbolic proof of the continuity, despite changing times, of their authority as spiritual leaders of the community of believers.

A degree of cultural awakening occurred toward the middle of the century and was fostered by the at least temporary cessation of civil conflicts. During the same years there occurred an interesting intellectual development in the monastic world, which became increasingly free of royal and episcopal control and less involved in social and political life. Both of these phenomena led to a considerable increase in suggestions for going more deeply, both methodologically and conceptually, into religious questions. Not infrequently, moreover, the monastic preference was for the more interior aspects of spiritual wisdom and problems connected with the intimate religious and existential relationship of the soul with God. This led to an open confrontation, in the area of the doctrinal development of dogmas, with the harshly critical bishops, who for their part were increasingly concerned to keep under control the ethical and practical conclusions drawn from theological theses and to check the rise of excessively individualistic religious attitudes.

On the other hand, the sovereigns persisted in their determination to proclaim themselves still the guardians responsible for the cultural and religious life of their territory. And while they continued to protect poets and masters of the liberal arts and to subsidize the embryonic schools at their courts, they did not hesitate to claim the role of judge also, and even especially, in debates of a theological kind. In particular, Charles the Bald, last son of Louis the Pious, king of the western part of the empire, and then emperor from 875 on, set himself up as heir to the leading cultural and religious role played by his grandfather Charlemagne. On several occasions he circulated lists of theological problems among representatives of the various classes of intellectual authorities of the day: bishops, monks, and masters of the liberal arts. The effect was to give rise to quarrels among them rather than to promote the emergence of peacemaking solutions.

As a result, in the middle years of the ninth century the kingdom of France became the setting for a densely interwoven complex of discussions of theological subjects, calling often for the publication of official positions and synodal decrees but almost never leading to open breaks, sanctions, or persistence in schism. The most complex and prolonged of these discussions, and one engaging a great many authors (the discussions often involved the same individuals as protagonists on various fronts), occurred precisely in the years around the middle of the century and had to do with the subject of divine predestination.

In 847, Noting, bishop of Verona, sent Rhabanus Maurus, archbishop of Mainz, a worried letter telling him of how Gottschalk, a German monk of the Mainz archdiocese, was traveling around northeastern Italy preaching a dubiously orthodox doctrine on predestination. Rhabanus was well acquainted with Gottschalk, who had been a monk of Fulda when Rhabanus was abbot there and had always shown a dangerous intolerance of ecclesiastical discipline. At Rhabanus' own request Gottschalk had been transferred by imperial decree to France, first to the monastery of Corbie, then to that of Orbais, which was under the uncompromising jurisdiction of Hincmar of Rheims. The dangerous preacher had evidently fled, perhaps on the pretext of a pilgrimage to Rome and, appealing to the thought of Augustine (so Noting said), was now teaching the inescapable effectiveness of the judgment by which God binds the saints to good and the wicked to evil.

In his reply to Noting, Rhabanus properly expresses his own puzzlement at this teaching, which comes dangerously close to theological determinism, but, without entering into the controversy, he limits himself to asserting the absolute simplicity, unity, and necessary goodness of the divine will. Rhabanus then saw to it that the rebellious monk should appear before him; he had him judged and condemned by a synod of Mainz and sent him back to the monastery in France to which he belonged, in order that he might be judged by his own metropolitan, Hincmar. Hincmar took direct and energetic steps to deal with the matter, which had serious implications for the problem of ecclesiastical jurisdiction and the moral responsibility of the individual. He convoked a synod of the bishops of northern France, which met in the royal palace of Quierzy in the presence of Charles the Bald. Gottschalk was condemned once again, publicly flogged, forced to burn his writings, and warned not to continue preaching the rejected doctrine. The rebellious monk was then locked up in the monastery of Hautvillers, under the supervision of Hincmar, and remained there until his death about twenty years later.

But from his prison Gottschalk began to publish and circulate short writings in defense of his thought. Among others there were a first *Confession*, known as the *Shorter*, a book on *Predestination* in several parts, and *A More Detailed Confession* in which he explains how the unity of the divine nature is not necessarily compromised by a division among the effects of God's will. In this new phase of the debate he thought up a further theoretical refinement of his teaching, this on the basis of a suggestion he derived from the writings of Isidore of Seville. According to the latter, divine predestination should be described in Latin as *gemina* ("twin," "twofold") or "looking in two directions": it is one in itself but double inasmuch as it is reflected in two effects that are equal but distinct. This clever grammatical artifice made it possible, by means of a predicate that is singular in number but has two meanings, to declare that in God there is a singleness of substance but a plurality of effects.

The sophisticated use of the rules of grammar was, in fact, Gottschalk's preferred means of explaining the innermost meanings of the words of revelation. He knew well the deductive methods of logic and the types of rhetorical argument, and he did not scorn their use, but his demonstrations concentrated on grammar, a preference surely due also to his strong personal inclination to base the understanding of the faith on the words of Scripture (an inclination typical of monasticism). In his opinion the rule-bound language of grammar was, because God had created it for this purpose, the most faithful mirror of the universal order of the cosmos, whose perfection and, at the same time, inviolability it reflects. But the compactness of that order is not only formal, because in the area of ethics it links moral values and the destinies of human individuals by establishing an immutable and eternal correspondence between particular actions and the rewards set by God.

Gottschalk constantly referred back to the Augustinian tradition and the theological methods tested during the first decades of the renaissance. For this reason the circulation of his writings elicited a good deal of sympathy among some important representatives of Frankish religious culture and led in a short time to the establishment of a real theological party on his behalf. Among these men were the elderly and learned philologist Lupus of Ferrières, Bishop Prudentius of Troyes, who fought to base the Christian cultural tradition on the authority of the Fathers, and Ratramnus of Corbie, a monk, theologian, and penetrating cultivator of the liberal arts. But a further, seemingly irrelevant factor linked these individuals despite their divergent interests and training: namely, a shared aversion to the lordly exercise of archiepiscopal authority of a pre-feudal kind. This authority, with the sovereign's support, strengthened the activity of the archbishop of Rheims and gave credibility to such a limited assembly as Quiercy, consisting as it did of aristocrats and prelates trained more to deal with legal and administrative matters than with the study of Christian truth.

In the face of these criticisms Hincmar counterattacked by writing a treatise/pastoral letter *To the Simple [Faithful] and Recluses* (i.e., religious). His purpose was to use citations from the Fathers to strengthen the theoretical positions already expressed by Rhabanus Maurus; he also strongly exhorted his readers to trust with optimistic confidence in the justice and cosmic governance of a God who is an absolute sovereign, provident, and guarantor of just rewards for good done. Hincmar was moved by fear of the consequences of Gottschalk's doctrinal views (fatalism, laxism, superstition) and was concerned to safeguard the church's role as distributor of grace. He therefore urged Gottschalk's supporters to distinguish between divine foreknowledge, which embraces equally both the good and the evil in the world, and predestination, which consists in the restoration of the order violated by human beings. Predestination therefore has for its object redemption and all its effects, that is, the salvation of the just but not the punishment of the wicked, who are solely responsible for their own damnation.

In support of this teaching, which seemed to him the only orthodox doctrine on predestination, Hincmar felt the need of winning the support of reason placed at the service of the faith. He needed also to reply to the abstruse subtleties of Gottschalk and his supporter Ratramnus. Therefore, in 851, probably by way of his ally Pardulus, bishop of Laon, he asked for an opinion on the teachings of Gottschalk from Master John Scotus, a thinker of Irish origin and a protégé of Charles the Bald, who taught and practiced the liberal arts at the school of the court.

In reply to the request John Scotus wrote the short work *Predestination* or *Divine Predestination*. From its very outset the atmosphere of this work is that of a religious Platonism, which is the foundation of an orderly hierarchic conception of created being and an unbroken aspiration to attain to theological knowledge through the stages of a gradual movement away from matter and from the accidentality of individuals. In this deeply and rationally optimistic setting John Scotus sees no place for the gloomy ethical pessimism of a predestination understood as a rigid and immutably necessary connection between cause and effect (that is, between goodness and reward, on the one hand, and between wickedness and damnation on the other). In his view such a conception cancels out the very effects of God's mercy and of the grace of the redemption, which Christ wrought in order to save from evil everything that, insofar as it is real, is a work of God and, by that very fact, good.

In a further step John starts with the assumption that, as far as the doctrinal aspects are concerned, the rejection of Gottschalk's error and the criticism of its distance from the authentic teaching of the Fathers are already clearly stated in the replies of Rhabanus and Hincmar. For his part, being, as he is, a master of liberal arts, he chooses to refute Gottschalk by coming down onto the ground of demonstrative method and rigorous argumentation. To the grammatical formalism of his adversary he opposes the (in his view) much more demanding and infallible tool of dialectic (that is, logic), the art of determining the truth and making it manifest.

In accord with a model of Neoplatonic origin (used also by John Damascene), the art contains four methodologies, agreement among which places beyond doubt the solidity of the results reached: division, definition, and deduction, followed by a reconstruction of the concepts being discussed. John also issues an urgent invitation to his readers to deepen their knowledge of Greek, for this will enable them to understand fully the authentic teaching of the Fathers and the effectiveness of the philosophical methodologies used by them. After the statement of its presuppositions, the text of Scotus's little work is divided into nineteen chapters that develop a series, with side-branches, of arguments and demonstrations. These make it possible to bring into focus all the rationally knowable aspects of the complex mystery of predestination and its effects on the destiny of individual souls.

In the process John brings to bear the hermeneutical power of almost all the logical tools available to a Latin thinker during these years: definitions, differences, etymologies, divisions, analyses, oppositions, distinctions, clarifications and checking of concepts and propositions, chains of syllogisms, major premises, and the *topoi* ("topics") or more general areas of thought from which these premises are derived.

The work on *Predestination* is, then, based frankly and effectively on the Augustinian premise (mentioned at the beginning of this book) that "the true philosophy" and "the true religion" are one and the same. The book is a complicated but clear and linear demonstrative structure that is very competently placed at the service of the fundamental principle on which, in the author's view, every possible grasp of the divine attributes, including foreknowledge and predestination, is based. This principle is that the unity of the divine is absolute and incontrovertible and that multiplicity and accidentality belong solely to the created world. The formal structure of the treatise, then, is that supplied by a rigorous set of arguments, all the conclusions of which are constantly supported by confirming citations from the Fathers. But the speculative scenario that is outlined and confirmed by the arguments is the very one that reciprocally supports it: the optimistic conception of a harmonious universe that is the work of a God who is a wise and provident architect, a universe that is a triumph of beauty and goodness, and whose truth is solidly guaranteed by the strict consistency of thought, language, and reality.

Foreknowledge and predestination or, better, knowledge and appointed destiny (for in God there is no temporal succession) are therefore a single reality in the one divine essence. But for the weak human intellect that is immersed in time they are two different ways in which it is forced to imagine, on the one hand, the natural relationship and, on the other, the moral relationship between created things and the divine arrangement that gives them existence and governs them. If evil exists, it is explicable only by the imperfection of the free creaturely will, which decides to orient its own choices and actions in a direction contrary to the cosmic order that God established, that is, predestined, in an eternal instant outside of time, and bodied forth in the eternal ideas in his Word. In fact, God never punishes the nature he himself created; he does, however, punish the wrong direction taken by the creaturely will. Indeed, the punishment is simply the outcome of the free human will's turning away from its natural object, which is God. It is precisely, and only, by desiring something other than God and what he wills that the sinner punishes himself by losing the good for which every creature is eternally and universally predestined by God.

As soon as John Scotus' little work appeared, its rational form and speculative boldness made it a ready target of theological attacks by representatives of the party opposed to Hincmar of Rheims. Prudentius of Troyes wrote a ferocious treatise, *Predestination: An Answer to John Scotus*, in which he accused the archbishop of having illicitly brought into a difficult religious discussion a "sophist" who was more familiar with Martianus Capella than with the Fathers of the Church and who introduced into the discussion dangerous philosophical ideas that could easily lead to immanentism or Neo-pelagianism. Prudentius was echoed by Florus of Lyons, a monk and author of a series of polemical statements against the decisions and procedures of the synod of Quierzy. In these he directs his arrows chiefly against the "nineteen chapters" of John Scotus (but shows that he had only an indirect and quite superficial knowledge of their contents). At this point Hincmar distanced himself from John Scotus, saying he had nothing in common with him.

In 853 a new teaching of Gottschalk, this time on the Trinity, raised further concerns for the archbishop, who convoked a council at Soissons and once again won a formal condemnation. This "new treachery," as Hincmar described it, consisted in a proposal to introduce the expression *trina deitas* ("triune Godhead") into the liturgy as being appropriate in invocations of the Trinity. It was clearly Gottschalk's intention to confirm, by means of this new formula, the correctness of the grammatical method he had already applied to predestination. The method was based on the use of singular adjectives that had a plural meaning: just as in the case of *gemina* the method served to express the "doubleness" of predestination within the single unity of the will, so now *trina* was used to ensure the "tripleness" of the divine persons within the unity of a single substance. As in the previous case of predestination, the council of Soissons formally rejected this new formula, which it regarded as a liturgical abuse, and asserted the impossibility of combining any multiplicative predicate with "Godhead," a word that expresses only the one divine substance.

Gottschalk replied to this new condemnation by composing a treatise, *The Triune Deity*, and asking his friend Ratramnus of Corbie, who had already spoken in his favor on predestination, to intervene again in the dispute over the Trinity. From this point on Ratramnus played a leading role in the group opposed to Hincmar and, shortly after receiving Gottschalk's request, composed a polemical *Divine Predestination* in two books, as well as an anthology of patristic texts in support of *trina deitas*. The archbishop answered in a short work, *The Godhead Is One and not Triune*.

Ratramnus was a trained and careful scholar and one convinced that the primary need was to base theological research on solid definitions and verifications of the reliability of the terminology being used. This methodological reminder was, as mentioned earlier, one that other thinkers also recalled during these years. Ratramnus saw a perfect example and therefore an important model in the *Answer to Eutyches*, the fifth of the short theological works of Boethius, an author who became a favorite source of his thought.

With great logical clarity and procedural consistency Ratramnus applied this methodology as he intervened in almost all the controversies that arose during the time of Charles the Bald; in these disputes he continually called on his opponents to respect the fundamental rule of conceptual clarity. In addition to debates on the subjects of Gottschalk's preaching, Ratramnus also involved himself in numerous other areas of disagreement. On two occasions he disagreed sharply with doctrines formulated and supported by his own abbot, Paschasius Radbertus of Corbie, one of them dealing with the reality of the eucharistic mystery, the other with the birth of Christ. On two other occasions he intervened in a resolute way on questions arising from the nature of the human soul.

The discussion of the Eucharist went back to the very year of the Treaty of Verdun (843) and was one of those arising directly from a query of Charles the Bald. The latter asked the monks of Corbie whether the eucharistic change of the bread and wine into the body and blood of Jesus takes place "in mystery," that is, symbolically, or "in truth," that is, in actual reality. The two monks, Paschasius and Ratramnus, were both convinced that the answer to the two alternatives should be "both" (the eucharistic change is symbolic *and* real), but they differed radically in their explanation of the "in reality." Paschasius Radbertus immediately championed a solution based on a definitely materialistic realism (real material body and real material blood) and sent the sovereign a treatise on *The Body and Blood of the Lord* that he had written a few years earlier.

Ratramnus responded with a treatise bearing the same title, in which he sees the sacrament as an act of high symbolico-spiritual meaning that produces a salvific food for the soul; in order to be such, the food must be separated from the accidents of space and time and from the corruptibility of matter.

Ten years later, in the very year of the Council of Soissons (853), Ratramnus wrote a short work, *The Birth of Christ*, after learning that someone, for the purpose of strengthening the doctrine of Mary's virginity "in the act of giving birth" (*in partu*), was spreading the idea that Christ's birth took place in a miraculous manner and not in the usual natural way. In Ratramnus' opinion these ideas risked detracting from the integrity of Christ's human nature, which can be guaranteed only by a normal and natural birth from the maternal womb. Paschasius Radbertus, for his part, in a document sent to the religious of a monastery of women that was under his protection, had pointed to Mary as the perfect model of virginal integrity, both spiritual and corporeal. He now recognized that he was the object of Ratramnus' attack and replied immediately by circulating his *The Childbirth of the Virgin*. Here he left to God's unqualified omnipotence the choice of the way in which the Virgin brought the Savior into the world. But he maintained a negative certainty: it was impossible that this way should have been a childbirth that compromised her purity, unlike the way in which other human beings, who are stained by original sin, are born.

It is easy to see that in both areas—the Eucharist and the virgin birth—Paschasius' theological choices were inspired by a deeply anti-Platonic and anti-dialectical approach, that is, by a refusal to admit that human reason could claim to describe a cosmic order willed by God and to which God himself had to submit. The concreteness of the presence of Christ's body and blood in the sacrament of the altar, as well as the certainty about his real birth in a way that fully respected his mother's virginity, were guaranteed solely by the unfathomable and unlimited omnipotence of God, and no exercise of logic could ever provide a sufficiently persuasive explanation.

Ratramnus, on the other hand, bore witness to a spiritualism of a completely opposite kind, one based on a careful definition and delimitation of the scope and effective power of human logic. The rules of dialectic strictly reflect the way in which natural things exist; this is due to the parallelism, established by God at the moment of creation, between the "order of things" and the "order of ideas." But when these rules are applied to something supernatural, such as everything that is an object of revelation, the powers of dialectic inevitably undergo a formal change as they are adapted to the object whose knowableness they intend to measure. (Once again Boethius had explained this in his *Short Sacred Works*, especially the one on the Trinity).

Thus the birth of Jesus is a bodily act belonging to the natural world and therefore takes place in accordance with the laws in force throughout the visible world. In contrast, the eucharistic change is not a material repetition, in time, of Christ's sacrifice, as though it were necessary on each occasion to renew the redemption of the human race. The change is therefore something purely spiritual and symbolic that cannot be subordinated to the rules of logic and of the natural sciences that depend on them. The measurement of human reason's ability to define, which is checked from time to time by taking into account the nature of the object to which it is applied, is therefore the fulcrum of Ratramnus' method.

This method also governs the first of his two treatises on psychology, a short *The Soul*, in which he maintains that the soul is non-corporeal and non-localizable, that is, that it cannot be conceptually defined according to the principles of the sciences of things visible and corporeal. (The treatise was probably a reply to Hincmar of Rheims, who had advanced contrary views in a short work *The Divine and Multiple Other Aspects of the Soul*.)

It was, however, chiefly in his final work (around 863) that Ratramnus produced the most mature speculative results of his method. The work was the *Book on the Soul*, addressed to bishop Odo of Beauvais, who had for some time been abbot of Corbie in succession to Paschasius. Its purpose was to challenge the teaching on anthropology that was being defended by an anonymous monk of the abbey of Fly, who attributed it to his respected teacher, a not-further-identifiable Macarius Scotus. According to the anonymous writer, Macarius had claimed that from the works of Augustine the idea could be correctly derived that all individual human beings participate in a single universal soul.

In validating the more common theological certainty about the concrete individuality of each personal soul Ratramnus found strong support in his own methodology: he maintained that a universal soul is conceivable only as a product of human logic and not as an actual reality. The reason: since the substance of souls is a primary, single, and real substance, it can only be individual; if it were universal it would be substantial in only a secondary sense, that is, as a sum of characteristics common to various individuals, and it could never be an actual reality, that is, a person endowed with his or her own will and intellect and therefore responsible for his or her moral choices.

Clear once again, in this discussion, is the theological and philosophical influence of Boethius; in fact, Ratramnus includes in his text, paraphrasing and analytically commenting on them, some pages of Boethius, especially from the *Answer to Eutyches* and from the commentaries on the *Isagoge* of Porphyrius. For the first time in the centuries of the early Middle Ages, Ratramnus gives special attention to the discussion of the nature of the universals; he solves the problem by coming out explicitly in favor of the concrete reality of the individual.

The *Book on the Soul* was one of the final products of the period of lively theological discussions that went on in the lands controlled by Charles the Bald. With the deaths of some of the most influential scholars involved in these discussions the more rigid forms of theoretical thought were toned down. In 860, at the Council of Douzy, after various reciprocal condemnations and refutations, the party of Hincmar and the party that had formed around Florus of Lyons reached a general agreement on predestination: in the final analysis both agreed to forget about Gottschalk and his arguments.

During these same years, in which John Scotus remained apart from theological controversies, Charles the Bald gave him the task of retranslating the works of Pseudo-Dionysius into Latin in order to replace the muddled version prepared by Hilduin of Saint-Denis about twenty-five years earlier. The maturation of John's skills and thought as a result of this encounter with Neoplatonic Christian theology from the East would lead him to work out a solid, complex, and coherent speculative system that seems today to have been the final and best success produced by the entire philosophical-religious literature of Carolingian civilization.

To the historian, due in part to that ending, the twenty years of theological production and passionate discussions that marked the long reign of Charles the Bald, from the Peace of Verdun to the Council of Douzy, appear to have been, in substance, a period in which the young but already vigorous world of Carolingian religious thought gave itself to study and an assessment of its own strengths. It was a large intellectual laboratory in which tools of research and critical appraisal were forged and improved amid the lively clash of doctrines, factions, and profoundly different ideologies. These tools allowed scholars to improve their cognitive powers and to acquire an ever-greater consciousness of belonging to a unanimous Christianity, within which dissent could have a place only insofar as it served as an incentive to shed light on what was still obscure and uncertain.

5. John Scotus Eriugena

The island origin of the master whom contemporaries called simply "Iohannes Scottus" is confirmed by a second name indicating origin, which he himself coined: at the beginning of his Latin translation of the *corpus areopagiticum* he describes himself by means of a place-name from ancient Irish combined with a Greek root: "Eriu-gena," that is, born in Ireland.

Neither the year of his birth nor the year of his death is known, nor is it easy to determine just when he entered the service of Charles the Bald. The only certain date is that of his intervention in the controversy over predestination: 851. His activity as teacher of the liberal arts at the court, as well as the basis for Prudentius of Troyes' rebuke that he was excessively familiar with the *Marriage* of Martianus Capella, are documented by his set of learned notes on that text. These show that even in his early years of teaching he possessed a very wide-ranging proficiency in matters scientific and philosophical.

After the composition of his *Predestination*, the depth of his learning and the resultant linguistic and hermeneutical clarity found a splendid opportunity for their application in the translation of the writings of Pseudo-Dionysius and later, approximately during the years 860–870, in other valuable translations of important works of Greek patristic thought. These included the *Ambigua* and the *Questions to Thallassius* of Maximus the Confessor and the *Creation of Man* of Gregory of Nyssa. This last was a treatise presenting a Platonic-Christian anthropology based on an allegorical exegesis of the biblical account of the creation of humanity in the image of God; John gave his translation the title *The Image*.

In the area of cultural growth and speculative penetration the first beneficiary of these translations was the author himself, whose familiarity with Greek-language writers was further increased by other texts already to be read in Latin or in any case rendered available during these same years. These included the *Homilies on the Hexaemeron* of Basil of Caesarea (which gave a physico-literal interpretation of the six days of creation, based on the author's philosophical and scientific knowledge), *The Man Well Anchored* (or *On the Faith*: a compendium of dogma) by Epiphanius of Salamis, the *On First Principles* of Origen, and, perhaps mediated by Maximus the Confessor, numerous passages from the sermons of Gregory of Nazianzus.

John Scotus made innovative use of these sources of eastern thought, his deeper knowledge of which, even by itself, gave his work exceptional originality in comparison to all the principal representatives of Carolingian culture. But in addition, John's growth in learning did not neglect the contribution derived from a good many careful readings of the works of the Latin Fathers: Augustine first and foremost, whom John consulted and reflected on with constant and devoted dedication, then Ambrose, Jerome, Gregory the Great, and Hilary of Poitiers. Finally, his cultural background also included, of course, the exemplars of late antique philosophical and literary erudition: in addition to Martianus Capella and Boethius there were the *Timaeus* as commented on by Chalcidius; Macrobius; and the classical Latin writers such as Cicero, Pliny, and Virgil.

During these years of his maturity, on the basis of this substantial and unusual fund of philosophical and theological knowledge John Scotus planned the composition of his major work, *Periphyseon* (*On Natures*), a title that is further evidence of the author's ease with the Greek language and that only in the modern period editors mistakenly replaced with the easier title *The Division of Nature*. This is a lengthy, structured dialogue, in five books, between a Master or Teacher and a Disciple or Pupil. Whereas the style of Alcuin's dialogues was essentially didactic, John's dialogues are marked by an alternation of lengthy and detailed interventions, characterized by a wide-ranging and analytic discussion of each argument or problem met by the two individuals in the course of their reasoning.

The text is full of lengthy extracts from the works of the Fathers (taken in good measure from John's own translations), thereby confirming the important part played in the formation of Eriugena's thought by the sapiential contribution of Greek and Latin patristic literature. The entire speculative plan contained in the work comes down in practice to an attempt to explain, with the tools available to the created intellect, all the varied manifestations of truth that the mind meets in the study of both visible and invisible realities.

More even than the ancient philosophers, the Fathers of the Church were witnesses to the very important results obtained by such study in the past, the reason for this being that their investigations were based on a complete complementarity between scientific knowledge and the knowledge of revelation. They were based, in other words, on the complete synthesis of "the true religion" and "the true philosophy" which, beginning with the first lines of his *Predestination*, John Scotus proclaimed, as we saw, to be the foundation and justification of all human knowing.

By applying a solid argumentative method based on the rules of liberal knowledge and on a richly expressive but also incisive and measured language, John now intended to take up and, as far as possible, complete this cognitive project. He did so by trying to show how every truth attainable by human beings, from the broadest and most general to the most specific and particular, is always a further insight into the divine. For though the divine is in itself unknowable and unfathomable, it has manifested itself in creation in an infinite number of revelations (or better, to use a favorite term of Maximus the Confessor, of "theophanies"), which the truly wise person is urged to investigate and understand.

The most profound and complete of all the theophanies is certainly God's revelation of his own truth in the Sacred Scriptures. For this reason the cognitive system of reality that Charles the Bald's philosopher put together could not but be from its very first expressions a theological system: i.e., a system that, first in the conceptual principles that are its starting point and then in every further development is supported by the necessary information that the sacred text offers to the human mind in order to help and direct it on the long and complicated journey toward the final discovery of truth. This consummation will therefore be the result not only of a sincere belief in the revealed datum but also of a definitive understanding of the truth that is attested by that datum and is an object of belief in it.

Not only, therefore, do a remarkable number of scriptural citations and references fill the pages of the *Periphyseon*; the entire formal approach that is taken in the work and lies behind the complexity of the demonstrative language and the continual developments on problems that present themselves, one after another, to the inquiring mind, is essentially that of an extensive, detailed, and very fruitful commentary on the words of Scripture, starting with those that open the book of Genesis: "In the beginning God made the heavens and the earth."

A. NATURE AND ITS DIVISIONS

In the opening lines of the *Periphyseon* the Master suggests a single word that is suitable for expressing to the human mind everything that is thinkable, or, in other words, all the things *that are* and, at the same time, all the things *that are not*. This all-embracing word is "nature." The Disciple cannot but agree:

> **Master.** When I think hard and when with more than ordinary effort I seek, as far as my powers allow me, to understand the fact that the first and supreme division of all the things that the intellect can perceive or that entirely surpass its powers of penetration is the division between *what is* and *what is not*, then the only word that presents itself to my mind as able, like a genus, to include all things is "nature" (in Greek, *physis*, in Latin, *natura*). Or do you think that this is not correct?
>
> **Disciple.** On the contrary, I am in complete agreement. Indeed, even I, who am taking my very first step on the way of rational thinking, find that that is the situation.

It is from this fundamental premise that human reason must begin its effort to understand what lies hidden within the wealth of meaning proper to the word "nature." The Master then sets out to demonstrate the knowableness of nature by using the rules established by logic: "nature" is a noun signifying a genus, but a genus to be regarded as the most inclusive one that can be thought. For this reason it is not possible to follow the instructions of Aristotle and formulate a *definition* of this genus, because it cannot be located within a still-more-inclusive semantic field (as "man" is included in "animal" and defined as "rational animal"). In cases of this kind, logic then suggests applying to such broad and complex concepts the opposite logical procedure, namely, *division*.

As a genus, then, nature can be divided into a number of species (or, to use Eriugena's term, "forms") through the identification of sufficient differences. It is, however, certainly a very complicated task for the human mind to identify strict distinctions within a concept that must embrace everything that is true, including, therefore, even the ineffable divine essence and its unknowable attributes. It becomes necessary at this point to fall back on the contribution of knowledge of the truth that comes from Christian revelation. In Scripture reason does in fact discover a conceptual factor that enables it to understand a logical and real difference, and therefore a division: the concept of creation. Once it becomes possible to predicate the verb "create" within the field covered by "nature" it also becomes possible to set up a logically correct division of nature.

> **Master.** Then *nature* is, as I said, the *general* name that includes everything that is and everything that is not?
>
> **Disciple.** It is. And indeed in an absolutely universal way, since nothing can come to mind that falls outside the meaning of that word.
>
> **Master.** Since, then, we agree that nature is a *general* term, I would like now to apply to it the rule dealing with the division into a number of *species* because of a number of *differences*. . . . It seems to me that on the basis of four differences nature is divided into four species. The first of these is *that which creates and is not created*; the second, *that which is created and creates*; the third, *that*

which is created and does not create; the fourth: *that which does not create and is not created.*

The unlimited extension of the term "nature" allows us to include within it all the possible ways in which the verb "create" can be predicated according to the rules of grammar and logic: affirmative and negative, active and passive. As a result, the division of the concept "nature" can be the strictest possible and at the same time the most exhaustive possible: a four-part division based on the Aristotelean square of oppositions.

An educated mind, formed by the reading of the Fathers of the Church, has no difficulty in recognizing at least the first three of the four identified species of "nature." *That which creates and is not created* is God, the uncaused universal cause. It is no less obvious that the third species, *that which is created and does not create*, a description that is symmetrically opposite to the first, corresponds to the world of multiple individuals, who are the remote effects of the divine creative causality. But the second kind of nature, *that which is created and creates*, is easily recognizable in the divine ideas, which are the primordial models and causes of the multiple individuals; the latter are created inasmuch as they are thought by the Father in the Word, but they are in turn creators of individual effects.

On the other hand, it is more difficult to single out and understand the truth of the fourth species, the nature *that is not created and does not create.* Yet the logical necessity of such a species is presupposed by the stringent argument used in the fourfold division itself. The reality here is divine inasmuch as it is not created, but such an ultimate reality must be something outside of created time and therefore thinkable as the goal of the entire history of being and creating, when God will be only God and all things will find their own truth in God at the end of the process of creation. But an adequate understanding of this ultimate level of reality is not yet possible for the moment. Only after a thorough inquiry into the meaning of the three preceding species and their succession will the human intellect perhaps be in a position to approach the profound truth of the fourth; for the moment, the necessity of this species must be postulated by the harmonious convergence of reason and revelation.

It is evident, on the other hand, that the fourfold division is only a means of moving into a cognitive explanation of the very general word "nature," which is so comprehensive and complex that the human intellect can aspire to achieve even a minimal understanding of it only at the end of a lengthy and complicated series of rational operations, of which division is but the first. The complexity is also shown by the fact that from the very first lines of *Periphyseon*, even before the fourfold division is given, John Scotus has introduced another and different division of the same concept, a bipartite division into *things that are* and *things that are not.*

When the Disciple expresses puzzlement at this division, the Master answers with an explanation of *that are* and *that are not* that seems to complicate the problem rather than resolve it. He gives a good five different ways of interpreting the pair, but these are apparently irreconcilable among themselves or at best are alternatives. (1) Things knowable *are*, those that elude creaturely knowledge *are not*. (2) Things located at a lower level in the hierarchy of reality *are*, while those that *are not* are superior to them. (3) Primordial causes *are not*, while their multiple, sensible effects *are*. (4) Spiritual entities *are*; accidental and corporeal things *are not*. (5) Human beings in their condition after original sin *are not*; *being* can be predicated only of the holiness that preceded sin and will follow upon redemption.

It is obvious that in comparison with the quadripartite division this bipartite division seems much less rigorous and effective, all the more so since the Master suggests the possibility that to the five interpretations given can be added other, perhaps countless attempts to explain it. But the explanation of this complicated superimposition of many different interpretations of a single reality comes from later in the work, during a recapitulation of the division of nature at the beginning of the second book. In an evident, even if not explicit reference to the Neoplatonic distinction of the powers of knowing (senses, reason, intellect)—a doctrine about which Eriugena was abundantly informed not only by Boethius but by the writings of Maximus the Confessor—John points to a gradation in logical steps that also justifies the distinction between three different kinds of "division" by means of which the knowing subject apprehends the same object in ways that are distinct but lead to the truth by different paths.

The bodily senses exercise a division of the "whole" into its "parts." This kind of division has to do solely with material things and lacks any formal accuracy (because the parts of a whole can be divided up at the pleasure of the subject); it is therefore obviously insufficient for explaining the universality of nature. The second form of division is division in the true and proper sense, which follows rules and is symmetrical because based on respect for the laws of logic. This is the work of dianoetic reason, which is capable of knowing, classifying, and deductively organizing the universal aspects of reality. The third form of division is of a supralogical kind. John Scotus describes it as "a kind of intellectual contemplation of the totality of things"; it springs from the intuitive and unmediated (therefore not discursive and deductive) knowledge proper to the highest faculty, the intellect (or *nous*) whose object is always the reality of the totality of things, which includes everything that can be thought.

It is now clear how at the beginning of the work the higher intellect made possible an intuitive perception of the deepest truth of the concept of "nature." Then, in a more accessible formulation, namely, the bipartite division into *things that are* and *things that are not*, the intellect passed this perception on to dianoetic reason; this last is an inferior instrument but also indispensable to the intellect for a discursive unfolding of its own inherently vague intuitions.

Starting with this initial participation in the highest truth that can be intuited by natural knowledge, reason must then face the task of giving a logical explanation of its contents and consequences. It is precisely in order to initiate and make possible the development of its slow and mediated demonstrative operations that reason, with the help of both the noetic intellect and faith, formulates its quadripartite division of nature; this division is more understandable and open to investigation because it is formally subject to the laws of logic. This task of dianoetic reason is precisely what Eriugena promises to undertake by tracing the complex structure of the quadripartite division in the course of the work's five books. In the process and by way of a mosaic of interconnected problems he advances toward the attainment of the maximum understanding available to reason of the content of the noetic intuition that was his point of departure.

B. The Knowableness of God and the Possibility of Making Predications about Him

The first book of *Periphyseon* is entirely given over to measuring the knowableness of the first kind of nature, *that which creates and is not created* or, in other words, the divine being as uncaused cause and therefore the cause of everything that is real.

As a cause that is not derived from another cause, God is eternal and immutable. He is therefore certainly not on the same level as anything that, being caused, is subject to change and accidentality. In God there are no "accidents," but, for this very reason, in his perfect simplicity there is nothing knowable that can be understood as "substance," since the human mind cannot conceive of substances that are not the actual or potential subjects of inhering accidents. It is therefore not possible to speak of God as like anything else or to speak of him as distinct from or unlike anything else. Evident here is the influence of the "negative theology" of Pseudo-Dionysius: God is utter simplicity and utter perfection, and as such he is utterly profound and impenetrable darkness, precisely because he is the fullness of being. For this reason any attempt by the created intellect to develop a concept matching the truth of the divine is illicit and bound to fail.

Nevertheless, revelation has spoken about God to humanity and in human language. And when human knowledge has endeavored to speak of God it has managed to say something true: as when it asserts that God is the cause of all things and the ultimate end of everything that is. It is therefore possible and appropriate, as Pseudo-Dionysius himself teaches, to develop a positive theology that makes up for the prohibition against formulating meaningful predications about God by introducing terms for the divine perfections that are suggested by revelation or human reason. Accompanying this introduction, however, must be a warning that these terms must always be given a purely metaphorical value and never a literal one.

John Scotus completes this necessary dynamic adaptation of positive theology and negative theology by introducing a third way of predicating about the truth of God. It is a way that results from a productive combination of the first two, namely, a superlative theology. This is effected by applying to God terms expressing his perfections but correcting them by the preceding addition of "more than" or the prefix "super-." The terms then assert a true meaning while denying any possible parallels or references to creaturely imperfections. Thus it can be said that God is neither an essence nor a non-essence, but rather is a more-than-essence, which is something that has more both of being and of nonbeing. God is more-than-truth, more-than-goodness, and so on, and even more-than-nature, more-than-creator, more-than-God.

In order to explain what the application of this new theological semantics really involves, John Scotus harks back to an example given by Augustine and Boethius and already picked up by other Carolingian writers. He tests the possibility of predicating of God the ten categories of Aristotle, which according to the philosophers subsume everything meaningful that can be expressed in human language. The result of the inquiry is that words correctly expressing the divine cannot be placed in any of the categories.

This is because, on the one hand, there can be nothing accidental in God and, on the other hand, even substance and relation cannot be predicated of God in a directly affirmative way (although such predications are implied by the patristic tradition in its explanation of the trinitarian formulas). All this means that in God there can be no predication of qualities (he is not "good," "just," and so on) or quantities (he is not "great") or actions (he does not really "love") or passions (he is not really "loved"); he is not truly "Father" or "Son" or "Holy Spirit" or "divinity" or "one" or "triune," or, in the final analysis, truly "God." Moreover, because knowledge itself seems to be in this context not a perfection but a consequence of creaturely imperfection, we can be pushed to the point of saying that God's perfect wisdom is simply a non-knowing, that is, a divine ignorance.

On the other hand, it is obvious that our intellect cannot avoid predicating the categories if it really wants to express and understand something, even in theological discourse. Eriugena confirms this fact especially by a careful analysis of the final two categories: space and time. There is no subject the human intellect can tackle in an appropriate way without locating it within the coordinates of space and time. This means that instead of being objective modes of being, space and time are *a priori* conditions required if any object at all is to be knowable by the mind. If, then, God is to be in any way thinkable in his utter conceptual indetermination, we must locate even him within spatio-temporal parameters that, according to the rules of superlative theology, have at the same time both a maximal positive and a maximal negative value. This we see when Scripture says that God is "always" (that is, not in a limited time or in any time at all) and "everywhere" (not a limited space or in any space at all).

This same situation can then be extended to the other categories, all of which, including substance, are not diverse modalities proper to the reality of the object in itself, but true and proper *a priori* forms for organizing the subject's capacity for knowledge; within these any external datum whatsoever must be placed if it is to be known.

Eriugena's comprehensive analysis of the possibilities of theological language boils down essentially to the recognition that all meaningful terms can be predicated of God not because they are required by God's nature in itself but because of the relationship knowledge establishes between the divine object and the creaturely subject. In complete agreement with the foundations of Neoplatonic gnoseology he confirms the fact that the modes of true knowledge are determined by the capacities of the knowing subject, who is forced to give coherent expression to the representation of the known object in accordance with his/her powers of receiving and representing it. Consequently, it is always true that God is God, is one and three, creator, good, just, great, and so on, not *in himself*, but *for us* who know him. A correct theology, the reliability of which is ensured by the authority of revelation, must always guide the mind in its operations, correcting it and warning it of its limitations and of the errors into which it may fall through excessive assumptions about reality.

c. The Knowableness of Creatures: The Substantial Triad

If the semantic grid of the ten categories provides the formal coordinates the mind necessarily uses in receiving into itself, knowing, and organizing the images of things that come from without, we must conclude that nothing is truly knowable by the human mind as it is in itself, in its underlying substance or *ousia*. Instead, its reality can show itself to our minds only insofar as it is enveloped in the phenomenal appearances given it by the accidents defined in the categories. No created substance is knowable in itself, but only by means of the network of spatio-temporal, qualitative, quantitative, and other relationships that, in order to know it, the knowing intellect establishes between this substance and other substances. This manifestation of the object under the veil of the accidents is always a product made within the subject, a phantasm. The substantial truth of things in themselves truly exists only in the eternal mind of God, that is, in the Word, who truly is the "beginning" in which, according to the words of Scripture, "God made the heavens and the earth," that is, all things.

The second species or kind of nature, namely *that which is created and creates*, is the subject of the second book of the *Periphyseon*. The words describe God insofar as he is the divine creative thought, and they describe a creature insofar as the ideas (or divine notions, the primordial, eternal, intelligible, and perfect causes) are the true being, changeless and preceding any accidental manifestation, or, in other words, the true substance of the multiple, individual, and visible effects derived from the ideas. Guided by the Neoplatonic metaphysics of Maximus the Confessor, Eriugena passes beyond the widespread Augustinianism of his age and engages in a penetrating study of the ideas as something more than simple immutable models on which God draws in his work of organizing the created world. The "reasons" (*rationes* or *logoi*) of the divine mind, although produced by the latter, are in their turn creative and productive of things insofar as these reasons are divine and connatural ("coeternal," says Eriugena) to the Word (the *Logos* or *Ratio* of God), a person in the Trinity whose activity consists in devoting himself to the planning and production of created reality.

It was Maximus, once again, who suggested to John Scotus a metaphysical key essential for a correct understanding of the relationship between God the creator, the mediating causes in creation, and visible created effects. According to the teaching of Maximus, in every created reality can be seen a perfect triad of metaphysical components that are the universal trace of the trinitarian manifestation of God: substance (*ousia*), potency or power (*dynamis*), and act (*energeia*). This threefoldness is manifested to human knowledge only in distinct and differentiated forms, due to which each substance seems to pass from an infinite series of unfulfilled potentialities to a no-less-infinite series of actuations that are only partial and are still laden with unfulfilled potentialities.

The third kind of nature, *that which is created and does not create*, is precisely these imperfect and fragmented manifestations of the multiplicity of potentialities that are activated; behind this manifestation the true original substantiality of the object is hidden and remains invisible. Even when the human creature turns to knowledge of itself, it finds itself in the presence only of imperfect external manifestations of its own *ousia*. In contrast, in the mind of God all things (including the "I" of each knowing individual) are completely gathered up in eternal and perfect ideas, in the complete harmony of potency and act, that is, in that complete and perfect actuality (Greek *entelecheia*) in which the substance fulfills all its potentialities without exception.

The ideas, then, are creation as known by God in the Word, which is the true place, that is, the place of original ideal existence, of all reality. The multiple effects are the same creation as known by the imperfect created intelligence. The third kind of nature, the world of pure actual appearances, is therefore only a phenomenal reality: the appearing of imperfect creaturely potentialities and actualities in the course of a history of reality that unfolds—but only for finite mind, which is itself part of that reality—in the multiplication of phenomenal spaces and times.

But since effects are the manifestation of divine causes to the creaturely mind, and since the divine causes are a manifestation of the divine thought, Eriugena can say that in everything that is and is true, without exception, there is a *theophany*, a manifestation of God: an appearing of that which is in itself invisible, a showing forth of God's perfect substantial subsistence in the imperfect succession of multiple potentialities and actualities. Any phantasm is deceptive only insofar as the subject regards it as the manifestation of something individual, separate from God, and self-subsisting as an individual thing. In fact, it is really a theophany, since it is an appearing of God in what comes from God. It can therefore be said that each thing is God, and this can be said without bringing any risk of an immanentist confusion of the divine and the creaturely because only in God is every manifestation of multiplicity and diversity reduced to unity, whereas creatures are creatures insofar as they perpetuate the division between potential being (that is, the pure possibility of being) and actual being.

D. CREATION AND PROCESSION: ERIUGENA'S HEXAEMERON

The history of God's work is, then, according to John Scotus, the description of a twofold process: a descent (or procession) from causes to effects and a return from actual multiplicity to the originating divine causality. This return is the result of the natural tendency of all things to the reunification of their being in perfect self-knowledge, which, for its part, is a participation in the pure divine knowledge that contemplates, in the eternal changelessness of the ideal substance, the perfect balance of potency and act.

The third book of the *Periphyseon* is devoted to a description of the procession, set in the framework of an extensive commentary on the six days of creation as narrated in Genesis. This is a Hexaemeron that Eriugena tackles with a great display of sophisticated knowledge in the areas of the sciences, physiology, and astronomy. Making his own the principle that Scripture contains an inexhaustible depth of meanings (like the limitless gleaming colors of a peacock's tail), he engages in a broad and structured exegesis that takes over patristic interpretations, even of the same verses, that may differ but are all true. Thus he advances from the naturalistic interpretation of Basil to the allegorical one of Augustine, and, finally, to the exposition of his personal interpretation, which enables him to take the divine work of creation and to find and develop therein the fundamental elements of his own system.

Thus the creation of light on the first day is for him an allusion to the descent of causes into their effects. On the second day the locating of the firmament between the upper and the lower waters describes the appearance of the four elements and of the spatio-temporal bounds that divide spiritual creatures from corporeal. The emergence of the dry land on the third day describes the combining of forms with matter that gives rise to individuals. In the exegesis of the fourth day John Scotus displays a noteworthy knowledge of astronomy as he describes a system that is geocentric but sees the planets circling the sun while the sun circles the earth. On the fifth day the multiplication of the corporeal, vegetable, and animal species on the face of the earth describes the appearance of the visible accidents that cover and hide the *ousia* of each thing, so that the created earth becomes a symbol of the original ideal substantiality of all things that is hidden by the appearance of imperfect creaturely potentialities and actualities.

The presentation of Eriugena's anthropology, which is introduced by the exegesis of the sixth day, is dominated by the conception of the human being as the central creature in the cosmos and the goal of the divine work, toward which all created reality is moving and in which everything is included and brought into harmony. The human being is the true middle or center of the cosmos and the metaphysical workshop of the world, in which all the creaturely lives—corporeal, sensible, imaginative, rational, and intellectual—are accounted for.

In the mind of the human being, whose knowledge is thus the most complex and therefore also the most complete of all creaturely kinds of knowledge, all creatures exist in the form of cognitive notions, although these are imperfect inasmuch as they reflect not the *ousia* in its original ideal state but the dispersion of these creatures in the accidental setting of space and time. In this sense, then, human beings are truly "images" of God to the extent that their intellect is modeled on the Word as its archetype. But whereas in God creatures are known in the ideal perfection of their full actuality (*entelecheia*), human knowledge is only a potential image of the divine knowledge. This is the "image of God" that the human person at its creation receives along with the task of actualizing it by one day attaining to the "likeness" of God; that achievement will mark the definitive convergence of human and divine knowledge.

E. ORIGINAL SIN AND THE INTERRUPTION OF THE CREATIVE PROCESS

By placing Adam in the earthly paradise Scripture tells us, in symbolic form, of this assignment to human beings of their central task in the economy of creation: to rise up from the world to God in order to acquire in him a perfect knowledge of the world and thereby aspire to the knowledge of God himself. By carrying out this duty, human beings would have been able to discover, in their true knowledge, the real essence of things. And when they reversed direction and traversed, while also unifying, the stages in the manifold diversification of created effects, this action was to be the very accomplishment of the definitive return (not only cognitive but real inasmuch as really known) of all multiplicity to the real unity of the divine ideal knowledge. It would mean the return from individuals to species, from species to genera and therefore from senses to reason, from reason to intellect, from created intellect to the divine Word, ending in the final reunification of all that is true in the peaceful divine contemplation of reality, that is, in the repose of the seventh day.

But the completion of this journey was possible only as the result of a free choice by the created will, a choice willed by God precisely because it meant a free decision to love him. But original sin, described in the pages of Genesis (to the exegesis of which the fifth book of the *Periphyseon* is devoted), interrupted and halted the divine plan, for it diverted human beings, and with them the entire creation that is recapitulated in them, from the course of action that was to lead them to the achievement of the "likeness to God," that is, of their own complete actualization and, at the same time, the complete actualization of the entire creation.

The loss of friendship with God thus brought with it a radical upheaval in the correct order of the human cognitive powers, an upheaval that was at the same time the cause and the definitive consequence of the sin itself and the reason for and result of the divine punishment.

Drawing in part on Ambrose's *Paradise* and in part on Gregory of Nyssa's *The Image*, John Scotus here gives an attractive exegesis of the biblical story of our first parents' sin. His exegesis explains the nature of the tragic interruption of the process that was to lead them to the ability to know the truth of all things in God. Adam is a symbol of the intellect, which is invited by God to contemplate the truth of creation; the invitation is contained in the promise that Adam will eat the fruit of the tree of Life, which is the Word himself in whom the eternal ideal substances have their existence.

But Eve, who represents the lower form of knowledge, allows herself to be infected and enthralled by the groundless outward appearances of sensuality. These are symbolized by the serpent, who urges her to pluck the fruit of the tree of the knowledge of good and evil. This fruit, however, God had forbidden because it represents the cognitive confusion that is at the source of the imperfect natural knowledge of human beings, who are continually looking for distinctions between truth and falsity. And instead of Adam's remaining submissive to the guidance of the noetic intellect, he allows Eve to involve him, too, in the loss of the intuitive contemplation of truth. As a result, the entire human soul is cast down into the deceitful phenomenological world of disordered particular, spatio-temporal, and accidental forms of knowledge.

Adam and Eve now realize that they are naked, for they have been stripped of the truth that protected them, like a clean tunic, from the iniquities of error. God covers them with clothes made of skins, that is, the sensible body, which henceforth rules the higher faculties of knowledge. The divine punishment solidifies this inversion of the cognitive order, for which human beings themselves are solely responsible, but at the same time the punishment includes the promise of a future redemption. God curses the serpent because the dominion of irrational sensuality over the soul is not part of the order of nature. Sensual passion will therefore creep along, feeding on earthly appetites, but only until the proper order of knowledge is restored and the serpent's head is crushed by the foot of the woman, that is, by the soul, which will once again correctly direct its own aspiration for knowledge.

Until that time comes, Eve will have to bring forth her individual acts of knowing with pain and toil (that is, her children or her *conceptus*, as the Latin of Genesis has it, an allusion to the particular "concepts" of the sciences, which are laboriously developed through dialectical investigation). Adam, for his part, will have to till the earth; the earth, as we have seen, signifies the *ousia* or true substance of things, which is covered by the thorns of cognitive appearances that no longer permit the intellect to approach the truth of the primordial essences. But, since Adam himself is earth (or the universal human, one of the eternal substantial ideas in the divine Word), his state of condemnation cannot change the hidden eternal perfection of the truth, which has only temporarily been lost.

It has been lost "until you return to the earth from which you were drawn" (Gen 3:19), says the divine voice, thereby solemnly prophesying the return of the human person to the changeless divine idea in which its truth resides.

F. REDEMPTION FROM SIN AND THE RETURN

The incarnation of Christ is the way, and the only possible one, that permits a reconciliation between creation, which has distanced itself from God, and the Word in which creation continues to be rooted in primordial truth. In fact only the Word, by a completely unmerited act of divine love, is able to turn around the dispersive thrust of creaturely knowledge by uniting his own divine nature to a human nature. And inasmuch as the Word takes flesh in a human being, who is the "workshop of the world," he recapitulates in himself not only the entire human race but the whole of creation.

The new Adam has thus made possible both the reversal of creation's descent and alienation from its divine cause and the beginning of the universal return to the true knowledge God has of the world and of himself, and therefore to the world's true reality in God. And precisely because this conclusion involves a return to the authentic order of knowledge, the formula at the beginning of the *Periphyseon* that alluded to this transcending of creaturely gnoseological coordinates could only find expression in a logically negative form: the nature *that is neither created nor creates* (to the complex treatment of which the fifth book of Eriugena's work is devoted). The fourth species or kind of nature, which will become a reality at the end of time, will in fact not be created, because the entire universe of things visible and invisible that God created will return to its primordial causes, which exist in God, and nothing further will be created. Nor will this fourth nature create anything, because it will be contained within its own fullness, and "God will be all in all things" (1 Cor 15:28).

The descent of Christ into creation occurred in order to heal the break caused by sin and to renew the possibility of beatitude for all human beings. Thanks to that descent, humanity will be able to traverse in the opposite direction the stages of the descent that alienated it from God. The risen body of Christ dissolved the bond with materiality and the chain of accidentality, and thereby anticipated within history the future condition of all the bodies that will arise in him at the end of historical time. This condition is that of a "spiritual body" in which corporeity is not eliminated but returns to the original perfection of its authentic substantiality.

This perfect body, which was that of Adam in paradise, will be united with the soul, which has been purified of all the dross of earthly multiplicity, and together with the soul will restore the unified truth of the human substance by reconstituting with it the perfection of the divine idea that created it. Together with the human being, who is "intermediary for the world," the whole of created nature will return to its causes and, as air is absorbed by light, will be united with the Word in the fulfillment of all its created potentialities. Nothing of the divine work will be lost, but it will be fulfilled in the triumph of its complete actualization, its *entelecheia*, the eschatological reunification of potency and act, which is that very "fullness of the stature (Greek *hēlikia*) of Christ" that Paul promises to all the resurrected.

In the final victory of nature over dispersion and separation from God the substance of sinners, too, will be redeemed. Those who continue to reject the universal offer of grace, if there are any such, will be punished not in their substance (*ousia*) but in their free will, which continues to remain persistently within the limits and imperfection of their individuality. Meanwhile, the entire cosmos will participate in the beatifying vision of God in all things. But among the redeemed there will be differences of personal condition in beatitude; these differences are consequences of the individual way of perfection each traveled during his or her earthly life. In a harmonious combination of the various forms of reward, the beatific vision will be granted in varying degrees, dependent on the greater or lesser completeness reached by the potential capacities of each person. Thus all will be caught up by the triumphant divine light in the eternal sabbath that will conclude the history of creation. Being in this situation will be for some (the damned) a source of torment, for others the source of complete happiness, but with varying degrees of intensity.

There is, then, a general return, the perfecting of all natural capacities that is shared by all. But, as John Scotus tells us in an inspired exegesis of the parable of the five foolish and the five wise virgins (Matt 25:1-13), he foresees some privileged individuals enjoying a mystical marriage with the Word. The possibility of contemplating God in God himself will be limited to the "special return" of the few chosen individuals who have fully merited a direct participation in a union of humanity and divinity that will repeat in eternity the historical condition of the incarnate Christ. As the Word really became a human being in history, so these true followers of Christ will really become God in eternity; as participants in the effects of Christ's humanization they will experience in themselves the final deification reserved to the elect (the *theōsis* spoken of by the most enlightened among the Greek Fathers).

G. BEYOND THEOLOGY

In the present life the theological intellect can reach an understanding of this ending of universal history, but only as a certainty that is necessary but incomprehensible. Only the deified human being can understand deification. But in the centuries-long course of the history of creation the cooperation of revelation and intelligence permits the searcher for truth at least to move, in the measure of his or her ability, toward an understanding of the mystery through the exercise of theological knowledge.

John Scotus never explains the concept of theology as something different from the highest form of philosophical knowledge. However, in three of his mature works he does provide some points useful in clarifying the role and finality of the knowledge with which human beings try, by a balancing of faith and reason, to anticipate in present theological understanding the content of the future beatific vision. The three are: an incomplete *Commentary* on the Gospel of John, his inspired *Homily* on the Prologue of the same Fourth Gospel (here we find his interpretation, which we saw earlier, of the race of Peter and John to the tomb as an allegory of the proper relation between reason and faith), and a commentary on the first treatise of Pseudo-Dionysius, the *Explanations of the Heavenly Hierarchy.*

This last-named work explains the various degrees of creaturely knowledge of the divine, a knowledge that is always imperfect and therefore of a theophanic kind. In the present condition of humanity after original sin the essential theophanic tool that enables human beings to achieve a theological knowledge is the reading of Scripture. But the effectiveness of revealed language in communicating is not of one kind only. At a lower level the divine Word (which John Scotus, like Dionysius, calls simply "theology") achieves expression by relying on the natural meanings of a language that can be understood and, with the help of the philosophical sciences, analyzed by dianoetic reason. We may say that to this order of theological knowledge belongs the entire effort to grasp scriptural truth, as attested by the complex speculative developments of the *Periphyseon.*

But in Scripture God also expresses himself in an alogical and artful way, using as it were a supernatural poetic art capable of raising created minds above the immediate literal meaning. Here symbolic expressions, parables, anagogical allusions, and even, at times, tetralogical (monstrous) images lift the intellect of the believer toward impenetrable mystical heights that human language is not capable of signifying directly. Finally, beyond the enjoyment of the revealed text that is written in human words there is the understanding of the divine that is reserved to angelic intellects that, in a more or less perfect way depending on their place in a hierarchic order, intuitively grasp the truth present in the countless theophanies scattered throughout creation.

Human beings manage only occasionally to reach this supremely perfect natural knowledge, when through the constant exercise of their lower faculties they are able to rise to the point of activating the intuitive and unifying power of the pure intellect. They reach, that is, the kind of knowing had by the angels themselves (thereby confirming the idea of human beings as occupying a middle place in the universe, capable, as they are, of rising from bodily sensation to angelic knowledge). At the same time, however, even this intellectual theological knowledge that is typical of the angels and attainable by perfect human beings is still indirect and incomplete inasmuch as it is based on theophanies. Such is the knowledge promised in Eriugena's *Periphyseon* to the blessed who share in the common or "general return." In the present life no one can anticipate the superlative conditions of the deifying beatific vision that is proper to the blessed for whom the "special return" is reserved.

But in a single instance in the entire history of the cosmos, by an exceptional and completely unmerited grant from God, it was possible for a created mind to rise to the vision in which God eternally contemplates himself and, in himself, all things. This privileged human being was John the evangelist, who was elevated to a state utterly transcending all creaturely limitations and to the vision of God in God and thus to an understanding of the divinity of the Word, who "was with God" and "was God" (John 1:1).

John Scotus celebrates this unique event with genuine speculative emotion, especially in his *Homily*, and then makes a thorough analysis of its theological content in his commentary on the Fourth Gospel. The supercelestial flight of the apostle John, a spiritual eagle who was able to fix his gaze on the sun of the divinity, ended with his return to earth in order to proclaim to humanity with prophetic voice the truth that "the Word became flesh" in space and time. By this proclamation he revealed that all who believe can someday reach the higher theological knowledge that he had been able to enjoy for a single instant outside of time.

6. Theological Learning and Thought in the Greek East of the Ninth Century and in the Late Carolingian West

A. THEOLOGICAL THOUGHT IN BYZANTIUM FROM THE NEW CONTROVERSY ON IMAGES TO THE PHOTIAN SCHISM

From the middle of the ninth century on, the frontier lands of Christianity, both Greek and Latin, experienced a new wave of attacks from outside peoples: the Normans from the Northwest, the Hungarians and Slavs from the East, the Arabs from the Mediterranean. In the West this new affliction became a further cause of serious social disorder within a political system that was obviously already weakened and subjected to a gradual feudal decentralization. This worked to the advantage of local lords to whom the populations looked for the defense of the territory and who saw to the maintenance of a limited but indispensable regional economic network.

In the Byzantine world the emperors reacted both to the intensifying internal tensions that had become endemic, as well as to the new increase in external pressures, by energetically tightening the screws in order to strengthen monarchical authority. Indeed, rather than representing a weakening of the office of the emperor, the frequency with which rapid successions to the throne occurred, often as the result of violence and depositions, was a sign of an impulse to strengthen the central authority, which sought to free itself, with the help of the army if necessary, from any interference by aristocrats, monks, and priests. As early as the first half of the ninth century this process of concentrating political power had important consequences, even in the religious sphere.

Leo V, the Armenian, was acclaimed emperor by the military in 813 because of the defeats the empire had suffered in war against the Bulgarians. Beginning in the first months of his rule, and with the specific intention of protecting the monarchy against increasing interference by monasteries, he inaugurated a second phase in the imperial imposition of iconoclasm. This return to the past promptly elicited a response from the two most important representatives of the ecclesiastical culture of the time: Nicephorus of Constantinople and Theodore of Studios. In contrast to the strongly polemical attitudes that marked the anti-iconoclastic literature of the previous century, both these men promoted a renewed commitment to theological research based on a methodical use of the argumentative tools originating in philosophy.

Nicephorus of Constantinople (d. 828/829) had been a collaborator of Patriarch Tarasius before succeeding him in 806. During an intense decade of eremitical withdrawal before becoming patriarch he had received a monastic formation, in the course of which he acquired a solid intellectual preparation. His official resistance to iconoclasm led to his deposition in 815 and then to an exile that lasted until his death. While far away from Constantinople he composed his most important works, among them his *Greater Defense* and three *Replies* or *Refutations*, in which he showed how iconoclasm and the ancient heresies, from Arianism to Monophysitism and Monotheletism, sprang from a common root. This he identified as the erroneous effort, made in order to facilitate reason's acceptance of the faith, to exaggerate the more spiritual aspects of the Christian religion by introducing into it a dangerous reduction of the physical concreteness of Christ's human nature.

Theodore (d. 826) was the founder and energizer of the monastery of Studios in Constantinople, which was for centuries an important study center with its own fruitful scriptorium and an increasingly well-stocked library. His works display an even more obvious familiarity with classical literature and the exercise of a theological reflection based on the collaboration of biblico-patristic culture and philosophical speculation. He became an outstanding figure in the iconophile party, especially after Nicephorus was exiled; he himself was later sent away from Constantinople. He was a prolific writer, whose works also supported his considerable activity as a reformer of monastic life. He wrote a great many *Letters*, *Homilies*, and poetic compositions; of special importance among his interventions against iconoclasm were his three *Refutations*, in which the use of philosophical tools in support of theological controversy was even more notable and effective than in the works of Nicephorus.

The renewal and perfecting of a methodology for the defense of religious truth was thus the common characteristic of the second generation of anti-iconoclastic polemicists. The interventions of Nicephorus and Theodore were solidly supported by an extensive biblical and patristic erudition that was energetically employed against theological error in order to defend the unity of the religious tradition. But precisely in order to ensure its stability, both men set this scriptural and patristic traditionalism within an unassailable logical and speculative framework. Thus the need of refinements, beyond those of the eighth-century writers, led these two writers to draw on the foundations laid by Aristotle for categories, definitions, and conceptual comparisons that were useful especially in defining an "image" and its relationship to its "archetype."

Nicephorus explained this relationship by appealing to the concepts of "participation" and "analogy"; Theophorus appealed rather to the principle of mimesis or imitation. But especially evident in both cases was the felt need to make clear that the legitimacy of the veneration of christological images in particular was based on the very theological justification of the mystery as a whole. Pictorial representations had in fact the function of recalling the Incarnation, which was the historical manifestation of the divinity of the Word in a corporeal and visible reality and, as such, could be represented in sufficiently meaningful expressions. Such expressions included both theological discourse and, even more, visual images that transcend linguistic and cultural boundaries and are universally understandable and therefore of high informational and educational value.

Motives of a political kind also led, under Michael III, to the definitive restoration of the veneration of images, which had been sanctioned by a solemn council in Constantinople in 843. When Michael attained his majority in 857 he made his uncle, Bardo, his associate in governing. Bardo favored a monarchic centralization and devoted himself to an attempt to remove the cultural monopoly held by religious and monastic parties. It seems that Bardo should be credited with having promoted the reorganization of studies at the university of Constantinople, where the study of mathematics and astronomy was combined with the reading of Plato and the Neoplatonic philosophers. The new consolidation of political authority, which was quickly stabilized when Basil I seized power in 867 and the Macedonian dynasty was founded, was thus accompanied by a new era of cultural stability, which fostered the systematization and erudite rethinking of the literary, but also the juridical, scientific, and religious patrimonies.

The foremost figure in the political and cultural life of those years was Photius (d. ca. 891), who came from an aristocratic family that had always had a hand in political and religious matters during the recent period. Photius was a layman, but in 858 Bardo raised him to the patriarchate after the deposition of Patriarch Ignatius for political reasons and despite the opposition of the episcopal party and the Roman church. As a result of the break between Rome and Constantinople and the reciprocal excommunications of Pope Nicholas I and Photius, 867 marked the beginning of a real schism (the "Photian schism"), with its aftermath of serious controversies between Latin and Greek Christianity. During this period, as often happens, the polemics shifted appreciably from the institutional level to other sensitive ecclesiological and theological areas. Two examples: the rivalry between western and eastern missionaries in the conversion of the Slavs and, for the first time, a difference in trinitarian formulas, especially due to the introduction of the *Filioque* into the Latin liturgy's description of the procession of the Holy Spirit ("from the Father" alone, according to the Greeks; "from the Father and from the Son," according to the Latins).

In 868 the new pope, Hadrian II, asked western theologians to take a position on this last subject of debate. The invitation was accepted by Bishop Aeneas of Paris and the now-elderly Ratramnus of Corbie, who wrote an *Answer to the Objections of the Greeks* in which he had an opportunity to make a final interesting application of his theological method. After his coronation Basil I initiated a policy of rapprochement with the Roman church and therefore deposed Photius. In 869 a council in Constantinople (regarded as the eighth ecumenical) ended the schism and restored Ignatius to his office.

In the years that followed, however, the papacy became involved in a serious internal crisis due to the hostility of the Roman aristocracy to John VIII; that group opted for antipope Formosus of Ostia. Photius profited by this situation and the death of Ignatius to have himself once again recognized as patriarch in 877. John VIII excommunicated him a second time, but then in 882 John was assassinated. Only a lengthy series of protests by John's increasingly weaker successors led finally to the definitive deposition of Photius in 886.

During his exile the elderly ex-patriarch devoted himself to the writing of a lengthy theological work in which he responded to the attacks made on him by Latin scholars: the work was his *Mystagogy* (that is, mystical teaching) *of the Holy Spirit*. Fed as it was by the author's great knowledge of philosophy (he knew and made extensive use of the writings of Aristotle, especially those on logic, and of works of the Neoplatonists), his defense of the eastern trinitarian formula was marked by a profound theological acumen, as he continually moved back and forth between scriptural citations and rational arguments. In rejecting the legitimacy of the *Filioque* he emphasized, above all, the fact that the coeternity of the divine persons is guaranteed by the procession of the Spirit from the Father alone, just as the Son is generated by the Father alone.

Yet, despite the insightful structure of the arguments, the tone had now become tranquil, and the writer's criticism did not become a direct attack on the authority of the church of Rome and the Latin patristic tradition. He knew the latter and cited it accurately. This was a sign of a conscious maturing of his own theological wisdom, which moved beyond the limits of the controversies of the moment and contributed to a renewed pride in his continuity with the age-old spiritual heritage of the Greek world and his independence of the Roman church and the criticisms of Latin scholars.

If we look at the man in this same perspective we must appreciate his extraordinary fertility as a writer, for he was the author not only of a large number of theological and homiletic works but also of some learned compilations, the purpose of which was to collect, organize, link together, and pass on to others the many-sided evidences of his vast erudition. Especially noteworthy here is the wide range of information about the books, secular or Christian, he claims to have read, and which he sets down in the elaborate collection he calls his *Library*. This is a real encyclopedia of notes on his reading; they take the form of summaries, comments, short extracts, and passages giving the historical, cultural, and philological setting of the books, and they cover an impressive number of works from the past. In not a few instances what Photius says supplies the only or at least the most authoritative evidence that has come down to us.

b. In the West: The Late Carolingian School

Learning and a wide range of books written in widely varying settings and widely varying genres are not always signs, as they were in Photius' case, of an increase in a generation's cultural efforts. They can also be a clear sign of a decadence in the intellectual sphere that in turn reflects a wider crisis of civic, spiritual, and moral identity.

In the last decades of the ninth century the Latin West saw a progressive and almost inevitable disintegration of the political ideals that maintained the structures of the Carolingian empire and, along with those ideals, of the cultural vitality that had likewise supported and accompanied the structures. The political breakup led to the intensification of open rivalries between corrupt and weak rulers who were no longer capable of controlling the foreign enemies who were infiltrating the territories of the empire. Moral corruption spread also among the representatives of the ecclesiastical hierarchy, which became involved in struggles for power, and even in the monastic world. The Roman church had for some time been subject to the arrogant activity of ambitious aristocrats.

Charles the Bald died in 877, a few months after sanctioning in the Capitulary of Quierzy the inheritability of the high offices and feudal possessions of the crown's most important collaborators. His death left the empire to be the booty in fierce struggles over the succession. The last attempt at territorial unification under a single emperor failed with the death of Charles the Fat in 888. Thereafter, while the Danes were storming the northern coasts, the empire broke up into various regional centers of power.

In this environment educated and religious individuals were no longer filled with the great enthusiasm for research that had marked the most fruitful minds of past years. The activity of the Palatine School ceased with the disappearance of the last heirs of Charlemagne, and the vitality of the episcopal schools likewise began to fade. Only the monasteries continued to be centers of intellectual life, but now in isolation and amid the monotony of their customary ways; thus the scriptoria continued and even intensified the copying of ancient and patristic texts and the libraries continued to grow, but the approach of educated men to these treasures was notably passive. In the writers of these years the search for wisdom soon degenerated into a voracious but often uncritical curiosity. The writers wandered about among ancient and recent literary documents in search of the elements of a basic learning that could be brought together in the form of brief, summary notes and then passed on in easily understood and available didactic forms.

The principal method of conveying this didactic erudition was the *glossa*: a brief, basic comment made up of more or less short notes placed between the lines, or in the margins, of literary, philosophical, or patristic classics and of manuals for the teaching of the liberal arts or the books of the Bible. From the point of view of form these were quite unorganized comments containing a very fluid and malleable material. So malleable, indeed, was the material that even if the inscription explicitly identified its author, or at least made him easily identifiable, the material could be continually recast from one manuscript to another, with completions, corrections, or additional notes. The reason for this adaptability was that the primary value of the comments was to supply information for use with the work being analyzed.

From the viewpoint of content the glossator's comments served not only to explain or clarify points in the text being commented on. They often took the occasion also to introduce other useful ideas, doctrinal additions, information, and sometimes even anecdotes having no direct connection with the subject. Such stories, however, contributed to the expansion of a comprehensive cultural patrimony the glossator wanted to pass on to his colleagues or disciples. It was as if, within a complicated system of reciprocal references, the elements of all this erudition were being set before the reader so as to complete the picture, with some of them explaining the true teaching contained in others, and vice versa.

The two most notable representatives of this cultural phenomenon, which was characterized precisely by its typical lack of originality, were Heiric and Remigius. Both belonged to the school that had developed at the Benedictine monastery of Saint-Germain in the episcopal city of Auxerre; this school, like those of Laon and Quierzy, reflected the last gleams of the culture of the Carolingian palace. Their cultural importance thus reflected the influence of the three types of study center that had vied among themselves for cultural primacy in mature Carolingian civilization: the urban, the monastic, and the curial. In their learned compilations Heiric and Remigius were the first witnesses to the initial spread of the philosophical and theological influence of John Scotus Eriugena; they may also have been his collaborators or his students.

Heiric of Auxerre (d. ca. 876) was certainly a pupil of Haymo, a renowned author of homilies and biblical commentaries and himself linked to the cultural personality of Eriugena. Heiric left direct evidence of the didactic activity of his teachers in his *Collectanea*, a collection of notes on his reading of the various texts that were the subject of commentary in the lectures he followed. In the kind of program it represents, although certainly not in the richness of its interests and the wide range of its contents, the *Collectanea* may be likened to the *Library* of Photius. The influence of Eriugena is evident in some of Heiric's *Homilies* and above all in a hagiographical work, the *Life*, in verse, of Germanus, patron of the monastery of Auxerre. Here the author is inspired by the *Periphyseon* when he describes the ascent of the saint toward the highest gnoseological and ontological goals of the "return," including even deification.

As an author of glosses, Heiric stands out especially for a commentary on the Pseudo-Augustinian *Ten Categories* (a Neoplatonic paraphrase of Aristotle's *Categories* that was especially esteemed in the Carolingian period). Here, again under the influence of John Scotus, Heiric propounds, among other things, a reintegration of all created reality into an ontological pyramid of genera and species that is dominated by the ten categories or supreme genera. At the apex of the pyramid is the all-inclusive concept of "nature," which includes both God and creatures. Heiric warns, however, that dianoetic reason, using its own logical tools (such as definition and univocity), is not able to capture such a maximal reunification of "all the things that are and those that are not" in a meaning supplied by a single mental concept. Such an action is rather the work of the higher noetic intuition of the intellect.

This passage makes clear the educational and popular role that the late Carolingian teachers assigned to their learned comments. In his glossa, Heiric in fact constructs a cosmic ladder of reality that is useful both for showing the classificatory effectiveness of Aristotelean logic (in this case, the doctrine of the ten categories) and for exemplifying the bold unifying vision of being that is proper to Eriugena's system, in which two doctrinal worlds are fused in a single instructive explanation of reality.

Remigius of Auxerre (d. 908), a student under Heiric, was the most prolific and representative author of glosses in the late Carolingian period. He was active both in the monastic sphere and in the urban schools, especially those at the cathedrals. He has left a large number of comments on texts from every discipline that was practiced in the scholastic curriculum of those years: Sacred Scripture, liturgy, liberal arts, logic, philosophy, and theology. These texts show clearly a plan to bring together in a usable summary of ideas and information the most important results reached by western wisdom during the century just ending. Thus Remigius does not disdain to set side by side, as plausible alternative yet complementary explanations of one and the same concept, doctrines that differ among themselves in origin and context or are even contradictory. For example, when commenting on the Latin text of the Mass he is not afraid to combine in a single gloss the most boldly allegorical interpretations of Amalarius of Metz and the moralizing and spiritual readings recommended by Florus of Lyons, who when living had been Amalarius' most implacable critic.

Above all, some of Remigius' best organized and most successful comments, such as those on the *Consolation* of Boethius and his short theological works, the one on the handbook of Martianus Capella on the liberal arts and the one on Genesis, make one point clear, namely, that this cultural irenicism allowed Remigius to combine information and suggestions produced by the wisdom of the various Carolingians and to develop a comprehensive conception of cosmic reality and of relations between creatures and creator. His glosses helped spread this conception widely in the Latin-language schools. At the center of this doctrine Remigius places the Platonic and Augustinian principle of the derivation of all things from the Ideas that God eternally thinks in his Word, who is the Art and Wisdom of the Father and the Life of everything that exists. This was the idea that Alcuin had made the foundation of Carolingian theology and that

John Scotus had turned into the core of his entire ontological system. Remigius, for his part, avoids all rationalistic excesses as he quietly makes this idea the basis of a comprehensive conception of the universe as the arrangement of things according to the order established by God.

In short, toward the end of the ninth century the late Carolingian cultural world displayed a gradual rigidification into a network of texts and related ideas within the framework of an institutional and mental structure that was decidedly technical and scholastic in its approach. Therein its cultivators, beginning with the elements of grammar in order with their aid to enter upon meditation on Scripture, made their own the classical desire to achieve the perfection of knowledge by ascending from corporeal realities to those that are intelligible. This scholastic mentality, then, was not a cage imprisoning the sapiential aspirations of the Latin West. It was a fertile soil that was arid and bare at the time, but in which, after a period of silence, there would spring up renewed thinking about the intelligibility of the world and of religious truth. Moreover, the thinkers of the following generations would have no difficulty in regarding this renewal as the natural development, without any break in continuity, of the speculative activity and intellectual productivity of the Carolingian period.

Chapter 2

The Contradictions of the Transitional Period: The Ancients versus the Moderns

I. Theological Platonism and Ecclesiastical Reform in the Tenth and Eleventh Centuries

1. The Renewal of Studies in the Ottonian Age

A. THE REFORM OF MONASTIC LIFE AND THE CLUNIAC MOVEMENT

During the years when Remigius of Auxerre was teaching in Paris he was also charged with reorganizing the cathedral school of Notre Dame, which in the following centuries would become the most important scholastic center in France. Among the young men who attended his courses was a canon of Tours named Odo. After being converted to a monastic life and having been elected abbot of Cluny, Odo became in the following years the principal force behind a reform movement in the Benedictine Order; in the tenth and eleventh centuries this movement gradually spread, first in France and then in the rest of Christian Europe.

During this lengthy period the Cluniac movement was not the only effective plan at work in the reconstruction of the monastic communities and the restoration of the moral and religious foundations on which the ascetical ideal of late antiquity was based. During the Carolingian period the work of reformers who were supported by the imperial structures, such as Benedict of Aniane, had given an energetic impulse toward uniformity and respect for the Benedictine *Rule*. Now, in the later period, some important monastic centers promoted an internal reorganization of the cenobitic system: two such were Brogne in Flanders and Gorze near Metz in Lorraine. Later, various eremitical movements developed in Italy due to the work of such individuals as Romuald of Ravenna (d. 1027), whose teaching gave rise in the eleventh century to the Camaldolese congregation, and John Gualbert (d. 1083), the founder of Vallombrosa near Florence.

In England the Danish invasions inflicted a hard blow on the first cultural revival, which in Wessex had as its patron King Alfred the Great (d. 899), the author of paraphrastic translations into Anglo-Saxon of such fundamental paragons of early medieval Christian culture as Gregory the Great, Bede, and Boethius. In the tenth century, however, a new impulse to spiritual fervor and the cultural vocation of monasticism sprang from the reorganizational work of Archbishop Dunstan of Canterbury (d. 988).

Nonetheless, the movement originating in Cluny became, at least until the beginning of the twelfth century, the most widespread and effective of the organized reform movements, due to its spread of religious and ethical ideals that were sincerely adopted and to its creation of a close-knit system of exchanges and surveillance among religious settlements. For the success of its planned reform the Cluniac religious movement relied on the direct submission of its communities to the protection of the church of Rome. It thereby removed itself from the direct control and interference of the local clergy and, as a result, over the decades it also made a useful contribution to the preservation of the spiritual unity of the Latin West, at least at the ideological and religious level. The work of the Cluniacs also gave an impulse to a considerable intensification of reflection on the contents of the faith. This was due above all to the fact that, among the activities the *Rule* saw as making up a monk's everyday life, it placed a special emphasis on prayer and on reading and meditating on Scripture, as compared with manual and economically productive activity.

We have very effective descriptions of the diligence shown by these monks in implementing and cultivating the practico-theological vocation that characterized their ideal of religious life. The descriptions are found both in the theoretical writings of some of the most important representatives of the movement and in a rich flowering of hagiographical writings. In the latter the lives of the saints and the founders of the most important centers became a means of calling the reader's attention to a persuasive model of the virtues and principal works of the perfect monk.

In addition, in his *Life of Gerald of Aurillac*, Odo (d. 942) described the exemplary life of a devout lay prince who, outside the cloister, embodied the heroic virtues of a soldier of Christ, fully making his own the commitment to a holy life and the struggle against evil that the monk was intended to exemplify in visible forms in the world. In three books of *Conferences* Odo subsequently wrote a gloomy denunciation of the vices of the society of his time. He also composed a large-scale religious poem in an epical and didactic style; this was titled *Occupation* (that is, a "meditation" on the truth that ought to "occupy" the mind of believers). In it he reviews, in a moral perspective, the entire history of creation, emphasizing the centrality of the Incarnation and explaining the monastic way of life as a continuation of the original evangelical community of the first redeemed Christians that was begun by the mysterious event of Pentecost.

Over against the distressing description of the moral corruption of the outside world Odo sets the spiritual orderliness of the ecclesiastical community. The authenticity of the latter is attested in monastic life by two tangible and irrefutable signs: asceticism and the practice of the liturgy, both of which draw human beings closer to higher realities. Among the central acts of worship Odo attributes great importance to the celebration of the Eucharist, which he interprets in a resolutely realistic manner in order to emphasize the serious sacrilege committed by priests and laypersons when they approach the rite in a state of mortal sin. In Odo's eyes the monastery is a perfect and exemplary ecclesial cell; correspondingly, the church is seen as a great universal monastery in which the way of moral perfection is traveled by the whole human race.

B. THE THEOLOGICAL COMPETENCE AND PRACTICAL WISDOM OF THE BISHOPS: ATTO OF VERCELLI AND RATHERIUS OF VERONA

In the tenth century the priority given to theological and moral concerns was not found exclusively in the monastic world. A successful process of partial political reunification had indeed culminated in the restoration of the empire by Otto I of Saxony (crowned in 962), yet a few of the scholars whom kings and feudal lords still liked to have around them (in imitation of the Carolingian model) saw clearly the distance separating them from the ideal uniformity that had sustained the social, economic, cultural, and moral revival in a political system now gone for good.

Typical, in particular, was the attitude of some churchmen who had administrative responsibilities and were therefore inevitably involved in political quarrels. In works not without a certain religious depth these men energetically stressed especially the desire for an ethical renewal of Christian society, which they considered an indispensable foundation for the restoration even of social interests, peace, and a solid resumption of productivity. Moreover, not infrequently their call for a moral reform of the clergy was inspired by their esteem for monastic life as a model and was accompanied by efficacious exhortations to a revival of intellectual activities and, in particular, of a reading of the Bible that was supported by liberal studies.

One such churchman was Atto, bishop of Vercelli (d. before 964), who worked in northern Italy during the decades that saw the most intense struggles for power prior to the coming of the Ottonians. He, for one, explicitly called for a return to meditation on the contents of the faith as the goal of a constructive program of education and saw in it a remedy for moral error. In a short work titled *Pressures on the Church*, while denouncing and condemning the plague of simoniacal priests, he points to a liberal education as the main way of leading monks and secular clergy to the restoration of their virtue.

It was, however, especially in his extensive *Explanation* of the letters of Paul that Atto showed in a paradigmatic way how competence in the mundane sciences could be fundamental for a correct approach to Sacred Scripture, but without ever yielding to the temptation of turning one's rational criticism into an unfettered investigation of the mysteries of the faith. It is of some interest to note in his reading of Scripture the presence, even if still only episodically, of methodological hints that would later lead to interesting developments in the formal organization of theological work: for example, the raising and discussion of the "question," the formulation of various "solutions" that can be found in the works of the Fathers, and the decisive judgment on which of these can be proposed as the most acceptable.

A few years later, Canon Ratherius was summoned by Otto I to administer the diocese of Verona; he subsequently returned to Germany as bishop of Liège (d. 974). Ratherius was one of the most active imperial bishops, both on the political and organizational levels and on the intellectual level, during the years when authority was being reorganized. He too was deeply grounded in the moral and contemplative ideals of reformed monastic spirituality and also possessed a good knowledge of Scripture. He wrote letters and sermons in which he unsparingly attacked an excessive devotion to literature, but he also showed a considerable philological competence as he discovered and annotated as yet little-known classical texts, among them the poems of Catullus, who was one of the glories of the diocese of Verona.

In his principal work, the six books of *Preliminary Remarks*, he justifies the cultivation of secular studies by showing how useful they are when the skills they produce are put at the service of the moral correction of administrators and, above all, of pastors. According to Ratherius, the latter in particular ought to have a solid knowledge of theology that would guide and assist them in their practical work in the area of the social government of the community of believers. Only a concrete knowledge of the truth, put forth not arrogantly but modestly and in subordination to the constructive interests of the church, makes it possible to bring the will of God to fruition in the world of human beings.

Ratherius also made an interesting concrete application of this principle in his explicit criticism of the mercantile economic system, which was beginning to flourish at this time in the northern Italian provinces as a reaction to the hardships of the civil wars. Here the self-centered acquisition of private gain was based on scorn for the neighbor. In response Ratherius proposes an ideal reorganization of Christian society, one based on the restoration of the kind of community life seen in the apostolic church. The seeming utopianism of this proposal is offset by pointing to the factual historical existence of a society truly based on altruism and the sharing of goods, namely, monastic society.

The need, then, was to have the true Christian charity exemplified by monks practiced by the other two classes as well. In an unwitting revival of the Platonic model of the state, Ratherius divides human society into the laity, who in the common interest ought to renounce the defense of private property, and churchmen, who ought (as Plato planned for philosophers) to be given a serious education of a theological kind, one based on knowledge of the Bible and of the works of the Fathers that will help them learn to govern the Christian people.

The evangelical "foolishness" that seems to triumph in this ideal of Christian living was then expressly celebrated by Ratherius in a short but polished work titled *Madness*, written to defend himself against enemies who called him "mad." It is not difficult to discern beneath the rhetorically convoluted surface of this work the radical nature of the Christian call to cultivate a truth, both theoretical and practical, that is not of this world. It is, however, a truth that, while solidly grounded in a literal acceptance of the Gospel, can be reinforced by the useful support of the wisdom of the ancients that is to be derived from the valuable manuscripts made available in civic archives and monastic libraries.

c. The Pride of Gunzo and the Humility of Hrosvit

The obligation of the bishops to reorganize the educational system, as well an initial consolidation of new concerns arising from a nascent bourgeoisie, called for the reappearance of the master of the liberal arts in the territories governed by Otto I. In most cases this master was a canon professionally involved in the restructuring of the urban schools but also having links with the monastic schools. With the latter these new masters established embryonic cultural relationships, exchanges of books and information, and at times competitive rivalries.

A good example of this last is the testimony of the *Letter to the Brothers of Reichenau*, written by a Lombard master named Gunzo (and known as Gunzo of Italy). It is an indignant response to an insult he suffered at St. Gall, where he was a guest while on his way to carry out a mission for the emperor in Germany. During a conversation at supper he committed a slight grammatical error, using an accusative instead of an ablative, and one of his hosts mocked him, using obscene language. Writing to the monks of Reichenau (a rival abbey on the other shore of Lake Constance), who had taken him in after his angry departure from St. Gall, Gunzo gave vent to his wrath as he defended his dignity as a master with a torrent of examples of his own competence. This defense gave him the opportunity of listing at length the books he had read and the extent of his training in the liberal arts.

His letter thus lets us know the texts an Italian master of the tenth century was reading: the classical authors (among them Horace, Cicero, and Virgil with Servius' commentary), the repertories and treatises on the liberal arts (with Boethius evidently outstanding among these), but also the ancient philosophers in Latin translations (the *Timaeus* of Plato and the *Organon* of Aristotle), the Fathers of the Church. A detailed knowledge of Scripture was foundational to all the rest.

But beneath this proud display of learning, an important concept of theological wisdom underlies Gunzo's attack on what he regards as a science that is immoral and corrupted by the same perverse arrogance as was shown in the unfortunate incident of which he was the victim. His point: even the most extensive and penetrating competence may not and never should foster the presumption that one possesses an exhaustive knowledge of the truth. For the rules of the liberal arts, even if appropriately accepted, as Augustine suggests, as useful instruments in understanding the signs that express various realities, will never be able to bring that goal to completion. Then, too, those who have mastered many rules must always expect that they must still learn many more, for, as Gunzo says mockingly, the rules are far too numerous to fit into the cowl of a monk of St. Gall.

In illustration of this fundamental certainty Gunzo draws on Boethius for the opposed opinions of Plato and Aristotle on the nature of universals, genera, and species, and slips in his own conviction that there are not sufficient reasons for preferring one opinion over the other. The question arises, therefore, of how it is possible that logic, a discipline for obtaining truth, is capable also of reasoning in defense of what is false. Gunzo continues in this vein: if it be true that arithmetic is the discipline whose task is to define quantity, why is it not able to determine how many numbers there are? The answer, the only possible one, is that the human sciences are useful in recording the facts presented by reality and allowing the knowing subject to get his bearings in the created world. However, they certainly cannot impose the truth of laws whose formulation, even if it claim the authority of the wisest scholars of antiquity, is always provisional and can soon be replaced by other norms and other rules that are no less instrumental but are further refined and made more accurate.

Gunzo was, in short, a witness to the opening up of a new perspective in human investigation, one that was in different ways nuanced in comparison with the unwavering certainties of Carolingian wisdom, which inevitably reflected the stability of the political and cultural order of the empire. Now, after the long period of confusion that followed upon the decline of that system and of the ideology that supported it, this tenth-century thinker preferred to state openly how inexhaustible was the task he undertook, and to do so even while making known the wide range of skills he had acquired through dedicated labor.

It is interesting to see how a similar conception of learning and statement of goals run through the literary work of Hrosvit of Gandersheim (d. after 973). This erudite nun is known chiefly as the author of the first medieval western dramatic works worthy of mention. These are comedies whose form is inspired by the plays of Terence, but whose edifying plots are drawn from the hagiographical literature of the time. The purpose, here again, is to offer perfect exemplars of piety and the Christian virtues, which always lead, for the greater glory of God, to the resolution of serious human vicissitudes.

The language used by Hrosvit's personages is refined and full of allusions to a liberal education. In speeches or prayers that draw on classical or recent sources from Augustine to John Scotus, such allusions are useful for concealing effective references to theological convictions rooted in the early medieval mentality. At times she uses her extensive training in the arts even to give a comic emphasis to one or other paradoxical situation in her plots. Some examples: Callimachus, a pagan, in confiding in his friends, runs rapidly through the logical rules governing the division and semantic definition of a concept, only to close his line of reasoning with a declaration of love for a chaste Christian spouse; the hermit Paphnutius, before telling his disciples of his intention to go to a brothel in order to convert a fearful courtesan, indulges in a lengthy and repetitious learned exposition of the beauty and harmony of the cosmos, which are sullied by the sins of human beings.

Yet, despite this seemingly gratuitous display of her acquired skills, her consciousness of her outstanding education (which she herself says was exceptional for a woman) is not a reason for her to be proud and overweening. She even feels obliged to justify her continuous and excessive use of the "debates of philosophers" by warning her readers, in the preface to her writings, not to fall into the error of thinking her to be a truly wise person. Her reason: not only her knowledge, which is a pale imitation of true knowledge, but all the ideas and rules discovered and established by the philosophers over the centuries are only drops of a wisdom that flows inexhaustibly from the bottomless well of truth. Applying to her own situation an idea from the *Periphyseon* of Eriugena, she also warns that all creaturely wisdom is always potential and that only in the life of beatitude will human beings have an actual knowledge of the truth. Knowledge and foolishness are equal in God's sight; only injustice and immorality are condemnable in human beings who do evil because they know less than they ought to know.

D. THE WISE ABBOT AND THE LEARNED POPE: ABBO OF FLEURY AND GERBERT OF AURILLAC

Like Gunzo and Ratherius, Hrosvit, who celebrated the *Deeds* of Otto I in a poem in hexameters that is almost hagiographical in tone, had connections with the aristocracy of the court, doubtless through the cultivated abbess Gerberga of Gandersheim, a niece of the emperor. All these authors were clearly aware of participating in a planned renewal of culture that was spurred on by the political restoration. The model for this renewal was the academy of scholars who had gathered around Charlemagne, but the troubled political situation of the current century turned scholars in a decisive way toward practical and spiritual goals that were useful for the moral advancement of souls rather than for celebrating the glories of the empire.

This did not mean, however, any lesser awareness of the close historical bond that in the final decades of the tenth century connected the two parallel plans for the renewal of the empire and the renewal of studies. The two principal agents in the intensification of the process of renewing philosophical, scientific, and theological studies during the reign of Otto II and especially of Otto III were Gerbert of Aurillac (d. 1003) and Abbo of Fleury (d. 1004). It is of interest to note that these men were also the two most eminent personalities, one in the ecclesiastical and episcopal world, the other in the monastic world. Both, moreover, had played an active part on the political stage, first in the process that gave birth to the French monarchy and culminated in the coming to power of Hugh Capet, and then in the formation of the Ottonian dynasty's program of pacification and consolidation of the imperial institution.

Abbo was a native of Orleans, educated at Rheims and Paris, and a friend and correspondent of Odilo, abbot of Cluny. As abbot of the great monastery of Fleury-sur-Loire, Abbo was one of the most energetic promoters of monastic reform in France and England.

Gerbert, originally a monk at Aurillac in the Auvergne, spent some time in Catalonia and was the first master of the Christian West to come in contact with the advanced scientific skills of the Arabs. He then served as master in Rheims, where he had among his students the future Otto II and the future Robert II of France, the son of Hugh Capet. He went on to be abbot of Bobbio, archbishop first of Rheims and then of Ravenna, and, at the imperial court, the tutor and adviser of the young Otto II. The latter wanted Gerbert at his side in carrying out his ambitious but ephemeral plan of restoring the ancient empire of the Romans. He also placed Gerbert on the chair of Peter, where the monk chose for himself the name Sylvester II as a symbol of continuity with the ancient alliance between state and church established by Constantine the Great and the first Pope Sylvester.

Abbo and Gerbert gave themselves fully to a reform of the broad spectrum of liberal studies. Both men regarded the latter as the natural starting point for rational investigation, which gives access to truth in the degree in which it succeeds in better understanding and reflecting the order God has established for creation. In other words, according to an image Abbo takes from Eriugena's Platonism, reason ascends from a description of *things that are* to an understanding of *things that are not*, that is, of the hidden divine causes, the spiritual and eternal forms governing creation.

As part of this project the two men established a prolific school of young disciples who then became active in following their teachers' scientific, philosophical, and theological example. The two fostered the formal restoration of the stylistic, graphic, and artistic habits of the Carolingian past as means of bringing the ideals and aspirations of that past back to life again. They were enthusiastic searchers for books containing as yet unknown sources of ancient and late antique science; they looked to these as ways of revitalizing studies that had become stuck in a tedious repetition of ideas from manuals and of bringing to light new problems that would stimulate intellectual activity.

In the study of logic, for example, one of their merits was to have rediscovered and put into circulation the monographs of Boethius and his commentaries on Aristotle. These would contribute to turning the attention of scholars from the rules of logic governing terms (definition and division, predication, categories, and so on, which had mainly captured the attention of the Carolingians, relying, as they did, primarily on the commentaries of Boethius on the *Isagoge* of Porphyry) to those governing the construction of discourse and argumentation (propositions and their relationships, syllogisms, topical arguments, and so on). According to the testimony of one of Gerbert's pupils, the historian Richer, a monk of Saint-Rémi in Rheims, the future pope gave courses in logic based on the reading, with commentary, of the entire Aristotelean-Boethean logical corpus, thereby introducing a technique that would later be given a definitive form by Abelard in the twelfth century.

Abbo, for his part, wrote an *Explanation of Categorical and Hypothetical Syllogisms*, which represented the first effort, based on the monographs of Boethius, to investigate more deeply the old Late Latin knowledge of syllogisms, which was scanty and purely schematic and formal and had come down from Martianus Capella and the *On Interpretation* of Apuleius. Abbo also composed a series of *Grammatical Questions*, which contain some interesting problems of semantics that force the reader to go beyond purely morphological considerations in judging the effective meaning of words. For example, of special interest from the point of view of theology is his explanation of how the seemingly equivalent terms "unbegotten" (*ingenitus*) and "not begotten" (*non genitus*) have rather different meanings in trinitarian doctrine, since the former expresses an unqualified negation while the latter expresses only a privation.

Another area of studies in which both these masters worked with valuable results was the disciplines of the quadrivium. Richer attributes to Gerbert the construction of an abacus, an astrolabe, and a map of the stars; he praises the didactic value of the latter, saying that even an uneducated person, given a correct starting point, would be able on his or her own to recognize in it "all the other parts and properties of the celestial sphere."

But it was Abbo, in particular, who brought out the close connection between the visible order of things and the divine wisdom that produced it. He did so in his most important piece of writing, a deeply speculative work that is both scientific and sapiential and combines scientific skills and theological reflection in a single elegant ideal of knowledge. The work is his commentary on the *Calculus* of Victor of Aquitaine; the author himself gives his work two meaningful titles: *Introduction to Arithmetic* and *Treatise on Number, Measure, and Weight*. After explicitly citing the words of Wisdom 11:21, which declare prophetically the mathematical perfection of creation, Abbo makes Victor's text, a summary list of the systems of measurement used in antiquity (weight, length, capacity, etc.), the starting point for an intricate numerological and theological meditation on the cosmic order established by God, who is supremely One, "according to number, measure, and weight."

The human mind is invited to use the tools of the liberal arts in making its way through the stages of a philosophy that embodies genuine cognitive love of the self-revelation of divine wisdom in creation. This philosophy works on both the practical and the theoretical levels and is supported in its operations at every point by reference to scriptural truth, but can also look forward to a continual, indeed inexhaustible progress in its own perfectibility because the created mind will never cease to draw ever nearer to the self-revelation of God in creatures. The understanding of "numbers," "measures," and "weights" respectively will become an understanding of the quantities, qualities, and substantial forms that determine the being of creatures. It will at that point become possible to ascend to the contemplation of these determinations in themselves that make beings determinate and that Abbo speaks of as "what Plato calls ideas."

Furthermore, by way of an elaborate philosophical and theological ascent that passes through the categories of the Aristoteleans, the mathematical essences of the Neopythagoreans, and the formal causes of the Augustinian and Eriugenean tradition, the human intellect attains to a glimpse of the eternal perfection of the three absolutely primordial things. The representation of these to itself marks the completion, and at the same time the exhaustion, of the mind's effort to reconstruct the harmony that reigns in reality. The three primordialities are: the "number" that can never be quantified, the "measure" that can never be qualified, and the "weight" that can never be substantially defined. The three "together are a unity and a trinity (they are *aequiterna*); they are always and everywhere distinct; they are always and everywhere a single God in all and through all."

As for Gerbert, a similar inspiration drawn from a theology of ascent that has a Platonic and Pythagorean flavor lies behind his compilation of a short work on logic, titled *On Rationality and the Use of Reason*. He wrote the work in an attempt to resolve a seeming inconsistency in Porphyry's rules for the definition of a concept, but he sees this limited technical problem simply as an occasion for pointing out to human reason the opportunity it has of going beyond the instrumental and artificial nature of the logical classifications worked out by the philosophers in an effort to move about more comfortably in the visible universe, and of advancing to the superior, true, and perfect divine logic that presides over the objective, orderly arrangement of things.

Porphyry teaches in his *Isagoge* that it is correct not only to predicate a "difference" of a "species" (for example, "the human being is rational"), but also to predicate a "difference" of another "difference" (for example, "what is rational uses reason"). But this seems to contradict another fundamental rule of Aristotelean logic, namely, that the predicate must have a greater extension than the subject (it is correct to say that "the human being is an animal," but not to say that "animals are human beings"). Yet "rational" has a greater extension than "uses reason," as is clear if we think of someone who is asleep and suspends the use of reason, but does not cease to be rational.

By way of a series of subtle formal clarifications Gerbert finds the solution in a correct application of the distinction between "potency" and "act": "rational," which signifies a potential capacity, seems in fact to have a greater extension than the "use of reason," which signifies the same function but in act, but this is simply because we presuppose, unjustifiably, that what exists in potency has a greater extension than what exists in act. This is indeed true, but only in the limited sphere of particular physical things, the world of corporeity, where what is true can also be actual. But in the world of intelligible realities, that is, in the eternal reality of the divine ideas, everything that is true is actual. In that theological state of perfection, what is "rational" is always a form "in act," and of that form it is always correct to predicate "uses reason."

Logic can also think up other rules and niceties in order to make up for the deficiencies and inconsistencies that persist at the level of natural imperfection. For example, the idea of an "indefinite predication" helps to a formal resolution of the problem that arises from admitting that the subject of a proposition can have a vague extension (thus not everything that is "rational," but "some rational beings," without saying how many, "use reason"). But this is only a loophole for escaping the incompleteness of our mental universe, which reflects all the imperfections of the material world, that lowest degree of reality. It is therefore fundamental for the human intellect to recognize exactly where it stands within the dynamic hierarchy of the created world. In fact, it stands on only an intermediate step of the pyramid of intelligible perfections that reaches up to God. It is to God's perfection that the intellect must always and unwearyingly move, even though in this life it will never reach a definitive, exhaustive, and satisfying understanding of it.

2. Cosmic Optimism and Criticism of Reason after the Year One Thousand

The legend of the Year One Thousand has it that humanity waited fearfully for the dawn of the new millennium because this signaled the end of time. Romantic historiography indeed painted exaggerated pictures of that age, but the legend does have some objective reality in the pages of some chroniclers at the beginning of the eleventh century. This is true especially of the highly figurative writing seen in the *Histories* of Rudolph Glaber (d. 1047), which are marked throughout by the intense apocalypticism of a visionary and filled with stories of miracles and other warning signs that urge sinners to repentance.

It is interesting to compare two anonymous autobiographical notes written at different times in the margins of two manuscripts from the cultural world of the abbey of Fleury. Both notes were probably written by the same individual; on the basis of the handwriting they seem to have been made by historian Ademar of Chabannes (d. 1034), a learned reader of the classics and a dedicated promotor of the religious renewal of the church in his day. The first note describes the succession of apocalyptic portents and prodigious events that occurred in 1003; the writer connects these with the unexpected and sensational disappearance of Sylvester II, which was preceded by the death of Otto III (Sylvester's "Constantine") a few months earlier and was followed a year later by the death of Abbo of Fleury.

In the second note, written exactly three decades later, Ademar tells of the helpless amazement caused by an eclipse of the sun on June 29, the feast of Saints Peter and Paul, in the year 1033 (the thousandth year since the redemption). He reports that many believers swore they had seen in a fiery circle around the darkened sun a half-length image of a human person, perhaps Christ himself returning for judgment. But this time Ademar is skeptical: "After looking long and attentively, I, for my part, saw nothing; and I am not lying."

During the thirty years that separated these two notes and saw a shift in Ademar's outlook from apocalyptic symbolism to a dispassionate recording of a collective illusion, something changed in the religious temper and cultural dynamics of Christian Europe. The seeds of intellectual inquiry that Gerbert and Abbo had sown began to bear fruit; so, too, the period saw the first results of the work of renewal of religious spirituality as it spread from the Cluniac monasteries to the entire church and nourished a lively ethico-religious consciousness even among the laity and the working classes. A subtle but growing humanistic and religious optimism spread from the schools and reached the centers of power and worship, in a climate favorable to a more intense activity of research and study.

The growing trust in the powers of scientific reason also gave a positive impulse to new attempts at a deeper understanding of religious subjects. This occurred in some writers who focused on a clearer understanding of important aspects of dogma but who also never lost sight of the needed impact of their meditations on the uninterrupted efforts at a moral improvement of monasticism and the secular clergy. It could happen, of course, that the study of the liberal arts took the form of an accentuated specialism that lost sight of the propaedeutic role of human knowledge in relation to theological truth. But in no case during this period did greater trust in the powers of reason lead to a split between distinct and noncommunicating spheres of knowledge. Despite their different emphases, the thinkers of the time never moved too far from a principle they all shared: that of organic complementarity, which ought always to combine the results of human science with what is given to us to understand, through the reading of Scripture and the study of natural reality, of the ordering perfection of the divine cause.

A. ORDER OF THOUGHT AND COSMIC ORDER: HERIGER OF LOBBES,
   ADALBOLD OF UTRECHT, AND FULBERT OF CHARTRES

The historians, too, felt the impact of this influential idea of the parallel between the created order and the divine law, and they sometimes tried to introduce it into their material by thinking up undeveloped theological divisions of history that allowed them to point out signs of providential government in the universe of human beings. For example, both Rudolph Glaber, already mentioned, and Heriger, abbot of Lobbes (d. 1007) and chronicler of the bishops of Liège, seem to have drawn inspiration from Eriugena's fourfold division of "nature." Thus they set the vicissitudes of humanity within a speculative framework that gave meaning to the seemingly irrational course of history and placed even the aspects of it that are least intelligible to practical reason in the perspective of government by the eternal divine will.

Others, following more closely the model given by Abbo and Gerbert, looked first and foremost to the study of nature for evidence that the workings of human reason and the providential order of creation could be brought into harmony. In a commentary on the cosmological hymn *O qui perpetua* in the third book of Boethius' *Consolation*, Adalbold, bishop of Utrecht (d. 1026), regards the study of the mathematical order of the visible universe as able to lead the intellect, through exacting syllogistic meditations, to an understanding of the derivation of everything from God. In this way he manages also to introduce a strictly rational proof of the existence of God based on the identification of the higher origin of the cosmic order. His argument: if every creature has a form that gives it a qualitative or quantitative individuality and if every form is good, there must be something good at the origin of the determinability of all these forms, and this something is not itself a form. If theologians nonetheless follow Boethius in saying that God is "the form of all things," this is only because "form" is predicated, by extension, of that which has no form in itself, being the source of everything that is formed.

Thus a particular speculative tendency of a Platonic kind spread in a perceptible way and touched and influenced many writers of this period. The tendency had filtered down from the teachings of Augustine and Pseudo-Dionysius and was strengthened by a palpable presence of Eriugenean influences. It seems to have been dominated on the whole by one general idea: that it is possible for human beings to become assimilated to divine truth through a careful study of the correspondence between the order of things in creation and the order of the ideas in the divine Word; this study is in turn made possible by an exploration of the order of words or, in other words, by a mature ability in using the rules of logic. In the early decades of the eleventh century the best representative of this approach was Fulbert, bishop of Chartres (d. 1028), who also helped spread it through the great success of his philosophical and theological teaching.

Fulbert was a disciple and admirer of Abbo of Fleury, whom he loved to address in his letters as "high priest and philosopher" and even as "god" (*deus*), because he had become like God in his ability to contemplate *the things that are* and *the things that are not*. Fulbert himself possessed a high degree of classical and patristic learning and, in his cathedral school at Chartres, encouraged studies that would develop in important ways during the following century. His persistent search for a solid rational control of intelligible truth is documented in his writings by the subtle lines of argument and the systematic way in which he takes up specific theological problems. For example, in his *Treatise in Answer to the Jews* he bases interreligious dialogue on an invitation to recognize in Christ the Word the source of universal rationality; he then makes willing use of logico-syllogistic arguments to explain the religious truth of Christianity.

Likewise based on a systematic way of arguing are some of his sermons on the "Mystery of Mary," which aim to show the logical consistency of the various fundamental aspects of Marian devotion.

Especially important is the way in which Fulbert's theological Platonism guided his thinking about the sacrament of the Eucharist. He was persuaded of the validity of the teaching of Pseudo-Dionysius and Eriugena according to which the substance of visible things (their true "being" = *esse*) is in itself invisible and can be grasped only by the intellect, whereas the outward appearance of the accidents (which are "not being" = *non esse*) is perceptible to the senses. Against this background he wrote two *Letters* on the Eucharist in which he maintains that the body and blood of Christ are truly present on the altar after the consecration, but as substances that are to be regarded as real precisely inasmuch as they are invisible and not subject to the variability of appearances.

The same approach is to be seen again in another interesting contemporary contribution on the Eucharist, *The Body and Blood of the Lord*, by Heriger of Lobbes, who was mentioned earlier. The author refers explicitly to the Carolingian controversy between the extreme realism of Paschasius Radbertus and the symbolism of Ratramnus of Corbie. Heriger offers a solution that reconciles these two teachings on the Eucharist, noting that while, even during the sacrifice, the bread and wine continue to be food for the "outer person" (*homo exterior*), the body and blood of Christ are a real and substantial nourishment for the "inner person" (*homo interior*), which is the spiritual and intellectual substance of the souls of believers, this being the real subject of redemption from sin.

B. THE BOUNDARY BETWEEN THE LIBERAL ARTS AND THEOLOGY: ANSELM OF BESATE AND ADALBERO OF LAON

During these same years a rich local tradition of juridical and rhetorical studies developed in northern Italy and produced some useful tools for research. One such was the successful encyclopedic lexicon titled *Elucidarium* and attributed to a certain Papia (or perhaps Papias, from the name of the city of Pavia). It was in this setting that the masters of the liberal arts first began to claim the right to separate the practice of these arts from their exclusively propaedeutic role in the improvement of theological knowledge.

Among the most spirited representatives of this new attitude was a Lombard, Anselm of Besate, known as "the Peripatetic." In a work with the odd title "Battle of Rhetors (or Speakers)" (*Rhetorimachia*) he says that his own scientific skills authorize him to avenge himself against his cousin Rotland, who was guilty of using Anselm's own oratorical gifts to portray him as a wicked practitioner of the most unlawful black magic. Under the veil of irony this claim, that his highly specialized knowledge exempted him from the fundamental obligation of every Christian to defend the truth, signaled an overly bold confidence in the distinction between the scope, goals, and particular traits of the various scientific disciplines. The discipline he was practicing and defending in this work was rhetoric, the natural purpose of which is to improve the human ability to speak, while it is for logic to distinguish expressions of truth from those of falsehood. And just as there should be no confusing of the tools and purposes of the various arts, so too all problems having to do with the explanation of the dogmas of the faith ought to be excluded from studies within the province of the arts.

Anselm seems to want to draft a manifesto for this autonomous practice of the human disciplines in a famous passage in which he tells of being transported in a dream into paradise. Here his mortal remains were the subject of a strange quarrel, both verbal and physical, between a group of the souls of his blessed relatives, who wanted to keep him with them in eternal happiness, and the personified arts of the trivium, which called for his return among the living lest they be abandoned by their best disciple. But just when these three young women were on the point of triumphing over the "saints," the dream was broken off, leaving Anselm consoled and at peace because he did not have to make such a difficult decision.

In France, during these same years, Adalbero, bishop of Laon (d. 1030/31), who had probably studied under Gerbert at Rheims, was another practitioner of the liberal arts who attested to the need to accurately define the areas of competence of each kind of knowledge. Unlike Anselm, however, his concern was to establish, in this way, the limitations of liberal studies in relation to the mysteries of the faith rather than to claim the right of free expression for the specific viewpoint of each of the arts. For example, in a dialogue titled *Correct Argumentation* he engages in a sophisticated syllogistic exercise dealing with the solution of the seemingly trivial question of why a she-mule is a useless creature. His purpose is to show in a concrete way the versatility and fruitfulness of the teachings of this art while freeing them from the claim to have an influence on theological questions of fundamental importance. In fact, the paradoxical conclusion reached in his display of so much technical skill (namely, that the uselessness of a she-mule can only be caused by the wickedness of demons) seems to have for its only purpose to show that rational judgments are limited to the world of the natural, beyond which only revelation has a right to speak.

The same approach is taken in Adalbero's better-known *Poem Addressed to King Robert*. This is a dialogue in verse between Robert II, king of France, and Adalbero himself, in which, as he exhorts the sovereign to promote peace among peoples, he sketches a pitiless description of the imperfections, injustices, and discords of the world and contrasts them with the organized perfection of the universe created by God. The conclusion of the work, however, explains that the entire first part of the poem, with its description of the horrors for which Adalbero boldly made the king himself responsible (eliciting the latter's contemptuous resentment), had been intentionally exaggerated by a generous use of rhetorical artifices. The purpose of these artifices was to describe not reality, but rather a likely outcome, so that the king might now understand what would happen if he did not intervene in a prudent way to make corrections and try to make the world of human actions conform to the mathematical perfection of the visible cosmos.

Therefore, while keeping the liberal arts within the boundaries of their real competence, their practitioners can and indeed should place themselves in the service of theological knowledge, but while remaining completely respectful of the absolute and higher truth of dogmas. This is the point Adalbero documents in another speculative poem with the pithy title *Summary of the Faith*. The explanation here of the contents of the Christian religion is explicitly aided by recourse to arguments from logic, but only to some extent and for the purpose of showing the reasonableness of some central aspects of the faith. The process then allows the mind to accept even that which, because it follows a logic of the supernatural order, inevitably eludes its grasp.

c. THE LIMITS OF THEOLOGICAL REASON ACCORDING TO GERARD OF CZANÁD

Reflection on the distance separating the results of earthly science from the true glory of God leads to markedly more pessimistic thoughts about the human condition in *A Study of the Hymn of the Three Young Men*, a commentary on the song of the three young men in the fiery furnace in the book of Daniel. Its author was Gerard of Venice, bishop of the distant city of Czanád in Hungary, whose inhabitants were recent converts to Christianity. Gerard writes an implacable condemnation of the arrogance of philosophers, such as those who think they can impose rational "divisions" on higher realities "by mistakenly classifying divine activities by means of their useless judgments" (the reference to John Scotus is clear, even if tacit).

Gerard, too, had a thorough understanding of the teachings of the liberal arts, had read the classical writers, and had some familiarity with the philosophical doctrines of the ancients, even if only indirectly. He was not an unperceptive enemy of philosophy and worldly learning, and he even had very clear ideas about the scientific character of the liberal arts. Each of these, as he knew well, is founded on intelligible, changeless, and true first principles that are therefore divine insofar as they are eternally engraved in nature by the will that created it. But he carried to an extreme a reductive assessment, evident in other contemporary writers as well, of the explanatory powers of reason, which is incapable by itself of attaining its own ends.

He therefore pronounces a merciless condemnation on an arrogant use of human intelligence, that is, a use not for legitimate specific and instrumental inquiries but for impossible investigations into the ultimate truths of the created world. Recalling the biblical metaphor that says that the words of God are "sweeter than honey" (Ps 118:103), he explains that instead it is human words that are honeyed; it is the arts of the trivium and quadrivium that are sweet but can cause nausea and can impair our salvation if we feed on them alone. The works of God are, paradoxically, at once searchable and incomprehensible. We human beings need to scrutinize them in order to develop the practical ability to live on them and by means of them, but we must always be certain that we shall never have an exhaustive and adequate understanding of them.

This duality comes surprisingly close to Gerard's rational criticism of the Platonizing dualism that to a great extent inspires the thinking of his contemporaries. Knowledge, in this case human philosophy, is in Gerard's view probable but changeable and imperfect, as are the realities of the corporeal, sensible world. Invisible realities, in contrast, are the subjects of a higher wisdom, a "heavenly philosophy"; this must be capable of being grafted onto the body of our knowledge of visible things, which are the image and trace of a higher reality. But the human intellectual ascent toward the divine will be advanced only if and when the arts are really placed at the service of theology, not by claiming to impose their own methodologies on theology but by agreeing gradually to renounce the supposed necessity of their rules after having used them fruitfully in investigating only what is within the scope of human judgment.

At the apex of this ascent toward truth the denial and transcending of natural judgment will, thanks to the pure simplicity of faith, yield the possibility of a judgment that is no longer dialectical but of a higher order, one that reveals the intelligibility of the mysteries in all its luminous splendor. Only at this highest level does the true voice of Christ-Wisdom do away with the unknowableness of the mysteries of the Trinity and the Incarnation, which will ultimately appear to the eyes of believers to be a true, possible "miracle of dialectic." In an important reversal of the usual methodology of theologians, Gerard sees in the simplicity of faith not the beginning of the ladder of knowledge but its highest rung. The rigid patterns that mark the use of intelligence have elevated the mind to the point at which it is able to do without their help; henceforth, belief is the best preparation for reaching the truth: "The deepest meanings of words are disclosed, and every human being becomes a true philosopher."

3. Humanistic Classicism and Religious Spiritualism at Byzantium in the Century of the Schism

A. Erudite Scholarship and Mystical Spiritualism in the Tenth and Eleventh Centuries

In Byzantium, too, in a way that was singularly parallel to what was happening in the Latin West, the active memory of the intellectual openness of the greatest thinkers of the ninth century, such as Nicephorus of Constantinople, Theodore of Studios, and Photius, was kept alive during the tenth century by the lively, though not original, work of erudite descendants who were engaged mainly in the disseminating, anthologizing, and annotating of ancient texts. Their work ensured the preservation and spread of the cultural synthesis of the past by freezing it, so to speak, within a system that was both lexicographical and encyclopedic. Exemplary from this point of view was the work of Arethas, metropolitan of Caesarea (d. 932), a Platonizing disciple of Photius; his name is connected with the preservation of a very rich, annotated library of philosophical and literary texts, both classical and late antique. Another exemplary work was the anonymous *Suidas*, a title not easily understood (perhaps equivalent to "palisade" or "bulwark"); it is a large lexicon of about 30,000 entries in alphabetical order and full of philosophical and historical definitions and ideas.

Contrasting with this learned conservatism was another conservative, though nonproductive trend: the appearance, chiefly in monastic circles, of an ardent religious spirit that emphasized the spiritual and was rooted in a radical return to the simplicity of faith and meditation on the gospels. As compared with the antiquarian tendency that marked the teachers at the so-called school of "higher education" in Constantinople, the mystical reaction of the monks took the form, oddly enough, of a trend that was in its own way innovative, even though claiming to be driven by an obedient return to the patristic heritage and a refusal to compromise with secular learning. This emphatic spiritualism was in fact a break with the recent past. Indeed, the very appeal that was made to the patristic tradition in controversies with those sympathetic to pagan philosophy proved to be not a call for them to revive the speculative models or scientific skills of the Fathers, but rather an exhortation to immerse themselves completely in the sincere experience of their faith.

Simeon the New Theologian (d. 1022) was a typical representative of an intense religious fervor that was practiced in a strongly individualistic perspective and in the intimacy of a personal dialogue of the soul with God. During his lifetime Simeon was opposed and persecuted for his intolerance of ecclesiastical and monastic structures, and indeed of every outside influence. He produced many writings marked by an intense mystical piety; outstanding among them are the three *Centuries* of *Theological, Gnostic, and Practical Chapters*, as well as numerous hymns. His preferred means of leading souls to a knowledge that participates in the truth of God was prayer. More particularly, prayer meant the interior experience of a total offering of the self, in the course of which the mind "strips itself of every thought"; it abandons the formal aspects and rules of thought and language and immerses itself, freely and without limiting ties, in the splendid power of divine love. His mysticism is indeed not without parallels of terminology and content with the intellectual asceticism of Platonism, but from secular wisdom he takes only such means of expression as are useful for shedding light on the ineffable contents of his own religious experiences.

There are clear reasons why certain attitudes of Simeon seemed excessive, and in fact his mysticism was revised in the direction of greater moderation by his greatest disciple, Nicetas Stethatos (d. ca. 1090), the superior at Studios. Nicetas was Simeon's biographer and saw to the publication of his works; he also modified the master's individualistic outlook by setting it within the framework of a cosmic process by which illumining grace is mediated; this correction, inspired by Pseudo-Dionysius, restored the continuity between the hierarchic order of the angelic intelligences and the hierarchic order of the organizing structures of the church.

B. MICHAEL CERULARIUS AND THE SCHISM

The new religious radicalism even took root at the very heart of institutional religion. This is shown by the work of the patriarch of Constantinople, Michael Cerularius (d. 1058), which is full of deep spirituality and marked by an unmistakable aversion to secular wisdom. He was an apostle of the autonomy and superiority of the patriarchate in relation both to western Christianity and the Roman See and to the entire ecclesiastical structure of the East. He was indeed a theologian only to the extent that he had to be in defense of the institution he represented, especially during the violent dispute with the representatives of the Latin church that broke out in 1054 over the western use of unleavened bread in the eucharistic sacrifice.

On this particular subject Michael and the eastern theologians who supported him, among them Nicetas Stethatos, went as far as possible in developing arguments against Rome, but they did it more as a formal duty than out of conviction. In fact, the search for demonstrative evidence for that specific liturgical usage would have had to be located within the broader framework of a systematic theological justification of positions on a variety of questions of custom and dogma on which disagreement between the two churches had been clear for some time. That would have been quite difficult for both sides, since their disagreement was obviously rooted in the immobilism of their respective traditions rather than being based on a real theoretical foundation.

That fact also explains why the confrontation with Humbert of Silva Candida, the papal legate charged with upholding the Latin position rather than promoting a constructive examination of the two different outlooks, ended in an irreconcilable break that caused the definitive schism between the Greek church and the Roman church. After reciprocal excommunications the debate continued, but the disputants were unable to hear one another. When Humbert returned to the West he wrote an *Answer to the Objections of the Greeks*, to which Cerularius replied with an official decree, a *Sēmeiōma*, of the so-called "permanent" synod. Both documents put greater emphasis on the untenableness of the opponent's position than on the justification of their own.

The quarrel with the West simply confirmed, by official acts that had no real practical consequences, a split based on historical and cultural disparities rooted by now in the centuries-long development of two worlds that had sprung from the religious heritage of the Roman empire. On the other hand, the unwillingness of the Greek ecclesiastical hierarchy to enter into a theoretical dialogue on the dogmatic questions pointed to a specific direction being taken by the new generations of Byzantine thinkers. The latter longed for a renewal of Christian spirituality and morality that would be brought about by a complete immersion in religious experience. In Michael's view (here he aligned himself with Simeon as corrected by Nicetas) this renewal was to be sought even on the community level, with a strong emphasis on the more external and communal aspects of the liturgy and, consequently, a rigid attachment to traditional formulas.

In light of this attitude we can see why it was precisely in these middle years of the eleventh century that the quarrel with the Roman church was unrestrained. In this same perspective we can also understand the heightening of internal disagreements between the defenders of the new religious radicalism and those who continued the cultural traditionalism of preceding centuries. The latter were better disposed to tackle ancient philosophy and more open to a synthesis of human wisdom and theological study.

c. MICHAEL PSELLUS

In the second half of the century the most important representative of this traditionalist humanism was Michael Psellus (d. after 1078). On several occasions he was opposed by representatives of the powerful movement for the renewal of Greek spirituality, chief among them Patriarch Michael Cerularius himself.

Psellus was a respected master of philosophy in the reorganized imperial school, but in 1055 he was compelled to make a profession of orthodox faith in order to escape suspicion of heresy because of his stated readiness to subscribe to the Neoplatonic interpretation of the trinitarian mystery. He withdrew to a monastery in Bithynia, together with John Xiphilinus, his companion in studies and in religious life, but returned later to Constantinople as an influential assistant to Emperor Isaac I Comnenus. He supported the emperor in a spirited dispute with Cerularius on questions of ecclesiastical policy. The patriarch was arrested in 1058, and Psellus wrote the indictment, but the patriarch's sudden death in prison led to a popular reaction that forced Isaac to abdicate. Yet it was Psellus who delivered the eulogy at Cerularius' funeral; in it he defended a laicist conception of imperial authority, which would be free of ecclesiastical interference but respectful of the religious and moral autonomy of the church.

In the years that followed, a new quarrel with the authorities brought Psellus the bitter opposition of his old friend, John Xiphilinus, who had become patriarch in 1063 with the name John VIII. In contrast to John's religious closed-mindedness, Michael claimed the right to be a follower of both Christ and Plato. The new and drawn-out disagreement kept the two men at bitter odds for a decade, until the final, only seemingly paradoxical public appearance of Psellus at the funeral service of his second great persecutor, who died in 1075.

Michael Psellus' adherence to the learning and philosophical classicism of the preceding centuries made him a thinker in open opposition to the recent tendencies prevalent in the Byzantine theological world of the eleventh century. Encouraged by the example of his teacher, John Mauropous, Psellus became a scholar, man of letters, poet, and humanist, but also a sensitive liturgist who possessed great religious depth (recall in particular one of his poems in which he pleads with God to rescue Plato and Plutarch from damnation). He was convinced that the speculative power of human thought could be used, in moderation, as a very practical help in explaining and confirming some theological themes communicated in revelation. He therefore urged a comprehensive retrieval of the best results of the ancient philosophical and sapiential tradition. In order to show the legitimacy of this step he placed at the center of his entire educational program the intellectual archetype provided by the work of Gregory of Nazianzus, the theologian *par excellence* among the Fathers and unanimously acknowledged by all Byzantine thinkers as an authoritative model.

Psellus' best-known work, *A Miscellany of Teachings*, which he dedicated to Emperor Michael VII in 1071, is in fact only an encyclopedic collection. The consistency and quality of his working method can best be seen in the extensive and valuable collection of his lesser theological writings, known as the *Theologica*. In these Psellus frequently introduces carefully chosen passages from the *Orations* of Gregory, subjecting them to commentary and interpretative refinements, thereby turning what the Greeks universally regarded as the most authoritative systematization of the faith against heretics into a tangible proof of the religious continuity between the Platonic philosophical tradition and Christianity.

On this foundation Psellus bases the orthodoxy of his own generous revaluation of the Platonic religious mind. Following the model of the late antique Neoplatonists and of Proclus in particular, he sets this reassessment in the framework of a graded classification of the philosophical sciences. This moves from the lower disciplines (codified by Aristotle: these first of all provide methodological help in reaching knowledge [logic] and then direct the description of the visible world [physics] and the ordering of norms for practice [ethics]), on to contemplation of intelligible principles (doctrine of the ideas), and finally to the peaks of higher intuition of theological truth. Psellus found all this expounded in the henadic metaphysics of the Neoplatonists and the theurgic symbolism of esoteric revelations (such as the *Orphic Fragments* and the so-called *Chaldean Oracles*, a second-century soteriological and metaphysical poem with Neopythagorean echoes on which Psellus wrote a philosophical commentary).

These classical testimonies are constantly compared with passages from Gregory and, less frequently, other Greek Fathers in order to arrange their contents to form a single undeviating line of theological speculation that is placed at the service of biblical exegesis and the interpretation of dogma. The goal of the philosophical ascent to the highest truths of theology is union (*henōsis*), that is, the mystical union of the intellectual soul with the divine mind (*nous*) in pure contemplation of the One. This union is the supreme state of the natural intellect in the Proclian system, but it coincides with the supreme results of the fruition of grace in the religious thought of the Fathers.

The speculative depth of Psellus' "humanistic" outlook is evident; it allows him to ascend from the elementary level of an erudite explanatory reading of the classical and patristic texts of his predecessors to the development, as he himself expressly claims, of a true and proper "philosophy" of the contents of theology. From the by no means simple text of Gregory's *Orations* he manages always to ferret out lines of thought that are consistently ruled by the norms of logic, of which he shows a complete and penetrating knowledge. Especially painstaking are his analyses of the semantic range of the concepts used in Gregory's religious language (nature, being, soul, time, eternity, and so on); these concepts he compares with the corresponding ideas developed by the philosophers.

Even his openness to the theurgy of the *Chaldean Oracles* and his comprehensive teaching on demons bear witness to his constant concern to graft these speculations with crystalline clarity onto the orthodox interpretation of the faith as ensured by the Fathers of the Church. (His teaching on demons was set forth in his anti-dualist dialogue, *Timothy, or on the Activity of Demons*; this was translated by Marsilius Ficino and has enjoyed some success in the West in the modern period.) It is indeed true that the teaching of the ancients has handed on many erroneous ideas to Christians, but if in avoiding these one makes a clear but unintelligent break and renounces the entire patrimony of philosophy, one loses completely the possibility of sharing a truth of great value for a better understanding of the faith and for advancing the salvation of the soul. In fact, according to a recurring image in Psellus' writings, "we ought to learn to recognize not only curative herbs but also those that are poisonous, so that we may heal ourselves with the first and keep away from the others."

D. JOHN THE ITALIAN AND THE EXHAUSTION OF SPECULATIVE THEOLOGY IN BYZANTIUM

Psellus' work remained the only authentic attempt at an original development of a theological method in the Byzantine world; its fate, moreover, was closely connected with the exceptional intellectual powers of its developer. Once Psellus left the scene, religious radicalism regained the upper hand over the last efforts to preserve the classicist tradition, for the radicals saw in the Platonic religious spirit only an impious survival of pagan superstition that was further contaminated by magico-theurgic practices. The only thing this criticism of the entire field of pagan philosophy left standing was the legitimacy of a purely instrumental use of Aristoteleanism, according to the model set down by Damascene.

This reaction against rational speculation in the Byzantine world is illustrated, above all, by the vicissitudes of John the Italian (d. after 1082). He was a student under Psellus and then the latter's successor in the chair of philosophy from 1072 on. He himself was the author of numerous scholastic treatises (manuals and questions, among them a series of "aporias and solutions," wrongly titled "Quodlibetal Questions" by the editors). In these, following the model of his teacher, he included many authoritative figures from among the ancient philosophers, but the number of citations of Aristotle was already far greater than those of Plato and the Neoplatonists.

John became the subject of a lengthy inquisitorial trial, carried out by the imperial tribunal but emphatically called for by the ecclesiastical authorities. This led first, in 1077, to a rejection of some philosophical propositions in his writings that were judged incompatible with the faith; it ended in 1082 with a formal condemnation for heresy. In fact, if we prescind from easy parallels with the case of Peter Abelard in the West, John the Italian does not seem to have held views any bolder than those of his teacher or to have introduced excessively rationalistic interpretations into his explanations of the trinitarian formulas or of the doctrine of the immortality of the soul. The discontent of his judges was due chiefly to the unprejudiced attitude with which he took up religious questions. In dealing with these he made methodical use of Aristotelean logic and of Neoplatonic definitions of the most important theological concepts, but without basing his own deliberately philosophical arguments on the solid foundation of the patristic and exegetical culture that had supported the bold moves of Psellus.

Beginning in 1107, the Patriarchal School of Constantinople made official the tendency of ecclesiastical thinkers to give a privileged place in the formation of the clergy to preparation for exegesis and a basic religious education. The study of philosophy soon ended as succeeding generations of teachers settled for simple commentary on the classics. Evidence of this are the commentaries on Aristotle by Eustratius of Nicaea, a pupil of John the Italian, and by Michael of Ephesus (which were translated into Latin by Robert Grosseteste in the thirteenth century). These men avoided any forays into the realm of dogma and concentrated increasingly on a proper approach to the text in the form of a thorough technical explanation of logical, physical, and ethical questions.

Eustratius was also a theologian esteemed by Alexius I Comnenus, and in his treatment of trinitarian themes was guided by the negative theology of Pseudo-Dionysius, but for this reason he too was condemned in 1117 after being accused of heresy by Nicetas, metropolitan of Heraclea. The latter commented on the *Orations* of Gregory of Nazianzus and was an energetic example of the henceforth incurable split in the Byzantine world between the kind of investigations proper to philosophy and the truth that was the province of religious wisdom.

With few exceptions, the desire to combine philosophical truth with the truths of faith continued to decline and became increasingly hard to find in the twelfth and thirteenth centuries. In addition, further enthusiastic efforts to reopen a theological dialogue between the ecclesiastical authorities of the East and those of the West would prove to be completely futile. Examples: the unionist council convoked by Urban II at Bari in 1098, in which Anselm of Aosta was a participant, was soon frustrated by discussions of the *Filioque*; or the debate that took place in Constantinople in 1111 between Eustratius of Nicaea and Peter Grossolanus, archbishop of Milan and legate of Paschal II. The Greeks' subsequent lack of interest in western culture was not only evidence of the increasingly closed character of their spiritual world; it was also a confirmation of the prejudicial tendency, typical of late Byzantine thought, to avoid any theological dialogue that was based, as they saw it, on obvious contaminations of religious tradition by philosophical reason.

4. The "Modern" Theologians

In times past all of the most authoritative students of medieval philosophy accepted the historiographical image of eleventh-century Latin thought as reducible to a controversy between "dialecticians" and "anti-dialecticians." Today, when seen in the light of a more penetrating reading of texts and historical documents, that image appears to be overly schematic and, in many respects, distorted. Authors like Berengarius of Tours declared and proved their intention of shedding light on the truths of faith by adopting Augustine's exhortation to make understanding precede faith. To describe them as radical dialecticians or, worse, "hyperdialecticians" is unjustifiably to make them seem pure rationalists; yet, given its overall cultural character, the Middle Ages could hardly have produced such a type.

On the other hand, those who adopted an attitude widespread in preceding centuries and refused to place too much trust in the definitional powers of human reason as applied to the mysteries of faith are often described as "antidialecticians." This simplification prevents a true appreciation of the real culture and skill in using the rules of the liberal arts that those writers possessed and, indeed, on the very basis of which they were able to set limits, regarded by them as insurmountable, on human cognitive investigation.

Also oversimplified is the idea that the debates of the time concerned only the liceity or nonliceity of a recourse to logic, for it is clear that what was at issue was not simply a more or less vigorous use of the forms of logical argument. The disagreement seems to have been rather over the greater or lesser trust to be placed in the approach reflecting Platonic theology. This perspective had been widely adopted by Christian thinkers even since the Carolingian age and had resurfaced to a significant degree between the era of the Ottonians and the beginning of the eleventh century. That approach urged scholars to apply their natural intelligence to understanding the reasonableness of a suggested parallelism between the order of things, the order of ideas, and the order of words, or, as we said earlier, between (1) the objective reality of the universal order of things as established by God at creation, (2) the divine ideas eternally thought in the divine Word, which are the ineffable sources of that order, and (3) the verbal tools of the human arts, which endeavor, on the basis of their respective rigorous methodologies, to reconstruct the harmony between things and the divine thought.

Those who were the ardent and most severe critics of this theological Platonism believed it led to the claim that the marvelous effects of divine power in creation could be reduced to the measure of human intelligence. It is especially significant that for the most part these same critics were also active in the movement for the moral and religious renewal of Christianity, which, during the dark period of the battle between papacy and empire over the issue of investiture, was linked with the cause of a radical and universal reform of the church. For this reason their attack on the theological optimism of the past seems in many respects to have been a reflection, at the theoretical level, of their practical struggle against the secularization, simony, concubinage, and immorality of the clergy, those tragic effects of the dreaded meddling of the political authorities in the spiritual life of the church. As seen in this light, the thinkers in question would have regarded the abuse of reason in theology as simply a further aspect of the harmful secularization that over the centuries had corrupted the purity of the primitive Christian virtues and the most authentic Christian ideals.

Precisely because they were promoting a radical renewal of religious life, the polemicists who banded together in defense of the reforming activity of the popes involved in the investiture controversy (from Clement II, d. 1047, to Gregory VII, d. 1086) were not infrequently described by their contemporaries as "modern." These men were part of a general battle against all aspects of a process of secularization of Christianity that seemed to them to have been dangerously increasing for many decades. The name "modern" can therefore rightly be given to these Christian scholars of the second half of the eleventh century who shared a "modern" attitude of rebellion against the "traditional" Platonic-Carolingian speculative approach. Meanwhile, the traditional approach lived on during these years in the teachers and cultivators of the liberal arts who still accepted the ideas that had prevailed in the recent past. Their speculative thinking shared the intention of using the rational powers they exercised in their studies to produce a theoretical reconstruction of the providential arrangement of the world.

A. Manegold of Lautenbach

If we accept the testimony of a contemporary chronicler who praises him as "the master of the modern masters," Manegold of Lautenbach (d. after 1103), a German, can be regarded as one of the chief representatives of the religious and intellectual outlook we have been describing. He explicitly pointed to Platonic philosophy as the root cause of the excesses of a human use of reason that boldly passes judgment on the mysteries of revelation. He taught the liberal arts during the last quarter of the century. We know little about him except for what he himself tells us in his writings, but his testimony is outstandingly important for a correct assessment of the intellectual outlook of the "moderns," since the polemical positions he takes show an explicit connection between the condemnation of Platonism and the militancy of the reformers.

Two authentic works of Manegold have come down to us. The first, *Book to Gebhard*, which was sent to Count Gebhard of Helfenstein, is of interest for its embryonic contractualist theory of the state. He starts with the presupposition, which he regards as beyond discussion, of papal authority's divine origin and of the pope's exclusive jurisdictional competence in all ecclesiastical matters. Then, and in contrast, he immediately calls on natural reason to ground and explain the mutual agreement that links the emperor with his subjects and can be canceled in a case in which one of the two parties fails to honor its commitments. This political naturalism obviously has for its purpose to exclude any right of earthly rulers to interfere in the conduct of divine business. On the theoretical side it is completely in line with the limiting of the claims of reason to intervene in the mysteries of the faith; in practice this limitation reduces the scope of the liberal arts to the investigation of natural phenomena.

This second aspect of Manegold's thought is the main theme of his other writing, *A Short Work in Answer to Wolfhelm*, in which he openly attacks one who presumes to rely on the systematic cosmology of Macrobius in answering questions about the origin of the universe. Here is confirmation of the fact that error begets error: Wolfhelm was an abbot who was also a philosopher and a supporter of Henry IV; as a result, just as he claims to crush the power of the pope under the weight of the secular yoke, so too he is not afraid to give Platonic doctrines priority over the truth narrated in Genesis.

Manegold lists the erroneous absurdities that follow from this contamination and emphasizes their complete incompatibility with the sure data of revelation: the preexistence of souls and the idea of bodies as their prison; the explanation of the nature of the soul as a composite of parts, which is the usual explanation of the being of bodies; the pagan doctrine of the world-soul; the claim to measure the distance to the sun and the moon. Even the definition of the human being as a "mortal rational animal" is contradicted by the clear fact of the resurrection of Christ, and the axiomatic statement used to express the logical rule of consequence, namely, "if she has given birth, then she has lain with a man," is contradicted by Mary's virginal conception of Christ.

But Manegold's denunciation of philosophical errors (a tactic valued and used profitably by the Fathers of the Church) should not be extended into a global condemnation. His intention is simply to urge philosophers to avoid competing with the Holy Spirit in the theoretical investigation of truth and, instead, docilely to return their discipline to the role proper to it as a useful and fruitful tool in the practical, moral, and political education of human beings.

B. THE DISPUTE OVER THE EUCHARIST: BERENGARIUS OF TOURS AND
   LANFRANC OF PAVIA

Theological Platonism was likewise the target, though less explicitly and directly, of the adversaries of Berengarius of Tours (d. 1088) during the prolonged debate over the interpretation of the eucharistic mystery. This was a debate that inflamed the spirits of many during the most impassioned years of the conflict between papacy and empire.

Berengarius was a pupil of Fulbert of Chartres at Liège and then master of the liberal arts in Tours, which was the heartland of Carolingian philosophical traditionalism. He took as his starting point a very genuine realism of essences (or of the universals or the divine ideas) and went on to assert the necessity of a symbolic-spiritual interpretation of the Eucharist.

His argument: since no transformation is possible in the world of corporeity without a becoming of substance, that is to say, in this particular instance, without the substances of bread and wine ceasing to exist and the substances of the body and blood of Christ coming into existence, it is absolutely necessary to deny that in this mystery a substantial change occurs, and to adopt the most radical possible eucharistic spiritualism. In fact, precisely because it is true that the body and blood present on the altar are those of the risen Christ they must be thought of as exempt from any kind of change and endowed with the eternal perfection that essences have and that, after the end of time, all risen bodies will have. Conversely, on the altar of the divine sacrifice, even after the consecration, the visible substances of the bread and wine continue to manifest themselves to sense knowledge. Consequently, to a Platonizing philosopher the real presence of the body and blood of Christ is the truest and most real presence possible: that of the eternal, invisible, and immutable essence that is the authentic sacramental "thing" (*res*) of which, after the consecration, the bread and wine are the sacred symbol.

Immediately after beginning to spread this teaching and making the express claim to have deduced it from the teaching of Fulbert, Berengarius was attacked as a denier of the reality of the sacrament. His attackers were Adelmann of Liège and Hugo of Bréteuil, two theologians who had been his companions during their studies and were bent on defending the memory of their common teacher. The two pointed out especially the excessive use of logical arguments and conceptualisms of which Berengarius was guilty as he presumed to give substantial status to essences thought up by the intellect, although the intellect ought to limit itself simply to searching out essences and knowing them.

In the library at Tours, Berengarius discovered a manuscript containing the book, *The Body and Blood of the Lord* by Ratramnus of Corbie, which until this point had not been widely known. Perhaps misled by an error in the cataloguing of the manuscript, Berengarius believed that it was the work of John Scotus and he thought of circulating it and thereby basing his own defense of eucharistic spiritualism on the authority of the greatest thinker of the recent Carolingian past. Then began a long series of attacks against both Berengarius and the supposed "John Scotus." Both men were met with energetic defenses of the strongly realistic position taken, in John's own time (against Ratramnus), by Paschasius Radbertus. Paschasius' work, unlike that of Ratramnus, was very widely read and esteemed in monastic reformist circles. It is easy to understand how effective eucharistic realism was both in the devotional influence it had on the minds of the faithful, whose emotions it strongly engaged, and, above all, as a weapon against the immorality of unworthy priests, since the accusation that their sinbesmirched hands touched the sacred material reality of the body and blood of Christ only made their sacrilege all the more serious.

Between 1049 and 1079 Berengarius, along with his "John Scotus," was condemned several times at a series of councils, many of them held in Rome with reforming popes presiding. He was compelled to repudiate his own teaching and formally profess the truth of highly realistic eucharistic formulas. Participants in the uprising against the new "heretic," either through their intervention in the conciliar assemblies or through the writing of theoretical treatises on the subject, were many of the principal representatives of the reformist party. Among them were Guitmund of Aversa (d. ca. 1095), Alberich of Montecassino (d. 1086), and Humbert of Silva Candida, who had been Michael Cerularius' adversary in the tragedy of the eastern schism. Among all these names one stands out: Lanfranc of Pavia (d. 1089), the prior of the abbey of Bec in Normandy, whom the Norman king of England, William the Conqueror, would call to the episcopal see of Canterbury in 1070.

After rashly allowing Berengarius to involve him in the controversy, Lanfranc fiercely attacked what he regarded as an inexcusable change in the true nature of the sacrament, which was made explicitly clear, without interpretive subtleties or loopholes, by the words of the gospels. With the intention, however, of cutting through the variety of interpretive nuances that were multiplying in the conciliar formulas and in the theses of the most intransigent supporters of realism, Lanfranc preferred to descend directly to the level of the adversary. This meant making a logical analysis of the text of revelation in order to show, on the basis of scientific and logical skills, what the real contribution of the liberal arts and philosophical learning could and ought to be in the explanation of the faith. The account of the direct opposition of the two men is to be found in their two most important works on the subject: *The Body and Blood of the Lord* of Lanfranc and the *Reply to Lanfranc* of Berengarius.

Lanfranc's contribution is in two parts: a negative critique of the heretic's extreme method and a correct application of a logic that is subordinated to the faith. He is convinced that not only the Fathers of the Church but even St. Paul had a good knowledge of logic, something he regularly brings out in the pages of his own detailed commentary on the Pauline letters. He therefore rebukes Berengarius for having given the truth of logic priority over the truth of the faith; in other words, for having first sought to use pure reason in determining the nature of the sacrament and then having imposed the results of his inquiry on revelation. By doing so Berengarius reversed the correct relationship between reason and faith, for the mystery is such precisely because it cannot be reconciled with the expectations of human knowledge; therefore the act of believing ought to be free of any logical or philosophical preconceptions.

On the other hand, once faith is born and solidly rooted in the believer, the use of the tools of reason becomes not only legitimate but necessary for describing exactly and consistently not *how* what the dogma says is indeed possible, but *what* the statement of it really means. Just as reason is able to say *what* happened at the moment of the change of water into wine at Cana, but without being able to explain how or why the change was possible, so the authentic theologian is one who can teach *what* happens at the eucharistic sacrifice, but not the conditions under which the reality actually becomes possible. To all other questions and curious inquiries that the desire for human knowledge raises, the only correct answer must be: it is divine omnipotence that makes the miracle possible.

Once the proper order that ought to exist between logic and faith has been restored, Lanfranc is able to move on to the constructive part of his indictment and apply his sophisticated powers of demonstration to explaining in a definitive and unambiguous way *what* happens when the bread and wine become the body and blood, as faith tells us they do and as is therefore certainly true.

In the books on logic available to him Lanfranc found the Aristotelean classification of the kinds of movement: once he excludes the idea that a generation-corruption takes place in the Eucharist, much less a transfer in space or an increase or diminution of quantity, there is no choice but to admit that the miracle consists in a change in the natural reality. According to the laws of the sensible world, however, such a change comes about through a change in the accidental aspects of the thing in question (as when water becomes ice or vapor), while its substance, which remains intrinsically invisible because the senses perceive only the accidents, does not change (otherwise there would be a process of generation-corruption). Given these premises, but relying on a prior acceptance of the datum of faith that proclaims an incomprehensible exception to the laws of nature, Lanfranc can conclude that through the action of a power superior to all natural powers and brought into play through sacramental grace, the substances of bread and wine are miraculously changed in the Eucharist, while their accidental appearances perdure and remain visible after the substantial change.

The teaching thus formulated by Lanfranc was definitively approved at the final anti-Berengarian synod, the Lateran synod of 1079, in the presence of Gregory VII. It was taken over by Thomas Aquinas, who more precisely defined the concept of transubstantiation, and was proclaimed as the official and authentic explanation of the eucharistic mystery by the Fourth Lateran Ecumenical Council in 1215 and, later, by the Council of Trent in 1551 against the Protestants. But Lanfranc's intervention, when seen in the correct historical environment that produced it, has value above all as a witness to the possibility of reaching a balanced middle position between opposite extremes: the claims of a rational activity not sufficiently subordinated to faith and the no-less-dangerous rigidities of a radical fideism (such as can often be seen in the works of other, less flexible representatives of the anti-Berengarian forces).

c. PETER DAMIAN

Peter Damian (d. 1072) was another who attacked the arrogant claim of reason that, by following the uncontradictable rules of the liberal arts, it could determine the presence and activity of the divine in the order of creation. He did so because of his dispassionate allegiance to the most authentically religious aspect of Christian truth. Peter was one of the most energetic supporters of a pontifical theocracy and one of the most unyielding promoters of the moral improvement of the clergy during the years preceding the pontificate of Gregory VII.

An unconditional commitment to the reform of the church was the dominant trait of Peter's life. As prior of the Camaldolese hermitage of Fonte Avellana he embodied in his monastic solitude the ideal of holiness and a perfect life even though he was frequently obliged, against his wishes, to leave this solitude in order to carry out responsibilities and missions for the popes in the fight against simony and the abuses and immorality of bishops. In 1057 he was appointed cardinal bishop of Ostia. His literary production was quite extensive: a *Life of Romuald*, many sermons, poetic compositions, and numerous treatises, chiefly in the form of letters, on dogmatic subjects, ecclesiology, exegesis, and the eremitical life and its characteristic virtues. His entire existence shows that for him holiness was a goal which monks must pursue throughout their entire earthly lives without ever being able to regard it as attained. Similarly, he conceived of the spiritual understanding of revealed truth in the Scriptures as the always incomplete result of a continuous journey that leads the Christian through the successive degrees of the deepening of faith to a mystical union with Christ as Spouse, according to the image in the Song of Songs.

This advance in knowledge was always to be entirely subordinated to faith, which must permeate the believer's whole soul, without yielding to compromises with the cognitive ambitions of human science. His condemnation of any theological abuse of the liberal arts was absolute and unequivocal. In his work *The Perfection of Monks* he says that a monk who practices the arts renders himself as unclean as a man who approached a woman who had not been purified from menstrual blood. Anyone yielding to the desire to know something not within his reach should remember this: the fall of Adam and Eve, which was caused by the serpent's invitation to "know" good and evil, was accompanied by an unrestrained use of grammar that was not controlled by faith and taught them to decline the name of God in the plural number: "You will be like *gods, knowing* good and evil" (Gen 3:5).

So, too, the beginning of the little work with the telling title *Holy Simplicity Is to Be Preferred to Knowledge that Puffs Up* warns the reader: the "reasons" supplied by a knowledge that is puffed up with pride should never prevail over the simplicity of faith. The arts are indeed necessary in order to read Scripture correctly just as they are necessary in order to orient the human race in the natural world, but they ought to fall silent before the revelation of divine truth, which is always beyond their reach.

Typical, for example, is the indignation at vain human curiosity that is voiced at the beginning of the little work, *The Lord Be With You.* Peter's monks have asked him what sense it makes for a monk praying alone in the silence of his cell to use dialogical formulas such as "The Lord be with you" and then answer himself: "And with your spirit."

Peter hotly rebukes this idle "common sense." Those who thus allow the doubts suggested by natural reason to play a part in questions of this kind will be unable later on to resist reason's claims when faced with the more impenetrable and important depths of the faith. Only if they clothe themselves in the pure foolishness of faith will holy simplicity save them when they rely on it and accept without discussion the formulas and ideas demanded by Scripture and the Fathers and by the continuity of the liturgical tradition. Only after first ensuring the solidity of their acceptance of Christian truth will believers be able to look for and find an answer to the initial question, an answer very favorable to a deeper understanding of the truth. That is to say, a monk praying alone is a living cell in the community of believers, and the use of traditional liturgical formulas gives voice, in his solitary prayer, to his spiritual membership in the church of Christ. The irremediable source of error, then, is not the growth of rational understanding of the faith as such, but the claim to make faith dependent on it.

Yet, like Manegold and Lanfranc, Peter Damian had a profound knowledge of the liberal arts, the abuse of which he challenges and rejects, and especially of logic. But he uses his skill not so much to formulate satisfactory explanations of dogmas (in his view a work already done in an outstanding way by the Fathers) as to define strictly the limits of human knowledge (a task that is his basic and almost obsessive theological concern).

His most important contribution in this area is also his work best known to historians of ideas, the treatise *Divine Omnipotence*. The necessity of anticipating and combating the temptation to raise questions and utter judgments on the supposed "reasonableness" of the incomprehensible divine truth is illustrated by an example in which the sinful attitude of unjustified intellectual curiosity is carried to the extreme. The opportunity was given to him at Montecassino by a discussion that went on during the evening meal between him and Abbot Desiderius, who was his host. The subject was a hyperbolic expression used by

Jerome in the reading at the meal, namely, that not even God could restore the purity of a fallen virgin. Since obviously no one would deny God's power to repair miraculously the physical sign of virginity, the question became: Can God, if he so wills, also remove the very reality of the event, thereby changing something that really happened in the past?

Fearing that, given this question, human reason might succumb to the temptation of asserting that there is something God cannot do or, in other words, setting limits or conditions of any kind on his freedom, Damian would have preferred not to be drawn into the toils of this intolerable discussion. In the end, however, he decided to accept the challenge with the intention of showing how worldly knowledge cannot presume to submit to its own laws and proofs those truths that are infinitely beyond its reach. He himself then pushes a logical analysis of the problem of divine omnipotence as far as possible in order to show at the end that, despite the extreme consistency and correctness of its formal applications, the logico-deductive method is useless when it speaks of supernatural realities. Then, generalizing and carrying to the extreme the confrontation between divine power and the laws of natural noncontradiction, he reaches the point of asking whether in the present God can, without qualification, will that things he willed in the past had never happened: if, for example, he can cause Rome and its empire never to have existed.

The human mind knows, thanks to the faith, that it cannot give a negative answer to this question, but it also knows, on the basis of the laws governing its own operations, that it cannot answer affirmatively. In fact, the rules of reason are valid only within a closed system of reality, the elements of which can all be subjected to verification, but ontologically God precedes creation and time, and his action is not subject to any temporal or modal conditions. Moreover, the simultaneous presence of contradictory aspects in his will (such as willing to make something exist and at the same time willing to make it not exist) is impossible only to our logic, which, within the truth system proper to it, has for its task to proclaim as false what cannot exist in created things, but not to proclaim the same of the higher nature that produced these things.

The duty of human logic is in fact to judge in what way that which God wills to be true or possible is indeed true or possible, just as in the moral realm our practical reason recognizes as evil that which is opposed to what God has ordained and willed as good. Consequently, it is correct to assert that the only allowable limit on divine omnipotence is the willing of evil, for if God were to will evil, the object of his will would be, by that very fact, inevitably something good. In the same way, God can do the impossible, because he himself, and he alone, has decided what is impossible; but if he were to will the impossible, the impossible would become possible, even by the norms of our logic.

God alone beholds all of reality in a comprehensive, unifying gaze and in an eternal present. Human logic—the "windy," that is, arrogant and useless dialectic that turns into heretics those who believe they can reach "inevitable conclusions" by means of it—is not comparable to that gaze or capable of the truth it beholds. Reason's questions about divine omnipotence are therefore unanswerable: they are simply mistaken and improperly formulated, or, better still, they are not formulatable at all. Once this radical conclusion has been reached, the recognition of the impossibility of coming to grips with divine omnipotence becomes for the human intellect a true and valid principle regulating its activity. It becomes a criterion of true theological knowledge and requires the construction of an "order of words" that becomes an inexhaustible way by which the creature approaches the objective but always higher and unreachable truth of the "order of things" and of the "order of ideas" that causes the order of things.

d. OTLOH OF ST. EMMERAN AND THE ANONYMOUS OF REGENSBURG

The conflict between investigative reason and the ardent desire for spiritual perfection remains completely unresolved in the writings of Otloh (d. 1070), a monk of St. Emmeran near Regensburg, all of which are filled with an intense and unintegrated religious feeling.

In his *Book of His Temptations* Otloh describes a soul devastated by contradictions in its unstable balance between the weakness of human fragility and the longing for monastic perfection. He speaks of how the sincerity of his faith is dangerously affected by the gnawing of rational doubt, which draws strength from an intelligence that is versatile and in love with the classical world. In a well-known dream he reports in another work, *The Book of Visions*, he gives expression to the fearful interior dissension between his faith and his mind: from a manuscript of Lucan he has placed under his pillow before sleeping there emerge monstrous demoniacal creatures that threaten to drag him down into hell if he does not repent of his love of pagan poetry and devote himself sincerely to a life of exclusive meditation on the sacred texts. And in another vision reported in the same work a group of devils afflicts him with bodily torments while insinuating into his mind a doubt that God exists and can come down to help and defend him against these devils.

But the atmosphere is less gloomy in *A Dialogue on Three Questions*, which Otloh expressly devotes to a moderate justification of reason in the solution of three sensitive problems of moral theology. These come up in the course of a calm discussion with a pilgrim named Henry, who is passing through and is welcomed by Otloh. In a world created by God why is there room for evil? How was it just to have the punishment of one man's sin inflicted on all his descendants? Can human beings do good in the state that followed on sin? A series of logical and rhetorical arguments leads to a cautious understanding (an acceptance due to persuasion rather than to a cognitive proof) of the best answers among those that reason and faith together can supply to the three questions. The effectiveness of these answers is seen as due explicitly to the fact that they allow only an approximation to the truth, an answer that is not definitive and exhaustive but only probable and, as such, satisfactory to a mind that can be content with probability.

Given these premises, it is possible to grasp the fact that a world in which good triumphs over evil is better, even to our limited imagination, than one in which good forces itself on creatures without their freely choosing it. Then: that God is surely just in punishing the descendants of Adam because he knows with certainty that any other human being would have committed the same sin. Finally: that in a universe harmoniously governed by contingent numerical proportions, human actions, too, depend on the conditions in which they are performed; therefore even human nature that has been turned from its proper course by sin is able to accomplish not an absolute good, but a partial good that is proportioned to its real possibilities.

These answers clearly show that Otloh's conception of knowledge is relativistic inasmuch as it too is only proportionate to the truth. So too, as in the case of Peter Damian, his theological relativism-probabilism is the natural consequence of a careful assessment of what the reduced, and therefore correct, function of logic and the other liberal arts ought to be. In the Prologue to his *Dialogue* Otloh expressly condemns not the practitioners of logic generally but what he calls "naive logicians," that is, those who want to be logicians and nothing more but who, concerned more with their discipline than with the truth, think they can demand universal and unquestioning acceptance of the truthfulness of their teachings. For this reason they also claim the right to impose their rules on the words of Scripture.

The theological error that lurks in this outlook is evident. It is indeed true that within a system of truth governed by logic every word has but a single meaning and every deduction reflects a single, univocal necessity. But revelation communicates to humanity truths that are far higher and more comprehensive than those that fall under the jurisdiction of the logicians. In this communication it uses words whose meaning is infinitely richer and more multiform than the human art of defining and arguing can claim to grasp and classify.

A few years after the death of Otloh, a manuscript composed around 1184 and preserved in the library of the abbey of St. Emmeran has kept for us a correspondence that was collected or more probably composed (under the pretext of reproducing a collection of letters) by an anonymous prelate of Regensburg. This writer represented the philoimperial party that was opposed to the Gregorian party, but the man was obviously bewildered and discouraged by the violent tone taken by the conflict between empire and papacy. Following the example of the "modern" theologians' reductive criticism of early medieval theological Platonism, this Anonymous of Regensburg offers his own way of mitigating and introducing balance into any possible conflict between faith and reason: he explicitly harks back to the probabilism of the Academics as defended by Cicero.

In an important return to the ancient denunciation of the contradictions that the entire history of pagan thought showed to exist in the "discordant philosophers" of antiquity, the Anonymous sees the fundamental error of false philosophy as consisting in its claim to know too much. He is not unacquainted with logic and the other arts, nor does he neglect them, but he does recognize that their only function is to exercise the mind, without any claim to lead the mind beyond conclusions of a merely probable kind. True philosophy, which lacks any ambition to systematize and claim theoretical absolutes, is a philosophy that is based on the principle of verisimilitude and enables persons to take their bearings in the moral sphere. The practical sphere, with its determination of the boundaries between good and evil and its distinction between vices and virtues, is the authentic realm for philosophical judgments. In this area, philosophy takes as its point of departure the undeniable truth of the Decalogue and the evangelical commandments and on that basis is able to pursue to the end its true task, which is to lead human beings to the only complete knowledge they can have in this life, namely, the knowledge of themselves.

E. MODERNS VS ANCIENTS: ROSCELLINUS OF COMPIÈGNE

The dismantling of Platonism as the theoretical foundation of philosophical and theological knowledge reached its extreme form a generation, more or less, after the authors thus far considered. It reached that point in the person of Roscellinus of Compiègne (d. 1120/1125). He is known chiefly for being, at different times, an adversary challenged by the two greatest thinkers of those years, first Anselm of Aosta and then Peter Abelard. They attacked him as a supporter of a radical nominalism in dealing with universals and voicing a sacrilegious view of trinitarian doctrine that led him, according to the criticisms leveled against him, to admit a dangerous tritheism. But an understanding of Roscellinus' real thought is to some extent made difficult by the fact that the most important information available to us comes from the writings of his adversaries. The only work of his own that has survived is a *Letter* to Abelard in which he defends his interpretation of the dogma of the Trinity.

In a *Letter on the Incarnation of the Word*, written to argue against that theological teaching, Anselm of Aosta bases his discussion of Roscellinus' errors on the untenableness of the latter's logico-ontological position. Roscellinus maintained, in fact, a purely verbal conception of universal substances (that is, genera and species), thereby reducing their reality to a mere "emission of sound" (*flatus vocis*) in which the corresponding names are uttered ("animal" or "man").

Later on, Abelard, both in his *Dialectic* and in a famous *Letter* to the bishop of Paris on the errors of Roscellinus, explains in detail that the latter's nominalism represented not only a position taken on the nature of universals; his reductive approach extended to all the teachings of logic and the other arts. It meant, therefore, a radical rupture of the correspondence between the order of things and the order of words that the early medieval theological tradition had asserted. Yet on this correspondence rests the very reliability of human beings' knowledge and their ability to describe objectively and consistently the manner of being of created things and the laws that govern their existence. According to Abelard this logical negativism led to an "insane" deontologization of all human knowledge or, in other words, to the impossibility of attributing to thought the capacity for an objective correspondence to reality. It did so by reducing every kind of knowledge to an organization of experiential data that is purely practical inasmuch as it is conventional and arbitrary.

According to the unanimous denunciations by Roscellinus' adversaries, the most serious consequence of this deconstruction of knowledge was that it made it utterly impossible for the intellect to grasp the reality meant by the theological formulas accepted in Christian teaching. As Anselm observed, if a person is unable to understand the unity of individual human beings in the species "human," how will he ever grasp what is meant by saying that three different persons are united in a single divinity, which they themselves constitute? And if a person cannot conceive of any reality other than that of individuals, how will he or she be able to admit that the individual Christ is the result of the coming together of two natures, human and divine?

This, then, according to Anselm, is the serious theological error made by the master from Compiègne, an error Anselm himself had denounced and caused to be condemned at a council at Soissons around 1092, where a public retraction by Roscellinus was demanded. The error: the assertion that the three divine persons are not a single reality (*res*) because then they could not perform different operations and would not be related to one another; therefore there are *three* different divine realities. A mischievous understanding of logic would thus lead Roscellinus to *tritheism*, making him, in Anselm's words, a "heretic through logic" and, according to Abelard, a "false Christian" just as he was a "false teacher of logic."

In his *Letter*, written some years later, Roscellinus justifies himself. Hurling back at his adversaries the accusations of ungodliness and asserting his own orthodoxy as an interpreter of Christian truth, he assures his readers that he is recognized throughout the world as a respected teacher and "defender of the faith," a man listened to as an authority and approved even in Rome. He also insists that his teaching on the Trinity is truly in harmony with the contents of revelation and that his and only his reading of the mystery can avoid the conclusions that the Father and the Holy Spirit were incarnated and suffered with the Son on the cross.

In his *Letter on the Incarnation of the Word* Anselm completed his indictment of Roscellinus by explicitly accusing him of belonging to the category of "modern dialecticians." He meant those who introduce serious errors into the understanding of the truth of the faith because they fail to realize the necessity of allowing in God, as in other natural realities, a distinction between the properties of individuals and the properties of their common substance. Anyone who says that the objects of logic are not only true but, as such, also real, and that human knowledge can have no other object or field of investigation than purely individual entities makes it impossible for himself or herself to accept such a distinction.

This reference of Anselm to the "modernity" of Roscellinus signifies, perhaps, something more than a mere emphasis on the "novelty" of the man's views on logic and, consequently, of his "heresy." Some light is shed here by the fact that other witnesses from this period recall the intense and sometimes overly intransigent zeal with which in subsequent years Roscellinus worked for the moral improvement of the clergy, thus continuing the work of the most energetic representatives of the Gregorian and anti-imperial party. His militancy among the "moderns" thus drew him in several respects toward the anti-systematic and anti-Platonic position of such radical reformers as Peter Damian and Otloh of St. Emmeran, who were committed not only to a moral renewal but also to the liberation of theology from the logical conceptions of the philosophers.

On the other hand, this self-alignment of Roscellinus with the modern theologians of the preceding generation fits in perfectly with his defense of a purely instrumental and verbal conception of logic. This was opposed to the traditional Platonic-Augustinian teaching that had been taken over and reinforced by the masters of early medieval classicism, from the Carolingians to Gerbert of Aurillac. According to them the teachings of the liberal arts are not an artifact of the human mind but an intellectual reflection of a necessary order imposed on all of creation by God. The moderns, in contrast, reduce human knowledge to the role of merely recording in an organized way what can be understood by means of experience. Therefore, as Anselm insists, "they believe only in what they can understand through inquiry by the senses."

There could not be a clearer expression of the contrast between two "ways" that emerged at the end of the eleventh century and the beginning of the twelfth. There was the "way" of the ancients (that is, a speculative and methodological approach), which based the very possibility of collaboration between reason and faith on the supposition that there is a connection, established by God in the creation of the universe, between logical truth and ontological truth. There was also the "way" of the moderns that, in opposition, was bent on defending the integrity of the faith against the lies of Platonic pan-logicism and on unconditionally removing objective correspondences between "names" and "things."

It was not an accident that in the period of transition between the centuries one of the firmest defenders of the realism of essences was Odo of Tournai (d. 1113), a theologian and master of the liberal arts who was considerably influenced by Anselm. According to the direct testimony of one of his pupils, the historian Hermann of Tournai, Odo taught logic as reflecting reality (*in re*), "according to the practice of Boethius and the ancient teachers," and for this reason got involved in a well-known dispute with nominalist master Raimbert of Lille, who taught logic as involving only sounds or words (*in voce*), "according to the teaching of the moderns."

A careful reading of the testimonies in our possession leads us, therefore, to state more accurately that Roscellinus was not, as many historians thought it necessary to infer from Anselm's strong words, a reckless rationalist and zealous imitator of Berengarius, one of the "naive dialecticians" whom Peter Damian and Otloh criticized for trying to impose the rules of the arts on the truths of the faith.

On the contrary, it seems clear that Roscellinus was a radical theologian who was opposed to any admixture of reason and faith but possessed great professional skill in the field of the liberal arts in general and of logic in particular, the disciplines he taught. From this serious scientific training he derived the conviction that the rules of the branches of human knowledge had always, and only, a relative value and a purely instrumental function. Their purpose, that is, was to give human beings their bearings in a dynamic and free physical reality made up of indivisible singularities and the effect of unsearchable divine causality. There was, then, a "nature of things" that could not be controlled by the organizing and deductive patterns of the intellect but was indeed the source of continual stimuli to empirico-deductive scientific observation.

Roscellinus' intellectual personality was thus characterized by two basic, distinct, but complementary components. On the one hand there was the master of liberal arts, skilled in consistently drawing the correct conclusions from the constitutive principles of his field of knowledge. On the other there was the intransigent defender of the faith, the theologian opposed to any imposition of rigid and anthropomorphic mental patterns on the free will of God. For him, too, therefore, as for Peter Damian, the unqualified affirmation of divine omnipotence was the only principle that allowed an explanation of the mysteries of the faith.

It is clear, then, that Roscellinus never maintained and preached a real tritheism or other erroneous and subversive theological novelties. When he asserted that human reason cannot represent to itself the reality of the divine except as a juxtaposition of three realities, his intention was to emphasize the human inability to express a judgment on the ineffable divine theological mysteries except by falling back on doctrinal explanations. But the role of these (as Otloh of St. Emmeran, too, had maintained) was purely instrumental and relative, since they were explaining something that surpasses and transcends all the limitations inherent in human knowledge.

In light of these conclusions we can also explain the readiness with which, at the end of the Council of Soissons, Roscellinus agreed to withdraw his own trinitarian formulas. The certainty of the shifting conventionality of human terminology, which was obvious above all in theology, was for him a more than sufficient reason for being ready to change his theological language and not to take a defensive position in religious questions based on the correctness of a word or its univocal correspondence to a concept, and on that alone.

II. Anselm of Aosta

Lanfranc of Pavia had for some years been archbishop of Canterbury when, around 1076, he received a manuscript from young Anselm, one of his best students and his successor as both master and prior of the monastery of Bec. The title of the work was *An Example of Meditating on the Meaning of the Faith.*

Before this first speculative work of Anselm reached Canterbury it was preceded by news of worried reactions on the part of some of the monks of Bec. Indeed, it had elements that could not fail to cause some puzzlement even in the elderly archbishop, who remembered the battle fought during the debate with Berengarius against the kind of logical reason that dares express judgments on the truths of the faith. Anselm's treatise was an investigation into the nature of the Christian God, his existence, and all his important characteristic features, from eternity to spirituality, from creation to the Trinity of persons. Yet these demonstrations, which were linked in such a way that one led on with necessity to another and did so with a fundamental simplicity, were carried out without any explicit support from the authority of Sacred Scripture or the teaching of the Fathers. From the very outset, indeed, Anselm declared his unconditional respect for the truth of revelation, but the unfolding of his whole discourse about God was an exercise in pure rationality that was independent of any external presuppositions and conditions ("by reason alone"—*sola ratione*).

This method led indeed to conclusions that were always in agreement with the contents of Christian catechesis. But the independence with which the human intellect here claimed to have reached them could not but seem to Lanfranc to be a worrisome reemergence of the rashness that claimed the right to develop, with the laws of logic, a complete mental reconstruction of reality and to assert that this reconstruction was in every respect and every way an image of the cosmic order eternally established by God.

Anselm immediately replied to his teacher's call for moderation. He urged Lanfranc to have the little work burned if he thought this necessary, but he begged him, before doing that, to verify the fact that no statement of his could be interpreted as an attempt to play down the superiority and priority of faith and the authority of the Scripture and the Fathers over all the ways and results of natural intelligence. He added that no one would ever be able to single out even one word in this text that was not confirmed in the doctrinal explanations of the Fathers and, in particular, in Augustine's *The Trinity.*

Anselm would subsequently repeat this justificatory interpretation of his own work in the Prologue to the definitive edition of the text:

Some of my brothers have often and insistently asked me to put into writing, in the form of a *model for their meditation,* some thoughts I had offered when conversing with them in everyday language about the way in which they ought to meditate on the essence of the divinity and on other subjects appropriate for this kind of meditation. When I wrote the requested meditation I forced myself to respect a particular form (something I tried to do solely in order to satisfy their desire and certainly not because it was easy to do or within the reach of possibility for me). The form was this: that *nothing in the text was to be based on convictions springing from the authority of Scripture,* but instead, using an elegant and clear style, understandable arguments, and a simple demonstrative process, I would see to it that, on the one hand, rational necessity (*rationis necessitas*) would compel acceptance and that, on the other, the light of truth itself (*veritatis claritas*) would show clearly how the unavoidable conclusions of varied and structured investigations are also true.

Lanfranc did not order the destruction of the short work. Hugh of Lyons, the papal legate, advised that, in order to avoid misunderstandings of the concept "meaning of the faith" (*ratio fidei*), Anselm should simply change the title later on to *Monologion,* a Hellenizing neologism meaning "reflection" or "interior meditation." His second work, which completed the speculative program of the first and which he had originally titled, in perhaps an overly frank way, *Faith Seeking Understanding,* became *Proslogion,* "conversation." The two new titles indicated the different formal approach in the two treatises: a direct explanation of mental processes in the first and the record of a spiritual dialogue between the author and God in the second.

Instead of seeing in Anselm's work an effort to submit the mysteries of the faith to the judgment of the rational mind, the archbishop of Canterbury must have realized the sincerity of Anselm's effort to lead the mind to a logical systematization of theological truths *without making this dependent on faith* (that is, on premises drawn from or confirmed by revelation) and yet *presupposing the truth of the faith* as a control and standard for constantly checking every mental step taken by reason alone.

1. Theological Truth as the Rectitude or Right Ordering of the Intellect to Faith

Anselm was born in Aosta around 1033. He entered Bec in 1059 specifically in order to study under the famous Lanfranc; in later years he experienced a rapid rise as a churchman: abbot of Bec in 1078, then archbishop of Canterbury from 1094 to his death in 1109. His many theological writings are marked by formal elegance and speculative depth and are permeated by a coherent systematic inspiration that undoubtedly offers the highest testimony to the maturation of western theological wisdom in the early Middle Ages. Looked at as a body of work, his treatises seem to mark the several phases, distinct but interconnected, of an organized and, on the whole, unified attempt to carry out the plan of theological research that is announced as early as the first two treatises.

At the beginning of the little work *Truth* Anselm defines the concept of "truth" and thereby makes clear the profound meaning of his close-knit theological plan, which in substance consists at every point and throughout in implementing his fundamental intention, namely, to bring out, confirm, and explain, by a prudent application of the intellect, the unqualified logical necessity of the statements of the faith. According to Anselm everything is "true" that possesses a formal rectitude, that is, that exists precisely in a way that is "right" or, in other words, "correctly ordered" in relation to the divine will in which everything has its proper origin. The "true" human being is human in the way in which God determined that he or she should be, and so on. Terms or propositions are true when they correctly express the agreement between thought and its corresponding reality.

In adopting this fundamental and foundational speculative presupposition Anselm shows himself to be a complete follower of the Platonizing and Augustinian conception of the true nature of understanding: namely that the latter is a reflection of the cosmic order willed by God from the very beginning of creation. Consequently, the liberal arts generally and logic in particular have as their task to ensure that the human intellect that respects their rules will be consistent and correct in its reconstruction of the truth, which is what it is because God willed it so.

For Anselm, therefore, logic is the science of the rectitude or right ordering of things known insofar as it guarantees the absolute correspondence between reality, the intellect (or interior thought that represents it), and the word or expression that signifies it in oral or written communication. Anselm's theological plan, which he began to implement in the *Monologion*, consists in continuing to its very end the attempt of the human intellect to speak of God: that is, to formulate the words and expressions or the signs that must express the manner of being of the perfect reality from which all true things derive and must ensure their complete correspondence to an intellect, that is, to a thought or set of thoughts with which the human mind is able to represent the truth of them.

But human reason is limited and always operates within a finite system of knowledge that is made available to it by experience and regulated by the laws of logic. It may not therefore presume to possess a natural ability to represent in a thought the truth of the reality corresponding to the word "God." So perfect a mind or thought would be identical with the divine mind itself: it would be identical with the Word, that is, with the Thought in which God knows not only all things but also himself. This explains why created reason, at the very moment in which it inquires into the reality of God, while at the same time drifting about in a system of knowledge that is for it infinite, must subordinate itself to the supreme truth that God alone knows but that God himself has put at reason's disposal through the gift of revelation. "I believe in order that I may understand":

belief precedes reasoning; the truth of revelation precedes the truth of philosophy.

But after establishing and acknowledging this order of things, the human mind realizes that it is able not only to believe but to believe *and* to understand the object of its belief. This is because once it has made its act of faith, reason is in a position to recognize the right order of its argumentative processes in relation to God, that is, the correspondence between them and the truth made known to it by faith. For this reason the intellect can now also develop purely logical proofs that lead the understanding subject to know the object of its belief, on the basis of faith and in harmony with faith but without using faith as a tool or source or support of these proofs: "I understand in order that I may believe."

Therefore at the beginning of his *Proslogion* Anselm addresses God as the one "who gives understanding to faith" because the understanding would not be possible if it were not preceded by faith. Yet this understanding is something different from and more than faith, something that adds to the fullness of the divine gift of truth the soul has already acquired through faith. And only because God grants it can the human being grasp the truth. Anselm's method of "reason on its own" consists therefore in advancing in the understanding of the contents of the faith while bracketing faith, in order to add to faith a knowledge that is something more but is never alternative or contradictory but always complementary and unifying in respect to what faith affirms.

If Lanfranc welcomed and approved this plan, he must have understood its ability to reconcile the aspirations of Platonizing traditionalists to organize their knowledge with the complete immersion in the faith that was called for by the reformers and theologians of the new era. It was a plan in which rational demonstration and emotional participation in prayer could once again be combined in one and the same movement of a thinking that was both logical and affective. In moving between the unqualified character of faith and the necessities of reason, Anselm's aim was in fact to pursue a truth that was at once absolute and necessary.

2. The Monologion, *Model of Meditation on the Truth of God*

Understanding of the rectitude of the word "God" is, then, the common purpose of the two short works that head the list of Anselm's writings: the *Monologion* and the *Proslogion*. In both cases the procedure consists in starting from the perception of a higher truth, or from an idea corresponding to the name of God and then moving from an understanding of its meaning to the determination of the further particular truths contained in it or legitimated by it. To use modern philosophical language, which is alien to Anselm's way of looking at things, we can say that his was an *a priori* procedure. It is obvious from its opening lines that the *Monologion* follows this procedure, despite the fact that not a few modern interpreters have thought the work had to be taken as an *a posteriori* "cosmological" discourse—obvious because the entire development of the argument starts with the "idea" of the divine as the mind is capable of receiving it, in order then to show how necessary it is to admit the existence of what the idea signifies.

Faith puts the believer in a position to know what God is. But, as established above, it is now necessary to bracket faith. Indeed, even a hypothetical mind that does not know what God is, either because this has never been communicated to it ("either because it has not heard") or because, having been told of God, it does not believe ("or because it does not believe") can nevertheless be led by reason alone to represent to itself what faith means when it speaks of God as the only, absolute, and common cause of all created substances. The demonstration consists in passing from this representation of God's existence to the necessity of admitting it. The mind hastens toward this goal by bringing its dialectical powers into play; it identifies more than one possible way of tackling it. And on each occasion the mind has hardly reached its goal when it returns to its starting point and identifies another possible approach that is no less correct and fruitful, and follows it to the end.

> If anyone, either because he has never heard God spoken of or because after hearing him spoken of, he did not believe it to be true, is ignorant of the fact that there is a single nature that transcends all the other things that are, that alone is self-sufficient in its eternal happiness, and that by means of its omnipotent goodness generously grants and sees to it that all other things exist and are what they are and are good, I believe it will nevertheless be possible for that person to have, at least in its broad lines, a perception of this truth even by means of his reason alone, provided he be endowed with at least an average degree of intelligence. And there are many ways in which this can happen.

The first and simplest of these ways consists in showing how the rectitude of the idea corresponding to the existence of God consists in God's being the supreme object of our desire. In fact, no matter what we desire, we do not desire the things themselves but their goodness. Therefore we desire what makes them good, namely, the good itself. And if we look for it in things, this is because it exists and causes us to recognize that all these things are imperfectly good, while it alone is the greatest good. In other words, it is *the good as such*, which exists because it makes things to be good and causes them to be desired because they are good. The supreme good, which is knowable because it exists and has need of nothing else in order to be desired, is God.

Immediately and relentlessly the ascent of the mind toward the idea of God begins again with a second search for its rectitude among finite and knowable things: all things possess a greatness, and in all we recognize their being great. Therefore in all things we know something that makes them great, and this something is not knowable as great because something else makes it great; instead, it is *greatness as such*. Since it is the greatness that makes everything else great, it is necessarily the greatest thing that is thinkable, and therefore the best of all that is thinkable. The supremely great is, then, nothing else but the supreme good; it necessarily exists because it makes great everything we know as great, and therefore it is God.

These first two arguments already show clearly the Platonic approach Anselm takes in his reasoning. The approach is this: the simple fact that the subject recognizes, in the finite objects of his knowledge, the truth of certain predications or, in other words, the rectitude of the subject's evaluation of these predicates, requires him to ascend to the very origin of this truth, that is, to the rectitude of their rectitude, to the truth-making source that makes true everything that is true, because it is the Truth as such. Thus the lines of argument in the *Monologion* do not spring from a chain of causative steps that proceed from the existence of what is certain (because experienced) to what is necessary (because presupposed by what is experienced). Instead, Anselm's theological mind starts from the knowableness of the finite in order to grasp that this knowableness would not be possible unless it derived from certainty regarding a higher truth that is perfect and fully actuated in its correspondence, in every respect and completely, to what it is and must be.

But the aspect of the text of the *Monologion* that makes even clearer the progressive unveiling of the truth is the rapidity with which the arguments succeed one another. There is a kind of process of gemmation that starts from the modes of predicability of particular truths and yields further aspects of the unitary understanding of the rectitude of the divine substantiality. It is therefore not by chance that in pursuing the manifestation of this substantiality the mind begins with its perception, in created things, of the first two predications that in Aristotle's list of the categories describe the ways in which substance manifests itself: *quality*, in the form of the best qualitative predicate (namely, the good), and *quantity*, in the form of the best quantitative predicate (namely, greatness). In both cases the mind ascends from predication "by way of something else"— that is, from the predication of a quality recognizable as such by reference to a higher quality, and from the predication of a quantity recognizable as such by reference to a higher quantity—to the predication of pure quality as such and of pure quantity as such, which are such because they are identical with the divine substance, with God in himself.

The third line of reasoning takes up the third category of things that affect substance, namely, *relation*, which focuses the mind precisely on creaturely predication of what is in God by its very nature. Everything the mind knows is something that is. But being can be predicated either because something else makes the thing exist (that is, it exists in relation to something else that is) or nothing causes this something else to exist (that is, it exists without relation to anything else that is). But what exists without relation to anything else is being as such or in itself, or God. All things that are not God exist, therefore, insofar as they are related to being as such. The latter will be the "power that makes to exist," the source of being for all the things that are; this source exists precisely because it exists of itself, while all other things exist due to something else, or in relation to being as such, which is therefore God.

But *relation* exists not only between substances, but also between the qualities or *perfections* of things. The fourth argument takes for its starting point the observation that it is possible to see, in the nature of multiple things, various *degrees of dignity*, and that whenever the mind considers things it sees them existing in a logical hierarchy of dignity or perfection. Thus it judges that a horse is superior in dignity or perfection to a tree or that a human being is superior to a horse. But if at the end of this hierarchy of perfections that depend on another there were not something whose perfection is superior to all the others because it is perfection as such or in itself, then the series of perfections would not be thinkable, because nothing would make it possible to see the relation as ascending from inferior perfections to those that are higher, rather than in the opposite direction. Therefore there exists a maximum degree of perfection, a *nature* that is superior to all the others and whose perfection is perfection as such or in itself, namely, God.

The rectitude of the concept corresponding to the word "God" implies, therefore, the truth of God's existence before any other truth.

But since God exists of himself and is perfect, the recognition of his existence can be achieved only if it is accompanied by an understanding of what the God is who is. Existence cannot but be the first of the attributes the mind discovers in a nature that is conceived as being the highest and most perfect of all natures. Such perfection exists, but if it exists it must be thought of as characterized by all those perfect properties that in the case of creatures are better predicated than denied. At the same time, however, it must possess these properties in a way unqualifiedly superior to that of finite substances, and it must be perfect *of itself*; otherwise it would be blended with the natural imperfection of creatures, which are perfect only due to another. Thus it must be denied that God possesses those attributes that best express the finiteness of creatures, because they define creatures as such (e.g., "body," "animal," "human," and so on). On the other hand, it is necessary to predicate of God, and in the highest degree, those properties that express a perfection of creatures but do so by relating it to something higher ("life," "knowledge," "justice," "truth," "happiness," "eternity," and so on).

After the first four demonstrations of God's existence (each demonstration complementing the preceding), and on the basis of these, Anselm takes up an organized series of predicable perfections, each of which follows from the one before it. Here he goes more thoroughly into his understanding of God, using further deductive arguments, all of which are so many necessary unfoldings of the reasoning that gradually shows its presence in all the affirmations of the faith.

Thus God is unbegotten because his existence cannot depend on another or preexisting cause, for then he would not be the supreme essence. In fact, he is "the supreme essence, the supreme existent, the supreme being," that is, the essence that can be everything (infinite potency) and is everything it can be (infinite act). It is eternal and omnipresent because it cannot be subjected to any spatio-temporal measurements, which are always relational. Furthermore, because all existing things exist insofar as they have being from God, every causality, material and formal, originates in God. He himself is neither matter nor form because he is not corruptible or multiple; he is therefore the source of all matter and all forms or, in other words, the creator of everything. In the history of Christian theology this was perhaps the first strictly rational demonstration of the necessity of "creation from nothing."

But the penetration of reason into the depths of the faith is henceforth unstoppable, and the mind sees the unqualified affirmation of the divine Trinity emerging from the necessity of its own arguments. "Creation from nothing" is in reality something incomprehensible and contradictory to the human intellect, since every word that means something must correspond to something that is. If, then, everything comes "from" nothing, even "nothing" must be "something," and this amounts to saying that things were something before being something. But only God was before things; therefore things were in God, but were not God.

Before existing, then, things were necessarily divine thoughts; that is to say, they were in the Logos or divine Word, the eternal mind or the "reason of the supreme nature," which planned their existence. The Word is the utterance, the word in which God expresses himself and the things he creates; as such, the Word is begotten by the Father. But the relationship between the begotten and the begetter is not one of either altereity or subordination, because the two are united by a love that is identical in both, a love that is perfect because in loving the beloved the lover loves himself. Such love is therefore one with the divine substance; it is itself God, the Holy Spirit who proceeds from the Father and from the Son.

3. The Proslogion: From Faith to Understanding of the Truth of God

The loving desire of the mind for God is thus progressively satisfied in a process that is at every point rendered certain by a rigorous respect for the laws of thought but is also structured as a series of successive cognitive increments and, running parallel, a series of unbroken possible comparisons of reason with faith. On the other hand, the composition of the *Proslogion* was stimulated by the subsequent emergence in Anselm of a desire to sum up knowledge of the divine in a single efficacious act of thought. This act will be unified and direct and will not require further deepening and confirmation by other argumentative procedures, as happens in the four demonstrations of God's existence, which are closely connected each with the others at the beginning of the *Monologion*.

Thus there arose in his mind the idea of a "single argument," one self-sufficient argument, "needing no other proof than itself, to prove that God really exists."[1]

The Latin word *argumentum* refers directly to the technical notion of *topos* ("place"), which in treatises on logic corresponds to those intuitive "places" of the mind, the perception of which makes possible the persuasive, intuitive unveiling of a general truth. The role of dianoetic reason is then to articulate this truth in an argumentative process in order thereby to make the logical necessity of the truth explicit in a discursive form. But the immediacy of an argument arises from its initial location at a primordial level of the intellect. The difficulty experienced in a "finding of an argument," that is, the mind's formulation of an argument still unknown to it, is due precisely to its primordial and intuitive character, which makes it difficult to reach by way of definition or induction or by means of a step-by-step chain of mental operations.

In the Preface to the *Proslogion* Anselm explains the extreme difficulty of the mental effort he had to make in order to attain to his goal. As he sought it he often seemed to glimpse, unexpectedly, the outline and logical clarity of the argument, but as soon as he tried to translate these into concepts and orderly mental steps the whole thing grew blurred and became elusive. Yet every time that he despaired of success and was on the point of giving up, the thought befitting the argument became present and filled his mind, preventing him from abandoning the project. Then one day, unexpectedly, right in the midst of this "conflict of my thoughts," the formulation of the argument suddenly became clear to him in a sure and communicable form.

This personal confession of Anselm is echoed in the hagiographical disguise used by Eadmer, his biographer, in narrating the moment of Anselm's intuition of the argument. According to Eadmer the intuition made itself known twice at night; Anselm quickly wrote it down on a wax tablet, but in the morning he inevitably found only illegible fragments of what he had written. Finally, one night Anselm awakened his copyist and asked him to transcribe his notes immediately and safeguard them. All this realistically describes the state of noetic intuition in which the understanding of the argument came about, prior to the discursive translation of the intuition by which the argument became a line of argument. But in this elevated state of prerational intuition the mingling of conceptual representation and faith could not but have played a decisive part in guiding the mental processes of the theologian.

Over the course of a long and varied reception in the modern age and today, Anselm's argument would become known as the "ontological argument." In fact, however, Anselm formulated it under speculative conditions that made it unqualifiedly medieval in character and differentiated it from all the postmedieval formulations of it, beginning with that of Descartes. The fundamental presupposition of an "ontological" argument, for good or for ill (that is, from the viewpoint of a defender or that of a refuter), is that the human mind is able to acquire by itself, by means of its natural powers of study, intuition, and definition, a concept that captures perfectly the nature of God, a concept from which the necessity of God's existence can be derived.

But in Anselm something more or, in any case, something radically different is involved: both here and in the *Monologion* the meaning of the name "God" is suggested to him, exclusively and with utter clarity, by faith. Anselm's formulation of the argument (which is therefore not "ontological") begins with reflection on an idea that is not and could not be the result of a human discovery, that does not depend on information derived from experience, and that is not the product of a conceptual abstraction but is communicated through the expression of the truth of faith, an expression that for the believer is antecedently endowed with rectitude. This means that only a believer is able to think the argument through, even though it is a rational argument with its own demonstrative power and without reference to faith. As a result, once Anselm the believer had thought out the argument and had measured its logical necessity, the argument became valid and unquestionable for every mind that grasps its meaning, even an unbelieving mind.

The formula "faith seeking understanding," which Anselm had originally chosen as a title for the *Proslogion*, confirms the fact that faith alone suggests to the mind the object it is to seek in its "dialogue" with God. It also gives the reason for what is undoubtedly one of the most beautiful passages in early medieval Latin literature: the very fine prayer or "Exhortation to the mind to contemplate God" with which the short work begins. This is an impassioned meditation on the state of the human intellect when faced with the truths of the faith; here the soul is urged to enter into the silence of its own "inner chamber," that is, into the spiritual perfection of monastic solitude in which it is possible to forget everything that is not God and in which the soul can turn to its creator, who gives understanding of the faith.

> Come now, little man (*homuncio*), turn aside for a while from your daily employment, escape for a moment from the tumult of your thoughts. . . . Free yourself awhile for God and rest awhile in him. Enter the inner chamber of your soul, shut out everything except God and that which can help you in seeking him.

Only in this silent rediscovery of interiority is it possible to ask God himself for the words with which to speak of him, because only by believing in their truth can the person grasp their meaning: "I do not seek to understand so that I may believe, but I believe so that I may understand."

See, then, what faith says God is, and how reason immediately and necessarily deduces from it that this something that faith says God is necessarily exists:

> Now, Lord, since it is you who gives understanding to faith, grant me to understand as well as you think fit, that you *exist as we believe*, and that you *are what we believe you to be*. *We believe* that you are that thing than which nothing greater can be thought (*aliquid quo nihil maius cogitari possit*). Or is there nothing of that kind in existence, since "the fool has said in his heart, there is no God" [Ps 13:1 and 53:11]? But when the fool hears me use this phrase, "something than which nothing greater can be thought," he understands what he hears; and what

he hears is in his understanding, even if he does not understand that it exists. . . . And certainly that than which nothing greater can be thought cannot exist only in the understanding. For if it exists only in the understanding, it is possible to think of it existing also in reality, and that is greater. If that than which nothing greater can be thought exists in the understanding alone, then this thing than which nothing greater can be thought is something than which a greater can be thought. And this is clearly impossible. Therefore there can be no doubt at all that something than which a greater cannot be thought exists both in the understanding and in reality.

The entire argument ends in the simplicity of the act of thought by which the argument's premise is understood, namely, the identity of God with "that than which no greater can be thought." This identity is a perfect expression of negative theology, which requires denying that any perfection at all can fail to exist in God or that God possesses any perfection in a lesser degree than other beings possess it. This identity, as such, is suggested to Anselm by faith. But the recognition of its truth is possible and even inevitable for everyone, since it is a primordial operation of the intellect, one that is intuitive and direct and so simple as to be self-evident.

Therefore no one can refute it: even the fool who asserts that "God" does not exist recognizes nonetheless that "God" implies "that than which no greater can be thought," because this identity is present in his intellect. But the intuition of the meaning of this statement ("God is that than which no greater can be thought") also implies the recognition of his existence: because if God did not exist, he would not be "that than which no greater can be thought," since something else would be thinkable that has all the perfections recognizable in "God" plus the perfection of existence. Then "that than which no greater can be thought" would in fact be "that than which something greater can be thought," which is a contradiction and therefore impossible. Consequently, God exists not only in the understanding but also in reality.

In the *Monologion* the mind traveled a number of affirmative paths in order to say what God is. Here, however, it quickly reaches the summit of the negative way and realizes that if God is truly God, he cannot but exist. One of the best interpreters of Anselm's argument was undoubtedly Bonaventure of Bagnoreggio, who reformulated it while emphasizing even more, if possible, the aspect of immediacy: "If God is God, God exists." The fool (*insipiens = non sapiens*) who continues to say that "God does not exist" can do so only because he is "not wise" (*non sapiens*); he is not only a nonbeliever but one who is not wise, a non-rational human being who does not understand the meaning of the words he utters and does not know the rules of logic that support and confirm what he says. Indeed, to say that "God does not exist" amounts to saying "that than which no greater can be thought *is not* that than which no greater can be thought."

In order to prove that Anselm's argument was not tenable, a monk named Gaunilo, belonging perhaps to the monastery of Marmoutier, wrote a *Book in*

Defense of the Fool, claiming the impossibility of establishing a real, that is, ontological, coincidence of existence in the understanding and existence in reality. It is not difficult to see a parallel between the speculative outlook of Gaunilo and the anti-Platonizing tendency peculiar to the monastic spirituality of the "modern" theologians, which in the name of an empirical and unconditioned conception of truth rejected the claim that any correspondence could be established between the logical procedures of thought and real existence, between the order of words and the order of reality.

Gaunilo held that the human intellect is able to grasp truth only in the information provided it by sensible experience, which gives concrete witness to the existence of things known. In the human mind, on the other hand, there are only words and meanings, not realities. To illustrate the fact that having something in the intellect does not necessarily imply the existence of that something in reality, Gaunilo gives the example of a legendary "lost island," full of perfections, which the mind can picture with great clarity and effectiveness without therefore being obliged to admit its real existence. In Gaunilo's view the true individual reality that is God can never be, as such, the object of human intellection. Therefore the Anselmian "that than which no greater" (the *quo maius*) is only a purely abstract and conceptual idea thought up by the human mind that will never capture what God is; hence, when all is said and done, not only does the *quo maius* not exist in reality, but it does not truly exist even in the mind.

Anselm replies to these objections in a response he himself appends to the *Proslogion*, along with Gaunilo's *Book*. It is obvious to him that Gaunilo has not understood the invitation to use the *quo maius* formula in order to reach one of the highest intuitive truths to which the human mind can attain, the understanding of which implies both the truths and the necessary reality of what they express. The mental representation, however perfect, of an island or any other limited creature can certainly not be considered such a truth.

It was no accident that when Gaunilo reproduced Anselm's definition of the concept, instead of correctly citing it as "that than which no greater can be thought," he came up with something quite different, speaking of *maius omnibus*, "the greatest thing among those that exist." Even a creature might seem to satisfy such a definition, being "the greatest thing in its genus," but some other reality, of the same or a different genus, could be thought of as superior to it in the order of perfection. In contrast, only the *quo maius* is something whose necessary existence is revealed by the fact that nothing more perfect can be thought, for its existence is necessarily implied in the fact that it is thinkable as *quo maius*; if it did not really exist, it could not even be thought.

Anselm then goes on directly to remind his adversary of the proper intellectual formation and correct speculative attitude of a believer. The refusal to recognize the truth is possible for a mind not informed by revelation, a mind such as that of the fool. But Gaunilo is a Christian and as such ought to admit the existence of a logical order of reality that is thought and willed by God in his Word and made available to be known, investigated, and reconstructed by the human intellect.

But Gaunilo is evidently not clear on the mental effort that leads to the working out of the argument; it is therefore necessary to have further recourse to the explanatory resources of logic and to show how the lucid movement of the reasoning that leads from the thinkableness of the *quo maius* to its reality is indeed linear and coherent for "those who through study have acquired even a minimal knowledge of the discipline of debate and argumentation." Therefore, as Anselm goes on to reply one by one to Gaunilo's remarks on the argument, he takes the time to turn the argument into a series of structured and interconnected argumentations. These take a primarily syllogistic form and compel the adversary to draw a series of necessary conclusions, all of which lead to the unavoidable impossibility of combining in a single complete proposition the subject "God" and the predicate "does not exist."

As was already the case with the demonstrations given in the *Monologion*, so too Anselm's meditation on the identity of meaning between the word "God" and the *quo maius* does not end with the demonstration of the existence of God. Here again, in fact, the established existence of God gives rise to a rapid but orderly explanation of all God's attributes, but in this case the explanation continues to follow the negative way opened up by the argument. Everything that implies any reduction at all of the perfections of the *quo maius* must be removed from its meaning and therefore from its reality.

Thus it can be said that God, being incorporeal, knows corporeal realities better than any other subject does; being unable to do anything imperfect, he is omnipotent; being impassible, he is supremely merciful; being incapable of injustice, he is supremely just; not being incapable of goodness, he is good even when he punishes. Furthermore: he is visible everywhere even though he is absolutely invisible; he is inaccessible light, a harmony that cannot be heard, a fragrance that cannot be smelled, a beauty that cannot be possessed, an inexhaustible presence and eternity that cannot be bounded by any space and any time. Yet these contradictions, which could be a restraint on created reason when it proceeds by way of comparison between various finite objects, are on the contrary a wonderful food for the intellect when it approaches God. This is because all the contradictions spring from the first, mysterious contradiction that defines in a unique way the existence that is necessary: the contradiction marking the supreme perfection, which necessarily exists but which it will never be possible to understand.

> Now arouse yourself, my soul, attend with all your mind, and think as much as you can about the nature and extent of so great a good. For if each good thing is delightful, think carefully how delightful must be that good that holds within it the joy of every good, and not such a good as we experience in created things, but as different as Creator is from creature. (Translation by Ward, 263)

4. The Theological System of Christian Truth

The works of Anselm's maturity as a speculative theologian run from *Truth* through *Free Will* and *The Fall of the Devil* (all three completed between 1080 and 1085), the *Letter on the Incarnation of the Word* in response to Roscellinus, *The Virginal Birth* and *The Procession of the Holy Spirit*, and on, finally, to the magnificent theological symphony of *Why Did God Become a Human Being?* (*Cur Deus homo*).

All of these methodically pursue the goal of a conceptual analysis of the principal topics of the faith that arise once the existence of God is recognized and once there has been an initial determination of God's fundamental natural attributes. After the *Monologion* and the *Proslogion* these further works do indeed seem to represent the successive stages in the sketch of a complete system of interconnected rational examinations of Christian theological truth in its entirety. If in fact the thought in which God knows himself and creation can only be a single, all-embracing act of true knowledge, then the human effort to develop an intelligible representation of that thought through the cooperation of faith and the intellect can only lead to an explanation that is organized, composed of diverse elements and phases, but proportionate to the source from which it comes and therefore necessarily uniform and harmonious in all its parts.

Once again, the achievement of such a systematic explanation of the reasonableness that ought to interconnect the particular true formulations of the Christian dogmas depends for Anselm on the correctness of a fundamental presupposition: namely, the theological usefulness of language when it is regulated by the laws of logic and guided by the directives of the faith. Respect for the rules of science renders human thought and the language that expresses it capable of possessing an adequate rectitude in dealing with finite natural objects. Faith ensures the extension of this capacity to everything God has established that must be true and necessary and that the human person as such should know, including therefore all the mysteries of the faith.

This twofold system of coordinates—logical rationality and faith—introduces the intellect of the theologian into a clear and certain system of truth. The intellect is not able to fathom this on its own because the system represents the superior vision that the divine *Logos* has of the created universe. But once introduced into this system the intellect can set to work, using its proper analytical and critical judgments, and can develop its own concrete operations. Something similar happens when the human intellect performs mathematical procedures by setting to work within the organized and coherent system of numbers: it cannot grasp this system completely and in all its parts, but it is capable of recognizing and outlining its necessary laws.

This antecedent requirement of Anselm's theological thought explains the energy with which, as we saw earlier, he opposed the nominalism of Roscellinus of Compiègne and did so precisely in the context of a discussion of trinitarian doctrine that is documented in the *Letter on the Incarnation of the Word*. Roscellinus' error was not essentially different from that of Gaunilo when the latter refused to acknowledge the objective reality of what human thought regards as true. In Roscellinus' view any logical predication is a purely mental fact, the use of which, in theology as in every other field, has only an instrumental value as a clarification and coordination of thought and language.

Anselm was convinced that this position compromised the reliability of scientific knowledge in general and theological knowledge in particular. For if all true logico-linguistic statements were only conventional and practical and signified no other reality than that of individual material things known through experience, they could never possess rectitude, that is, correspond to the true and changeless mode of existence of the divine ideas and the realities these ideas govern. It would therefore not be possible for human beings to have knowledge of anything, much less of the divine nature, that is, the Creator's modes of being.

In contrast, in a short logico-grammatical dialogue titled *Grammar*, Anselm expressly sought to defend the human ability to express immutable and eternal truths through a correct organization of language. He made the same point several times in other pages of his writings down to his final treatise, which remained incomplete under the provisional title *Power and Powerlessness, Possibility and Impossibility, Necessity and Freedom*. He also explained that all meaningful logical terms (for example, "man," "horse," "animal," but also "large," "good," and so on) can point either to individual things ("a particular man," "a particular animal," "a particular size") or to realities that are more or less universal ("human existence," "animal existence," "largeness").

Furthermore, it is up to propositional logic, which decides what relationships are possible between different terms, to say to which level the meaning of each term belongs, depending on the use being made of it. For example, "this human being" (individual) "is an animal" (universal); or: "this man" (individual) "is Socrates" (individual); or: "the human being" (universal) "is an animal" (universal); and so on. Thus every reality, whether individual or universal, is true and can be used as a predicate within a discourse consisting of propositions (that is, a true discourse) only if and because in this form it is made to correspond to the relationship between different truths that exists in the divine mind; in other words, if it has its own rectitude.

In summary, in its own argumentative processes human reason must always and only use logically defined elements, the rectitude of which has been established by preceding mental operations and that have thus become a correct reflection of the eternal truth of the corresponding meanings in the thought of God. Throughout his entire systematic description of knowledge of the faith Anselm continually summons up and, as it were, pursues these eternal sources of truth, which he calls "necessary reasons": "reasons" because they determine the temporal truth of things by referring these to the immutable truth of their causes in the Word, and "necessary" because they determine this temporal truth in the necessary and eternal way established by God when he created.

Since the divine Word is an *utterance*, he too possesses a supreme rectitude, or correspondence with the reality of the things he speaks forth. To the extent that he speaks the divine nature, the Word has an absolute rectitude. To the extent that he speaks created things and is the source that by speaking them makes them exist, these will be things that come from the Word and have their own rectitude in the measure in which they make real in themselves what has been decreed for them in the necessary reasons of the divine archetype.

The systematic acquisition of theological truth consists, therefore, in tracking down, after the existence of God, further necessary reasons, connected with that existence, that ensure the objective correspondence between human thought and both the eternal divine will in the Word and the revealed description of this will that Sacred Scripture provides under the dictation of the Holy Spirit. Anselm's theology comes down essentially to the effort, rendered possible by the convergence of understanding and belief, to make our thinking about God correspond to what God is in his own thought and to what in that same thought are his own eternal nature, created nature, the human being, sin, forgiveness, and, finally, redemption and the Incarnation that made redemption possible.

The problem of the reality of evil is one of the first that Anselm considers, one reason being that it offers him a possible way of indirectly verifying his own conception of truth. For, in the theological universe thus outlined, what reality can something have that God neither thinks nor wills? And what logical and ontological necessity can the cause have that produced this thing (or, according to the title of the short work devoted to the subject, *The Fall of the Devil*)?

Effectively turning the argument of the *Proslogion* on its head, Anselm shows that evil does not exist because it is not thinkable and because no necessary reason for its reality can be found in the divine Word. The thinkableness of "that than which a greater cannot be found" forced the intellect to acknowledge the necessary existence of the corresponding reality. In contrast, the definition of evil as "that which cannot possibly be thought of as a good," or "that than which a better or greater can always be thought" is a definition utterly deprived of rectitude in the sense that no reality willed by God can correspond to it and the only conclusion to be reached is the necessity of the nonexistence of what it signifies.

Clearly, then, just as when one speaks of nothing (provided this word is not assigned a theological value of excellence in relation to being, as in the *Monologion*, but is equivalent to "something that absolutely does not exist"), so too when one speaks of evil, our human language does not in any way express a meaning corresponding to something positive and real, but only a negation of a corresponding positive. Thus, when one says "blindness" one is in fact saying "privation of sight," or when one speaks of "darkness" one can only mean "privation of light"; so too "evil" or "nothing" can only mean "privation of good" and "privation of being."

Consequently, it cannot be said that God is the cause of evil except in the sense that he made the consequences of sin a reality, just as when "I make naked" someone whom I do not cover with my cloak I am not the cause of his or her nakedness, but I do cause it to perdure. In like manner God made good even the nails that pierced the hands and feet of the Redeemer because they did what by their nature God called upon them to do. But it is equally obvious that not even the fall of the devil or the subsequent fall and punishment of humanity were the cause of evil, for evil is not a "thing" and therefore does not have a cause of which it is the effect. Sin, on the other hand, is the actuation of something's non-rectitude, its being different from what God wants it to be, for a necessary reason established by God for intelligent creatures wills that the latter be endowed with freedom, which is a fundamental requirement if they are to be happy as a result of a voluntary adherence to the divine order.

God has, therefore, not imposed any necessity on the freedom of creatures, as Anselm explains especially in the short work *The Harmony of God's Foreknowledge, Predestination, and Grace with Free Will.* The only necessity he has imposed is that the free choices of creatures should lead to what is good if these choices are morally right, or to the absence of good if they are morally wrong.

For while in the divine mind the order of reality is eternal and eternally true, in creation this order is an order that is coming to pass. In the latter the realities God wills as potential must be actualized in the course of a history of gradual developments, some of which are conditioned by nature while others, such as the free choices made by intelligent creatures, are completely unconditioned. In his work on *Free Will* Anselm explains further that freedom is not a possibility of sinning or not sinning, but is rather the possibility of deliberately making real or failing to make real the perfections foreseen by the "necessary reasons" of rational creatures. This possibility, which in the ethical realm corresponds to the possibility that in the logical sphere thought and language have of being true, is likewise called a "rectitude." Freedom is the possibility of maintaining the rectitude or right order of a will determined solely by the will to rectitude and not by any other motive.

5. *The* Cur Deus homo: *From Faith to Understanding of the Mystery of Christ*

God, too, is free with a freedom that is its own cause inasmuch as the will to maintain the rectitude that is adherence to his own will is natural in him. On the basis of these thoughts Anselm, who had now for some years been archbishop of Canterbury, had to face the crucial point in his speculations on the nature of God. That is, he could not avoid asking, in the name of the internal consistency of the faith, what God's motives were and what freedom God exercised in bringing about the redemption of the human race. It is in his work *Why Did God Become a Human Being?* (*Cur Deus homo*) that he demonstrates how the rational mind can find even the Incarnation, the central mystery of the Christian faith, to be consistent with his theological system, which accepts both the universal efficacy of God's "eternal reasons" and his absolute freedom from any limiting conditions. The *Cur Deus homo* was a work of Anselm's mature years and won the almost-universal approval of contemporary theologians; his reputation in subsequent generations depended mainly on this work.

The method followed here is substantially the same as in the early works. Anselm sets himself to bring to light the "reasons" of the central mystery of Christianity, and to do so on the basis of a purely mental inquiry, while bracketing the truth known by faith even though it is this act of faith that launched the inquiry: "acting with the mind and detaching the latter from Christ as though he had never been" and "as if the mind knew nothing of him." He then postulates, as a fact already known, that human beings alienated themselves from God by a free choice through which the will failed to fulfill its own rectitude and, consequently, violated God's planned order of universal perfections.

But if there was even the slightest possibility of repairing this rupture, the rupture could not be permanent, because God is the Good, and the universal actualization of the good is inevitably the actualization of God's will. For this very same reason the possibility in question existed because, as part of his purpose of bringing the good in creation to its completion, he could and therefore did will the repair of the disorder caused by sin.

It was necessary, however, that forgiveness be petitioned by someone who had sinned and therefore by a human being. But at the same time no human being could ever have won forgiveness for a sin freely committed by a will opposed to the divine will. Consequently, only a human being who was also God could successfully obtain forgiveness for humanity. Since such a situation was possible and was good, God could not fail to will it; therefore the Incarnation of Christ was necessary. The redemption of humanity, which could not fail to occur, could not have happened in any other way. Yet even though necessary, the choice of the Incarnation of his own Son for the redemption of humanity was an absolutely free choice on God's part, because the true freedom of God consists in the necessary fulfillment of his will. Thus, as the good is not chosen by God because it is good, but rather is good because God chooses it, so too everything that is necessary is such because God wills it, and God can do everything except what he does not will.

When Anselm's argumentation is thus reduced to its essential elements it risks being impoverished. As in the *Monologion*, so here the possibilities of formulating the same method of bringing to light a rational necessity for the truth of the dogma of the Incarnation flow each from the others. For example, Anselm makes lucidly clear that the mediator could not have been an angel or some other creature nearer to God than the human being is, because this would have meant the subjection of humanity to its liberator and not to the Lord alone, whose service is not dependence but is the only true freedom of any creature whatsoever. In addition to the *Cur Deus homo*, Anselm also wrote a short work titled *The Virginal Conception* that has for its explicit purpose to point out others of the "many reasons" or lines of argumentation that enable the intellect to draw near to the mystery of the incarnate Word and to receive it in an increasingly adequate way and with an ever-increasing intellectual and affective participation in it.

6. Truth, Necessity, and Prayer: Faith as a Cognitive Experience

In short, Anselm's limpidly clear demonstration of the necessity of the divine activity is anything but a proof that there is necessity in God. In fact, the multiplication of rational argumentations makes it possible to emphasize even more clearly how defective a procedure it is to apply to God any theological claim of *necessity* or *possibility* or *impossibility*. The reason: these procedures are applicable solely to the imperfect and in itself ineffective way of acting of creatures.

Anselm therefore pauses for a timely explanation of what such terms mean when it comes to creaturely activity. He distinguishes two kinds of necessity and two meanings for this concept. There is an antecedent necessity, that of a cause that inevitably produces its effect; for example, the force that presides over the movement of the heavens. There is also a consequent necessity, that of an effect that inevitably follows upon the action of a cause; for example, the sound of words that follows the action of speaking. But an antecedent necessity always involves a consequent necessity; thus the heavens move as the causality that moves them determines them to move. In contrast, a consequent necessity is not always inevitable and determined by an antecedent necessity; thus it is not necessary for a human being to speak, because he or she is free to do so, but if he or she does speak, the words must sound. In conclusion, the Son of God was not obliged by any antecedent necessity to become incarnate, but only by his spontaneous free choice; therefore the necessity that determined his choice was exclusively consequent.

But this decisive distinction yields an explanation and justification of Anselm's entire theological method, since this is based on a logic that claims to assert a rational necessity in our knowledge of God but without presuming to impose on God's way of being and action the necessities that rule our knowledge. In relation, therefore, to the truth of the faith the necessity involved in dialectical argumentation is only a consequent necessity, whereas the objective truth of the things God creates and wills in accordance with his "necessary reasons" is an antecedent necessity in relation to logical truth. It is not the rules of logic that render necessary the nature of things; on the contrary, it is the nature of things that renders necessary the rules of logic. Furthermore, it is not logic that renders the faith necessary; it is the objective truth of reality, which the faith sets forth and which is eternally thought and willed by the divine *Logos*, that renders necessary the truth reached by logic.

From another point of view all this brings out the importance and efficacy of a further constitutive and no less important element of Anselm's theological thought (in addition to the rational and investigative element): namely, the element of prayer that runs through the entire body of his writings and enables him to write especially inspired and literarily splendid passages in his collection of *Meditations* and *Prayers*. In fact, in these an even greater intensity and effectiveness mark the interior approach to truth that is made possible by the complementarity (something not programmed but fully realized) of intellectual understanding and interior participation through faith.

If true knowledge always produces an experience of the truth, then when faith (which already involves a direct participation in revealed truth) is united to rational knowledge, it ensures the possibility of an even deeper experience of the truth, one that is organized, based on, and confirmed both by spiritual emotion and by the interiority of understanding. To the extent, indeed, that faith is the intensely grasped object of a total and engrossing belief, one without questions and without the felt need of inquiry, it becomes for the human soul the highest, most deeply personal, and most intense *cognitive experience of the truth* that is possible. Moreover, to the extent that it captivates, engages, and fills the human intellect this experience of faith activates its capacity for undertaking a scientific knowledge of the true, because the experience enables it to participate indirectly in the knowledge God has of himself and his creation.

It was not possible to formulate, in terms logically more accurate and religiously more coherent with the divine plan governing the universe, a better implementation of the Augustinian principle, "I believe in order that I may understand."

Endnote

1. This and the following passages of the *Proslogion* are taken from *The Prayers and Meditations of Saint Anselm with the Proslogion*, trans. Sr. Benedicta Ward (London and New York: Penguin Books, 1973) 238, 239, 244–45.

Chapter 3

The Century of the Schools

I. New Movements and New Study Centers in France

1. Anselm's Heritage

The historical development of the twelfth century in western Europe was clearly marked from its early decades onward by several factors: a general improvement in economic and social conditions, a new productive and organizational vitality in urban centers, and a greater openness in commercial relations, as well as a perceptible parallel increase in intellectual activity and literary production in every field. Historians describe this period as an age of renaissance or rebirth. Apart from the overall improvement in living conditions and the many clear signs of social and political progress, the correctness of the description is further confirmed in the cultural sphere by effective signs of a real increase in activities connected with study and research. This awakening was to a great extent fostered, as in all renaissances, by a return to antiquity that included the rediscovery of philosophical, logico-grammatical, and scientific texts, whether classical or late antique, but also of theological and exegetical works of the patristic period. These had lain forgotten on the shelves of monastic libraries; now, in addition, works hitherto unknown to the West began to be imported from the Byzantine and Arabian worlds and translated.

This expansion of materials for reading and study did not, however, bring about a radical change in the methods, principles, and mental frameworks that had until now inspired and ruled the philosophical and theological speculation of the early Middle Ages. On the contrary, this century was shaped, on the one hand, by the still-fundamental Carolingian restoration and, on the other, by the intense period of intellectual growth that was produced, during the run-up to the thirteenth century, by contact with the Arabs. As a result, the cultural rebirth of the twelfth century proves to be the central link in a homogeneous and continuous growth of Christian thought, a growth based on the integration into

theology of the store of thought deriving from classical antiquity. The fundamental problem during this central phase in the history of western abstract
thought was still that of keeping alive, despite difficulties arising from historical
circumstances, the uniformity of religious consciousness on which the Carolingian ideal of Christianity as the spiritual unity binding believers had been
founded and that had survived even the political downfall of the Frankish
empire.

As a matter of fact, there had been a notable widespread weakening of this
ancient ideal. The factors contributing to this weakening included the gradually
increasing differentiation between opposing national identities; the tendencies
of civil and ecclesiastical structures to claim autonomy, tendencies exacerbated
by conflicts between the church, the empire, and the new monarchies; and not
least the shadows cast on western religious consciousness by the practical acceptance of the breach with the Orthodox Church. In this sense, and precisely
to the extent that it was a "renewal," the renaissance was also the result of a
critical challenge to this foundational aspect of Christian wisdom. The latter
had for its purpose to restore or at least to give a new authority and a new solidity
to the principle, now obviously weakened and becoming obsolete, that there
should be unanimity in religious and speculative thought.

In the common view of Christians the revitalization of religious consciousness was due in the first place to the fact that at the end of the eleventh century
the plan for a crusade to liberate the Holy Land became a concrete reality. And
indeed, in the echo produced by the strong call of the crusade movement for the
unification of Latin Christian civilization we can sense a clear sign of the widespread longing for a renewal of the ideological certainties that would ensure
conformity and thereby the spiritual unity of the Christian world.

In the specific area of the history of theological thought the practical success
and the triumphal fortunes of the speculative system of Anselm of Aosta had a
similar unifying effect among the Christian scholars of the twelfth century.
Anselm's systematic theology offered a complete rational explanation of Christian doctrine, one available to all believers in their effort to confirm their certainties and defend these against the enemies of the true faith, whether within or
outside the church. It therefore seemed to many to be the best "learned" response
to the need for a fundamental renewal of a Christian consciousness that would
be based on unquestionable certainty regarding the common possession of the
truth.

During the same months of late 1094 and early 1095 when the crusade
movement was passing from the planning stage to one of concrete organization,
Archbishop Anselm at Canterbury was beginning to write his *Cur Deus homo*.
Perhaps this represented only a coincidence of dates, but the fact is not lacking
in significance. For Anselm's work had brought to completion and placed a seal
on a systematic collaboration of reason and faith that allowed one to grasp the
intelligibility of the central mystery, the Incarnation. Now it seemed to acquire

an apologetic value as well, one rich in symbolic meaning. This was because it was useful in showing to all human beings, even those of other religious confessions, the persuasive, inescapable truth and the essential comprehensiveness of the Christian faith. During the first years of the new century this model exerted a strong influence on the direction taken by the better-trained and better-informed Christian theologians.

In fact, the element of systematization clearly marked the very approach taken to the curriculum of theological studies, especially at the urban study centers that were dependent on the episcopal courts; the last-named were themselves characterized during this period by a new and fruitful vitality. Back in 1079, in the general climate created by the call to arms against interference by lay politicians, a decree of Gregory VII had strengthened the obligation laid on all the chapters of episcopal sees to open schools, where lacking, or to restore and directly manage the schools already attached to them for the training of young prelates; these schools were to be supervised and controlled by a chancellor or an archdeacon. The more talented graduates of these episcopal study centers became "masters" (*magistri*: teachers) in their turn and had the right to teach within territorial limits.

These limits were gradually extended by further canonical interventions and then were settled, exactly a century later, by the third Lateran Council of 1179. The twelfth century was thus the period when the cathedral schools were revitalized and reached their flowering. Especially in the kingdom of France and in Italy these schools acquired a place alongside monastic schools and gradually gained the upper hand over them. The new approach to studies promoted the circulation of masters and students; the more famous cathedral schools attracted students eager to learn and desirous of a training that would enable them to advance rapidly as ecclesiastical and civil officials.

In the first decades of the twelfth century the first urban center that became an important place of theological training was the school of Laon. Two of the teachers there were Anselm (d. 1117), who as a young man had studied at Bec under the guidance of the greater Anselm, and his brother Radulf (d. ca. 1131–33). Many renowned scholars of the twelfth century received their education at this school, to which they were drawn by the reputation of its masters. They were drawn also by the special character of its theological teaching, which was based on a methodical explanatory and interpretative reading of Scripture and the Fathers and accompanied by the identification and analytical resolution (but one always based on the patristic sources) of possible theological problems suggested by the text or easily arising from the unrestricted course of the masters' lectures.

As a result of his own teaching, and with the collaboration of young William of Champeaux and other masters, Anselm has left a number of treatises that take the name *Sententiae* or "Statements" because they are characterized by a methodical discussion of opinions drawn from the writings of the Fathers. The influence of the model provided by Anselm of Aosta on the genesis of these collections is evident in the very idea of a comprehensive systematic framework within which are located various questions or further, deeper reflections, often without any particular order but never losing sight of the framework as a whole.

The success of this methodology led in a short time to the flowering, which continued throughout the century, of many systematic collections of this type. The order within these was dictated by the course of sacred history or by other organizational patterns inspired by religious doctrine, such as the list of the sacraments or other liturgico-catechetical frames of reference; the aim was always a clarification and orderly understanding of revealed truth.

At some centers of study, on the other hand, preference was gradually given to "questions" posed in the form of problems that required for their solution a balanced consideration of the scriptural and patristic authorities, on the one hand, and, on the other, a rational method based on the teachings of the trivium. This tendency was already clear in the school of Rheims, which was directed for at least fifteen years by Alberic, who had been a student under Anselm of Laon and later became archbishop of Bourges (d. 1141); his contemporaries described him as a skilled practitioner of the art of disputation. The tendency was strengthened by the composition of the first collections of theological questions by masters working in Paris, such as Robert of Melun.

Elsewhere, as at Chartres or, later, at Orleans, there emerged a greater interest in contemplation of natural realities, along with a tendency to give a theological direction to the solutions of questions about physics and nature. Finally, in Italy and especially at Bologna, it was studies in law, dealing with the tensions between papacy and empire, that stimulated a deeper interest in religious problems in the area of political ethics.

Not lacking, especially in the monastic world, were negative reactions to this extensive flowering of cultural interests; some regarded this phenomenon as being supported by an excessive confidence in a tainted combination of methods and perspectives of a secular and a religious kind. It was no accident that this traditionalist resistance was accompanied by scattered instances of distrust of Anselm's theological methodology.

Indicative, for example, is a story told by Rupert of Deutz, who (as we shall see further on) was a typical representative of Benedictine monastic traditionalism. He reports that in a lively public debate he had with Anselm of Laon and William of Champeaux on the problem of how evil and providence were to be reconciled, the two masters resolved the difficulty by introducing a distinction between the permissive will of God and the positive will, which was evidently modeled on similar conceptual distinctions of Anselm of Aosta. In Rupert's view the sole purpose of these useless subtleties was to describe the divine will in anthropomorphic terms and, by means of vague mental tricks, to water down the tragic harshness of the tension between human sin and the justice and mercy of God.

Again it is no accident that Rupert's was one of the few dissenting voices raised against Anselm and the chorus of praise lavished on the *Cur Deus homo* during those years. In fact, in commenting on his debate with the masters from Laon, Rupert cited Anselm's masterpiece as an example of the excesses to which an illicit human curiosity can lead, inasmuch as the latter does not draw back even from the mystery of the sacrifice of the Son of God.

I may mention here that the only other theologian known to us during these years who expressed a similar criticism of the *Cur Deus homo* was the elderly Roscellinus of Compiègne. In a *Letter* to Abelard, written after the death of the archbishop of Canterbury, Roscellinus levels at his former, now-deceased adversary the charge of excessive rationalistic presumptuousness: "His opinion that God could not have saved humanity except in the way in which he actually did so is forcefully contradicted by the words of the holy doctors who enlighten the church by their teaching." Anselm's heritage thus had its opponents, men following in the steps of those "modern" theologians in the monastic world who had made the rejection of the intellectualism of the "ancients" the main target of their polemics in favor of the simplicity of faith. But the new vitality acquired by the synthesis of reason and faith due to the celebrated contribution of the archbishop of Canterbury was not lessened by these criticisms. In fact, on many sides there were increasingly signs of the enthusiastic fervor of new imitators of the general model provided by Anselm's teaching and method, his spirituality, and his religious charism.

Anselm was thus the common master of almost all the theologians who, from the beginning of the century and for several decades thereafter, each proclaimed himself the heir to Anselm's teaching, despite the notable differences among them in doctrinal approach and methodology. They regarded themselves as disciples in the "school of Anselm," the correct interpreters of his works, and the legitimate defenders of his thought against unfavorable explanations. This multiplication and diversification of spiritual sons who claimed the right to call themselves the descendants of a common source of doctrine and spirituality was probably also due to the possibility of reading the body of Anselm's writings as a witness to two different theological needs.

On the one hand there were those who sought an immersion in the spirituality of faith; for them both logical argument and prayer were only formal externalizations, both imperfect and complementary. On the other hand there were those strongly driven by the ambition to expand the realm of reason; they sought, step-by-step, an ever more concrete and satisfying explanation and interlinking of the various subjects of revelation. Without raising the question of excessively rigid schematizations we may note that in the twelfth century this double inspiration behind theological approaches distinguished the several ways in which Anselm's complex heritage was received and used, despite the shared desire to renew the spiritual unity of Christendom.

The explanation of the conceptual symmetries among the various parts of the Christian creed was addressed even to nonbelievers and infidels in an effort to urge them to a conversion based on intellectual persuasion. This explains why, as early as the years linking the two centuries, the writings of various authors more or less directly influenced by the archbishop of Canterbury displayed a new interest in the literary genre of dialogue among the various religions, especially in the form of anti-Jewish polemics. Thus the proof of the "logical" necessity of the mystery of the Incarnation is basic in the *Argument against a Jew Named Leo* by Odo of Tournai, who was mentioned earlier, in the *Debate of a Jew with a Christian* by Gilbert Crispin (d. 1117), abbot of Westminster and a friend and disciple of Anselm at Bec, and in the *Treatise on the Incarnation in Answer to the Jews* by Gilbert of Nogent (d. ca. 1121).

In the following decades the same rational-apologetic methodology was applied to the debate with Muslims and heretics, the result being that the literary genre of dialogue enjoyed further success. It attracted important authors such as Abelard, whose *Dialogue of a Philosopher, a Jew, and a Christian* is perhaps the most intelligent and best-known interreligious dialogue of the Middle Ages. Others were Peter of Blois, who wrote an *Answer to the Faithlessness of the Jews*, and Peter the Venerable of Cluny, who wrote treatises against the Jews and the Moors.

Anselm, bishop of Havelberg (d. 1158), who had been a pupil of Radulf of Laon, was another example of recourse to a contrast with the teachings of outsiders as a way of proving the consistency and effectiveness of the Christian doctrinal system. After engaging in a debate at Constantinople with Nicetas of Nicomedia and Basil of Acrida on the superiority of the Roman church, Anselm put his report of it in writing in his *Dialogues in Answer to the Greeks*. Here his refutation of the Easterners' positions provided a model for an argumentative explanation of the true faith in answer to others.

In these various works, then, the challenge to the infidels provided, by way of contrast, the occasion and argumentative basis for bringing out the internal unity of authentic Christian wisdom. But, once rediscovered, the consistency and solidity of the doctrinal system also served as a powerful instrument in the debate with internal adversaries. By the latter are meant those theologians who in their debates displayed an excessive reliance on the application of dialectical tools to reflection on the faith. According to those who challenged these theologians, the latter ended up in obvious and indefensible doctrinal errors. It was customary in these cases to base a reply on the demonstration of the consistency uniting the data of Scripture and all the authentic teachings of the Fathers and to reject the formulations of erroneous doctrines by showing their isolation and the impossibility of giving them a place in the complete, organic system of the common doctrinal truth.

At the center of these debates, then, was the problem of the correct interpretation and best use to be made of Anselm's principle, the understanding of the faith. Amid the variety of nuances and interpretations of it, the point the various implementations of the Anselmian program for the intellectual systematization of the content of the faith had in common was essentially and fundamentally an apologetical purpose. This apologetical aim was pursued not in order to feed disagreement and opposition, but always to contribute to the strengthening of the common patrimony of religious truth. Such was the purpose that in the last analysis sincerely animated the writings of each of the participants in the collective work of research based on a methodical advance through the phases of *lectio* and disputation. And yet, in the long run, it would seem no longer possible to pursue this kind of work without embarking on a labyrinthine sea of discussions, debates, and arguments on the benches of the most famous schools, both monastic and urban, and, not infrequently, in lively synodal assemblies that quite often ended with solemn proclamations of condemnations and anathemas.

2. Peter Abelard

When Abelard published the first version of his *Treatise on the Unity and Trinity of God* he began to circulate it under the more general title of *Theology* and continued to do so through the years, even when the name referred to successive editions to which he himself gave differently worded titles. Even in the final years of his life, in his last work, the above-mentioned *Dialogue of a Philosopher, a Jew, and a Christian*, he described what he considered his basic work as "that wonderful work of Theology that others in their envy could neither endure nor successfully tear down and that their persecutions rendered even more glorious." Bernard of Clairvaux, his most implacable adversary, speaks of it as "the book by Peter Abelard that he calls *Theology*."

In the author's mind this title may initially have represented only a linguistic term similar to the Graecisms coined by Anselm in the titles *Monologion* and *Prologion*. That is, "theology" might be taken as simply the proper name given to a particular piece of writing and would mean "A Discourse about God." But Abelard himself gave the word a new meaning when, in the title of the second edition of the work, he added the adjective "Christian." The word "theology" had hitherto been used rarely, and when it was (as in Boethius or John Scotus) had meant, as in the ancient philosophers, a superior kind of natural knowledge. Now, due to Abelard, the word made its definitive entrance into the history of western thought as signifying the intellectual understanding of the truth revealed by God to his prophets, preserved in the dictated words of the sacred books, and handed on in the church's tradition.

This specification of the nature of theological knowledge was not important solely for the history of terminology. The syntactic unit "Christian theology" implicitly refers to the factual convergence of understanding and belief and carries the specific meaning of "knowledge of God" (that is, a "theology" or knowledge of God in the objective sense). But if this knowledge is to be truly such it must be based on a participation, by way of the revelation of Christ, of the creature's mind in the true "knowledge God has" of himself and his creation (that is, a "theology" or knowledge of God in the subjective sense). In comparison with the always incomplete and insufficient rational study of the divine, the true theology of Christians offers itself as a possible way for them and them alone to know the truth in the perfect way in which God knows it.

In conceiving the matter in this way, Abelard (after Boethius and John Scotus) accepts the gnoseological principles of Neoplatonism and contributes to the introduction and spread of these in the religious thought of the twelfth century. In fact, it is not knowledge that conforms to the nature of the object; rather, it is the object that makes itself known in various ways depending on the various cognitive faculties activated by the knowing subject. Christian theology can therefore be born of the illumination by means of which God allows the human person to ascend to his vision of the truth, in a still-imperfect way in the present life, but in the state of blessedness in proportion to the merits of each individual.

This interpretation of Abelard's thought is confirmed by a passage in the *Dialogue*, which is this author's real spiritual testament. Here the Christian is given the task of showing to the Philosopher (perhaps an Arab, but in any case a proponent of natural rationality) the perfect convergence between the truths of the intellect and the higher truths of revelation. In answer to an objection of the Philosopher as to how the beatific vision is possible, given that God, the supreme good, is unknowable by creatures, the Christian points out that every object of knowledge, whether spiritual or material, is always perceived in many and varied ways by the faculties and the subjects who approach it ("the thing known is always one and the same, but all do not know it in the same way").

It is clear, then, that for Abelard the knowledge of the Supreme Good that the philosophers seek during their earthly lives with the tools provided by their natural doctrines can lead them only to a creaturely understanding of the divine. This does not mean that this understanding is false (provided it is not erroneous), but rather that it is not yet "true" because it is grasped by a mind inherently incapable of grasping the essential nature of the object. The Philosopher himself must therefore accept that the human desire to know God can be completely satisfied only by one who relies on the grace of revelation, but with the important proviso that unless even this utterly unmerited divine gift is accepted with an appropriate intellectual commitment to understanding it, it cannot bear fruit.

This commitment is to a dialectical study that, in light of the gospel exhortation "Ask, and it will be given you; seek, and you will find" (Matt 7:7), means studying the meaning and contents of the "sacred reading" (the text of Scripture) for the purpose of bringing creaturely understanding closer to the divine understanding (or to the Word, the divine Wisdom). Dialectical reason can thus lead to a still more convinced acceptance of revelation by giving rise to a more solid and better-grounded faith. This interpretation of Abelard's thought is confirmed when, on the same page of the *Dialogue*, he recalls the Ciceronian-Boethian definition of the dialectical *topos* or argument as "a reason that convinces in a matter still in doubt."

He thus thinks that to the entirety of the logic that guides the human search for an understanding of the faith he can attribute the same effectiveness Anselm in the *Proslogion* finally attributed to one, and only one, of the higher operations of the mind. Better still, "theology" itself ought to be understood as an "argument for faith," an activity of the rational order that is intended in the first place to give rise to and foster the assent of the intellect to the faith and then to support, develop, and defend it.

A. THE UNIVERSALS AND THE TRUTH OF KNOWING

Abelard was born around 1079 at Le Pallet in Brittany, whence the title "Palatine Master." Around 1095 he came to Paris after making the rounds of various cities in search of schools in which to learn logic, "the scaffolding of all knowledge," as he tells us in his autobiographical *Consolatory Letter* to a friend, a work better known as *The Story of My Misfortunes*. At the cathedral school of Notre Dame he followed the lectures of William of Champeaux, who had recently moved there from Laon, but he soon earned censure for the boldness with which he, a young student, dared to contradict the master publicly "in debate" (*in disputando*). The annoyance (he calls it "envy") felt by William, and by Abelard's older fellow students, led him to depart and to devote himself, when only a little more than twenty years old, to teaching first at Melun and then at Corbeil, not far from Paris, where he achieved successes that increased his reputation as a teacher of logic.

When he returned to the capital after a short illness he learned that William had withdrawn to the abbey of St. Victor, on the left bank of the Seine, not far from Notre Dame but outside the city walls. There William had taken the habit of the Clerics Regular (who followed a modified kind of monastic life inspired by the *Rule* of Augustine); he had also established a school of rhetoric in which he gave lectures that were open to students from outside the community. Abelard did not fail to attend them and to renew his old attack on the elderly master. In particular, as he says in the *Story of My Misfortunes*, he criticized William's "old view of universals." Rather than meaning by this that William still maintained the doctrines he had taught a few years earlier, Abelard's words more probably mean that William had adopted the realistic views of the "ancients" as opposed to the nominalism of the "moderns." In a few sentences, with ill-concealed pride, Abelard tells of his new victories in arguments with William, who was twice forced by his adversary's attacks to change his teaching and explain it in detail, but always in vain.

It is a fact that emphasis on the problem of the universals was encouraged chiefly by the discussions in classrooms where lectures on logic were held, specifically on the work that introduced logic to the Middle Ages, namely Boethius' commentary on Porphyry's *Isagoge*. But during these years the problem of universals was not regarded as a pure question of logic because it was closely connected with the very foundations of the epistemological criterion that made it possible to distinguish scientific and true knowledge from false. The question was: What accord, whether existing or not in reality, between "the order of reality and the order of words" makes it possible to attribute or not attribute an objective reality to logical conceptual definitions, thus guaranteeing the truthfulness of the scientific statements in which these definitions are involved?

At the beginning of the *Isagoge* Porphyry asks three basic questions that are clearly of the metaphysical and not the logical order and from which arise the entire problematic nature of the subject: Do universals exist, and are they therefore a reality? If they do exist, are they separated from their individual embodiments? If they are separated, are they knowable without reference to individuals? It is clear, then, that for Abelard the justification and very possibility of all human scientific knowledge, not least of theological knowledge itself, depended on the answers to these three questions.

It was in this perspective that the Palatine Master chose first of all to make himself heir to Anselm of Aosta by continuing Anselm's fight against Roscellinus of Compiègne. Abelard refers to the latter with great contempt when mentioning him as one of the first masters of logic whose lectures were attended before Abelard's own arrival in Paris.

Abelard was fully aware, as we know, that the nominalism of his former teacher, William of Champeaux, was not limited simply to the problem of the subsistence of genera and species, but was extended perilously to the effective correspondence to reality of the entire teaching of logic, from term to proposition and from syllogism to topical argument. On the other hand, Abelard understood perfectly how the very standardization of William's exaggerated realism, based as it was on a naïve and figurative presentation of traditionalist theological Platonism, was open to criticisms of anthropomorphism and of reducing the universe to a mental image (criticisms put forward in recent decades by the "moderns").

Abelard had personal experience of the way in which this view could have unfavorable consequences even at the theological level. This happened when (I am still following the narrative in the *Story of My Misfortunes*), after the quarrel with William, he decided to go and study theology in the school of Anselm of Laon, another representative of the trend seen among the ancients. Here again he was deeply disappointed by the speculative triteness of the teaching he received, which was entirely lacking in real scientific vigor.

William, whose thinking was deeply rooted in early medieval theological Platonism, maintained that the universal is to be regarded as the underlying ontological basis of individuals and therefore as a real substance. That is, it is a reality of the spiritual order inasmuch as it is not subject to accidental determinations and variations and, in the graduated hierarchy of being, is superior to bodies, which also participate in it. In this hierarchy of reality, species is the substantial substratum common to all individuals and genus is the substantial substratum of the species. Some of William's short theological writings, which have been preserved in only a fragmentary form, make clear this metaphysical formulation of his logical views. In a short text on the Eucharist, for example, his justification for the refusal of communion under both kinds to the laity is that if, after the resurrection, the true essence of the individual Christ is a single spiritual and indivisible reality, then the believer who receives the consecrated host is united spiritually with the whole reality of Christ and therefore with his risen body and blood, but also with the soul and the very divinity of the Redeemer.

Abelard's criticism of William was refined in the sets of lectures he delivered in Paris during the years after his return from Laon, first at the school of Mont-Sainte-Geneviève near the gates of the city and then, as his reputation soared triumphantly, in the capitular school of Notre Dame itself. The criticism focused directly on the untenableness of realism from the viewpoint of logic. William had first set forth a simplified theory according to which the universal as a sub-stratum would be a kind of noncorporeal material element of the individual. Then, after the student's first critical remarks, he fell back on a second solution by defining the universal as a reality characterized by an "indifference" in rela-tion to the resulting individuals instead of by a multiplication of differences, as the logicians asserted. But, Abelard commented, a reality cannot be predicated of other realities. Moreover, the science that studies and describes things, namely physics, must presuppose and use the rules of logic in determining how language is to express the truth of the predicates that give information about the being of things. These rules and predicates are logical universals and therefore not things.

Yet the nominalists were wrong in denying that logic is a science of some-thing real. For if it is a scientific knowledge of truth and not simply of words (as grammar is), it must necessarily base its own claims on the reality of some-thing (that is, it must be a scientific knowledge of the truth of things) and, more accurately, of something that does not change, is not born and does not die, and is permanently real. To bring out his point Abelard adds a fourth question to Porphyry's three: "Would the universal continue to be real even if the corre-sponding individuals no longer existed?" He gives an example: Would the term "rose" have the same meaning even if no roses still existed? The answer is nec-essarily in the affirmative, since the statement "There are no longer any roses" would always be true. Therefore universals are real, but not in the way that individuals are real; that is, they do not connote individual existence.

The Palatine Master was reasoning in accordance with the ancient Platonic-Augustinian conception of logic as the art of interiorly reconstructing the truth established by God when he created. In his view truth is always the outcome of a relationship established between a knowing subject and a known object. And this is the correct answer to questions about the reality of universals: a universal is *the reality of such a relationship* when the relationship is true, that is, when the intellect or the interior act of intellection, the act in which the intellect recognizes a mode of existence of a thing, corresponds really and fully to the status or condition in which the thing exists outside the mind.

For Abelard, then, logic is "knowledge of things grasped by the intellect," that is, an accurate knowledge that permits thought to discern in things, and to express with corresponding words, the forms that compose their true mode of being and their relationships. This conclusion permeates Abelard's entire body of writings on logic, while allowing for further refinements in successive versions of it (from *Logic for Beginners* to *Logic in Response to a Request from Our Colleagues*, and finally to *Dialectic*, which was completed between 1135 and 1137).

But behind the technical language and the variations elicited by controversy it is not difficult to discern the metaphysical and theological background that inspired Abelard's conclusion. In order for them to be true, the universals or, in other words, the understandings proper to the human mind must reflect with the greatest possible consistency the true manner of being of things, that is, the laws that govern God's creation. For Abelard, then, as for Augustine, Boethius, and Anselm, the ultimate truth of universals is that of the divine ideas, the real models of the entire creation, models eternally existing in the Word and reproduced by the creaturely mind through the development of its own objective concepts of created things.

B. True Logicians and True Philosophers

The metaphysical implications of logic thus justified the growth of Abelard's didactic and speculative interest in theological study.

The result of this study was the already mentioned courageous reflection on the subject of the Trinity. His thoughts were continually revised and set down in three different works. The first was *Theology of the Supreme Good*, written to challenge the trinitarian teaching of Roscellinus but quickly criticized for its bold methodological originality and condemned in 1121 at a provincial synod in Soissons at which papal legate Conon of Palestrina presided. The second was *Christian Theology*, composed in the years that followed in order to set forth his own theses in a more systematic way. The third was the mature *Theology for Students*, which was completed in the second half of the thirties; its success worried the Cistercian William of Saint-Thierry and then the more authoritative Bernard of Clairvaux, whom William asked to intervene and who got a council at Sens in 1140 to issue a summary condemnation of propositions taken from the work.

The tragic story of Abelard's love for Heloise meant a total involvement not only of two bodies but also of two minds possessing great spiritual depth and marked by advanced intellectual training. Their love was ferociously punished when the guilty Abelard was castrated by hired thugs in the service of the girl's uncle and tutor. These events took place during the years in which Abelard's thought was maturing, and they laid a heavy burden on the course of his career. Driven by suffering and shame to embrace the monastic life, he also rescued his beloved from the constraints placed on her by relatives and gave her refuge in the monastery of women at Argenteuil. He himself seems vainly to have sought peace amid the continuous opposition and persecution roused by his writings, while he made an unsuccessful attempt to find a definitive place for himself in a suitable monastic setting. Finally he established the spiritual school of the Most Holy Trinity, which he renamed the Paraclete; here the female part of the foundation later received Heloise and some of her fellow nuns who had fled Argenteuil.

Given this background of personal tragedy, it is striking to see the clarity of mind with which the Palatine Master transposed his own conception of human knowledge of the truth from the realm of logic to that of theology. In fact, the legitimation of the creaturely claim to speak of God (in theology) and to speak with God (in prayer) is consistently derived from the science of logic. This is a certainty Abelard expresses with great clarity in the Prologue of his fourth treatise on logic, namely, *Dialectic*. Some adversaries, convinced that Christians were not permitted to occupy themselves with anything unrelated to the faith, accused Abelard of having offended against religion by introducing logical arguments in support or clarification of dogmas.

But, Abelard replied, if logic is a science, then it deals with truth no less than does faith itself; in fact, the faith even produces scientific knowledge because it makes it possible to know the truth. In addition, two truths can never be contradictory, just as two sciences cannot if both of them are true. On the other hand, a true science can never be false even if its object is something false, nor can it be evil even if its object is something evil, because the scientific knowledge of what is false enables us to know truth just as the scientific knowledge of what is evil enables us to do what is good. The use of logic in theology is therefore not only licit but indispensable, because by applying one science it enables us to direct and increase another science, thereby striving for a common goal, namely the cognitive acquisition of the true and the good, which brings human beings closer to God.

Knowledge of the true, knowledge of the good. While Abelard was the second founder (Boethius being the first) of medieval logic, he was also the first writer of the Christian West to have explicitly thought out a speculative justification of ethics. From the patristic period on, Christian moral wisdom had always taken the form of a penetrating reflection on the application of the laws of the Gospel, even including elements of profound existential self-awareness, as in Gregory the Great. Abelard was the first to have felt the need to establish within the human consciousness principles that ensure a substantial and not merely formal allegiance to the laws of Christ. It was not by chance that he gave to his first work on the subject the title *Ethics* or *Know Thyself*. Why? Since for a human being to sin means that he is locating the goal of his actions in himself rather than in God, it is fundamental, if sin is to be avoided, to grasp the goodness of the divine law and to correctly order one's attitude to it.

The principle that inspires this regulation of human action is in substantial agreement with the criticism Abelard himself would level later on, in his *Dialogue*, against Jewish legalism, namely: it is not simply the form the action takes, but the intention behind it that determines the responsibility of a human individual. Killing is evil, but only an intentional killing is a sin, whereas an unintended killing is not. On the other hand, the mere intention of killing, even without performing the act, is a sin.

It is clear, in the final analysis, that this emphasis on the value of the intention as a norm of moral judgment is directly symmetrical with the emphasis on the value of understanding (which is also a form of intention or of attention of the mind to the object) on the logical and cognitive level. But just as no good action can fail to tend or cause a tendency toward the Good, so too no understanding of truth can fail to be directed, or cause others to be directed, toward the one, immutable, and absolute Truth in itself, namely, the knowledge of himself and his works God has in his thought, which is the *Logos*. Thus true logicians are always truly philosophers and truly theologians. It is even the case that, as Abelard several times insists in his writings, true logicians and true philosophers are the true Christians, being followers of the *Logos*, on whose arrangement of things and whose truth logic is based, and being also lovers of the true Sophia, which is the divine Wisdom, namely, Christ.

In fact, from the moment when Wisdom shared itself with human beings through revelation, logic was authorized, precisely because it is a "science of the truth," to investigate the truth of what is read in Scripture. After all, even the words of the Bible, inasmuch as they are meaningful and, on better grounds, inasmuch as they are true, produce an act of understanding in the mind, a cognitive relationship between the manner of being of the known object and the representation of it that the subject is in a position to develop. But because the object in this case is so perfect as to remain, inevitably, beyond the human powers of understanding, the representation will be produced through recourse to similes and metaphors, these being signs that refer allusively to the ineffable corresponding reality. As a result, beginning with his first attempt at a logical analysis of the contents of the sacred text and even as he takes advantage of the riches and beauty of the figurative language of revelation, the theologian immediately comes up against the superimposed and interwoven meanings of Scripture. These he must then necessarily attempt, with the help of a solid method of interpretation, to turn into a consistent, unambiguous, and constructive possession of the true contents of the faith.

Abelard provides productive examples of this methodology in his comments on the Hexaemeron and the letter to the Romans. More important, he has set forth the theory of this methodology as well as a coherent application of it in his famous work *Yes and No* (*Sic et non*). This is a collection of statements chosen and brought together in such a way as to make clear not so much an organized teaching of the Fathers as obvious contradictions among the positions of the Fathers on one and the same theological subject. The author's intention, however, is not to tear down, for his sincere purpose in making these comparisons is not to bewilder the readers but to urge them to set their minds to resolving the contradictions in a methodical way by rising to a higher interpretive level where the multiplicity of opinions will make way for the undeniable unity of truth.

According to the specific directions given in the Prologue, the interpreter must carefully apply a graduated series of rules. First of all, he must submit the correctness and authenticity of the discordant texts to a rigorous philological examination. He must then take into account a possible evolution of each author's thought and a possible variation in the expressions he uses, depending on the literary genre in which he is writing and the preparation of the audience to which he is speaking. Next, he must check on the potential impact of the various possible ambiguities and multiple meanings of human language generally and of theological language in particular, given the necessarily figurative character of the latter.

The final rule is the trickiest, but also the most important: if all this study does not yet yield a clue useful for resolving the contradictions, then, given that the positions taken by the various patristic writers are always imperfect attempts (though deserving respect) to determine the difficult understanding of the scriptural text, the reader is authorized by their very disagreement to introduce a definitive factor, namely, dialectical reason, into this debate over the reading of the biblical text. Thanks to the objectivity of the dialectical method as presented in treatises on logic, such an unavoidable choice will not be subjective and debatable but, as far as possible, necessary and will lead to the most rigorous and persuasive manifestation of truth.

c. The Logic of the Trinity

Scientific rationality, thus legitimized, was brought into theological meditation as a means of further ensuring, and certainly not of playing down or discounting, the truthfulness of the faith.

The composition of the *Theology* was perhaps initially spurred by the need to react to Roscellinus' discrediting of logic in the area of theology and in particular in relation to the trinitarian mystery. Here Abelard uses all his skill in an attempt to bring home the fact that only a consistent regulation of thought and its processes can enable the human intellect to approach the image that is perhaps the supreme and most complex of those used in the scriptural text in speaking of God to humanity. The aim, then, is to explain *to* human reason, but also *by means of* human reason, the possibility of the coexistence of a plurality of relations within the absolute purity of the divine form.

The wise men of antiquity, especially the Platonists, had advanced a good distance in their search for some degree of natural understanding "of the utterly profound and incomprehensible philosophy of the divine," and had been able to do so by starting from the knowableness of the created world. This was possible only because, as even Paul allowed ("for what can be *known* about God is plain to them," Rom 1:19), they had available to them in finite nature a conception of God, a manifestation in nature of the essence of the Creator. They believed, moreover, that they could further explain this idea by speaking of the distinction and unity in God of *power, wisdom,* and *goodness.* Abelard's theology sets out to bring this philosophical idea of God, insofar as it is true, into harmony with the scriptural explanation of the mystery. It is as if the whole of ancient philosophy, on the one hand, and the whole of the Bible, on the other, had no other ultimate purpose than to speak to human beings of the power, the wisdom, and the goodness of God and of the unity of all three.

Abelard thus courageously linked the philosophers with the prophets as being able, both of them, to see God manifesting himself as one and three and to express what they had learned in images and allegories. These pointed all the more to the divine unity in proportion as they also identified the triadic properties of God and sketched the outlines of their meaning. But Abelard's censors, and especially William of St. Thierry, saw in Abelard's move a revival of the worst heresies of the early centuries. For if reason left to itself were to make an excessive distinction among the divine operations, the result would be the reappearance of subordinationism, which violates the unity of the divine substance. If, on the other hand, reason were to emphasize the divine unity to the point of regarding the persons as simply different ways in which the one God acts and manifests himself, the result would be a revival of modalism.

In fact, however, precisely in order to avoid these dangers Abelard explains in his theology that the trinitarian determinants do not point to "relations" but to properties of the substance, which is therefore not defined by something impressed on it from outside. Power, wisdom, and goodness are three distinct terms whose meaning cannot be understood apart from the semantic context in which they belong, and the context here is the one substance. But they do not reflect a single definition of the substance (and therefore are not simply "modalities" of it), even though all three are identical with the substance. Turning to the language of logic, Abelard explains that each of the three properties corresponds to a different state of the one divine substance; consequently, on the one hand each has its own definition; on the other, each completely expresses the one reality.

The progress beyond Augustine's and Boethius' teaching on the Trinity (which speaks of "relations" within the one divine "substance") can be measured by the fact that Abelard has transposed the problem from the logic of terms to the logic of propositions. In the former, "God is God," "the Father is God," "the Son is God," and "the Holy Spirit is God," because among these signifiers only identities can be established, without adding anything further. But at the level of the logic of propositions it is possible to show the correctness of such state-ments as "that which the Father is the Son also is," and to prohibit statements such as "the Father is the Son." The reason: the semantic context of "that which the Father is" or "that which the Son is" is that of the one substance, whereas the semantic context of "Father" and of "Son" is that of properties distinguished by different definitions inasmuch as each corresponds to a different state, which causes the imposition of the respective names.

This new semantic contextualization of the trinitarian problem makes it possible now to proceed in the same way when speaking of the three divine properties intuited by the ancient philosophers: God is Power, God is Wisdom, God is Goodness. The reason: that which is Power is also Wisdom and Good-ness; it is true, therefore, that Power, Wisdom, and Goodness are predicates of the substance and not of the divine persons. But it is also true that Power is not Wisdom or Goodness, and so on, because these three properties correspond objectively to three states of the divine substance and produce in the inquiring mind three different concepts or, in other words, the distinction among three properties that are linked respectively to the three divine persons.

These three properties are not simply representations within the knowing subject but arise in the mind from the real manner of being of the known object, which is God. Nonetheless, the state to which each of the properties corresponds is not a "thing" and is therefore not to be understood as a principle of division within the one utterly simple reality, which is indivisible inasmuch as it is the complete subject of the several properties, namely, God.

In an effort to attenuate the contrast between his "new" logical clarifications and the conceptual definitions hitherto urged by Augustine and Boethius (which he does not mean either to scorn or to change), Abelard offers a new image that is apt for expressing the dogma of the Trinity in a figurative form while bringing out the compatibility of the two solutions. He suggests the metaphor of a bronze seal in which the mind recognizes the presence of three different modes of being, namely that it is bronze, is able to seal, and is actually sealing. He then develops three different conceptions, corresponding to the three modes, that make pos-sible a better understanding of the complex reality of the object.

The image also makes it possible to go more deeply into the reality of the mystery and to realize, for example, that just as the act of sealing can derive simultaneously from the bronzeness and the ability to seal, so too the Latins are right, over against the Greeks, in defending the introduction of the *Filioque* in speaking of the procession of the Holy Spirit. At the same time, however, this illustration, which cannot say everything, is open to further improvements. In fact, taking other investigative paths Abelard explains that in the same context he regards the expression "through the Son," which had been attested and recommended even by authoritative exponents of Latin and Greek patristic thought, as more effective even than "from the Son."

In support of this improvement he once again invokes the studies of the di-vine principle that had been made by the Neoplatonic philosophers, these being known to him from Macrobius. They had taught that the "World Soul," or the effective agent of the divine action throughout matter, had proceeded from the One, the higher principle, *through* the mediation of the Mind or *Nous*. In this teaching, while exercising pure reason like Abelard himself, they had produced a very effective likeness of the doctrine of the Trinity; the Christian theologian can make use of this likeness because revelation extensively confirms its exceptional representational value.

The Neoplatonic invention of the World Soul thus became the final precious image in support of the theological knowledge developed by the human intellect in the course of its philosophical studies. It is still a very effective image for expressing not only the trinitarian relations but also the relationship of God with creation. Like all images, it is deficient inasmuch as it expresses something true under the veil of a fiction, a figment, although the fiction enables the human mind to perceive the mysterious universal presence of the divine Pneuma in creation as a Goodness that forms and regulates everything in accordance with the eternal laws of the *Logos*, but without being mistaken for finite things themselves.

3. The Schools of Paris

A. ABELARD'S HERITAGE AND THE SCHOOLS OF LOGIC

The vigorous attack by Bernard of Clairvaux on the trinitarian views of the *Theology for Students* at the Council of Sens led to a hurried condemnation of many propositions taken from that work. Abelard was unable even to speak freely in his own defense. While he was on the way to Rome in order to appeal to the authority of the pope, Bernard, for his part, composed a work, *Answer to the Main Points of Abelard's Errors*, and used every available means to secure the author's excommunication, even writing fiery letters to the principal representatives of the Roman curia. The Palatine Master, now seriously ill, stopped at Cluny in about 1142. The abbot, Peter, later to be called the Venerable, invited him to remain there; he wrote to the pope interceding for his guest and aided him materially and spiritually during his last days. Peter himself would carry his friend's remains to the Paraclete and hand them to Heloise, thus joining the two lovers at least in the peace of death.

Peter's attitude showed that among his contemporaries there existed a current of sympathy for the person and work of Abelard. Even more, it highlights, by contrast, the persecutorial rage of Abelard's enemies, who feared the spread of his excessively bold theological ideas. Many other names, even of important members of the curia, showed up among the sympathizers and defenders of the memory of the Palatine Master; the majority of them had in their youth listened to his teaching in the schools of Paris.

Thus it was not by accident that, as an element in the pressure Bernard brought to bear on the Roman curia to win the condemnation of Abelard, he

linked the latter's name with that of Arnold of Brescia. Arnold was a young reformist preacher who in 1145 had fomented the rebellion of the Roman populace
against the pope; according to some testimonies he had listened to Abelard's
lectures and then was one of his successors in the chair at Mont-Sainte-Geneviève
in Paris. The connection between the two did not, however, signify a real connection in their teaching, but seems rather to have referred to the rebellious and
uncontrollable attitude attributed to both men.

It is easy to understand, moreover, that Abelard's influence found its natural
sphere more in the schools of the liberal arts than in those of theology. And indeed it was in Paris, the place especially linked to his teaching on logic, that the
arrows of his enemies were still aimed at him even after his death. An example:
the anonymous author of the satirical little poem *The Metamorphoses of Golias*
laments that the capital of the world of studies is afflicted by a swarm of little
schools that produce giants who lay siege to the church by grafting the evil plant
of bad theology onto the practice of logic.

The new Parisian schools of the liberal arts were indeed numerous and not
easily controlled by episcopal authority; not infrequently contemporaries described them as places of empty logical debates. Moreover, as often happens,
the division of the heritage of a single master soon gave rise to forms of disagreement and a further division of currents of thought. Thus from Alberic of
Paris, Abelard's first successor at Mont-Sainte-Geneviève, arose the group
known as Montanists (or Albericians); from Robert of Melun, his second successor, the Melidunensians (or Robertini). And these were only some of the
factions that devoted themselves during those years to resolving the problems
of the relation between understanding and state or mode, while also pointing
up the slide toward the predominance of propositional logic.

B. The School of Saint Victor

Alongside these centers of the study chiefly of logic, however, and likewise
in the shadow of Notre Dame, another school focusing on theological studies
arose and flourished. This was the school of Saint Victor, founded in 1108 by
William of Champeaux for a community that was characterized by a manner of
life halfway between that of canons and that of monks. Through the direction
taken by its studies this school was already legitimizing in principle the possibility of combining the temporal skills of the secular clergy with the biblical and
ascetical spiritual outlook of the monastic world, melding the cultural tradition
and working methods typical of Laon and Chartres with those of Bec.

A thoughtful dialogue with the representatives of the theology of the world
was the mark especially of the writings of Hugh of St. Victor (d. 1141), the pupil
and first successor of William in the administration of the school, and later prior
of the community. In his collection of *Statements about the Divinity*, Hugh never
expressed an overt sympathy with Abelard, but he had no qualms about following the latter in his certainty that the great thinkers of antiquity, Plato at their

head, had been able to grasp by reason alone the truths involved in the trinitarian mystery.

Even Hugh's most important and wide-ranging educational work, the *Didascalicon on the Art of Reading*, takes the form of a great storehouse of elements of Christian teaching that were collected following the two lines of the *Institutes of Divine Literature* and the *Institutes of Human Literature*. But in contrast to Augustine and in comparison with the skimpy Cassiodorean models, both of which Hugh obviously presupposes, his work is noteworthy for its extensive documentation and, at the same time, its keen attention to methodology. The latter leads him to design and describe the successive steps of a systematic intellectual education for clerics, one that prepares the way for meditation on spiritual truth.

Knowledge is an ongoing process, and for that very reason it must observe a law of ascent: it is not possible to reach higher levels except by rising from lower ones that prepare the way for them and are proved true in them; the final result is the contemplative life. We need to learn everything, because nothing is superfluous and the more we learn the easier it becomes for us to learn: "Learn everything, and some day you will realize that nothing is superfluous, because knowledge that is limited and curtailed does not reach its goal and does not satisfy."

Hugh's teaching was greatly valued by the university masters of the following century, who praised it as an example of a complete and systematic pedagogy of knowledge. The birth of "philosophy" arose out of the development of a twofold historical process: the loss of knowledge, which began with the fall of Adam, and its mirror image, the restoration of true knowledge. With humanity's expulsion from paradise it lost the three gifts that were meant to enable it to reach the perfection to which it was predestined: namely, its creation in the "image" and "likeness" of God and its endowment with immortality. At the same time it fell into ignorance of the good, the desire of evil, and bodily infirmity. In order to enable humanity to begin its return to its original condition, God gave it the gift of philosophy, which provides the remedies needed for the three evils and to this end requires a complete study of each of the disciplines into which it is divided; none of these can be sacrificed.

The first remedy, namely, the art of acquiring truth, thus making it possible to build up a body of wisdom, is taught by *theoretical* philosophy. The second remedy, the exercise of virtue for the attainment of goodness, is taught by *practical* philosophy. The third, the discovery of practical tools to combat the weakness of human nature, is taught by *mechanical* philosophy. The fourth but not final philosophical discipline is *logic*, which provides a correct method for all human acquisitions of knowledge, natural and revealed; the study of logic is therefore at the foundation of the wise person's formation.

These four disciplines then have their own internal subdivisions and interconnections; here we have the seven liberal arts and other more or less scattered divisions of knowledge. Of special interest is the openness to the mechanical sciences, which are conceived as symmetrical with the liberal arts and geared to the indispensable organizational and economic side of human life. This was something new, and it began the pragmatic reassessment of the scientific knowledge of nature that would in the next century characterize many representatives of English Franciscanism.

Most important, however, is the ascensional direction given to this entire systematization of knowledge, which always puts the inferior disciplines at the service of the higher goals of knowledge, thus confirming the view, typical of Hugh, of the secular sciences as preparation for the understanding of divine truth. In this context Augustine played a definitive role through his teaching that all the things or realities thus far studied for their own sake could and should become signs, visible pointers to invisible realities.

It was clear, however, on the one hand, that the accomplishment of this cognitive movement could be undertaken only by the highest part of theoretical philosophy, namely, natural or "this-worldly" theology, and on the other hand that the complete success of the movement demanded the self-revelatory initiative of God. Thus one ascends from a "theology of the world" to the "theology of God" by means of a careful change in cognitive procedures, in keeping with a conception developed by Hugh. The latter discusses this conception in greater depth in his own commentary on *The Celestial Hierarchy* of Pseudo-Dionysius and in another work, *The Mysteries of the Christian Faith*, a summary of Christian dogma organized in light of the recognition of God's manifestations in creation; to the whole of these manifestations Hugh gives the name "mysteries" (*sacramenta*).

The relationship between faith and reason is likewise evidently formulated in the ethical perspective of the consequences of original sin. After that sin the soul is no longer capable of seeing nature, itself, and God (with the three eyes of the flesh, reason, and contemplation); therefore "faith is needed in order to believe things unseen." But natural theology can anticipate faith, thanks to a participation in a divine illumination that, according to Hugh, who learned from Augustine, is actuated when human beings contemplate their own likeness to spiritual things, while in their knowledge of the sensible world they make use of their own likeness to corporeal realities. The human being, who is thus located halfway between spirit and matter, is the principal mystery (*sacramentum*), the primary manifestation of the divine. The first form of natural theological knowledge in the human intellect is therefore self-knowledge. From the knowledge of his or her own soul as contingent the person is in fact able to rise up—always in a way that is natural but also with the increasing strength given by interior enlightenment—to a consideration of the immutable existence of the Creator.

At this point the abilities of a theology of the world are exhausted, and a subordination of understanding to believing is needed. The expression "theology of God" signifies for Hugh, as for others, a knowledge that is organized and completed by a faith based on revelation, together with its consequences and proofs. But the expression also appears often in his writings (surely in imitation of Dionysius and John Scotus) as a synonym for "Sacred Scripture," because the theology of God comes down to an understanding of what God makes known of himself in the Bible. This applies especially to God's arrangement or ordering of his work, which he makes effective by the direction he gives to the history of salvation.

In addition, this primary role of exegesis as a constitutive element of theological knowledge explains the fact that the reading (*lectio*) of the Bible was a fundamental exercise in the program of studies followed by all the masters in the school of St. Victor. Here again, in this fundamental part of his study of the divine the theologian makes use of the liberal arts, because these are essential in enabling one to understand the scriptural text: the trivium for understanding the literal, historical, and demonstrative meaning, the quadrivium for dealing with the symbolic, allegorical, tropological or moral, and mystical meanings.

Moreover, just as the secular disciplines follow a pedagogical sequence, so the spiritual understanding of Scripture can only come after the understanding of the "letter," thus confirming the importance of the historical dimension and of the fact that, as far as religion is concerned, the providential presence of the divine in the events of created time is fundamental. Penetration into the mystical meaning of Scripture comes at the end of the soul's pursuit of knowledge, when it enters upon an intuitive and ecstatic vision of the divine; the latter is the supreme human participation in truth and an anticipation of the beatifying restoration of the likeness to God that occurs in the unrepeatable moment of the deepest possible interior recollection.

Hugh's theological writings exerted an important influence during the second half of the twelfth century, especially, though not exclusively, within his community. The historico-literal understanding is central to the vast exegetical works of Englishman Andrew of St. Victor (d. 1175). This scholar did not think himself above studying even the tradition of Old Testament interpretation represented by the contemporary rabbinical schools. He went so far as to introduce innovative exegetical proposals that did not fail to cause puzzlement even within the Victorine community (for example, the nonchristological explanation of the prophecy concerning the virginal birth in Isa 7:14).

Andrew justifies these choices on the basis of his conviction of the appropriateness of accepting multiple exegetical solutions, even on the same plane, namely, the reading of historico-literal sense. For example, in addition to directly historical readings of the text it is permissible to accept others of a naturalistic and scientific kind, since these too are literal meanings. Moreover, this method (based on an idea that cannot fail to remind us of Abelard) makes it possible to get beyond possible disparities among different interpretations to be found in the writings of the Fathers of the Church; these can all be accepted and combined, provided they do not contradict the fundamental teachings of the faith.

Another direct disciple of Hugh, a man endowed with more insightful speculative powers and a greater consciousness of methodology, was Richard of St. Victor (d. 1173); he was prior of the community from 1162 and the author both of encyclopedic educational works and of treatises on mystical theology. In both types of work he shows an overt acceptance of his teacher's conception of the hierarchy of the human sciences as a primary means of bringing about, at the end of a complete course of cognitive formation, the understanding of the faith as urged by Anselm of Aosta.

Richard, too, takes biblical exegesis as the starting point of theological knowledge, but he gives pride of place to allegorico-spiritual interpretation (in direct opposition at times to Andrew, as, for example, in his little work *Emmanuel* when he discusses the christological prophecy of Isaiah). The deeper understanding of the symbolism in revealed truth, once this understanding has been stripped of the excesses of the imagination, is not opposed to the literal sense, but is always its complement. For Richard this deeper grasp of symbolism is the basic tool for a deeper doctrinal understanding of revelation. This approach is evident in his *Book of Qualifications*, an introduction in handbook form to the reading of Scripture; the second part of this work circulated separately under the title *Allegories in the Old and New Testaments* and enjoyed great success in the following century.

Another work of Richard that was much cited by the university masters was his *Trinity*, in which the ascensional theory of knowledge was combined with the Anselmian practice of seeking out the "necessary reasons" with particular reference to the problem of the Trinity. With the *Monologion* and *Proslogion* evidently in mind, Richard first introduces some arguments that compel the human mind to admit the existence of God; he prefaces these arguments by assuming the idea of God that comes from faith and then entrusting its justification to reason alone.

Worthy of mention among these arguments is that arising from the division of being into "noneternal and not self-originated," "eternal but not self-originated," and "eternal and self-originated." Once the reality of the first two kinds, which are necessarily derived from something else, has been acknowledged, it follows that their origin is certainly the third, which therefore exists. Similar from the standpoint of form is the procedure Richard uses to lead the reader to a possible understanding of the trinitarian mystery. The argument runs as follows: if God exists, we must attribute to him the best that is found in the best creatures; the soul, which is among the most excellent creatures, has among its supreme powers the power of loving; God must therefore love, but to love always means loving another and loving this other as oneself; we must therefore admit in God a trinity of persons, the first two being necessary to account for the love with which God loves himself, and the third to account for the love with which God loves as himself whatever is derived from him.

Consequently, Richard sets forth a similar fusion of love and understanding (a human imitation of the divine life) in his highly esteemed works of mystical theology: *The Greater Benjamin* or *The Grace of Contemplation* and *The Lesser Benjamin* or *The Preparation of the Soul for Contemplation*. This fusion is seen as the core element in the process (which is the reverse of the descent of things from God) by which the soul is led from the consideration of finite things to the contemplation of the divine. In the first of the two works cognitive activity supports the soul in its ascent through the three phases of imagination, reason, and understanding, each of these preparing for the next and all three being necessary but not sufficient conditions for introducing the soul to the intellectual vision.

The second work takes the form of a tropological commentary on the prefigurative persons of Jacob's twelve sons, each of whom is the symbol of a virtue. The emphasis here is on the practical aspect, namely, the purification of the soul leading to mystical ecstasy. The ethical virtues, which are the daughters of the affections (symbolized by Leah, first wife of Jacob), will be governed by discernment (= Joseph), born of the first daughter of reason (= Rachel, the patriarch's second wife), which will die giving birth to contemplation (Benjamin). The reason for this death is that the human ability to understand and define must faint away, as it were, in the utterly negative although ardently affective and supercognitive moment of final access to the divine.

A similar demand for distinctions among, and understanding of, the cognitive courses leading to the completion of this ascetical advance led other Victorine masters to expand the classification of the soul's faculties and, as an aid, to immerse themselves in the study of the anthropological doctrines of the late antique and patristic period. Achard of St. Victor (d. 1170/71) had been prior before Richard and was likewise the author of exegetical sermons and an interesting *Trinity*, which has come down to us in fragmentary form. In all likelihood he also composed a work, *The Distinction of Soul, Spirit, and Mind*, that circulated anonymously in the university world. This work suggests a tripartite hierarchy (soul, spirit, mind) of the powers of the interior human substance and, applying a procedure already shown to be valid in connection with the divine Trinity, endeavors to ensure the unity and simplicity of this hierarchy amid the diversity of cognitive functions.

In the writings of Geoffrey (d. after 1194), another, younger Victorine master, similar descriptions of the natural powers and abilities of the human soul are accompanied by a decidedly optimistic anthropological view that allows him to free himself from the negative prejudgments about the senses and the other inferior degrees of knowledge that were typical of medieval Augustinianism. In his *Well of Philosophy*, a didactic poem on the hierarchy of the philosophical disciplines, and especially in his *Microcosm*, an allegorical commentary on the creation story, Geoffrey depicts the human person as a miniature universe combining in itself the best potentialities of the macrocosm. He achieves a real celebration of the human being's psycho-physical harmony and the power given it by the natural, ethical, and intellectual virtues. Following Abelard and Hugh, he claims that the credit for this discovery can be given to the best of the ancient philosophers, such as Socrates and Seneca.

C. READING OF THE BIBLE AND READING OF THE FATHERS

Geoffrey's dedication of his *Well of Philosophy* to Abbot Stephen of Saint-Geneviève is evidence of, if nothing else, some degree of circulation of theological ideas and writings in the educated and religious circles of Northern France. In fact, the teaching of the Victorine masters generally, and not of Hugh alone, was widely echoed in cultivated Parisian circles. In particular, the Victorines' effort to validate the exegetical approach to revelation contributed directly and rather effectively to the basic training of the masters of theology who were active in Paris in the second half of the century.

Two Parisians are indeed to be counted among the most important teachers of biblical exegesis in the pre-university period. One was Peter Comestor (d. 1178/79), who withdrew to Saint Victor in the last years of his life after abandoning teaching. He composed a continuous gloss on the Bible, titled *Scholastic History*, which he offers as a wide-ranging aid to a basic reading of the Scriptures and an introduction to any further exegetical approach; the work is rich in historical and geographical information that would be useful in learning sacred history. The second of these Parisians was Peter Cantor (d. 1197), who died a Cistercian. The first of his best-known works is *The Abridged Word*, a handbook of moral theology based on exegesis. The second is the *Summa, "Abel,"* another useful tool in dealing with biblical tropology; this is an alphabetical repertory (beginning with "Abel") containing over a thousand terms used in the sacred text or useful in tackling biblical studies.

These two masters educated Stephen Langton (d. 1128), whose career is a perfect example of the passage, in Paris, from multiple schools to the establishment of a new institution, the university, of which he was chancellor.

But if we are to describe correctly the cultural and institutional process leading from the fertile soil of the schools of exegesis that sprang up during those years in the shadow of Notre Dame to the formation of the great Parisian Faculty of Theology in the next century, we cannot overlook the contribution of Peter Lombard (d. 1160). He composed biblical commentaries, especially on the Psalms and St. Paul, but his most important work was the *Book of Sentences*, which would in the next century be universally accepted as the fundamental text for the teaching of theology in the universities.

Peter, from northern Italy, arrived in France while still young and came in contact with the Victorines thanks to a letter of introduction from Bernard of Clairvaux. He heard Abelard's lectures, became a master himself, perhaps in the cathedral school, and finally became bishop of Paris. His collection of *Sentences* was inspired, in principle, by the same purpose as Abelard's *Yes and No*: to enable him to go more deeply into the subjects of his own study at the precise point at which the possible overlapping of different authorities risked introducing confusions or misunderstandings unless it was faced head-on and settled with the tools of a satisfactory hermeneutic: "The livelier the debate over the truth, the greater the need of inquiry."

But unlike Abelard (from whose followers Peter distanced himself, criticizing them as "long-winded logicians") he committed himself openly to the purpose of not radicalizing but rather surmounting and removing any opposition between the patristic authorities by resolving it at the theoretical level. His task thus became that of a scholarly compiler who was charged with selecting and organizing various statements in the works of the Fathers so as to produce a complete and coherent explanation of Christian doctrine.

The *Book of Sentences* is thus strictly marked by a strong sense of the whole, which is set forth in a well-defined, thematic organization of the contents of the faith; Peter's model is the Anselmian system, and in the background lies sacred history. The first of the four books that make up the work has for its subject God in himself, therefore his unity and trinity and his attributes. The second deals with God as creator of the angels and human beings and then with sin and the promise of grace. The third book is about God as redeemer, and therefore about the Law, christology, and pneumatology. The fourth treats of God as distributor of grace, and therefore of sacramental doctrine and eschatology. No less effectively, the author superimposes on this quadripartite division an ordering of the texts according to the Augustinian distinction, already adopted by Hugh of St. Victor, between realities (to which the first three books are devoted) and signs (the subject of the fourth book).

The selection of sources is wide-ranging and, in many instances, original as compared with other collections made during these years, although Peter himself often knew these sources only at second hand from anthologies and collections. An example worth noting is his use of John Damascene's *The Orthodox Faith*, a work recently translated by Burgundio of Pisa. For the most part the authority of the pagan philosophers falls outside Peter Lombard's cultural vision, because it could not be subordinated to the interpretation of revelation. He was convinced that whatever philosophy might have that was useful for theological knowledge had already been acquired and developed by the Fathers; the rest was only worthless human opinion.

In contrast to the philosophers and in accord with his own premises, Peter presents the tradition of Christian wisdom in such a way as to make it seem free of contradictions and unjustifiable disagreements. He cites the patristic sources as a harmonious sequence, stresses the point that problems arising from their testimonies are inherent not in their teaching but in the subjects of which they speak, limits his own critical role to the linking of their texts, and tends to make their style his own by imitating the authors' language and expressions so as to blend and merge with them in the service of their truth.

Among the many emulators or imitators of Peter Lombard's *Book* the one most deserving of note was his direct disciple, Peter of Poitiers (d. 1205), who likewise taught theology in Paris and finally became chancellor of the cathedral school in the last years of the twelfth century. In addition to sermons and to exegetical works that urge a full explanation of the four senses of Scripture,

Peter composed a collection of *Sentences* in five books, in imitation of his teacher. But in contrast to his model he clearly emphasizes the introduction of logical criticism, alongside the citation of the Bible or the Fathers, in the study of points open to dispute—that is, all the subjects of revelation the meaning of which is not immediately clear. In this way Peter takes a decisive step toward the creation of the university's theological treatises, in which the views of the "authorities" are regarded as the source of problems and debate.

This development of methodology was obviously due also to the gradual increase of philosophical skills during the second half of the twelfth century. Some writers endeavored more explicitly to imitate the model supplied by Abelard. One such was the anonymous author of the *Introduction to Theology* in three books (dealing respectively with humanity, with redemption and the sacraments, and with the angels and the divine nature). Here we see a quite un-prejudiced use of the dialectical method in presenting, evaluating, and approving divergent interpretive opinions while using the "question" method in a still-crude but clearly defined manner. Another example is the again anonymous collection known as the *Parisian Sentences*; in its three sections (faith, sacraments, charity) the compiler alternates citations from the authorities and rational arguments that support or challenge the authorities.

Some traditionalists were inevitably shocked by the arrogance with which some masters went to exaggerated lengths in works of this kind. The indictments were eventually aimed first and foremost at those successful authors who, intentionally or not, seemed to be the models who had opened the way for the excessive freedom shown in the interpretive experiments of the schools. In addition to an obvious target, Abelard, who continued to be demonized by the most critical opponents of a rational approach to the faith, Peter Lombard also paid a price, chiefly because of the direction he seems to take in some of the choices he makes in tackling the texts of the Fathers.

In particular, it was the christology of the *Book of Sentences* that aroused the greatest suspicion because it allowed as legitimate an interpretation of the hypostatic union in Christ according to which he has a human nature due to an "assumption." The debate over the "assumed human being" (*assumptus homo*) broke out as soon as Peter's work began to circulate; to many, this expression seemed to herald the serious theological error commonly known as "christologi-cal nihilism," according to which Christ "as man," or in his humanity, was not a definite subsisting reality. They argued that according to the terminology in-troduced by Boethius in his *Answer to Eutyches* a formal definition of the person of Christ can result only from his participation in both the divine and human natures.

The formula taken from the *Sentences* asserting "that Christ as man is not something," was condemned after Lombard's death, first at the general Council of Tours in 1163 and then at a synod of the province of Sens that was held in Paris in 1170. Theologian John of Cornwall (d. before 1200) dedicated a work on the subject to Pope Alexander under the title *Eulogium* (later summarized in his *Defense of the Incarnate Word*; in it he attacked the *Book of Sentences* as the bastard offspring of the theological errors of both Abelard and Gilbert of Poitiers.

The second half of the century saw many manifestations of the traditionalist reaction against the "garrulous teachers" who dared treat of the Trinity and the Incarnation with the useless superficiality characteristic of the schools. But the most violent display came around 1177 and from the very abbey of St. Victor that had made one of the chief contributions to the formalization of the methodical use of understanding as applied to the faith. The one responsible for the attack was Walter, Richard's successor as prior, who wrote a strongly worded little book with the expressive title *Against the Four Labyrinths of France*, in which he showed a radical intolerance of anyone who sought or showed favor to the entrance of philosophical reason within the solid walls of Christian truth.

The work was probably not without the polemical intention of putting down Geoffrey, a fellow religious, whom Walter during these years forced to leave St. Victor. On the surface, however, his explicit primary target was the four dangerous monsters who were undermining the peace of Christ's church by dragging believers into the deceitful "labyrinths" of false philosophy and logic. The four labyrinths were four masters: Gilbert of Poitiers, Peter Lombard, Peter of Poitiers, and Peter Abelard (although in fact the object in the section attacking Abelard was the *Sentences on Divinity* of the Poitiers school, which Walter mistakenly attributed to the Palatine Master). Walter condemns wholesale all the witnesses to ancient pagan philosophy, who were to be disapproved not only for their conceptual errors but also and above all for their depraved immoral behavior. But he also rejects and looks with suspicion on all theological novelties not authorized by tradition: such, for example, as the work of "the not more clearly identifiable John Damascene" who suggested to his disciple, Peter Lombard, a great many errors contrary to authentic Augustinian teaching.

4. Gilbert of Poitiers

A. A DIALECTICAL COMMENTARY ON THE THEOLOGY OF BOETHIUS

Gilbert of Poitiers was born around 1180 and as a young man attended first the school of Laon and then that of Chartres, where he remained as a teacher in the cathedral school for over a decade, while also serving as chancellor. Then, in Paris, he held for a long time the chair of "logic and divinity," as John of Salisbury puts it in his *Pontifical History*; John had been one of Gilbert's most enthusiastic listeners. Finally, in 1042, Gilbert returned to his native Poitiers as its bishop. The world of Laon had familiarized him with the exemplaristic realism of Augustine; from Chartres he derived an interest in the Platonizing naturalism of the late antique encyclopedists and Boethius; in the world of the

Parisian schools he had occasion to compare himself with the best-known masters of logic of that time.

John of Salisbury emphasizes Gilbert's subtle intelligence and the great number of scientific and patristic works he had read and studied, to the point that "no one was his superior in any area of study, while he always seemed to be a little superior to anyone else in any area of study." John adds that a few decades after Gilbert's death in 1154 "all in the schools were now readily repeating formulas and teachings that, when Gilbert first enunciated them, all thought of as utterly new and unheard of."

And yet the very "novelty" of his doctrinal language caused problems for not a few of the more traditionalist theologians; these problems were voiced during the years in which Gilbert was reaching the heights of his ecclesiastical career. Two zealous archdeacons of the diocese of Poitiers asked Bernard of Clairvaux to investigate some of their bishop's statements about the trinitarian mystery.

Bernard first managed to have Gilbert summoned to a fact-finding synod in Paris that ended after lengthy discussions without any concrete results. Then, in 1148, Bernard brought Gilbert before a solemn council at Rheims, in the presence of Pope Eugene III; here Gilbert was required to retract four heretical propositions extracted from his writings. Gilbert submitted and was acquitted, but was ordered to stop teaching and spreading his own theological ideas. The attacks on him did not cease, however, even after his death. Not only Walter of St. Victor but other representatives of monastic thought brought together into a single condemnation not only Gilbert's theological innovations but also those of Abelard and Peter Lombard. Among these accusers were the already-mentioned John of Cornwall, and Gerhoh of Reichersberg, a German Benedictine who wrote a pamphlet with the telling title *The Novelties of the Present Age*.

While Gilbert also composed some interesting works of biblical exegesis and a correspondence, the anger of his adversaries focused on his principal theological work: his analytical commentary on the five *Sacred Works* of Boethius or, as Gilbert calls them in his Prologue, *Anicius' Books of Questions*. In that same introduction Gilbert sets forth his conception of theology as a very lofty form of knowledge that attempts to render intelligible the inscrutable depths of the divinity, which as such are unknowable and beyond expression. But theology also takes into account that in this area human reason must trust in the complexity of scriptural language and will never be able to claim to reach other than "probable" and never truly conclusive results.

In Gilbert's view Boethius was one of the most careful and accurate of theologians. While his intention was only to prevent the spread of heresies, he in fact set forth in the concise language of his books a series of fundamental rational explanations. These were based on the laws of the liberal arts, although inevitably falling short of the natural precision of those laws, and were intended to determine how much intelligible truth was hidden in dogmas. From Boethius' example we learn that, in order to make the faith understandable, everyone, teachers and students alike, must be both skilled and ignorant, proud and humble, and able to apply the rules of scientific language while at the same time recognizing their inevitable breakdown and moderating their semantic and definitional value in face of the greater ineffableness of the divinity.

Boethius was an "author," that is, a writer on sacred things who was acknowledged to possess an "authority" less than that of a prophet but subordinated to the latter and supported by it and therefore, as such, incontrovertible. Gilbert thinks of himself as a "reader," a commentator whose task is to complete the work of the "author" by correctly explaining the meaning of his words and making his intentions clear. A commentator will therefore not limit himself to explaining and mechanically repeating Boethius' teaching, but will be a real interpreter, one who is able to go more deeply into that teaching and explain, whenever necessary, the contents of the author's writings. He will do this by using the author's tools, that is, his rational skills, especially those that are logical and grammatical, and while adopting his readiness to be corrected, if need be, by the church's magisterium. Boethius' contribution to the interpretation of the faith, which he set forth in language difficult to understand, is thus made available by the commentator to all the faithful in a form they can understand, one that resists misunderstandings and mystifications.

Here, then, we have a commentary that is intended to be an explanation of the arguments used and therefore a clarification, interpretation, and evaluation of the speculative basis on which Boethius' theological formulas are grounded. It is obvious that such a commentary must necessarily be based on a strict methodology that Gilbert intends to follow closely in order to avoid errors or deviations from the original approach but at the same time to further refine and enrich it, thus making himself both its defender and its reinventor. The character of this method of study is suggested to him by Boethius himself when, at the beginning of the first of the short works, he describes the problem of the Trinity as "a question that has long been debated."

Commenting on these words, Gilbert explains that a "question" arises whenever it becomes necessary to resolve a contradiction between two theses (affirmations or negations), both of which seem to have valid reasons in their favor—that is, when, in context, there seem to be arguments both for and against a particular doctrinal claim. For a solution to be reached it must be presupposed that, since two contradictory theses cannot both be true, one of them is only seemingly true; this means that there is a semantic ambiguity that must be identified and eliminated. The ascertainment of such an error always involves a distinction, which is a means of showing that the two theses, and therefore the terms used in them, belong to different semantic and argumentative genres or orders or to different lines of argument. The distinction makes it possible to see which of the two theses really reflects the specific context in which they arose, and thus to acknowledge it as true.

With the help of this method, which he thinks is valid for explaining the speculative content of any text whatsoever, that is, of any scientific text that needs to be examined, Gilbert regards himself as able to carry out his own analysis of the questions raised by a theological text, that is, by a passage of Scripture or of the Fathers, or indeed any text the entire Christian tradition recognizes as authoritative. This represents a notable advance (even beyond Abelard's contribution) on the path leading theology to the status of scientific knowledge and to a worthy place in the system of human sciences. The reason is that it explains how the sphere of knowledge of the contents of the faith can be open to rational study and penetration, provided the latter are supported by a correct set of tools, thereby guaranteeing the consistency and necessity of the course followed. The conclusions reached must always be inherent in the premises and consonant with what is already explicit in revelation.

B. A Theological Method: The Shifting of Meaning

Such a correct set of tools, like those used in all the other scientific disciplines, will be consistent with the normative principles of logic; in their use, however, it is appropriate to take into account the specific nature of the kind of investigation proper to theological knowledge. This means that it will always be necessary to identify, acknowledge, and keep in mind the special changes that dialectical rules undergo when applied to formulas explaining Christian revelation. The language of logic will inevitably take on a specific nuance that is not indeed substantially different but does in some measure diverge from that language's original finalities when it is adapted to theological knowledge, the subject of which is a reality superior to any natural reality.

According to the report given by historian Otto of Freising, a devoted admirer, Gilbert himself expatiated on this situation at the Council of Rheims when, in explaining to his accusers his conception of the relationships between the divine persons, he asserted that the logical use of the term "person" is different in theology than in the other disciplines. Thus it is legitimate to say that the Father, the Son, and the Holy Spirit are three persons without one's being obliged to admit that they exist as three individual and separate realities, as the ordinary meaning of person (*persona* = *per se una*) requires. Only in the case of the three divine persons is each of them God and distinct from the other two, yet each is not God in ways that differ from the one to the others. If the conciliar tradition authorizes the use of the word "person" in expressing the meaning of the trinitarian relations, the reason is that among the words supplied by human language the customary meaning of the word is the one best adapted to express the paradoxical reality of this mystery. But a theologian must know how to distinguish correctly between the value of the word when used to signify a created reality and its value when it proves useful for expressing the mode of being of the divine.

It is therefore indispensable that the theologian clearly define the subject, the extent, the limits, and the satisfactory procedures of his own discipline. In the second chapter of Boethius' first short theological work (*The Trinity*), the author divides theoretical philosophy into three sciences: physics (natural philosophy), mathematics, and theology. These study three different fields: respectively natural reality, the immutable but not separated forms of bodies, and the one and only immutable and separated form, which is God. Each, moreover, has a different way of organizing its content or (in Gilbert's terminology) has its own specific guiding principle (*ratio*), which Boethius describes respectively with the adverbs *rationabiliter* (rationally), *disciplinaliter* (systematically), and *intellectualiter* (intuitively).

It is, of course, not difficult to accept that there are conceptual tools peculiar to each of the three fields, with their usage being strictly dependent on their respective scientific guiding principles. Thus a concept such as "corporeity," along with its definition, will apply only in the material world, in which one proceeds rationally, that is, by way of definitions, divisions, and lines of argument. In like manner, only in the theological realm is it possible to grasp and apply the meaning of the idea of "simplicity of being," such as God alone has; the real value of the idea emerges only when one proceeds *intellectualiter*, that is, by using the intuitive capacity of the higher, contemplative intellect.

In most cases, however, theological knowledge does not have satisfactory instruments proper to it. Therefore, just as Scripture itself uses images and metaphors, that is, words subjected to a partial shift away from their original meaning, so too theology must fall back on the tools of the lower sciences (mathematics and physics), but must at the same time subject these to a change or shift (*transumptio*) in their semantic use.

It is precisely because they do not take this kind of shift into account that heretics fall into errors. They claim to discuss the mysteries of faith, such as the Trinity or the Incarnation, while using nothing but reason, that is, the methodology suited for investigating natural realities. But if one takes into account the changes the other methodologies inevitably undergo when applied to divine realities we will understand that in theology, and only there, the use of ideas such as "person" or "trinity" can be valid provided they are subjected to a sufficient shift of meaning, away from the natural meaning of the one (person) and the mathematical meaning of the other (trinity). They thereby become suited to explaining the mode of being of something that is distinct and yet at the same time is one with that from which it is distinguished.

This proposed adaptation of scientific discourse to the peculiarities of the objects Gilbert was investigating was obviously one of the principal reasons why the traditionalist theologians, chiefly in the monastic world, criticized his thinking. They thought they could derive from the example of Anselm of Aosta the lesson that theological language was always to be regarded as univocal in comparison with the customary speech of human beings. Their argument: theological language was, at one and the same time, true and had immediate reference to the truth it expressed (as Anselm himself had vigorously asserted in response to the nominalistic conventionalism of Roscellinus). Gilbert was, however, sincerely convinced of the need to move away from a primitive conception of theology as simply a reflection of the *discourse of faith* in the human mind and toward a careful definition of the suitability of the instrumentalities that make possible a correct grasp of truth through the formulation of a complete *discourse on faith.*

c. ONTOLOGICAL COMPOSITION AND THE REALITY OF THE SINGULAR

To the extent that Gilbert's conception of knowledge was based on the distinction between the special natures of the objects proper to each of three disciplines, as signaled by Boethius, it became necessary to investigate each of these disciplines. The purpose of this investigation was to prove, in a comparative study, the reality and true character of the modes of being proper to individual things (studied by physics), to universal entities (studied by mathematics), and to the supreme, simple, transcendent substance (contemplated in theology). Gilbert was thereby forced to take a position on the debated question of the reality of universals. He had to be careful, however, to regard a universal not as a modality of the knowledge of the knowing subject but as a true and proper mode of being of something real that is located at an intermediate level of the ontological hierarchy uniting creation with God.

Consequently, as Otto of Freising expressly says, Abelard's solution to the problem of universals was, from Gilbert's point of view, too close to the nominalism of Roscellinus and, by dragging in clever but empty formalities, could jeopardize the understanding of theological realities. In fact, Gilbert's "realism" (if we may properly use this perhaps overly general term) consists in having identified a particular kind of subsistence proper to the object of each of the theoretical sciences: the natural individual, the universals, and the divine, and then having applied to each of these three objects the logical cognitive procedure that befits it and is suitable for defining and studying it.

The answer, then, to Porphyry's questions about the nature of universals should arise first from the acceptance of their reality and then from the recognition that, since everything existing as a reality is something singular, that is, distinct from everything else, not only individuals but also the universals and, for that matter, even the divine substance are always singular realities. Every individual is singular, but not every singular is an individual, since the universals too, and even God (who does not belong to a species) are singulars: "for whatever is is singular." It is therefore possible to complete Boethius' terminology and give a new description of the hierarchy of real substances: at the apex, the simple substance; then universal substances, which Gilbert suggests describing as "dividuals" (that is, "divisibles," allowing participation); and finally individual substances, which are indivisible ("individual," which is grammatically the opposite of "dividual"). The individual can be either irrational or rational; in the second case it is called "person."

It is peculiar to the individual that it does not share its form with anything else, but exists in a particular, non-repeatable way that results from the coming together of a part of matter with a form. As such, the individual, that which does not share its form with anything else, is described by Boethius in his *Weeks* as "that which is" [henceforth here: *id quod est*), that which exists by being what it is. On the other hand, the decisive factor, "that by means of which [henceforth here: *quo est*] the 'that which is'" exists in the way in which it actually does exist, is the form, one of many possible, that determines the manner in which the matter in the individual exists. This form is that "by which the individual exists," a reality like others inasmuch as it is exactly alike in all the individuals informed by it.

If the non-sharing of its form is a peculiarity of the *id quod est* or individual, similarity of form is the peculiarity of the *quo est* or *dividuum* (that is, of the universal). The non-sharing of its form is one of the set of characteristics proper to an individual and to no one else (for example, everything that characterizes the being of Plato, distinguishing it from that of Socrates and describable, if usage allowed, as his "Platonicity"). On the other hand, a shared likeness is proper to the other set of characteristics that displays its likeness to other individuals (genus, species, properties, and so on) and therefore constitutes its *quo est*.

It is difficult to make intelligible how the *quo est* can be a real subsistence, that is, a singular, while being shared in a constitutive way by several individuals. Gilbert resolves the difficulty by recourse to the doctrine of the "innate forms," which are incorruptible models of being (the same in many individuals), but distinct from the ideas that are eternally thought in the Word, and intermediate between these ideas and individual entities (which do not share their form). The divine ideas, which Gilbert calls *sincerae substantiae* = "substances that are true and unimpaired," are the eternal universals and not distinct from the mind and will of God. The "innate forms," on the other hand, are singular universal realities, forms that reproduce higher models and in turn become the models, that is, the formative forms, of inferior realities. The forms exist inasmuch as they are *dividua*, and they are the being of subsistent things, of inferior subsisting realities; in other words, they are the *quo est* of the individual things that participate in them on the basis of their shared forms.

We have here a clear example of a difference between Boethius and Gilbert. The language of the former is terse, almost obscure; he limits himself to a bare distinction between *id quod est* (that "which can also have something over and above what it is") and "being" (*esse*: that which "is not combined with anything but itself").

The commentator, for his part, has tried to make the teaching more explicit by offering a precise explanation of the mental processes by which the philosopher knows the various degrees of real existence. The structures of the three theoretical sciences correspond to the knowledge of this diversity. Physics studies those forms of corporeal individuals that have been conjoined to matter, by comparing them with the innate forms that subsist in these individuals, that is, are not separated from them. Mathematics studies the innate forms insofar as these are universals, as if they were abstracted from the individuals for study in order to evaluate their ability to determine the individuals. Theology, on the other hand, must move beyond all created forms, whether individual or universal, in order to focus its gaze on the simple being of God and of the exemplary forms (or *sincerae substantiae*) in God's Word.

D. The Trinitarian "Distinction"

The task, object, and procedure proper to theological knowledge are now clear. In order to understand the nature of God, theologians must inevitably use scientific language drawn from the lower-level disciplines (for example, from mathematics when they speak of God's nature or qualities; from physics when they fall back on the term "person"). The theologian must also, however, endeavor to move beyond all the limiting forms belonging to concrete created things, whether physical or mathematical, that is, whether individual or universal. All of Gilbert's theses, including those most criticized and censured, must be understood in the light of this careful articulation of cognitive levels and theological shifts of meaning.

God is a singular and therefore an *id quod est*, but a singular that is identical with the *quo est* that makes him to be God. For this reason theological language distinguishes between "God" and "divinity" (as the language of physics distinguishes between "human being" and "humanity") and asserts that God is God in virtue of his divinity. At Rheims Bernard pointed out that such formulas risked introducing composition into the divine being, and he persuaded the council to approve the opposite principle: "Everything in God is God," a principle that made it illicit to speak of a reality that could be called "divinity," as though it were different from God himself.

In subsequent years, despite Gilbert's official retraction in order to avoid condemnation, his disciples and supporters continued to defend him on the same lines and on the same basis. The defense was rooted in the certainty that theological language was a tool, useful in explaining to the intellect the element of the faith it had a duty to understand. In other words, the difference in the modes of signifying or ways of conveying meaning corresponds to a distinction in our modes or ways of understanding and not to a real distinction in the divine mode or way of existing. The distinctions we draw reflect a functional necessity of our imperfect way of speaking about and understanding God. The defenders endeavored to show that this change in human discourse when it becomes theological discourse was widely accepted by the Fathers and in particular by Hilary, Gilbert's ancient predecessor in the episcopal chair of Poitiers.

It is obvious, once again, that the sign of the speculative distance between Gilbert and his opponents is to be seen in their different conceptions of the relationship between human language and the reality of its objects. It is necessary, however, to point out that this functional interpretation of language does not lead, as it did in Roscellinus, to a fluctuating and optional view of theological discourse, as if one formula were as good as another in the human attempt to gain a rational grasp of what is in itself ineffable. Thanks to the constructive support provided by the acquisitions of truth in the lower-level sciences, the formulas of Gilbert's theology make necessary and carefully devised statements about the divine reality even while acknowledging their ultimate inadequacy.

The statement that "God is" cannot but be equivalent to the assertion that "God is by reason of his essence," that is "his divinity." This is because human thought can understand the being of anything only thanks to a logical distinction between what is predicated (the divinity, but also the "is" of God) and that of which it is predicated (God), as Boethius urges and as the grammarians teach, Priscian first among them (according to whom every noun always co-signifies, that is, also signifies, a substance and a quality). Otherwise it would be impossible to introduce any other qualification or determinant into the divine being—for example, to distinguish between goodness and greatness or wisdom, and so on, that is, to make all the distinctions valid for the knowing subject but corresponding to realities not distinct from one another in the object known.

Supremely important among these distinctions is the predication "triune," because without the possibility of distinguishing between "God" and "divinity" it would not be possible to ensure the unity of the three persons. Only because human reason recognizes that "the Father is God thanks to the divinity that makes him God" and that the same is true of the Son and the Spirit, can it understand that the divine substance is one and the same in all three divine persons; for only in theology do the *quo est* and the *id quod est* point to one single, identical reality.

The shift (*transumptio*) from the fragmented and multiplicitous level of scientific distinctions (which are required if we are to understand God's mode of being) to the higher level of God's absolute simplicity and unity is thus ensured by an ascent of the mind from the level of discursive reason to the direct, intuitive level of the intellect or intelligence (a level Boethius introduces when he uses the adverb *intellectualiter* to describe the method proper to theology). Gilbert has no difficulty, therefore, in agreeing with his opponents that any predication made of God is always and only a way of predicating his divine being. But in Gilbert's view the reason for their misunderstanding of his teaching and their refusal to acknowledge his orthodoxy was their failure to understand that this statement is made possible precisely by the analogical passage from one level of knowledge to another.

E. THE GILBERTAN OR PORRETAN THEOLOGIANS

The followers of Gilbert likewise emphasized chiefly the necessity of explaining the use of logical distinctions in theology, to the point of making this a sign, as it were, of ideological identification. The historians have overgeneralized in gathering all these men together as "Porretans" (theologians following the man from Poitiers) or the "School of Gilbert." In fact, there is reason to perceive different attitudes among his most fervent admirers and defenders. At one end of the spectrum were those who maintained their own doctrinal autonomy and combined his remembered teaching with that of other masters of theology and logic (this group included John of Salisbury and Otto of Freising, but also Alan of Lille and Rudolph Glaber = "Rudolph the fervent"). Then there were disciples who were more open to his influence, but not in a consistent way (such as Simon of Tournai or Stephen Langton). Finally, there were the closest and most faithful disciples, men solidly dedicated to his teaching, which inspired them in the writing of theological treatises; many of these followers have remained anonymous.

In general, then, given the lack of detailed information and of allegiance to a common institution, it is preferable, in dealing with these three types, to speak simply of a Gilbertan "current" or a "trend" that marks some aspects of the theological study done by different writers who were influenced in varying degrees by the Gilbertan model.

In any case, as I have already noted, their work is characterized by acceptance of the division of theoretical knowledge into distinct levels and by the resultant acceptance of the need to make a theological shift of meaning in using terms from the lower-level scientific fields. On the basis of this fundamental principle they were committed to continuing the work begun by the master, explaining dogma with the help of Aristotelean-Boethian logic; this they combined with more strictly exegetical work, which for these writers remained the foundation and essential presupposition of theological speculation. As a result, these masters felt it a special duty to develop a new theory of the divine names that combined the ancient Pseudo-Dionysian model with the logico-grammatical accuracy given by the special small change the meaning of each term undergoes when predicated of God.

Another dominant element in the works of many "Gilbertans" was recourse to the authority of the Fathers, which was supported by means of a large number of verbatim citations and was intended mainly to denounce the straying of Gilbert's opponents into the Arian (or Sabellian) heresy. For example, Canon Ademar of St. Rufus (Valence) made a methodical search for patristic citations consistent with Gilbert's teaching; these he gathered into a *Collection of Authorities* that he divided into twenty-four "distinctions" or thematic chapters, each devoted to a specific area of theological terminology relating to the various dogmas, mysteries, and sacraments of the faith.

For their part, Hugo Eterianus and his brother, Leo the Tuscan, moved to Constantinople in the second half of the century and through their translations of the Greek Fathers helped to augment the collection of texts that might be cited in defense of the master. At the request of German prelate Hugh of Honau, another Gilbertan of the strict observance, Hugh Eterianus composed a *Book on the Distinction between Nature and Person*; this was modeled on Boethius' fifth short theological work and in it he explains, among other things, how in the Trinity the terms designating the personal properties are identical in meaning but different in their signifying function in relation to the names of the persons.

Using the short work of Hugh Eterianus, Hugh of Honau himself composed a *Book on the Difference between Nature and Person*. Also devoted to trinitarian terminology were the anonymous treatise beginning with the words *The Invisible Things of God*, and the *Dialogue between Ratius and Everard*, the author of which was almost certainly Everard, bishop of Ypres and a Cistercian. The anonymous *Sentences of Master Gislebert*, the work of a disciple who labored while the master was still alive, spend an entire fourteen books showing the special character of theological language in still other areas of Christian dogmatics.

Meanwhile, another anonymous work, the *Book on True Philosophy*, was an effort to strengthen Gilbertan theology by showing the logical untenability of the formulas with which Bernard opposed Gilbert at the council of Rheims and in his own polemical writings. In contrast, the author of the so-called *Compendium of Porretan Logic*, composed in Paris after 1155, was concerned to promote Gilbertan theology by providing such knowledge of logic as was essential for the clarification of the controversies that arose around Gilbert and were caused by the incompetence of his opponents.

These various statements of the Gilbertan ideal of knowledge were unconnected with one another, autonomous, and to a large extent separated in time and space, yet they were at one in their defense and development of a common methodological ideal. It is impossible to overestimate their importance, given their impact on the subsequent development of medieval theological thought. In expectation, as it were, of the imminent introduction of a more complete and systematic Aristotelean epistemology into the West, these writings that sprang from the perseverance of the Gilbertan school helped to prepare the ground and did so without a great deal of outcry, but certainly with a palpable influence on the cultural predisposition of those years. They prepared the way for an initial determination of the epistemological status of theology by their extended effort to ensure for the study of the "sacred page," no less than for the other branches of knowledge, its own special methodology and its own recognized autonomy and status.

5. The School of Chartres

The doctrine of divine exemplarism was one of the foundational elements of the Christian Platonism that dominated the philosophical and theological culture of the early Middle Ages. It led to the thinking of authors who based on it their acceptance, in the logical and metaphysical areas, of the principles of realism regarding universals. In addition, it gave rise during the twelfth century to another important current of thought, one more directly concerned with the study of nature. Nature was regarded as being the other book (alongside Scripture) written by God and placed at the disposal of the human intellect so that it might ascend from visible realities to invisible, perfect realities.

In this perspective the link between the order of things and the order of ideas was investigated not so much by looking for a correspondence of the order of words with both, but by a more direct study of the forms of natural entities and the relationships among them, a study requiring competence in the arts of the quadrivium. Especially important in this context was the attribution to the human intellect of the ability to penetrate the veil of sensible appearances and discover the immutable aspects of reality, those regarded by the mathematical sciences as eternal quantitative forms that preside over the ordering and hierarchical distribution of visible things. This veil was often called an "outer wrapping" or "cover," a term already used by Abelard in describing the allegorical function of the bronze seal or the image of the "world soul." Its removal was therefore an indispensable moment in the development of true philosophy, that is, the understanding of the ultimate truth of things.

The ability of the philosopher to remove the veil and contemplate the higher truth hidden by it can bear fruit both in his reflection on natural phenomena and in his reading of the scriptural texts that contain true wisdom. It bears fruit first and primarily in the reading of the Bible, which hides the depths of the allegorical/spiritual meaning under the veil of the literal or historical meaning. But it also bears fruit in the writings of the ancient philosophers and poets who were able solely by their intellectual powers to rise above the appearances of the visible world; they were unable, however, to express their insights in the unambiguous language of reason and therefore set them forth in their writings in the form of mythical or allusive images.

This view of the matter explains, in particular, the great interest many masters, like Abelard before them, had in Plato's *Timaeus*, which Chalcidius had translated and commented on. This text is in fact a very representative example of how the pagan philosophers successfully intuited and expressed something of the true nature of God, whom they saw as a wise builder who draws on eternal ideal models and in an orderly way shapes the primordial matter in which all natural things have their origin. From the teaching of Plato as presented in the mythological wrapping of this account the theologian, whose mind has been formed by the higher truth of the faith, can draw some reliable philosophical ideas. These are especially valuable as he or she moves on to the understanding of another "outer wrapping," a theological one this time: the one that in the Genesis story veils the utterly incomprehensible depths of the divine creative activity.

The Platonic-Chalcidian work was not, however, the only classical philosophical document that could yield fruit once it was subjected to a hermeneutical treatment of this kind. Two ideas—that of the cosmic order established by God who created everything according to "measure and number and weight" (Wis 11:21), and that of the cognitive ascent of the soul from the sensible world to the suprasensible fed an interest in Macrobius' commentary on the dream of Scipio. The Christian need to reconcile this cosmic order produced by divine providence with the mechanical and unavoidable sequence of causal events within the world and its time also inspired a new appreciation of the poems and prose passages of Boethius' *Consolation*. But Aulus Gellius among the prose writers and Virgil and Ovid among the poets were also accepted as transmitters of a set of important cosmologico-theological doctrines that they hid, to a greater or lesser extent, beneath the veil of pagan mythology and literary symbolism.

These teachings expanded the cognitive range of the liberal arts and aided the human intellect in explaining the process of the formation of the universe and the ethical role of the human creature. The human being was, after all, at the center not only of the physiological order but also, and above all, of the order of the higher ethical and aesthetic values of creation.

The Christian interpretation of these two books thus facilitated the linking of "heavenly philosophy" with the "wisdom of the world" or "mundane philosophy," the latter being now made accessible to Christian scholars in part through the preparation of a new and ever-richer collection of philosophical and scientific documents. Thanks to the allegorical explanation of Genesis the researches of the philosophers into the "work of nature" could be reconciled, at least partially, with theological meditations on the "work of the Creator," that is, the divine activity that produced the things told of in revelation.

Furthermore, an abundant set of helpful principles and ideas developed by philosophical reason could now be acquired and used in continuing the studies of the theologians as they described and pondered the causal connections within the visible world. The latter they viewed as a system of signs making it possible to access the inaccessible and perfect creative will of God as it manifested itself in the book of nature. As a result, the whole of visible reality was seen as exhibiting the "signs" Augustine had seen as contained only in written revelation and in the liturgical and sacramental tradition of the Christian church.

A. BERNARD OF CHARTRES AND THE "INNATE FORMS"

Christians turned now to the search for useful signs of the active presence of God in the universe. During this period they enriched their specifically Christian store of important images with a new and very abundant set of signs and allusions, symbols capable of calling to mind invisible principles and active forces hidden behind what is accessible to the senses. Features of vegetation, the animal world, and the heavens worked along with traditional biblical and liturgical symbols to suggest traces of the activity of the living God in the living world he had created and was governing. The doors, altars, and naves of the Romanesque cathedrals were adorned with bas-reliefs and sculpted ornaments that imitated the natural world and competed with it in multiplying endlessly the signs pointing to the life and productive action of the divine goodness in the universe. Stone docilely submitted to the hand of the sculptor in order that these artists might imitate skilled poets and wise philosophers in concealing with magnificent veils the mysterious depths of created beauty.

Outstanding among the most imposing religious edifices built in French territory during these years was the splendid cathedral in the city of Chartres. Its construction was begun in 1020, during the episcopacy of Fulbert, a Platonist. In the course of the twelfth century, alongside the cathedral, there was a flourishing episcopal school that became the center of this kind of theological speculation on nature, thanks to the work of an important series of masters who succeeded one another in administration and teaching. The first to promote the modernization of the school was Bishop Yves, who died in 1116; he was a prominent canonist who as a young man had studied under Lanfranc of Bec and who left behind two influential collections of ecclesiastical legislation: the *Decretum* and the *Panormia*.

Yves recruited for his school the best-known masters of the liberal arts of that period. Among them was Bernard of Chartres (d. ca. 1124), who would later become chancellor and whom subsequent important members of the school regarded as their common teacher. According to John of Salisbury, who in his *Book in Defense of Logic* (*Metalogicon*) provides the little information that has reached us about the man, Bernard himself turned the attention of the masters of Chartres to the problem of exemplarism, as he tried to combine ontology and theology, both of which were implied in the teaching on the realism of essences.

He started with the fact that in the Latin *Timaeus* the ideal principle was designated, depending on the case, by two different terms: "example" and "exemplar." But he also saw the difficulty of allowing that the divine ideas, which are connatural in God, could be combined with "raw material" (that is, again in the language of the *Timaeus*, unformed matter) in giving rise to visible things. He therefore introduced (he was the first to do so) the distinction between the divine or uncreated and eternal ideas and the created ideas, which are likewise eternal but (according to an expression used earlier by John Scotus) "not completely coeternal" and therefore not completely identical with God.

In addition, he found in Chalcidius the idea of "innate forms," which for that commentator in late antiquity meant forms combined with matter; Bernard used the term to signify the ideal principles that are intermediate between the divine principles (which they imitate) and the material element. "From those forms that are completely separated from matter descend those that are in matter and give reality to bodies"; thus John of Salisbury describes the teaching of Bernard, whom he regards as "the supreme Platonist of our time."

Again according to John of Salisbury, in order to explain this doctrine Bernard took an example from the capacity of human language for signifying.

On the basis of the previously mentioned grammatical theory of Priscian, who maintained that in every predication there are two elements, substance and quality, Bernard pointed out that some nouns such as "whiteness" can express the possibility of qualifying a substance without at the same time mixing the two together, and he likened the substance here to a virgin still spotless. The verb "to whiten," which signifies the addition of the quality to the substance, would suggest a virgin on the point of entering her wedding chamber. Finally, the descriptive adjective "white" describes a quality united to a substance that is thereby "corrupted," as is a virgin who has had intercourse with a man.

This image attests to Bernard's native ability to make distinctions between various linguistic functions (thereby anticipating, as it were, the theory of supposition). But it also introduces an idea of great importance for the Chartrian conception of nature, namely, the metaphysical distinction between potency and act, which correspond, on the one hand, to ideal perfection (potency) and, on the other, to contamination by matter (act). This distinction was especially useful in the Christian explanation of the creative process, because it made it possible to explain natural becoming and the derivation of finite things from God without compromising God's immutability and transcendence. Natural becoming is thus understood as a process of the actuation (and therefore the corruption), in the particular or individual, of the original potentiality of the form. But the form remains uncontaminated (it is therefore virginal) inasmuch as in actuating matter it does not lose its proper nature as pure potentiality, which is a reflection of the immutability of the eternal divine ideas.

This admittedly primitive doctrinal development of Chartrian naturalistic exemplarism clearly represents a first effective introduction of the idea that every visible creature "covers" a higher reality that is hidden and active in it (in this case the intermediate efficacy of second causes). As John tells us elsewhere in his *Metalogicon*, when Bernard addressed listeners who possessed philosophical talent he was able, with the help of the liberal arts, to show them the hidden depths in the texts of the ancient authors. To this context belongs the very famous image (perhaps the most noteworthy of Bernard's ideas) that says that in relation to the great authors of past centuries the scholars of the present time are to be regarded "as dwarves sitting on the shoulders of giants." The reason (it is still John speaking): "As compared with those authors, they are able to see things much more numerous and remote: not, however, because their gaze is acute or because of their eminence, but because those great giants have lifted them up and elevated them."

B. WILLIAM OF CONCHES AND THE PHILOSOPHY OF THE WORLD

After Bernard's death Gilbert of Poitiers served as chancellor for about twenty years. But the seeds of the theological naturalism present in the teaching of the first chancellor were brought together chiefly by the man who can be regarded as the most representative of his disciples: William of Conches in Normandy (d. after 1154).

William, a well-known master who was esteemed in both Paris and Chartres, boldly sought to bring out the continuity of Christian theology with the writings and thought of the ancient pagan authors as well as the anticipations of it therein, thus carrying forward the ideas of Bernard. But this effort roused first the suspicions and then the implacable hostility of William of St. Thierry, who in 1141 wrote a strong indictment of what he regarded as the other William's theological errors. These, in his opinion, sprang from an improper combination of pagan naturalism with the truths of faith and from a desire to explain creation "according to the principles of physics." It was perhaps to escape that kind of hostility that William of Conches returned to his native Normandy, where he became the tutor of Geoffrey Plantagenet's young son, who would later take the throne of England as Henry II.

William of Conches' works include, first, three systematic treatises: *Philosophy of the World* (or *of Creation*), *Philosophical Sheaves*, and *Teaching of the Moral Philosophers* (a handbook of moral instruction based on the thought of the Roman philosophers, especially Cicero and Seneca). William also wrote a series of glosses and comments on earlier authors; especially useful for an understanding of his theological method are those on the *Consolation* of Boethius, on Macrobius' commentary on the *Dream of Scipio*, and on the *Timaeus*.

In this last-named work and in the improved version of his *Philosophy of the World* the controlling programmatic aim is to remove the veil of the Platonic myth in order to reach a correct scientific explanation of the origin of the cosmos, to show its agreement with the story of creation in Genesis (which is likewise rich in symbolic and allusive images), and to reveal thereby how the statements of the philosophers can be consonant or harmonizable with the words of the prophets. The tools that make it possible to carry out this twofold hermeneutical operation are the teachings of the liberal arts, and especially of the quadrivium, which may be learned not only from Martianus Capella and Chalcidius but also from the Neopythagorean doctrines explained in Boethius' *The Teaching of Arithmetic* and *The Teaching of Music*.

When, in these Boethean texts, William comes upon the assertion of the existence of purely quantitative, foundational, immutable, and authentically eternal realities, he explains that the object of the physico-mathematical analysis accomplished by reason cannot be these pure principles, which are divine in nature. The object must rather be "second causes," which are Bernard's innate forms, intermediate between God and creation, mathematical structures that have power over physical realities and that order and govern the entire visible world. The role of the innate forms, then, is to bring to completion what William calls the work of nature, which is distinct from the work of God and subject to it. This completion consists in effecting and preserving the "adornment of nature," that is, the external adornment of the natural order. According to William, then, on the basis of this mechanistic conception, which has a vaguely Presocratic ring to it, nature is endowed with its own special causative power derived from the divine will, but God remains distinct from and untouched by this power's mobility and many-sided efficacy.

The mythical image Plato uses in the *Timaeus* to express the self-organizing power of nature is that of the world-soul. On more than one occasion William seemed to agree with Abelard's suggestion that the world-soul be identified with the Holy Spirit, but the mechanical approach taken in his theory of natural becoming perhaps held him back from formulating this identification too explicitly. It was essential that he avoid any danger of confusing the Creator, or even the world-soul, with created nature or the intermediate principles that govern it. To this end he makes a careful distinction between eternity and perpetuity in order to emphasize the separation between, on the one hand, the truly eternal divine causes and, on the other, second causes and matter, which have a causal beginning that makes them derivatives of the higher power of what is divine and eternal.

Despite, then, the watchful doubts of his critic, William of St. Thierry, William of Conches is convinced that his distinction enables him, without at all diminishing the power of God, to attribute a real and direct causative efficacy to natural principles, which are arranged in a descending hierarchy from the innate forms to the four elements and finally to the last individual entities or "atoms" (i.e., "indivisibles").

In spite of the fact that William of Conches develops his physics by superimposing the theories and naturalistic descriptions of the philosophers and pagan writers on the story in Genesis, he does not at all think of it as a doctrinal alternative to Christian theological understanding. On the contrary, he expressly sees the knowledge of nature as helping to produce a cosmological understanding of God that can confirm the truth of revealed dogma. In fact, he does not follow a systematically articulated demonstrative program and even allows himself, here and there, to be drawn aside by the text on which he is commenting. Nevertheless, he follows reason step-by-step in its inquiry through the various stages in which philosophical understanding makes its contribution to faith.

Here again, these stages show a clear dependence on the heritage of Anselm, which was shared by the better theologians of the twelfth century. First he uses reason to demonstrate, on the basis of the natural order of causes, the existence of God as supernatural efficient cause (this being a specific prerogative of the Father). He then shows how Plato's world of eternal divine ideas is identical with the divine intellect, which is the second person of the Trinity and the formal cause of the universe. Finally he shows that the divine goodness, and therefore the Holy Spirit, is the final cause the entire created order seeks and is therefore the principle that, without affecting its own immutability, renders the innate forms effective and, through them, moves the world and the souls of living beings (and can therefore be identified with the world-soul). By adding the philosophical doctrine of the four elements, which are the material cause of everything corporeal, philosophy is able to discover, through the world, not only the existence of God but the full dynamic of the trinitarian relations, while incorporating this dynamic into a complete and effective description of its connection with the formation of the visible world.

As William expressly says when commenting on the appearance of Philosophy in Boethius' *Consolation*, there is no contradiction at all, but always and only a fruitful continuity, between a philosophy of the world and theology or "discourse about things divine." There is a full and reciprocal relationship between the ancient philosophers and the Christian sages: as the Fathers teach, ancient wisdom aids the exegete in explaining and making clear the mysteries of dogma, while faith sheds light on, confirms, and consolidates the rational procedures developed by the philosophers. And while there are aspects of ultimate truth that the philosophers have been unable to reach by their unaided efforts and that they have even endeavored to prove impossible (creation from nothing or the virginal birth of Christ), this fact confirms their authority even while limiting it. For when they refuse to consider possible, from the viewpoint of a natural analysis of things, what is accomplished by a causality superior to that at work in the natural world, they only demonstrate that this causality is more effective than all the laws, whether of physics or of logic; it is a superiority that is absolute and beyond the reach of any criticism.

Human science, then, can only shed light on but never contradict the truths of the faith, precisely because the truths of the faith belong to a different order of truth than the truths of science.

All this is undeniable, despite the fact that some ignorant "modern theologians" (an expression that is, quite significantly, peculiar to William) cry scandal whenever they hear scientists affirm something not to be found in the texts of the sacred writers. These men do not take into account that this absence is due solely to the fact that such statements "are not pertinent to the building up of the faith, which was the concern of those writers."

C. THEODORIC OF CHARTRES AND THE PHYSICS OF CREATION

After Gilbert of Poitiers had been called to the episcopal chair of his native city, the new chancellor of the school of Chartres was Theodoric (d. after 1156), another disciple of Bernard (or, according to some, his brother, but the claim is in all probability unfounded). Theodoric was a writer and teacher esteemed by his contemporaries; indeed, his disciple, Clarembald of Arras, described him as "the greatest philosopher in all of Europe." After the middle of the century he left the school and retreated into monastic life, perhaps donning the Cistercian habit.

Prominent among his writings are the *Heptateuch*, a wide-ranging handbook for the seven liberal arts, and the *Hexaemeron* or "The Works of the Six Days," a commentary on the opening pages of Genesis, which are interpreted "according to an explanation inspired by the principles of natural philosophy and based on a detailed analysis of the entire structure of the text." Theodoric also left behind collections of glosses on Cicero's rhetorical works as well as an especially interesting collection on the *Short Sacred Works* of Boethius.

The typical Chartrean method of harking back to the philosophers of the past and linking theological reflection with their writings is seen again in Theodoric, with special attention this time to the disciplines of the quadrivium, which make up natural science or "physics." In his opinion these were precisely the disciplines Chalcidius used in his commentary on the *Timaeus*. In Theodoric's view the perspective afforded by natural philosophy was the only correct one for understanding the relationship between creation and its creator. This approach caused him not only to return to the ancient sources (such as Varro, Pliny the Elder, Martianus Capella, and Boethius), but also to hark back to more recent, early medieval texts that combined a theological and a mathematical approach (for example, the writings of Gerbert of Aurillac).

Ultimately it led him to an interest in works of ancient science recently introduced into the West. These included magical-astrological and esoteric writings such as the *Asclepius* of Hermes Trismegistus, scientific treatises such as the *Elements* of Euclid (recently translated by Adelard of Bath) and the *Planisphere* of Ptolemy (the Latin translation was the work of Theodoric's disciple, Herman of Carinthia, who in his dedication described Theodoric as "a Plato come back to life" [*Plato redivivus*]).

This unbiased attitude toward the scholars of antiquity was justified by the fact that, like Bernard of Chartres, Theodoric was convinced that human wisdom is essentially the sum total of the shared advances human reason has made in the scientific understanding of nature since the beginning of history. He was convinced, too, that the possession of this wisdom is indispensable for moving beyond the simple narrative level of the Genesis story, as well as beyond the purely ethical and spiritual interpretation of it, and engaging in a satisfactory reading of the scientific meaning of the text—that is, a reading of what revelation tells us, in the rhythmic pattern of God's six days' work, about the origin of both the invisible and the visible universes.

If, then, we are to understand the importance Theodoric assigns to this wisdom in studying the physics of creation, it is fundamental that we grasp the conception of knowledge he, like Gilbert of Poitiers, sets forth when commenting on the division of the philosophical disciplines as set down in the second chapter of Boethius' *Trinity*. Unlike Gilbert, Theodoric tends to play down the distinctions of methodology in the various disciplines because he prefers to adhere more closely to the Augustinian tradition and to subordinate all of them, insofar as they are explanations of the single truth that God is, to a common process of argumentation. Following the Platonico-hierarchical conception of reality he shared with the other Chartreans, Theodoric holds that this methodology common to the various branches of knowledge must follow two paths of study that are inversely symmetrical and complementary and are valid in all the fields of knowledge. The two paths are the ascending process of bringing together (*compositio*), in which the entire realm of multiplicity is reduced to unity in the truth, and the descending process of "unravelling" (*resolutio*), which follows the breakup of the primordial unity through a graduated series of intermediate principles that leads finally to individuals.

The distinct sciences classified by Boethius do not, therefore, correspond to different and contrasting ways of approaching the truth, as the Porretan theologians maintained. In harmony rather with the teaching of William of Conches, Theodoric sees them as corresponding to successive steps in the unified cognitive journey toward a single object of philosophical knowledge. Given the human inability to reach to the divine principle (that is, the One) as such, this final goal of reason is to discover the primordial principles (or "reasons") that are the formal causes presiding over the entire structure of real being, those to which every truth attainable by the human intellect must be traced. The structure of the sciences depends therefore on the distinction of steps or degrees through which the eternal higher truth manifests itself: in sensible things that are divisible into corporeal parts (physics), in the ordered and symmetrical rejoining of such beings in entities of a higher order (mathematics), and in the tracing back of every kind of multiplicity to the One (theology).

The *Heptateuch*, which is a wide-ranging and elaborate encyclopedia of texts and information on the study of the liberal arts, also goes into greater detail on the differentiation of the procedures specific to the various ways in which human knowledge is organized. Yet it never loses sight of the fundamental methodological unity of the intellectual activity that makes its way through these graded disciplines in order to reconstruct the order existing in created reality. The arts of the trivium ensure respectively the correctness, the consistency, and the stylistic adornment of the language in which human knowledge finds expression. The arts of the quadrivium provide this language with its informational content, the purpose of which is to reduce multiplicity to simplicity as each of these arts applies a specific probative method to the numerical forms identifiable in nature.

Inasmuch as God is Unity he is the formative truth of all knowledge, precisely because he is the form that gives being to everything that he has created and that exists. An organized knowledge of the Creator is thus essential for directing the mind to a correct understanding of creation. For this reason, and in order to complete his own exegesis of the six days, Theodoric in his *Hexaemeron* offers a rational demonstration of God's existence, highly mathematical in its approach. Just as the multiple presupposes the simple and numbers presuppose a unit, so the universe proves to be an all-embracing return of every being to the undifferentiated and immutable principle in which everything participates and from which everything derives. That principle is the One that produces the infinity of numbers and therefore as such "suffers no limits to its power." The principle is infinite precisely because it is one; it is omnipotent precisely because it is the creator of everything that is numerical and numerable. And inasmuch as it is this kind of being, it exists necessarily and in the supreme degree.

But scientific reason can delve even more deeply in its thinking about the relation between the divine and the created. Every number presupposes a unit, and the unit multiplied by any number produces an infinite numerical series: all things, therefore, are in God, but inasmuch as God is One. This shows the rightness of admitting the existence in God of the ideas, the eternal modes of everything real, yet without any lessening of God's essential, absolute simplicity. Moreover, the unit multiplied by itself always produces a unit: therefore the presence of the unit in the unit is also the presence of the multiple in the unit and, at the same time, the presence of the unit in the multiple.

From this it follows that the mind can see that which is not distinguishable as nonetheless distinguished within the unit: the unit identical with itself is the Father, the knowledge of the multiple within the oneness is the Son, and the active presence of the oneness in the multiple is the Holy Spirit. For this reason, moreover, the Father is absolute and limitless power. The Son or the Word is the wisdom that contains within itself the ideas of all things, the wisdom to which all things are conformed at the very moment in which they are all defined by it. Finally, the Spirit with its quick and unhesitating action (which does not sacrifice the divine simplicity and transcendence) is expressly identified with the world-soul of the Platonists, the principle that forms all of multiplicity in obedience to the eternal plan of the divine ideas in the Word.

Since the pagan philosophers have contributed in this way to a clarification of the highest degrees of knowledge of the faith, it is not difficult to accept also their teachings on physics, at least those that are more profound and more useful in bringing out the true meaning of the words in the story of the six days. According to Theodoric it is therefore permissible and even indispensable to offer an exclusively physical, that is, historical and literal reading of that text now that its allegorical, spiritual, and moral depths have been sufficiently studied and explained by the Fathers of the Church.

We see, then, that in this physical perspective the "beginning" mentioned in the first verse of Genesis ("in the beginning God created the heavens and the earth") is certainly the instant marking the historical beginning of creation: the separation of the effects from the changeless eternity of the divinity and their being launched out into the differentiated succession of temporal periods. Theodoric thus introduces a structuring (similar to that proposed by William of Conches) of the divine causality based on the Aristotelean differentiation of the four causes. He establishes the true and proper start of the creative process as consisting in the introduction of the material cause, that is, the four elements, signified by Scripture in the pair "heavens and earth." At the same time he points to the cessation, at this first moment, of the direct causative action of God, whose nature due to its simplicity remains apart from spatio-temporal limitations.

Thus making his own the mechanistic approach typical of the Chartreans, Theodoric tells how the physical development of creation originates in the very nature of the four elements: the movement of the heavens being caused by the mobility of fire, the formation of the stars by the condensation of watery vapors, the emergence of the land due to the heat circulated by the stars, a heat that, as it spreads farther and thickens, is transformed into a vital heat and gives rise to living beings. The intermediate causes present throughout the universe direct and regulate all the forms of development; even miracles and seeming interruptions of the laws of nature are the result of the potentialities located in the seminal principles which the efficacy of the first Cause actuates everywhere in the form of multiplicity.

If the mind then attempts to produce a conception of this first Cause itself, it can do so only by thinking of it as pure and absolute simplicity and as unformed form and, consequently, as "Being as such" (*ipsum esse*), to use the words of Boethius in his treatise on *Weeks*. Theodoric was present at the Council of Rheims that condemned Gilbert of Poitiers; we do not know whether he was one of those who directly attacked his predecessor in the chancellorship, but in his commentary on the *Short Sacred Works*, even if he does not directly criticize, he certainly distances himself from the distinction between God and Godhead the Porretans defended.

The simplicity of the divine form is assured by the fact that it is absolutely not formed by anything else; this means that in the divine nature no distinction can be made between what is formed and what forms, just as one cannot be made between the eternal One and his eternity or between the good One and his goodness or, therefore, between God and his divinity. The existence of God is not the actuation of a precise possibility, even of one that is not an alternative in relation to other possibilities. His existence is rather an act involving no potentiality, for it is a pure act of existing, the "I am who am" who revealed himself at Sinai, thereby asserting that in him there is an absolute identity, both logical and ontological, of *esse* and *quod est*.

The hierarchically structured universe of Chartrean theology could not exist unless it was subject to the absolute perfection of an unoriginated origin that, precisely because it has no form, is the form of everything that exists.

D. HERMAN OF CARINTHIA AND BERNARD SILVESTRIS: NATURE AND THE THEOLOGICO-POETIC VEIL

The influence of Theodoric led to a further emphasis, in the Chartrean conception of the world, on the role of nature understood as a single entity, a fruitful source of movement that disseminates the efficacious divine power throughout the universe while itself remaining distinct from and subordinate to that power. Herman of Carinthia dedicated to Theodoric a treatise of his own on *Essences*, in which he sets forth a cosmology based on the operation of second causes and on the conception of nature as itself a universal second cause whose efficacious action reduces all other action to unity. In his description of the physical cosmos Herman develops further the image of a harmonious system of causal concatenations and correspondences.

Not surprisingly, then, his text also gives a great deal of space to ideas and concepts that are frankly of a magical and astrological kind; these he discovers in the Platonic, Pythagorean, and hermetic sources of late antiquity. Herman gives them a generous welcome in order to emphasize the parallelism between macrocosm and microcosm by accentuating the reciprocal influences and affinities between the elements of the world and those of the human body. The apparent inconsistency between such teachings and the theological principle of the divine governance of the world is eliminated by developing to an extreme the idea, prevalent in Theodoric, of the autonomy that second causes enjoy once they have been created by God and set in charge by him over everything that happens in the world.

There is also extant a true and proper introduction to astrology in which the author carefully harmonizes the subject matter with Christian teaching by presenting the heavenly bodies as docile instruments of the divine omnipotence. This work, the *Book on Experiments,* may be attributed to another master with links to the world of Chartres, namely, Bernard Silvestris (d. after 1160). He produced many other writings, among them poems and commentaries on the *Timaeus,* the *Aeneid,* and Martianus Capella. All these are strewn with figurative images, used to represent in a veiled and indirect way the nature of second causes, which are intermediate causes and therefore cannot be studied directly by the physical scientist. Worthy of mention here is Bernard's interpretation, in his commentary on the *Aeneid,* of Aeneas' journey and especially of his descent into the lower world: Bernard takes this as an allegory of the ethical and cognitive formation of the human person culminating in the high point of theological knowledge, namely, the contemplation of the divine.

Bernard's best-known work is his *Cosmography,* also titled *The Whole World, or the Megacosm and the Microcosm,* which is dedicated once again to Theodoric of Chartres. It is composed, as the *Consolation* of Boethius had been, in the literary genre of the prosimetrum, in which prose passages alternate with poems written in elegiac distichs. The work is a dialogue in two parts between two allegorical personifications: Nature and Providence or *Nous.* In the first part, which employs imagery-laden and allegorical language, Nature (as understood by the Chartreans, that is, the totality of efficacious causes placed in the universe by God) explains the creation of the universe or the megacosm, which follows upon the primordial chaos of prime matter and consists in the establishment of a perfect order preordained by *Nous,* which is the supreme divine mind.

In a lengthy series of analogies and parallelisms, the second part of the work tells of the formation of the human being, or microcosm, which is the completion and ultimate goal of the created world, all of whose perfections it recapitulates in itself. Other figures are located at the intermediate levels of the process by which Nature is derived from *Nous*; for example, Entelechy or Soul, which represents the Platonic world-soul and carries with it the vestiges of the divine ideas (or "innate forms"), Urania, which gives order to the heavenly sphere, and Physis, the principle of physical life. Urania and Physis arrange the parts of the human being, that is, soul and body, which Nature itself combines into a living unit. Even God, the absolute source of everything real, is described as one of the actors in the mythical account, where he is given the resounding name of Tugaton, that is, Supreme Good.

Bernard's language is thus packed full of allusions and references to the classical myths, to history, and to the wisdom of the ancients. Behind the words lie numerous, more or less similar philosophical, cosmological, and anthropological influences that take their place in his vision as the result of texts, new and old, made available to him in the library at Chartres. In Bernard the Chartrean method of removing the veils present in the words of past sages is reversed by the formation of new allegorical veils that, under the cover of poetic allusion, conceal and at the same time make more vivid what the other masters of that time were setting forth in abstract form in the speculative language of the theology of the schools. Thus understood, Bernard's work is rightly regarded as the first, but already mature, example of medieval poetic theology.

E. CLAREMBALD OF ARRAS AND THE LIMITS OF THEORETICAL THEOLOGY

The introduction, just described, of mythological images and secular scientific ideas into a rereading of the revealed data reached limits that could not fail to puzzle theologians, especially in the monastic world. The monastic theologians stood for a much more traditional approach to religious discourse and were certainly much less familiar with the bold images of Platonic physiology. Thus, when commenting on the beginning of Genesis in his *Notes on the Pentateuch*, even Hugh of St. Victor spoke proudly of the distance between, on the one hand, the philosophers, who thought of God as simply one of the three sources of the universe (along with matter and the ideas) and turned him into a commonplace worker and, on the other hand, "our authors," who "recognize that there is but a single source of everything and that this is God." In addition, the extensive limitation Chartrean physiology placed on the direct efficacy of God's activity in creation due to the introduction of numerous intermediaries could not fail to perplex those who feared that this meant a philosophical lessening of the absolute and limitless omnipotence of God.

Clarembald of Arras (d. ca. 1187) was a devoted disciple of both Theodoric of Chartres and Hugh of St. Victor. As a result we see in his theological thought an unusual commingling of, on the one hand, the Chartrean desire to produce, with the help of reason, an orderly systematization of the hierarchy of the scientific disciplines and the forms of created being and, on the other, the rejection of an unjustified intrusion of excessive conceptual distinctions into theological meditation on the divine mysteries. Clarembald taught in his native Arras and in the school of Laon. This explains his closeness to a theological realism that took a systematic approach directly dependent on the Anselmian model. At the same time, however, he maintained good relations with Theodoric, whose naturalism has left clear traces in the two commentaries that Clarembald devoted to two of Boethius' *Short Sacred Works*, the first and third respectively.

It was these two theological treatises that led Clarembald to an interest first in the epistemologico-cognitive problem (as he commented on the division of the sciences in the first treatise) and then in the question of the composition of *id quod est* and *esse* (as he commented on the third treatise). In his introduction Clarembald tells us that he has two purposes in writing his own interpretation of these texts: on the one hand to show the correctness and orthodoxy of Boethius' use of logic in theology and, on the other, to criticize the excesses into which his contemporaries, whether Abelard or Gilbert of Poitiers, have fallen in this very attempt at a formal organization of the understanding of dogma.

He conducts his campaign with the weapons of the Platonizing gnoseology that was widespread in the early medieval world, due in no small part to Boethius and his *Consolation*. In his view theology consists in a direct contemplation of intelligible truth by the intellect, a cognitive faculty superior to dialectical reason and capable of contemplating its object directly and not in a mediated way, this object being the forms of all things as they originally exist in the mind of God before entering into union with bodies.

This approach has two important consequences: on the one hand it allows the theologian to accept the Chartrean hierarchization of the formal intermediaries between God and visible creatures, but on the other hand it demands that this scientific theology be identified with that which is only the highest degree of theoretical philosophy (that is, of natural knowledge) and distinguished from direct knowledge of the divine, which revelation alone makes possible.

This means that scientific theology has for its object not God as such, but the eternal forms, to the extent that these are directed toward creation; therefore all the conceptual distinctions and structurings the human mind introduces into theological knowledge always have to do solely with the effects of the supreme Cause and not with the Cause's existence as pure unformed form and pure self-positing being. In order to speak of God as he is, human beings can only have recourse to the Pseudo-Dionysian negative approach and strip the intellect of all its formal structures and argumentative claims, thereby leaving it free to contemplate directly, and without any rational mediations, the simple content of revealed truth.

This position enables Clarembald to decry two views. The first is the absurd claim to introduce into trinitarian dogma conceptual distinctions that can be predicated of each of the three persons separately; an example was Abelard, whom Clarembald sharply criticizes while accepting the positions defended by Bernard. The second is the absurdity of introducing into the supreme and absolutely simple being of God formal distinctions such as those proposed by Gilbert (but here the theologian of Arras speaks with a degree of respectful caution). All these tools of logic have value in the scientific disciplines dealing with the world of nature. Moreover, as Plato himself says in the *Timaeus*, in a sentence repeated verbatim by Boethius in the *Consolation*: "It is absolutely indispensable that the words we use be closely connected with the things of which we are speaking."

II. The Monastic Schools

The Concordat of Worms in 1122 and the promulgation of the agreements between pope and emperor, which were approved in the following year by the first Council of the Lateran (the ninth of the ecumenical councils and the first in the West), marked the end of the investiture conflict. What could not be regarded as finished, however, was the struggle for the moral reformation of the clergy. The best soil in which this struggle could be established and grow was the monastic world, permeated as it was by spirited exhortations to the renewal of the original spiritual and ascetical calling, which seemed to have been overshadowed by prolonged contacts with secular interests and the importunities of secular culture during the lengthy crisis just ended.

The desire to establish new and stricter forms of ascetical discipline increased in monastic institutions, along with the need to foster a theological reflection that was completely spiritual and interiorized and geared to the conquest of mystical contemplation. The impulse to a spiritual reform and the exhortation to return to the original ideals were characteristic, indeed, of the communities that had retained their original Benedictine obedience. But they were also found in Cluniac communities and, finally, in the first centers to welcome the new reform currents with their emphasis on asceticism and a rigorous practice of poverty. Outstanding among these last, both for the rapidity with which it spread and for the highly spiritual individuals who represented it, was the Cistercian movement that began with the foundation of Cîteaux (*Cistercium*) by Robert of Molesmes in 1098.

1. Reading of the Bible, Theology of History, and Visionaries in the German Area

Perhaps due precisely to the continuity of the reform movement that had sprung from the investiture conflict, it was above all in the German region that the monastic world experienced a period of fruitful theological revival. Here the twelfth century saw the activity of such individuals as Manegold of Lautenbach and Otloh of St. Emmeran, who were following in the footsteps of Rhabanus Maurus. The first author in this area who had a noteworthy influence even outside his own monastery was Rupert, a Benedictine and abbot of Deutz (d. 1129).

Rupert was a native of Liège and was educated in an atmosphere still inflamed by the struggle over investiture. He has left us an extensive body of work consisting of commentaries on Scripture and theological treatises; he presents himself to his readers as primarily a master of biblical exegesis and claims that through a special gift of the Holy Spirit he had a unique ability to interpret the revealed message.

Being convinced that theological knowledge could only take the form of a correct reading of the Bible, he was always sincerely hostile toward the idea of using in explanations of the faith the theoretical tools or interpretative conventions that marked the work of the "masters of the schools." In particular, he regularly had fiery words for the lovers of logic who vainly lift their weak voices solely to impose terms and concepts from worldly wisdom on the eternal words of the "God who speaks." Thus in his treatise *Divine Omnipotence*, when telling the story of his previously mentioned dispute with the theologians of the Laon school, he exclaims: "Even if I were really skilled in that art [logic], I would never take the time to employ it unless I were compelled to do so or were led to use it spontaneously due to its practical value."

In contrast, religious truth can be heard only in the silence of cloistered contemplation, where the idle chatter of the urban schools finally dies away. Rupert does not scorn the use of human reason as such, but he does condemn any commingling of it with contemplation of the mysteries of faith. Nothing keeps him from sometimes allowing the value of some teachings of the "philosophers of the world," for example their numerology, which led them to an understanding of the superiority of the number three, the primordial source of the truth of the unequal numbers (from which the equal numbers are likewise generated) and of the prime, indivisible, and therefore eternal numbers. But the real value of philosophy is to bring the mind to a recognition of both the abilities of the created intellect and its limitations. Thus only one who savors the pure truth of the faith is capable, in fact, of understanding the profound symbolism of the threeness of the days between Christ's death and his resurrection, a threeness that refers in an inexplicable way to the incomprehensible trinitarian mystery.

On the other hand, Rupert acknowledges the presence in Sacred Scripture of rhetorical and grammatical figures and even of metaphorical and fabulous images, but in his view true wisdom consists not in decoding these literary embellishments and removing their effectiveness but in being able to appreciate and enter deeply into the inner meaning that these adornments barely hide. Rupert was convinced, then, that in general the liberal arts were useless or at least inadequate for understanding the sacred text. It is not surprising, therefore, that in his exegetical writings he showed a degree of independence, unusual at that period, even from the works of the Fathers of the Church. He respected the authority of the Fathers, but he regarded them as inferior to the inspired writers. The latter were, he said, the only sources from which he wanted to draw; this meant that for him the only tool for interpreting Scripture was Scripture itself.

In Rupert's view an authentic understanding of the biblical text produces an entirely interior, inexplicable, and profound illumination, as it were an enjoyment of the vision of the blessed. For this reason his main interests were in sacramental theology and christology, and all his excursions into themes connected with the liturgy, Mariology, sacred history, and eschatology were presented as ways of entering more deeply into the central mystery of the Incarnation and the distribution of redemptive grace.

Given this perspective, we can understand his forceful disagreement, mentioned earlier, with the central thesis of Anselm's *Cur Deus homo*. The birth of the God-man, which is at the heart of the gradual approximation of the divine and the human that reveals itself as going on throughout the whole of sacred history, cannot, in his view, be regarded as subject to any rational necessity grasped by scientific reason. The truth of it must be accepted by faith as the result of a free act of supreme divine generosity that has for its purpose the glorification not of human beings but of God himself. Absolutely basic, therefore, in the historical life of the church is the daily representation of that mystery in the eucharistic action. This action Rupert interprets, in line with the theses of Berengarius' most radical opponents, as an "in-breading" (*impanatio*), a real union of the substance of the body of Christ with the substance of the bread. This in-breading is as incomprehensible and supernatural as the union of the divine person with human flesh in the incarnation of the Word.

A good idea of Rupert's program of scriptural theology can be gained from the full treatment of the Trinity in his *The Holy Trinity and Its Works*, which he composed between 1112 and 1117. This is a spacious summa of trinitarian dogma in the form of a commentary on the basic books of the Old Testament and the theological principles of the Gospel. Sacred Scripture enlightens believers for an understanding of the trinitarian mystery, while faith in the Trinity brings out in turn the most authentic meaning of the Scriptures. Indeed, the whole of sacred history is seen as a celebration of the Trinity, whose saving activity enters human time in three periods that contain the work of the Father from the creation to the sin of the first human being, of the Son from the fall to the redemption of humanity, and of the Spirit, who travels with humanity toward the final celebration of supraterrestrial glory.

Rupert's biblical radicalism often gave rise to sharp debates and challenges. Even when he was but a simple monk his interpretation of the Eucharist brought him into open conflict with the clergy of Liège, while later doubts and suspicions also circulated among the Cistercians, so much so that William of Saint Thierry himself wrote to him, asking politely but firmly that he explain his sacramental teaching. Norbert of Xanten, founder of the Premonstratensians, another reformed branch of Benedictine monasticism, claimed that by his distribution of functions among the three persons Rupert lessened the real power of the Holy Spirit, since according to him the Spirit began to work as distributor of grace only after the Passion of Christ. Rupert always made one and the same reply:

his teaching was that to be learned in the only true school, the school of Christ. This was the only school monks could and ought to attend if they were to become authentic witnesses of the "true life proper to the apostles," the disciples of the true Master. (*The Truly Apostolic Life* was the title of another of Rupert's important works on monastic piety.)

During these years other monks in the German world accepted in a significant measure the dominant themes of Rupert's theological thinking. In particular they agreed with his direct reading of the Bible, one based on an interiorized esteem for the symbolic efficacy of the images by means of which the Bible gives voice to the message of grace and divides the history of salvation into a series of phases that manifest suprahistorical truth. So marked is this approach that recent scholars have spoken of a "German symbolist school." This name has value, however, only as describing a tendency shared, with various nuances, by writers of the monastic world; these same writers differed in their formation and temperament as they sought paths of knowledge different from the scientifico-rational ways dominant in many urban schools.

One author who seems quite close to Rupert was Gerhoh (or Ghero) of Reichersberg (d. 1169), who belonged to one of the many Augustinian congregations that experienced a revival during these same years due to a fuller participation in the monastic reform. Gerhoh was likewise a convinced supporter of a return to the vocation of the apostles, out of which monastic life had developed. He made this idea part of a comprehensive reform of the church, which he, too, placed in the setting of a tripartite theology of history. He added, however, the proclamation of the apocalyptic coming of the Antichrist, for which the monastic world ought to prepare through increased rigorism and the pursuit of moral perfection.

In his *Book on God's Edifice* Gerhoh describes such a reconstruction of the church of Christ, and in it adopts a cosmic-theological perspective that is very powerful. The materials that go into the building of Christ's church are twofold: human beings, who are the agents in the search for the way to the heavenly city, but also every other creature in the entire universe, because everything that God has created is a basic and never worthless part of his city. The true church, the true city of God, is therefore the entire world.

The deep intimacy with the revealed message that supports Gerhoh in this longing for the sanctification of the world also explains his deep-rooted intolerance of the excessive scholasticism of the secular theologians. "If my writings should fall into the hands of readers intoxicated from drinking far more scholastic wine than theological wine, they must simply excuse them." These words occur in the dedication of Gerhoh's *The Glory and Honor of the Son of Man*, which was written during a debate with Demetrius of Lampé, a Byzantine teacher who accused the Latins of regarding the Son as simultaneously inferior to the Father and of equal dignity with him. Especially lengthy was Gerhoh's battle, in which he was joined by his brother, Arno of Reichersberg (d. 1175), against provost Volmar of Triefenstein, who attempted to give a rational explanation of the mystery of the Incarnation, but whose arguments caused him to succumb to adoptionism.

This intransigent opposition to the methods of the schoolmen (stressed especially in his earlier-mentioned *The Novelties of the Present Age*) was likewise due to his acceptance of one of Rupert's ideas that could ultimately be traced back to the ancient position of Gregory the Great, namely that true and truly meritorious faith is "faith as judged by faith," that is, faith that is explained solely by itself and with the aid of itself and does not ask "human reason" for any confirming argument.

In the previously mentioned *Dialogues in Response to the Greeks*, which Anselm of Havelberg, a Premonstratensian, wrote in 1136 after returning from a failed apostolic mission to Constantinople, the author likewise justifies the primacy of the church of Rome by directly locating it in a theologico-historical perspective. According to Anselm the revelatory communication of truth did not end with the coming of Christ, as the dogmatic and institutional immobilism of the Greeks would have it, but continues, by the action of the Holy Spirit, in the gradually increasing closeness to the truth on the part of ecclesial tradition, a process supported by the monastic Orders, the workers to whom God has entrusted the fleshing out of his pedagogy of salvation.

But the most representative spokesman for the connection, typical of this cultural world, between the theology of history and monastic revival was the Benedictine Honorius Augustodunensis, a very learned man and a prolific writer. In many of his writings, but especially in his *Complete Summa of Every Kind of History*, he proposed a rewriting of universal history in a Christian perspective, from the creation of the angels down to the most recent chronicles of the German empire and of the investiture conflict. In other pages of his works he multiplies symbolic keys for the interpretation and theological organization of history, while always taking biblical images as his starting point. Thus in his *Jewel of the Soul* he establishes a symbolic parallelism between the events foretold for apocalyptic times, the events of the Passion, and the rites of Holy Week; in his *"Glory" Summa* the parallelism between biblical personages and worldly authorities is used to determine their hierarchy.

But a still more expansive, constant, and variegated phenomenon in Honorius' extensive writings is the assemblage of the aspects of created reality into a complex structure of symbolic signs and allegories. The best key to this systematic universal symbolism is given to us in a passage of the *Book of Twelve Questions*: here the entire world is represented as a great cithara, of which all creatures are the strings, each producing, according to laws established by God, a single sound contributing to a universal harmony. All the seeming contraries of the visible world thus come together in a cosmic harmony that is also beautiful (yielding great pleasure) and useful. Every created thing serves some purpose: to cure sicknesses, to serve as food, or even simply to give joy by the sight of it; all are capable of providing meaningful symbols of divine truth.

This symbolism is remarkably close in its results to the nature-based exemplarism of Chartres, but it is pervaded by aesthetic sensibilities and religious sentiment and is completely free of any intellectualism. Everything is a symbol, whether in Scripture or in nature: animals, garments, herbs, weapons, and above all the human being, who is the symbolic key to all history and all created reality. Carrying his search for harmonies to an extreme, Honorius describes a detailed correspondence between the organs, parts, and functions of the human being and those of the world, as well as between the six ages of the human being, from infancy to old age, and an equal number of historical eras, represented by the biblical patriarchs from Adam to Christ.

Honorius is in some respects still a relatively unknown individual, beginning with the place of origin that gave him his name (probably not the French city of Autun, as used to be thought, but possibly the German Augusta = Augsburg). He entered the monastery of St. Emmeran in Regensburg at a somewhat advanced age and after having spent time in England, where he was probably in contact with Anselm in Canterbury. His conception of a universal harmony was culturally derived from the many ancient and early medieval sources he used boldly and liberally: Augustinian, Pseudo-Dionysian, Eriugenean, and Hermetic works, but also those of Chartres and the Victorines, and other contemporary authors accepted as witnesses on problems discussed, even if not always resolved.

His philosophical education, which he got from Anselm of Aosta, and his career as an encyclopedist provided fruitful access to the wisdom of past and present: this by comparison with the unyielding intransigence of Rupert and Gerhoh. He was convinced that an "authority" was simply a "truth proved by reason," a truth so confirmed with the help of the intellect that the teachings of someone deserving to be regarded as an "author" were to be accepted not simply out of loyalty or respect for his name, but because they were truly persuasive and trustworthy. As a result, whether expressly stating this or not, he draws freely on his sources whenever he feels the need.

His *Mirror of the Church* and his *Knowledge of Life* show the influence of Anselm throughout. His *Key to Physics* is really a rewriting of John Scotus' *Periphyseon* in a cosmological perspective, and contains lengthy unaltered passages from this source. His *Image of the World* is a learned catalogue of information about nature, theology, and history, collected through a systematic excerpting and simplification of an immense number of encyclopedic sources at his disposal. Even his more strictly theological proficiencies were developed on the basis of a similar program of cultural absorption, although in this case the solidity of the activity cannot but be attributed to the unshakable support of its biblical foundation. This fact is amply attested by his main work in this field, his *Exposition*, a summary of Christian knowledge understood as a universal knowledge; the very title expresses the writer's intention of presenting with pedagogical clarity even the most complex subjects of contemporary theological speculation, by way of a series of concise questions and answers.

In a much more spiritual and interiorized climate, a similar erudite theological syncretism was put at the service of religious meditation in the *Garden of Delights*, an unusual visionary work by Herrad (d. 1196), abbess of Hohenburg (Mont-Saint-Odile in Alsace) and her fellow nuns. The work brings together a very large number of excerpts from scientific and theological works by authors chosen chiefly from among the most recent and renowned. These might belong to the same cultural world—for example, Rhabanus Maurus, Honorius, and Rupert—but they might also be from elsewhere: for example, the Victorine, Cistercian, and Chartrean writers, and even the Parisian masters of exegesis and the liberal arts. The elegant pictorial art in the work cannot but remind us of the mosaic of images and theological poetry on Rhabanus' cross.

Alongside the theoretical expositions supplied by the anthology of texts the nuns of Hohenburg set splendid miniatures laden with both scientific and religious symbols. The purpose of these is to conduct the soul of the reader through a rich course of interior meditation that leads from the beginning of the world, through the missions of the prophets, Christ, and the church, to the eschatological completion of redemption. This fulfillment will take place in the earthly paradise, the "garden of delights," which is both the starting point and the ultimate goal of all of history.

The work, several decades earlier, of another great representative of female mystical theology during this period, Hildegard (1098–1179), noble-born abbess of Rupertsberg near Bingen, can be set alongside that of Herrad. In Hildegard there is a similar use of visual and symbolic elements along with theoretical meditation, but in her case the result is quite special due to the depth of her visionary inspiration and the solidity of her theological speculation.

According to the testimony of her biographers and some personal references scattered throughout her work, Hildegard began at an early age to experience visions that, as an adult, she expounded with an intense religious feeling but also with great theological skill and a profound ability to grasp the innermost meanings of revelation. The complexity and conceptual depth of her language openly contradict her express protestations of incompetence and simplicity. These claims are typical of female intellectual writings in the Middle Ages (think of Hrosvit) and therefore seem intended primarily to forestall criticism and censure and to highlight the metarational nature and supernatural origin of her visions. Hildegard in fact describes her mystical experience as involving her entire being; it enables her to *see* with the eyes of the soul the deepest meaning of the words of the prophets, something far beyond the grasp of the unaided intellect. The truth grasped was so far beyond her intellectual powers that she could not possibly have communicated it and put it into writing if the divine Spirit had not given her efficacious human words, so that she in turn became a prophet.

In the introduction (or preliminary statement) of her major work, the *Scivias* ("Know the Ways" of truth and salvation), Hildegard insists on the authentically revelatory character of the "visions I saw." These, then, are not dreams or ecstatic transports or a concealment under sensible appearances of something intrinsically undecipherable or incomprehensible. Rather, without any temporal process for acquiring knowledge, a divine illumination is given to the passive soul of the visionary. Without any intermediate understanding of concepts, any use of words, or any analytic descriptions of images, this illumination gives the soul a complete understanding of the Scriptures: "the Psalms, the gospels, all the books of the Old and New Testaments."

But Hildegard was well aware that since God is truth and will he is a "great philosopher" as well as a "very skilled artisan." For this reason philosophy and the arts, which, from the Fathers of the Church to the most recent masters of her day, have always been the life-giving nourishers of theological language, provide her, too, with help in the communication of the truths she has intuited in her visions. In the *Scivias* and in the other two works that make up her trilogy of visions—the *Book of the Merits of Life* and the *Book of Divine Works*—a sophisticated methodology enables her to interweave psychological and scientific ideas from many philosophical and erudite sources with theological doctrines and biblical allegories, thereby giving concrete and vivid form to the contents of her extracorporeal and extra-mental visions.

This synthesis is at bottom nothing more than a mystical sublimation of the basic Augustinian realism that pervades much of medieval monastic theology. Accordingly, the real source of the truth of prophetic language is the same divine Wisdom that is the eternal source of the order in created things and of the truthfulness of the sciences and arts that search out that order. If, then, the power of the divine mind that produced and governs the world of visible and invisible realities works interiorly and efficaciously in the soul of Hildegard of Bingen, it follows that her knowledge of this world springs from her knowledge of the divine. In turn, the manifestation of the divine made known to her becomes possible through recourse to the words and fruits of created reason that have been codified by the investigators of nature whose works are available on the shelves of her monastic library.

2. Peter the Venerable and Cluniac Theology

The expansion of Cluniac monasticism was hindered by the progress made by other reformed Orders. Nevertheless it maintained, at least until the thirteenth century, an internal cohesiveness ensured by its centralized organization, which placed the appointment of priors and the administrative control of all the dependent monasteries in the hands of the abbot of Cluny.

The desire for an interior renewal combined with a strong emphasis on the Order's tradition characterized especially the vigorous rule of abbot Peter (d. 1156), whom his contemporaries honored with the title "Venerable." (We met Peter earlier as the host, protector, and moral defender of Abelard.) He possessed a noteworthy practical mind, which he tested in his astute handling of the administrative and ideological problems, whether internal or external, of Cluniac monasticism. He showed it also in meeting the attacks and claims of excessive secularism and compromise with worldly interests that were made by representatives of the new currents of reformed monasticism, and especially by the Cistercians. Bernard, the principal spokesman of the last-named group, carried on a lively epistolary debate with Peter about the fulfillment of the Benedictine ideal.

In defense of the Cluniac model of religious life Peter wrote his *Answer to the Followers of Peter of Bruys*, a strong response to a heresy widespread in the lower ranks of Peter's followers. These individuals denied the validity of liturgical forms, of infant baptism, of good works offered in intercession, and of prayers. They did so in the name of a pure spirituality that was in open opposition to many of the activities in which the involvement of the Cluniacs with the laity took concrete form.

Of particular importance in the history of civilization was Peter's attitude toward Islam. His initial interest led him, during a mission to Spain in 1141–42, to ask for translations of works useful in telling the Christian West about Muhammad and his teaching; these works included the Qu'ran, which Herman of Carinthia translated at the abbot's request. Peter then planned to convert Muslims to Christianity, using the weapons of persuasion. He laid down his program in a work that, despite its aggressive title, *Against the Accursed Saracen Sect*, seems to be an effort to translate into apologetics and missionary preaching the dialogue that Abelard proposed to carry on among the various confessions. The dialogue was to be an open defense of the reasonableness of the Christian faith and an alternative to the military missions of the Crusaders in the Holy Land.

3. Bernard of Clairvaux: Cistercian Theology and Spirituality

Everyone knows, on the other hand, how forceful and impassioned was the dedication of Bernard the Cistercian to the promotion of the second Crusade, which he called for with an almost obsessive insistence as the means of keeping the Christian states of the East from falling under the yoke of the Turks.

Bernard exerted great influence even outside the monastic and clerical worlds. In his modest position as abbot of Clairvaux, a daughter of Cîteaux that he himself had established in 1115, he was almost a pope without a tiara. He practically says this of himself when writing in 1145 to Eugene III, who had been his disciple, in order to congratulate him on his election: "They say that I, and not you, am the pope." He served not infrequently as mediator between popes and emperors, as spiritual guide of bishops and cardinals, and as an unyielding bulwark against the enemies of the Roman church. He also combined an ever-vigilant commitment to the life of the Western church with a deep faith and a meditative spirituality that he set down in an elegant style, deeply permeated by scriptural wisdom, in a series of writings marked by a lofty theology.

Deserving of mention among his many works are those that document his commitment to ecclesial reform, such as *The Conduct and Office of Bishops*, *Praise of the New Band of Soldiers*, and the mature work *Consideration* (or *Meditation*). There are also theological treatises such as *Grace and Free Will* and *Baptism*, handbooks on preaching and apologetics such as *To Clerics on Conversion*, and detailed guides on spiritual asceticism such as the *Book on Loving God*.

In addition there are some collections of sermons, among these being the work infused with the greatest theological depth, the collection of *Sermons on the Song of Songs*. This is devoted to the praise of faith as a pure and disinterested reaching for God; it was occasioned by the liturgy's meditation on the allegorical song about the mutual love between Christ and his church. This relationship is necessarily reciprocal, since the suppression of one of the two poles would mean the dissolution of the other; in fact, true faith is impossible without love for the object of one's faith, and there is no other object more worthy than revealed truth.

The synthesis of love and faith, that is, the act that reaches the point of being its own deepest and exclusive motivation, cannot but mean the radical referral of all human knowledge and aspiration to religious devotion, which is the sole way for the human person to be united with the truth. Moreover, anything that does not lead to the highest truth is not necessary for salvation. One example would be stopping to dwell on intermediate and partial truths that, being incomplete, are subject to doubt and discussion, such as the truths of the arts and sciences. Indeed, such discussion can do harm to the soul by distracting it from true knowledge (which is knowledge of the Bible, the Fathers, and the tradition of the church), and claiming to be a substitute for this true knowledge. Reason ought to be used not to investigate but to expound and shed light on what in revelation is indeed not uncertain (since nothing revealed can be subject to doubt) but may well be obscure and not evident. Theological reason, thus understood, has been made to yield its greatest results by the Fathers of the Church.

For this reason Bernard does not like to answer those who ask him subtle but useless theological questions; it is enough to seek light in the works of the Fathers, since "we are certainly not wiser than they." If there is disagreement among the patristic sources, he prefers simply to admit his own ignorance and not adopt any position. If he is forced to take part in controversies triggered by lovers of debate, he does so only to give explicit witness to the faith and certainly not to set forth his personal opinions: "We do not seek to engage in verbal contests." These principles, deeply ingrained in his mind, explain the open hostility with which he fiercely repudiated the theological teachings first of Abelard and then of Gilbert of Poitiers, and sought to have them condemned.

John of Salisbury, who had studied under Gilbert but also greatly admired Bernard, paints a loving comparative portrait of the two but, while doing it, tells of his distress at having witnessed such a violent conflict between two men of such high intelligence. Both were very well educated and eloquent, but very different in the direction they took in their studies. The words of this young witness make quite clear the fine intellectual preparation of the bishop of Poitiers, but also the great familiarity with the text of the Scriptures that was shown by Bernard, an exceptionally fine preacher and very skilled in penetrating the mysteries hidden in the language of revelation. "Although many have sought to imitate each of them in his special area of study, no one has ever succeeded in reaching the same greatness."

To Bernard's contemporaries, then, even to those most supportive of the teachers he opposed and persecuted, he appeared to be a well-trained scholar, gifted with a capacity for theology that was constructive but based specifically on his deep interior familiarity with the Scriptures and inspired by an irrepressible love for the truths of the faith. It was a love that in his writings he never wearied of urging as the sole and essential driving force behind a devout knowledge of the object of belief.

His, then, was a gift of theological penetration of the depths of dogma, without displays of subtle logic but with a deep interiorization of these truths that did not exclude the presence of a moderate and loyal use of interpretative reason. A clear example of this penetration is to be seen in the special interest Bernard developed in Mariology; it was this that caused Dante to celebrate him in the *Paradiso* as the saint most qualified to address prayers to the Mother of God. He penetrated to the innermost truth of the Marian dogmas, not in order to attempt conceptual clarifications of them but rather, accepting a tendency already obvious in the earliest theoreticians of the western monastic tradition, only in order to present the Virgin as the absolutely best and unblemished model of a perfect monastic life.

According to Bernard, Mary's virginity was not only physical and moral but the effect of a total participation in the Son's unique and unifying love. This love she returned in a form so wholehearted and enveloping that it could only be the result of an incomprehensible, indissoluble, but also fruitful concentration of contradictions: virginity and motherhood, obedience and free choice, love and suffering, compassion and joy, human weakness and supernatural strength. Mary was thus the repository and guardian of all the virtues that, through the perfect living of the monastic state, bring the human being ever closer to the state of eternal blessedness in which those supreme contradictories, the finite and the infinite, are fused, each melting into the other.

In Bernard's view, then, given these presuppositions and these goals, theological knowledge can only end in a state of mystical contemplation of the truth that faith alone can make intelligible and interiorly vitalizing to the soul of the believer. If it be correct to speak of mysticism in connection with this profound contemplative spirituality, the reason is that it interprets monastic asceticism as a progress from the "land of unlikeness," in which human beings find themselves as a result of original sin, to the recovery of the lost "likeness to God." This recovery is possible for them because, despite sin, they have retained the "image of God," which is identical with the foundational characteristics of human nature and therefore with free will.

The soul is promised that at the end of a journey through the successive degrees of interior perfection, which correspond to the monastic virtues, it will enjoy a direct and unqualified encounter, "through the ecstasy of contemplation," with the object of its hope. In this final embrace between the love that directs the creature's free will and the love that inspires the Creator's free distribution of grace, those who have reached the highest degree of perfection attain to the supreme degree of mystical experience (something no creaturely merit can acquire). Their souls will be completely ready to enjoy the beloved object and therefore to become one with it or, as the earliest witnesses to patristic asceticism teach, to be "deified."

4. William of Saint-Thierry

The other great persecutor of the "philosophizers" in the first half of the century was William (d. 1148), who was appointed abbot of the Benedictine monastery of Saint-Thierry in 1112. In about that same year he wrote his first treatise on mystical love, his *Contemplation of God*. Although he was not yet a Cistercian (for a long time Bernard wanted him to remain a Benedictine in order that he might help in grafting the reform onto the original stock of western monasticism), even in this first work on contemplation he showed his full acceptance of Bernard's spiritual ideals. These came down to the exhortation to seek, through prayer and the loving raptures of religious meditation, the indwelling of God in the soul, a state that links the creature with the Creator by allowing the former to find and know the latter in a direct way by knowing itself.

In 1135 William decided at last to relinquish his office as abbot and enter the reformed Order, becoming a simple monk in the monastery of Signy. About ten years later he wrote his most important work, *A Letter to the Brothers at Mont-Dieu*, which he composed as a thank-you to the Carthusians of the monastery of Mont-Dieu who had given him hospitality.

William was convinced that human discourse about God is necessarily inadequate for expressing the true meaning of its object. At the same time, however, he held that, once human reason drops the arrogant claims of an extreme logicism and a materialistic naturalism, it can and ought to be used as much as possible by believers in defending their true faith against errors and heresies. Theological reason, properly understood, is not an inquirer into the faith or a judge of it, but a support and sustainer of faith, to which it is always subordinate; it is therefore not a reasoning that leads to faith but a reasoning about faith that is able to produce a reasonable faith. "It is one thing to have the faith of the simple, another to understand what is believed and to be always ready to identify the reasons for one's faith."

In taking this stance William was supported by the Platonizing model of the Fathers of the Church, whose works formed him intellectually as a young man in the urban schools he attended before becoming a monk: those of his native Liège, then Rheims, and perhaps Laon. The Fathers in question were chiefly Pseudo-Dionysius and Augustine, but also Gregory of Nyssa, who taught him the Platonic hierarchy of the faculties of the soul, which sin has reversed and redemption must restore. Another was Origen, whom he cites extensively and who confirmed him in the conviction that knowledge, by producing love of the object known, leads the soul by stages to mystical contemplation, which is an anticipation of blessedness here on earth. Finally, there was Maximus the Confessor, whom he knew as filtered through John Scotus' interpretation. Maximus gave him the idea of locating this cognitive asceticism in the framework of a Platonizing eschatology that climaxes in the next life with the "special return" of perfect believers or, in other words, the authentic "face-to-face" vision of God that is reserved for them.

At the heart of this plan of ascensional knowledge is William's certainty that the divine image remains in the innermost depths of human nature despite the corruption caused by original sin. This is the trinitarian image that Augustine found in the dynamic interplay of memory, will, and intellect, which are three different manifestations of reason, the unifying principle of knowledge that God bestowed on Adam so that he might direct himself to inquiry and the contemplation of divine truth.

But this image is also the image (likewise trinitarian) that can be seen in the gradual development of the theological virtues of faith, hope, and charity. These are three different and successive articulations of the one fundamental perfection of a Christian, namely, faith, but in the most comprehensive and truest sense (inasmuch as this faith is the convergence in the soul of belief that the revealed God exists, of hope that he gives himself, and of love without intermediaries). The coming together of memory and will in reason corresponds to the coming together of hope and love in faith. Moreover, reason and faith, made perfect by the fusion of the lesser parts that support them, must turn each to the other and unite in supporting one another in leading the soul toward its true goal.

Obviously this idea of the convergence of faith and reason in a joint cognitive ascent was incompatible with the "perverse" trickery of Abelard's logic (which William refutes in his *Argument against Peter Abelard*) and with the reduction of revelation to a treatise on physiology inspired by Chartrean naturalism (condemned in *The Errors of William of Conches*).

On the contrary, a true philosophy is one that is ready to learn and put into practice the Platonic rule that like knows like and like loves like. This is why, when reason and faith discover that each is like the other and that each attracts the other, they unite each in the other and together guide the soul toward the truth. Here they teach each other how to discover the soul's most authentic and original "likeness": the likeness of Adam to God that was obscured and hidden (in a different way than the "image" was) by the consequences of sin. Reason and faith, now in harmony, teach the soul to cultivate a disinterested love, to the point of accomplishing a cognitive union with the one object of its desires, the object that divinizes it by loving it with a love that is one with the love of the beloved and unites the beloved with the lover.

Two closely written short works, *The Mirror of Faith* and *The Obscurity of Faith*, take their titles from Paul's description of the knowledge proper to faith during life in this world (1 Cor 13:12). Here the foundational love that supports reason in assenting to and defending the faith becomes ever more intense and strong precisely in view of the ultimate incomprehensibility of the object of belief. Henceforth reason no longer asks questions except in the interests of believing, like Mary's question to the angel ("How can this take place?"), questions bearing witness that intelligence has become faith and a grateful acknowledgment of the truth of the mystery. Faced with the inscrutability of God's reasons for acting, human beings are able to believe thanks to their will ("you believe, if you will to do so"), but only if the will is enlightened by grace ("but you do not will it unless you are enlightened by grace").

5. Spiritual Friendship and the Psychology of the Mystical Ascent

In a surprising agreement with the classicism of their century, the Cistercians who dealt with the subject of divine love rediscovered the Ciceronian principle of friendship, that is, the sentiment of one who finds that the reasons for a disinterested affective enthusiasm are traceable to a familiarity with someone fundamentally like oneself in nature and disposition. Not only did the Cistercians use this idea of spiritual friendship as a symbol of the final union with God; they also made it basic for monastic society itself. In this setting it is a sentiment of disinterested love that unites, in a communion of virtues and prayer, those who share the same experience of ascetical perfection, which is an image and anticipation of and preparation for that same final union.

William of Saint-Thierry explicitly contrasts this monastic friendship with Ovidian eroticism and combines it with his own theory of the meeting of faith and reason in the likeness to God. In keeping with this concept Aelred of Rievaulx (d. 1167), an English Cistercian, wrote a work on *Spiritual Friendship* in which he shows how true friendship can be the key to the fulfillment, in the cloistered life, of the Christian commandment of perfect love of God and neighbor. The reason? "God is friendship," and true charity is a participation in the divine truth. Moreover, friendship among human beings is only an introduction to the attainment of their friendship with God: "When you and I are together, I hope that Christ is the third with us." Aelred is echoed later on by Peter of Blois (d. 1200), who had been a pupil of John of Salisbury and who, in agreement with Cicero, maintains in his own work on *Spiritual Friendship* that love springs indeed from instinct but can be purified by reason before being sublimated by the descent of divine grace.

The idea that reason is an instrument for balancing the lower instincts aroused in the soul through contact with the body was an idea widespread in Cistercian circles, in contrast to the pessimistic dualism of Augustine, which was traditionally based on the tension between soul and body and was typical of the Benedictine environment. The division of the soul's functions into irascibility, concupiscence, and rationality was taken over from patristic sources (which in turn derived it from the Platonic myth of the winged chariot). To the third function was entrusted the task of pointing out to the first two their respective good purposes.

This conception appears in a letter on *The Soul* that Isaac (d. 1178), abbot of Stella near Poitiers and a Cistercian, wrote in 1162 to another Cistercian, Alcher of Clairvaux. It comes up again in the anonymous treatise *Spirit and Soul*, which for practical purposes is a compilation of various patristic and early medieval texts. It makes ample use of Isaac's letter, which enjoyed great success in following centuries because it was falsely attributed to Augustine (some have suggested that the letter was actually the work of Alcher himself).

Both writings offer a detailed structuring of the human cognitive faculties; the structure derives its rich nomenclature from the psychological treatises of the Fathers and recent authors (such as Hugh of St. Victor), but also from newly available late antique and Arabic anthropological and medical sources.

Isaac describes five stages in a cognitive ascent, the result of which is an advance toward and a participation in the divine wisdom. The ascent involves the senses, which deal with things corporeal; the imagination, which grasps "a kind of body"; reason, which abstracts what is "quasi-incorporeal"; the intellect, which is directed to what is "truly incorporeal"; and the intelligence, which grasps what is "purely incorporeal" and is therefore "immediately subject to God." The work *Spirit and Soul* adopts pretty much the same distribution of degrees, but places at the top the "spirit," which is, as it were, "the spark of the soul," the highest degree of "mind." During these same years other writers give this highest degree the name *synderesis* (spark of conscience, a term taken from a passage in Jerome). Here the original "image of God" is located, and here alone is true knowledge of God possible by means of the purified eye of contemplation, a knowledge that anticipates the supreme joy of the blessed.

The earthly foretaste of the beatific vision in the contemplative life of monks is thus a constant element in Cistercian mysticism, but Isaac of Stella investigates it, justifies its possibility, and describes its achievement, even in his many renowned *Sermons*. Here, quite unusually in comparison with the majority of monks during these years, Isaac shows himself ready to take useful information from logic, ethics, psychology, and physiology, and even from works of the schools, those of the ancient philosophers, and the practice of the liberal arts. These sources serve as guides in defining more closely the shape of the cognitive ascent of the soul by way of its faculties. A privileged place is given to the attainment of the highest intellectual level (described sometimes as "mind," sometimes as "intellect," sometimes as "intelligence"): a suprarational knowledge that uses reason as a kind of springboard in order to immerse itself in a higher intuitive activity in which theoretical and practical knowledge, understanding, and love are joined in an indivisible unity.

But Isaac also thinks it extremely important to specify the essential condition for the attainment of this perfect intellectual activity, namely, the experience of solitude of the most complete kind, the absolute isolation that he himself decided to experience personally and concretely by withdrawing for many years to the deserted little island of Ré, off the coast of La Rochelle. The contemplative intelligence is so superior to reason that its exercise brings the soul to the point at which any kind of discursive thought or verbal communication among human beings is impossible. The reason for this is that it raises the soul to the sphere in which, as the mystical theology of Pseudo-Dionysius teaches, only a sacred silence permits it to speak directly to God, who is hidden in the utterly light-filled darkness of ineffability.

III. The English Schools and John of Salisbury

The first important name in the history of English Christian thought after the death of Anselm of Canterbury (in 1109) is that of Adelard, master at Bath in Somerset (d. before 1160). Like many other Englishmen of his times, Adelard lived his formative years in France, studying at Tours and perhaps Laon. He spent a good deal of time in traveling, visiting southern Italy, where he was probably in contact with the medical school in Salerno, as well as Sicily and perhaps the Middle East. In any case, he learned Arabic and gained a knowledge of scientific circles in that distant world that awakened his admiration and interest. This encounter led to fruitful work in the form of translations of Greek and Arabic books on mathematics, geometry (including the *Elements* of Euclid), and astrology, as well as to the composition of his two chief speculative works: *The Same and the Different* and *Questions about Nature*.

In its title, *The Same and the Different* mentions the two elements (*same* or the ideal immutable, and *different*, the accidental mutability of matter) of which the universe is composed according to Plato's *Timaeus*. The work is an allegorical dialogue between the author and two female personifications who try together to carry on their side of the dialogue; the two are Philosophia, the science of the identical, and Philocosmia, the investigation of what is different.

Philocosmia is the incarnation of the art of constructive investigation into the realities of the natural world; its object is singular things, and it must take sensible knowledge as its starting point. Philosophia, on the other hand, defends the exercise of reason, which alone is capable of understanding what is identical and immutable; it rises from opinion to the knowledge that contemplates the pure ideal essences. The author intervenes in the debate with a prudent moderation:

he acknowledges the right of each to exercise judgment in its different areas of competence. It would be a mistake, he says, to try to claim that the individual alone is real while universals are unreal, and vice versa. One and the same entity is an individual or a genus (or species) depending on the viewpoint from which it is considered. But in the last analysis it is against a theological background that Adelard justifies this harmonization of the two different perspectives. For neither of these can claim an exclusive right, and God alone, in the perfection of his supra-terrestrial thought (or *nous*), grasps in a single gaze the shared truth of individuals and of forms, or, in other words, of matter, but also of genera and species.

In his *Questions about Nature*, which is certainly later than his intense work of study and translation of the Arabic sciences, Adelard's interest tends more toward naturalism, which henceforth is simply identified with Arabic science ("the science of the Saracens"). In this work the author answers seventy-six questions on physiology a nephew raises as a result of his curiosity about every-day experiences. For the most part Adelard gives mechanistic and experiment-based explanations of the phenomena; these bring out the natural causes directly involved and do so with a resoluteness that seems to prepare the ground in England for the scientism that will be characteristic of the Oxford masters in the following century.

The nephew, for his part, expresses his own conviction that every natural event, including the growth of the grass, depends solely on the omnipotent will of God and should be attributed to the latter as its cause. Adelard responds that he himself has no doubts on this point: "I am taking nothing away from God, because everything that exists certainly comes from him (*ex ipso*) and through his action (*per ipsum*)." But everything that God causes to happen happens according to a law and is part of a natural order God himself has established. It is therefore the task of reason to investigate this order and to pursue its inquiries until the study of causes makes possible the explanation of their effects. Certainty has a limit that prevents it from turning into rashness and arrogance; this fact justifies the greatest possible development of science. Who, for example, could ever explain how it is possible to speak of a creation of matter, of a passage from nonbeing to being of the first element of creation, that which then gives substance to everything else? "Discussion of such matters transcends all other studies both because the concepts involved are so subtle and because discourse about them is so difficult."

There is, then, no opposition between science and religion, but only a distinction that allows each to make up for the limitations of the other: of religion, which does not have the task of explaining minimal natural phenomena, and of science, which is not able to achieve understanding of the highest truths. More-over, just as no one can do without the faith that enlightens human beings about the supraterrestrial order, neither can one do without the intellect that gives us direction within the order of the things of this world. As Adelard puts it succinctly in the preface of his final work, *The Astrolabe*: someone living in a beautiful house who does not take the trouble to recognize its wonderful beauty deserves to be evicted from it; so too, Christians who do not investigate and appreciate the harmony and beauty of the "noble palace of this world" in which they live are not worthy of dwelling in it and deserve to be expelled from it.

The Astrolabe, which remained unfinished, was dedicated to Henry II Plantagenet, the heir to the English throne, who was living in Normandy, where he had as tutor William of Conches. Some years later William dedicated to Henry a work entitled *Teachings of the Moral Philosophers*. Institutional links and the circulation of writings and ideas between the English and continental schools occurred frequently throughout the twelfth century and involved not only the secular schools, whose masters often traveled back and forth across the English Channel, but the monastic schools as well. As a result we find, here again, masters who took a traditional approach and others, like Adelard of Bath, who paid more attention to the results of the recent theological studies that fed discussions in France and Germany.

Those masters who mostly stayed in England retained closer ties to the tradition of the previous century. One such was Gilbert the Universal (d. 1134), bishop of London, who commented on various books of the Scriptures. Another was Eadmer of St. Andrews (d. 1141), a Benedictine, secretary and biographer of Anselm of Aosta; he applied the method of bringing out the reasonableness of the mystery of faith in his *Treatise on the Conception of the Blessed Virgin Mary*, in which he defended the Immaculate Conception.

Other scholars who had been educated in France and done some of their teaching there were more open to new methodologies. From this point of view a personage of some interest was Robert Pullus (d. 1146), who studied and taught in Paris and became a cardinal in the Roman curia. While he shared with Bernard (a personal friend of his) a dislike of the introduction of dialectical method into theological questions, he did not hesitate, in his *Eight Books of Sentences*, to attempt, in full confidence, a conceptual organization of the truths of the faith; indeed, he offered a systematic explanation that shows some critical insight.

Both in Adelard of Bath's more accurate application of method in the various areas of study and in Robert Pullus' cautious effort at a theological system we can see a tendency toward the reconciliation of the various cultural approaches and even a synthesis of them. This was perhaps rendered easier in the English world by the greater distance of the latter from the polemics on the continent. But it was due, above all, to the reassuring blessing given to these studies by the authoritative balance of faith and reason as seen in the Anselmian model, the memory of which was still alive and highly esteemed by scholars.

In this climate of quiet conciliation, based on a calm critique of the capacities of reason, a special and indeed paradigmatic value is to be assigned to the intellectual contribution of John of Salisbury (d. 1180). His name is connected chiefly with his important effort to revive for the medieval Christian world the philosophical probabilism of the ancient Academics, which Cicero urged in his philosophico-theological writings.

It is not irrelevant that the emergence of this effort in John of Salisbury was the result of his lengthy training as a young man, in which he savored the teaching of almost all the dominant personalities in the intellectual world of the twelfth century. He moved from England to Paris because he was attracted by the reputation of Abelard, whose lectures he attended with admiration and apprehension during that scholar's stormiest years. He went on to study under Alberic of Paris and Robert of Melun at Mont-Sainte-Geneviève; then he stayed in Chartres as a pupil of William of Conches and Theodoric, then in Paris again, where he studied logic and grammar and followed the theological lectures of Robert Pullus. John admired and loved both Gilbert of Poitiers, whose lectures on logic and divinity he attended, and Bernard of Clairvaux, whom he esteemed as a powerful preacher and a wise master of the Scriptures.

When John returned to England he became, at Bernard's recommendation, the secretary first of archbishop Theobald of Canterbury and then of the latter's successor, Thomas Becket. John was exiled in 1164 during the most heated phase of the conflict between Henry II and the church, a conflict that ended with the assassination of John's protector by the king's hired killers. In 1176 John was appointed bishop of his beloved city of Chartres, where he remained until his death.

The dramatic events of John's public life gave him a strong interest in the ethico-practical area of philosophical thought, an interest that culminated in the composition of his *Policraticus* (1159), which was dedicated to Becket. This was a deeply thoughtful handbook on the education and moral reform of earthly rulers, and was permeated by a solid ethical and political philosophy that was grounded in Christian practical wisdom. The same inspiration was at work in the broad historical picture given in his *History of the Popes* as well as in his *Life of Anselm* (1163, based on the life by Eadmer) and his *Life of Becket* (1176). The purpose of the two *Lives* was to defend the memory and secure the canonization of the two primates, both of whom had been persecuted by the political authorities.

In giving preference to the ethical dimension of Christian thought John was obviously influenced by the writings of Cicero, which he read and reflected on with diligence. So great was this influence that John even took over from Cicero a literary style unusual at that time: elegant, refined, and carefully accompanied by a sensible use of rhetoric. He combines the ancient idea of virtuousness with the fundamental principles of Christian morality and makes a practical perfection the goal of all human intellectual activity and philosophical study. This outlook shows in his conviction that abstract theorizing is useless and fruitless; it appears even in his more strictly philosophical and less directly political writings, namely, his poem *Entheticus* (or *On the Opinions of the Philosophers*), an enlightened collection of the opinions of the ancient philosophers, and above all in his *Metalogicon*.

The titles of his works reflect the Graecizing tendency in neoclassical learning, already to be seen in John Scotus and Anselm. *Polykratikos* is the person "who has supreme power," that is, the ruler; *Enthetikos*, "one who puts into," is in practice the "sower" of the wisdom of the ancient philosophers; *Metalogicon*, finally, is "a book in defense of logic." But this defense of logic, which helps the intellect to ready itself for acquisition of the truth by distinguishing it from its opposite, does not justify an uncontrolled and unrestrained indulgence in dialectic. John shows the same methodological moderation we saw earlier in Abelard; he is convinced that, like every other science, logic draws its real strength from the recognition of its own limitations. The first and fundamental limitation on the exercise of logic comes from the fact that, like every other philosophical discipline, it cannot refuse to have a practical usefulness, and must seek the moral perfection and reconciliation of humanity.

Above all the rules and conceptual structures it uses, logic will therefore place the principle at work in all practical wisdom, namely, the Supreme Good, which is divine and supernatural. This Good can certainly never be grasped and detected by rigorously applied methods of definition, for these only imprison their object in images that are partial or reductive and thus cause serious errors, both theoretical and ethical (such as the materialism of the Stoics or the Epicureans).

John thus distances himself from all those who think it the task of logic to ensure the possession of incontrovertible knowledge on the basis of necessitating proofs. He prefers to say that logic, and therefore science, is all the truer and more fruitful the more it acknowledges, like Cicero, that its task is to attain to a probability, a seemingly likely demonstration of that which can never be grasped in a definitive way: "As a trained scholar, when faced with anything that a wise man agrees is subject to doubt, I do not claim that what I say is true; rather, whether it be true or false, I am satisfied simply that it is probable."

The occasion for this reform of logic that John intends to complete was the attack on followers of an unidentified master who hid behind the pseudonym "Cornificius." (According to a statement by Philargius, a late antique scholiast, this was the name of an envious slanderer of Virgil.) Starting with the recognition of the insufficiency of logic, the Cornificians disparaged the entire study of language ("eloquence"), regarding it as mere verbal formalism and thus impoverishing the entire study of the arts of the trivium. This depreciation was in favor of knowledge based rather on sensible experience and on the immediate value of everyday language, both of which put the wise person in direct contact with reality.

These "new teachers" were especially opposed to the course of studies given at the school of Chartres during the period when Gilbert and then Theodoric were chancellors. They instilled dangerous doubts in the young about the ability of reason to establish a necessary and consistent correspondence between words and the things these signified. Their criticisms were nit-picking, being based on fallacies that were as trivial as they were dangerous. They asked, for example, whether a pig being led to be sold in the market is being taken by the man or by the rope to which it is tied; or whether one who buys a cloak also buys the hood that is part of it.

Their critique evidently attacked the entire Platonico-Augustinian tradition of Christian wisdom and could not fail to remind scholars of the similar attempt to drain logic of its truthfulness that had, according to Anselm, marked the attacks of the "moderns" in the time of Roscellinus. John of Salisbury, with an eye on the practical foundations of his own thinking, saw the Cornificians as primarily endangering the very morality that is the basis of human life in community, since this is based on the truthful communication of thought and volition. "When, therefore, Cornificius ignores and wrongly opposes the study of eloquence he is not besieging only one city [Chartres] in order to destroy it, or even a few cities, but all human communities and the whole of political life."

When John thus personally takes up the defense of medieval Christianity itself he is following his own teachers, from Anselm to Abelard, from Gilbert to the Chartreans, in launching a war in defense of the Christian theological system. In his own work he intends to bring back to logic the capacity for real demonstration that has belonged to it by its nature ever since the entire creation was placed at the disposition of human beings as a reality to be understood before being used. To defend logic is to ensure the semantic capacity of language and its correspondence to things, that is, its ability to seek what is true. To defend logic is therefore also to defend the whole of philosophy with its goal of understanding truth and to defend even the higher truth of the Christian faith, which has been put in meaningful words that communicate to believers the prophetic inspiration of the sacred writers.

A defense of logic necessarily requires, to begin with, a sufficient understanding of its true nature, in order, among other things, to keep it from becoming a prey to fallacies and ungrounded criticisms by second-rate teachers. Above all, it must be said that if logic is to be the science of the correct meaning of words it must begin with the study of meaningful terms and then cover the entire field of rules basic to the correct construction of a discourse, which is made up of propositions containing several terms and of reasonings containing several propositions.

Peter Abelard, especially in his *Logic*, had already surveyed this broad area of logic, from the opening discipline in which terms are defined to the teaching of correct reasoning. He had based his work especially on the model provided by Boethius, but John of Salisbury now had at his disposal a much better-stocked and varied library that had also been enriched by new translations. A reading of the complete *Organon* of Aristotle, and especially of the *Topics* and *Posterior Analytics* (both translated into Latin by James of Venice) enabled him to make his own a much more detailed and accurate conception of the constitutive parts of logic.

In reading these Aristotelean works, John learned that Latin writers had wrongfully given the name "dialectic" to the entire field of logic, whereas it originally signified only one of the three possible kinds within the art of proof or demonstration. According to Aristotle, the first of the three is the science of probable demonstration, to which belongs the name "dialectic" and that argues correctly but looks only to the formal aspect of the premises of an argument without verifying their actual correspondence with reality (for example: "All men have wings, therefore Greeks have wings"). The second is the science of necessary demonstration, or "apodictic," which studies reasoning from the viewpoint not only of its correctness but also of its truthfulness. The third is the science of imperfect demonstration, or "sophistic," which shows how error arises from transgressions of the rules of apodictic.

In a departure from his source, John prefers to give the name "probable" to the first of these three disciplines (the one Aristotle calls "dialectic"), dividing it into a section called "rhetoric" and another called "dialectic" in the strict sense. He then gives "apodictic" a new designation, namely, "demonstrative." Since, however, the aim of this discipline is to ensure the complete correspondence between its conclusions and truth, it will find a use exclusively in mathematics, where the necessary correspondence between definitions and the conceptual realities they signify ensures also the necessity of conclusions drawn about them. Finally, "sophistic," a discipline that likewise builds up knowledge and is not deceitful, intentionally falsifies the structure of its own demonstrations in order to show how logical error consists in changing the correspondence between words and reality.

So then, "dialectic," as distinct from "probable rhetorical argumentation," which is not concerned with the truth or falsity of its contents, appears only at the end of this entire structure of the forms of logical knowledge. Here it signifies essentially the discipline that yields "probable argumentation that moves toward the truth," although it will never be able to reach it definitively. At this point John remarks on the striking and noteworthy fact that the term "dialectic" is the one that for centuries, right down to the present period of western culture, has signified the entire art of debate with its sets of rules and principles, or, in other words, the entire art of regulating thought that is at work in every form of scientific knowledge.

John is saying, in effect, that not only the abstractions of mathematics but every investigation into the truth of things (whether finite creaturely things or the infinite perfection of divine reality) must be regulated solely by the laws of dialectic (in the new form given it by John himself). For dialectic is the discipline concerned with probability and ensures the necessity and veracity of argumentation, precisely to the extent that it prohibits one from pushing on to a complete, absolute, and necessary definition of the knowableness of its object. To John's mind, then, knowledge of reality is always a knowledge of probability. In addition, every act of scientific understanding always aims at a result that is probable and is accepted as an approximation to the truth but is, as such, always perfectible and always heralds further acts of probable knowledge. "To prove truly and probably" is, therefore, the only seemingly contradictory formula that, according to John, describes the only course possible for philosophy, since philosophy constantly seeks its proper object even at the very moment in which it finds it, and truly finds this object only if it continues to seek it.

Human beings will never be true philosophers if they delude themselves that they can utter necessary judgments on something whose necessity is, in the final analysis, known only to God. John gives an enlightening example of this principle when he gathers together and comments on the varied, subtle, but empty solutions (a real truckload of new, tormenting "disagreements among the philosophers") that his contemporaries, including the most highly respected, have given to the question of universals. John dismisses this question as a false problem on which "more time has been wasted than it took the Caesars to conquer the world." In fact, in his view, error is already at the heart of the presumption that human beings can make a metaphysical entity (be this a "concept," an "idea," an "image," or even simply a "sound") out of what is for us only an object of intellection, that is, an act of the mind by which we endeavor to draw close to a truth that is in itself eternal and immutable and that infinitely eludes our perfectible ability to know and define.

In this perspective, which was new and truly revolutionary in the cultural setting of the time, John of Salisbury sees dialectic, i.e., the science of the probable, as the only instrument making it possible to establish an authentically theological knowledge. Just as, and much more than, in the case of the universals, only provisional answers can be given to all the questions human beings raise about the suprasensible realities whose existence is made known to us by revelation: for example, the nature of the soul, eternal life, the manner of existence of the angels.

The same is even more true of questions about the mysteries of faith, which are mysteries precisely inasmuch they cannot be penetrated by following the normal laws of logic: the nature and perfections of God, the Incarnation of Christ, his virginal birth, the Eucharist. Quite correctly, therefore, does Aristotle define faith as an "opinion," not as implying a depreciation of faith in comparison with certain knowledge, but as meaning that everything a human being believes with certainty is debatable. In a similar way, as we watch the sun go down in the evening we have a deep conviction that it will rise again on the following day; this conviction is not a scientific certainty but a deeply rooted confidence in what seems to us to be the truth. So solid a faith gives the appearance of being certain knowledge.

As a matter of fact, Christian faith, which relies on what God has revealed to human beings about himself and their destiny, gives rise to a kind of knowledge—theological knowledge—that is truly halfway between imperfect, probable human knowledge and God's knowledge, which is perfect and beyond our reach. This intermediate knowledge is a knowledge of the eternal "reasons" that, as Anselm teaches, are accessible to human beings only through freely given revelation.

Yet, precisely for this reason, theological knowledge based on revelation can be regarded as a science, and even as the "queen of the sciences," and can be described as "divine" inasmuch as it makes its lovers like God. Why? Because it enables them to know sufficiently the truth that God alone knows. Only by allowing itself to be guided by faith can the human intellect pass, as the Platonists taught, from the conceptual universe of reason (which distinguishes and defines its objects through probability-yielding processes of dianoetic inquiry) to a direct participation in that "supreme spiritual power" that (with the help of a direct communication by God) directly contemplates the divine reasons of all things and that therefore, without knowing, truly tastes them, with God and in God.

Chapter 4

Between Two Worlds

I. The Maturation of Theological Method in the Age of Philip Augustus

In the final decades of the twelfth century and the first of the thirteenth the intellectual world of Latin Europe experienced one of its most intense phases of growth and maturation, both in regard to the means and information at its disposal and in regard to the economic and institutional conditions that permitted and defined the development of its cultural life. Chronologically this period coincided with the term of government of Philip II, known as Augustus, king of France from 1180 to 1223—that is, the span of time from the end of the third Lateran Council (convoked in 1179) to the definitive approval of the *Rule* of Francis of Assisi by Honorius III. It was also the period that saw, especially in the heart of France (Paris), the definitive shift from the cultural dominance of the educational structure of the cathedral school, which the bishop controlled, to the union of various establishments in a single organized association that became known as the university (*universitas studiorum* = the totality of studies).

On the one hand the scholars of this period who concerned themselves with the expansion of theological thought often bore witness to the continuation and further development of the intellectual efforts that had been tested during the twelfth century. On the other hand they bore witness also to the first signs of the imminent global transformation of speculative thought into a profession geared to a demanding and practical teaching activity, the mark of a university. But of no less importance in the religious activity of this period was the apologetical commitment, which was intensified both by increasing cultural relations with the Islamic and Jewish worlds and by the spread of popular heresy. These were, in fact, the years that saw the greatest spread in Southern France and the Rhineland of the Neomanichean doctrines of the Cathars, who were repeatedly condemned by councils and finally were subjected to violent military repression beginning in 1209. This military enterprise was known as the "crusade" against the Albigensians (so named from the city of Albi in Southern France, which was the heart of the movement).

1. Alan of Lille

Alan of Lille was perhaps the figure most representative of these various factors, which produced a phase of consolidation but, at the same time, of transformation of the work of a medieval theologian. Alan, who was born in the twenties of this century, studied as a young man in the schools of Paris and then perhaps also at Chartres under Gilbert of Poitiers. He then spent a period of training in southern France, partly in the school of medicine at Montpellier, where he made contact with the world of eastern physiology and medicine, which for quite some time had already been practiced in the area of Salerno in southern Italy and to some extent also at the Benedictine abbey of Saint-Gilles. From 1160 to 1180 he taught liberal arts and theology in Paris, following in the wake of Peter Cantor and Peter Lombard.

After the first condemnation of the Cathars at the third Lateran Council, Alan wrote a treatise on *The Catholic Faith in Response to Heretics*, which he dedicated to the Count of Montpellier. This work locates its attack on the new popular heresies of the second half of the twelfth century (for example, the Albigensians and Waldensians) in the post-Anselmian literary stream of religious debate with the Jews and the Arabs. The work is also a prototype of the apologetical and missionary treatise that would reach its flowering in the thirteenth century. In the last years of his life Alan entered the Cistercian Order and in 1195 withdrew to Cîteaux, where he died in 1203. His life was thus coextensive with the intellectual world of the second half of the twelfth century and dealt in practice with all the most important aspects of religion and thought. With this as background, he developed during his mature years a wide-ranging synthesis of philosophical and theological thought in which the many stimuli from the recent past came together in an effort at a new kind of systematics.

His many-sided interests and abilities can be seen in the diverse genres of his writings, as he experimented with all the principal didactic and literary forms of that time and tried to update the study of the faith by means of very varied methods and perspectives. In addition to *The Catholic Faith*, which brings together and alternates rational arguments and citations from the Fathers, some other works deserve mention. The *Summa "Because Human Beings"* is a never-completed systematic treatise on the entire Christian faith; it is organized according to a sequence of subjects that is typical of the collections of *Sentences* (Creator, creation, and re-creation: that is, redemption and eschatology). The *Rules of Heavenly Law* is an explanation of the truths of the faith that proceeds by axioms of a Euclidean type. The *Distinctions Among Theological Terms*, which also circulated under the title *Summa "In how many ways,"* is a collection, with explanations, of terms useful in theology, namely, words and expressions from the vocabulary of the Bible but also from philosophy or the sciences, or simply words for concepts susceptible to an allegorical exegesis.

There are also a commentary on the Song of Songs, various sermons, and other exegetical writings that show a prevailing preference for symbolical interpretations: *The Art of Preaching* or *Summa on the Art of Preaching*; a *Treatise on the Virtues and the Vices*; two works of a visionary, allegorical kind, namely *Nature's Lament* and *Anticlaudianus*; other poetical and hymnological texts, among them a *Poem on the Incarnation and the Seven Arts*, the title of which points to the compatibility of Christian faith and the secular sciences.

This very diversified body of work won for Alan the title "Universal Doctor" (before this was later given to Albert the Great). But amid its diversity it shows at every point a constant concern to identify the language best suited for expressing theological knowledge; this central idea justifies Alan's experimentation with many kinds of methodology and literary genres. And yet Alan was not a restless spirit continually in search of new outlets for his longing for the divine. On the contrary, each of his works seems to be carefully composed and to exemplify a complete model of an "understanding of the faith," even when the work has not been completed.

It seems as if he wanted to make available to his readers a series of individual programs, each with its specific characteristics and merits, in order that these readers might decide which one to choose, depending on cases and timeliness. Among these formal proposals of his some in fact had a following in the theological schools of the ensuing decades while others attracted no imitators. This may be an indication that his work as a writer was really a transitional cultural activity, a reflection of a past that from this moment forward could either become part of a living tradition or be forgotten once and for all.

Alan had long since shown a great familiarity with the technical use of the term "theology" to designate a particular form of knowledge distinct from the other disciplines. Now, in the first chapter of his *Art of Preaching*, he proposes a division of theology into two parts, both of which are to be practiced and used by skilled preachers. The latter, like the angels in Jacob's vision, ascend and descend along the paths of these two kinds of study: rational theology, which seeks a true and proper knowledge of divine things, and moral theology, the object of which is to establish the normative principles of Christian ethics. Alan's theological writings effectively document his commitment to both kinds of theology.

In the area of moral theology, and chiefly but not exclusively in the *Treatise on the Virtues and Vices*, Alan tries above all to revive the practice, widespread in the early Middle Ages, of formally classifying the Christian virtues and the vices. Also concerned with this field of reflection are his two poetico-literary works, which are perhaps his best-known writings. In his hortatory explanation of the concrete ways in which good and evil manifest themselves in the moral life the author deliberately harks back to the method of "veils" used by Abelard and the Chartreans. He also makes use again of the model tried by Bernard Silvestris and indulges freely in a rich, allegorical mythopoetry whose purpose is to celebrate the virtues and the cosmic dignity of the human person.

In *Nature's Lament* Alan also follows Bernard in using the Boethean prosimetrum or combination of verse and prose. The work begins with an introductory lament by the author over human immorality, which has overturned the natural laws governing sexuality. He then tells of seeing in a dream a personification of Nature, that unwearying and fruitful continuator of the divine work; she explains to him the way in which, through her activity, the laws of God govern creation. The narrative widens with the introduction of further symbolical personifications celebrating the laws of the love that allows reproduction. They also condemn all deviant sexual behavior (with an evident polemical reference to the sensuality of the Cathar religious spirit) and proclaim the need to cultivate the virtues and reject the vices. The reason for this proclamation is that the supreme will of the first Cause is fulfilled in the universe through the sanctification of human beings.

More structured and complex is the theologico-poetical vision of the *Anticlaudianus de Antirufino* (meaning something like "Against Claudian and his Attack on Rufinus"), which contains a prologue and nine books. The title refers to the poem *Against Rufinus* by the late antique poet Claudian, who called upon all the vices *en masse* to rush off and corrupt the soul of Rufinus, prefect of the East and an adversary of Claudian's protector, Stilicho. Here, in contrast, a personified Nature summons all the Virtues to its palace in order that with their gifts they may contribute to the formation of a perfect human being who will serve as a model for the entire human race.

But because Nature does not have the power to give this new creature a soul, Prudence is charged with asking God to complete the task; for this purpose she goes up to heaven on a winged chariot, the work of the seven liberal Arts; the chariot is drawn by five horses, which are the Senses, and driven by a charioteer, who is Reason. After a lengthy journey among the heavenly spheres the pilgrims are welcomed into the presence of the Virgin, but their access to God is made possible with the help of Theology and Faith, which show God to them in a great mirror. God then bids *Nous* (the Word) to search among the already existing forms for a soul that may be given to the human being; the latter, in an alliance with the Virtues (which defeat the Vices), will be master of the universe and leader of the new golden age.

The great suggestive power of this symbolic theological language exerted a widespread influence on the literature of the following centuries, from the *Roman de la Rose* to Dante himself. Some decades later, John of Garland in his *The Triumphs of the Church* would praise Alan as a "poet greater than Homer and Virgil." But no less influential on following generations were Alan's works that were explicitly devoted to the theoretical systematization of theological knowledge, that is, the "science of things divine."

In his *Summa "Because Human Beings,"* which he wrote around 1160, Alan distinguishes two courses of thought proper to rational theology; to these the two books of the work are respectively devoted. The first deals with "supercelestial apothetic theology" ("apothetic" = "setting aside"), which is developed by the higher intuitive intellect; when the latter shapes the work of discursive reason it can only express in a negative form the content of its perceptions of the first causes, since these are as such unknowable and ineffable. The second book, which is incomplete, deals with "subcelestial hypothetical theology." This is a rational inquiry into the efficacy of second causes on the basis of the observation of natural phenomena; it is a process that advances through affirmations but is able to describe the divine power at work therein only by means of hypotheses.

For a correct investigation in both fields Alan expressly harks back to the Porretan norm, that is, the "transferral" or "transumption" of the semantic efficacy of language and the tools of the liberal arts. This is to say that when the logical and grammatical categories typical of human thinking are transferred from the world of created nature to that of the divine nature their significance is necessarily distorted, if not completely overturned. Priscian, after all, teaches that every noun always expresses a substance or a quantity; but in God there can be no distinction between the subject and its formal determinations. As a result, every term used in theological discourse must become "formless," as it were, as though it had completely lost its ability to signify a property the meaning of which is distinct from that of the essence. The only guarantee, then, of the correctness of the semantic transferrals made by theologians must be the regulatory power of Sacred Scripture, which authoritatively tells the human intellect what the end result of all its inquiries must be.

In a kind of cadence at the end of each stanza of his *Poem on the Incarnation*, at the point when the intellect is faced with the revealed mystery, Alan repeats that there are no other formal rules that permit an understanding of this mystery: "In the presence of this union established by the Word/every rule falls dumb."

The need to alter the efficacy of natural language in a positive way is fundamentally at work even in the distortion of meaningful images of the truths of the faith that is effected by poetical theology in its appeal to "veils." But if this kind of semantic transferral is to have the indispensable consistency that speculative theology requires, it must be accompanied by the establishment of a new value for the terms involved that will be in effect only in this context. Reason must therefore endeavor to purify its own language of any contamination by elements of meaning that belong exclusively to finite creatures and to endow these with a new but strictly determined expressiveness.

This principle can be seen at work in the theological use, attested in Scripture, of ideas that specify a temporal condition, even one peculiar to the divinity, such as eternity. The way in which philosophers usually solve this problem, that is, by equating eternity with an inexhaustible present moment, is not acceptable in theology because it always implies a comparison with other forms of temporal flow proper to things corruptible. But the authentic scriptural "now" of God must not be understood as a correction or sublimation of the forms of creaturely temporality. On the contrary, it signifies a complete negation of such forms: God's time is simply the absence of time. Thus concepts such as creation or incarnation do not signify a beginning or a change in God, but solely in the creature involved in these activities.

Only by means of such corrections can theology be placed on the semantic foundation that it requires and that allows it to be considered a science. In fact, only on these conditions can the arts apply their rules here. Moreover, theology can also borrow from other fields of demonstration methodologies that ordinarily do not belong to it. This is the case with the method of "concentration" or the "question" (*quaestio*), which had already been tried in the legal and scientific fields but thus far only episodically in theology. Alan makes extensive use of it in the *Summa*: it consists in formulating hypotheses that, one after the other, are tested and judged, positively or negatively, over against other, opposed claims, but also against the patristic authorities frequently cited in order properly to direct the line of argument.

But the same method is used, with entirely different formal results, in the short work titled *Rules of Heavenly Law*, in which, as mentioned earlier, Alan applies the axiomatic method of Euclidean geometry to theological knowledge. Alan was not the only one in his day to attempt a project of this kind, but his was probably the most successful since it yielded a complete exposition of the truths of the faith in a broadly structured but strictly deductive form.

The applicability of the geometric method to all other forms of scientific knowledge and to theological research in particular had first been asserted in the West by Boethius in his third short theological work, *Weeks*. But, as we pointed out, he offered only an example in connection with a particular problem, that of the substantial goodness of the created world. His effort there began with the presupposition, also made by Aristotelean epistemology, that at the highest point of any science there are always some indisputable first principles having to do with content (definitions, postulates, general premises) or the form of argumentation (rules, common topics).

The peculiarity of the axiomatic method resides in the fact that deductive demonstrations start from these premises alone and constantly refer to them in a process of continual comparisons and linkages among them. Commenting on Boethius' short work, Gilbert of Poitiers then showed how, given the completely intuitive (that is, intellectual and suprarational) character of the axioms, the deductions made from them by discursive, dianoetic reason should not take the form of successive conceptual mediations (if every A is B and every B is C, then every A is C); this is the form of reasoning typical of scientific proof and is based on experimental verification. The process here is rather the mind's progress in knowledge by way of setting successive mental conditions, a real "cloning" of the contents needed for thought (if A is necessary, the necessity of B springs from A, the necessity of C from B, and so on).

Gilbert's methodological clarification helped foster the idea of a possible new systematization of all revealed truth along geometric lines. Perhaps the first to take up the challenge was Nicholas of Amiens (d. after 1203). In a short work titled *The Art of the Catholic Faith* he gives a succinct explanation of Christian truth in five books, in each of which a list of premises (axioms, definitions, common ideas) is made to yield a linked series of propositions or theorems and the proofs of each. This same approach "after the manner of an art" marks Alan's *Rules*, but in a less rigid and stripped-down form. In his Prologue the author says that he has taken it upon himself to "introduce order among the demonstrable logical necessities having to do with the faith." He accomplishes this by linking these necessities among themselves on the basis of a series of proofs that make the necessity clear. In the course of the work he tracks down the generation of each necessary notion taught by Scripture from a necessity prior to it and produces a succession that reflects the natural links among the truths of the faith. Each truth that flows from another is also a clarification of that other and a further specification of it; finally, all of them are brought together in a coherent comprehensive unity that is ensured both by the efficacy of understanding and by the certainty of faith.

In short, the consistency and solidity of the line of argument evidently characterize both the *Rules* and the *Summa "Because Human Beings,"* despite the fact that the two works are directed by very different and incompatible methodologies. In the author's mind the two works are meant to lead by different paths to results that are equivalent inasmuch as they match the order within the truths of faith. The two works follow, in practice, the same thematic path, with a frequent identity of content, but always in obedience to two different expository procedures. Both works, therefore, reflect the shared apologetical presupposition that directs Alan's whole theological calling: namely, his constant ambition to bolster the truth of the faith through theological explanation and to defend it against the attacks of skeptics, infidels, and heretics.

The axiomatic method of the *Rules* did not win many followers in the university world of the following century, which preferred the technically more flexible method of the "question." The reason for the lack of later success may have been that the method was formally dissociated from any confrontation with patristic authority and advanced in an overly autonomous way in bringing to light the necessary identity between the results of reason and the propositions of faith. Despite this lack of a following, when seen in the overall setting of Alan's theological production as one of his most effective ways of organizing and communicating theological truth the geometric formalization of the contents of the faith is certainly significant evidence of a conviction he now shared with many of his contemporaries: that learning about God was to be treated as a well-defined science with its own field of investigation and its own object and therefore requiring the exactitude of a specific methodology to ensure the consistency of its procedures and the necessity of the results.

2. Organization of Knowledge and Definition of Theological Knowledge

This kind of progress toward the achievement of a strict definition of theological knowledge and the determination of its scientific status (allowing it to be compared with the other sciences) can also be seen in the writings of other masters active in France at the end of the twelfth century and the beginning of the thirteenth. In many instances this tendency led well-known masters of theology to suggest and experiment with several ways of classifying and subdividing theological knowledge for the purpose of clarifying its object and systematizing its contents. Simon of Tournai (d. ca. 1201), for example, in his *Theological Summa* works with a distinction between discourse on the literal sense of Scripture and discourse on its figurative sense. Stephen Langton (d. 1228) in his *Theological Summa* combines the Gilbertan method of "transumption" with Peter Cantor's method of exegetical distinctions; he groups important terms dealing with God into various semantic groups corresponding to the various functions peculiar to theological language.

Praepositinus (Prévostin) of Cremona was chancellor of the Paris school from 1206 to 1210, that is, during the years that saw the transformation of the school into a university. In his *Summa Based on the Psalter* he preferred to use the method of the distinction in organizing the art of preaching on the basis of the various hermeneutical tools available. Robert of Courçon (d. 1219), a cardinal legate of Innocent III and well known for having issued the first statutes of the University of Paris, wrote a *Summa* in which for the first time he proposed the division of theological material into a branch dealing with faith and another dealing with morality; he would be followed in this by many scholastic writers.

Other masters with greater confidence in their ability to identify a scientific method common to all areas of learning went on to test the applicability of this method even to theology. As a result they placed theology (and not simply because of the dignity of its contents) at the summit of an encyclopedic systematization of the sciences along the lines of the model shown by Hugh of St. Victor.

Radulf Ardens (d. ca. 1200) was the author of many sermons whose liveliness of expression won him the nickname "burning (*ardens*)." He also wrote a *Universal Mirror* or *Summa on the Virtues and Vices*. Here theology is located within a systematic organization of the sciences (a move justified on the grounds of methodological uniformity) and described even visually in a series of summarizing tables or "trees" of knowledge. This approach ensured the place of theology as a discipline that explained the faith and was thus a source of the doctrinal information indispensable for the subsequent explanation of the specifically moral ideas that, as the second title showed, were the main subject of the work.

While taking into account the necessary transumption that marks the extension of natural language into the realm of theology, Radulf rejected the Gilbertan disparagement of continuity between philosophical and theological knowledge and was convinced of the suitability of regarding theology as the goal and completion of philosophical knowledge; on this point he was in agreement with the Augustinianism of many early medieval theologians. Not only did he urge a systematic application of the specific terminology of the human sciences to theological questions: he also said he was convinced that the use of creaturely language in speaking of God (a point he exemplifies in regard to the Trinity) represented the only possibility for human beings to understand the truth of things that would otherwise be completely unknown to us and beyond our powers to investigate.

Alexander Neckam (or Nequam; d. 1217) likewise wrote an encyclopedia of theological ethics, *The Natures of Things*. This combines an erudite moralizing description of created nature with (in the second part of the work) a commentary on the book of Ecclesiastes. Later, as a mature thinker, Alexander published another ambitious encyclopedic work of theology titled *Mirror of Speculations*, the explicit purpose of which was to safeguard the contents of Christian teaching against the deviant interpretations of new heretics, the Cathars. He refutes them with the constant help of a quite advanced competence in logic based (as in the case of John of Salisbury) on a knowledge of the entire collection of texts that make up the *Organon*.

Alexander was very familiar with the world of the logicians of Paris, where he had studied as a young man. He distrusted the useless curiosity displayed in their debates, but he nonetheless regarded logic as essential in forming theological proofs, which he, like Radulf, understood to be the completion of philosophy and therefore in continuity with its procedures. It was no accident that for this English master one of the most effective models of this method of demonstrating the truths of the faith was to be seen in the work of Anselm of Aosta, the last witness to the unified conception of systematic reason that was dominant in the early medieval centuries.

3. Joachim of Fiore

During the final twenty years of the twelfth century Joachim of Celico (d. 1202), a monk of Calabria in southern Italy, had spiritual experiences that were destined to have a notable influence on the religious world and the theological ideas of the following century.

This phase of the history of religious thought coincided with the early years of the reign of Philip Augustus, which also saw the definitive establishment of the Norman kingdom in the Italian South and its involvement in the destinies of the Swabian imperial dynasty. The beginning of the phase was marked by the convergence, on the one hand, of tendencies and attitudes originating in the recent monastic past and, on the other, of impulses and innovative approaches emerging from the contemporary intellectual world. In fact, while Joachim's religious experience was linked to early medieval aspirations toward the moral improvement of the church, the monastic world, and Christian society, it also led to a radical disdain, supported by a convinced and charismatic prophetism, for the revival of religious ideals and the reform of theological studies as these had been taking shape for some time in the arid debates of the schools. A true revival and reform had to lead once again to a vitalizing, interiorized kind of knowledge that would bear fruit in the everyday life of believers.

Many factors, including his own immediate personal experiences, fused to produce Joachim's unique spiritual and prophetic vocation. These were the missionary spirit of the crusader ideal, the longing for monastic perfection, and the pauperism of the popular religious movements and the impulse to evangelical revival that inspired them. But there were also influences from the lively movement of reform that swept through Byzantine monasticism in the eleventh and twelfth centuries and from the Jewish cabalist tradition, which was to be encountered in the theological writing of a Jewish convert, Peter Alfonsi (d. ca. 1140). A detailed knowledge of the Fathers and of the early monastic ascetical tradition served to unify the several elements of this synthesis by rooting them directly in the fruitful, integrative earth that feeds all of Christian truth, namely, the words of Sacred Scripture.

Joachim developed his own language on the basis of the sacred text; from it he derived all of his theological ideals as well as the skills needed to explain them; the thematic ideas of all his works are grafted onto it. This unalloyed primacy of biblical wisdom is quite evident in all the many writings that make up his theological production, the composition of which began when, in 1177, he was elected abbot of the monastery of Corazzo, which had been Benedictine but under his influence shifted to the Cistercian obedience. (In 1190 he founded the monastery of San Giovanni in Fiore, in Calabria. — Tr.)

The primacy of Scripture is especially clear in the three great works of his maturity, which he never ceased to rework over the years: *Harmony of the New and Old Testaments*, *Explanation of the Apocalypse*, and *The Ten-Stringed Psaltery*. That same primacy inspired his final, uncompleted work, *Treatise on the Four Gospels*. Joachim's reading of the Scriptures is not of a rational and conceptual kind; rather, it adheres closely to the revealed truth and is therefore profoundly visionary. This is why he gives a great deal of room in his writings to his visual imagination, which makes his understanding of biblical truth immediately accessible; he even had skilled illuminators produce the splendid images, rich in symbolism, that illustrate his exegetical texts. In the last years of his life he himself began a *Book of Images* that would bring them all together; a disciple completed the work after Joachim's death.

It is again an image of scriptural origin, the loftiest and most symbolic of all (since it represents the trinitarian mystery), that is the focal point of Joachim's most important and direct visionary experience, the one that represents the highest development of his vocation as a prophet. This is the vision of the ten-stringed psaltery, of which he speaks in the work bearing that title.

At the time Joachim was a guest at the Cistercian abbey of Casamari, and on the morning of Pentecost 1183 (or 1184), as he was about to enter the oratory for prayer, he felt surfacing within him a "kind of wavering" with regard to the truth of the divine unity and Trinity. Then the silence of both understanding and belief was answered by the appearance within his mind of a psaltery (a triangular musical instrument) with ten strings, which was "obviously a clear symbol of the Holy Trinity." The explanation of the symbolism is basic, yet also very difficult to grasp simply by using "appropriate words." The psalter, Joachim says, is made up of parts that, if separated, destroy the instrument; the undivided unity springs from the very distinction between parts that cannot be separated. But whereas words and concepts do not add knowledge, the image revealed in this charming symbolical language sheds in the soul an unexpected light on the revealed truth.

The very nature of this new communication is enough to explain Joachim's intense dislike of everything characteristic of "scholastic science," but also of a spirituality he regarded as a threadbare mysticism based on an affective participation in the propositions of faith and not on a real understanding of the mystery. It was this thinking that gave rise to his decision to leave the Cistercian Order and led to a fierce battle with its representatives and in particular with Adam of Perseigne (d. 1221), whom the general chapter of 1190 appointed to investigate Joachim's doctrinal views. It was also in this context that he made his attacks on the intellectualism of the schools, an outlook he identified in particular with the work of Peter Lombard, whom he accused of "blasphemy" for accepting the formula "There is a supreme reality that is the Father and the Son and the Holy Spirit." In Joachim's view this introduction into God of a reality produced by the human mind—a reality that neither "begets" nor "is begotten" nor "proceeds"—amounts to maintaining a divine quaternity, a heresy produced by the rationalist mind.

The idea of the communication of truth through symbols certainly did not come to Joachim from a single image or a single vision, but rather from the combination and interaction of several intuitions arising from the pages of Scripture. His conviction that every word or image of the sacred text not only has an immediate meaning but always possesses a further symbolic richness gave rise to an inexhaustible flood of truths that ran from vision to vision amid constant references to ever better ways for the soul to draw near to the divine. The root of this multiplication of symbolic meanings (itself an aspect of Scripture) is to be found in the words of Jesus when he advises his disciples that many things are still to be made known to them but that they will not be able to understand them until the Spirit is in their midst (John 16:12-13). As a result, not only do Old Testament images become symbols and prophetic foreshadowings of truths made known in the Gospel, but the entire Old Testament becomes a symbol of the New.

In addition, the truths of the New Testament become in their turn symbols and prophesies of further meanings. And just as the truth of the Father foretold that of the Son, so the truth of the Son is an anticipation of the truth of the Spirit. Onto this new prospect is grafted the construction of a new theological law governing history, a law that is concrete and about to come into operation. The law is that as the truth of the Father was fulfilled during the period of the Law that preceded the Incarnation and as the truth of the Son came to humanity beginning at the Incarnation, so this same truth of the Son, or the Gospel, foretold and brought into being the age of the Spirit, which will bring humanity a future of peace and of understanding of the divine will through an "understanding" that is "spiritual" because given by the Spirit.

As the Law was transcended by the grace of the Gospel, so the Gospel will reveal its truth still more through the "even greater" grace of spiritual understanding. Joachim did not predict the replacement of the New Testament by a "third" testament of the Spirit. On the other hand, there was a clear and revolutionary shift in his thinking from the Christocentrism of the traditional Platonic-Augustinian conception of history (Christ as mediator of the passage from the old Adam to the New Adam and from the resurrection of the latter to the resurrection of the entire human race) to a triadic pneumatological vision wholly focused on the expectation of the eschatological fulfillment of the truth. Further divisions of the historical process could then be added and superimposed on the tripartite pattern, provided they preserved the indispensable eschatological orientation. An example: connected with the symbol of the seven seals of the Apocalypse or the symbol of the days of creation is the sevenfold division of history, which by adding the end of time completes the theory of the six ages in Augustine's *City of God*; for Joachim, five ages belong to the era of the Father and one each to those of the Son and the Spirit.

Therefore and in any case the age of the Spirit is the goal and resolution of the entire theology of history. The discouraging sight of the violence and instability of his time, the decadence of the church, and the conflicts within Christianity were all signs to Joachim of an irreversible crisis that was bringing the world headlong under the temporary domination of the Antichrist predicted by the book of Revelation. But these same realities were also signs foretelling the new reign of the Spirit that was to arise from the wreckage of a corrupt human race and bring the definitive victory of Christ along with the complete fulfillment of his words. A complex system of calculations based on the data of Scripture, together with an authentic interpretation of the Old and New Testament prophecies, led the prophet to foretell the end of wars, punitive coercions, and earthly sovereignties and the triumph of peace through the establishment of a new order, that of spiritual human beings who find their true freedom in the truth, after the model of Christ.

4. Amalric of Bène

In 1215 the fourth Lateran Council rejected Joachim's teaching on the Trinity as turning the divine unity into something "collective and analogous," while at the same time the council affirmed the orthodoxy of Peter Lombard. The condemnation was inspired by a desire to rein in the spread of unauthorized interpretations of Christian dogma. To the latter it opposed, as a solid bulwark based on the authentic theses of the Fathers of the Church, the consistency and coherence of the syncretic interpretation of dogma in Lombard's *Books of Sentences*, which the context in the decree recommends as a basic text for theological lectures in the schools.

At the same session the council forcefully condemned not only the errors of the Cathars and Albigensians but also the theological teaching of Paris master Amalric of Bène (d. ca. 1206/7) and his "followers." They taught that the works of the Trinity are not eternal but separated in time, in a succession that corresponds to their revelation in three distinct periods of history: the Old Testament, the New Testament, and the present age.

We know little about Amalric, and that little is distorted by the hostile attitudes of the sources. Perhaps as a young man he had some connection with Chartres (Bène was in that diocese), and then studied in Paris, where he later taught the arts and theology. It is difficult to confirm the claim that he was for a time a tutor of the sons of Philip Augustus. In 1204 his theological theses elicited a first censure from some Parisian theologians, especially the thesis, seemingly anchored in Pauline christology, that "in order to be saved, every human being must believe himself to be a member of Christ." Amalric went to Rome and appealed to Innocent III, but the pope confirmed the condemnation.

After returning to Paris, Amalric seems to have retracted his teachings before he died, but they were kept alive by some of his disciples, who were soon accused of spreading their teaching among the lower classes. On being discovered and denounced to the bishop of Paris, they were condemned at a council of the province of Sens, which met in the capital in 1210 in the presence of the masters of theology. This council also condemned vernacular translations of the sacred texts, the reading of Aristotle's "new" books of natural theology (probably the *Physics* and *Metaphysics*), together with commentaries on them (perhaps those of Alfarabi and Avicenna), and the teachings of David of Dinant, another Parisian master accused of pantheism. The punishment included the exhumation and posthumous excommunication of Amalric's corpse and the dispersion of his disciples; it was confirmed in 1215 by papal legate Robert of Courçon and also formally by the ecumenical council. Stubborn Amalricians were searched out, interrogated, and sometimes executed by the secular arm, as in the case of a man named Godino who was burned at Amiens.

During the following decades, when Peripatetic doctrines had for some time been included in the teaching of theology at the universities, the linking of Aristotle's works with the condemnation of Amalric and David led to a series of reconstructions of that event and of the teaching of those two masters. The purpose of these reconstructions was clearly to defend the thought of the Stagirite against any connection with the two condemnations. Attempts were made, in fact, to connect the condemnations with the Neoplatonic immanentism of John Scotus Eriugena (whose *Periphyseon* was also the object of various censures in the early years of the thirteenth century). Even highly intelligent theologians such as Albert the Great and Thomas Aquinas contributed to this interpretation of the incident, which was then emphasized by other representatives of the Dominican Order.

And indeed, on the basis of our modern reconstruction of events, David of Dinant does seem to have built his thought on an accentuated Neoplatonic immanentism. His pantheism sprang from his division of being into three fundamental elements: mind or *nous*, matter or *hylē*, and the separated essence or substance. In the final analysis all three are formal manifestations of the single, indivisible divine entity: while the essence is in fact God, mind is God as the subject and matter is God as the object of the formation of the essence, that is, of the single principle that carries out the many functions that give life and reality to everything that is.

As far, however, as the thought of Amalric of Bène is concerned, the inconsistency of connecting that thinking in any way with Eriugenism or other forms of Christian Platonism has today been demonstrated beyond any doubt. To the contrary, it is clear that the conceptual system of the Amalricians shows analogies with the theology of history that was widespread among the symbolist monks of the Germanic world (such men as Gerhoh of Reichersberg and Honorius Augustodunensis) and, above all, with the eschatological prophetism of Joachim of Fiore. Whether or not Amalric had any direct connection with Joachim, he did emphasize, but in an unrecognizable way, the longing for moral reform and cosmic renewal that are found in Joachimism, as he directly grafted God's action onto created action, something that is inherently alien to biblico-Christian wisdom.

According to this teaching, each of the divine Persons works in history separately from the other two: the Father acted first; then, until the present time, the Son has been acting; from now on the Spirit will act. The three periods correspond to the phases of a progressive self-revelation of God during which, in a process of universal incarnation, each of the divine Persons has manifested himself in several human creatures. Thus the Father has been incarnated in Abraham and the other patriarchs of the Old Testament, the Son in Christ and the other saints, the Holy Spirit in all those at the present time who believe in him. Incarnation is thus the common form of the relationship of God to humanity in the various phases of history. All human beings are God incarnate, and in the life journey of each the divinity of God's being can be perceived: the body of Christ is in every human being as it is in all bread, which is always eucharistic bread.

In a characteristically gnostic perspective, the salvation of human beings consists in knowledge of the truth, which at the present time means the revelation and incarnation of the Spirit who breathes in all, leading them to the fullness of self-knowledge, that is, to the realization that they are God. Paradise will consist of knowledge, hell of ignorance, and the duty of the believer in the present life is to struggle against error. Knowledge of the truth is, therefore, the real resurrection: Christ did not rise from the dead, nor will other human beings rise from the dead. Nor is there another world to which humanity can look forward, since the divine is in this world, and true resurrection takes place in this life and in the courage to accept the divinely inspired knowledge that enables us to recognize our divine being.

The Amalricians were skilled dialecticians who shored up their teaching by an exaggerated application of logical rules in support of a literal interpretation of the biblical texts they invoked. For example, when Paul says that human beings are saved when they acknowledge themselves to be members of Christ, the Amalricians interpreted this as referring to the duty believers have of recognizing in themselves the incarnated nature of God; and when the apostle proclaims that "God will be all in all things" (1 Cor 15:28), they deduced syllogistically from this formula their theory of a universal incarnation. It became clear that in both David of Dinant and Amalric an extremist linking of logic and theology led to or at least supported monism.

One contemporary theologian clearly realized how especially dangerous Amalric's methodology was, since all of his errors sprang from it. The theologian was Garnerius of Rochefort (d. after 1225), a Cistercian, abbot of Clairvaux until 1192 and then bishop of Langres, and author of an analytical refutation entitled *Response to the Amalricians*.

Not by chance does Garnerius see the eucharistic symbolism defended by the new heretics as descending from the error of Berengarius. Adopting a position not unlike that of Lanfranc of Pavia, he focuses his criticism on a denunciation of the excessive logicism that led the heretics to formulate their absurd teachings. Garnerius shows the absurdity of their method by demonstrating its ultimate consequences: when the Amalricians take literally the Pauline statement that "God will be all in all things," they ought not to call a halt in their deductions from it. Thus, since there is no change in God, the future is identical with the present and the past, so that God "is and has always been in all things"; therefore "God is stone in the stone, and Godino in Godino," and "Godino is to be worshiped not only with expressions of veneration but also with expressions of adoration, since he is God." And "even the mole and the bat" are to be adored, "since God is a bat in the bat and a mole in the mole."

Garnerius was a prudent laborer in the theological workshop of his day; that is, he does not turn his critique into a call for renouncing scientific method in theology, but instead, in face of the pride of the new masters, he recalls the ancient rule that the arts are subordinate to the truth of the faith. Aristotelean philosophy can help us to understand and correct the error of the heretics. The latter do not understand that in using the verb "to be" they ought to be able to distinguish between a causal presence and a substantial presence. As a result they fail to realize that God's presence in all things is that of a formal cause, not an efficient cause; consequently, the divine causality as such remains transcendent and separated from its effects. This is a well-chosen indication of how the "new" philosophy can be used to overcome errors and not to produce them.

Garnerius therefore proposes a methodology of his own, which he considers to be more solid than the overly confident logical approach taken by too many of his contemporaries. He focuses attention on the formal meticulousness that marks the disciplines of the quadrivium and proposes to find in these an instrument of proof that is an alternative to logic and grammar; the mind can grasp the solidity of this new method through its immediate perception of the visual images analyzed in geometry. In this idea, which runs through some of his *Sermons*, especially the twenty-second on the Trinity, we can hear an extraordinary echo of recently suggested theological methodologies such as the axiomatic method of Alan of Lille and the visionary method of Joachim. For geometrical propositions reflect in their inherent necessity the traces of the divine Trinity, and geometrical images allow the mind to have even a visual perception of these traces; this is especially true of triangular figures, the truth of which arises out of the reduction of a plurality of lines to the unity of the figure.

In short, it was only right that philosophy as a whole, including physics and logic, should begin to show its usefulness at the very time when it was returning to life in the lecture halls of the schools and enjoying all the dignity of being a specific, autonomous area of certain knowledge—provided it accept being adopted as a servant, that is, as a handmaid of theology.

II. The Encounter with Greco-Arabic and Jewish Philosophical and Theological Thought

In one perspective the history of medieval thought is the history of many successive transfers of studies (*translationes studiorum*)—or, perhaps, of a single continuous transfer of the knowledge possessed by the ancient world, a transfer that began during the same years that saw the disintegration of the imperial institution in the West and the definitive interruption of cultural contacts with the Greek East. It began with the work of Boethius, whose translations of and commentaries on the books of the *Organon* provided the Latin West with its first and, for a long time, its only direct contact with Aristotelean philosophy.

But in fact the historical process of the medieval transmission of philosophical, scientific, and theological knowledge was a segmented and complex one that was prolonged over time and progressive, even if discontinuous. Even in the works of the Fathers of the Church, and then in those of the late antique encyclopedists, the abridgment and anthologization of the cultural documents of antiquity often had the further function of preserving those documents and transmitting them to later generations. This work was then continued and intensified by new discoveries and translations of texts, first during the Carolingian period, then in the Ottonian revival, and later still during the mature development of intellectual activity in the urban schools.

But the most important and effective rebirth of culture in the Middle Ages was the one that, from the beginning of the thirteenth century on, seemed to alter radically the face of Latin intellectual civilization and imprint on it new, indelible features. However, this final important instance of cultural transmission in the Middle Ages would not be comprehensible if we did not grasp how it was the result of the interaction of other historical processes. I am referring to the earlier transferrals of philosophical wisdom that took place at various times as classical Greek culture was transplanted from the late Roman world to the Near East and the ancient Middle East, first during the Sassanid civilization and then, in an even more radical implantation, into Islamic culture.

When the school of Athens was shut down in 529 by decree of Justinian, the last Greek Neoplatonists (Simplicius, Damascius, and their companions) found a new home in the Mesopotamian city of Haran. Here they opened a study center at which they continued to use and copy the basic texts of classical philosophical thought, especially those of Aristotle and Plato. The Arab conquest of Syria and Persia in the seventh century brought Islamic civilization into contact with this pagan philosophical heritage.

One result was the start of an enthusiastic work of translating these texts, often involving two steps: from Greek to Persian and from Persian to Arabic. The activity of translating was subsequently extended to include other texts that were tracked down and imported directly from Byzantine territories: philosophical books, of course, but also scientific, mathematical, astronomical, and medical writings. This eastern transfer of studies, which was fostered by the political consolidation of the Islamic state in a definitively nonmigratory form, reached its high point in the establishment of the House of Wisdom in Baghdad under Caliph al-Mamun (who reigned from 811 to 833): the House consisted of a large library and an attached center for the copying and translation of books.

This mass of scientific and philosophical knowledge from the classical world was studied, commented on, and often reworked and made to include aspects and elements of religious culture and Arabic anthropology; it then spread throughout the Islamic world, from the Persian East to the Iberian peninsula. It remained, however, a specialized patrimony reserved for an elite of skilled men of letters. One reason for this was that its origin in a world alien to Islam caused traditionalist theologians to regard it with suspicion; many of them soon showed an open and radical hostility to what they regarded as contamination of revealed truth by philosophico-scientific wisdom. As a result, rational study or, to give it a generic name, philosophy (which even kept the Grecizing name of *falsafa*) retained in the Muslim world its original lay character, which marked it as a study focused on specific areas and having nothing to do with the object of faith.

In the Islamic world, then, from the very beginning, purpose, approaches, and expository procedures differentiated philosophical reflection from meditation on the contents of the faith. This created a cultural situation very different from that typical of early medieval Latin thought, which ever since the patristic age had been characterized by a ceaseless search for a harmony between understanding and faith and for the permeation of each by the other. In Islam, rational study investigated the finite, visible world, took experience as its starting point, proceeded by way of inexorable demonstration, and respected the rules governing the logico-mathematical codification of thought. The knowledge of faith had for its first and exclusive object the omnipotent will of God. Faith sought evidence of this will in the sacred text, the Qur'an, which was the prophetic word dictated by God himself. Faith was also guided by the principle of authority in that it respected the inspiration of the Prophet and his first followers and interpreters.

It is clearly advantageous that we understand and properly judge the significance and consequences of this situation, which was typical of the medieval Arab world. One reason is that we can then gauge the disruptive effects the introduction of such a different view of the relationship between faith and reason and therefore of the importance and autonomy of the two areas of study and research had on the world of western culture. This introduction occurred in the second half of the twelfth century, when the transfer of studies to the Islamic world crossed the Pyrenees and spread its contents at an increasingly rapid pace throughout the Latin-speaking Christian world.

1. Islamic Theology or kalam

What we call Islamic "theology" was in fact not thought of by its founders and cultivators as a "science of the faith," since the religion of Muhammad claims to be a wisdom accessible to all and allowing no disagreement or variant interpretation of its elementary teachings. In its original approach, and especially in its opposition to Christianity, Islam offered itself to believers as a faith uncomplicated by mysteries that can cause doubts or puzzlement in their minds and feed a desire for some further kind of intelligibility or rational explanation. Islamic theological knowledge, called *kalam*, is therefore primarily an apologetical exposition of revealed truth and the law contained in it. Its main objective is a true understanding of the foundation, namely, the divine unity (which is the first and constitutive tenet of the Islamic faith, *tawhid* in Arabic). This understanding allows for proofs and persuasive arguments, which are based, however, not on external means but simply on the sacred text.

The *kalam* came into existence at Medina in the first decades of the spread and study of the Qur'an, that is, in a country, Arabia, that had no prior cultural tradition. Its setting explains why it developed in complete independence of other forms of knowledge and, in any case, drew into its own orbit of influence the first disciplines to be developed in Arabic civilization, such as grammar, rhetoric, and jurisprudence. From the very outset these studies were directed respectively to the reading of the Book, the appreciation of its beauty, and the correct systematization of the moral principles taught in it.

Even during the first period of the formation of the *kalam* there was, however, a certain openness to a constructive acceptance of suggestions coming from the other two great monotheistic religions (Christianity and Judaism), which were likewise based on the communication of a written revelation. This was true at least to the extent that these other religions did not contradict the foundations of Islam; examples of acceptability were the story of creation and accounts of eschatological events. The encounter especially with the Christian religion and the forms of theological study that had developed within it intensified with the installation of the Ummayad caliphate and the transfer of its capital to Damascus in Syria in the seventh/eighth centuries.

Islam was a universal religion and, like Christianity but unlike Judaism, was characterized from the outset by a politico-religious totalitarianism in which temporal rule was not something different from the spiritual leadership given to believers. Being universal, Islam contained the idea of a "holy war," that is, the mission, binding permanently on every believer, of extending this true religion to the entire world. But this holy war also included an obligation to promote the development of political and social conditions required for the conversion of infidels and not to impose conversion by force.

As a result, especially in relation to the followers of the "religions of the Book" (Christians and Jews), the Muslim state practiced tolerance, but only relatively: these other religionists had to accept a state of juridical and economic inferiority and subjection to Muslims and were not to proselytize in any way. Especially in the early centuries, these demands led in fact to a subjection of nonbelievers that was so intolerable as to amount in practice to forced mass conversions. Later on, however, the principle of religious coexistence finally won out, favoring especially the Jewish communities settled in Muslim territories (these were by their own tradition not inclined to proselytism), but granting a relative cultural autonomy to Christians as well. As we know, during the Ummayad period John Damascene lived and worked both in Damascus and in the Holy Land; in addition, some Christians and Jews became important persons and officials of the court.

Thus a degree of interreligious dialogue was established, though this was always under the political and ideological domination of Islam. The dialogue consisted in part of some reciprocal scrutiny of the participants and in part of lively apologetical debates. These last made an important contribution to the development of the constitutive doctrines of the *kalam* in the area of theological ideas common to all three confessions.

Especially the encounter with the speculative mentality of Christian theologians and the necessity of being armed against the danger of heterodox infiltrations into Islam's defense of its revelation soon led Muslims to feel the need of developing theoretically based justifications of their faith. This in turn played an important part in producing a systematic and argumentative form of the *kalam*. This tendency grew stronger after the transfer of the religious and political center of the caliphate to Baghdad on the Tigris and the shift from the Umayyad dynasty to the Abbasid in the eighth century. The shift marked the transformation of the Islamic world into a multiethnic civilization founded on an equality, based solely on the faith, of all believers, whether Arabs or not. In this new phase of their work some practitioners of the *kalam* began to look with interest at the nonreligious culture and gradually to take over such intellectual tools as seemed useful for their work. Thus the Islamic *falsafa* came into contact first with grammar and law (Arabic *fiqh*) and then with logic (as an instrument of knowledge) and metaphysics.

The theologians who, to give credence to their theses, courageously used tools of thought derived from settings alien to religious piety took the name of "Mu'tazilites." They formed a broad religious and intellectual movement that was active especially during the ninth century in Basra and Baghdad. The movement promoted the introduction into Islamic religious thought of some fundamental theoretical positions and ideas in the area of morality and thereby made an important contribution to the translation of *kalam* into an organized system of knowledge, the essential nucleus of which was the principle of the absolute unity and transcendence of God (that is, the *tawhid*).

This principle was known by way of a negative theology in which all the divine attributes of an anthropological or material kind were excluded, even those of which the Qur'an speaks and that are to be understood as having only a symbolic value. From this first principle further fundamental theological theses followed logically: the created nature of the divine word (since God is immutable and the Qur'an exists in time); the radical assertion of the justice of God, who wills and does only what is good; eternal reward or eternal punishment from God for the actions of human beings, who alone are responsible for the goodness or wickedness of these actions; the obligation of believers to condemn evil explicitly and publicly.

The Mu'tazilites were often rigid and intransigent defenders of this theology of theirs, especially against the "literalists" who held fast to the simple traditional interpretation of the data of the faith and were opposed to raising subtle speculative questions. Beginning in the second half of the ninth century this attitude of the Mu'tazilites gave rise to numerous tensions that often led to an open rejection of their teachings; as a result the movement was weakened and scattered until it was finally exhausted. In the generations that followed, moderate theologians promoted a middle ground between radical orthodoxy and some of the Mu'tazilite positions; this shift was especially fruitful in further developments of *kalam* and in its theoretical maturation.

An outstanding figure here was al-Ashari of Basra (d. ca. 932), the real founder of the theological teaching of orthodox Islam. His principal work,

Explanation of the Principles of Religion, takes a prudent middle ground between an exaggerated literalism and the inflexible theoretical and moral views of the Mu'tazilites: the divine attributes are real, but of a different kind than human attributes; the Qur'an is the eternal and uncreated word of God, but its historical manifestation in ink and letters is created; sin is necessarily punished, but the divine mercy can lessen the application of the divine justice. As a result of al-Ashari's work, *kalam* moved to an important degree toward an apologetical and moderately rationalized explanation of the revealed data. Al-Ashari's thought, although not exempt from challenges, was destined by its moderate and conciliatory character to become widespread during the tenth and eleventh centuries, especially in the East and in Africa.

The names of other important scholars are associated with further stages in this ongoing development of Islamic theological wisdom. It is appropriate to mention at least al-Baquillani, likewise a native of Basra, who contributed to the introduction of atomist teaching into Islamic thought, a teaching corrected, however, in light of the dogma of creation and used to explain both the efficacy and the absolute freedom of the divine omnipotence. The atomist approach to the created world made it possible to adopt an occasionalism that denied efficacy to any second cause while attributing every action to the first cause alone, which is God. A similar but more penetrating constructive introduction of speculative elements into *kalam* came with the thinking of al-Giuwayni (d. 1085) and then, above all, in that of his immediate disciple, al-Ghazali (d. 1111), who was beyond a doubt the most representative and insightful exponent of medieval Arabic theological thought.

The thinker whom the Latins would later call Algazel (or Algazali) was born at Tus in eastern Persia and trained in *fiqh* and *kalam* under al-Giuwayni at Nishapur. After a period of youthful skepticism he turned to *falsafa*, but as an intermediate stage in a personal journey that would lead him, by way of a complex religious experience, to the attainment of pure ecstatic contemplation; this for him was the ultimate and exclusive goal of all human study, including even *kalam*. He became a lecturer in Baghdad, then a hermit devoted to mystical contemplation in Syria, and then a pilgrim in Palestine and Arabia. He then returned to teach at Nishapur, but finally retired to a hermit's life in his native Tus, where he died with a reputation for great holiness.

For al-Ghazali, *kalam* is knowledge that has God for its object: God in himself, in his attributes, in his actions, and in his prophets, and that is based on what Muhammad taught on these subjects. This knowledge is not faith nor is it, like faith, sufficient for salvation. It is, however, necessary, relatively speaking, in the way in which remedies are necessary for the sick. It is therefore not to be transmitted to simple believers, who have no need of it, or to unbelievers and heretics, for whom rational discussion is useless and only strengthens their stubbornness. *Kalam* is indeed useful, on the other hand, for good believers who are in difficulties due to intellectual doubts and must be preserved from heretical errors. It is also useful for those unbelievers who are well-disposed toward the truth and can be taught by persuasive rational discourse. This curative aspect of theological thought was brought out in his *Book on Moderation in Belief* and then explained in detail in another famous work of his with the expressive title *The Rejuvenation of the Sciences of Religion*.

Al-Ghazali's writings are truly treatises on dogma; in them religious thought based on revelation takes the form of an organized body of knowledge that has a specific place in the global assemblage of human knowledge. But the author is convinced that the most important part of this religious thought is what he calls the science of "the unveiling," which is a pure knowledge of the divine object in a mystical contemplation that is not communicable through lectures or books. He has, therefore, a decidedly negative attitude toward any overly unbiased exercise of a *kalam* based on free rational inquiry; the latter, in his view, leads only to a quarrelsome curiosity and empty discussions.

In fact, in his several writings al-Ghazali displays different attitudes toward human rationality, even in relation to his personal development in the search for truth. He often speaks of it in a way that borders on contempt; at other times, in a mood of greater moderation, he is himself disposed to use the tools of logic in order to demonstrate the existence of God *a posteriori*, distinguishing that existence from the modes of being of finite things, and to analyze the reality of the divine attributes. But any such use is always accompanied by the conviction that any intellectual grasp of the divine truth is secondary to God's own direct communication of that truth. So, then, his contribution to the history and development of *kalam* consists in his restrictive reminder of the real tasks and areas of competence proper to theologians. These scholars are to use logical reasoning only as a useful aid in defending the truths of the faith; they are never to yield to the temptation of arrogantly seeking to make their own opinions prevail.

It was not by chance, then, that this writer's most successful work was his *The Self-Destruction* (or *Incoherence*) *of the Philosophers*, in which he directly attacks the proponents of a *falsafa* that claims to be not a tool but an autonomous knowledge of truth. The critique takes the form of twenty questions covering the three fundamental problems of metaphysics (the soul, the world, God) and showing that when Greek philosophy is used to assert rather than simply explain it leads to conclusions irreconcilable with religious truth and is utterly incapable of confirming the faith. But the defectiveness and therefore the falsity of such philosophical theses emerge even more clearly in the fact that when these theses are brought face-to-face they refute each other and cancel each other out. Appealing to a juridical principle constantly used by Islamic theologians, al-Ghazali maintains that an exposition of doctrine is evidently false if it contains contradictions and internal inconsistencies. This argument suffices to refute and thus to show the godlessness of all the teachings the philosophers tried to formulate on religious matters.

As a preparation for the writing of his *Self-Destruction* the author also composed a synthetic presentation of the philosophical doctrines he intended to refute; this he titled *The Intentions of the Philosophers* and circulated as the first part of his work. In 1145, as we know, only a part of *The Intentions* was translated into Latin and circulated in the West under the title *The Metaphysics of al-Ghazali*. But it lacked the prologue that explained the introductory character of the work, with the result that by a strange irony of history al-Ghazali was regarded as a supporter of teachings that he explained only in order subsequently to demonstrate their falsity.

2. Arabic Philosophy

A. The Formation of *Falsafa* from al-Kindi to al-Farabi

Al-Ghazali regarded the philosophy he attacked in his *Self-Destruction* as a corrupt totality to which many doctrinal influences contributed, all of them originating in ancient Greek wisdom. In fact, the main work done by cultivators of philosophy in the Arabic world (the so-called "Hellenizers" or *falasifa*, that is, "philosophers") was to develop a syncretistic reading of the most reliable information gained from many ancient Greek sources. It is obvious that this procedure continued the synthesizing activity the late antique Neoplatonists had already carried on, based on the principle of "harmony" among witnesses to the truth and, in particular, between Plato and Aristotle, the two greatest philosophers of antiquity. This principle allowed them to develop a systematic conception of truth that could, by means of coherent doctrines, explain both the world of visible things and the world of intelligible realities. Clearly, then, al-Ghazali's critique was aimed in part at rejecting the internal unity of that synthesis.

The philosophical library available to Arabic scholars showed a conspicuous presence of the witnesses to Neoplatonic thought. In addition to having the collected writings of Plato and Aristotle, these scholars rather quickly gained access, in Arabic translations, to other important works of metaphysics such as the *Enneads* of Plotinus and the *Elements of Theology* of Proclus, and then to the treatises and commentaries of many other exponents of the late Platonic and Aristotelean tradition.

Of the Platonic dialogues, the special success the *Timaeus* enjoyed even in the Islamic world favored the acceptance of the idea of a fundamental distinction between the visible and imperfect world of bodies and the intelligible world of the eternal exemplars. From Aristotle's *The Soul*, which the Arabic *falasifa* read through the commentary by Alexander of Aphrodisias, they derived the idea of the possibility of introducing Aristotelean psychology into the hierarchic conception, Platonic in origin, of the cosmic distribution of the heavenly intelligences, which transmit knowledge from degree to degree. They identified the agent intellect of which Aristotle speaks in the third book of *The Soul* with the ultimate separate intelligence, which is one and the same for all human individuals, distinct from their individual intellects, and not subject to becoming. From the combination of these suggestions the Arabic writers soon conceived and circulated a complicated synthesis of physics and metaphysics that resulted, strangely enough, from the harmonization of Platonic and Aristotelean ideas and principles.

The majority of the translations and adaptations of Neoplatonic texts that helped to bolster this philosophical syncretism came from the "circle" of scholars led by al-Kindi (d. ca. 865), one of the first important teachers active in Baghdad during the period when the Abbasid civilization reached its intellectual maturity. It is very likely that this same environment produced two compilations of Neoplatonic metaphysics that circulated under the name of Aristotle. One was the *Theology of Aristotle*, of which two versions are known (one shorter and more verbose, the other longer); it is in fact a paraphrase of the fourth, fifth, and sixth *Enneads* of Plotinus. The false attribution of the work promoted the grafting of a systematico-hierarchic explanation of the derivation of the multiple from God onto the physico-teleological conception of the divine in Book Lambda of Aristotle's *Metaphysics*.

The other compilation was the *Book on Causes* or *Aristotle's Discourse on the Pure Good* (especially valued in the West, where it would be known as the *Book on Causes*). This work combined texts of varied origins (Plotinus, the *Theology of Aristotle*, mentioned above, and sometimes even Pseudo-Dionysius), but the *Elements of Theology* by Proclus played the dominant role. This work thus contributed to the spread of the conviction that the separated intelligible substances existed and had a causal and mediating function.

First Philosophy, al-Kindi's principal work, which he dedicated to Caliph al-Mutasim, begins with a defense of *falsafa* that seeks to bring out the nature of unified knowledge, which is basically directed toward knowledge of suprasensible and intelligible truth insofar as such knowledge is permitted to the human race. The author's exposition of this teaching in the course of the work makes his intentions clear: these come down to a desire to outline, with the help of classical speculation, the basic rational consequences of the theological assertion of the *tawhid*.

Accordingly, the first Cause is the sole and unchangeable source of all the movement in the universe, beginning (there is here an obvious correction of Greek thought, due probably to the influence of John Philoponus) with the very first movement of beings, namely, the passage from nonbeing to actual being. Since, then, the divine principle is utterly simple and absolutely one, it is in its totality causal and therefore also creative. By the very fact that they are moved, created-caused beings are multiple: that is, their unity is not inherent, but is born of their limitation and from comparison with other units. The first caused being is the first intellectual principle, which, since it is capable of thinking, contains within itself the intelligible models of all things. It is not possible to show a direct influence of al-Kindi on the thought of al-Farabi or Avicenna, but there is no doubt that the combination of Aristotelean theology and Neoplatonism effected by al-Kindi's "circle" produced the essential frame of reference for Arabic philosophical study, at least down to Averroes.

The synthesis of philosophical causality and creationism is likewise the dominant element in the thinking of al-Farabi (d. 950). This author came from the region of Farab in Turkestan; he was active as a teacher of logic, first at Baghdad and then in Syria at Aleppo and Damascus, where he seems to have lived a secluded life as a mystic (*sufi*). Later Arabic sources regarded him as the "second Master," and inferior therefore only to Aristotle. In a book titled *The Agreement of the Opinions of the Two Wise Men, the Divine Plato and Aristotle*, al-Farabi (Alfarabi or Alfarabius to the Latins) continued the work of showing the fundamental unity of Greek thought.

Al-Farabi focused his attention chiefly on the problem of explaining the origin of the world. Following an interpretation of the *Timaeus* that was widely held in the Islamic world, he was convinced that Plato thought the universe had begun in time and was therefore created by an intelligent cause. When he found it necessary to harmonize this thesis with Aristotle's denial of a temporal beginning of movement (in his work on *Heaven*), he confidently told his readers that Aristotle's real view was that both time and the world were produced and began simultaneously; there was therefore no time prior to the world, even one created by God. Al-Farabi argues for the correctness of this interpretation on the basis of other works of Aristotle, in particular the *Physics* and, significantly, the (pseudo-Aristotelean) *Theology*.

The agreement thus reached between the theologies of Aristotle and Plato was in practice the clear sign of a now-achieved syncretistic assimilation of Greek metaphysics, which was not only translated into a way of thinking and of inspiring scientific and philosophical studies, but also had now been definitively turned into an organized doctrinal whole. On the basis of this unity, al-Farabi, in his *Catalogue of the Sciences* (known to the Latins as *On the Sciences*), proposes a reordering of Aristotle's division of the scientific disciplines and an adaptation of these to Islamic culture. But the basic lines of this al-Farabian organic *falsifa* are clearest in his masterwork, the treatise on *The Opinions of the Inhabitants of the Perfect City*, an original reinterpretation of Plato's *Republic* as adapted to Islam's conception of the politico-religious order.

This ideal society is founded on a harmonious distribution of productive, moral, and intellectual functions that allows the human community to imitate the harmony existing among the separated intelligences, which are themselves more or less perfect depending on their greater or lesser likeness to God. The citizens of this ideal society accept the theological ideas of the philosophers, which offer the best explanation of the foundations of their religion and especially of *tawhid*. The uniformity of the teaching of the *falasifa* starts, as in al-Kindi, from the single premise of the acknowledgment of the first Cause as the "first existent" and source of the existence of everything else that exists. But this basic identity of the foundations of theology with those of metaphysics imposes on philosophers the necessity of explaining the derivation of other beings and of universal movement through the distribution and sequence of second causes, without compromising the perfect unity, immutability, and permanence of their source.

Al-Farabi completely changes the terms of the problem as he advances a subtle and penetrating argument in which he shows how the very fact of the derivation of multiplicity proves the simplicity and self-sufficiency of the first Cause, since these characteristics cannot but be attached to an inexhaustible productive power. As Aristotle claims, the fundamental characteristic of the divinity is that it is an intelligible being because it contains no matter. But that which is always and only intelligible can only be intelligible in act, and a purely actual intelligible reality is also a pure act of intellection, that is, it is intelligent. Aristotle's God-who-is-thought is thus wonderfully identical with the Neoplatonists' God-who-is-One, for inasmuch as God is self-sufficient he need not think something other than himself in order to be Thought, but is the Thought of his own essence, that is, of the best possible intelligible object, and as such lives a life of eternal blessedness. But inasmuch as it is perfect, such Thought cannot but reach out beyond its own essence and communicate the perfect result of its thinking, that is, its unity.

So, then, as the source of light sheds light on everything around it without any diminution of itself, the Thought-Unity of God, by the very fact of being what it is, produces the many derived unities, the existence of which adds nothing to its perfection but all of which "proceed" from its essence. And while the essence of God, as such, exists simply and wholly in act, all derived beings actually exist only in an always incomplete fulfillment of their essences. Here we see the first statement of the distinction between essence and existence that, when filtered through Avicenna, would considerably influence Latin theological thinking in the thirteenth century.

As for al-Kindi, so for al-Farabi the first created reality is the first Intellect, an immaterial substance that is distinct from God because it accepts the thinkableness of something other than itself and therefore the possibility of multiplicity in the sense of potential ideas. But the fact that, as compared with previous philosophers, al-Farabi emphasizes God's role as intelligent being allows him to conceive the entire movement within creation as a reception of knowledge from God and a movement toward God as the ultimate object of this knowledge. Every intelligence lesser than God thinks its own essence and, in doing so, thinks God from whom it derives, but insofar as it thinks God, its own thought becomes an emanating source and gives rise to a further intelligible substance that is inferior to it.

The result is the hierarchical distribution of a series of perfections that decrease because the further effects of intellectual activity are more and more distant from the first Cause. Inferior intellects in their turn think themselves and tend to imitate the perfection of the divine thought; by thinking, they in turn give rise to other intelligibles and, by subordinating these to their efficacious knowledge, move the bodies that are the result of their ability to produce beings, namely, the various heavenly spheres; then on to the lowest degree of matter, which is the ultimate effect of the creative and conserving power of the first Thought, because this lowest degree is not gifted with the ability to know.

Even the human intelligence is subject to a similar degradation of its cognitive efficacy; al-Farabi speaks of this in a *Letter* on the intellect, a text imported into the Latin West under the title of *The Intellect and What Is Understood*. Basing his thinking on the interpretation of Aristotle's *The Soul* by Alexander of Aphrodisias, al-Farabi distinguishes within the intellectual soul: the possible intellect, understood as the propensity of the soul to know; the intellect in act, that is, the activity of acquiring new knowledge; and the acquired intellect, which translates such acts of knowing into intelligible representations and entrusts these to memory.

He then subordinates the functioning of these faculties, and therefore the insertion of actual knowing into the potentiality of the soul, to a separated agent or active intellect, which is the last of the separated intelligences (and therefore the intelligence that presides over the heavenly sphere of the moon) and acts on all human souls as the common efficient cause of their knowing. This teaching ensures the objectivity of the true knowledge acquired by individual human minds; it also provides adequate grounds for maintaining the immortality of individual souls because, unlike the passive intellect, the intellect in act and the acquired intellect are true sources of knowledge and therefore intelligible, incorruptible realities.

B. METAPHYSICS AND THEOLOGY: AVICENNA (IBN SINA)

Ibn Sina (d. 1037), whose name would be Latinized as Avicenna, set forth his theological ideas in many writings, but above all in a special section on the "science of God" in his major work, *Book on Healing*. This section was translated into Latin and circulated under the title *The Metaphysics of Avicenna*, thus guaranteeing it would be known to the masters of western scholasticism and exert an exceptional influence on them. Avicenna was born in Afshana near Bukhara, where he was appointed court physician at an early age; he later became a teacher of the sciences and law and was then given a variety of public and political missions in various cities of Persia. He was a man of vast and many-sided learning; his *Canon of Medicine* played an important role in the history of the sciences.

The *Book on Healing* is an imposing encyclopedia of philosophy and science that essentially takes the form of an elaborate paraphrase of the writings of the *falasifa*, and of Aristotle in particular. It is divided into four parts dealing respectively with logic, physics, mathematics, and first philosophy or metaphysics. The author openly declares his debt to al-Farabi for his understanding of metaphysics, but his exposition of it is a great deal more organized (following the Aristotelean model). He endeavors, moreover, to introduce some thematic order:

the object of metaphysics, the doctrine on substance and its predicates, and the doctrine on causality.

The first Cause appears, therefore, at the end of this course of studies as a first principle that must be postulated to avoid an infinite regress that would jeopardize its efficacity. (If there were no first Cause, it would be impossible to traverse the infinite series of causes needed in order for the causal activity to reach a given cause before the latter could itself produce an effect.) It is at this point that Avicenna, too, is faced with the necessity of solving the problem, raised by religious truth, of the passage of second causes from nonbeing to being: that is, the problem of creation. For if in fact the first Cause is essentially and therefore necessarily causative, how can that which exists emerge from nonbeing, that is, from a state, prior to being, in which God is not causing?

Avicenna's solution to this problem consists of introducing into theology the Aristotelean distinction between potency and act. If God is the source of being and the point reached in the regress from cause to cause, then he is a necessary being, because his existence as first Cause is the very existence of the necessity of being, and as such he is necessarily in act. A creature, on the other hand, is "that which acquires being from another" and therefore is not necessarily in act. It is a possible being, whose essence is this very possibility and whose existence becomes actual through the efficient causality of the necessary principle. Every being after God is therefore a possible being that becomes actual through creation and in this way becomes necessary (that is, it is necessarily what it actually is) due to its relationship with the first Cause.

This distinction between essence and existence or between the (potential and therefore possible) quiddity of each thing and its actual (that is, necessary) existence applies to all creatures, but not to God, whose simplicity requires that his essence be understood as that which necessarily exists. In contrast, whatever does not necessarily exist is composed of a quiddity that is possible (or not necessary) and an existence that is necessary, being made such as the effect of the causality exercised by the divine necessity. The fact that nothing can be predicated of God follows from his simplicity, which in turn is guaranteed by the identity of his essence and existence. Since he does not have a quiddity that is distinct from his existence, there is no antecedent genus that can be predicated of him; he cannot, therefore, be placed in any category (substance, quality, quantity, place, time) or be made part of any pairs of opposites (like-different, true-false, and so on). Consequently one can speak of God only by denying any and every likeness to the being of creatures.

Like his predecessors al-Kindi and al-Farabi, Avicenna thinks of God, insofar as he is pure act, as a pure act of thought. For since intelligibility is the condition of everything exempt from matter, that is, from potentiality, that which is fully and necessarily in act will be perfectly intelligible (and therefore pure intellect). A pure intellect does not depend on any intelligible object outside itself and is therefore itself the object of its own intellection. In God, then, intelligence does not involve any division or multiplication, and the fact that he is a cause is not the result of an activity outside himself, but rather of a drawing of the universe to himself as to the goal of every creaturely desire. But the intellect of the necessary being cannot ignore all the beings that derive their existence from his necessity: Avicenna's first principle (unlike Aristotle's disinterested divine thought) knows all things in his own necessity. He knows them, therefore, in a universal way, not as particular individuals that exist separately from himself, but as effects linked in their existence to the chain of causes that produces them and, therefore, in the final analysis to the knowledge the ultimate Cause has of them. God knows things as universals in himself.

As in al-Farabi but in a superior way, in Avicenna's metaphysics the Aristotelean model harmonizes perfectly with Neoplatonic emanationism when the author turns to the explanation of how created beings are derived from God. God did not "decide" to create, for that would mean a dependence on external goals and would imply multiplicity. But neither did he create because he was "free" to do so or because in some sense he "had to" do so. For his essence is in fact identical with his necessity and his necessity with his essence. God creates because he is God, and good springs from him in an outflow that is as inexorable and inevitable as it is absolutely unconditioned, since it is not caused by another. This means, further, that the act of creating cannot take place without God's being aware of it and giving his assent, because his knowing and willing are identical with the simplicity of his essence. In simple terms, in God there is no opposition between freedom and necessity or between knowledge and non-knowledge or between will and compulsion, because there are no creaturely distinctions in God.

In contrast, all second causes, which are necessary as causes but possible as creatures, are causes only because God makes them necessary, that is, makes them pass from possible existence to necessary actual existence. The first effect produced by the first principle can only be a first Intellect that is pure and completely separated from matter and is identical with its own intelligible content, which is to say with the intellectual activity of all lesser beings. This first Intellect gazes upon God, who makes it necessary, and as a result knows itself as such and generates a lesser intelligence, that is, the second Intellect, which derives from its generator the necessity/actuality of its own being and, seeing itself to be created, realizes that it is capable of making actual something outside itself. This second Intellect then generates a first Soul in order that this may ensoul the object of its intellection. A heavenly body is then made subject to the efficacious causality of the Soul; this body moves with a perfect (that is, circular) motion in which it tends toward the Soul.

In a progressive descent through the hierarchical order each intelligence, knowing itself first as necessary and then as possible, generates a soul and a heavenly body animated by it, that is, a heavenly sphere that responds to the act generating it by moving toward it. In Avicennian Neoplatonism, as the author continues to carry out al-Farabi's plan, there emerges a prodigious cosmic architecture of causal mediations consisting of ten successive intellects, each of which generates a soul and a body, and leading to the final emanation, the one that governs the heavenly sphere of the Moon. The intelligence and separated active intellect of this sphere continually cause the imperfect, inferior intelligences of individual human beings to move from potency to acquired actuality.

Finally, corporeal, visible, and non-intelligent beings, which are placed in the sublunary world and subject to the realm of accidents and of continual change, exist only as possible and not as necessary. Thus the body, even that of a human being, is a pure potentiality that is destined to decompose and leave behind it only the intelligible immortality of the acquired intellect.

C. THE AGREEMENT OF PHILOSOPHY WITH RELIGION: AVERROES (IBN RUSHD)

It is by now obvious that Avicenna's thought had to become the direct object of theological attack and the accusation of "ungodliness," which was made against him by al-Ghazali at the beginning of the twelfth century in his *The Self-Destruction of the Philosophers*. But this controversy had a decisive effect on the subsequent development of *falsafa*, because as a result of the accusation of having improperly intruded, with their method and conceptual tools, into the sphere of truth having to do strictly with revelation, the *falasifa* thenceforth devoted themselves to establishing for their speculation and studies an object and area of investigation that were autonomous and strictly distinct from those of faith. Their ultimate intention was to prove that reason and religion could not possibly be contradictory, being knowledges of different orders, and that therefore in the final analysis they were in basic agreement.

Perhaps because of the theological authority al-Ghazali enjoyed in all the eastern territories of Islam, it was not by chance that the first works illustrating this new development were by writers working in the Iberian world, that is, in the independent emirate and later caliphate of Cordoba that was ruled from 756 on by the surviving branch of the Umayyads. For example, Ibn Baggia of Saragossa (d. 1138), whom the Latins would later call Avempace, wrote a famous ethico-political treatise, *The Rule of the Solitary*. In it he defended mystical knowledge as the goal of a journey begun by rational activity, a journey that ends, at the height of the abstractive ascent and in agreement with the aspirations of the speculative religious current known as Sufism, in a cognitive union of the wise person with the separated agent Intellect.

Especially significant, next, was the contribution of Abu Bakr ibn Tufayl (d. 1185; known to the Latins as Abubacer); he was born near Granada but moved to Morocco and the court of the Almohads, who in the second half of the century united the territories of western Islam into a great empire. His *Letter of Hayy ibn Yaqzan* takes its inspiration from a short novel by Ibn Sina about the same personage. Abu Bakr makes him the hero of a real "philosophical novel about education," the author's intention being to set forth in an allegorical but persuasive way the great Persian philosopher's "philosophy of enlightenment." Hayy is born on a deserted island from clay heated by the sun, without father or mother; he grows up, having been nursed by a gazelle, and quickly comes to know things by developing his natural faculties. After discovering the truths of physics and the order of the universe, he solves the problems of metaphysics and reaches the heights of mystical intuition in his desire to be united with the agent Intellect.

In the second part of the novel Hayy meets a devout theologian named Asal who shows him that the discoveries he has made using only his natural faculties are in perfect harmony with the contents of the Qur'an. The two men then plan to make known to others the results of their studies and the great mystery of the complete convergence of reason and faith. The effort is useless, however, since the highest truths cannot be grasped by all human beings and simple believers must be molded solely by the letter of revelation.

Philosopher Ibn Rushd of Cordoba (d. 1198; known to the Latin world as Averroes) was a physician at the court of the Almohads. He above all others deserves praise for trying to direct the question of the relations between philosophical knowledge and knowledge based on the revealed word toward a concordist solution that he offers as certain and "decisive" in his *Decisive Treatise on the Accord between Religion and Philosophy*. This short work is part of a series of monographs about which the Latins knew little, since only one of them was translated and this at a late date (1328); this work, titled *The Self-Destruction of the Self-Destruction*, is an answer to al-Ghazali's criticisms of philosophy. The successful spread of Ibn Rushd's thought, especially in the Latin world, was due to his great commentary on the entire body of Aristotle's writings (except for the *Politics*), a work that caused the scholastics to call him "the Commentator" *par excellence* on the thinker known to them simply as "the Philosopher."

The task of writing these commentaries, with their explicit purpose of making known Aristotle's authentic thought, was officially entrusted to Averroes by Caliph al-Mumin at the request of Ibn Tufayl. The commentaries belong to formally different genres, traditionally classified as "short," "long," and "medium." The "short" ones are really "synopses" or original paraphrases of the disciplines corresponding to the titles of Aristotle's main works. The "long" commentaries, for their part, establish the genre of the literal analytical gloss, with direct citations of the text. The "medium," finally, are more concise, organized by questions, and less explicit in distinguishing the thought of the author from that of the commentator. Only a few of Aristotle's works, those of greater relevance to theological problems (the *Metaphysics*, *Physics*, *Heaven*, and *The Soul*) and to the determination of the status of scientific knowledge (the *Posterior Analytics*), are given all three kinds of commentary.

In all these texts the interpretation of Aristoteleanism is accompanied by the commentator's fundamental intention to take every possible opportunity to explain and define the range, purpose, and results of human rational speculation, for he is convinced that Aristotle's philosophy provides the historically most perfect expression of such speculation. To this end Ibn Rushd regards it as indispensable to identify and eliminate the contaminations of Platonic and Neoplatonic thought that over the centuries have been imposed on the original spirit of Aristoteleanism. In his view the thought of Avicenna is a typical example of such hermeneutical deviations, its main defect being that that author did not sufficiently understand and respect the distinction between philosophy and theology and the mutual limitations of the two. But in making this point Ibn Rushd does not seek simply to claim the rights of an autonomous rational thinking that is free to roam unhindered into subjects connected with the truths of the faith. This attitude ran counter to that of many Islamic theologians of his day, who raised serious claims that he was an atheist and unbeliever; this was probably the reason for his being disgraced and exiled until his death, first to a village in Andalusia and then to Marrakesh.

But Ibn Rushd was also in fact a convinced champion of the possibility and even the fundamental necessity of a harmony between faith and reason: that is, between, on the one hand, an understanding of the true depths of the Qur'an and, on the other, a purely rational interpretation of knowable created reality. This is possible and even necessary if both faith and reason are ways of attaining to truth; the harmony depends, therefore, on the recognition that there is a strict distinction among the areas of activity, the method used in each, and the goals of the theological and scientifico-philosophical fields of study. This is to say that al-Ghazali was basically correct in rebuking those *falasifa* who, like Ibn Sina, disregarded such limits and presumed to venture into explanations of the divine mysteries. Human reason is unable and lacks the skill to describe and understand the ways of salvation that are open only to those who respect the divine word. The deepest meaning of the *tawhid*, which is the foundation of Islamic truth, is that God is absolutely one and therefore absolutely other than the world. The claim of philosophers to plumb this mystery is, for Ibn Rushd as for al-Ghazali, the primary source of their errors.

Philosophy ought therefore to be practiced exclusively by those who, through sufficient education and personal talent, are in a position to understand its contents, all of which have to do with knowledge of the created world. Harking back to Ibn Baggia's suggested division of human beings into three classes (believers, theologians, and philosophers), Ibn Rushd makes these correspond to the three types of reasoning listed by Aristotle in his *Topics*: rhetoric, logic, and apodictic (in Latin Christianity John of Salisbury was making the same discovery during these same decades).

The vast majority of human beings understand only rhetorical arguments— that is, are open only to persuasive discourse. Logicians are those who, by nature or by profession, are satisfied to exercise their rational skills in constructing probable proofs that are reliable in their demonstrative method but certain only if their starting point is premises whose necessity comes from outside and is not guaranteed by the reasoning process itself. It is to this class of human beings that all theologians, whether Asharites or Mu'tazilites, belong; they are logicians or "dialecticians" in the Aristotelean sense, inasmuch as all of them argue with rigorous logic, but only on the basis of the words of the Qur'an. These words are inherently true to believers but still only "probable" from the viewpoint of logic, since reason does not prove them to be necessary. The apodictics or demonstrators are those alone who, again whether by nature or by profession (that is, by exercise), have mastered the art of philosophizing; their reasonings are always necessary because they start from scientifically ensured premises or from preceding demonstrations or because the conclusions flow from undemonstrable first truths (the first principles of Aristotelean logic).

The *falasifa* are not true to their profession when their arguments take them beyond their proper borders into doctrines concerned with the final salvation of human beings, for on these it is not possible to formulate scientifico-rational arguments that are certain. But neither are the practitioners of *kalam* true to their profession whenever they act as philosophers and claim to utter judgments on natural truths that are not contained in the words of revelation, for God's purpose in speaking to humanity is to lead them toward respect for his will and certainly not to substitute his word for the uses of reason, thereby abolishing the latter.

The function of philosophers is to lead reason, through valid demonstrations, to the necessary conclusions that make up the inherited body of scientific knowledge. Aristotle long ago made an important contribution to the formation of this body of knowledge, the certainty of which is indisputable because it is acquired through demonstrations. At the same time, however, he introduced into the body of human knowledge some theses he regarded as necessary but that contradict religious truth. The most serious of these are the assertion of the eternity of the world and the denial of individual immortality. The reason why the Philosopher thought the world to be eternal is that, in his view, to postulate a beginning of God's efficacious activity would mean a change in God's immutable perfection.

In contrast, the thesis on individual immortality arose out of a necessary correction of the psychology of earlier *falasifa*, a correction that, according to Ibn Rushd, goes back to a correct reading of Aristotle's *The Soul*. The knowledge acquired by an individual is owing to the efficacious action of the separated agent intellect on the passive intellect and takes concrete form in the actuation of the speculative intellect. To the extent, however, that the speculative intellect (which as such is the same as the acquired intellect of al-Farabi and Ibn Sina) is contaminated by the sensible imagination, it is mortal and disappears with the death of the body (as Alexander of Aphrodisias teaches). Insofar as the speculative intellect knows a truth of a higher order, it is united with the agent Intellect. It is only in such a union (as Ibn Baggia and Ibn Tufayl agree) that the passive intellect achieves supreme happiness, that is, human blessedness. On the other hand, this means that in the degree to which it is immortal the passive intellect melts, as it were, into the agent intellect and is no longer individual.

According to Ibn Rushd, then, the basic argument against an individual immortality is that this would mean an infinite number of individual living souls, that is, an actual infinite, which is logically impossible. Moreover, if matter is (following Aristotle) the source of individuation, a soul separated from the body and therefore from matter returns to the purity of its intelligible form and can no longer be an individual.

Because in his commentary on Aristotle Ibn Rushd maintains that these theses are scientifically true and necessary, he and his followers were accused of legitimizing the obviously absurd coexistence of two contradictory truths (this became generally known as the "double truth" doctrine). But as the distinction among the three classes of human beings makes clear, the separation of reason from faith is only a distinction between varying expressions of the same truth; it is impossible, therefore, that they should contradict one another. This means, first and foremost, that the statements of faith are often not exactly identical with what theologians teach, and can be understood in ways much less opposed to the results of the demonstration of what those statements are not really asserting. For example, the statement attributed to Ibn Sina and so harshly criticized by al-Ghazali, namely that God knows only universals and not particulars, was simply an unsatisfactory way in which theologians explained a higher philosophical truth: that God also knows particulars but in a different way than do human beings (whose knowledge is conditioned by the mode of being of its object).

But there is also a deeper truth at work when the theologians maintain that a logical conclusion demands acknowledgment of its necessity yet also say that the faith ought to be accepted by human beings for their salvation. At work is the clear idea that truth, which in the final analysis is known only to God, can be expressed and interpreted in different degrees by the human mind. The acknowledgment of the trustworthiness of the faith is necessary even on civil and political grounds, while acknowledgment of the necessity of rational demonstration is essential for the pursuit of science. But human knowledge is never exhaustive and is constantly perfectible, at least until the knower attains to an identity with a higher intelligence. If, then, scientific truths can be opposed to revelation, the reason is that God has a knowledge and wisdom greater than those of human beings. In addition, what human beings know, either by investigating nature or by interpreting revelation, is true, but with a truth proportioned to their condition as knowers. Both the truths of reason (stripped of all mythical and allegorical language) and the practical truths of the faith (imposed by the demands of civil coexistence) are always relative to the human way of knowing.

God alone knows completely, exhaustively, and without qualification. In contrast, the cognitive faculties of human beings are incapable of tackling problems for whose solution neither nature nor the divine law provides. Faith can and should come strongly into play where reason is unable, either because human beings are incapable of properly directing the activity of reason or because the truth is inexhaustible. An example here is miracles, which are true even though we do not understand how they occur; in fact, philosophy has little to say about them except that they are miraculous! Even though science says miracles are impossible, faith can recognize and accept them. The same holds for the gift of prophecy, which is a form of knowledge that is all the truer the more it evades the grasp of reason. Because of this gift the prophet is able to foresee things that have not yet happened, to command actions, or to communicate knowledge that does not depend on a scientific grasp of reality.

3. Jewish Theological and Philosophical Thought

In the "transfer of studies" (*translatio studiorum*) to the medieval West there was still another fundamental stage that likewise followed indirect paths through the Mediterranean civilizations. In this case the transfer was effected by way of translations, beginning in the second half of the twelfth century, of theological and scientific works produced by the great rabbinical schools of the Jewish communities scattered throughout countries under the political control of Islam.

Fundamental here was the mission of ensuring the preservation, transmission, and correct interpretation of the Law (or Torah). Medieval Jewish theology developed in service of this mission, as a result of the layering and interweaving of various hermeneutical traditions that came together over the centuries and in different geographical locales to form a shared fabric of assured teachings. The uniformity here was guaranteed by the strength of rabbinical culture. A basic factor in the cohesiveness of this tradition was the establishment and spread, beginning in the third century C.E., of the text of the Talmud; this organized explanation of the Torah, both as a whole and in its many applications to daily life, was understood to be a systematic body of teachings by which the divine will in its totality was communicated to the chosen people. Reference to the spiritual teaching of the Talmud was a constant characteristic of the theological work of the medieval Jews; the Talmud became, in practice, the solid ground under the thinking of the rabbis about the cognitive ascent of human beings toward the ultimate truth of the Law and the interpretive tools that could and should be used to achieve this ascent.

As a matter of fact, in its first phase of development Talmudic wisdom refrained from speculations about God, creation, and the destiny of human beings and gave its primary attention to the juridical and narrative aspects of the text of Scripture. A first example of intellectual reflection on the ways in which God accomplished the creative work described in the first pages of revelation was the *Book of Creation*, a short and compact work marked by a Gnostic approach and showing the influence of Greek arithmology. This work appeared in Hebrew between the second and fifth centuries; it was later subjected to interpolations and reworked during the Islamic period, around the tenth century.

The book describes the thirty-two *Sefirot* or formal principles that translate God's free creative act into effective operation; the thirty-two are symbolized by the twenty-four letters of the Hebrew alphabet and the ten principal numbers of the Pythagoreans. Insofar as the *Sefirot* are constitutive elements of the Scriptures in which the divine word is embodied in order to communicate itself to humanity, they are the foundations of the created universe. Just as the text of the Bible is composed of letters and numbers, so too the universe is effectively organized and governed by these eternal intelligible principles that have emanated from the divine will in order to activate the divine creative power. Some human beings, due to the perfection of their knowledge, are able, as Abraham was, to achieve a higher contemplation of God in the fullness of these manifestations of mystery; such persons can be said to share in the creative action.

In Jewish theological thinking the *Book of Creation* was a first sign of the desire to make a consistent whole of the mental processes that human reason uses in studying the order of reality and the mysterious depths of revelation. In fact, the contribution made by a rational mind trained in science but also strengthened by the cognitive support of the divine truth provided in Scripture soon came to appear indispensable as a tool for defending the tradition against the first worrying signs of trends away from orthodoxy. These trends arose from the encounter with Islam and the lack of communication among the communities of the diaspora. The agreement between faith and reason, based on the presupposition that the Torah expresses the truth in a way that harmonizes with the expectations of the rational mind, runs through, for example, the work of one of the first important Jewish theologians, Saadyah Gaon. This writer, who was born in Egypt but lived in Mesopotamia and Syria in the first half of the tenth century (d. 942), shows a degree of influence by Mu'tazilite *kalam*.

On the other hand, the Neoplatonism of the *falasifa* (in particular the pseudo-Aristotelean *Theology*) was the main source of the two works of Isaac Israeli of Kairouan in Tunisia, who was known and often cited by the Latins as Isaac Judeus (d. between 932 and 955). The two works are the *Book of Definitions* and the *Book of the Elements*; these are extensive collections of solutions (some of which would be widely circulated among Christian theologians) and of philosophical principles and conceptual developments that take over some interesting Plotinian ideas with a view to a theological systematization of the biblical universe.

The most important example of a mature Jewish theological Platonism is a dialogue between Teacher and Disciple called *The Book of the Fountain of Life*. This had already been translated into Latin before 1150 (as *The Fountain of Life*) and was especially valued by Christian teachers of theology, who knew it as the work of a master named Avicebron (or Avencebrol); only in modern times has this writer been identified as a famous Jewish poet of Saragossa, Shlomo ibn Gebirol (d. 1058). While this writer's poetry is explicitly inspired by religion, *The Fountain of Life* lacks biblical citations and references to revelation, the intention evidently being to offer a celebration of God and his relations with creation that is of a purely philosophical kind, parallel with but distinct from the faith-inspired glorification of God in Scripture and liturgy.

The characteristic element of Ibn Gebirol's thought, from the very beginning of the work's five books, is what philosophers call "universal hylomorphism." That is: every substance except the divine is composite, not simple, and always springs from the meeting of matter with a form and even, in most cases, with a plurality of forms. Even the intelligible substances and the simplest of created substances are made up of matter, however elusive, and form. According to the principles of Platonic emanationism, universal matter and universal form are the first two creatures and the closest to the perfect and simple creative will of God, who is the only "fountain of life." From the combination of these two spring all other composed realities in a descending hierarchy. The task of the human soul is to reascend the ladder through knowledge, which is always a recognition of the hylomorphic compositions, until it reaches an understanding of the universal matter and universal form. This understanding is the highest form of natural knowledge available to the soul; the perception of "what is beyond these things" and the final reunion with the will of God are possible only as the effect of a gift that cannot be merited, but only hoped for.

The doctrine of the plurality of forms has special implications for psychology, since it introduces into the human individual a plurality of souls that, depending on the degree of illumination available to each, preside over the different types of knowledge relative to different objects. This approach is also to be seen in another Jewish writer who lived under the Almohads at the beginning of the twelfth century. This was Yehudah ha-Levi or Judah Ha-Levi, who was born in Andalusia, then moved to Toledo in Christian territory, and finally journeyed to the Holy Land, where he perhaps died in Jerusalem at the end of his pilgrimage (in 1140/1141). He composed a work titled *Kuzari*, a splendid, balanced interreligious dialogue of a philosopher, a Christian, a Muslim, and a rabbi. The king of the Khazars (the personage who gives his name to the work) asks these individuals questions about metaphysics and religion; at the end of the discussion he declares his own preference for the strict monotheism of the Jews, which transcends any and every attempt at anthropomorphic rationalism, and he converts to that faith.

The most famous Jewish philosopher and theologian of the twelfth century was Moses ben Maimon, known to the Latins as Moses Maimonides (d. 1204). Like Ibn Rushd, he was born in Cordoba, Spain (in 1135), and like him was compelled by the anti-Jewish persecutions of the Almohads to emigrate to Morocco and finally to settle in Egypt. He served as a distinguished physician and jurist at the court of Saladin, sultan of Egypt and Syria, who in 1187 wrested

Jerusalem from the crusaders. During the second half of his life, and despite his many official duties, Maimonides was able to devote himself to the composition of his main theological writings, the *Code of Precepts* and the more famous *Guide for the Perplexed*; the latter was written in Arabic but was almost immediately translated into Hebrew.

The "perplexed" (or "uncertain" and even "confused," "gone astray") whose guidance Maimonides undertakes are interpreters of the Bible who, after studying the works of the philosophers, did not know how to act correctly in building up their faith. Such people wavered between the two opposed dangers of disbelief and excessive literalism.

In order to help them the author develops a complex and seemingly (but only seemingly) disorderly synthesis of Talmudic traditionalism, rabbinical theology, and Greco-Arabic philosophical thought. The purpose is to teach believers how to make their way to the allegorical meaning of the sacred text without losing sight of the fundamental principles of their faith: the existence of God, his attributes, creation, providence, and human freedom. The entire operation is based on a special esteem for prophetic wisdom, which is the foundation of revelation insofar as the latter offers the only possible contact between the knowledge God has of the truth and that which human beings can have. Insofar as the expression of this contact is found in the perfection of the Law, to which human beings have access through faith and understanding, the gift of prophecy represents the culminating point in the process of reciprocal convergence of reason and faith. This process is identical with the journey of the Jewish people toward the God who has called them.

In contrast, the philosophical arguments Maimonides frequently uses to explain the meaning and practice of the divine commandments can never ensure either an understanding or any kind of justification of the will of God. The necessary but unprovable premise of all human thought is that the Torah is an undeniable, free, and unqualified gift that was given on Mount Sinai at a particular moment in history. Everything that reason can base on this foundation, from the proof of God's existence to an understanding of his attributes, is a consequence of this gift. An authentic thinker is one who, instead of pursuing the truth through philosophical study and then trying to show its agreement with the Bible, succeeds in deriving philosophy from revelation. The application of scientific reason certainly enjoys its own autonomy as long as it investigates the created world. Among the many "sayings" of Maimonides that were often repeated by medieval Latin thinkers, one of the best known was that "Aristotle was never deceived about anything existing under the heavenly sphere of the moon"; in other words, philosophers will not make mistakes as long as they remain within their field of competence, which is the world of visible, physical realities.

But natural reason is inherently weak, and if it wishes to ensure the truthfulness of its processes it must necessarily let itself be instructed by biblical truth, taking the latter as a source of corroboration and confirmation of all the steps it thinks it can take on its own. The constructive aspect of this biblical training of reason comes in the realm of interpretation: reason must learn to understand correctly the terminology of Scripture and to judge correctly allegorical expressions that, if taken literally, would lead to utter confusion. But even more constructive is the element of self-criticism: having once been told by the Bible of its inadequacy in dealing with the truth, reason must acknowledge its own limits, that is, its natural inability to rise to the insurmountable level of the divine transcendence. In a further confirmation of this position, Maimonides strictly confines any rational-scientific claims about the nature of God's attributes within the limits of negative theology. He rejects without qualification any possibility of using the language of science to express the transcendent reality that no created intellect can ever grasp by means of its complicated and inadequate definitions.

Maimonides' teaching, then, like that of Averroes, involves a careful division of the areas of study proper to the several kinds of knowing, but without sharing the reductive valuation of theology as compared with philosophy. On the contrary, knowledge of the true faith is placed here at the top of the ladder of the forms of human knowledge. As philosophy ascends from one kind of knowledge to another it is in a position, with the help of the loftiest metaphysical speculations, even to intuit the identity of the source of all human thought with the very foundation of the faith, namely, "the existence of the first Being who gives existence to everything that exists."

It is in this supreme insight that philosophy reaches its crowning point, which is the same as the beginning of asceticism and a genuine religious life, inasmuch as by knowing God the human person is finally ready to love in the purest and most disinterested way. Moreover, faith, which has hitherto directed and coordinated the movements of knowledge and helped it not to get lost amid doubts and uncertainties, is now perfectly ready to blossom in the living of a virtuous life directed solely by love. But this purification of the intelligence leads persons only to a state of mental acquiescence and a possession of wisdom that are the necessary but insufficient conditions for receiving the gift of prophecy, which God alone grants, freely and without human merit.

The circle is thus closed: prophecy has given expression to the word of God in the Law, and knowledge of the Law leads human beings to the state of being in which they are able to receive prophetic powers. Moses was at once the greatest prophet and the greatest philosopher. But as a prophet he was more than a philosopher, because by a supreme act of abandonment of all his cognitive powers to the divine attraction that was mediated by the heavenly intelligences he was able to intuit and then reformulate the past, present, and future truth about humanity, reducing it to symbolic terms that made it available to all. He was thus able to tell all believers that God is the source of everything, that he is in everything, that every being that receives existence from God moves toward him, that God knows the universe he has created and in which he exercises his providential care, and that creatures, from the heavenly intelligences to human beings, are urged to know and love, here in the universe, the God who created it and loves it.

4. The Introduction of Greek and Arabic-Jewish Thought into the West: The Latin Translations

Historians of medieval western philosophy have spoken of "the rising tide of Aristoteleanism," but in fact, as we can see from what has been said, the reality was a complicated and labyrinthine world of contacts, forms of openness, and communications of knowledge. These took place through the direct medium of books, which could travel with their contents beyond the lives of individuals and social communities and cross the political and religious borders of the several civilizations from whose internal traditions such books emerged.

An uninterrupted labor (over about two centuries) by active schools of translators and then also of commentators began first in southern Italy and Sicily, Spain, and southern France. Beginning in the middle of the twelfth century this labor poured its products into the libraries and scriptoria of the Latin world, in a rising flood that began in the middle of the twelfth century, intensified especially during the decades of passage into the next century, and then continued throughout the thirteenth. The new learning was not only philosophical and theological; it was a well-developed scientific body of knowledge that included original texts, commentaries, and reworkings from antiquity and the more recent Arabic and Jewish past, in the areas of logic, metaphysics, ethics, and theology, but also of physics and psychology, arithmetic and algebra, geometry, optics, astronomy, medicine, and alchemy. So broad a movement that was renewing the overall intellectual patrimony of the West could not help but change radically the mentality and speculative parameters of medieval Latin thought and, above all, give new direction to the conception of knowledge and a new esteem for the value and conditions of scientific learning.

Toledo was a privileged place for the study, acquisition, and spread of the learning of the Islamic "Hellenizers." The city poured out upon Europe many literal translations from Arabic, usually the collaborative work of two individuals, one of whom translated the Arabic text into the vernacular while the other translated the vernacular into the Latin of educated people. It is clear, of course, how defective these first versions must have been from the philological point of view, especially when we reflect that in the case of the Greek classics the texts had already passed through linguistic filters in the pre-Islamic period. Yet we cannot underestimate the enthusiasm with which Latin scholars welcomed this new availability of authoritative tools and sources of thought.

Among the first works to be translated in Toledo were the scientific and logical writings of al-Kindi and al-Farabi and the writings of both on the nature of the intellect; these provided the Christian world with a first and decisive look at the psychology of Aristotle's *The Soul*. The translation of Avicenna's *Metaphysics* and of al-Ghazali's *Metaphysics* (that is, the expository section of his *The Intentions of the Philosophers*), then of the *Book on Causes* (thought to be Aristotle's work) and of Alexander of Aphrodisias' *The Intellect*—all these helped make the highly developed contents of the Islamic synthesis of classical philosophy and theology increasingly well known.

Some of the translators also contributed by original works (but always based on the new sources) to the melding of the existing system of western thought with the Greco-Arabic system. In particular, there was Dominic Gundisalvi (or Gundissalino). He worked in Toledo in the first half of the twelfth century and with his collaborator, John of Seville (or John Hispanus), translated works of Avicenna and *The Fountain of Life* by Avicebron. He also wrote two treatises on theological cosmology that were basically a combination of Avicennian and Jewish Neoplatonism: these were *On Unity* (falsely attributed to Boethius) and *The Procession of the World*. Another work was *The Division of the Sciences*, in which he began to deal with the problem of how to classify the new sciences introduced through contact with the Arabs and how to systematize their contents. Finally, there was attributed to Dominic an *On the Soul* that contributed to the grafting of the psychological theory of Aristotle and Avicenna onto the tree of the Platonic gnoseology transmitted by medieval monastic sources.

From the same Toledan environment came other, anonymous treatises on theological psychology and cosmology, for the most part compilations and minglings of Arabic and Christian sources. One such was the *Book on First and Second Causes and on the Stream of Things that Flow from Them*, which likewise became known as *On Intelligences*. It was composed in the decades ending the twelfth century and beginning the thirteenth and circulated at Paris and Oxford during the early years of the formation of the universities. It fuses Avicenna, the pseudo-Aristotelean *On Causes*, and citations from John Scotus.

The history of the translations of Greco-Arabic literature is complicated by the work of new individuals and the opening of further centers for the diffusion of the new culture. Some of these individuals are of special interest in the subsequent development of medieval theological thought. After coming to Toledo in about 1160, Gerard of Cremona, an indefatigable translator of Aristotelean, Arabic, and Jewish works, completed the process of making the *Organon* available in Latin by his translation of the *Posterior Analytics*, both in its original form and in Themistius' paraphrase of it. This work made it possible to grasp Aristotle's theory of science as a strictly deductive demonstration having necessary premises and objects that are always universal. In the twelfth century the *Posterior Analytics* was again translated, this time from Greek, by James of Venice, who lived for a long time in Constantinople with Burgundione of Pisa, a translator of patristic texts, among them the *Orthodox Faith* of Damascene. At the Norman court in Palermo, Henry Aristippus translated Plato's *Phaedo* and *Meno* from the Greek, but his work did not circulate in any important measure.

Later on, after 1220, Michael Scotus, a Scotsman living at the court of Frederick II, began the introduction of the writings of Averroes into the West with his translations of the major commentaries on Aristotle's *Heaven, The Soul, Metaphysics,* and *Physics,* as well as of some shorter commentaries and paraphrases, chiefly of texts on nature. Direct contacts with the East increased as scholars, philosophers, and translators into Latin traveled to Constantinople in search of original texts. The first half of the thirteenth century saw the beginning of a revision of translations from Arabic and the preparation of new versions based on the original Greek and bypassing the Arabic versions. In this area we must note the contributions made by Robert Grosseteste (d. 1253), a Franciscan philosopher and theologian, in the fields of science, philosophy, and patristics; and those as well of Dominican William of Moerbeke (d. ca. 1286), who played a noteworthy part in the enrichment of the library of classical philosophy on which Thomas Aquinas would later draw extensively.

III. The Civilization of the University

1. The Birth of the Universities

"The wisdom" of God the Father "has, then, built a house for herself" (see Prov 9:1) at the study center in Paris. The city of Athens was the original mother of studies. The city was divided into three main sections: . . . that in which the merchants and the ordinary people lived . . . that of the rulers and the nobility . . . and that in which the philosophers lived and in which the schools for students were. . . . Then St. Dionysius came to the city of Paris in order to make it the mother of studies in place of Athens. As a matter of fact, Paris, like Athens, is divided into three sections, namely, that of the merchants, artisans, and ordinary people, which is called the "residential area"; then the section of the nobility, in which the royal court and the cathedral church are located and which is called the "organized community"; and finally the section of the students and colleges, which is called the "university." The center of studies was thus moved first from Greece to Rome and then, in the time of Charlemagne, that is, around 800, from Rome to Paris.

That is how Parisian master Thomas of Ireland, at the beginning of the fourteenth century, combines history and legend in celebrating the final stage in the transfer of studies from the ancient Greek world to the Christian world. He traces back to Charlemagne the foundation of the center of human studies in what would be the most important university city in the West throughout the later Middle Ages.

In fact, the term *universitas studiorum* (place where all the branches of study are concentrated) appears first in the royal, episcopal, and pontifical documents that at the beginning of the thirteenth century recognized the juridical autonomy of the newborn corporation of teachers and students. The documents also regulated the educational process within a new structure of international scope. This structure was the urban study center, soon to be called the general study center as distinct from other more or less specialized schools outside the university. It was, then, a single center for studies or, better, a community, a scholastic city in a true and proper sense, born from the coming together of several institutes into a single juridical body that included scholars, but also experts who saw to practical and organizational matters. The different fields of competence of the teachers led to a division into a number of faculties that provided different possibilities in the choice of disciplines to be pursued. The faculties were coordinated by means of a set of regulations or general statutes and differentiated, not by working methods or the organization of careers as masters, but solely by the objects of the respective disciplines.

The method of teaching was the one that had been more or less settled in the age of Philip Augustus. It consisted of the "reading" of (or lecture on) a fundamental text in a particular area of learning. The text was approached by asking a "question," which was then developed through a structured "disputation" involving several persons. In ordinary teaching, the latter were a teacher and his students; these took on the roles of "answerer" and "objector," since the former proposed answers to the questions while the latter raised objections to these answers. This teaching method gave rise to the literary genre of "disputed questions," the material now being revised and published by the teacher.

The disputed questions might be "everyday" (or ordinary) or "in the schools" if intended as a didactic exercise within a faculty, or they might be "on any subject" (*de quodlibet*) and described as "quodlibetal" when occasioned by questions raised outside the regular classes and when the exercise was attended by many of the teaching body. The texts of this literature that have come down to us were often the results of a "report," that is, of notes taken by students or fellow teachers during the event and not infrequently revised by the master.

It is obvious that the various faculties used different texts. In the Faculty of Arts—that is, of the liberal arts—the reading of texts of Aristotle (which would cause the name to be changed later on to Faculty of Philosophy) gradually replaced the reading of the ancient manuals for the several disciplines. The Faculty of Law was divided into two subject areas: Civil Law, in which Justinian's *Corpus iuris* was read, and Canon Law, in which Gratian's *Decretum* was read. In the Faculty of Medicine the basic text was the collection of Hippocrates' writings as translated and re-edited at the various centers of the early medieval medical tradition, from Salerno to Montpellier. Finally, in the Faculty of Theology the text *par excellence* was Scripture, but this was soon accompanied by analysis of the manuals of systematic theology, among which the *Book of Sentences* of Peter Lombard quickly took first place.

If we leave aside Bologna, whose schools had already been recognized by Frederick Barbarossa as an independent body of masters, the first center of studies that evidenced the full development of all these elements was undoubtedly that of Paris. In 1200, after a gory brawl between the students and the civil police, Philip Augustus decided to grant to the masters and students of the schools of Paris the right to be judged only by the bishop and the university authorities. This act marked the beginning of an increasing autonomy that led in 1215 to the solemn approval of the first official statutes of the University of Paris by Cardinal Robert of Courçon, legate of Innocent III. In 1231 Gregory IX issued new statutes in his bull *Parens scientiarum*: the study center was regarded thenceforth as an institution directly at the service of the church, with the result that all the disciplines except Civil Law were taught there.

During these same years the schools of Oxford combined to form an organized institution that was recognized by Innocent III in 1214 and was the only one that from the very beginning foresaw the active presence of all the Faculties. A secession from Oxford gave rise in 1209 to the University of Cambridge (but this was recognized only in 1319). In Italy, a similar migration of masters from Bologna gave birth in 1222 to the study center in Padua. The center of studies in Naples became the first university established by the civil authorities on the initiative of Frederick II. In 1245 Innocent IV opened the curial study center, located at the papal court; this was devoted specifically to the study of theology. In France, the University of Toulouse was established in 1229 as a result of a lengthy interruption of teaching decreed by the masters of Paris during a conflict with the bishop there; next came Orleans, where the study of law was promoted, and Montpellier, which followed the tradition of Salerno and gave primacy to medicine. On the Iberian Peninsula the oldest university was established at Palencia in 1208, but Salamanca, founded in 1230, became the more famous institution.

The average student entered the university at the age of fourteen or fifteen and was obliged to start in the Faculty of Arts, where in accord with the traditional propaideutic character of philosophical studies he had to spend about four years learning the common foundations before passing on to other Faculties. At the end of this first cycle the better students were promoted to the degree of bachelor (baccalaureate) and could deliver introductory or complementary lectures and oversee the disputations, in which their task was to ask the questions and decide on the answers (in Latin, *determinare*). Having passed the test for the "license to teach," the bachelor became a "master" and began his lectures as a master with a solemn ceremony known as a "commencement" (*inceptio*). He then had to teach the Arts for at least two years. The few who did not leave the university in order to go and teach in schools of a lower standing then began the next, longer, and more demanding cycle of studies in other Faculties.

In theology, which was regarded as the highest level of university training, the student had to follow lectures on the Bible and the *Sentences* for seven years; he then became a "biblical bachelor" for two years, his duty being to lecture on the scriptural text, and then a "Sententiary bachelor" with the obligation of lecturing for a further two years on Lombard's work. Only after an apprenticeship of at least four more years as a "trained bachelor" could he, at about the age of forty, achieve the title "Master of Theology." The curriculum of studies culminated in the acquisition of the "license to teach anywhere," that is, the authorization to teach in any university of the Christian world (initially the granting of such a license was the prerogative solely of the Faculty of Theology in Paris).

The university was on the whole a strictly communal institution: personal initiatives were quite limited in the setting of an internal democratic form of government that ensured a comprehensive organization and control of all teaching activities. The chancellor was the chief authority and the immediate representative of the bishop. His mandate, which was to safeguard the normal exercise of teaching and to mediate internal disagreements, came from the General Council of Masters, which in turn reflected the thinking of the Councils of the individual Faculties, each headed by its own Rector.

2. Philosophers and Theologians

In point of fact, agreements and disagreements about the scope of the authority to determine the subjects and problems to be studied arose very quickly, especially in relations between the Faculty of Theology and the Faculty of Arts. This was due especially to the extension of the competencies and range of philosophical research allowed to the "artists," who were the first to profit from the new texts provided by Greco-Arabic scholarship. The teaching program of the Arts shifted gradually as this Faculty turned rhetoric over to the Faculty of Law and neglected literary studies for a fervent pursuit of logico-linguistic researches and of teaching on subjects dealing with nature.

A special interest in Aristotle's "apodictic" and in the binding character of his epistemological principles often led the artists to think of themselves as authorized to impose the fundamental rules that every other discipline, including theology, was obliged to respect if it wanted its propositions to have scientific value. On the other hand, the broadening of the quadrivium through the introduction of Aristotelean physics led, in a similar way, to an extension of its practitioners' claim to pass judgment not only on visible realities but also on the invisible aspects of created reality. So far did they go that, in an only seemingly taken-for-granted extension of their field of competence, they soon laid claim to the right to teach the *Metaphysics* and the *Ethics*.

It is easy to see how this development of philosophical studies in the Faculty of Arts, with its corresponding sharp distinction from the areas of competence of the other Faculties, resulted in reopening, in a new and in many respects more dramatic way, the problem of the relations between reason and faith and the compatibility of the two. Philosophy returned to the West as an area of robust research, freed of contradictions among its representatives. As the Arabic *falasifa* had learned from the later Neoplatonists and had then taught the Latins, so too the western philosophers rethought their discipline, seeing it now as a homogeneous, unified science rigorously organized for study of the truth of things and of their first and second causes.

Thus in the space of two decades the masters of the Faculty of Arts had taken a qualitative leap in their philosophical and scientific researches, but also in dealing with the fundamental problems of natural theology, a leap normally taking several centuries of concentrated thought and theoretical acquisitions. In light of this it is obvious that the masters of the Faculty of Arts could well feel authorized to carry their researches beyond the realm of nature into the realm of beyond-nature, with the intention of coming up with objective and exhaustive answers to the ultimate questions about the causes and order of creation.

In this perspective we can understand the initial, overt positions taken by the theologians not only toward the new sources of knowledge and philosophy in general and Aristotle's writings in particular, but more especially toward the kind of use being made of these by their colleagues on the Faculty of Arts. Due to the influence of theologians on the bishop, the first calls to order came from the ecclesiastical authorities and soon took concrete form in a series of censures and condemnations. I mentioned earlier how the council of the province of Sens, held in Paris in 1210 and chaired by Peter of Corbeil, a master of theology, not only found David of Dinant and the followers of Amalric of Bène to be guilty of heresy but also prohibited, under pain of excommunication, the use of Aristotle's work on natural philosophy and of the commentaries on these. Then, in 1215, when Cardinal Legate Robert of Courçon, likewise a former master of theology, came to Paris with a mandate to approve the statutes of the University, he confirmed the regulation of the Faculty of Arts that excluded the *Metaphysics* of Aristotle and his works on natural philosophy from its curriculum. The curriculum was to include only works dealing with the teaching of the seven liberal arts and of the foundations of ethics (that is, the first three books of the *Nichomachean Ethics*). This limitation was an important indication that the target of censure was not Aristoteleanism as such but rather the intrusions of the philosophers into the field of theology. Perhaps because these censures applied only to the public use and not the private reading of the prohibited works, they did not in fact hinder the circulation of the latter, which continued to elicit the interest and curiosity even of a good many theologians.

The problematic character of the new conflict between philosophy and faith was increased by another fact: since the teaching of the Arts was meant to be a preparation for theology, as set down in the University statutes, the practical effect was that all the masters of theology were, in principle, already well acquainted with philosophical arguments and would have found it hard to avoid using and applying them in their "questions." In 1228 Pope Gregory IX sent the masters of the Faculty of Theology a letter warning against those who, according to information reaching Rome, dared "to cross the boundaries set by the Fathers by making the understanding of the heavenly text depend on the requirements of natural philosophy" instead of "tracing all doctrines back to that Queen." In doing so they were acting not as authentic "theologians" or spokesmen for divine truth, but as "theophants" ("revealers of God"), charlatans who out of pure vanity circulated empty opinions about God.

The following year, as mentioned earlier, saw episodes of violence between students and civilians and a resultant interruption of classes that was decided on by a coalition of all the teachers in defense of their right of exemption from the civil courts. The newly established, rival University of Toulouse let students and masters everywhere know that in the name of academic freedom they could read all of Aristotle in their several curricula. Meanwhile, Gregory IX took a number of steps to settle the crisis in Paris, ending it with the publication of his bull *Parens scientiarum* in 1231. In this he permitted access to the books of Aristotle on natural philosophy, but only after a commission of prudent men, appointed by him, should have first examined them and purged them of all errors.

Despite the warnings not to mingle the teaching of theology with the doctrines of the philosophers but, in keeping with the classical allegory of the gold of the Egyptians, to maintain the subordinate role of the arts in relation to sacred doctrine, these interventions of Gregory IX revealed the urgent need of taking into account the fact that for years the different disciplines taught in the universities had already acquired their own special features and attained to the autonomy and dignity of sciences. It was clear to those who controlled and worried about the fate of Christian culture that the distinction between the arts and theology had no legitimacy except as signaling a hierarchical relationship between the areas of knowledge; theology had necessarily to be placed at the summit and not subordinated to other forms of knowledge.

On the other hand, given the complete description of the fields and boundaries and of the specific objects and methodologies of the scientific disciplines as determined by Greco-Arabic scholarship, it was now essential to undertake an equally rigorous definition of the object, language, and autonomy of theological knowledge, precisely in order that this discipline might retain its prerogative of being source and guide of other forms of knowledge. When Gregory IX warned theologians in *Parens scientiarum* not to confuse their "methods" with those of the philosophers, he was at the same time urging them to fashion their own.

At Paris in particular the masters of theology were committed to this task from the very beginning. Their aim was to introduce into a comprehensive revision of the tools and approaches of Christian doctrine some important ideas developed in the schools of the twelfth century as scholars there delved more deeply into the truths of the faith. These ideas became so many foundational principles of a new theological epistemology. There was the idea (dominant among the Victorines) that the reading of the Bible was fundamental as the source of any further acquisition of knowledge; the idea (spread by Gilbert of Poitiers and the Poitiers school) that if theology were to be regarded as a science it had to subject the expression of its contents to a "transumption," that is, the shifting of natural language in the direction of a meaning adaptable to the contents of revelation; the idea (originating with Abelard but applied chiefly by the writers of "sentences" and the encyclopedists) that the fundamental contents of the faith can be organized systematically in accordance with the unitary course of the history of salvation.

These different models had already come together to form a rich and original synthesis in the years bridging the two centuries, as is evidenced especially by the writings of Alan of Lille. But this same synthesis seemed suited for coping with the new scientific aspirations that were being encouraged by the new developments in philosophy. The doctrine that emerged from this synthesis, that is, the sacred doctrine that was identified with the very truth of Sacred Scripture as set forth in a didactic form, was therefore, in practice, a knowledge organized according to firm methodological principles and with respect for binding rules. In the early years of the century Robert of Courçon expressed his esteem for the results of this working program when he wrote with some exaggeration in the margin of his *Summa*: "Anyone who lectures publicly on Sacred Scripture sets out on a journey to a perfection more demanding than that of any Cistercian monk at Clairvaux."

3. The New Psychology and the Shift in Cognitive Parameters

The description of the tasks and limitations of each philosophical discipline was thus imposed by the necessity of organizing the new and complicated material found in books and used in teaching. From a certain point on, the description was also influenced by the models offered by Averroes and Maimonides. The task here was rather quickly accepted by the scholars of Latin Christianity, for whom it included theology as well and gave urgency to the formation of a new system of wisdom whose pinnacle, the "science of things divine," ensured the soundness of all the lesser sciences. But in this process of rethinking the cognitive parameters that condition and make feasible the genesis of a science, it is not possible to overestimate the important role played by Aristotle's philosophy and especially his conception of the kinds and potentialities of human knowledge. When Greco-Arabic psychology, which was based on the text of Aristotle's *The Soul* and the commentaries on it, was grafted onto the Platonico-Augustinian gnoseology that had been accepted and tested by early medieval monastic culture, it introduced not only a new terminology but also a shift in perspectives regarding the very conception of what knowing is and how it comes about.

As was mentioned earlier, in the twelfth century the Platonic division of the powers or faculties of the soul, which were originally three (senses, reason, intellect), was complicated, especially among the Cistercians, by the introduction of numerous more specific stages that were arranged hierarchically and were, in ascending order: senses, imagination, reason, intellect, intelligence, mind, spirit, and synderesis. The combination of Aristotelico-Arabic psychology with this detailed structure brought a new distribution of the operations performed by the different parts or functions of the intellect. But "intellect" was now taken as the inclusive name for the entire intellectual part of the soul, which Aristotle located at the third level of psychic activity, after the vegetative and the sensible. "Intellect" therefore no longer meant a faculty superior to that of logical and discursive reasoning, a faculty itself alogical and intuitive; for "intellect" thus understood the term "intelligence" was used at this period.

As a result the various aspects of the individual intellect—possible, abstract, acquired, accommodated—had to find a suitable place within the preexisting hierarchy of psychological faculties. As a reading of the first Latin treatises dealing with the new Aristotelean psychology will show (for example, the anonymous *On Intelligences*, the *On the Soul* of Dominic Gundisalvi, or the *Treatise on the Soul* of John Blund [d. 1248]), this new synthesis ran into difficulty when it came to reconciling the two different approaches of the soul to the source of knowledge as seen in the teaching of Plato and that of Aristotle. According to the former, the soul was drawn toward the pure forms of truth by an illumination from on high; according to the latter, the soul was importuned by the senses, which provided, from below, information about the external world.

The authors just mentioned solved the problem by recourse to the psychological teaching of Avicenna, which suggested a useful complementarity between the two origins of knowledge: on the one hand knowledge is activated, by way of abstraction, through external contact with the data of the senses, but on the other hand truth itself, through an illumination, exerts on the soul an enlightening attraction as a result of the mediating and ministerial function of the heavenly intelligences. These two different approaches to truth were complementary, and the Latins began to use the terminology of Augustine and call them respectively "knowledge" (*scientia*) and "wisdom" (*sapientia*).

But this very solution introduced in turn an important change of perspective in dealing with the past; it was a change the majority of Latin thinkers soon accepted, in most cases without any clear awareness. The Platonic-Augustinian approach to gnoseology involved the idea, dominant throughout the entire early Middle Ages, that knowing is always the result of an appropriation of the object by the subject, in forms that varied with the various faculties—senses, reason, intellect, and so on—which the self puts in motion in order to achieve this appropriation.

In this perspective truth is known unqualifiedly and perfectly by God alone. In contrast, the human faculties work, in various and necessarily limited ways, toward a subjective reconstruction of the object, grasping its nature in the ways developed from time to time by the various faculties: corporeally by the senses, conceptually and through definition by reason, and intuitively and completely by the intellect. But the true nature of any "thing" remains knowable to God alone, who contemplates its ideal presence in his own Intellect. Participation in this kind of true contemplation is possible for the created soul only when it is united with God at the supreme level of mystical asceticism, that is, in beatitude.

Aristotelean-Avicennian psychology, however, makes knowledge depend on the introduction of data that always come from outside, whether through the senses, which place the soul in contact with the inferior reality of bodies, or through an illumination, which brings it a formal representation of the truth that descends through the mediating heavenly intelligences. But this subordination of knowledge means a radical and unavoidable reversal of relations between subject and object in the act of knowing and, consequently, a subtle but decisive change in the very conception of knowledge, a change that will display its consequences from the beginning of the thirteenth century on. For, in this new perspective, true knowledge is not the result of each of the subject's faculties developing in its own fashion its perception of the objective datum. Rather, true knowing consists in making clear to the soul, in the most direct form possible, the real mode of being of the object in itself.

In other words, truth arises from an adaptation of the knower to the mode of being of the object known, and knowledge will be all the truer and more accurate the more unequivocally the soul is disposed to reflect the forms of things passively, as in a mirror, without any active enhancement on its part.

The technical formula "truth is the correspondence of object and intellect" seemed to be the best expression of this new conception of the relationship between subject and object in the act of knowing. It was accepted by many Latin writers of the thirteenth century, Thomas Aquinas among them, and attributed to Isaac Israeli (in his *Book on Definitions*), although it probably went back to Avicennian sources. In fact, the principle of a truthful correspondence between the intellect and the mode of being of the object presupposes that this mode of being is objectively true in itself as a created thing that really exists in the way in which it is known. The truth of the entity is not found in the idea in which God knows it or in the effort made by each of the soul's faculties to attain to a correspondence with that idea; it exists in the entity itself, regarded as in itself real and existent.

There was thus a transition from early medieval theological realism about the universals to a new, object-centered realism that was typical, in its original form, of Peripatetic-Arabic thought. According to Thomas' comments on the formula attributed to Isaac (*Summa Theologiae* I, q. 21, a. 2), it was now necessary to distinguish between, on the one hand, the creative action of the divine Intellect, which is the "cause" of the being of things that are and is itself the "rule and measure" of their truth and, on the other, the cognitive action of the created intellect, which must, in contrast, achieve a correspondence with the mode of being of things and find in it the "rule and measure" of its truthfulness.

The reversal or at least the revision of cognitive parameters through the adoption of an Aristotelean perspective thus ended by exerting a special influence both on the new psychological teachings and on the search for the stability and autonomy of each of the scientific disciplines. Every science, including philosophy, could now claim the right to pursue its own researches into its own characteristic object, which is always one or other of the real modes of being of things. Theology, too, being a science or at least true knowledge, could claim its own proper object, which is the divine reality or its real mode of existence, that is, its attributes and their operations.

Beginning in the twenties of the new century, access to Averroes' paraphrases of and commentaries on the works of Aristotle gave rise to new debates and qualifications. On the one hand there was a series of proposals for correcting the Avicennian hierarchization of the faculties of the soul and restoring the authentic Aristotelean conception of how human knowledge came about. On the other hand there was resistance from masters more bent on defending the Augustinian tradition, which meant preserving the synthesis of illumination and abstraction begun by psychological treatises in the first decades of the twelfth century. It is obvious, however, that the Christian masters of the new century, no matter what their area of teaching or their cultural inclination, could not fail to cope with the consequences both of the new clarification and definition of the boundaries between the disciplines and of the change that had taken place, along decidedly Aristotelean lines, in the conception of relations between subject and object in true knowing.

In fact, however, perhaps due to the now-ongoing absorption of the new doctrines and their basic spirit by Latin culture, the work of the commission charged by Gregory IX with removing from the texts on natural philosophy any potential causes of theological error was never completed. In 1245 Innocent IV extended to Toulouse the prohibition against reading Aristotle on natural philosophy, but what was involved henceforth was simply precautionary measures aimed at avoiding excesses and having little effect on ordinary administration. In the statutes of the Parisian Faculty of Arts that were promulgated toward the middle of the fifties the reading of all the works of Aristotle was made obligatory in the curriculum, with no warnings or limits any longer attached.

Chapter 5

The Golden Age of University Theology

I. Genesis and Formation of University Theological Thought: The Work of the First Masters of Theology

1. The Standard-Bearers of University Theology: Secular Masters and Masters from the Mendicant Orders

The thirty years between the fourth Lateran Council and the first Council of Lyons (the twelfth and thirteenth ecumenical councils respectively) were set off by two important dates in the history of university theology. The first was 1215, the year in which Cardinal Legate Robert of Courçon issued the first statutes of the University of Paris. The second was 1245, the year in which, again at Paris, chairs of theology were filled by Odo Rigaldi of the Franciscan Order and Albert of Cologne of the Dominican Order.

Repeating and improving on a series of measures already taken at the third Lateran Council (1179), the fourth, which Innocent IV convoked in 1215, confirmed the determination of the popes to strengthen their leadership role in controlling the cultural development of the Christian world. In carrying out this plan the church during these years found useful support in the preaching activity of two recently established Mendicant Orders: one founded in Spain by Dominic Guzmán (d. 1221), the other in Italy by Francis of Assisi (d. 1226). Within a short time, thanks to a solid organization that was centralized and independent of episcopal authority, these Orders became effective and disciplined representatives of the ardent ideals of spiritual and moral renewal that were at this time shaking the religious world to its foundations.

The Dominican Order, or Order of Preachers, which Honorius III approved in 1216, was established in order to help defend the orthodox faith and the unity of the Christian world against the spread of heresies, especially among the masses of the people. This goal naturally called for the extensive education of the members and a familiarity with intellectual tools useful for the attainment of this apostolic purpose.

In contrast, the Franciscans, or Friars Minor, whose manner of life was approved by Innocent III in 1209 and their definitive *Rule* by Honorius III in 1223, were motivated by the ethical and religious desire to promote a universal return of Christendom to the spiritual perfection and evangelical poverty of the first apostolic community. But the need for a theoretical justification of the Christian authenticity of such a mission led the Franciscans, too, to involve themselves with the instruction given at the new educational structures. Representatives of both Orders did not delay in stepping forward on the stage of university life. This life had initially been the exclusive possession of the urban secular clergy; meanwhile, the monastic world remained permanently apart from the universities, both in fidelity to its tradition and in obedience to the explicit prohibitions in the various *Rules* against working in the "world."

Beginning in the first decades of the new century, Dominic himself sent his friars to study in Paris, where he gathered them at the convent of Saint-Jacques in a house of studies reserved to the Order. During the crisis in the operation of the University that began in 1229, William of Auvergne, bishop of Paris and a former master in the Faculty of Theology, strengthened the study center at Saint-Jacques and promoted its integration into the university (that is, its curriculum was merged into that of the university). Then, to counter the refusal of the secular masters to teach, he urged the chancellor to assign a chair of theology to Dominican Raymond of Cremona. At almost the same time the Dominicans acquired a second chair when secular master John of Saint-Gilles entered the Order.

Relations between the Franciscans and the university were more difficult at the beginning, especially because of their evangelism, which made them appear similar to popular movements that were suspected of heresy. In 1236, however, due again to the conversion of a secular master, Alexander of Hales, they too had their first chair of theology in Paris. Only a few years later, Friar John of La Rochelle was added to the faculty, and the Franciscan study center was likewise integrated into the program of studies of the faculty of theology.

The authorities of each Order fostered in their representatives a definite uniformity of spirit and a homogeneity of doctrine in the teaching of this discipline. The same outlook was adopted when new Mendicant Orders, founded later in the thirteenth century, acquired their own masters at the university, for these took over the approach and ideals of the Dominicans and Franciscans. These new Orders included the Carmelites, recognized by Innocent IV in 1245, and the Hermits of St. Augustine, or Augustinians, who emerged, by decree of Alexander IV in 1256, from the union of various congregations that had revived the monastic rule of Augustine of Hippo. The conspicuous internal identity in the doctrinal direction taken by the Orders became more noticeable after the early decades.

But the subverting of the strike at the university and, later, the successes achieved by the proselytizing of the Mendicants, which brought frequent conversions of both students and masters, soon became the causes of ideological conflict with the secular masters. The latter wanted to protect the autonomy proper to their university corporation and feared being infected by and becoming subordinated to outside institutions. A further reason for the obstinacy of the seculars was the strong ideological cast given by the Mendicants to their teaching of theology, since they intended this teaching to serve their goal, the religious renewal of the Christian world. To this end the Mendicants sometimes called upon the university authorities to grant them special privileges in the exercise of their instructional activities.

The conflict came to a head in 1254 when a secular master, William of Saint-Amour, sent the pope his *Book on the Antichrist* in which he denounced as perverse and full of errors against orthodoxy the teachings Franciscan Gerard of Borgo San Donnino set down in his *Introduction to the Eternal Gospel*, where he located the Franciscan ideal of the moral renewal of Christianity in the historico-theological perspective of Joachim of Fiore and prophesied the imminent coming of a new spiritual kingdom and the triumph of evangelical poverty.

The controversy intensified, gradually involving even the popes and important members of the Roman curia, and William reacted by himself adopting an apocalyptic tone in his reply, *The Dangers of the Last Times*. Here he made himself the spokesman for a deep dissatisfaction with the Mendicants, accusing them of deviating from ecclesiastical principles that reserved to priests alone the mission of preaching and therefore also of teaching. The Mendicants thereby showed themselves true followers of the Antichrist who were undermining the stability of the ecclesiastical hierarchy. An immediate reply came from the most eminent masters of the two Orders, in particular Bonaventure of Bagnoreggio, who responded for the Franciscans in his *Questions about Evangelical Perfection*, and Dominican Thomas Aquinas, who wrote a strongly worded little work, *Answer to Those Who Attack the Worship of God and Religious Life*.

The authoritative character of these responses, together with the solid position the Mendicants had gained within the ecclesiastical organization, led to a first conclusion of the dispute with William's suspension from teaching and his exile. But this did not suppress the controversy, which was renewed by Gerard of Abbeville (d. 1272) and continued by other secular masters until the beginning of the fourteenth century. Gerard elicited new replies, both from Thomas in his *The Perfection of the Spiritual Life* and *Answer to the Teaching of Those Who Turn People Away from Religious Life* and from Bonaventure in his *Defense of the Poor*.

2. The First Secular Masters

The prolongation of this controversy was the most obvious reflection of the ideological, moral, and institutional differences that from the outset separated the seculars and the Mendicants. There was, on the one hand, the educational vocation of the secular clerics, who were the real founders of the University of Paris, and, on the other, the ambition of the Mendicant masters to introduce the energizing principles at work in their way of life into the systematization of theological knowledge.

In fact, the program of work that characterized the secular masters, beginning with their first representatives in the thirteenth century, showed clearly that their professional interests were in continuity, despite obvious formal differences, with the general problems tackled by the western thinkers who were active in the transition between the two centuries (such men, for example, as Alan of Lille and Simon of Tournai). But when confronted with the unforeseen expansion of didactic material and the resultant unexpected complexity of the new disciplinary divisions of knowledge, these masters had to react primarily by ensuring the consistency of their teaching with the formal presuppositions of the synthesis of reason and faith they inherited from the preceding scholastic tradition. They also had to make clear the superiority of theology over the other disciplines of learning.

An interesting example of this progress amid continuity may be seen in the further step taken by one of the first secular masters of Paris, William of Auxerre, in regard to the position of Simon of Tournai on the natural reasonableness of theological knowledge. In a deduction seemingly bold but fully in line with Anselm of Aosta's long-term theological plan, Simon taught the following in his *Explanation of the Creed*: in philosophy the line of argument (or *topos*) is, according to the Aristotelico-Boethian definition, an "argument that produces assurance about what is doubtful," but in theology the terms are reversed and the foundational principle of true knowledge will be a "faith that makes reasonable."

In the Prologue of William's *Golden Summa*, when speaking of Paul's statement that faith is "the conviction (*argumentum*) of things not seen" (Heb 11:1), the author refers to Simon's theory and makes one point even clearer: that the reversal of the relationship, which is fundamental for encouraging the faithful, refuting heretics, and guiding the ignorant or "the simple," constitutes a true and proper method that is specific to theological discourse as opposed to the method of philosophy. The purpose of the former method is to bring the believing soul closer to the divine mysteries (a closeness that is always and in every case a form of understanding).

The special merit of the Parisian secular masters was to have harmonized this ancient conception of rationality in the service of faith with the new methodological and speculative exactitude made necessary by the appearance of new and still unmastered lines of philosophical thought. In other words, they studied and identified the possibility of discoursing on the major problems of Christian thought while adding new solutions made possible by the recent acquisition of philosophical tools, which they boldly derived from books on metaphysics or natural philosophy.

A. WILLIAM OF AUXERRE

William of Auxerre (d. 1231) was teaching theology in Paris when, during the crisis of 1229, he was sent to Rome, along with Franciscan Alexander of Hales, to secure the support of Gregory IX for the university. The pope made him a member of the commission charged with purging the writings of Aristotle on physics, but death kept William from finishing this work.

His *Golden Summa* consists of a series of questions, loosely organized and collected by treatise according to a doctrinal outline similar to that of Lombard's *Sentences*. The dynamic parallelism between "reason producing assurance" and "faith making reasonable" provides the supporting structure of the work and makes it possible to exploit a productive formal analogy between theology and the other sciences. In this approach the "articles of faith" (that is, the dogmatic formulations that make up the creed) can be regarded as equivalent to the "self-evident first principles" characteristic of scientific knowledge. But, William says, any attempt to base on this analogy a deductive type of explanation of the contents of revelation is contrived.

In his opinion, theological reasoning advances rather in the fragmented thematic manner of the question. The reason for this choice is the fact that the foundations or principles of theological knowledge possess a quite special kind of lucidity that is based on the act of faith: they are evident because they have no need of any "external proof," and they enlighten the mind, but in the way that faith, and not knowledge, does. Thus while William has not taken the decisive step toward the idea of basing theological knowledge on its first principles, he has nevertheless moved in that direction by granting them a fundamental validity (but one peculiar to studies presupposing the truth of the faith) in controlling the argumentative method that must characterize theological knowledge in relation to the other sciences.

But in William's case the successful fusion of Augustinianism and the new philosophy is the result of his obvious conceptual debt to Avicenna, from whose thought he derives the distinction between the being in and of itself (*per se*) of the first essence, which is God, and the derived being of all creatures. The first of the articles of faith that produce a rational necessity in the mind is the article on the existence of God. Given this first premise, the finite being of created things is not understandable as such unless it is somehow connected with the idea of the divine essence, the absolute source of being. From this it follows, on the one hand, that any being that is not God can be conceived of only as "existing through another" and therefore as "being" in an indeterminate sense as compared with the divine being. On the other hand, it also follows that the intrinsic divine being can only be conceived as transcendent and unknowable, and yet intuitable by ascending toward it through rational reflection on the limitations of creatures.

Starting from this central idea, William in his *Golden Summa* is able freely to develop his synthesis of naturalistic rationalism and theological traditionalism as he turns to the various problems connected with the thinkableness of the first essence. He begins with the very problem of knowing God, a knowledge that, after original sin, is only possible either "in a mirror" (*per speculum*), that is, by contemplating the divine image in the soul, or "in a riddle" (*in aenigmate*), that is, rising up to God from the contemplation of created things and with the aid of arguments accessible to everyone because based on universally known principles (such as "everything that is caused and because it is caused needs another in order to exist"). In this same context he harks back to the "single argument" of Anselm's *Proslogion* and to Richard of St. Victor's studies of the "necessary reasons" for the trinitarian mystery.

William is also able to tackle the philosophical problem of the eternity of the world by drawing on Augustine's thinking on the nature of time. According to Augustine, the impossibility of reason's conceiving a "before" the world is due to the necessity of admitting that time, too, had its own beginning after that first "beginning." In psychology the distinction made by the Aristoteleans between active intellect and material intellect can very well be explained as corresponding to the Augustinian distinction between higher reason and lower reason.

B. THE THEORY OF THE TRANSCENDENTALS

The emphasis on the thinkableness of God as first essence and of creatures as derived beings led to an initial reflection on a theme that had a dominant place in the typical synthesis of novelty and theological tradition of these first masters; the synthesis, that is, of Avicennianism, Augustinianism, Areopagism, monastic spirituality, and Porretan logic. That theme was the theory of the transcendentals. The complicated elaboration of this theory, which was to undergo important developments throughout the history of scholastic theology, captured the interest not only of William of Auxerre, but also of two other secular masters of this first generation: William of Auvergne, who was, as we have seen, bishop of Paris, and Philip the Chancellor.

As a matter of fact, the term "transcendentals" appeared for the first time a few years later in the *Summa* of Dominican Roland of Cremona. Philip the Chancellor was, however, the first to deal specifically with them in his *Summa on the Good*, where they are described as "concomitant conditions of existence." They are, that is, the most universal possible notions that are part of the thinkableness of being. They are, then, as it might be put by Pseudo-Dionysius, the highest and all-embracing among the divine Names but also the most general of creaturely names. Since they are in fact the primary ideas that allow the mind to understand what being is, the grasp of their meaning leads the human mind from the knowableness of creatures to the cognitive limit represented by transcendence, beyond which such ideas disappear, since they necessarily combine to form an indivisible unity. They are therefore "transcendentals" because knowledge cannot advance beyond them: beyond existence there is only the transcendent and therefore the unknowable.

Because of their supreme universality, the list of such properties must necessarily be limited: according to Philip they are being, one, true, and good; William of Auvergne adds "beautiful" (a transcendental of special importance in the theological universe of Pseudo-Dionysius). Their names correspond to the simplest distinctions available to knowledge or, as Philip describes them, to the "primary basic conceptions of the mind." The latter are the most basic terms and the ultimate goal of every process of abstraction of the human mind in dealing with being and, conversely, the first possible ways in which the transcendent divine can be known.

In his study of these fundamental ideas William of Auvergne takes as his starting point the admission that it is impossible to think pure existence except as one, inasmuch as it is necessarily identical with itself. From this admission springs the necessity that "one" be recognized as a property of transcendent being. Continuing this line of thought, one must accept that simple being is also self-sufficient and is therefore good in itself, that is, identical with its goodness. And from the fact that one and good are identical it necessarily follows that this identity is true and is even the very truth of trueness and that therefore "true" is an absolutely necessary aspect of the thinkableness of the divine.

In this way the secular masters show how all the transcendentals condition theological knowledge, since they are presupposed by any truth of the faith. But at the same time, with the help of Avicennian ontology, the secular masters show the necessity of appealing to their meaning in explaining the being of what is created, because anything that exists in a limited way can only be a "being" insofar as it is "something good" and "something true." Here, too, we find a cognitive principle that is essential for the understanding of revelation, since the data of the faith are all knowable only as truths of faith, that is, as "something true," and as pointers to the virtuous action of human beings, that is, as "something good."

The theory of the transcendentals thus became the irreplaceable speculative link connecting the truths of theoretical philosophy, ethics, and theology, since without a correct understanding of the transcendentals no further specific knowledge is possible.

C. PHILIP THE CHANCELLOR

The making of this connection is especially clear in Philip, who was a master of theology and chancellor of the university from 1218 to 1236, the year of his death. As he makes explicit in the Prologue of his *Summa on the Good*, he takes the transcendentals as the foundation of the explanatory structure of theological wisdom.

In fact, as the title of his work indicates, Philip is principally interested in the range of signification of the term "good," since he is concerned to harmonize the ontology and psychology of the new Aristoteleanizing philosophy with the soul's moral situation. This point of view links him to the most important twelfth-century representatives of monastic theological anthropology.

But an understanding of the transcendentals is not to be had by isolating them and studying them separately, since their truth consists in a continuous interaction of their reciprocal thinkableness. This is why the initial introduction of the doctrine of the transcendentals in all its complexity determines the approach taken to the problems faced in the work, for it allows the author to make the divine essence the source not only of finite existence but also of the particular goodness proper to creatures and therefore of their natural ordination to the good; this last is a fundamental condition for the moral evaluation of human activity. This position is possible only if one accepts that in God being-*one*, being-*true*, and being-*good* cannot be thought of as a projection onto God, in however superlative a degree, of the corresponding qualities in creatures. On the contrary, it is creaturely limitations that give rise to a multiplication of knowable aspects of creaturely being. These aspects arise from the graduated succession of distinctions and limitations that characterize beings insofar as they are different and, at the same time, insofar as they have their origin in God. For his efficacious causality leaves a different real imprint on each of them.

Using a formula the substance of which is Avicennian but the logical form of which depends on the Boethean-Porretan tradition, Philip says that "truth is the lack of division between existence and that which is." In his interpretation of these words, the meaning is that in God the relationship between his several modes of being is the relationship among things that are not distinct, and that each of the modes is convertible into the others because in God there is no distinction among potential modalities that could lead to an existence in act that would be different from his essence.

Philip thus introduces for the first time a fruitful reflection on the lack of distinction in God between being and existence. He is therefore able to assert that if in God being-*true* is not one thing, being-*good* another, and being-*one*, or self-contained existence, still another, then the reaching out of human minds toward the truth of logic and the good of ethics is simply a different modality (but different only from the creature's point of view) of the constant reaching of minds toward the one, that is, the divine being of theology. Furthermore, thanks precisely to the light in which this divine being reveals himself in the Scriptures it is possible to build up a satisfactory knowledge of the true and the good that will influence both theoretical knowledge and moral discipline.

D. WILLIAM OF AUVERGNE

In 1228 Philip was a candidate for election as bishop of Paris (he lost); his competitor was another secular master, William of Auvergne, who carried the burden of episcopal office until his death in 1249. The major work in his wide-ranging collection of theological, exegetical, and pastoral writings is his *Teaching on Wisdom and Divinity*. This is an organized explanation of the faith set in the framework, once again, of a synthesis of traditional early medieval Platonism-Augustinianism (Augustine, Boethius, Anselm) and the enticing aspects of the new eastern Platonism-Aristoteleanism (Avicenna and *On Causes*, but also Avicebron, "noblest of all the philosophers").

In the order imposed on the thematic sections of the work, which were composed at different times and often published separately, it again shows its dependence on the systematic approach taken in the twelfth century: from trinitarian theology to christology and religious anthropology ("The Reasons Why God Became Incarnate") and from sacramental theology to theological cosmology (in which the approach is still that of the physics of the *Timaeus*). Once again, a combination of the old and the new justifies the identification of theology (which in the early Middle Ages was the "true philosophy" or the "heavenly philosophy") with the "first philosophy" of the Aristoteleans.

According to William, the philosophers had insights into many natural truths but also into supernatural truth. It was therefore necessary to learn how to distinguish between their constructive contributions, made when they were speculating in harmony with the truths of the faith, and their errors, on which they must be openly contradicted. William's own well-developed philosophical sensibilities, deeply influenced by Anselm, led him to identify theological reason as the sole instrument of such a critique: that is, a dialectical intelligence able, on the basis of converging faith and philosophy, to show the falsity of the demonstrative excesses of nontheological reason. Thus it is possible to respond to the claimed eternity of the world or the introduction of intermediaries between God and creation with the theological assertion (which becomes a real criterion for recognizing the truth) of the unqualified omnipotence of God's free will. This principle can in fact not only be derived from the Bible and religious tradition; it has also been solidly demonstrated by theological reason on the basis simply of reflection on the nature of the divinity. Witnesses to this fact are not only Augustine and the theologians of early medieval monasticism, but also the best of the "new" philosophers, chief among them Avicebron, who has shown how "will" is the first characteristic of the divine being to manifest itself in creation.

Moreover, the influence of Avicebron allows William of Auvergne, who likewise grounds his thinking in reflection on the nature of the transcendentals, to correct Avicenna's teaching on ontology. The latter's distinction between necessary being and possible-derived being was for the most part understood by the Latins as equivalent to Boethius' distinction between existence and that which is. But Avicebron, who always interprets the individual's nature as a composition of matter and a plurality of forms inhering in matter, explains that derived being is not to be understood (as a superficial reading of Boethius and Avicenna might suggest) as the result of a pure and simple participation of particulars in the higher divine form, since such an understanding of derived being would lead to pantheism and emanationism. But neither is it to be understood as a participation in a single inferior form, the last in a long chain of intermediate forms, for this view, given the priority of the efficacious action of the heavenly intelligences on the activity of individuals, would have serious consequences of a mechanist and determinist kind.

Creaturely reality is therefore the fruit rather of the complex participation of each individual both in the divine form, which is present in every created entity insofar as it gives it its existence, and in a series of inferior accidental forms that condition the fulfillment of its whatness or actual being. Acted on and moved by an unmediated divine love, creatures return this love by moving toward it in a variety of ways that are conditioned precisely by the existential determinants of each creature. Thus the angelic substances, which have the contemplation of God as their sole existential orientation, are exempt from composition with matter (contrary in this case to the teaching of Avicebron) and are individualized solely by divine love and their own formal elements.

Only in God is existence the identifying characteristic of his very essence, since pure essence can in fact only be a necessary essence. The reason is that a perfectly complete being can only be a perfectly existent being as well as perfectly transcendent and completely causative, precisely because necessary, of every composite being (evident here is an interesting combination of Avicenna and Maimonides with the speculative foundations of Anselm's *Proslogion*). God's existence, then, is pure, absolute, and perfect, and is identical with the perfect true and the perfect good, so that in God to exist is also to know perfectly and to will perfectly.

But then, precisely to the extent that God gives creatures their actual existence, he also grants them the existential acts of knowing and willing, which are then conditioned in each particular being by the influence of accidental forms in contacts between individuals. In contrast, the only conditioning factor possible in the divine action is the free act of love by which the supreme being gives creatures their individual existences. The freedom of this act, being pure nondetermination in relation to others, also guarantees God's unqualified immutability and his pure pre-temporal, unmediated knowledge of all the things he creates, orders, and preserves in being.

The human soul (according to still another combination of Augustinianism and Aristoteleanism) is a purely spiritual substance like the angelic intelligences, but in this case there can be no denying that it is also the formal principle of the body. In order to avoid any kind of composition in the soul, William rejects the distinction between agent intellect and possible intellect (which he regards as a defective Arabic interpretation of Aristotelean psychology) and reduces all the faculties listed in both Aristoteleanism and early medieval Platonic gnoseology to the operations of a single substance. The production of intelligible forms in the intellect cannot be the work of an external cause: not the senses, which could never lead to abstraction, but also not of a higher intelligence, since, like all creaturely operations, knowledge is the direct effect of the unmediated, deliberate, and providential action of God. Knowledge can therefore be due only to an illumination, an act that efficaciously forms knowledge, which comes, in the measure proper to each soul, from God alone, who is the "light of knowledge" and the "exemplar and mirror" of all truth.

God's action in the soul thus creates a reciprocity. Insofar as he is existence he gives the soul its existence, which consists in its being ordered to the actuation of its being. Insofar as he is true and good he gives the soul intelligence and love, which are its very life ("love is the life of the spirit"). This life achieves its authentic actuation only in ascending, through the exercise of knowledge and the virtues (therefore cognitively and ethically), to the closest possible contact with the first principle and ultimate end of all knowledge and love. This ascent ends in the union and deification proper to ecstatic and prophetic vision in this life and to the beatifying vision in the life to come.

3. The Franciscan Masters of Paris:
Alexander of Hales and John of La Rochelle

The doctrinal teachings of the first masters from the Mendicant Orders must be assessed in light of the entire cultural context in which the first university theology had come to birth. Thematic parallels and shared cultural conditions do not permit us to trace back to the beginnings any very marked divisions and trends of thought. The umbilical cord linking these men to the patristic and monastic traditions and, in addition, their encounter with the new Greco-Arabic philosophy gave a homogeneous cast to the thinking of the secular, Franciscan, and Dominican masters during the first decades. On the other hand, it is legitimate to follow the gradual emergence of some preferred trends of thought that were spurred by current debates in the scholarly world. These trends were also given direction by the different motivations that, on the basis of the fundamental vocation of the Order in question, justified the acceptance of divergent ways of conceiving truth with its manifestation in Scripture and in nature and its hiddenness in the transcendent.

Thus in a first phase the Franciscans and Dominicans went along with the synthesis of monastic Augustinianism-Platonism and ideas coming from the "new" philosophical sources. It has been suggested that this synthesis be given the perhaps incorrect but nonetheless meaningful name of "Avicennianizing Augustinianism," inasmuch as it was fostered especially by its being set within the speculative framework provided by Avicenna's system (with subsequent corrections drawn from Avicebron). In harmony with the speculative course adopted by the first secular masters, the Franciscans in particular opted for a degree of conciliation with philosophical learning, their express intention being that, in response to the triumphal success of currently popular teachings, they would restore the solid bulwark of theological certainties inherited from the Fathers of the Church and their medieval interpreters. Their purpose here was to defend and fortify the citadel of the faith.

By common agreement they therefore set out to learn and use Aristotelean-ism to the extent that it was useful and did not alter the Christian vision of reality and, above all, did not undermine certainty about the origins and supernatural goals of human life. When these limits were transgressed, the Mendicants' typical and constant recourse was to the thought of Augustine. He was regarded as a veritable storehouse of philosophical ideas that he had already adapted for the effective support of the truths of revelation and that through a new and laborious inspection and application of their speculative range could be combined with the best ideas coming from Aristotelean thought and from the Arabic and Jewish interpretation of it.

Anthony of Padua (d. 1231) was one of the first Franciscans to devote himself to the intellectual life; he was a master in Bologna and then in various French cities during the twenties. His *Sermons* already show clearly the desire to take over and make the most of the Christian theological tradition of earlier centuries, from the Fathers to the Victorines, the Cistercians, and Peter Lombard. The primary goal was to shape an exegetical method that was solid and could be profitably used in apologetics. At the same time, however, the aim was to build up a process of theological understanding that allows the soul to ascend from the reading of revelation to contemplation of the christological mysteries and even to rediscovery within itself of the lost truth about the image of God. Such a rediscovery was to be made possible by divine love and divine grace in a reciprocal convergence of the intellect and the loving will (that is, of the understanding that gives rise to love and the love that directs understanding).

It seems that the introduction of the *Book of Sentences* as the ordinary text for advanced lectures in theology was due to Alexander of Hales (d. 1245), the first secular master to put on the Franciscan habit. One result of his own reading was the *Gloss on the Four Books of Sentences*, which he composed between 1223 and 1227 while still a secular. His theological method then led to the writing of a lengthy series of *Disputed Questions*, which formed two collections known respectively as "first" and "after becoming a friar," that is, before and after his conversion, which took place in 1236 when he was about fifty. In both series the author applies the analytico-demonstrative method rigorously and consistently. He appeals regularly to the authority of the Fathers and confronts a series of doctrinal problems, at times in a critical spirit, at times in a conciliatory spirit, in order finally to formulate a thesis resulting from what has preceded. He reaches positions that often combine different schools of thought, but are not completely lacking in originality.

For example: In order to give a definition of the nature of the soul, Alexander lists first the opinions of the Fathers and then the more recent views of the philosophers (namely, the Aristotelean doctrine of the soul as the form of the body).

From the latter, however, he accepts only what is compatible with Platonico-Augustinian teaching, and ends by developing a conception of the soul as a substance created by God but capable in addition of giving form and activity to the body.

Another example: he takes over the distinction and analogy between divine being and created being, which he regards as indispensable for demonstrating the existence of God on the basis of the ontological incompleteness of the finite. But (like William of Auvergne) he combines into a single concept the Avicennian distinction between what is necessary in itself and what is necessary due to another, the Boethean-Porretan distinction between that which is and that by which it is, and hylomorphic composition in all creatures whether earthly or heavenly (the latter according to Avicebron, but not William of Auvergne).

These examples show what Alexander means when he repeats Anselm's idea that theology has as its object every mental act by which an understanding of the faith is acquired, in order then to establish a "science of God" based on revelation. This science is an essential means of leading human beings to a true share in the divine life, just as God through the Incarnation shares in human life. In this perspective the ultimate goal of the Incarnation, achieved by means of the restoration from sin but also by what lies beyond that restoration, is to bring humanity close to God. Anselm was therefore correct in maintaining that the Incarnation would have taken place even if there had been no original sin. In effect this amounts to saying that the ultimate purpose of the Incarnation is "theology" itself, which brings the conversion or "turning" of humanity to God to its highest degree of perfection. This conversion is made possible by grace and guided by faith; it culminates in the direct experience of the divine, which can already be savored in this life (by a free gift of the Holy Spirit, as Alexander read in the Cistercian mystics) through the "spiritual senses" of the soul.

This last observation introduced into Franciscan thought the need to explain how knowledge—sensible, rational-scientific, and finally theological-contemplative —is produced in the human soul, while safeguarding the soul's nature as a single substance that is free and capable of autonomous life despite its relationship with corporeity. This subject was tackled directly by John of La Rochelle (d. 1645), the leading spirit at the Franciscan house of studies in Paris until Alexander's entrance into the Order led to the study center being incorporated into the university; at that point John became Alexander's colleague and collaborator.

John, who was influenced by the teaching of the first secular masters, has left works of scriptural exegesis, sermons, and various treatises in which he shows once again the express intention of systematizing and harmonizing ideas circulating in Parisian theological reflection during the first decades. It is in light of this concordist attitude that we ought to assess John's conception of anthropology, which is documented in a preparatory *Treatise on the Complex Division of the Soul's Powers* and then by the more organized and extensive *Summa on the Soul*, which was composed after 1236, that is, after he began teaching.

In the *Summa on the Soul* all the definitions and divisions of the soul, whether coming from the early medieval Platonic-Augustinian tradition or from the "new" Peripatetic tradition, are subjected to a critical examination. The result is a view of the soul as a "perfection," a term that in this context is synonymous with "act" or "form." The soul is thus seen as a formal principle of the body but, at the same time, as the subject of the fulfillment of the human individual's capacity for intellection and ethical activity. The soul is thus able to attain a perfection of its own due to the work of grace, which orders it to its supernatural end and leads it to beatitude.

This idea, which John derives, while refining it, from the work *Spirit and Soul*, which was composed in the Cistercian world (though he believed it to be by Augustine), enables him to harmonize Aristoteleanism and Augustinianism by means of the concordist position anticipated by Alexander of Hales. That is: in the single psychic substance, which is an intelligible individual entity (a "this something"), it is possible to discern a functional direction downward as mover and as vitalizing, vegetative, and sensitive form of the body (this is why it is called "soul"), but also a higher tension (this is why it is called "spirit") that constantly draws it toward contact with God. This contact is made possible by the image of the Trinity (memory, understanding, and will) that is impressed upon the soul.

As substantially transcending the body even while functionally immanent in it, the soul is capable of ascending to intellectual knowledge with the aid of the two powers the Aristoteleans called the possible intellect and the agent intellect, though this knowledge is always limited to natural and finite objects. But when it comes to knowledge of the suprasensible world, the agent intellect (which is a possession of the person) is unable to provide any idea of it through abstraction. All of supernatural truth can therefore be made comprehensible only by a higher agency, external to the soul, which can only be God himself. In order to ensure human understanding of revelation, which has to do with suprasensible realities, God intervenes with his enlightening grace and renders the human intellect able to participate in a truth that is learned through the senses (the words of Scripture), but to do so on a level of understanding that is infinitely beyond its creaturely capacities.

Since God is enlightener, he was regarded by the Franciscan masters as both the subject and the object of theological knowledge. In this perspective they gradually developed an awareness of how a deeper study of theology could have a special and unique meaning for them, one more directly reflecting their basic vocation as preachers working within history for the moral reformation and sanctification of humanity. Making clear the truths of the faith to believers meant showing them the ways of leading a true Christian life. John of La Rochelle therefore found it essential to describe and foster the correct ordering of the soul to the attainment of its anthropological perfection, because this goal could and should be the same as the Franciscan ideal of evangelical perfection.

A Franciscan theologian should, then, devote himself to developing a new teaching in response to the speculative novelties introduced into Christian education by the philosophers. Then he ought to make this teaching bear fruit in defense of historical revelation and the traditional patrimony of Christian culture that had been applied down the centuries in support of revelation. Thus it became increasingly clear that the Friars Minor needed to devote themselves to the development of a theological learning that did not reject solid philosophical argument, while being based on the absolute truthfulness of revelation. Thus they would achieve in their "sacred reading" a complete synthesis "of knowledge, life, and doctrine," as John himself said explicitly when he published his first two lectures on the Bible under the title *General Introduction to Sacred Doctrine*.

The desire to bring together into a single systematic doctrinal corpus the positions that proved most characteristic of this special theological project led the Franciscan masters to undertake the compilation of a great *Summa*. Later generations attributed this work to Alexander of Hales (as the *Summa of Friar Alexander*), but it was in fact the result of the collaboration of many scholars close to him, under the direction especially of John of La Rochelle. These scholars drew to some extent on the authentic writings or classroom materials of Alexander, and the work was later brought to completion, under commission of Pope Alexander IV, by the English friar William of Meliton, who was a master in Paris beginning in 1248.

This work, to which scholars nowadays prefer to give the general name *Summa of [Alexander of] Hales* (or *Summa of the Friars Minor*), contains a complete, structured collection of the fundamental theological doctrines accepted by the first theologians of the Order and acknowledged as characteristic of speculative trends among the Franciscans even in later generations. These doctrines were: the distinction between being and existence, universal hylomorphism, a gnoseology of illumination, the divine knowledge of particular realities and an emphasis on themes dealing with the affections and the will in God, the divine government of created nature by means of the seminal reasons, and the conception of the soul as both form and substance. The chief merit of the *Hales Summa* was that it brought these various theses together in the framework of a comprehensive and organized conception of natural and supernatural reality that was to become a true and proper manifesto of the Franciscan way of thinking.

The idea of theology as a fusion of life and doctrine has an important place in the program of work in the *Summa*, especially in the Prologue to the third book (which certainly incorporates a teaching of John). This Prologue gives a comprehensive statement of theological material that later enjoyed a certain success. Knowledge of the truth about things divine includes teachings that are broken down into two sections: faith and morals. The first part includes "the faith that is believed," that is, the dogmas contained in revelation and to which assent is given, and then the simple enunciation of these; and then "the faith by which one believes," that is, an argued rational explanation of this same content, the goal being persuasion. The section on morality is likewise divided into two parts: an explanation of the vices, that is, a description of the various sins, and then a rational analysis of the remedies for sin and their effectiveness (commandments, virtues, gifts of the Holy Spirit, sacraments).

4. The Franciscan Masters of Oxford: Robert Grosseteste

The teaching of the Franciscans in the schools and study centers of England displayed an outlook all its own. Here, from the beginning of the century, the absence of prohibitions aimed at the books of Aristotle was combined with an emphasis (already to be seen in John of Salisbury) on the limitations of reason's claim to compete with faith in the discovery of truth. The combination led to a definite stress on the cognitive role of experience as well as a new openness to the physical-naturalistic aspect of scientific study. In contrast to the dominance of logical methodology at the universities of the continent, English scholars preferred to look to the disciplines of the quadrivium and to medico-astrological experience for ideas on a methodology useful for knowing and organizing visible reality. This was especially the case in view of the deficiencies of reason in going beyond the data of revelation and investigating the modalities and conditions of invisible reality.

The English Friars Minor were at ease with this naturalistic approach, especially because it could reflect the celebration of creation as a choral witness to God's work, as Francis himself had urged. But they preferred it also because it reflected the tendency (in opposition to Greco-Arabic philosophy) that gradually became characteristic of the Order's thinkers, to reduce the excesses of systematic rationalism and the unjustified all-embracing ambitions of metaphysics.

It was not by chance, then, that the masters of arts at Oxford and Cambridge in the first half of the century devoted special attention to the *Posterior Analytics*. This work had already been known there for several decades (as John of Salisbury bears witness) and was made more accessible by Gerard of Cremona's translation of Themistius' paraphrase. In this work the Latin-language masters found detailed information on Aristotle's conception of science. They were thus able to determine the conditions under which knowledge could henceforth be described as "scientific."

These conditions were: (1) that this knowledge start with the acquisition of experimental data through the senses, (2) that the understanding of it be ensured through abstraction of universal data not subject to accidental change (as information about particular aspects of things is) and therefore objectively true in their determination of a meaning that is always the same, (3) that it be structured through deductions based on definitions and sets of ideas that are strictly universal, and, finally, (4) that it always be a knowledge through causes, because only then can it be based on necessary linkages of truths that correspond to universal ideas.

The first Latin commentary on the *Posterior Analytics* was composed around 1230 by Robert Grosseteste (d. 1253). Beginning in the previous year he taught theology at the Franciscan house of studies in Oxford; in 1235 he became bishop of Lincoln. In a key question of his commentary he deals with Aristotle's first instruction, that scientific knowledge must always be based on data provided by the senses. He corrects this and even completes it with a remark that is essentially drawn from Christian theology, namely, that without being dependent on sensible experience the divine intellect has an eternal knowledge of all things, universal and individual, and that it is therefore appropriate to show a greater gnoseological openness to Aristoteleanism once one accepts that it is always possible for any finite intelligence to receive knowledge of truth from the higher divine source.

The idea of a complementarity of experience and illumination in the human soul had already been accepted by the secular masters and the first Franciscans in Paris. Here, however, it is fruitfully introduced into the codification of the epistemological claims of human knowledge. Aristotle was right in saying that the only knowledge truly certain and informative about the nature of its object is knowledge connecting that object with universality. It is therefore necessary that through the process of abstraction the mind take all ideas coming from sense experience and express them in universal terms, that is, in terms purged of contingency and particularity.

In order to ensure the objectivity of this process the philosophers have, without sufficient reason, introduced the activity of an agent intellect that, in a manner that is the same for all particular intellects, abstracts forms from sense data. In order for the agent intellect to do this it must (they argue) be separate from individual souls and be one and the same for the entire human race. In contrast, the Christian perspective offers much more solid reasons for sticking to a simpler, more effective, and therefore truer solution. Grosseteste's position: since cognitive certainty can also come through divine illumination, abstraction from the empirical data indispensable for the production of scientific knowledge must be subordinate to the intervention of the interior light from on high. As a result, the particular truth of any completely scientific idea will depend on its effective participation in the divine Truth, that is, in the eternal ideas that govern creation and subsist eternally in the intellect of God.

But these are only the theological premises of a correct epistemology. Grosseteste must now explain the meaning and possibility of the production of intelligible universals in the human mind through the establishment of a direct communion between the mind and the divine ideas, which are the causes and formal reasons of everything created. It is impossible, indeed, to admit a direct participation of creaturely intellects in the absolute and ineffable superiority that truth has in God. It is therefore necessary to identify a cognitive connection between the truth of the exemplary ideas and sensible experience, a connection that will explain and ensure the participation of human knowledge in both realities: that is, preserving both the necessity and changelessness of the former and the informational capacity of the latter.

According to Grosseteste, mathematics provides such a perfect model of knowledge and of a true connection between divine illumination and sense experience. In mathematical knowledge the empirical data are always raised to an abstractive level on which they give information about the true nature of the corresponding reality, information that is complete but also rigorous and necessary, this being a sign that the knowledge is the effect of a true illumination from on high. In contrast, no other creaturely science is able, as mathematics is, to justify its claims from relationships among natural phenomena by showing their cause-effect links, thereby fully adhering to Aristotle's ultimate epistemological criterion, namely, knowledge through causes. Physics, which considers nature in its mutability, is unable to meet that standard; neither can logic or metaphysics, the objects of which are too elusive and abstract and lack a correspondence to visible reality.

In his commentary on the *Analytics* Robert therefore concludes that "only in mathematics do we have science and demonstration in the proper sense." This is because only in mathematical knowledge is the object accurately known as resulting from a convergence of experiential knowledge and the formation of abstractions that is made possible by the divine illumination.

This teaching of Grosseteste, which has been dubbed a "metaphysics of light," reflects ideas quite widespread in the world of Oxford (and not only there), in which hints from the Bible are combined with philosophical ideas from Avicenna and the *On Causes*, but also from Avicebron. In any case the teaching clearly shows a definite interaction of mathematics and theology, emerging naturally from the twofold nature of light itself, which is internal to creation inasmuch as it is the first creature, and external to it inasmuch as it is supernatural and comes directly from God. Especially important, then, for the development of Grosseteste's teaching was his encounter with the works of Pseudo-Dionysius (which he himself translated anew and commented on). Since all intelligent creatures, both angels and human beings, know the truth by participating in the divine light and recognizing the presence of this light in creation, and since everything that God makes receives the imprint of his mode of being, God himself is therefore knowable as light.

Thus, in a reversal of the process whereby light descends from God, the human intelligence, by its understanding of the nature of light, is enabled to draw near, in the highest degree allowed it, to the truth of the divine nature and of the trinitarian mystery. With the aid of an analogy with visible light and the active production of light, clarity, and warmth, which spring simultaneously one from another and reflect one another with complete reciprocity amid the distinction of functions, God is conceivable, "through an example" and in the highest possible degree, as unity in trinity. Since God is in fact light, and since light is the source of knowledge, the aspects of God's essence are likewise sources of his intelligibility.

The influence of Anselm of Aosta, which was still quite strong in the English world at the beginning of the thirteenth century, added a final essential element in the conception of theology that Grosseteste set alongside his rigorous interpretation of the scientific knowledge of nature. According to his gnoseological principles the ascent of human knowledge toward the encounter with divine illumination can start only from some experiential datum. But, as Anselm taught, *faith* in revelation is a direct source of an *experience of truth*; therefore only by taking this experience as a starting point can the mind reach the complete illumination in which theological truth attains its perfect form.

Thus, for example, in Robert's treatise on *The Relaxation of Laws* he explains his own understanding of the christological mystery by drawing openly on *Cur deus homo*. Revelation, he says, tells us of the historical event of the Incarnation, and faith accepts this as true; theology goes further and understands that the Incarnation was not occasioned by the need for redemption from Adam's sin, but was eternally preordained in the will of God, who from the moment he created human beings wanted to be united with them. When God made human beings the heart of his universe, inasmuch as they are capable of accepting everything coming from him, God also made them the principal object of his love and the beings most worthy of receiving a divine person among them in order that this person might give the highest possible expression to the active presence of the Creator in his creation. Robert then turns to the Scriptures in order to show that the suitableness of the Incarnation is everywhere present in it and in all the inspired words, which always celebrate God's self-revelation to humanity, of which the Incarnation is the supreme act.

5. The First Dominican Masters

The Dominican masters of the first generation were less united in their speculative choices than were the Franciscans, and for the most part adopted individual doctrinal positions under the influence, to a greater or lesser degree, of the more prominent trends among the secular masters.

As noted earlier, Roland of Cremona (d. 1250), an Italian, was appointed master of theology in Paris by William of Auvergne at the time of the strike. He later moved to Toulouse and finally returned to Italy as a papal inquisitor. In the thirties he composed a *Summa* that did not enjoy any great success. It is a work inspired by Augustine; in it philosophical and scientific information makes a sporadic appearance as complementary to theology and subordinate to it.

John of Saint-Gilles (d. after 1258), who competes with Roland for the title of first Dominican master in Paris, has left us only some sermons. In one of these, delivered at the university, he complains in a somewhat general way about the outlook of masters of arts when they move into theology: "They have great difficulty in distancing themselves from their previous sciences, as can be seen in some of them who are unable to leave Aristotle aside in their theology, but fill it with philosophical questions and opinions, thus stuffing it with brass which they pass off as gold."

Hugh of St. Cher (d. 1263) succeeded Roland in Paris and then became a cardinal in 1244. He has left us numerous exegetical contributions based for the most part on the literal sense, some disputed questions, and one of the first commentaries on Lombard's *Sentences*, in which he takes up in an uncertain manner only a few particular questions of sacramental theology. Of greater interest is his effort to improve the biblical text by offering various *Corrections* as well as the first composition of a biblical concordance in Latin. He is truly dependent on the patristic tradition and does not hide his liking for the Greek Fathers, whose thought was to some extent being rediscovered and newly translated during these years.

This leads him at times to adopt some odd positions. In particular, in one of his notes on the Fourth Gospel and in a question on the same subject he formulates a teaching on the beatific vision that he says he has gotten from *The Orthodox Faith* of John Damascene but that also shows a clear acceptance of Pseudo-Dionysian teaching on theophanies. He says that in eternal life God will be visible to the blessed immediately and through illumination, "not however in his essence but only insofar as he is glory, goodness, and truth." In other words, even the eschatological vision of God will not be of his essence, but only of the effects of his power; this holds not only for human beings but also for the angels.

Guerric of St. Quentin (d. 1245) succeeded John of Saint-Gilles in Paris from 1233 on and is known chiefly as the author of some literal commentaries on the Bible. In some *Quodlibetal Questions* he takes up the same subject as Hugh and adopts the latter's position, going so far as to say that even the soul of Christ does not see the divine essence as such "since this vision belongs to the Trinity alone."

It is worth noting that this position, which would have been quietly accepted in the cultural world of the early Middle Ages, took on a special and in some ways dangerous character in this new century, now that Aristotelean epistemology had become widely known. The reason: In the Aristotelean perspective, which regards true knowledge as the appearance of the known object in the intellect, the assertion that the blessed have only an indirect knowledge of the supreme object of their blessedness could sound like a denial of the truth of the beatific vision. As a result, in 1241 bishop William of Auvergne and chancellor Odo of Châteauroux issued a solemn prohibition against the public teaching in Paris of a beatific vision that is indirect and made possible only through intermediaries (theophanies). The authorities condemned, among its supporters, a friar named Stephen (probably Stephen of Vénizy, a Dominican).

As a result of the condemnation, Guerric returned to the subject in another question, where he changed his thesis and followed the directives of the authorities. As this action shows, even in the Order there was fear that the introduction of philosophical ideas on the nature of theological knowledge that differed from current trends could give rise to quite serious misunderstandings.

At the beginning the Dominicans of Oxford were likewise characterized by a strict adherence to theological traditionalism. This is especially clear in the case of Richard Fishacre (d. ca. 1248), a student under and successor to Robert Bacon (who also died in 1248), who had held the first Dominican chair of theology in England. Fishacre wrote a commentary on the *Sentences* in which he clearly accepts the Avicennian-Augustinian ideas shared by the masters of Paris and Oxford during the first three decades of the century: universal hylomorphism, exemplarism, and a gnoseology based on divine illumination. Like Grosseteste, Fishacre does not hide his debt to Anselm of Aosta, whose "one argument" he explicitly repeats and whose example he follows in using reason to explain dogma.

He adopts, however, a new model of the use of reason derived from his knowledge of Aristotelean and Arabic thought. He thus uses the new philosophy not as the carrier of a conception of metaphysics but, following the example of dialectic in the Augustinian tradition, as a storehouse of argumentation tools helpful in explaining the more important theological ideas. All this shows the completely "ancillary" role of philosophical studies in relation to theology; Fishacre explicitly harks back to the most reductive meaning of "ancillary," making it equivalent to "introductory."

This instrumental use of Aristoteleanism emerges most clearly in the way in which Fishacre, in the prologue to his commentary, tackles the question of theological knowledge by appealing to philosophical principles and conventions without at all taking into consideration the Aristotelean idea of science and comparing it with theological wisdom. Thus, in order to explain what theology is he brings in the four causes and uses them as a set of arguments showing that all theological knowledge comes essentially from God. From the viewpoint of final causality, theology is an answer to the human being's innate desire to know the truth, a desire raised to its highest degree; from that of efficient causality, theology is produced by God, who reveals himself; from that of material causality, the subject of theology is God as One and Triune and therefore, in God, the work of redemption, the church, and the sacraments; from that of formal causality, the entire explanation of theological doctrine, with the parts that constitute it, permits the union of humanity with God.

From these premises it becomes clear that by its nature this knowledge is purely apologetical and not scientific, and the task of the theologian cannot consist in demonstrating what transcends all demonstrability, but is simply to explain the truths of the faith in intelligible language. It follows that faith and theology are and must remain identical: the assent of the believer and the speculation of the theologian are two aspects of the same exercise of knowledge, the purpose of which is essentially the attainment of salvation.

II. Birth and Systematization of Theology as a Science: Odo Rigaldi and Albert the Great

The refinement of the formal definition of theology as a scientific knowledge was advanced in the central decade of the thirteenth century by Odo Rigaldi (d. 1276), a Franciscan, and Albert of Lauingen or of Cologne (d. 1280), a Dominican. These two were the masters' best representative of the maturation of the speculative choices being adopted in the two Mendicant Orders. Both men became university professors in Paris when in 1245 they succeeded the masters of their respective Orders, Odo taking over from John of La Rochelle and Alexander of Hales, and Albert from Guerric of St. Quentin. In that same year both began their glosses on the *Sentences* and, in their prologues, faced for the first time the problem of theology as a science. In their handling of this problem they touched on all the fundamental themes and solutions that would characterize their thinking.

Both Odo and Albert remained for only a short time as masters at the University of Paris. Odo, whom the Franciscan chronicler, Salimbene of Parma, describes as "one of the world's greatest clerics," became archbishop of Rouen in 1248. There he was drawn into political affairs and into diplomatic missions involving the kingdom of France, the kingdom of England, and the Holy See; he played an active role in the organization and carrying out of the seventh crusade. He died in 1276 after attending the second council of Lyons.

Albert, who was known to his contemporaries as "the German" but would within a few years after his death be called "the Great," was assigned in 1248 to set up the general house of studies of the Dominicans in Cologne. He was Provincial Prior of Germany from 1254 to 1257 and bishop of Regensburg from 1260 to 1264. But he continually interrupted these institutional activities to devote himself again to teaching and the composition of his own works, with which he busied himself until his death in 1280. Odo and Albert outlived their two greatest disciples, Bonaventure and Thomas, both of whom died in 1274. The place Odo and Albert earned in the history of theological thought can be judged only as preparatory to the coming of the two disciples.

The speculative depth of Albert the Great and his influence, not only theological but also scientifico-philosophical, on later generations were certainly greater and more extensive than Odo's contribution, which was more limited and concerned only with theological problems. It is nonetheless useful to set the two men side by side and speak of their work as parallel, and this not simply because of biographical or chronological coincidence. In fact, both of them, each in the speculative history of his Order, were the prime representatives of

and the ones chiefly responsible for the development of a first formal organization of the theological doctrines on which the university masters of the first half
of the century were focusing their attention. They were responsible, therefore,
for a first consistent and foundational definition (foundational at least for each
group of followers) of the very special nature of a knowledge based on a balance, which had to be unchanging, between knowledge based on revelation and
knowledge acquired by the efforts of unaided natural reason.

1. Odo Rigaldi and the Theory of Theology as a Science

The problem of the nature and purposes of theological knowledge was first
tackled by the Franciscans in the *Hales Summa*. Here, in the "Introductory
Treatise," there is a question on theological doctrine that certainly depended on
the thinking of Alexander "after he became a friar" but also reflects the revision
of Alexander's thought by John of La Rochelle.

Theology has two functions: it is knowledge to be appropriated by the
learned, but it is also, and above all, knowledge in the service of the salvation
of souls. From the outset and on the basis of these two functions the question
claims for theology the right to be regarded as a discipline that is both theoretical, supported by natural reason as its servant, and practical inasmuch as it
implies a deliberate, affective act of the soul when it accepts the truths of faith
("moving the affections to embrace goodness"). This evidently contradicts the
Aristotelean position, according to which theoretical knowledge is necessarily
distinguished from practical knowledge by the fact that for the knowing subject
the former is a disinterested knowledge.

This difficulty is then overcome by a peremptory enlargement of the very concept of "science," which is extended to include the affective component and the
possibility of a divine illumination at the beginning of the process of knowing.
Taken as it stands, this action represents a resistance against facing the problem
on the terms suitable to it. That is, although the author of the question has an
accurate knowledge of the factors that characterize and condition science according to Aristotle, he does not ask whether these are verifiable in theology.

But the development of university teaching emphasized the urgency of a
more rigorous solution. Once the reading of the *Sentences* was introduced into
the schools of theology and once the *Posterior Analytics* became the subject of
lectures in the schools of the arts (through which all candidates for the study of
theology had to pass), it was no longer possible to avoid a careful examination
of the conditions for theological knowledge. The latter, after all, claimed to be
a systematic treatment of the knowableness of dogmas and the problems they
raised.

Aristotelean epistemology provided the criteria for a reorganization of
knowledge that permitted the inclusion of the new natural philosophy and of
metaphysics and the ethico-practical disciplines among the by-now-antiquated

liberal arts. But, as Robert Grosseteste realized, this epistemology also set the necessary conditions for the inclusion within it of any form of knowledge. Even theology, then, especially if it aspired to the title of "queen of sciences" and a place at the head of the new system of disciplines, had to show itself able to take its place within these limits.

Seen in this light, the position on theological knowledge taken by the author of the question in the *Hales Summa* represented a first deliberate resistance on the part of theologians against subjecting theology to the demands of the Aristotelean method. The impossibility of adapting theology's investigations into the "Cause of causes" to the investigations of all the other sciences into things that are caused—that is, secondary causes and their effects—suggested to them that they should place "the science of God or theology" on a higher level, that of wisdom. Wisdom (*sapientia*) meant a "flavorful or savory knowledge" (*sapida scientia*), a knowledge that involves the affections of the knower, turning his desires toward the good, but that can be considered "scientific" only by violating the limits of Aristotle's definition.

Other masters of the first generation, and not only the Franciscans, were no less baffled. William of Auxerre, like Grosseteste, shows the tendency to place sacred doctrine on a higher level than any philosophical knowledge. With Augustine he regarded this doctrine more as wisdom than as a science, while at the same time tending to reduce its speculative scope and its ability to produce arguments. Roland of Cremona adopts the same view in the prologue of his *Summa*, but he is more explicit in denying that theology as wisdom can also be regarded as a science, especially because it does not proceed exclusively by deduction. It is indeed possible to derive a great number of other truths from a single concept provided by revelation, but this procedure violates the principle, followed in all the sciences, that syllogistic demonstration always emerges from two premises ("nothing is proved from a single premise").

These problems were also faced by William of Meliton (d. 1257), an English Franciscan who would succeed Odo Rigaldi in the chair at Paris in 1248 and was charged by papal decree with finishing the composition of the *Hales Summa*. He faced the problems in a question on the knowledge of God in which he appeals to the negative theology of Pseudo-Dionysius in order to prove that knowledge from a supernatural source could not be fitted into the overly rigid schemata of Aristoteleanism.

Stimulated by these difficulties, Odo Rigaldi then decided to develop a personal synthesis that would safeguard the authentic peculiarities of theological knowledge. Such knowledge enjoys a truthfulness that is of prophetic origin and that affects history and operates within it. At the same time, a series of cognitive conditions it has in common with the other sciences urges it to claim the right to use rational "arguments" in the field proper to it. After a first explanation in the prologue to his *Reading of the Sentences*, Odo's contribution is set forth in a question on theological knowledge.

The basic framework in which the problem is to be tackled and resolved had first to be explained by showing what it means for knowledge to be formulated in terms proper to a strict, certain, and definitive science. Odo therefore explains the criteria set down in Aristotelean epistemology (although as compared with the Latin commentators on the *Posterior Analytics*, such as Grosseteste, his explanation is reduced to the essentials).

The criteria are: first, every science must have an object and be based on the acquisition of the relevant data from outside (that is, experientially but not necessarily through the senses), which is to say that it must be based on things knowable and experienced. Second, it can embrace only the intelligible, necessary, and changeless aspects of the object (it must be knowledge of intelligibles and universals). Third, it must proceed by way of argument from the necessity of an initial datum to the necessity of a conclusion (it must lead to a "necessary conclusion derived from necessary premises"). Fourth, it must therefore start with something already known as necessary, that is, either from conclusions already reached or from unquestionable first principles. Fifth, this deductive procedure (or "technical mode") can develop in three and only three possible ways: through definition, division, or syllogistic conclusion.

It is obvious that these conditions do not seem at first sight to be verified in theological knowledge. The revealed datum is always fundamentally historical and therefore singular. In addition, it is set forth in Scripture in language that is poetic, rhetorical, and narrative, and it therefore takes a form that is now preceptive, now illustrative, now hortatory, but always distinct from the deductive form. The truthfulness of faith as a cognitive experience is therefore based on an affective assent, even if later mental reflection on this truth claims to produce a theoretical knowledge, as we see happening in the most authoritative patristic and monastic sources. It is therefore necessary to focus attention directly on the basic relationship between believing and understanding if we are to show the possibility of considering the understanding of the faith as an act of knowing to which a theoretical value can be assigned.

Odo then explains that inasmuch as believing does, on any accounting, produce an understanding, it is in its deepest reality an act of the rational order. In the very moment in which grace produces an assent in the believer, this act leads immediately to the transformation of what is believed into something known. The affections, therefore, are the condition for an emotional involvement—consequent upon the understanding—which believers see as a consequence and not a premise of their cognitive assent to the faith. To this participation of rational consciousness in the effecting of a complete relationship between knowing subject and object known Odo gives the name "intention" (*intentio*), a term destined to have a lengthy and important place in the subsequent history of medieval gnoseology.

The term came from Augustine. In the *Confessions*, for example, when he speaks of time the word signifies an interior attention (*intentio*) of the subject to the perceived object, an attention that has implications on both theoretical and practical levels. But then it is obvious that "intention" is not something peculiar to theological knowledge; rather, as is clear from the teaching of Augustine, every act of human reason is an intentional act involving all the cognitive and affective forces of the soul. Every intellectual act, therefore, implies an affective participation to a greater or lesser degree. Now theology, in comparison with other forms of knowledge, is characterized by the fact that essential to it is a complete fusion of knowledge and desire in a single "intention." All the more, therefore, is it truly a science in a more complete way than is any of the lesser sciences.

As the *Hales Summa* had already intuited, all this demands the introduction of a distinction within the very concept of "science." Theology is not a science in the strict sense because it is not based on certainties acquired exclusively through the activity of reason, as metaphysics is; otherwise even nonbelievers could theologize. Instead, theology is a science in a broad sense, in the same sense in which "any certain intellectual knowledge" is scientific. Theology is a science inasmuch as (1) it is based on principles that are certain, and (2) it is developed on the basis of those principles and by following a consistent procedure.

The first principles of theology are also its object (its "subject matter"): concretely, as William of Auxerre had already noted, they are the articles of faith. Drawing on the terminology used in Boethius' translation of the *Analytics*, but combining it with terms from the axiomatic literature of the late twelfth century (Gilbert of Poitiers, Alan of Lille, and Nicholas of Amiens), the first university masters allowed for three types of scientific first principles: First, *dignitates* (the term is a direct translation of the Greek *axiomata*), that is, formal rules of a most general, intuitive, and axiomatic kind (such as the principle of identity and noncontradiction); second, presuppositions, that is, general statements of truths universally accepted but proper to the area of investigation of a given science (such as the postulates of geometry; for example, "the shortest distance between two points is a straight line"); third, conclusions drawn from principles of the first two kinds.

It is clear to Odo that theology has its axioms (*dignitates*), which are intuitively known to all (apart from faith) and whose truth is "written in our hearts"; for example, that "God is the Supreme Good," that "he is to be loved more than anything else," or that "he is supremely just." It is obvious, too, that there are conclusions that can be drawn from the preceding. But then it is possible, and therefore necessary, that the articles of faith play the role of presuppositions, that is, primordial and indemonstrable truths peculiar to theology. It is these articles that make possible the cognitive grafting of the affective element in belief onto understanding. They are not evident to reason (they are not intrinsically evident or intuitively known), but they are indeed evident to faith and through the action of grace are communicated to the intellect, becoming presuppositions for the science (in the broad sense) of theology.

It can therefore be said that the method of theology as a science both is and is not deductive. It is not, because the special nature of theological presuppositions does not allow it to be regarded as identical with the method of the other sciences. And yet it cannot be denied that, starting from such premises, theology develops a correct rational procedure for reaching its goal, namely, a sapiential understanding that is loftier and more trustworthy than scientific demonstration precisely because the way in which it reaches its goal is loftier and more trustworthy. Thus wisdom and science are harmonized in theology as Odo conceives of it inasmuch it combines two fundamental requirements: the supernatural origin and therefore the affective character of such knowledge, and the use of a structure of demonstration that can become systematic when organized into a complete rational explanation of all the aspects of the truth that grace makes the object of belief.

In his *Disputed Questions* Odo proves that a systematic establishment of theological knowledge is concretely possible. In this work he records his lectures on theological subjects, wherein he tackles some fundamental themes: for example, the relationship between Creator and creatures, the derivation of being from God, and exemplarism (that is, the refusal to allow that sin was the motive for the Incarnation). He deals with all these theological issues in an organized and consistent way against a background of all the fundamental doctrinal themes and through analyses conducted by applying in a concrete and detailed way methodological tools he has described at a theoretical level.

2. Albert the Great (or: of Cologne)

A. ARISTOTELEAN PHILOSOPHY AND CHRISTIAN THEOLOGY

The thought and writings of Albert the Great are marked in an important measure by the desire for a complete systematization of all the best results of human thought and the identification of a solid scientific methodology common to the various fields of study.

The desire "to make Aristotle intelligible to Latin readers" nourishes and characterizes especially his contribution in the area of philosophy. He pursued this goal with strong commitment from 1250 on, that is, during the period he spent in Cologne after having taught theology in Paris. He planned to read, paraphrase, and comment systematically on all of Aristotle's works, beginning with the *Nicomachean Ethics* but then following the classic succession of individual works. He thought of this order as reflecting Aristotle's original organization of philosophical instruction, culminating in metaphysics and in natural theology which, in his view, had been given its most complete explanation in the *Book on Causes*.

Albert was indeed working on ground prepared by many anonymous Latin commentators (mostly workers in the arts). But he was also the first master who no longer looked upon Aristotelean speculation as a storehouse of more or less coordinated ideas and information on which to draw from time to time as an occasionally helpful tool. Instead, he understood it as a complete expression of the inherent organization of philosophico-scientific knowledge. It was a system of thought that had its own special methodology (logic) and that embraced all the areas, theoretical and practical, of human study.

This systematic conception of philosophy was certainly guided by an interpretation of Aristotle that was still Neoplatonizing in tendency, an interpretation fostered especially by the influence of Avicenna. But Albert was convinced that the systematic character of Aristotle's thought was its most important quality, so much so that he proposed to make original additions of his own, when necessary, in order to fill possible gaps (even in books the Philosopher never wrote or that had not been handed down!). These additions allowed him also to criticize Aristotle's thought when necessary—since "even he could err, just like us"—that is, when one or other of his statements was inconsistent with the overall movement of his true philosophy.

It was precisely this perspective that allowed Albert to regard philosophy as a field of studies preparatory and complementary to theological wisdom. The latter was the area in which he had worked effectively before 1250 as a university teacher and scholar especially during his years in Paris, when he composed some very important works, such as a treatise on *The Nature of the Good*, an impressive *Summa on Creatures*, numerous commentaries on the Bible, and an official commentary on the *Sentences*.

Thus Albert's professional and speculative development was marked by a strange inversion as compared with the official sequence of studies according to university regulations. That is to say, when this already renowned and skilled theologian moved to Germany he devoted himself methodically to the study of philosophy. To this study he dedicated many years of his life, but without ever losing sight of the place of theological wisdom as the goal of every form of human intellectual development. Furthermore, it is not without significance that precisely during the months bridging the two phases of his life, months spent partly in Paris, partly in Cologne (where one of his listeners was the young Thomas Aquinas), Albert lectured on the *Corpus areopagiticum*, subsequently publishing a complete commentary on it. This was an important novelty in the world of the university (we know of no earlier lectures on Pseudo-Dionysius), and one that, not accidentally, dealt with the work of a theologian traditionally regarded as the last great pagan philosopher, a man converted by St. Paul.

This revaluation of natural knowledge as essentially preparatory to theology is completely in line with the decisions taken in 1259 by a commission of Dominican scholars gathered in Valenciennes; the group included Albert and Thomas. The commission imposed on the entire Order the obligation to regard the Aristoteleanism of the arts faculty as a study preparatory for theology. Thus the valuable result of the Cologne experiment was that for a good many theologians of the West the study of the arts became, once and for all, the study of philosophy, which was distinct from theological research but an essential introduction to it. In the final years of his career Albert returned to the study of theology, after having been a bishop and having returned to Cologne to end his life as a student and scholar. Here he composed his last great work, the *Summa of Theology* (left unfinished), as the crown of the speculative project he had planned.

B. THE PHILOSOPHICAL SYSTEM OF REALITY

According to Albert, metaphysics shares with logic the title of the organized knowledge, or science, of first principles. But whereas the purpose of logic is to clarify these principles and set them forth as premises and formal repositories of subsequent articulations of true discourse, metaphysics or "first philosophy" studies them in order to make known to reason the immutable, primordial, and fundamental laws governing the natural order. It explains these, however, as natural causes, that is, without appealing to the free divine will that created them. Thus the scope of metaphysics allows philosophy, whose reach is that of reason itself and of which metaphysics is therefore the natural crown, to present itself as a true, autonomous science that is completely independent of faith in its scientific (= rigorous and objective) assertions.

This position is clearly consistent with the reading of Aristotle given by Averroes, with whom Albert was familiar and to whom he imputes the support of "many heresies" because the Arabic philosopher stubbornly defended his philosophical positions *against* the faith. Albert himself openly defends the necessity of accepting that according to the laws of nature movement and, consequently, generation and corruption had no beginning and will never end, even though this view is in contrast to the truths of the faith and therefore *despite* the faith. It was perfectly clear to Albert that scientific-demonstrative discourse is the only kind that philosophy can and should consider: "When dealing with natural realities, we do not think of divine miracles."

In order, then, to be true, philosophy must enjoy absolute freedom of judgment and not be obliged to submit to any external authority. But it can legitimately so submit itself precisely because it recognizes its own limitations and can dispassionately accept the fact that a force external to nature, namely, the divine will, can break into the course of nature and put an end to the universe, just as it was able to give it its beginning. This is to put brackets around the field of competence of philosophical judgment by allowing the possibility of miracles as an external interruption (not an alteration) of its legitimate role. But, at the same time, this admission enables philosophy to safeguard its own autonomy and protects it from theological error. In Albert's view this is the first and most important peculiarity, and the principal advantage, of the philosopher who is a believer, as compared with a pagan philosopher.

This presupposition makes it possible, in fact, for ancient philosophy, when transplanted into the Christian mental universe, to achieve a further development and completion of its original results. Thanks to its encounter with the certainties of the faith, philosophy is now able to make correct choices among the accurate and the mistaken teachings of the philosophers, even while exercising this critique on the basis of a purely rational analysis and the greater or lesser consistency with the overall systematic explanation of nature that Christian philosophy has worked out. Thus, for example, Albert can reject the universal hylomorphism of Avicebron because it readily turns into immanentism. Such a result can be seen clearly in the case of the heretical thought of David of Dinant, which Albert studied in order to defend Aristoteleanism against the charge that it had produced David's thinking.

Encouraged by this assumption that philosophy can be corrected "philosophically" when it errs, Albert develops his own rational system of reality. This system is structured according to the various disciplines and follows methodologies specific to the several particular sciences that, when combined into an organic whole, constitute scientific philosophy. In his close study of the various disciplines he makes personal contributions spread out over numerous treatises on physics, psychology, and metaphysics (down to one of his final writings, the commentary on the *On Causes*, to which he gives the title *Causes and the Development of the Universe*), as well as paraphrases of the writings of Aristotle. It was this last-named extensive and multiform material that, taken as a whole, justified later generations of masters in calling him "Universal Doctor" when they appealed to his authority.

Albert took over from Arabic sources the concept of being as descending through the universe; he justified this acceptance because of the (false) attribution of the *On Causes* to Aristotle. He then places at the summit of his philosophical system of reality a God whose existence is identical with his essence and who is, therefore, pure intellect and operative free will and is, consequently, very like the Creator God of religion. The universal first causality is transmitted to the created world through an ordered hierarchy of secondary causes. In order to ensure the systematic consistency of the created universe by means of the transmission of efficacious causality from the first mover to the natural world, Albert thinks it necessary to specify (as he frequently does from the commentaries on physics down to the *Summa of Theology*) in what this mediatory role of secondary causes consists. The secondary causes in question are heavenly beings and (with Aristotle and Avicenna and contrary to Avicebron) absolutely immaterial, that is, intelligible and intelligent. Their mediatory role consists in the transmission of purely formal influences that determine the being of inferior realities by manifesting this being as a detailed "that which is" or essence.

In order to explain how this formal influence is exercised without changing the nature of the Causer, but only that of what is caused, Albert introduces the idea of a potentiality for being formed. In his view this potentiality is proper to any determinate being whatsoever; he calls it a "beginning of a form" or "inchoative form." By this is meant an openness to form that can be seen even in corporeal beings and that directs all of created nature, on the basis of its specific potentialities, toward the attainment of the forms that in each finite being are activated by the higher causes. God is therefore the pure Intelligence that contains the exemplary forms; to him all the particular forms of created things, present in matter in a disorderly and confused way, necessarily tend due to the attraction exercised by the higher causes.

By means of this attraction God regulates the entire order of the universe: "The work that is nature is the work of an intelligence." The movement of bodies is subordinated to that of the heavens; the latter in turn move according to the arrangements made by the secondary intelligences, which in turn are subordinated to the perfection of the first Intelligence. The universe is thus a system dependent on the causality exercised by a supreme form that acts on its own and in complete freedom without presupposing any preexisting subject on which to act.

From the viewpoint of philosophy this universal systematic intertwining of causes can also be given the name of "fate" (*fatum* or *hymarmene*, a transliteration of the Greek term Albert found in the hermetic literature). But the name *fatum*—fate or destiny—need not stir any fear of determinism. True, the formal influences coming from on high are in themselves necessitating, but the very diverse receptivities caused by material imperfections receive these influences and make them efficacious in ways that are completely unforeseeable and contingent. Thus the influence of astral causes can be analyzed by the discipline the ancients called astronomy or astrology, but this study can by no means imply any lessening of God's autonomous, formative freedom or any removal of the contingency and original indeterminacy of the world. For, just as the influence of the sun's rays gives rise to the endless and unrestricted germination of the forms scattered throughout nature, so too the efficacy of secondary causes activates, in ways no less dynamic and variegated, the inexhaustible potentialities of the "inchoative forms" in material things.

C. ANTHROPOLOGY AND THE COGNITIVE ASCENT

Human beings, too, are plunged from birth into this universal system of formal actions and reactions. Not only their bodies but their souls as well are, at least in part, "educed" from the potentiality of matter, because astral influences cause matter to give rise to the vegetative and sensitive functions, which are "inchoatively" present in the paternal seed. The vegetative soul is potentially present in the "formative power" of the seed and is actualized by natural agents; the sensitive soul, in turn, is potentially present in the vegetative and will develop as soon as the fetus forms suitable organs.

The intellective function, however, in which according to Aristotle the true nature of human beings is actualized, is indeed potentially present in the sensitive soul but cannot originate simply in the readiness of the body to receive its proper form. The reason: it is endowed with a freedom to know and to act that ensure its independence of the causal system thus far described. Its actual formation, then, is directly due to the efficacious action of the first, that is, divine

Intellect, which pours its light into the soul. The human soul thus originates partly "from within" and partly "from without"; it has its place "on the horizon separating eternity from time" and is absolutely free in relation to fate, being partly dependent on and partly independent of the various corporeal functions. Albert explains this doctrine (attested also by Dante in *The Divine Comedy*) in his book *The Nature and Origin of the Soul*.

Like the separated intelligences, the human soul must have the ability to know the universals objectively. The activation of this ability consists in an intellective production of forms in order then to know them, a production directed by the attraction of the higher intelligences: this activity is what Aristotle calls the agent intellect. But the human soul is united to the body, which immerses it in spatio-temporal accidentality, so that it cannot contemplate the forms directly, as the higher intelligences do. Within the soul, therefore, the agent intellect must ask, as it were, that an interior capacity for representation receive the forms and activate them in particular intellective acts: this receptivity of the soul is called the passive or possible intellect. Albert lists the arguments of the Aristoteleans for one universal active intellect, but here again theology corrects philosophy and requires that we accept instead the equally strong reasons for admitting that the active intellect is singular, that is, an operative part of the individual soul.

But the distinction between active and passive intellects not only serves to explain how knowledge comes about and to give reason for the co-presence in knowledge of universal data and particular operations. It also has an important ethical implication inasmuch as it urges all human beings gradually to free the passive intellect from the limitations of corporeity and to lead it, through deeper study and theoretical activity, toward an assimilation to the agent intellect, "the intellect as intellect," which is the true substance of the human being. The process of ascent does not stop at this level of pure intelligibility because the agent intellect is drawn, via the natural desire to know, by the formal source of its knowledge, namely the separated intelligences and, through them, the divine Intellect. The desire to know, which motivates all of philosophy, can reach its goal only by advancing from the intelligibility of that which exists within spatio-temporal coordinates to that of the separated substances and, finally, to the first Cause.

The end result of this philosophical ascent (a result in harmony with the explicit aspirations of the Arabic thinkers) is therefore a union with God in the true and proper sense. It is the realization of a vision in which, thanks to a supremely developed cognitive exercise, the soul can gaze into the very fountainhead of truth and intelligibility. Thus the highest perfection of the intellectual activity described by Aristotle is surprisingly identical with the contemplative solutions of the purest theological Platonism, which is characterized by explicit references to Pseudo-Dionysius and (indirectly) to Eriugena.

Albert's anthropology thus leads to a complete identification of philosophical science and theological wisdom and to the mystical crown of a knowledge that will be perfect from both points of view. But this crown, which the soul seeks with all its natural powers, is in the present life dependent on a concession by the divine Intellect that can only be free and unmerited. It is therefore the task of theology to make manifest now the other side of this perfection, once rational study has reached the described goal. This goal becomes the point of departure for human reflection on the innermost meaning of the verse of Genesis that describes the beginning of the human being's dependence on God and the task of moving ceaselessly toward God as the absolute end of its every act: "Let us make humankind in our image, according to our likeness" (Gen 1:26).

D. THE SYSTEM OF THEOLOGICAL TRUTH

The authority of Pseudo-Dionysius the Areopagite evidently played a leading role in Albert's effort to distinguish, correlate, and harmonize philosophical and theological knowledge. In the universities of the thirteenth century, as attested especially in Paris during these years, there was in circulation a scholarly edition of the entire Dionysian corpus. This was furnished with marginal glosses and with a selection of passages from Maximus the Confessor and other interpreters among which were included, anonymously, a number of passages from the works of John Scotus. When commenting specifically on *The Divine Names* Albert stops to give a description, which agrees with the early medieval theological tradition, of the stages of the ladder-like ascent of the soul toward knowledge of the truth; it places the acceptance of the contents of revelation at the summit and as the completion of natural studies.

But in the third book of his commentary on the *Sentences* the reader's attention is already drawn to a sentence of Pseudo-Dionysius that Albert often cites in others of his writings. The sentence is accompanied by a remark attributed by Albert to a certain John the Bishop whom he believes to have been a little-known commentator on the Dionysian corpus but who was in fact no other than John Scotus (who was transformed into a bishop—*episcopus*—by a mistaken transliteration of the first three Greek letters of the name "Eriugena").

Dionysius says: "Faith is the sole foundation for believers; it places them in the truth and the truth in them," and the commentator adds: ". . . as an immutable source of supreme truth." The words "immutable source" in this text had a decisive meaning for Albert. The point was not simply to accept the faith as the highest source of truth, but also to make it the source and foundation of any kind of argumentative development of it. That is, the infused light of the assent to faith functions as a regulative principle, a real *a priori* form, of theological knowledge. The truth of the latter transcends the rational grasp of truth (as when theology says that "God is one," but is such "in a plurality of persons") but also regulates and governs all of its applications (as when reason explains the intelligibility of the trinitarian mystery).

The first task of theology is to understand the way in which the descent of truth from that source of faith into the human soul can be regarded as an acquisition of knowledge—immutable, universally communicable, and spelled out in all its aspects—of the contents of faith or, in short, as a science. In an inversion of the regulative use made of it in philosophy, the meeting of faith and philosophy here immediately raises the question of the compatibility between, on the one hand, the epistemological norms used by philosophers in their organization of the sciences and, on the other, the special character of a discipline that locates its source *a priori* in the transcendent and unverifiable nature of revelation. Apart from many allusions in various writings, Albert answers this question, in more or less the same terms, in his commentary on the *Sentences* and in his *Summa of Theology* (thus showing that his idea of theological science did not change during his long development as a scholar, whether before or after his prolonged intellectual grappling with the "system" of Aristotelean thought).

It is therefore appropriate, before all else, to distinguish theology from the other sciences in terms of their respective subject matters. The term "subject" (which appears in all medieval discussions of the rank of the sciences in general and of theology in particular) signifies the subject matter spoken of in the various divisions of a particular form of knowledge. In fact, logic teaches that all "predicates" are always predicates "about something" or "about a subject"; the subject matter is therefore the substratum or substance of the act of knowing, the content, at once informative and formative, of the knowledge that springs from that act.

In light of this explanation we understand why Albert thinks himself authorized to say unhesitatingly that theology, in keeping with the very meaning of its name, has as its very first subject (its "special subject") God himself directly. This is the ultimate goal toward which the understanding of the faith moves, even though it will never reach it completely in this life. In the second place ("the subject more particularly"), theology seeks to know God by describing his characteristic properties; in other words, it has as its subject matter everything that is an object of belief (the *credibilia*), and therefore all the articles of the faith. Finally, reaching out even farther ("the subject more generally"), theology deals with everything that in any way expresses the truths of the faith; therefore all the things and signs contained in revelation (according to the Augustinian division taken over by Hugh of St. Victor and Peter Lombard). In this general sense the Scriptures are the subject matter of theology.

Despite this multiplication of contents, theological science is always dealing with a single reality inasmuch as God is the sole cause, efficient and final, of everything having to do with credibility; theology is therefore a single science. Thus precisely from the perfect unity of theological discourse there emerges the complementarity of its relationships to the truth of God both as efficient cause and as final cause. In this it differs from metaphysics, which seeks knowledge of God solely as end, a limitation that prevents it from attaining to that knowledge completely. This distinction between beginning or source and end in theology is reflected in its content, though without detracting from the unity of the science. The full extent of theological teaching reaches from the understanding of God as creator from whom everything comes to the understanding of God as goal of the universal process of the return of being to its source.

This circularity of truth is the reason for its systematic character; moreover, it is completely adaptable both to the order of doctrinal explanation in Lombard's *Sentences* and to the descent-and-return pattern within which the patristic sources, both Augustine and Dionysius (with his "commentator," John Scotus), locate all of created reality in relation to the creative Word.

But the fact that God, understood as universal end, is the subject, and therefore the goal, of all the divisions of theological science also includes the assertion of the eminently practical nature of this knowledge. In fact, just as God is not evident to faith, so too he is not a rationally evident principle for theology. Since, then, theology does not have an object that is knowable as such, but rather has an end on which all its assertions converge, it is a practical and not a speculative science. It is a truly "affective knowledge" that informs as it attracts, as was made clear by the mystical reflections of the Cistercian monks of the preceding century, by the practical tendency of the Victorines, by Philip the Chancellor's idea that "good" is the transcendental most revelatory of the divine, and, above all, by the rich tradition of theological Platonism from the Pseudo-Dionysian tradition down to the very recent approach of Avicenna. Theology therefore bids us seek the truth of the faith in the final union with God that, if it is to be achieved, must involve the entire substance of the believer, that is, both intellect and will.

As the loftiest results of philosophical speculation had already suggested, the science of this kind of truth must produce the perfection of both the intellect and the affections; moreover, if it is to be such it "must not ignore the reasons for the good." But theology assures us that this is not simply an inspiration but rather the sure goal of knowledge of the faith. In Albert's mind the contradiction seemingly inherent in the concept of an "affective science" (which is knowledge, but of a practical kind) is resolved in the eschatological understanding of the attainment of this perfection in the beatific vision, for which it is the task of this science to prepare us. The vision will beatify because it is a knowledge, both fully intellectual and fully affective, of God as the final end; it is intellectual precisely because it is affective, and vice versa.

It is therefore possible to maintain theology's status as a speculative science even as one asserts it to be a practical science, but it is clear that the first is subordinate to the second. That is, even in the beatific vision God will be knowable not as an essence in itself and as such but as the goal of the affections of every creature, a goal reached through a manifestation of his essence as attractive goodness. This explanation amounts to an explicit defense of the theophany thesis adopted, as was mentioned above, by other representatives of the Dominican Order and condemned in 1241 by William of Auvergne. But the defense is accompanied by a qualification: the theophanies are not to be understood as a form of indirect knowledge transmitted through the veil of creaturely intermediaries, but rather as a knowledge of the divine goodness (which in God is identical with his essence) exactly "as he is," as the Scriptures promise.

When theology is thus truly situated at the point of arrival of the work that the lower disciplines of knowledge prepare for and support it can lead the intellect even to an immersion in the joy that flows only from this fullness of truth known and desired. That fullness is a participation in the Word himself and is made possible by the descent of the Word into the soul. It is the absolute and universal end of knowledge and the beginning of blessedness. All this shows how, above and beyond philosophy and as a result of the illumination given by grace, mystical contemplation characterizes, radically guides, and completes Albert's entire conception of theology.

III. Bonaventure of Bagnoreggio

> Theology is a discourse about God and the first principle; as the supreme science and doctrine it traces everything back to God as its first and highest source. Therefore in defining the reasons for everything contained, from beginning to end, in this short work or little treatise I have endeavored to ground every demonstration in the first principle. I will thus be able to show that the truth of the Sacred Scriptures is from God, is about God, is according to God, and has God as its goal and to let this science correctly show itself to be "one" and "organized" and to merit justly the name "theology."

Bonaventure wrote these words in the margin of the Prologue of the *Breviloqium* in 1257, that is, during the months when he was ending his academic activity in order to become General of the Franciscan Order with the task of leading it at one of the most difficult moments in its young history. In these words he summed up his program for the construction of a theological science. The passage is short but especially full of substance, for its function is to introduce the reader to a work the author intends as an instructional compendium of Franciscan theological thought. It therefore gives the impression of being a short summary of the fundamental characteristics of and conditions for theology.

According to this passage theological learning seems to combine the strict form of the secular sciences with the sapiential character of Christian doctrine. It is "the supreme science and doctrine," supreme both absolutely and relatively since it expresses both the mind's highest capacity for knowledge and its superiority over other forms of human knowledge. It is in fact a "discourse about God," since the God of revelation is the subject matter of its study and therefore its "object," and this makes it a form of doctrine. It is also a discourse about the first and supreme source of everything that is, and this makes it a science. But, unlike metaphysics (which is only a science and not a doctrine), its purpose is to show that this source is God.

As a science its duty is to bring out the conditions making it possible to reach a rational judgment about the divine object's mode of being; in other words, to define the reasons for this judgment. Theology must do this in an analytical way by investigating the many concepts the faith proposes for the attention of believers. It must follow the fundamental rule that the reasons for each concept, which have been brought out by the argumentative and demonstrative method of the philosophers, must be traced back to the fundamental certainty that was its starting point; in other words, it must constantly show how every theological truth can be traced back to the first principle, which is God, and to God's self-manifestation, which is Sacred Scripture.

Thus theology is always and in every respect reducible to God: it has God as its source, it expresses God's nature, it is regulated and conditioned by the truth that is God, and it has God as its final goal. As other theologians of this same period also realized, all the truths of theology are recapitulated in God, because the four causes, which according to Aristotelean metaphysics underlie the truth of anything whatsoever, are verified in God: efficacious, material, formal, and final. If, then, God recapitulates in himself all the causes that make theology exist, theology exists only insofar as it is the science of God. It is therefore one (both unified and sole), since God is one; it has an order, that is, is organized and has a methodological discipline thanks to the logical reasons, or arguments, that are reducible to the first and supreme "reason" for everything; and it is truly "theo-logy," because it has God for both its object and its subject and therefore is, in the full sense of the genitive, "the science of God."

But in this exposition of the characteristics of theology Bonaventure also explains what truth is for Christians. Theology is true if its way of knowing is true: that is, if it starts with what is true and is ordered to what is true. Now, that which is intrinsically true is undeniably superior to the truth of any particular thing since it is what makes that particular truth exist. But, as Augustine teaches, the truth in itself is God, and therefore theology, as the science of God, is the science of the truth in itself. It is this that makes theology unqualifiedly superior to all the other sciences, which are sciences dealing with the truth of some particular thing, of particular beings and their manifestations. It is in this triumph of Augustinianism over Aristoteleanism that we see the ultimate meaning of the Franciscan way of theologizing, which finds its best expression in the extensive and subtly profound work of Bonaventure. It is a triumph that does not end in the destruction of the defeated adversary but rather lifts up even the conquered to share in the glorification of the victor.

The manner in which Bonaventure grounds theology also signifies a reform of philosophical knowledge, since theology aims at a comprehensive renewal of human life. As he writes in the first of his *Conferences on the Hexaemeron*, which he composed nonstop in the spring of 1273, it is no longer possible to postpone the mission of the true theologian, namely, "to lead spiritual human beings from worldly wisdom to Christian wisdom." The ungodliness of too many theologians denies the life of Christ on the moral level; the ambiguity of too many of the "artists" denies his teaching with theses that cannot be defended on the speculative level. And since the life and teaching of Christ are the sole concern of the Christian, Bonaventure takes upon himself the task "of showing that 'all the treasures of the wisdom and knowledge' of God are hidden (Col 2:3) in Christ and he is therefore the center on which all the sciences converge." It is only by standing at this center that a true Christian will attain to the "fullness of wisdom and understanding."

These are words he spoke in his formal presentation of the *Conferences* at the University of Paris a year before his death (which came to him while he was taking part in the second Council of Lyons in his capacity as Cardinal Bishop of Albano). But in the Prologue of his commentary on the *Sentences* he had already signaled the loftiest of theology's apologetical aims in the area of true Christian life: "The use of rational procedures is helpful in theology because the purpose of the latter is first of all to confound the enemies of the faith . . . second, to heal and restore weak and sickly believers . . . and, third, to give pleasure to those already made perfect in this faith." "To give pleasure to the perfect" is the highest and noblest justification of Bonaventure's own activity as a theologian: in other words, to help those who have made faith the basis of their lives and the pledge of their salvation so that they may enjoy the reward of this faith even during the present life through participation in the wisdom of Christ.

Everywhere in Bonaventure's theological works this ideal always remained the most authentic and therefore the only way of accomplishing in his own life the "imitation of Christ" that Francis of Assisi had urged.

1. Theological Science as the Unification of All Truth, and Its Scriptural Basis

The final reference to unity ("one") in the Prologue of the *Breviloquium* is not simply about the application to theology of one of the most important elements of Aristotelean epistemology in order to ensure the scientific character of the discipline. Beginning with the commentary on the *Sentences*, Bonaventure displayed an anxious fear that the dissension that had torn ancient philosophy apart when it was not illumined by the truth might return and spread among true believers. The reason for his fear was the renewed claim to autonomy that worldly wisdom thought it could base on the new and rigorous methodologies it now possessed. But theology had precisely the opposite task: to ensure unity not only among opinions about the faith but among all opinions about truth. And it could successfully carry out this task by conforming itself to the perfect unified wisdom of Christ while leaving out what is superfluous and improving everything that is useful but poorly formulated.

Bonaventure was born in 1217 at Città di Bagnoreggio near Viterbo and was dedicated to Francis by his mother after she had been cured of a fatal disease. He studied under Alexander of Hales and Odo Rigaldi and served as a Bachelor on the Faculty of Theology under William of Meliton. In his eyes being a Franciscan was not only a way of life but an ever-expanding vocation that constantly drove him to devote himself entirely to serving the ideal of universal peace. He became a theologian because the study of theology was the best tool for drawing men and women to the Truth and for effecting, in continuity with past tradition, the tracing back of all knowledge and volition to "one." Moreover, in complete agreement with the spirituality of Francis, this "one" could only be Christ, who unites the divine and the human and joins human beings with his own divinity, as Francis learned in his vision on Mount Alverna.

Intelligibility and love are the forces at work in this shared theological journey: the entire universe is intelligible because created by the divine Logos, and what is known as good is the object of love. Therefore it is not only by having recourse to the authority of the Fathers or the excellence of tradition or, worse, to the arguments of the philosophers that we may legitimately accept or reject a thesis or an interpretation. Rather, we should show unequivocally the real agreement or essential disagreement of the thesis with the organic system of Christian wisdom. This approach may indeed make it necessary to deal in an innovative way with the theological wisdom of the past when this is required in order to obtain the assent of wise persons of the present time. But this assent will be given only when the theologian's original position is so solid as to make possible the harmonization with it of all other conflicting opinions.

If such a project is to be carried through there is but a single certainty that helps the theologian in his work: namely, certainty about the truthfulness of Scripture. Only in revelation is divine truth present with all of its profound stability and inexhaustible fruitfulness. Once again, it is in the Prologue of the *Breviloquium* that Bonaventure gives an influential description of his plan for basing the search for truth on Scripture, which, being the "word of God," is truly "theo-logy" (as suggested also by the terminology of the Pseudo-Dionysian tradition: "Scripture, which is called theology"). As St. Paul says (Eph 3:14-19) in words that are both plain and full of mystery, Scripture includes the entire universe as measured by the four dimensions of the cross: breadth, length, height, and depth. It is "the cross made intelligible; in it the entire fabric of the world" (that is, all truth) "is described and in a way becomes visible in the light given to the mind."

The breadth of the truth consists of the parts, the Old and New Testaments, that make up the Bible. Its length consists of sacred history, which embraces all the ages of the world from creation to the final judgment. Its height is found in the Pseudo-Dionysian hierarchies, which are here reduced to three: ecclesiastical, celestial, and supracelestial, in order of increasing inaccessibility, for while the angels form the celestial hierarchy, the supracelestial is the most holy triadic nature of the divinity in its trinitarian manifestation. Its depth, finally, is given by the multiplication of the mystical senses of the scriptural word: literal, allegorical, moral, and anagogical.

In connection with the first sense, the literal, which supplies the material of faith, the question arises of the "subject" of Scripture, that is, of theology. For this problem, too, which was so much discussed by the university theologians in light of subtle epistemological niceties, the solution derives, for Bonaventure, from an illumination that comes down from the Trinity and was accepted by the Fathers. A teaching of Pseudo-Dionysius (one that, as we saw, was accepted into the system of John Scotus) sees the most obvious trace of the trinitarian nature of truth in the universal composition of all things: in all there is a unity of essence, power (*virtus*), and act.

The subject of theology, therefore, is the substance of God, the power of Christ, and the activity of redemption. Since all three are distinct within an absolute unity, then, given the combining of these three realities in one, the subject of theology is the datum of faith, that is, what is believable. Threeness and fourness are thus combined, the allusion being to the ineffable compenetration of the divine and the human that is realized in the central mystery: namely, the cross (the divine Trinity on the four arms of the created universe). Once again Bonaventure's understanding of the truth comes from Francis' contemplation of the stigmata on the christological Seraph; here we see the heart of Bonaventure's search for God, which earned for him the title of "Seraphic Doctor."

This doctrinal meditation provides us with an excellent example of Bonaventure's method of reasoning. Over and over in his works we see him almost obsessively basing his thought on a formal schema; the elements of this spring from a richly equipped religious mind rooted in the Bible, catechesis, sacred numerology, ecclesiastical tradition, and patristic and early medieval literature. In a continuous interweaving of images, lists of terms, and organized structures that lead in turn to new lists and new structures, Bonaventure explains his own way of understanding the speculative synthesis of reason and faith as laid out by his two primary models, Augustine and Anselm. This synthesis has for its purpose to help the human mind grasp the efficacy of the message of salvation as made known in revelation. Bonaventure's way of proceeding is not simply a matter of style but a methodology in the true and proper sense, its goal being to produce a mental organization of scriptural truth that will make it easier for reason to accept this truth. The procedure is constantly present in all his doctrinal works and finds its best expression in *The Journey of the Mind into God*, a masterpiece combining strict form with spiritual depth.

2. Theology as a "Solution That Leads Elsewhere"

The goal sought in the search for the understanding of Sacred Scripture is the knowledge of Christ. This knowledge of Christ is the true theology that will bring to completion the synthesis of reason (or understanding) and faith (scripture). The meditative reading of the biblical text is the preliminary and essential starting point.

The first stage of Bonaventure's theological journey thus coincides with the work he produced during his time as a Bachelor, first as a Biblical Bachelor (1248–50) and then as a Sententiary Bachelor. The fruit of this period of teaching was various series of notes (*Postillae*) on the Gospel of Luke, Ecclesiastes, and the Fourth Gospel; these would undergo successive revisions during the years when he was teaching theology. These exegetical notes were inserted into the text, but gradually they tended to become marginal comments and take the form of "questions."

When these exegeses are compared with the greater literalism of contemporary Dominican glossators such as Hugh of Saint-Cher and Guerric of Saint-Quentin they already show clearly an organization of the theological material in accordance with the specific understanding that inspires Bonaventure's reading of revelation. In this understanding the journey of the theologian toward the knowledge to be had in eternity is located between human knowledge and God's knowledge and begins with and is guided by the manifestation of the Word. This manifestation is twofold: an eternal intratrinitarian revelation of the divine nature (the uncreated Word) and a historical revelation to the created world in the Incarnation (the incarnate Word).

During the phase immediately following this first stage Bonaventure composed his own commentary on the *Sentences*; here he subjects the results of the schools' reading of Lombard to a formal, organic revision. Even on the level of method and internal organization we see now the beginning of the movement from the scriptural basis to a theological understanding of revelation. The reading of the Bible and the theological "solution" of questions (their "determination" in the contemporary language of the schools) have the same object: revealed truth. But the former yields an explanatory exposition, aimed at communicating this truth to believers and explaining it to them. The latter, on the other hand, produces a scientific understanding that goes beyond a simple statement of what is to be believed because it transforms it, through the concomitant work of grace (which reveals) and human reason (which "solves"), into something intelligible.

Thus seen, theological knowledge turns out to be a "solution that somehow leads elsewhere" (*determinatio quodam modo distrahens*) according to a well-known Bonaventuran formula, in which *distrahens* does not signify a removal or confusion of judgment but rather "something leading elsewhere," since the cognitive domains of the intelligible and the credible differ from one another. Moreover, while in the text of Scripture the credible is found as such ("Scripture deals with the credible as credible"), in the solution proposed by the master the credible is as it were transformed into an object of intellectual knowledge ("the credible becomes intelligible") and, consequently, into something that draws the will. Yet, while theological knowledge as knowledge penetrates deeper than Scripture does, revelation, which is based on a certainty that transcends every rational activity, has first place epistemologically as the primary source of that which is subjected in theology to a re-cognition by means of rational activity. revelation is "subordinating" (*subalternans*), while theology is "subordinated" (*subalternata*).

The rational power that works on revelation in order to learn the content of faith, make it cohesive, and vouch for its correctness is the same instrument used by the philosophers, both ancient and Arabic. In addition, this intervention of something that is outside of faith but aims at the completion of faith explains the "dis-tracting" nature of theology. This justifies Bonaventure's position that philosophy, which is epistemologically inferior to theology, since of itself it cannot fully satisfy the human longing for knowledge, nonetheless becomes the second stage in the cognitive process that leads from Scripture to theology, or the knowledge of Christ, while passing through the imperfect but necessary knowledge of the human person.

3. From Science to Wisdom

According to Bonaventure the rank of the sciences human beings can aspire to possess is proportionate to the specific influence each can have on their lives and on their desire to attain to happiness. The only science that fully satisfies this requirement is the science or knowledge of Christ. The latter therefore has an exclusive right to the name "wisdom" because it achieves a perfect synthesis of understanding and action in the complete knowledge of the Supreme Good, who is also the Supreme Truth.

In contrast, the human sciences, and therefore philosophy as a whole, presume that they can pursue their own investigations in an autonomous way; as a result they introduce into learning both a diversification of subject matters and an imperfection in their results. The philosophers start with the distinction, which Bonaventure regards as contrary to nature, between theoretical and practical disciplines, and must then pursue the varied and limited outcomes of individual cognitive acts; as a result the knowledge they seek is necessarily incomplete.

While still in paradise and in the original human condition, the mind of Adam, who had been created in the image and likeness of God, participated indirectly in the form of the truth (became "deiform") and was able therefore to grasp, clearly but only partially (partially but not obscurely), its eternal and supracreaturely nature. After sin and the corruption of the divine image human beings were condemned to an indirect and fragmentary knowledge of truth (to a "deformity"), a knowledge that was not only partial but also uncertain (partial and obscure); this is the kind of knowledge characteristic of natural science. But the very awareness of this condition does not allow human beings to remain in it; it rather demands that they strive with all their powers to attain to the knowledge promised in the state of blessedness, a knowledge that is neither partial nor uncertain, that lacks any "deformity" and is full of "deiformity."

After original sin human beings became incapable of reading the book of nature, which God had created in order to make himself known. Now, however, they cannot and may not refuse to subordinate their inquiries about God to the superior communication of his truth contained in the book of Scripture. It is therefore not only good and legitimate but also necessary and natural for an intelligent being not to be satisfied with philosophy, but rather to be ready to correct philosophy with the aid of faith in order then to strengthen faith with the aid of philosophy. If one understands as a philosopher the real nature of the human person, one cannot but be a theologian.

It was in these terms that Bonaventure tackled the problem of the role of philosophy in his *Disputed Questions on the Knowledge of Christ*, especially the fourth. After his discussion of this subject had won him his teacher's license in 1253 he repeated its main lines in the sermon with which he began his teaching: *Christ the One Teacher of All*. Here he formally sets forth the foundational theme of his entire teaching: the idea of the unity of knowledge through a shared participation in the wisdom of the Word. Philosophy is here seen in its servant role and as a science to be transcended through the acquisition of the highest knowledge possible to human beings in this life. Twenty years later he returns to the same subject in his earlier mentioned *Conferences on the Hexaemeron*, but approaches it from the opposite point of view; that is, he condemns the claim to autonomy made by rational science, which, "being left to its own judgment" and being imprisoned in its reflection on nature as such, prevents itself from seeing the traces of the divinity in nature.

In the thirteenth century the word *collatio* (conference) originally meant, in the Mendicant Orders, the recapitulation in the evening of a sermon delivered that morning. But during the years in which Bonaventure and Thomas were teaching, the word was extended to signify also the approved edition of official sermons delivered by the masters before the teaching body or the students; the final version was often the fruit of a stenographer's notes (a *reportatio*). In addition to those on the *Hexaemeron*, Bonaventure has left us two other series of *Conferences*, which during the years of his generalate served as a sign of the continuity of his teaching activity; in them he frequently urges that the human search for truth be definitively satisfied through the acceptance of revelation.

The first of these series is the *Conferences on the Ten Commandments*, in which he exhorts his readers to make philosophical morality concrete through the morality of the Gospel, which is founded on the theological commandment of love for God and neighbor. The other series is the *Conferences on the Gifts of the Holy Spirit*; here the author reflects on the many gifts of grace that dispose human beings for an experiential knowledge of the divine. In a continual counterpoint to these exhortations on theoretical and practical perfection, Bonaventure bitterly denounces the inversion of the order of truth by which the university theologians have sullied themselves as they allow themselves to be drawn by the empty curiosity of the philosophers.

If Christ is the only true teacher, then after him the title "master," of which the teachers in modern universities boast, belongs in fact only to those who follow Christian teaching and make it their own. The Faculty of Theology ought to be truly the new house of Wisdom, over against the false schools of human philosophy. Provided they obey the basic norm prescribing "in what order and following what authority wisdom is to be reached," Christian masters lecturing in these university halls may also draw profit from the research tools invented by ancient wisdom. Nor is there question any longer of the old, now harmless secular learning that was limited to the rules for organizing knowledge taken from the books on the liberal arts or of the "new logic." Recent philosophy embraces also the complex explanatory descriptions of reality offered by physics, metaphysics, psychology, and the practical sciences of the encyclopedic Greco-Arabic system. Theologians may avail themselves of all these contributions whenever they can profitably use them to organize, support, or give rational explanations of various aspects of Christ's teaching.

Like the secular and Franciscan masters of his youth, Bonaventure knows, for example, how to use Peripatetic teaching on the intellect in explaining with greater technical accuracy the distinction, discerned by Augustine, between "lower reason" and "higher reason." He is able likewise to join the Platonists in distinguishing the powers of the soul on the basis of their different objects of knowledge, but without ever losing sight of the radical oneness of knowledge and of the attraction exerted by higher, eternal, and unquestionable truths such as the transcendental properties of God.

Above all, the theory of illumination allows Bonaventure to accept and complete the teaching of the philosophers on the function of the agent intellect, while applying it to Christian truth in a more satisfactory way. That function is to receive and make its own, thanks to an illumination from on high, the fundamental rules of universal knowledge of particulars: the being that is the source of all that is, the goodness that makes every thing good, the greatness that makes every creature great, and the perfection that brings everything imperfect to its completion. The reference is, in short, to all the bases of the abstractive intelligence that produces scientific learning (we can see here, even if in a different order, the lines of argument in Anselm's *Monologion*).

Illumination guarantees the objectivity of knowledge. Moreover, the agent intellect and the possible intellect are not two separate substances, but two distinct faculties of the soul. The former is not without some degree of passivity, for otherwise it could not receive the illumination, and the latter is not completely inactive, since it is in a position to apply the abstract forms it receives to the information coming to it from the experience of the senses. Thus together with this thesis on cognitive illumination Bonaventure has acquired the doctrine of exemplarism, one of the most valuable achievements of the philosophers, thanks to the genius of Plato. The latter, while using reason alone, did not confine himself to the lower realms of cognitive activity, as Aristotle did, but succeeded in discovering the necessity of an eternal intermediary between visible things and God, an intermediary in which are mirrored the eternal laws established for nature at its creation and, at the same time, for the rational mind that studies nature.

Philosophy can therefore be acknowledged as bringing truth, but always and only insofar as it accepts being integrated into the higher unity of theology. This strict law governing the order among forms of knowledge has, however, been violated by the radical Aristoteleans or Averroists who, in their pride as theorists, deny the unicity and therefore the univocity of truth and propose instead that there are many different and mutually opposed "truths." These are the objects of disciplines that are erroneous precisely because they claim to be disconnected and special. They differ, it is said, because the objects they study are different, so that they can lead to contradictory results, as though truth varies when located within cognitive parameters that have been adapted to suit each different object. Bonaventure, for his part, makes his own the Augustinian perspective that embraces the scalarity of knowledge: here each truth is such only in subordination to a higher truth, and all truths are true only in subordination to the highest truth of all: the truth of revelation.

When, therefore, philosophy is left to its own resources it is a source of error. We must not abide with the philosophers, but go farther toward the higher truth they glimpsed and to which they pointed the way, but that they were unable or unwilling to accept. Moreover, the eyes of the theologian behold with horror the attraction arrogant philosophers have for those who ought to be teaching the true doctrine of Christ. In the fourth conference on the *Hexaemeron* the writer describes the invasion of the new philosophers in strong terms meant to warn readers against the plagues of the book of Revelation, against the "shaft of the bottomless pit" from which arises the smoke that darkens the sun of truth and the locusts that destroy whatever they find (Rev 9:1-3). True (and authentically Franciscan) philosophy is reducible, therefore, to a theological critique of reason, a reduction of reason's aspirations to the measure of its possibilities. "The soul would like to embrace all things within itself," but without the unifying light of Christ it is unable to grasp even the truth of a single thing.

This judgment holds even for Plato, who failed in his courageous effort to set aside the illusion that we know the natural world in an adequate and autonomous way and to replace it with the intuition of a transcendent truth; he discovered that such truth exists, but reason was not capable of grasping it. As we read in the seventh conference, Plato begot Cicero, who was also an "enlightened philosopher" but was forced to renounce reason's ability to lay hold of higher truth that subsists in itself. In fact, both men lacked an authentic illumination, which is purely divine in origin and is reserved for those who believe in the Scriptures. For this reason Aristotle was justified in criticizing Plato and reminding him of the evidence for natural truth, but his own reform of philosophy was deficient and destined to remain incomplete.

According to a well-known passage of *Christ the One teacher of All*, Plato spoke "the language of wisdom": that is, he realized the infinity of transcendent truth, but in the process he undermined the language of the science that seeks to understand the essences of creatures. Aristotle restored this language, the "discourse of science," by developing suitable tools for studying it, but he abandoned the higher way. "But both languages, that of wisdom and that of science, have been given by the Holy Spirit as a single entity, and in a superlative way, to Augustine, the foremost expositor of the Scriptures in their entirety."

4. Speculative Theology

Bonaventure's anxious attack on the purveyors of Aristoteleanism does not, therefore, signify a rejection of philosophy. It is even the foundation of a new speculative project based on a full appreciation of genuine intellectual activity in its most authentic form: theology. The Seraphic Doctor had already written in his commentary on the *Sentences*: "Things that remained hidden from the philosophers have now been made known to the simplest Christians." During his most mature years as a university master Bonaventure debated and published the eight *Disputed Questions on the Mystery of the Trinity*. While fully adapting his material to the formal structure of a scholastic disputation, Bonaventure here gives a perfect example of his theologico-speculative methodology, that is, of reason applied to knowledge of the faith.

Not only does the author decisively emphasize the limits of natural thought. He also takes over from the teaching of his master, Odo Rigaldi, the certainty that a complete and exhaustive application of Aristotelean apodictic to the discussion of dogmas is impossible. The guiding idea in the questions on the Trinity is therefore the indispensable complementarity of demonstration and faith in the pursuit (following the model of Anselm) of the "necessary reasons" that underlie the formulation of the dogma. The fruitful convergence of "indisputable rational knowledge" and "knowledge through faith," with a view to their reciprocal consolidation, is made clear in each question by two successive articles.

In the first question the first article demonstrates the existence of God from the evidence available to reason; the second explains that the credibility of the trinitarian dogma is unavoidably clear due to its own inner necessity. The proof in the first article is the immediate recognition of the evidence inherent in what one thinks when one thinks the God of faith. This is Anselm's argument, reduced (as we noted earlier in explaining the *Proslogion*) to its most immediate, essential, and genuine formula, because reason cannot fail to recognize the undeniable foundational reality of the being that, if it is God, must be like God and therefore must, first and foremost, exist: "If God is God, God exists." In the second article the intelligibility of the principle of divine activity flows no less immediately from the acceptance of the trinitarian dogma as credible; this principle cannot be reached except through belief, which makes it possible, through the application of a consistent process of reasoning, to understand the single origin of all other beings from the being whom the philosophers (such as Plotinus) were unable to describe except by introducing multiplicity and otherness into that original unity.

The second question tackles the unity of God, seen first as following from the acceptance of a first principle that cannot but be one, and then by showing the compatibility of unity and trinity in God. The same procedure is followed in the third question, which deals with the subject of the simplicity of God; in the fourth, on his infinity; in the fifth, on his eternity; in the sixth, on his immutability; and in the seventh, on his necessity. In the eighth question Bonaventure concludes the twofold course followed thus far by showing in a single article how the complete convergence of reason and faith produces an "intelligible circle"; this is due to the knowable presence in the universe of the same God who reveals himself to belief. Here Bonaventure also notes how the trinitarian mystery is no longer a mystery because it is now the evident outcome of an intellectual process that has shown that to think the faith is to know it and to seek the truth is to recognize its presence in faith.

The basis of Bonaventure's speculative theology thus clearly displays the recurring presence of a foundational intellectual principle that has obviously emerged from the convergence just explained of reason and faith and is accepted as a constitutive element in the whole of Christian thought. This principle is the "firstness" of God.

The primacy of God resides in God's existence as the being that cannot be thought of as other than it is. This is shown first and foremost by rational reflection on the dogma of the Trinity, where this primacy is seen as the reason for the production of the second and third persons from the eternal existence of the first. It is also made clear by the entirely metaphysical inevitability of acknowledging in this source of being a perfect identity of "being" and "being something"; this acknowledgment is the presupposition, in turn, for understanding the distinction between these two ontological aspects in all things that are less than God.

This truth is therefore the unquestionable "first" in the soul, where it is the source of every further certainty, whether theological, metaphysical, or physical. It is the first principle of being and also the first principle of knowledge, since the only beings that can be known are those that participate in the antecedent existence of the perfect being. This participation is in fact the first form the agent intellect receives from the divine illumination, which takes concrete shape in its capacity for recognizing the forms that come to the passive intellect from experience. This is the principle, located at the foundation of human mental activity, that allows these creatures to recognize *being* in other things and in themselves and to acknowledge it as a dynamic co-presence of the existential triad: essence, potency, and act. They recognize it, but do not understand it. They know that they exist, and they must search elsewhere for the reason for their existence. Thus the consideration of its own finite being drives the created intelligence to look for the divine perfection; this, however, can be conceived only as first and therefore as existent and productive.

In its perfection as first, the divine being cannot fail to be productive, precisely in order to be first in respect to all else. This production is activated necessarily in the perfect knowledge of what is to be produced; this knowledge reflects love for what is produced, and the production entails the secondary primacy of the Word and the Holy Spirit. This production involving the perfection of the first necessarily brings with it the coeternity and consubstantiality and therefore the equality of the three persons who carry it out. The firstness of God therefore explains the further divine properties treated in the successive themes of the *Questions* on the trinitarian mystery: unity, simplicity, infinity, eternity, immutability, and necessity. Present in the source is the knowable form of the ideas included in it and corresponding to it.

But in this knowableness the finite mind immediately recognizes also the goal of its every desire, the force that tirelessly inspires its longing for affective contemplation. For the believing mind, then, to reason's "book of nature" and faith's "book of Scripture" there is added the third evidence of God's self-manifestation, the "book of life." In this last the mind recognizes that the divine perfection is not an acquired state, but a power that expresses itself eternally in a vital activity that never ceases. All the modalities the intellect discovers in the realities of nature have their perfect embodiment in the eternal life of the Word, who is God. All the mind's ideas are reflections of the perfect exemplars that exist in the Word. All its actions ought to be fulfillments of the eternal law the Father has inscribed in his Word.

The "book of life," then, records the perfection of the intellect and the perfection of the will, of understanding and faith. Like the book of nature and the book of Scripture, it too is inscribed in the eternal trinitarian mystery by the Word, who has defined himself as "way, truth, and life" (John 14:6). He is teacher, therefore, of the knowledge of faith, of the knowledge gained by reason, and, finally, of that affective contemplation that is the supreme knowledge promised to the blessed but that can be anticipated in the lives of Christians who reach a complete fusion of belief and understanding.

During the pilgrimage toward God, which human beings know as their mortal life, the truly Franciscan way of living, which has Christ as its real and eternal model, has for its sole aim to attain to the much more authentic and immortal life that Christian life is. In a valuable little work titled *The Tree of Life* and marked by a profound spirituality, Bonaventure combines two images: the image of the tree that stood in the middle of the earthly Paradise and symbolizes the generation of the Word and the source of created life, and the image of the cross, which symbolizes redemption and the source of life everlasting. With the help of the imagination, which supports and aids understanding, the author meditates on the three central mysteries in the history of Christ (birth, passion, glorification); these are the three parts of the tree, from each of which spring four branches, each loaded with four fruits. Thus Bonaventure inextricably connects to the life of the Redeemer the lives of those who contemplate it.

5. *The Theological Reduction of Philosophy and the Itinerary of Theology*

In a sermon for the feast of the Epiphany, Bonaventure draws his inspiration from the image of the road traveled by the Magi in order to reach Christ as he reveals himself. He describes the ladder climbed by philosophical reason as a historical journey of the human mind toward the truth communicated through revelation. There are nine rungs corresponding to as many particular sciences and divided into the three general categories as distinguished in the classical division of the philosophical sciences: natural (physics, mechanics, mathematics), rational (grammar, rhetoric, logic), and moral (monastic, political, and economic).

Bonaventure takes up the same idea in the third of the *Conferences on the Hexaemeron*. Here the division is a little different, but there are still nine steps that are combined into triads according to the division of "things," "signs," and "actions"; thus there is an outline parallel to the outline of the parts of philosophy. These and other Bonaventuran schemata of the sciences have in common a vertical perspective representing a gradual ascent through a hierarchy toward the highest step, which is located above every human form of knowledge, namely, theology. Theology is the tenth coin that the gospel parable describes as lost because scorned by those who came to a halt on lower rungs of the ladder.

"The science of philosophy is the way to every other science, but anyone deciding to stay there falls into darkness," says Bonaventure in the fourth *Conference* on the gifts of the Holy Spirit. He thus, as it were, makes a doctrinal precept out of the university regulation that prohibited masters from continuing to work unprofitably in the Faculty of the Arts. But, to speak more accurately, the "staying" or "remaining" of the philosophers in the land of error is a descent toward dispersion and multiplicity: "the descent into philosophy is the greatest of dangers," he exclaims in the fourth conference on the *Hexaemeron*. The descent from the one into multiplicity through the splitting up of the sciences is, he says, the sojourn of Adam in the "region of unlikeness"; it is the captivity of the chosen people in Egypt, where the human arts were born, and their refusal to go to the promised land, where the arts lead into theology.

Bonaventure's theology reaches its highest level in two very compressed short works: *The Reduction of the Arts to Theology* and *The Journey of the Soul to God*. Here the premise that all knowledge forms a unity returns to complete and define the entire process of the search for truth as a journey the mind undertakes, to the point of rising above itself and unifying its multiple investigations into particular objects.

The "reduction" to theology is the exact reverse of the "descent into philosophy." As is clear by now, in Bonaventure's vocabulary the Latin word *reducere* does not mean "reduce," that is, diminish, but "lead back" or "bring back." Thus "reduction" implies not an undervaluation and repression of the cognitive possibilities of human reason, but rather a real exaltation of the human intellectual capacities, which are enabled through the cooperation of grace and reason to return to the condition natural to them before the sin of Adam. The sciences are many because when the divine light is diffused throughout creation it produces various reflections of itself due to the many and varied conditions that permit creatures to receive it. But these are not distinct lights flowing from different sources. Bonaventure reminds us of this fact when in the inscription of the little work he cites the same verse from the letter of James (1:17) that is cited at the beginning of the *Corpus Dionysianum* to illustrate the hierarchic transmission of divine truth: "Every best gift and every perfect gift comes from above, coming down from the Father of lights."

With an irrepressible cognitive impetus that is its very life, the human intellect sets out in the opposite direction, rising up from the various appearances of the light in the lower levels of science to the divine source in order to rediscover in the latter not only the origin of a particular truth but originating Truth itself. Nature alone could not sustain the effort required for this laborious reunification, but it is strengthened by the manifestation of this Truth, first in the whole of Nature and then in the Scriptures.

As the intellect ascends, the lights begin to show an order and to distinguish themselves from one another in a visible form that springs from the mutual collaboration of lights. There is the external light that leads to the study of the mechanical arts, which deal with outward things and can transform objects into means of satisfying the necessities of the body. There is the inferior light, which is that of the five senses and makes bodies known not in order to use them but in order to understand them. There is the interior light, which is philosophical knowledge: this investigates causes, formulates the principles of the disciplines, and structures these according to the rational order followed in discourse: natural discourse about things and moral discourse about actions. Finally, there is the superior light, which springs from the salvific truth in the Sacred Scriptures. In the course of moving from the lower levels to the highest, knowledge takes concrete form in the various arts and sciences in order to bring human thought ever closer to the divine Wisdom.

The *Journey* is a masterpiece of Bonaventuran theology that gathers up the entire cognitive, active, and contemplative life of the human person in a web of hierarchically ordered images. This work, too, begins with an invocation of the "Father of lights" in order then to lead the author and his reader from the scattered lights in which human beings participate while on their journey to the fullness of light that the citizens of the heavenly Jerusalem enjoy in the mystical peace of the divine unity. Bonaventure then immediately adds the example to be followed, that of Francis of Assisi, the father of all those who desire union with Christ:

> Following the example of the most blessed father Francis, I too, a sinner, sought this peace with eager spirit. Though utterly unworthy, I am the seventh after his death to succeed him in taking over the general government of the friars. It so happened, by God's will, that around the thirty-third anniversary of his passing into heaven I withdrew to Mount Alverna, hoping in this quiet place to satisfy my desire to seek peace. While I was there I tried to think out some intellectual ways of ascending to God and, behold, among other things there came to my mind the miracle that had happened to blessed Francis on this very spot, that is, the vision

of a winged Seraph in the likeness of the Crucified One. While I gazed on this image I suddenly realized how this vision led father Francis into ecstatic contemplation, and what the way was of reaching that state.

Thirty-three years later (the same number of years as from Christ's birth to the end of his life), Francis' ecstatic experience of the Truth became the common patrimony of the human race, thanks to the careful guidance of his interpreter. Peace, the goal of this quest, had during this passage through time been the object of an inquiry, of a "question"; now, at the end of a mental journey of ascent to God, it becomes the object of a contemplation. The goal is that to which Francis has already come: his "passing," which for him took the form of entry into the life of the blessed. For his mystical follower the goal will be the savoring, during a momentary ecstasy, of a full contemplative enjoyment, at once intellectual and volitional, of the peace that truth brings. The journey described in the subsequent pages of the little work is told in simple language that is, however, very complex in its stringing together of images. The *Journey* is a compendium, a narrative guide through the course followed by the intellect in its search for a mystical "likeness to God" ("deiformity").

It is impossible to recapitulate this journey by summarizing its main stages, because each stage is the result of countless other phases in the course of the ascent. The *Journey*—a book to be read not in order to know its contents but to put them into practice—is itself already a recapitulative description of a course to be run. It is, indeed, always possible to summarize this course even further, but in doing so one runs the risk of losing all the work's contemplative depth and all of its anagogical effectiveness.

It will be enough, therefore, simply by way of introduction to glance through the order of the chapters as the author describes them at the beginning of the work. There are seven of these chapters, which are as it were the necessary stages in an ascent leading to a contemplation that is initially indirect and then reaches its full form only at the end when the soul passes into God. The first six stages, which mount toward that goal, are linked in pairs like the six wings of the seraph, and correspond to three different cognitive levels and attitudes that are attained through three manifestations of light: external, interior, and superior. Using the language of Augustine and the Bible, the author describes the knowledge of God on the first level as a visible trace, on the second as an image, and on the third as a likeness.

The first level is that of the senses, which track God down, so to speak, outside ourselves, through traces he has left in the visible world. The second level is that of the imagination, which still looks for God outside ourselves by endeavoring to identify him in these same traces. The third level is that of reason, which seeks knowledge of God within us through reflection on the image of himself he has imprinted in the natural faculties of the human being. A fourth level is that of the intellect, which contemplates him still within ourselves but in that same image as renewed by the gifts of grace. On a fifth level, by means of the understanding, the soul attains to a contemplation of the Oneness of God in the likeness of the interior illumination, which enables the soul to grasp "above ourselves" the meaning of God's first name, which is Being. On a sixth level the Trinity grants a vision of itself, still above ourselves, that is, "in the Light itself," that is, in gazing on the perfect likeness of God's supreme name, which is Good. Here we are at the highest point of the mind, the "apex of the mind."

On a seventh level, beyond all knowledge, the rapture of the soul takes place in a mental and mystical ecstasy or going forth from itself. Here, like God at the end of his creative work, the intellect ends its work and reaches its rest. In the affections flowing from this rest the soul can completely abandon itself to ecstasy.

> And if you want to know how such things can be, look to grace, not doctrine; to desire, not the intellect; to the groaning of prayer, not to the effort of learning; to the bridegroom, not the teacher; to God, not man; to darkness, not clarity; no longer to the light, but to the fire that burns you up completely and transports you completely into God, in a sacramental rapture and the most passionate affections.

IV. Thomas Aquinas

"All human beings naturally desire to know the truth." Thomas begins his work *On the Oneness of the Intellect in Answer to the Averroists* with this not insignificant variation on the opening words of Aristotle's *Metaphysics* ("all human beings naturally desire to know"). The work is one of those in which he discusses erroneous and tendentious interpretations of Aristoteleanism and thereby makes clear his own confidence in the possibilities of human reason.

But what does it mean to "know truth"? Does it always mean, as Augustine would have it, to know God? Or is it possible to know particular forms of truth without moving onto the terrain of theology? Thomas' answer to this question explains the unique character of the position he took in the contemporary debate on the definition of science in general and of theological science in particular; it also explains the influence this position had on the thinkers of the thirteenth century.

In commenting on the first of Boethius' short works, *The Trinity*, Thomas came upon the expression: "to the extent that light from God enables us to understand." He asked at this point whether the human mind is able to know truth only if it participates in an illumination from God. He answers that, if we read correctly the teachings of the philosopher, that is, of Aristotle, we are given to understand that human beings naturally possess an innate light, one that is identical with the power of the agent intellect, and that the soul is therefore able to lay hold of truth.

But, "since it [the agent intellect] is a created and finite power, its capacity is limited to certain areas." That is, it is able to know many intelligible truths that are within the range of the agent intellect, such as first principles and the conclusions that follow from them; to do this it does not need another intelligible light in addition to the natural light. But there are aspects of truth that are beyond the range of these principles of knowledge. Such, for example, are future contingents and other matters of that kind. This is true especially of all the truths of the faith, which lie beyond the capacities of reason: "All these truths the human mind cannot know unless God illumines it by a new light that is added to the natural light."

In the first of the *Disputed Questions on Truth*, Thomas then explains, on the basis of the very definition of truth, that the qualification "true" is always related to something, since, according to the formula attributed to Isaac Israeli, truth consists in a conformity between reality and intellect, that is, in an affirmative or negative realization of the "agreement of the object with the intellect" or, in other words, of the fact that the thing possesses being in such a way that it can be recognized by the intellect. There are, therefore, as many truths as there are things the intellect can know, since no reality can be false in itself, for falsity consists simply in a lack of equality (instead of conformity) between thing and intellect.

We understand now how for Thomas theology, like every other science, is true if it permits human beings to see with their intellects the things that are the objects of theological assertions. In the case of theology this means knowing with the intellect the thing that is the object of faith and recognizing that it is true, or, in other words, grasping, as far as possible, the cognitive agreement with it. Curiosity, or the human mind's desire to know (of which Aristotle speaks), finds here, in this challenge that represents both a working program and a promise, a most inviting opportunity for measuring, as far as possible, both the intellect's own capacity for desiring to know truth and, at the same time, the real possibilities for satisfying this desire. In Thomas' mind theological science will succeed in this endeavor only by continuing on the way opened by Albert the Great and fulfilling the aspirations of philosophy to know the truth not only by understanding created things but also by moving beyond natural knowledge and discovering the foundations of revealed truth.

1. Master of the Sacred Page

Thomas was born around 1224–25 in Roccasecca, on the border between Latium and the Campagna, into the family of the Counts of Aquino. He received his early instruction as an oblate in the nearby monastery of Montecassino; in 1239 he was enrolled in the Faculty of Arts of the University of Naples, recently founded by Frederick II, where he studied grammar and logic and read Aristotle's works on the natural sciences. His conversion to the Dominican Order met with hostility from his family and especially from his mother, who wanted to see him become abbot of Montecassino. His brothers forced him to return to the paternal home, where he profited by his enforced stay to continue studying, reading the Bible in an analytical way, and beginning to reflect on the *Sentences*.

His stubbornness, however, overcame all resistance, and in 1245 he was able to return to the Dominican convent in Naples. In that same year he was sent to Paris, where his superiors made an exception and allowed him to follow a double course for three years, studying the arts both at the university and at Saint-Jacques and at the same time also following some courses in theology in the convent's house of studies. The master to whom he listened and whose lectures on the *Celestial Hierarchy* of Pseudo-Dionysius he copied down to some extent was Albert the Great.

From 1248 to 1252 he was that master's assistant and collaborator and followed him to Cologne. There he attended Albert's lectures both on theology and on the *Ethics* of Aristotle; for the latter he compiled a lexicographical table, based for the most part on Albert's citations from it. The early biographers tell a story about the first sign of appreciation for Thomas' intellectual powers during those years: Thomas was nicknamed "the dumb ox of Sicily" because of his taciturnity and imposing size, but Albert supposedly prophesied that the "lowing" of Thomas' teaching would soon be heard throughout the world.

To this period belong the first biblical glosses, those initial evidences of exegetical work that would continue in further scriptural commentaries composed during all the subsequent phases of Thomas' career, right up to the months immediately preceding his death. The first works in this area were notes on texts of the prophets: Jeremiah and Lamentations and, to some extent, Isaiah. A copy of these glosses has come down from his own hand, written, like all the autographs, in a cursive script so difficult to read that it became known as "illegible writing." The basic character of these notes, consisting as they do primarily in comparisons between the words of the prophets and other biblical passages, suggests that they were preparations for a course of lectures.

Later, after becoming a master of theology and having in mind his professorial duties, Thomas would comment in a more analytical way on the sacred page, both Old and New Testaments, and compose fuller explanations. These commentaries are connected with the various stages of his career. There is a literal commentary on the book of Job, which he uses as a scriptural basis for tackling the problem of reconciling divine providence with the presence of evil in history. It seems that this problem was being raised once more in a dramatic way by the Averroist teachings circulating in the Faculties of Arts, teachings that rejected the personal survival of the soul and therefore the possibility of a remunerative justice after death.

There is a commentary on the book of Psalms on which Thomas perhaps worked even during the last months of his life; in his prologue he says that the Psalter is justifiably among the biblical books most commented by Christian interpreters because, while all the other books have their specific themes, the Psalter "has an inclusive subject matter, that is, all of theology" and even "contains the whole of Scripture." There is a *Reading of Matthew* and a *Reading of John*, the latter devoted to a deeper theological understanding of the divine mystery of Christ. Of the latter the concluding gloss says that "even if the world were to last a hundred thousand years and [people] were to continue to write books, they would never succeed in understanding completely the individual meanings of all the things he did and said," because "even an infinite number of human words cannot come close to the one Word of God."

There is, finally, an extensive and elaborate commentary on the letters of Paul, which are viewed as a whole; the commentary shows a marvelous capacity for interpretive organization, making the work a kind of orderly exposition of systematic christology. In addition there is a *Continuous Gloss* on the gospels, which Thomas undertook by assignment from Pope Urban IV for the purpose of coping with theological differences from the Byzantines. The work provides an intelligent selection of patristic exegeses, both Greek and Latin, for each verse and was widely circulated under the title *Catena aurea* ("Golden Chain").

As was true of the majority of his fellow Masters of the Sacred Page, Thomas' wide-ranging theological treatises, such as the *Summae*, and his shorter works devoted to specific problems were always based on a solid knowledge of Scripture. This biblical learning not only provided a general inspiration or particular starting points for the thematic organization of theological science but was also the very reason for the existence of this science; it provided and defined its content and was its ultimate and essential goal.

During those years this deep grounding in Scripture characterized and fully justified the work produced at the university by the representatives of the Mendicant Orders. These scholars did not turn aside from their fundamental call to serve the Gospel, but rather endeavored to make their entire intellectual commitment to theological study produce forms of preaching and acts of prayer that would guide and support believers in their dealings with revelation. In particular, Thomas' whole body of work would be inexplicable if we were to focus our attention solely on the strict formalities of his mental procedures and his arguments and lose sight of this basic hermeneutical perspective.

The acceptance of reading of the Bible as the foundation of theological speculation justified the decisive importance Thomas assigned to the literal sense, an importance explicitly asserted in the first question of the *Summa of Theology*. This did not mean playing down the figurative (that is, the symbolic and allegorical) meaning of the sacred text, recommended by the most authoritative exegetes down the centuries and regarded by Thomas himself as a natural and therefore "necessary" characteristic of Scripture. But the historical and literal sense had to be the basis for the first and indispensable theological understanding of revelation.

Thomas had already left some interesting remarks on the usefulness of Scripture in theology in his notes on Isaiah, commenting on the verse "I teach you profitable things" (Vg). It is useful because it enlightens the intellect, as every true teaching does, because the aesthetic enjoyment of the divine words brings pleasure even to the ear, because it inflames the heart by eliciting the spiritual affections that are inseparable from theological knowledge, because it directs human moral activity, leading it toward the good, because it teaches how to instruct others, a final but essential part of a preacher's vocation. In his *Conferences* on the creed, produced some years later, Thomas stipulates the same program of constant meditative study of the Scriptures as a fundamental condition for faith and gives the Virgin Mary credit for having fully implemented this program with her readiness to listen to the divine word at the mystical moment of the annunciation and the conception of the divine Word.

In the Prologue of the commentary on the Psalms, with its more organized teaching, Thomas emphasizes the usefulness of reading the Bible for theological study. Here he takes as his basis the Aristotelean theory of the four causes. The matter or subject of Scripture is the work of salvation accomplished by Christ through his incarnation, a work first prophesied and then narrated or in any case explained throughout the entire series of biblical books. The efficient cause is God himself, who dictated the material to the biblical writers. The final cause is prayer and the raising of the soul to God. Finally, the form is fundamental for an understanding of the difference between revelation and theological discourse, which are essentially distinguished by the diversity of their respective ways of setting forth the truths of the faith. Scripture has, in fact, numerous ways, "commemorative, hortatory and prescriptive, argumentative, critical or laudatory," none of which can be said to describe the rational exposition proper to theological science.

Around the beginning of 1252, John the German, General of the Dominicans, asked Albert the Great to let him know of some young theologian worthy of possibly being appointed a Sententiary Bachelor in Paris. Thanks to the intercession of now-cardinal Hugh of Saint-Cher, Albert was able to overcome the hesitations caused by Thomas' youthfulness. Thus September of that same year saw the beginning of the Parisian career of the man whom posterity would call the "Common Doctor" or even the "Angelic Doctor." In 1256, after less than three years, he was appointed "Master of the Sacred Page" by Chancellor Henry of Veyre.

2. Saints and Philosophers

The *Commentary on the Sentences* was the fruit of Thomas' lectures as a Bachelor but was completed after his inauguration as Master. It is his first great theological synthesis, anticipating and in many instances already developing in a masterful way some of the principal theses of his later works. With a greater feel for the systematic than the majority of contemporary authors possessed, he takes his "reading" of the *Sentences* as an opportunity to produce, by way of numerous "questions," an organic presentation of the subject matter of theology, while adopting original doctrinal positions.

One of the elements marking the novelty of his projected work is his use of philosophical authorities to advance the theological discussion. This is a clear sign of his conviction that the search for wisdom should, if possible, be supported by all available tools useful for bolstering that work, and his certainty that there can be no contradictions between different manifestations of the truth, which is one. In the pages of the *Commentary* the dialogue Thomas inaugurates between the sources of Christian doctrine and those of Greek and Arabic-Jewish philosophy is very open, substantial, and productive. In number, the citations from the works of Aristotle, especially from the *Nicomachean Ethics* but also, to a lesser degree, from the *Metaphysics*, the *Physics*, and *On the Soul* are twice as many as those from Augustine, four times as many as those from Pseudo-Dionysius, and eight times as many as those from Gregory the Great and John Damascene. But these figures make no difference as to substance: the constant respect Thomas shows for the thought of the Fathers is not less than the debt that, despite the celebrated "novelty" of his work, he owes to contemporary theologians, chiefly Albert and Bonaventure, who are often cited as unnamed "someone's."

The role of philosophical sources in Thomas is therefore justified by the conviction that the theological system provided in Lombard's *Sentences* is an organic one. Within the framework of the four sections of the *Books of the Sentences*, which are devoted respectively to God, creation, redemption, and sacramental doctrine, Lombard's real purpose is to propose a unified organization of the subject matter of theology, its center being God as origin and end of reality and of the truth of the created universe. According to Thomas this unified organization means that there is an important connection between production within the Trinity and the creative and redemptive divine work. That is to say, the production of creatures as the effect of a higher cause is simply a consequence of the generation of the Word in whom the Father plans creation, just as the return of creatures to God through the work of grace is the result of the procession of the Spirit who spreads sanctification everywhere in the created world.

This teaching, which is deeply theological in its innermost truth, is able therefore to take over the rational explanation that Neoplatonic philosophy (as read especially through the lens of Avicenna's thought) offers in speaking of the descent of the many from the One and the return of the many to the One. As a matter of fact, the light thrown by philosophy on the productive energy at work in the divine causality, both in the process of things coming into existence through secondary causes and in the metaphysical explanation of the composition and structure of being, can be especially useful to theologians in their reflection on the parallelism between the trinitarian productions within God and the missions of the divine persons within creation.

In this conception of the relations between reason and faith (a conception truly innovative in that period), the contribution of the philosophical patrimony is no longer simply to identify organizational categories or a method for developing and sustaining theological arguments. It also serves as a way of acquiring and evaluating a rational analysis of reality (one of the objectives of theology) that allows theologians to compare solutions coming from various sources but frequently compatible with one another and reciprocally functional. This process is made possible by the succession of questions and answers, sometimes philosophical, sometimes theological, that the technique of the question produces. In short, for Thomas the philosophers begin to be a legitimate source of thought alongside the saints, the Fathers, and the theologians of the past; this is true also, and even above all, of the plan for a systematic body of knowledge that is authentically theological.

However, this act of assigning to the metaphysics of the philosophers the rank of an autonomous search for the truth about the created order and its causes cannot be simply a step without further consequences for so deeply theological a speculative thinker as Thomas. His appropriation of ancient philosophy does not result in a merely occasional use of it when this seems opportune. Such a minimal use is not possible for him, given his organic view of truth in itself as unitary and indestructible, a view on which he bases his acceptance of particular truths proposed by reason.

Indeed, given the very centrality of the self-revelation of the divine being, which supports the theological system sketched out in the *Commentary on the Sentences*, a theologian cannot simply ignore the metaphysics of the philosophers, and then use it later on only when he finds it handy and depending on the specific reliability of some of its assertions. Precisely because the possession of absolute truth is assured to him by revelation, Thomas, as a Christian, cannot but devote all his energies to establishing a new foundation for metaphysics. This will in turn ensure a solid, organic system of truths freely investigated with the resources of natural reason but deeply grounded in a basic compatibility with the other truth the Christian philosopher knows he can constantly and freely use without any need on his part to discover it.

Love of truth authorizes one to seek it and recognize it wherever it may manifest itself, but love also demands that one accept as its manifestations only those that are really objective and universal. If, then, metaphysics were to be a science, it could not remain tied to the varied and incomplete forms in which the numerous ancient philosophers and their Greek and Arabic interpreters passed it on to the medieval West. Thomas felt that, to be an authentic theologian, he had also to be an authentic metaphysician. This meant completing in an utterly rigorous way the systematic organization of the truth available to reason, thus, and only thus, allowing reason to enter into a real and fruitful dialogue with the certainties of the faith and the teaching of the Fathers of the Church.

3. The Fundamental Concepts of Metaphysics: Existence and Essence

According to the early biographers, during the period in which Thomas was commenting on the *Sentences* he also composed two short philosophical works that have been traditionally known as *The Principles of Nature* and *Being and Essence*.

The Principles can be regarded as a preparation for the thematic approach and developments in *Being and Essence*. The work is a concise explanation of the fundamental interpretive concepts introduced by Aristotle to explain the being and becoming of things. These are: the pairs consisting of act and potency, substance and accident, matter and form; then the divisions of genera into species and individuals; furthermore, the doctrine of the four causes, two extrinsic (efficient and final) and two intrinsic (matter and form), and of the three sources of becoming, namely, the same two intrinsic causes of being (matter and form) along with privation, an accidental cause.

These many and varied structures considerably complicate the rational explanation of the nature of being. It is necessary, therefore, to try to reduce these structures by means of a further conceptual distinction that is prior to all of them and makes possible a more direct approach to the reality of being by tracing the latter back, in an unmediated way, to the efficacy of the absolutely first principle from which everything derives, that is, the first Cause of which theology speaks. In other words, while the structured compositions of natural being can be deduced from Averroes' explanation of Aristotelean naturalism in dealing with becoming in the sublunary world, it is to Avicenna that we must look for a more general and exhaustive explanation of the thinkableness of derived being in relation to the absolute simplicity of the One.

Being and Essence begins with Aristotle's warning that "a small error at the beginning always leads to a large error at the end," and with Avicenna's observation that, since the first concepts known to the intellect are being and essence, it is necessary to be clear once and for all on their meaning, which is not easily grasped. "Being" has in fact many meanings, as seen not only in the rigid schema of the ten categories but also and above all in the different degrees of existence and hierarchical rank that substances have, from the lowest in the world of material imperfections to the highest simplicity of the divine perfection. "Essence" signifies the truth of that of which being is predicated. Therefore it always has a set definition, provided this definition is correct. *Esse* ("to be"), on the other hand, is that of which this definition is predicated. Therefore essence (also called *quidditas*, "whatness" by the philosophers) is predicated of that which is or, in other words, a being (*ens*). Therefore *ens* (the present participle of *esse*) is properly applied to everything of which the act of existence is correctly predicated, that is, to everything that is (*est*) and is something (*est aliquid*). This "something" that an *ens* is in act, or in a particular way that excludes other somethings, is the essence. *Ens*, that is, *esse* as act, and *essentia* are present in all substances, whether composed or simple.

Composite substances are those resulting from a combination of form and matter, so that their essence includes both. The combination of matter and form does not always produce an individual, but only when the matter is marked or sealed by quantity (*signata quantitate*), that is, when a determined quantity of matter, in composition with the form, permits the actuation of the *ens*. Thus, for example, Socrates is an individual because in him the form "human being" enters into combination with a quantitatively "determined" (*signata*) amount of matter. But part of the definition of "human being" is also, in combination with the form, matter (that of bones and flesh) that is not *signata*. Both Socrates and human being, then, are essences, but only Socrates is a quiddity (or essence) determined for existence in act, that is, an *ens*.

Even more important is the distinction between essence and existence in separated substances such as the soul and the separated intelligences. Some indeed (namely, Avicebron and his followers) claim that a combination of form and matter must be admitted even in the soul and the separated intelligences. But Thomas denies that intellectual power, which is the fundamental character-istic feature of the intelligences and is therefore their very mode of being, can be affected by matter, for if it were, it would not be able to grasp universality. At the same time, however, some composition must be present in souls and the intelligences, for otherwise they would be identical with the first Cause, who is supreme simplicity. Matter having been excluded, it becomes necessary to ac-knowledge in separated created substances a composition of form and existence, as we read in *On Causes*. These will then have as their essence the form alone, but a form with a specific mode of actual being that is not identical with the es-sence as such. Therefore they actualize their essences only partially, since these are affected by potentiality, which is the source of becoming. Their existence is not absolute but "received" and, as such, limited and finite.

The same is true of the human soul, but the soul is predisposed to union with a body; this being the case, it is in union with the body of which it is the form that the soul acquires its actual existence. This is true even though the body does not individuate the soul as though it were the soul's matter, for the union of soul and body (which has form and matter) individuates not the soul but the human being. Like the intelligences, the soul is individual inasmuch as it is composed of essence and existence. Unlike the intelligences, however, the soul is individual because its act of existing is predisposed to make the essence real only in union with an individual body. Once the body breaks down, the soul keeps its own individuality because of the fact that it has been formed for existence in this particular way. The individuation of the soul, then, depends on the individuality of the body for its beginning, but not for its end.

In contrast, only the first and universal Cause has an *esse* that makes its es-sence exist in the fullest and most absolute way; it is *ens* totally and completely, without any unfulfilled potentiality. To Avicenna and the logico-ontological teaching of Boethius and the Porretans there is added here the profound theo-logical inspiration of Pseudo-Dionysius, whose treatise on *The Divine Names* continues the unveiling of the incomprehensible divine essence and of its exis-tence as pure, actual perfection. This it does by the progressive stripping away of any limitation whatsoever. In God essence and existence are identical: "his essence is his very existence, and for this reason there are philosophers who say that God has no quiddity or essence, because his essence is nothing else but his existence."

The godhead is in fact not a genus made actual in a species or an individual but is actual existence. And precisely because the godhead is existence that actuates its own complete essence and because its essence lacks nothing that could be added to its being, it cannot possibly be thought of as a universal existence that makes other things exist, as a kind of shared existence that implies in its very concept the addition of something else if it is to be an existent being. Inasmuch as God is existence in act he possesses all the perfections that can actually exist, and therefore he lacks no attribute that signifies a perfection, "because all attributes belong to him that are in accord with his utterly simple being."

Up to this point Thomas has analyzed the essence of substances: the divine substance, which is simple because its essence is identical with its existence; the separated substances, whose essence is determined by their existence; and composite substances, whose essence is determined by the combination of matter and form. He now moves on to study the essence of accidents, because these, too, have definitions, so that it is natural for them to have essences. But since accidents always exist insofar as they inhere in a substance, their definition must include something of the other in which they inhere as in a subject. As a result, the definitions of accidents are always imperfect, and their essences are incomplete and relative. It is obvious, above all, that existence is not an accident of an essence, since even accidents have their essences; rather, then, *esse* is an actual existential determination or, in short, an existence.

In conclusion, the distinction between *esse* and essence allows Thomas to outline a complete, structured architecture of reality, both metaphysical and logical. Within it the author reintegrates and establishes all the principles fundamental for the philosophical explanation of the meaning of being; from it no further physical or metaphysical determinant can deviate. Included are: first and foremost, the absolute divine simplicity, which must remain fundamental for any development within the discipline of theology; next, the composite nature of essence (the possibility of existing) and existence (the act of existing) in all created beings; then the combination of matter and form in composite substances and the combination of substance and accident as different actualizations of essence in real existence, the one component being complete and fully definable (substance) and the other imperfect, unstable, and accessory (accident). In the coming years, the Angelic Doctor will build his entire philosophical and theological body of work on these foundations.

4. Philosophy and Theology: From the Commentaries on Boethius to the Summa against Unbelievers

The years (1256 to 1259) of Thomas' first period of teaching in Paris were especially busy ones, both for his teaching activity and for its impact on his theological productivity. In the classroom, along with the "reading" of the Bible, the dominant focus was on the disputation. It was this period that saw the composition of some of the *Quodlibetal Questions*, the *Disputed Questions on Truth*, and two important commentaries on Boethius. One of these, the already mentioned *On Boethius' "Trinity,"* took the form of questions; the other, *Explanation of Boethius' Book "Weeks,"* was in the form of literal glosses.

The first commentary, in accordance with Boethius' text, is devoted in large measure to an analysis of the relations between reason and faith and to the classification of the speculative sciences. Here Thomas chiefly takes the opportunity to bring out the distinction between metaphysics, which Aristotle calls "First Philosophy" but is also known as "the science of God" and then as "theology," and theology more fittingly so called: that is, Christian theology. The latter is also known as "sacred page" (because it comes down to an understanding of revelation) and "sacred teaching."

The full scope of the problem emerges in the fourth article of the fifth question. The task of metaphysics—the science proper to philosophers and whose subject matter is being as being—is to deal with the divine reality. It treats it, however, not as such, since God's being, which is utterly simple and identical in act with his essence, is not knowable, but rather as a reality from which the created intellect is able to derive the first principles of truth, which are supremely knowable but indemonstrable. In that sense metaphysics garners these principles from their effects, that is, from the "principiated" realities that are the knowable entities of the sensible world. It is therefore necessary to avoid all ambiguity in using the term "theology," since divine realities can also be the subject of another kind of theological reflection, according to which the first principles manifest themselves directly and not in their effects:

> See, then, that theology or the science of God is twofold. In one, things divine are looked upon not as the subject matter of this theology as a science, but rather as the principles of its subject matter; this is the theology studied by philosophers and is also known as metaphysics. The other theology, in contrast, considers things divine as such to be its subject matter as a science; this is the theology communicated in Sacred Scripture. Both sciences deal with things that in their being are separated from matter and movement, but they do so in different ways, because there are two ways in which things can be in their being separated from matter and movement. In the first case separation from matter and movement is inherent in those things of which being is predicated, inasmuch as they cannot in any manner be affected by matter and movement; it is in this sense that God and the angels are separated from matter and movement. In the second case separation from matter and movement is not inherently true of those things of which it is predicated, with the result that they can exist without matter or movement even if they are sometimes found in matter and movement; in this sense being, substance, potency, and act are said to be separated from matter and movement. . . .
>
> Philosophical theology, then, has as its proper subject things separated in the second sense and has as the principles of its subject matter things separated in the second sense. The theology of Sacred Scripture, on the other hand, has as its subject things separated in the first sense, although it also deals with those that exist in matter and movement, but only to the extent that this is required by the manifestation of things divine.[1]

Theology, then, can be either philosophical or based on faith. The former has as its subject being as such, and it studies things divine as the source of this subject, as Avicenna teaches. The latter has the divine in itself as its subject. As Boethius says, theology is concerned with "that which is separated from matter and is immovable." This is true of the subject of both sciences, but philosophical theology or metaphysics deals with it by considering the principles of being as separable, that is, as manifested in their effects, because God as such cannot be grasped by the human mind. The other theology exists because faith brings knowledge of God in himself, as separated and immovable.

This section is fundamental for Thomas' mature understanding of theological science and it brings to light something very important that shows his position to be decidedly original in comparison with all his contemporaries. The meeting between Christian theology and Arabic-Aristotelean metaphysics has at this point produced its revolutionary effects. If theology is to be a science, it is no longer enough to base its truths on its adherence in principle to the truth of revelation, this being accepted as believable before it can become intelligible. It must now be shown that theology's right to be a science is due to it not because it is based on faith but despite the fact that it is based on faith.

It will even be necessary henceforth, if Christian theology is truly to be a science, to show how its revealed nature is compatible with Aristotelean epistemology, despite the fact that theology's claim to be a knowledge of truth does not spring from reason. But that theology is necessarily a science is assured by the fact that it has a subject matter of its own: namely, the divine reality as principle or source, and considered not in the light of its effects but precisely as principle or source. The effects of the divine causality will enter into the study of theology only insofar as this is required by the fact that they are manifestations of the divine.

After bringing metaphysics within the realm of Christian knowledge of the truth, Thomas now faces the more difficult task, but one central for his system, of applying the paradigm of the human rational sciences to Christian knowledge of the truth and, at the same time, showing that this knowledge transcends the rational sciences.

In 1259 Thomas left Paris and went first to Valenciennes, where he took part in the work of the commission of Dominican scholars, Albert the Great among them, that had been given the task of promoting studies in the Order. This group left to the General Chapter the decision to make the study of the arts a prerequisite for the basic training of the friars. Thomas then went back to Italy, where in 1261 he was appointed Reader at the house of studies that was located in the Dominican convent of Orvieto, the city to which Urban IV had temporarily transferred his court. It was during these months that he worked on the composition of the *Summa contra Gentiles* or *Summa Against Unbelievers*.

This work may be regarded as the final product of the scholastic development of the genre "dialogue with other religions." This genre had emerged at the beginning of the twelfth century out of Anselm's idea of the possibility of producing a model of theological rationality that is completely identical with the eternal "necessary reasons" that justify the entire Christian revelation. This would be a rational apologetical tool for convincing those belonging to other religious confessions (persons here given the general name of "Gentiles") that it was right for them to convert, and for strengthening, in those already belonging to the religion of Christ, their certainty of possessing the truth. In the third article of the second question of the commentary on Boethius' *Trinity* this same program had already been described in words that even Anselm or Peter Abelard could have accepted, although they were dealing with a very different and less sophisticated conception of philosophical reasoning:

> Just as sacred doctrine depends on the light of faith, so philosophy depends on the natural light of reason. It is therefore impossible that matters proper to philosophy should be contrary to matters with which faith deals: the former are certainly on a lower level, and yet they contain some likenesses and some anticipations ("preambles") of the latter, just as nature in general is full of anticipations of grace. And if the words of the philosophers assert something contrary to the faith, this is certainly due not to the nature of philosophy but rather to its abuse through defective reasoning. Moreover, it is even possible, starting with the very principles of philosophy itself, to combat this kind of errors by showing that they express theses that are impossible or completely unnecessary. . . .
>
> In sacred doctrine, therefore, we can use philosophy in three ways: First and foremost, to bring to light the anticipations of the faith; these must necessarily be known, in coming to faith, as things about God that are proved by natural arguments, for example that God exists or that God is one or other of the kinds of things proved in philosophy by natural reasoning; these are presupposed by faith. Second, to make known through similitudes things proper to faith, as Augustine does in his work on *The Trinity*, where he uses many similitudes taken from philosophical doctrines in order to make the Trinity known. Third, to combat all the points made against the faith by showing that these are false or not necessary.[2]

The preambles to faith are anticipations of truths of faith that can be grasped by the use of natural reason alone, which thus precedes the steps subsequently taken by the understanding of believers when they accept the faith. The idea of the preambles will return in the second question of the first part of the *Summa of Theology* (a question devoted to the five ways of proving the existence of God). The definition of the preambles is the same there, as are the examples ("the existence of God and other like truths about God, which can be known by natural reason": *ST* I, q. 2, a. 2, ad 1; Dominican translation), to which is added the corroborative statement: "for faith presupposes natural knowledge, even as grace presupposes nature, and perfection supposes something that can be perfected."

This last clarification is very important because it amounts to saying not only that theology completes what philosophy begins, but also that this kind of beginning accounts perfectly for the authentic purposes of theology, just as grace cannot be effective except on a nature that needs redemption, and perfection cannot be reached except where there is imperfection to begin with. And just as nothing prevents those incapable of being philosophers from accepting by faith as credible truths attainable by reason, it must in the same way be permissible for theologians to use the ability of reason to bring such truths to light simply and purely as intelligible, for the purpose of dialoguing with unbelievers on the basis of what they have in common with believers, namely, pure reason, "to which all are compelled to assent."

This is precisely the purpose Thomas seeks to fulfill by composing the *Summa Against Unbelievers*, his first gigantic effort to produce a possible rational understanding of the same truths Christians believe and to locate it within a framework that on the whole parallels a systematic exposition of the faith. And yet from the outset the author explicitly claims that, despite this rational approach, the *Summa* is an eminently theological work:

> And so, in the name of the divine Mercy, I have the confidence to embark on the work of a wise man, even though this may surpass my powers, and I have set myself the task of making known, as far as my limited powers will allow, the truth that the Catholic faith professes, and of setting aside the errors that are opposed to it.[3]

The "wise (person)" of whom Thomas speaks in this sentence from a programmatic passage in chapter 2 of Book I is one who searches out the first causes of truth and therefore is at once a metaphysician and a theologian, at once an Aristotelean and a Christian, who enjoys by a higher right the support of God's word. The truth of things divine is in fact twofold, not in itself (that is, as seen from God's side) inasmuch as for him truth is one and simple, but in the way in which human beings are in a position to receive it (that is, from the viewpoint of our knowledge). For it is necessary to distinguish in our knowledge between, on the one hand, truth demonstrated by reason and useful in convincing adversaries through argument and, on the other, truth to which one attains only by faith, although reason is useful here in refuting errors that falsify this truth or prevent its reception.

The first three parts of the *Summa* have for their subject first God in himself, then the relationship between God as Creator and the created world, and, finally, the relationship between God as good and the moral life. These three open the way to the fourth part, which deals directly with the mysteries of revelation; these are explained, as is proper in theological procedure, with, on the one hand, the help of rational arguments, although at this level such arguments become only "probable," and on the other hand with the aid of Christian authorities. Thus reason, which in the first three books had followed its own courses that precede faith, is transcended in the fourth book by faith and agrees to follow in its steps in order to be taught, as in Eriugena's old allegory of the race of the two apostles to the tomb of Christ.

So at the beginning and end of the work Thomas places the fundamental *topos*, namely, the celebration of the "pursuit of wisdom," the ancient name for philosophy but the name given also to the theology that rises out of the best possible use of philosophical reason. Of all human activities theology is the most perfect because it permits human beings to share in blessedness, the most sublime because it transports them into the likeness of God and into friendship with God, the most useful because it leads them into the kingdom of immortality, and the most pleasant (a thought that occurs often in Thomas) because from all this there can spring only joy, pleasure, and delight.

The existence of God is the first basic truth about God in himself that can be demonstrated by reason; it is, therefore, "the necessary foundation of the whole work. For if we do not demonstrate that God exists, all consideration of divine things is necessarily suppressed" (I, ch. 9). The arguments to demonstrate God's existence that are introduced in the thirteenth chapter of the first book anticipate in their structure, if not in their exact formulation, those that in the *Summa of Theology* will, with a more clear-cut and direct manner of reasoning, become the five ways, with a special emphasis on the idea of God as prime mover behind all creaturely change.

Then, in a procedure that shows an impressive parallelism to the development of the meditation on the divine nature in Anselm's *Monologion* but is also based on a much more solid knowledge of what philosophy has to say on the metaphysical elements of being, Thomas goes on to show how from the existence of God—that is, from the realization that God is the "first being"—a swift chain of reasonings brings out the other fundamental conditions of his knowableness. Thus: if he is mover, he is immovable; if he is immovable, he is eternal; he is therefore free of all potentiality and therefore of all matter; he is therefore pure spirit, without any compositeness, passivity, or corporeity. There is no accident in God, no substantial distinction. God does not fall into any genus; he is not a form of things; he is absolute perfection. According to the (new) Christian metaphysics, God simply *is* his *essence*.

As is obvious, the logical premise underlying the possibility of thus conjoining rational theology with a theology based on faith is the principle that everything predicable of God is always and only expressible negatively (the "negative way" or "way of elimination"). As Pseudo-Dionysius taught (remember that during these same years Thomas commented on *The Divine Names*), both revealed discourse and philosophical discourse can speak of God only while presupposing a radical change in the original semantic value of the terms they use. This does not mean, however, as Maimonides thought, that names common to God and creatures are purely equivocal: that is, that in theological discourse they have a meaning completely different from their natural meaning (for example: just as between the animal "dog" and the constellation "dog," so too between the words used in theology and words for the natural world there is nothing in common except the empty enunciation of the same word).

To accept such a position would amount, in Thomas' thinking, to a denial of the very efficacy of the Pseudo-Dionysian negative way, since it is from the polarity between the positive meaning of the attribute and the denial of its attribution to God that Pseudo-Dionysius derives the possibility of an approach to the understanding of the divine. Then, too, to deny such a position would amount to denying any possibility whatever of a theological discourse that is logically meaningful. Theological predication, then, can be neither univocal nor purely equivocal, but given that there is nonetheless some likeness between God and things that justifies the very possibility of reasoning about the divine perfections on the basis of the created world, the conclusion must be drawn that every theological predication—that is, every divine name that is shared with creatures—is always and only applied analogically.

According to Aristotelean logic, analogy implies the possibility of predicating the same term of distinct things for reasons that are different but can be traced back to a common semantic purpose. Thus we say that a body is "healthy" or that a food is "healthy" or that a medicine is "healthy"; we make the same predication for different reasons, but all of them have to do with health. The meaning, then, is not the same, but in each case is ordered to the one truth. The way for the introduction of analogy into theological discourse was prepared by the studies of the Porretan schools and improved through contact with Arabic and Jewish thought.

In Thomas' theology analogy becomes a very powerful means of arguing, inasmuch as it permits an easier recourse to the tools and expressive terms of natural philosophy or of metaphysics in order to describe divine perfection. Thus it becomes possible to speak of goodness, unity, infinity, will, and truth in God. It is possible to speak of the divine intelligence, but analogously as compared with the natural intellectual capacities of human beings, so that it makes no sense to ask whether God can or cannot know contingent futures or things that are infinite or filthy, or even whether God can know evil. It then becomes possible to take problem after problem and speak analytically of God's relationship to creation as cause, as end, and as organizer and goal of the redemption promised to the human race.

5. Rome and Paris: Aristoteleanism versus Averroism;
Angelology and Anthropology

In September of 1265 the Chapter of the Roman Province, meeting in Anagni, appointed Thomas to inaugurate and direct a Dominican house of theological studies, probably at Santa Sabina. The beginning of work on the *Summa of Theology* goes back to this period; Thomas thought of it as providing students with a complete text for theological studies, better suited for learning than his commentary on the *Sentences*. But during the three years of his stay in Rome his activity as teacher and writer covered a good deal more than the *Summa*. Some important *Disputed Questions* were written at this time, among them those *On the Soul* and *On Spiritual Creatures*, both of them dealing with theological solutions to problems of psychology, anthropology, and angelology. Above all, in the area of philosophy he formed his plan for publishing a complete commentary on the writings of Aristotle based on the new translations from the Greek that his confrère, William of Moerbeke (d. ca. 1286), was producing during these same years; Thomas began with a commentary on the *De Anima* (*On the Soul*).

The work of commenting on the works of Aristotle continued during the years after 1268 when Thomas returned to Paris to continue his teaching there and to take part in the numerous doctrinal controversies that were stirring up the world of the university, especially on anthropological questions raised by the teachings of the Averroists. Thomas gave his answer to these in 1270, in his *The Oneness of the Intellect*. Here, once again, reason was put at the service of the faith by correcting the errors of incompetent philosophers. In this regard the Averroist conception of the intellect as a separated substance and the consequent rejection of the immortality of the soul were an attack on the truth of the entire Christian theology of redemption, the purpose of which was to lead humanity to the attainment of blessedness. This was why Thomas laid such stress on the subject, whether in the setting of the theological disputation or in a separate monograph or, finally but no less importantly, in the form of an accurate commentary on the philosophical texts on which the harmful Averroist doctrine was based, first and foremost Aristotle's *On the Soul*.

Although Thomas was deeply influenced by Aristotelean thought, he developed an anthropological doctrine his own contemporaries would hail as "new." This philosophico-Christian conception of the human person would later affect the entire *Summa Against Unbelievers* and then the *Summa of Theology*. It is consistently based on the foundational themes of his metaphysics: signed matter as principle of individuation, the rejection of universal hylomorphism, and the universal combination of essence and the act of existing.

In the course of the *Summa of Theology*, where he is not tied down by a text to be commented on, Thomas takes up the anthropological problem in the place proper to theology: that is, in the context of the divine six-day creation and the creation of the angels, which precedes that of human beings. Since the entire divine plan has as its goal the assimilation of creatures to the Creator, this assimilation must be accomplished in all its possible actuations. And because intelligence is not a function of the body, there surely exist creatures that can effect their assimilation to God by means of a completely spiritual intellect. Such are the angels: pure intellectual substances, exempt from composition with matter and corporeity. Even when commenting on the *On Causes* during the same years in Paris, Thomas says he is convinced that the nature of angelic substances is the principal proof of the hierarchical order of the universe freely willed by God as a ladder of perfections in order to realize all the forms of creaturely participation in his perfection. (Thomas understood that *On Causes* was not an authentically Aristotelean work because he was able to compare the text with the *Elementatio theologica* of Proclus, which Moerbeke had translated.)

This same perspective explains his rejection of the universal hylomorphism of Avicebron. This theory is erroneous because when dealing with the composition of created being it ends by giving a privileged place to the material cause, that is, to indeterminacy and particularity, as compared with the perfection given by form, thus turning upside down the order of Aristotelean metaphysics. As Thomas had already made clear in his *Being and Essence*, the determinacy of angelic substances, which are endowed with will and intellect, is produced by the composition of essence and existence, which does not allow accidental change. Furthermore, if, as Scripture reports, the angels appear in corporeal and visible forms, this is due solely to a limitation of the imagination of the human beings to whom they show themselves. Since they are not subject to the principle of individuation they are distinguished only by their species (in other words, each angel is a species, as Avicebron teaches, and "there are as many species as there are individuals"). Moreover, they are countless (as Pseudo-Dionysius claims), because since their number is decided solely by their form there is a greater and more perfect exercise of the divine creative activity than occurs with corporeal individualities.

Human beings are certainly endowed with a soul, that is, an intellectual and spiritual substance, as the angels are, because while with their bodies they exercise certain vital functions, they share only with the angels those activities connected with knowledge. At least those operations that the soul performs insofar as it is "intellectual" are not dependent on matter, just as the universal, which is the object of these operations, is not corporeal. Therefore the subject that performs them must be incorporeal. In addition, among these operations of the intellect there is also self-knowledge, which takes place without any corporeal intermediary. Therefore, like the angelic substances, the human soul is a "subsistent form." It is important to note that this character of the soul is deducible as a characteristic of its intellectual nature and not as an effect of its ability to inform the body, for the latter is not the reason for but a consequence of its being as form. The soul is a form because it knows as an intellectual substance. Moreover, as such, like all intellectual substances, it is incorruptible; it is endowed with will and intellect; and its definition as a substance is given by the composition of essence and existence.

Since each celestial substance is a different species, human souls do not belong to the same species as the angels. On the other hand, since intellection differs in each human individual as a singular subject ("it is this particular human being who understands"), it must be that each soul enters into composition with an individual body, contrary to the opinion of the Averroists. The latter, in order to safeguard the spiritual nature and objectivity of human intellection, claim that the source of intellection is one and the same for the entire human species. The answer to the Averroists is now simple: intellectual knowledge, the formative principle of humanity, is what makes a human being a human being; therefore if the source of intellection were one and the same for all human beings there would be but one human being. In conclusion, since a human being is individuated by the body, the source of intellection must be present in each human individual and is the form that makes a human being an individual body. Therefore the soul is the substantial form of human beings insofar as they are individuals.

The most important clarification introduced by Thomas at this point is that being a substance does not contradict being a form, but even springs from the perfection of the form. In the hierarchy of corporeal beings we see in fact a progressive predominance of form over matter: from the four elements (matter with a very simple form) to the mixed things resulting from their combination, and on to the plants and animals, the various qualities and therefore the various activities that arrive with the form are not the result of an accidental super-imposition of various forms that inhere in a single matter. Such a superimposition would lead to a contradictory multiplication of individualities in a single individual substance (since each form that combines with matter becomes an individual). On the contrary, there is but a single substantial form that shapes the matter proper to each individual.

Thus, in opposition to the tendency seen in Augustinian Platonism, Thomas thinks of soul and body not as two substances accidentally united and continuing to exist in act when they are separated, but as the constitutive principles of the single individual substance actually existing. Furthermore, contrary to the pluralist perspective adopted in *Spirit and Soul* (the attribution of which to Augustine Thomas rejects), the several faculties of the soul are powers belonging to a single form. In fact, every higher form is more complex and includes all the formative capacities of lower and more simple forms. Thus plants have only a vegetative soul; the sensitive souls of non-intelligent animals also carry on the vegetative functions; and finally in the human being the intellectual soul carries out the sensitive and vegetative functions.

In fact, this is true throughout nature. To use a comparison introduced by Aristotle, substantial forms, like numbers, are organized into a hierarchy of preordained perfections, so that some forms possess a lesser perfection, others a greater perfection that includes all the lesser perfections. And, according to Thomas, this hierarchical distribution of forms is in complete harmony with the universal hierarchy of which Avicenna, the *On Causes*, and the Dionysian theological tradition speak with one voice.

From the intellectual soul, its only substantial form, the human composite thus also has its being as sensitive, living, and corporeal, as well as the fact that it is a substance and a being. It is precisely this complex unity of the substantial form that ensures the unity of the human individual, which would be compromised if we were to think, along the lines of Plato, of the soul being united to a body-substance already formed without it. On the contrary, the union of soul and body is complete and perfect at the moment of the human being's conception in the maternal womb.

The conception of the intellect as a form free of the influences and determinations of bodily matter is also the foundation of free voluntary choice or, in other words, of the exercise of a practical judgment in which the will guides itself by the knowledge provided by the intellectual function, for there is no act of the will that is not preceded by an act of knowledge. But this primacy of the intellect over the will does not lead to an intellectualist determinism: the will is moved in a manner "conformed with" but not necessarily "subordinated to" the action of the intellect. The will can freely direct itself toward its object because of the simple fact that it always knows that object to be a good that is only partial and finite and therefore only more or less desirable. It would be completely determined or necessitated in its choice only if the intellect were in a position to present the object as the Supreme Good. In fact, the immutability of beatific contemplation in eternal life is guaranteed because souls there are confronted with a completely good object of knowledge they cannot fail to desire.

Furthermore, the immortality of the individual soul, with the resultant possibility of individual requital for the good or evil deeds done during earthly life, can be argued from the ability of the intellective form to know abstract forms independently of the corporeal representations that give rise to them during earthly life. To wit, when the soul separates from the body it continues to know by taking the needed "species" directly from the intelligible world, something it was previously kept from doing by its link with the body. Not only, then, does the incorruptible soul not lose its own individuality through bodily death; it also retains its nature as a form, that is, its ability to give life, movement, and knowledge to the body even when it is separated from the body by a purely accidental state of affairs that is a consequence of original sin, namely, the cessation of earthly life. This means that since all of creation is ordered to the achievement of the conditions for perfection that God wills for creatures, and since the perfection of the soul includes the ability to form the body, the state of separation of soul from body is unnatural and cannot be permanent.

With this insight Thomistic anthropology reaches one of the highest evidences of the compatibility of faith and reason inasmuch as the resurrection of the body, a dogma presented by revelation purely as credible and seemingly irreconcilable with natural philosophy, becomes instead a corollary perfectly deducible from the Aristotelean conception of the soul.

6. *The* Summa of Theology *and the "Theology of the Exodus"*

The fact that philosophical analysis has shown the reasonableness of some dogmas such as the resurrection of the body strengthens the certainty of Thomas' view that there is a univocal and complete convergence of rational truth and theological truth. It is evident, nonetheless, that even when the narrowing of the gap between understanding and faith is taken as far as possible, as seems to be the case in the *Summa of Theology*, there are limitations, thereby proving how indispensable is the completion of natural knowledge by revelation. Take the clear borderline case of creation: however possible it is to demonstrate (as Thomas does in the First Part of the *Summa*) that every being other than God is created by God, reason does not make it evident that the world had a beginning, as the Bible says it does. On this point the arguments of the adversaries are irrefutable: if creaturely movement had a beginning, this would mean a beginning in the mover as well and therefore a change in his complete immutability.

Thomas contributes to the discussion of this problem (on which Averroism based its claim of the autonomy of reason over against faith) in a short work, *The Eternity of the World*, published around 1271. Here he adopts a neutral position, accepting the impossibility of working up definitive philosophical arguments either in favor of or against the eternity of the world, even while he argues the possibility of solving the disagreement theologically on the basis of God's absolute freedom and omnipotence. This amounts to saying that philosophical reason can claim the right to assert its own truths in the field of research proper to it, without presuming, however, to veto contrary positions based on faith.

The impact of this borderline case strengthens rather than weakens the synthesis of reason and faith because it ensures that each remains distinct and autonomous even at the moment when the possibility of recognizing their convergence is given its extreme test. Even more meaningful, therefore, will be the ascertainment of the concurrence of philosophy and theology in defining the most fundamental of the preambles to the faith: namely, the rational affirmations and demonstrations of the truth about the nature of God. The opening questions of the *Summa* are expressly aimed at bringing out this fact.

As I said earlier, the composition of the *Summa of Theology* began during the academic year 1265–66. Without hindering further additions to his seemingly relentless production of questions, commentaries, and short works on individual subjects, Thomas continued work on the *Summa* throughout the last seven years of his life. During the Roman period he composed Part I, which deals with God, his nature, the Trinity, creation, and then the nature of creatures (with an extensive section on anthropology). During the second stay in Paris he wrote Part II, which in turn is divided into two parts (*Prima secundae* and *Secunda secundae*) in which he studies the relationship of rational creatures to God, and therefore beatitude and the means of attaining it (with a lengthy treatise on the passions, the sins, and the virtues). Part III, in which he speaks of redemption and grace, was begun in Paris around the beginning of 1272 and continued in Naples.

In the spring of that same year and during the following year Thomas was in the capital of southern Italy, where he was assigned to organize a general house of studies for the Order and where he did his final teaching. In the fall of 1273 he interrupted his teaching for reasons of health and did no more writing. He died a few months later, on March 7, 1274, at the abbey of Fossanova, where he was given shelter because his condition was deteriorating; at the time he was on his way to the Council of Lyons. The *Summa* remained incomplete at the ninetieth question of Part III, on the sacrament of penance. His disciples and friends, working as a team, completed the text according to his original plan by composing a Supplement (based essentially on his commentary on the *Sentences*) that finished the questions on sacramental theology and ended the entire plan with questions on eschatology and the final resurrection.

The work is a perfect example of the program designated by the word *Summa* in the Latin world of the twelfth and thirteenth centuries: namely, a complete, detailed, yet synthetic exposition of the field of study and research in question—in this case, of theology. In a very careful and unembellished style Thomas works through the entire discipline, following a methodology based on the procedure known as the "disputation": posing of the question, listing of objections (*videtur*—"it seems") to the anticipated answer of the author, a response that justifies the answer, and a reply to each objection. The systematic approach on an encyclopedic scale explains the fact that all of Thomas' more important doctrinal ideas find here their most accurate and complete explanation, serving as stones that form the entire new structure of theological knowledge.

The harmonization of philosophical clarity and the truth of the faith is especially effective in the first questions of the first part, which deal with problems concerning the nature of God "as he is in himself" and in which the philosophical preambles of the faith are explained with such rational completeness that they can be accepted as part of theological learning. Philosophy is able, above all, to demonstrate the existence of God with such a logical consistency that it supports, points up, and clarifies the very source of the faith as proclaimed beginning with the opening words of Scripture.

It is here, in the second question of the first part, that Thomas explains rapidly and clearly the five "ways" of impressing on the mind the unquestionableness of an assertion that is indeed not intrinsically evident but does flow necessarily from the knowledge of, and necessity of justifying what is known to us: that is, creatures, which are always and only knowable as being the result of something else. Because what appears to the mind as an effect cannot be thought of as absolute, the principle of causality demands that we acknowledge the existence of a "first," which if it is to be such must be transcendent. For it is impossible to accept an infinite regress in the transmission of any kind of efficacy, since an infinite series of actual causal links could never reach its end (being infinite) and therefore would never lead to a particular ultimate effect. In the response of the third article of the question "Does God Exist?" Thomas lists the five ways, which, since they take as their starting points data that are different and seen in different perspectives, are distinct and not reducible to one another.

The first way, which is presented as the clearest (and had already been emphasized in the *Summa Against Unbelievers*), is the way that begins with movement: everything that moves (or, more generally, that becomes) passes from potency to act and therefore cannot be moved by itself but, in all cases, only by something in act (as fire, which is actually hot, heats the wood that is only potentially hot). Consequently, in one and the same process of becoming, nothing can be simultaneously mover and moved, but, further, one cannot regress endlessly from mover to mover, because unless there is a first mover there would not be a second mover and so on. Therefore one must halt at a first mover, which is not moved by another but is purely a mover in act and not in potency; this mover is God.

The second way is that of efficient causality. All things depend on the effective action of some efficient cause of their being; nothing, however, can be the efficient cause of its own being, for otherwise it would precede itself, which is impossible. Here again an infinite regress is excluded because if there were not a first efficient cause there would also be no intermediate cause or a last cause directly linked to the effect. It is therefore necessary to suppose a first efficient cause, which everyone calls "God."

The third way proceeds from the possible to the necessary. Some things are possible: that is, they can be or not be. But if all things were possible, then, since what is possible can at some time not exist, we would have to admit the possibility of a moment in which nothing was. Being, however, springs only from something; therefore there is something that exists necessarily. Necessary things can derive their necessity from something other or from themselves. If only those necessary things existed that as such depend on something else we would once again be caught up in an infinite regression. We must therefore admit that something exists that derives its necessity from itself and is the cause of the possibility and necessity of everything else. Everyone names this cause "God."

The fourth way proceeds from the degrees found in things. Things are more or less good, true, noble, and so on; but "more or less" always supposes a greater closeness to or distance from something that exists in the greatest possible degree. Therefore there exists something that is supremely true, good, and noble, and therefore is being in the supreme degree. Moreover, since that which is the greatest in each genus is the cause of the membership of those things that belong to that genus (as that which is good in itself is the cause of the goodness in good things), the supreme being is therefore the cause of the being, the goodness, and the other perfections in things. This supreme being is God.

The fifth way proceeds from the governance of the world. All created things, and not only those endowed with the ability to know, always act to attain an end defined by their nature (for example, the solidity of a stone or the heat of a fire). In the universe, therefore, there is nothing that occurs by chance, but everything is ordered to an end. But things lacking knowledge never move toward an end unless someone endowed with knowledge and intelligence directs them to it, as is clear from the example of an arrow that does not reach the target unless someone shoots it. Therefore, given the constancy of finalized behavior throughout the universe, there is something intelligent that orders all natural things to their ends (and therefore makes stone solid, fire hot, human beings intelligent, and so on). This "something" we call "God."

This God, the "First" to which all causality in the universe leads back, is therefore an infinite power that moves, orders, and governs the whole of reality.

He is the maximum reached by unaided philosophical reason, but such knowledge is not yet a knowledge of the "what" of God, of what God is. By means of the interaction of the way of elimination and analogy that has already been pointed out in the *Summa Against Unbelievers* this maximum theological idea can now be completed by adding the characteristics that belong to it and bring it ever closer to the foundation of scriptural truth. Namely: this First lacks any kind of composition, such as cause and effect, matter and form, potency and act, essence and existence, and is therefore supremely simple. As such it is supremely good and infinite and therefore exists in all things, not indeed as part of their essences (as the Amalricians and David of Dinant would have it), but in the same way as a cause is in its effects: that is, it is the cause of the being of everything else that is. As such it is everywhere and always and therefore immutable and eternal; it is also one, indeed one in the highest possible degree, not because it lacks anything else but because its complete and most perfect nature is fully in act.

Therefore as reason endeavors to take these fundamental and necessary steps in order to reach the knowledge of how God exists, it is at the same time enlightened by faith in its inspection of these data and is therefore obliged to refer their entire semantic validity to an active power superior to any influence found in nature. That is, it makes all theological knowledge dependent on analogical discourse and so, at the very moment in which it grasps the divine perfections, it grasps them as "things invisible," as St. Paul teaches (Rom 1:20). Even if some terms are more effective and meaningful, such as intelligence, will, life, or efficient and creative cause, no concept formed on the basis of what is visible can claim to exhaust the meaning of what is invisible.

At this point we have reached the threshold of what has been described as Thomas' "Exodus theology," the reference being to the sole name God gave for himself when replying to the question of who he was: "I am who I am" (Exod 3:14). It is a name that hides rather than reveals; it exhausts our capacity for forming true propositions about the subject in question because it does not allow us formally to grasp and define its content but allows us only to turn toward it. The formula in Exodus asserts at one and the same time both the existence of God and his absolute simplicity: a being lacking in limitations or qualifications because it exists absolutely and is therefore absolutely prior to all the orders of specification or qualification of existence.

A being that is pure act is not one that actualizes an essence distinct from its existence, a divinity distinct from the divine existence; instead, such a being necessarily exists because it is unqualified existence. This is the only name that can be given to God as signifying what God is. The name is universal (because everything in God is contained in this name) and common (because there is no difference between this name and God). Everything true that is said in theology, in the analysis both of God's internal relationships with his essence and of his external relationships with his creatures, is always and solely the complex and varied but organic and substantially unified actualization of this one foundational principle. Here is what Thomas says in the eleventh and twelfth articles of the thirteenth question of the First Part:

> This name, *HE WHO IS*, is most properly applied to God, for three reasons:—
>
> First because of its signification, for it does not signify form, but simply existence itself. Hence, since the existence of God is His essence itself, which can be said of no other (Q. 3, A. 4), it is clear that among other names this one specially denominates God, for everything is denominated by its form.
>
> Second, on account of its universality. For all other names are either less universal or, if convertible with it, add something above it at least in idea; hence in a certain way they inform and determine it. Now our intellect cannot know the essence of God itself in this life, as it is in itself, but whatever mode it applies in determining what it understands about God, it falls short of the mode of what God is in Himself. . . . By any other name some mode of substance is determined, whereas this name *HE WHO IS* determines no mode of being, but is indeterminate in all. . . .
>
> Third, from its consignification, for it signifies present existence; and this above all applies properly to God, whose existence knows not past or future, as Augustine says (*De Trin.* V). . . .
>
> God, as considered in Himself, is altogether one and simple, yet our intellect knows Him by different conceptions because it cannot see Him as He is in Himself. Nevertheless, although it understands Him under different conceptions, it knows that one and the same simple object corresponds to its conceptions.[4]

7. Theology as a Science

As a true knowledge of reality—of the supreme, unique reality that is always identical with itself, and of secondary realities insofar as they are related to the supreme reality—theology is a science.

There is an ultimate and fundamental speculative question that Thomas' theological thinking must answer and that, insofar as it contains within itself all other questions, puts an end to the debates and arguments arising out of meditation on the realities of faith set before us as credible. That question is undoubtedly the one that he, like so many contemporary masters, places first: the question of the *what?* of theology, its *why?*, its nature as a science, its possible existence as a science. This is the question with which the Prologue of the commentary on the *Sentences* began and that was then raised again in the commentary on Boethius' *Trinity* and subsequently placed at the beginning of the *Summa of Theology* with the title: "The nature and extent of sacred doctrine." Can there be a science of the credible? To what extent is it really possible to speak of sacred doctrine as a science?

Posed in this way, the question is equivalent to asking whether it is possible to locate theology within the Aristotelian conception of science and, if so, definitively to include in the realm of demonstrative reason the patrimony and management of the religious knowledge that presupposes faith. Thomas also deals with the epistemological foundations of such an operation in a commentary on the *Posterior Analytics*. This was composed around 1272 and is marked by great expository clarity; here Thomas made use of the extensive interpretive writings on this text that were available in the second half of the century: the paraphrase by Themistius, the fragments of a commentary attributed to Alexander of Aphrodisias but coming in fact from John Philoponus, Grosseteste's commentary, and other recently translated Arabic texts, among them a commentary by Alfarabi.

Given this background, Thomas knows several things: First, that scientific knowledge has to do solely with the understanding of universal truths; then, that such truths are always expressed in demonstrated propositions, that is, propositions obtained as conclusions of apodictic syllogisms, the validity of which depends on the validity of the premises and the logic of the deduction; third, that the premises in turn must be demonstrated propositions, that is, derived from other syllogisms; further, that, in order here again to avoid an infinite regress that would render meaningless the entire chain of inferences, it is always necessary to admit, as the starting point of the demonstrations, some basic truths that are evident and therefore universally known, but undemonstrable. These are the first principles that preside over the scientific field within which the demonstration is valid and that are expressed in intrinsically evident propositions.

Finally, he knows that the truth of such propositions is ensured by the fact that in them the predicate is contained in the definition of the subject and therefore expresses either the subject's genus or its differentiating note (for example: "all human beings are animals" or "all human beings are rational"). These are therefore absolutely necessary propositions that convey with certainty the structure of reality, on the basis of the principle of conformity between the knowing intellect and the reality that is the object of scientific knowledge.

This ideal of Aristotelean science is, however, not perfectly attained in all the disciplines. In fact, apart from pure mathematics and logic the sciences depend on the introduction of data provided by experience. Insofar as such data are linked to particulars they do not always ensure an absolute correspondence between intellect and reality, but supply rather a factual knowledge that may be more concrete (giving some information about the cause) but in which the causal nexuses between the objects known are less directly evident.

This situation entails a lessening of the strictness of the basic epistemological criteria but is inevitable in all the forms of knowledge that have to do with the world of contingency, such as the natural sciences and even metaphysics. In each of these it is necessary to conjecture the impact of particular conditions that bring out the limits of human intellectual knowledge and compel the mind to alter and in a reasonable way adapt the model of a perfect science. According to Thomas, the observation of this alteration in the basic epistemological framework helps in defining theology as a science.

As a result, the question about sacred doctrine takes on the features of a real and proper "discourse on theological method." It is a method that helps render an account of the entire exercise of the theologian's art, whether in explaining and commenting on the words of the scriptural text or offering hypothetical solutions of speculative problems raised in preaching and meditating on the Bible. It is essential, first of all, to define the concept, content, and extension of this art or science, which Thomas calls not only "sacred doctrine" but even simply "Sacred Scripture," thereby intending something beyond what his contemporaries, Albert the Great in particular, describe as "theology." In his view this field of knowledge includes all the possible forms of Christian teaching that are strictly dependent on revelation: from interpretation of the Bible to solutions by masters that then, but only to a limited extent, are concretized in an organized and communicable body of teachings (such as the body that is the *Summa of Theology*). As a result, the question of whether theology is a science is rephrased in a more precise way: Does sacred doctrine, the knowledge indispensable for salvation, possess in one of its forms (specifically in what Thomas calls "theology that has to do with sacred doctrine" as distinct from the "theology that is part of philosophy") the qualities characteristic of scientific knowledge?

The first condition for an affirmative reply is that sacred doctrine be derived from self-evident principles. The problem resides not so much in admitting that theology has the articles of faith as its first principles (an idea shared by almost all the theologians of the time). It is rather in the appropriateness of allowing that these certainties, the starting points of theological knowledge, are principles of a knowledge flowing from them as from something intrinsically evident. But reflection on the already mentioned conditioning factors Aristotelean epistemology encounters in the various scientific fields aids Thomas in explaining that from the viewpoint of theological science the articles of faith do effectively function as first principles. In this field of knowledge, faith plays exactly the same role as the insight into principles does in the other sciences: that is, it produces inherently evident propositions, although in this case they are rendered such not by an intrinsic evidence provided by the agent intellect but by an extrinsic evidence provided by a divine light infused into the mind through the action of grace.

At this point we are introduced to the theory of subalternation. Some sciences, such as arithmetic and geometry, start from principles made known by the light of the natural intellect; others, however, begin from principles made known by light coming from a higher science: optics, for example, derives from principles supplied by geometry, and music from principles supplied by mathematics. Sacred doctrine is a science of this second kind because it starts from principles made known by light coming from a higher science to which it is "subalternated." This higher science, however, is not a human science superior to theology, but is the very knowledge possessed by God and the blessed and communicated to humanity through revelation. And just as a musician "believes" in the principles transmitted by arithmetic, so the theologian "believes" in the principles revealed to him by God.

The fact, therefore, that theology is based on a knowledge coming from an external source does not lessen its scientific character any more than the fact that a traveler is accompanied by a guide who has a better knowledge of the way lessens his vision of the goal when he has reached it. Furthermore, non-believers, who lack the habitual knowledge of faith's principles, are in the same position with regard to theological knowledge as uneducated people are with regard to other forms of knowledge.

All this confirms the fact that the method of theology is "kind-specific," that is, adapted solely to the matter with which it deals, and yet essential to it. It is therefore permissible to accept into sacred doctrine a series of procedures peculiar to it, such as metaphor, symbol, narrative, precept, promise, and so on, as well as the numerous levels of scriptural meaning. All this, however, does not negate but rather confirms the legitimacy of the argumentative method proper to theology in the strict sense.

Another peculiarity of theological knowledge is that sacred doctrine seems to deal with particular truths, such as the events of sacred history, thereby negating the universal nature of scientific knowledge. Here again, however, the unique status of theological knowledge, in that it is subordinated to God's knowledge, explains that particular data are not accepted as such into theology, that is, as happenings determined by physical accident, but for their exemplary nature (examples always have a universal value, as in the moral disciplines).

In the same perspective, finally, Thomas explains that sacred doctrine is undoubtedly a practical science inasmuch as it influences the ethical behavior of human beings in order to enable them to share in the fruits of redemption. But before being practical, theology is also a speculative science, concerned as it is with eternal realities insofar as these are made knowable by a divine illumination. This duality does not, however, detract from the unity of theology, because it is unique among the human disciplines in that it can serve as both a theoretical and a practical discipline. It does so inasmuch as it makes God known and his laws respected on the basis of that higher knowledge with which God knows himself and his works.

In any case, the unity of theological science is ensured, first of all, by the fact that it alone is based on revelation and has for its object everything based on revelation, to the extent that all this falls within the scope of its investigation and judgment. Also clear at this point is the distinction between sacred theology and philosophical theology: both have God as their subject but not according to the same formal viewpoint, since philosophical theology does not take the presuppositions of faith as its starting point. Here we must distinguish between the subject and the object of theology. As we know, every science is always a science "of something," and this something is called its subject. To grasp this subject means to carry out the investigation of it in a complete and exhaustive way. In contrast, the object is whatever is attainable and actually attained as the result of studies by the knower during the course of this earthly life. We see, then, that sacred theology and philosophical theology have, in practice, the same subject but differ by reason of the formal viewpoint under which they approach their respective objects inasmuch as the results obtained by each discipline in dealing with this subject vary due to the radically different methodologies of each, since the one is based on revelation while the other is not.

Thomas can say, therefore, that the subject of sacred doctrine is everywhere and always God. Just as color is a subject of sight and all colored objects are, as such, connected with sight, so too sacred doctrine pursues the knowledge of all objects knowable in relation to God, either because they are God or because they are ordered to God as their source and their end. Thus the entire study of theology and the entire body of doctrines developed by Christian theologians throughout history take concrete form in the series of cognitive acquisitions that are the object of theology and that are always in the service of the truth about the subject, a truth they will never totally grasp. Thus, even while valuing the attainment of their goals, theologians also and at the same time acknowledge their limits, and while perceiving the infinite nature of their task they also admit that it is inexhaustible.

When theologians claim the right to use the philosophical disciplines in achieving their purposes they must never lose sight of the humility urged upon them by the awareness of their limitations. They ought to be ready to accept the changes in the laws of nature that the rational sciences describe, so as to admit, when the faith requires it, a new or different application of these laws that will make it possible to explain, not indeed how the revealed datum can be true, but rather what is true in it, and similarly, in the presence of an event that is miraculous or contrary to the laws of logic, to explain not how such an event can happen but rather what has in fact happened.

For example, in one instance Thomas adopts a position symmetrically opposite to that which he took in the problem of creation. This is his theological explanation of the eucharistic mystery, that is, the doctrine of "transubstantiation" which (as we saw earlier in connection with Lanfranc of Pavia) would later be accepted and approved by the Council of Trent. According to this doctrine, whereas in every kind of natural mutation the substance remains the same while the accidents change, in the eucharistic sacrament there is change (or "conversion") of the substances of the bread and wine into those of the body and blood of Christ while the visible accidents of the transformed substances remain the same (a situation that is unintelligible because contrary to nature, but in this form nonetheless accessible to the human mind).

The advantages accruing from this strict definition of the relations between philosophical knowledge and theological knowledge are evident on both sides. In the readiness of the human sciences to offer their collaboration, theology finds new tools and the actuation of the epistemological criteria that ratify its aspiration to be recognized as a science. On the other hand, when philosophy sees its limits and aspirations, but also its own rights, thus defined in relation to the supreme truthfulness of the faith, it gains a superior recognition of its autonomy and its right to its own judgments. At the same time, however, although fully conscious of the service it shows it can render to theology, and while being able to make very profitable use for itself of the truth-revealing light granted to human beings by the grace of God, philosophy must recognize the impossibility of grasping in a definitory and definitive way the higher reality that, even in revealing itself, has made itself knowable and searchable only in the necessarily limited measure possible to the human intellect.

Endnotes

1. *The Summa of St. Thomas Aquinas, Literally Translated by Fathers of the English Dominican Province* (New York: Benziger, 1947) I, 12.

2. St. Thomas Aquinas, *On the Truth of the Catholic Faith (Summa contra Gentiles)* I, trans. Anton C. Pegis (Garden City, NY: Doubleday Image Books, 1955) 62.

3. Ibid., 78.

4. *The Summa of St. Thomas Aquinas* (see n. 1 above) I, 70–71.

Chapter 6

The Theological Workshop of the Late Middle Ages

I. Multiple Truths: Debates and Currents of Thought Bridging Two Centuries

On May 7, 1274, Gregory X inaugurated the labors of the fourteenth ecumenical council, which had been convoked in Lyons at the suggestion of that city's archbishop, Peter of Tarentaise (formerly a Dominican master of theology in Paris). Thomas Aquinas had died two months earlier. Bonaventure of Bagnoreggio, who had shared in the preparation for the council, died on July 15, two days before the council ended. The main purpose of the council, as requested by the patriarch of Constantinople, was a rapprochement with the Eastern church. This was in fact achieved, though without any concrete results at the ecclesiological level, by the approval of a compromise trinitarian formula according to which the Spirit proceeds from the Father and from the Son, not as from two sources but from one and through a single "spiration." This solution echoed a proposal put forth by Thomas in his treatise, *Answer to the Error of the Greeks*.

Almost forty years later, in October of 1311, Clement V, the first Avignon pope, convoked the fifteenth ecumenical council to meet in Vienne, a short distance from Lyons. This council was devoted to the moral and financial reform of the church. Among other documents the council issued the dogmatic decree *The Foundation of the Catholic Faith*, which condemned as a heretic anyone asserting that "the substance of the rational or intellectual soul is not of itself and essentially the form of the human body." Like the statement of Lyons on the dogma of the Trinity, this clarification of an anthropological doctrine in language obviously borrowed from Aristotelean speculation shows us the degree to which university theology exerted a cultural and religious influence during these years. The schools were henceforth the smithy in which were forged the forms for the doctrinal clarifications that supported the dogmatic magisterium of the Christian church.

And yet, during the almost forty years separating the two councils the Latin intellectual world experienced the increasing rise of conflicts between currents, parties, and representatives of differing conceptual systems, a phenomenon marked by strident voices and very radical ideological contrasts. Profound differences in tendencies and approaches had for some time separated the various paths followed since the beginning of the century in the effort to moderate or overcome the lack of harmony between secular knowledge and the theological tradition; this discord had been intensified by the introduction of Greco-Arabic thought into the West. These differences seemed to be increasingly transformed into boundaries and even insuperable theoretical barriers. A variety of dissonant voices echoed in the lecture rooms of the universities; there was not only the opposition of well-defined parties but also the movement of ideas and doctrines from one group to another, resulting in an increasingly complicated interplay of adulterations and fusions among the initial different approaches. Thus there began a slow but seemingly incurable breakdown of the unanimity on which the truth and communicability of Christian wisdom had for centuries been based.

The tenth to the fourteenth cantos of Dante Alighieri's *Paradise* tell of the fourth heaven, that of the Sun. Here are to be found the choruses comprising the souls of those wise Christians who have become capable, in the state of blessedness, of feeding with one mind on the truth of the trinitarian mystery ("The fourth family/of the supreme Father who always satisfies it/by showing it how He spirates and generates"). The poet, moved by the disappointed bitterness of the external observer, evidently means to contrast the harmonious unity of the blessed theologians and the disintegration of the earthly house of Wisdom, which is being torn apart by increasingly incurable oppositions and disagreements.

Dante's vision is authenticated by the harmony of the song in which the saints, arranged in two rings, one within the other, join their voices "in a timbre and sweetness" that can be heard only in heaven. The poet reflects on the contrast between, on the one hand, the orderly dance of the two garlands of saints, which become one through the union of their varying lights, and, on the other, the accentuated contrast on earth among the peculiarities and cultivated idiosyncracies of the several schools. As he does, he can only deplore "the senseless concern of mortals" who through their formulation of "defective syllogisms" lose sight of the higher unity of truth and thus undermine, instead of exalting, the cognitive longings of human beings.

As a century of social, political, and ecclesiastical upheavals was beginning, the leading representatives of theological thought certainly did not turn away from the desire to formulate, each in his own way, answers that were as far as possible objective and universally valid to human questions about the nature of God and his presence in the created universe and in human life. But the very increase in their scientific skills and speculative abilities, as well as the resultant complex vitality of the intellectual world, instead of promoting the resolution of conflicts only increased the emphasis on the differences and incompatibilities of the different theological "ways."

As a result, these ways appeared to contemporary witnesses as ongoing research projects rather than as permanent solutions that could overcome the doubts and insecurities of the people of that time. During these decades, then, more than ever before, the world of theological study with its controversies and conflicts took on the look of a "workshop of wisdom." That world seemed to be a research laboratory in which every idea and every theoretical proposal served primarily as a basis for experiments and as an occasion for further thought and in which, with increasingly diversified outcomes, tools old and new were improved and further directions for thought were prepared, entered on, and tested.

1. Henry of Ghent and the Secular Masters

The nostalgic longing for theological harmony that Dante celebrated in poetic form was also echoed by other witnesses whose lives bridged the two centuries. For example, many authors of university sermons lamented the paralysis of university activity that was caused by the prominence of ideological and doctrinal disagreements. In an anonymous sermon for Epiphany (preserved in a Paris manuscript, lat. 15952) the university masters are compared to the stars, which must follow their ordained courses and not break out of their proper trajectories: "Nowhere have we ever read that star battles star; in like manner, a religious ought not do battle against a good secular nor a secular against a religious." In this instance the writer points his finger at the opposition between seculars and the Mendicant Orders. As we saw, around the middle of the thirteenth century this opposition changed from a matter of institutional rivalry into a fierce controversy over the ideals of evangelical life and poverty-centered spirituality that had from the beginning nourished the thinking and action of the Preachers and the Franciscans.

After the first phase of this conflict, which was fed by the positions of William of Saint-Amour and Gerard of Abbeville, new controversies broke out in Paris after Martin IV (1281–84) granted new privileges to the Mendicants in the areas of preaching and confession. (Around 1258, Robert de la Sorbonne founded the university college named after him, for the service of students and secular masters.) Amid the flood of debates a commission of theologians was charged with analyzing and challenging the privileges; one of the commissioners was the best-known secular master of those years, Henry of Ghent, a Belgian, who was supported by a fellow countryman, Geoffrey of Fontaines. The conflict inevitably extended to more strictly doctrinal and speculative subjects; it was above all the most Aristoteleanizing theses of the Dominicans that were the first object of criticism. In particular, Thomas' distinction between essence and existence was attacked as coming too close to the metaphysical necessitarianism of the Arabs, while his psychology was accused of straying into Averroist gnoseology.

A, THEOLOGICAL FOUNDATIONS OF THE THOUGHT OF HENRY OF GHENT

The theological production of Henry of Ghent (d. 1293), whom his followers would call the "Awe-inspiring Doctor" (*Doctor Sollemnis*), clearly reflects the direction just described, beginning with his energizing principles. Henry was the master in charge of the theological school of Paris from 1277 on; he composed various *Quodlibetal Questions*, some commentaries (on Genesis and on the *Physics* of Aristotle), and later a *Summa of Everyday Questions*.

This last-named work implements the plan of basing the scientific character of theological knowledge on an epistemological method entirely different from the Aristotelean, which the masters of arts had imposed on the philosophical sciences. The explicit goal of this establishment of an authentic Christian epistemology was to make intelligible the contents of the *credibilia* accepted by faith. It was thus openly opposed to Thomas' theory of theology as a subalternate science located within a graduated order of knowledge including everything that fits the Aristotelean definition of scientific knowledge. But Henry's epistemology was also opposed to the Franciscan conception of theology as a wisdom that transcended the realm of the natural sciences and represented an epistemology too vague for it to be considered a science.

In Henry's view, Thomas' position meant that the cognitive possibilities ensured by revelation are unjustifiably limited by mental schemata alien to it. Theological deductions (he thought) certainly did not need to base their certainty on requirements of argumentation. On the other hand, the inclusion of theology in a system valid for the natural sciences imposes an unjustifiable opposition between the data of faith and naturalistic teachings that could give rise to serious doubts and errors in the minds of the faithful when faced with absolutely certain religious truths such as God's freedom in creating, the immersion of individuals in time, the moral responsibility of the will, and everlasting blessedness.

The reliability of these and similar assertions cannot be made to depend on their compatibility with a philosophical system. The reason: their true foundation, evident only to believers, consists in their being part of a system of thought that contains its own justification inasmuch as the thought is that by which God knows himself and that he communicates to human beings in order that they may know him. It is in this sense—and not according to Peripatetic methodology, which distinguishes between acquired and acquirable knowledge—that God is both the subject and the object of theology, for it is God who knows and makes known what ought to be known about him.

Furthermore, the superiority that for these same reasons theological knowledge must be acknowledged as having over the other sciences entails the admission of its ability to direct and delimit the latter, since it provides a higher criterion for determining their truthfulness. But this approach is hardly compatible with the Franciscan ideal according to which the particular sciences are transcended and resolved into theological knowledge; here resolution may prove to be a dissolution. The fundamental problem faced by Henry of Ghent is, therefore, essentially this: to bring theology down successfully to the level of human beings or, in other words, with the aid of revelation to make usable, and actually used, by the human intellect the knowledge God has of himself and of the truth. Given the absolute character of his truth, this also means it is usable as a source of regulation for the lesser sciences.

B. THE "INTENTIONAL" COMPOSITION OF BEING

The problem of reconstructing the entire architecture of theological science and the philosophical sciences that ought to depend on it can be solved only in the light of an accurate definition of the nature of the "things" that are the object of science. Henry is therefore compelled to broaden his discourse to provide a new clarification of what being is and how it is knowable.

The metaphysical distinction between "being in itself" and "being through something else" arose in the thinking of the first secular masters as the result of an erroneous combination of, on the one hand, Boethian-Porretan reflection on the different ways in which being is predicated of God and creatures and, on the other, the dual structure of the descent of the possible from the necessary as found in Avicennean metaphysics. Thomas then believed he could clarify and correct that initial approach by introducing the distinction between essence and being, that is, between essence in itself and essence actually existing through the addition of some formal perfection not given in essence as such.

Henry of Ghent tackled this subject in the ninth question of his first *Quodlibet*, which was debated in the winter of 1276. He feared that Thomas' distinction was overly dependent on Avicenna's metaphysics and could be understood as a juxtaposition of two "things," one necessary in itself (the essence) and the other possible and derived from the essence (the being or existent reality). Accordingly, God, whose essence is the only one existing perfectly, would have to be conceived of as pure necessity while creatures, being possible essences brought into existence by God, would have to be thought of as the result of a necessary emanation that actualizes their imperfect potentiality. Thus Thomas' teaching collapses into a deterministic necessitarianism, which, in Henry's view, is one of the worst errors of philosophy.

The reason for this judgment is that, according to Henry, Thomas' teaching jeopardizes not only God's freedom but the very reality of finite things as such, which in the light of authentic Christian metaphysics should be thought of as realities endowed with a complete ontological dignity and willed by God, one by one, as unrepeatable individual products of his divine omnipotence. The composition of being is therefore not to be understood as a differentiation between something that authentically exists and something that exists in only a derived and secondary way, but rather as the conceptual distinction between two equally authentic ways of being: the being of God, who exists because he is being in himself, and the being of creatures, which is what it is to the extent that God considers right and appropriate.

The human mind comes to know the being of God and therefore his existence from the simplest consideration of the idea of being as such. For in its most immediate conceptual form this idea presents itself to the mind as that which exists by the simple fact of being, and therefore as "something that is being itself." This something is God. From this consideration another flows directly, but in the opposite direction: the idea of everything that exists not by the simple fact of being but because being is in some manner bestowed on it from outside and is adapted to it. These other beings are "something to which being comes, and comes in an appropriate way" (*aliquid cui convenit esse: con-venit*, inasmuch as it "comes" from another, but also because it "suits" its aspiration to be in a certain way).

The "everything" embraces creatures, none of them excluded. Being is thus predicated in a non-univocal way: in God there is something that is simply being and can therefore also be called Good or True because it is Being by the fullest possible right. In creatures, on the other hand, being is the result of a creative process that may be instantaneous but is always temporal, a being that can take many forms and that among its various traits, which correspond to the categorical distinctions, always includes being (though not only that). That which is Being-in-itself is therefore not only the "first thing known" but also the cause of the being of everything that exists through another. This means, essentially, that what makes the created reality exist is simply the fact that the uncreated and necessary reality makes it exist.

Consequently, the distinction between essence and existence in creatures does not mean a distinction between two "things," one of which is added to the other. Every creative act of the divine will produces a single individual thing that exists as autonomous, unrepeatable, and distinct. Its existential unity makes it a subject, a reality capable of differentiating itself as such from everything else through a "twofold negation": the negation of any difference within itself and the negation of any identity with others. But if the distinction between essence and existence is not real, it is simply an operation of the cognitive order or an "intentional distinction." That is: it is the intellect that recognizes, and distinguishes, within the existential unity of the created reality, but only in theory and not concretely, two "intentions" or, in other words, two direct perceptions of the essential content of the thing as its constitutive marks.

Henry's solution has a theological consistency that renders it even more solid, for, in the very act of creating, the essence and existence of each creature are, in the mind of God, two distinct intentions. Such, in fact, is the meaning of the theological exemplarism recommended by the Fathers of the Church, since to accept the ideas as intermediaries of creation in the divine mind is equivalent to saying that the Creator first thinks an essence and then actuates its existence through the exercise of his omnipotent creative will.

C. TEACHING ON KNOWLEDGE AND THE SPECIAL ILLUMINATION

The extent to which these metaphysical premises could have directed Henry's gnoseology is obvious. In addition to being the cause of being, that is, the formal cause in the order of essences and the efficient first cause in the order of existences, the divine source is also the universal cause of understanding or knowing.

In order to "know the truth," that is, of created things, whose being is only "suitable," the human mind must be able to grasp directly the correspondence between their essence, ascertained as existing through sensation, and the divine idea from which the essence is derived. Above and beyond natural knowledge there is a higher order of necessary certainties on which the scientific character of every further field of knowledge depends. The more these certainties correspond to the divine ideas, the truer they are; it is evident that a human being can possess them precisely to the extent that they derive from the divine ideas themselves. Therefore for human beings to know the truth requires an intervention from on high in which God himself shows the human mind the truthfulness of something known by comparing it with a higher truth.

This position calls for a philosophically grounded reconsideration of the doctrine of illumination, which will not be a function regulating human thought, as the majority of Franciscan authors held, but an indispensable formal and constitutive condition for true knowledge. It will also operate in the practical sphere and make the will autonomous over against the intellect due to a transmission of active efficiency that comes directly from God. The illumination amounts to an aprioristic direction given knowledge and action; it is made possible by a mystical connection of the soul with the Word, an unmerited connection God freely grants in accordance with his incomprehensible judgment.

To this *a priori* principle governing knowledge Henry gives the name "special illumination" and makes it the basis of a radical and universal cognitive realism; it ensures the convergence in the mind of the notion of an existing thing, known through the senses, with the idea of its essence, which comes from God. Every science, therefore, is such to the extent that in its particular field of knowledge the special illumination ensures the continuity between the truths that the illumination makes formally known in the intellect and the eternal law represented by the divine universals.

D. THEOLOGICAL SCIENCE AND THE NEW CHRISTIAN EPISTEMOLOGY

The doctrinal positions taken by Henry of Ghent in metaphysics and gnoseology now allowed him to pass a fair judgment on the scientific character and normative superiority he claimed for theology over the other sciences.

The doctrine of illumination explains the insufficiency of Aristotelean epistemological criteria, which are based on the principle of abstraction and are therefore suitable solely for the sciences of the natural world, where they produce results that are only partial and uncertain and only gradually verifiable. In contrast, the science made available by an illumination from on high that can put the mind in contact with supernatural reality is decidedly superior to science attainable only through abstraction and demonstration.

This higher science is theology, the subject of which, namely God, is certainly not knowable or searchable with the tools of natural scientific knowledge. The entire structure of theological knowledge depends on faith in revelation, through which God has communicated to humankind what he himself knows. Thanks to this special character, only in theology is an absolute epistemological perfection guaranteed by the convergence of both the material element of knowledge, namely the data of Scripture, which are acquired experientially (that is, *a posteriori*), and the element of formal verification (*a priori*), that is, the knowledge God has of himself. The epistemological perfection is guaranteed because the continuity between the information gathered by the human mind and the exemplarity of the divine mind is here absolutely certain. Therefore the subject of theology is completely identical with its object.

Because of this unqualified superiority, the science of theology can also function as regulator of all lesser acquisitions of scientific knowledge; this is because the truth of theology is so certain and complete that it can be extended to cover all other knowable objects. Meanwhile, theology is superior to faith itself because it enriches the simple acquisition of information through belief with the addition of an understanding guaranteed by the intervention of the higher illumination that renders the truths of faith intelligible. At the lower levels of natural knowledge, then, natural reason receives from theology a ceaseless contribution of divine illumination, which helps reason in directing itself toward the truth of finite and particular objects.

Henry thus does not differentiate between theology and scientific knowledge as do the traditionalist theologians (including the Franciscans) who distinguish even formally between science and wisdom. Rather, he proposes to regard theology as an absolutely truthful science that enables human beings to participate in the essentially imparticipatible divine truth, which acts here in the way in which the inspiration of the Holy Spirit illumined the prophets in writing the sacred texts. This means that unlike any other form of human knowing, human theology can achieve the gnoseological perfection that makes it speculative in an absolutely perfect way (which according to Aristotle himself only God's knowledge can be).

E. GEOFFREY OF FONTAINES AND PETER OF ALVERNIA

The other secular master from Belgium, Geoffrey of Fontaines (d. 1306 or 1309), was Henry's colleague in charge of the school of theology in Paris. He

380 The Theological Workshop of the Late Middle Ages

worked along the same lines as Henry in dealing with questions arising in the attack on the juridical and scholastic privileges of Mendicants. He did not, however, go along with Henry's effort to depart, in metaphysics and gnoseology, from the strict Aristoteleanism that Thomas applied to Christian philosophy. He considered Henry's attempt to attribute to theology a scientific character superior to that of the natural sciences to be a failure. He challenged as baseless the idea of considering as "scientific" a knowledge springing from a higher illumination, because the incommensurability of divine inspiration, even though the latter does produce knowledge, turns upside down all the measures, proportions, and limitations that support human reasoning.

The thinking of Geoffrey, the "Venerable Doctor" (*Doctor Venerabilis* or *Venerandus*), is set down not only in some "ordinary" questions and some sermons but also, and especially, in fifteen *Quodlibeta*. These show his desire to establish theology as a profession while at the same time not detracting from the intellectual respect due to Aristoteleanism in the realm of nature. In open disagreement with Henry of Ghent, Geoffrey finds fault especially with the latter's depreciation of Aristotelean epistemology, which, to Geoffrey's mind, not only describes but establishes the very conditions of scientific work. Without respect for the normative criteria set down by Aristotle—the abstraction of concepts, the role of first principles specific to each field, the deductive and syllogistic nature of argumentation—there is no demonstrative science, although there may be other kinds of true but not scientific knowledge.

Theology, for its part, does not support its claims with any stipulations based on rational evidence; it is based on principles that are no more than credible, precisely because they are in no way evident; it cannot ensure that even its conclusions have any scientific certainty. Theology is therefore not a demonstrative science and is not to be placed either within or at the summit of the hierarchy of human sciences.

Yet theology need not, for that reason, give up completely on regarding itself as a discipline of a speculative kind. It need only recognize that the specific nature of its field of study, which is based on faith, makes it a kind of knowledge that is utterly distinct and autonomous and certainly not parallel to the knowledge gained by the philosophical sciences. Philosophical demonstration, being necessarily imperfect due to the limitations of human reason, leads the knowing subject to receive some (always incomplete) truths. Knowledge gained through faith, deepened by faith, and aimed at an intellectual appropriation of the content of the *credibilia* brings the knowing subject other truths that are different and have no formal analogy with philosophical truths. For this reason they do not necessarily contradict the latter; they are simply different. And in many cases, given the natural incompleteness of the philosophical truths that complement those of theology, Geoffrey is able to make his own the conception of theology as wisdom, that is, a knowledge both speculative and practical that represents the vertical completion of faith, science, and the increased understanding bestowed by grace.

The only philosophical matter on which Geoffrey seems on the whole to go along with Henry in a joint attack on the thought of Thomas is a rejection of the composition of being. In fact, his acceptance of Aristotelean gnoseology does not allow him to admit that existence (*esse*) can be conceived as a real object without immediately taking the form of a concrete existent reality. In order, then, to avoid making existence and essence two different "things," Geoffrey, too, excludes any real distinction between essence and existence; these are simply conceptual tools belonging to the order of abstract meaning proper to the intellect.

The same line of thought is followed by Peter of Alvernia (d. 1304), likewise a secular. He had been a student under Henry and Geoffrey, then a master, and finally, in 1275, was chosen, because of his moderation, to be rector of the Faculty of Arts in Paris in order that he might heal a schism caused by controversies over Averroism. He takes over, with subtle variations, doctrines of each of his two teachers, but in tendency he seems to favor mainly an ordered acceptance of many of Thomas' speculative positions. And yet in his *Quodlibeta*, where he is certainly influenced by the gnoseology of Geoffrey of Fontaines, he takes a position of radical opposition to the real distinction between essence and existence, to the point of rejecting the intentional distinction made by Henry of Ghent. His reason: that position is overly essentialist. For his part he accepts only a rational distinction between essence and existence as two terms that signify one and the same reality according to different ways of signifying.

2. Giles of Rome, Augustinian Master

The emphasis these three secular masters at the end of the thirteenth century placed on the question of the distinction between essence and existence seems to have been dictated not so much by the intention of distancing themselves from Thomas and his followers as by the need to reply to the thesis of another writer. Beginning in the first years of his activity as a Bachelor in Paris this other writer had, with genuine speculative originality, made the distinction a key element in his own philosophical and theological thought. The writer was Giles of Rome (d. 1316), who in 1297, while he was still alive, was proclaimed the official teacher of a new Mendicant Order, the Hermits of St. Augustine (or, more simply, the Augustinians).

Giles was born into the Colonna family, probably in Rome, between 1243 and 1247. He entered the new Order in 1258, two years after its foundation, and was sent to study in Paris, where he followed Thomas' lectures on theology. While still a Bachelor he wrote commentaries on Aristotle and the *On Causes* and began to publish his own theses in the form of commentary on the *Sentences*. He took part in the struggles against Averroism by composing a treatise on *The Plurification of the Possible Intellect* and a list of *The Errors of the Philosophers*. Then, in controversy with the adversaries of theological Aristoteleanism, he explained his own positions in the work *Rejection of the Degrees and Plurality of Forms*. In 1285, with his *Quodlibeta* debates, he became the Order's first master of theology. He was elected General of the Order in 1292 and archbishop of Bourges in 1295; he died at Avignon in 1316.

Contrary interpretations have been given of his speculative contribution: in some respects his thought seems to have developed in an emphatic dependence on the teaching of Aquinas; in others he seems to be a determined opponent of Thomism. In fact, however, neither interpretation takes account of the real originality of his thought. This emerges only when that thought is placed in a perspective that Giles himself says shows its sole purpose: namely, to establish a body of knowledge that is authentically Augustinian but is made speculatively solid by the contribution of philosophical reason. For showing the compatibility of faith and philosophical reason, Thomas' contribution was essential.

This revival and restoration of Augustinianism therefore had to be accomplished not only on the level of theology but also on that of philosophy. This is because if Augustinian theology, which is based on a synthesis of believing and understanding, is to be new and complete it must be rethought in light of the possibilities for the human intellect that have been opened up by pagan philosophy and that Augustine did not have at his disposal. It is therefore essential to reappraise the extreme Aristoteleanism of the Averroists, which has been left to itself and not weighed in the light of a constructive comparison with revelation.

But also to be reappraised is the trite Augustinianism of some secular and Franciscan masters who are unresponsive to philosophical speculation and are content to wander about in a befuddled world of vague illuminist spiritualism. Giles then undertakes to amend the Aristoteleanism in question, correcting its metaphysical imperfections through a constructive comparison with the foundations of Augustine's philosophy, especially its Platonizing exemplarism. One's understanding of the latter could at the present time be improved because it was now possible for Latins to read Proclus' *Rudiments of Theology* as well as the *On Causes*, which, as Thomas realized, is closely connected with the *Rudiments*.

These premises justify the strongly realistic emphasis Giles places on the Thomistic distinction between essence and existence, pushing it in the direction of a radical ontologism. Having traced the distinction back, by way of Avicenna, to its Platonic presuppositions, Giles asserts that the two elements of which every creature is composed are two created realities in the true and proper sense and that their union does not produce a true unity but rather a compound *per accidens* (like the union Augustine thinks exists between soul and body in the human composite). The divine act of creation from nothing is an unmediated, uniform action and is directly identifiable with the linking of existence to essence. This entire conception throws a clear explanatory light on the basic principle of Proclean theological ontology: namely, that the first thing created is existence.

Giles subjected his teaching to successive corrections and clarifications over the years and in connection with the increasingly bitter controversy with the seculars, from the first book of his commentary on the *Sentences* to his *Investi-*

gations into Being and Essence and on to his *Questions* on the same subject. Yet the teaching did not change substantially: while emphasizing Thomas' idea of essence as potentiality and existence as its actuation, he is constant in his insistence on reifying both the *esse* of essence and the *esse* of existence as successive stages in the process whereby created things are derived from the simplicity of the divine being, in which there is no composition.

It would, however, be trivializing and wrong to reduce essences to the eternal exemplars and existences to the effects that participate in them. In fact it is clear, given the foundations of Thomistic metaphysics, that the composition of essence and existence must be predicated of every creaturely reality and that the former may not be regarded as something self-sufficient and therefore necessary and eternal. This position also excludes any danger of a necessitarian emanationism of the Avicennian kind.

It is in gnoseology, above all, that Giles draws the most important conclusions from his own metaphysics since, in his view, true knowledge cannot be anything but the expression of a judgment on the real composition of essence and existence in every created being. But God alone is able to have a complete knowledge of this composition or, in other words, the real existence of an essence. In contrast, for human subjects, whose knowledge always moves from experience of the singular to the abstraction of universals and the formulation of their own judgments on these, the perception of the real existence of an essence is possible only through the mediation of the bodily senses. But the latter are, in themselves, incapable of bringing to light the presence of the idea of essence in the thing known. Therefore human thought is never able to grasp the actual composition of essence and existence in a particular thing, but can only describe various degrees of the manifestation of that composition; these degrees correspond to a structured multiplication of levels in the process of knowing.

Giles is thus clearly inclined to accept the Platonic-Augustinian conception of knowledge and to distance himself from the realism of Aristotelean gnoseology. The soul possesses numerous powers, each of which addresses the object with a different intentional capacity. This doctrine does not contradict, but even reinforces the philosophical conception of the soul as the form of the body, because the soul, with its various degrees of capacity for knowledge, is the principle that (existentially) actuates the many potentialities (of the essence). In his description of the several cognitive faculties Giles comes close to the synthesis of Aristotelean and Augustinian psychology put into circulation by the various treatises on the soul at the beginning of the thirteenth century (vegetative soul, then sensitive soul including common sense, imagination, fancy, evaluation, memory, and motive power, and finally the intellectual soul comprising the active and passive intellects).

Each power or faculty is able to issue its own appropriate judgment on the real composition in beings, but its truthfulness is relative, bound up as it is with the specific area in which it is expressed. These areas comprise the senses, which produce the phantasm; the passive intellect, which introduces the phantasm into the process of intellection; the active intellect, which is fully a part of the soul's nature and is therefore completely individual and that multiplies the acts of intellection by guiding the passive intellect in the formulation of judgments. Each cognitive act is concerned with the same object, but grasps in it the different kinds of presence the essence has in the existing being.

In brief, knowledge takes the form of a continuous acquisition of ideas in the presence of which the soul is completely passive. It does not have as its starting point (as Thomas would have it) the actual truth of the existing thing to which the intellect can achieve a correspondence by reflecting on it. But neither is any innate factor at work in the cognitive act or, as Henry of Ghent claims, any aprioristic presupposition coming from on high. The rejection of illumination as a transcendent cognitive function and the restoration of this function to the active intellect are seen by Giles as a recovery of the true Augustinian gnoseology. The latter is based on the multiplication and distinction of cognitive faculties and the resultant return (against Aristoteleanism) to a reversal of relations between the knowing subject and the known object. In other words, the same object shows itself under varying forms to the several cognitive powers, from bodily sensation to angelic intelligence. Finally, it appears in its complete reality in the pure originating contemplation of the divine intellect.

Giles' theory of theological knowledge clearly depends on the Platonizing approach taken in his gnoseology. His view is that, like every cognitive act, every science has its particular way of representing its object. Metaphysics and theology are both concerned with God, the former, however, only insofar as he is the universal cause of beings, but the latter insofar as he is the cause of the restoration and glorification of the human race. Yet neither metaphysics nor theology can aspire to a perfect grasp of the actuality of God, because every knowledge is always a reduction of the truth of the object to the subject's capacity to receive it. This is true even of beatitude, since none of the blessed will ever be able to grasp the divine perfection in all its aspects, but only in the measure in which the knowableness of that perfection can fill up the natural capacity for assimilation to the object, that is, the capacity to be one of the blessed. This is all the more true of theology in the present life, for it considers God and his infinite attributes in a way always proportionate to the limited capacity of the knower.

Giles thus regards it as essential to distance himself openly from the claim, common to the majority of his contemporaries, that they can make God the subject of theological knowledge as if he were just any knowable reality. This conclusion is already clearly drawn in his commentary on the Prologue of the *Sentences* and is clearly stated again in a *Question* on the theme of the "subject" of theology in which he opposes Henry of Ghent. God is, he says, the unreachable goal of the human soul's continual search for knowledge and its constant desire. Theology, then, which directs, guides, and accompanies this search and desire, has the exclusive peculiarity of being an "affective science." For while all the other sciences are, according to Aristotelean epistemology, either speculative or practical, theology has in fact something in common with both. That is, its goal is a speculation that at the same time produces an "operation," both of these being directed to a higher goal, which is love. Theology is therefore speculative insofar as it is practical, and practical insofar as it is speculative.

Thus theology's very nature as an affective science places it above all the other sciences and causes its results to be seen in an eschatological perspective, since only in the state of beatitude and due to the presence of the beloved can love of God reach a degree of completeness that brings knowledge to its limited fullness. As Giles says in his fifth *Quodlibet*, we may with our understanding be united to God as he is in us and according to our potentialities, but by love alone shall we be united with him as he is in himself and in a divine way.

3. The Aristoteleanism of the Arts Faculty and the Condemnation of 1277

A. THE CONTROVERSY AND THE CONDEMNATIONS

The Plurification of the Possible Intellect and *The Errors of the Philosophers* by Giles of Rome were written in a specific context, namely, the second half of the sixties and the first half of the seventies. This period saw numerous attacks by the teachers in the Faculty of Theology on the intellectual unscrupulousness of their colleagues in the Faculty of Arts (henceforth: the Artists). Bonaventure's *Conferences on the Ten Commandments* (1267), the *Conferences on the Gifts of the Spirit* (1268), especially the eighth on the gift of understanding, and then, in an even harsher tone, the *Conferences on the Hexaemeron* (1273), and Thomas' *The Unity of the Intellect* (1270) and *The Eternity of the World* (probably 1271): all these marked only salient moments in a more varied and lengthier series of adversarial interventions. Here the secular, Franciscan, and Dominican theologians joined forces in a consistent attack on the demonstrations offered by the Parisian Artists that led them, with no sense of shame, to conclusions incompatible with Christian revelation: the eternity of the world, creation through intermediaries, a deterministic fatalism irreconcilable with divine Providence, the oneness of the agent intellect, and the denial of individual immortality and the resurrection of the body.

The formulation and defense of such theses had in fact for some time characterized the Averroist trend among the masters of arts; this was true in Paris at least from the middle of the thirteenth century and later also at Padua and Bologna in Italy. The first worried references to the spread of monopsychism and its connection with the teaching of Averroes came in the lectures of Albert the Great in 1250 and in the second book of Bonaventure's commentary on the *Sentences*, composed between 1250 and 1253. Further attacks came in the following years again from Albert (in a work called *The Unity of the Intellect* [1256] and in many other passages on the nature of the soul), from Gerard of Abbeville (especially in a question on the oneness of the intellect in his eighth *Quodlibet*), and finally in the acclaimed denunciations by Thomas and Bonaventure.

In less than twenty years, then, the positions of the Averroists were gradually consolidated and radicalized and were ever more openly publicized along with radical claims for the "freedom to philosophize." What was clearer than the reliability of the results they reached in their logical demonstrations was their attitude: they showed a strong determination to defend the autonomy and liceity of their speculative activity.

The climactic point in the development of this program was Siger of Brabant's *Questions* on the third book of Aristotle's *On the Soul*; Siger was a master of arts from the Walloon area and was probably the direct target of Thomas' *The Unity of the Intellect*. The record of Siger's work that has come down to us shows a teaching divided into solid demonstrations with conclusions that are deliberately proposed as necessary without any relation to the theological foundations of Christian psychology. These conclusions are: (1) the intellect by which a human being knows, that is, the possible intellect, cannot be thought to be the form of the body in a full and univocal way, as the vegetative and sensitive souls are, for otherwise it would be incapable of detaching itself from sensible images; (2) if it is to be directed by the agent intellect in the formation of concepts, the possible intellect must be separated from the body; (3) it is part, therefore, of the purely spiritual nature of the higher Intellect and is universal because common to all individuals.

In December 1270, Stephen Tempier, bishop of Paris and a former master of theology, relying on the theological advice of Gerard of Abbeville, issued a decree prohibiting the teaching of thirteen philosophical theses. All of them were inspired by Averroes and were in essence reducible to a root set of three fundamental ideas: the eternity of the world and of the human species, determinism and the denial of Providence, and the oneness of the intellectual soul. While the immediate targets of the condemnation were specific positions that could be documented in the teaching of Siger and perhaps of others among his Artist colleagues, it arose in a broader context of discussions and controversies that enlivened university life during those years and had to do with the place of "purely" philosophical research and its compatibility with the Christian faith.

The request for episcopal intervention was probably not due solely to the need to rein in the uncontrolled expansion of philosophy's prerogatives into the area of subjects that should have been reserved to the theologians. It was time to rein in the theologians, too, with their adoption of attitudes that were too relaxed and conciliatory in their recourse to worldly wisdom, and especially to Aristoteleanism, as a means of developing Christian doctrine. A strong assertion of the religious authorities could also contribute to a clear answer to other internal questions of university life that had too long been left unresolved and were connected with the autonomy of the teachers. Some such questions had to do with the rivalry between the secular masters and the Mendicants, the disagreement over the areas of competence of the several Faculties, and internal juridico-institutional imbalances caused by partiality shown in the management of administrative duties.

In the next year Siger was caught up in an outbreak of disturbances in the Faculty of Arts caused by dissatisfaction over the election of a French master named Alberic of Rheims as rector. Against him the Norman "nation" of faculty members pushed the candidacy of Siger, a man from Picardy. Given an atmosphere already heated by Tempier's decree, this choice could not but be a sign of the determination of some of the Artists to show their autonomy against the theologians' claims of doctrinal and institutional supremacy. In 1272, during the ongoing division, new statutes for the Faculty of Arts were promulgated; in them the masters of arts were expressly forbidden to "issue decisions or even simply to hold disputations" on purely theological matters such as the Incarnation or the Trinity. A logical deduction from this decree is that it had become necessary explicitly to put down a practice that was appearing with excessive frequency.

In 1272–73 Siger published *The Intellectual Soul*, in which he showed a degree of respect for the authority of Albert and Thomas and partially revised his own psychology. But the unrest within the Faculty of Arts continued. In 1275 a new intervention by ecclesiastical authority imposed the appointment as rector of Peter of Alvernia, a man known for his moderation and his devotion to the recently deceased Thomas. The measure did not, however, suppress the resistance of the challengers. Thus, in 1276, a decree of the board of the Faculty of Arts forbade the holding of lectures in private places, thereby showing that some masters were continuing to lecture on the natural philosophy of Aristotle, but outside the university, thereby evading the control of the authorities. Two months later Siger, along with some colleagues, was summoned before the court of the Inquisition as being responsible for the unrest, but he seems to have left France before the censure was published.

Stronger and more radical interventions were needed. In 1277, Pope John XXI, formerly called Peter the Spaniard, a well-known teacher of logic in Paris and author of *Summaries of Logic*, the most widely used thirteenth-century handbook of logic, urged Stephen Tempier to again investigate the errors being spread at the University of Paris. A commission of sixteen theologians, Henry of Ghent among them, worked quickly to prepare an analytical list of doctrinal errors and suspect texts. On March 7 the bishop issued a decree condemning as heretics those who taught as true a series of 219 philosophical propositions.

The condemnation was leveled against all those who, while carrying on their intellectual activity in the Faculty of Arts, "boldly transgress the limits proper to their Faculty in order to discuss and debate in the schools certain obvious and abominable errors and even empty and misleading foolishness," thereby rending the unity among believers. Worse still, in trying to justify their error they produce another that is even more dangerous, because they say that their teachings "are true according to philosophy but not according to the Catholic faith, as if there could be two contradictory truths and as if the writings of the accursed pagans could yield a truth contrary to the truth in Sacred Scripture."

The decree then explicitly prohibited a series of books, among them *On Love* by Andreas Cappellanus (a treatise on courtly, that is, extraconjugal, love) and some short works on geomancy and necromancy. Next came a list (in practice a disorganized inventory that followed no internal order) of prohibited propositions, which even in their form (they sound like titles of *Questions*) seem to be direct echoes of the texts of authors or lecture notes circulating in the university libraries during those years.

Some of these theses were immediately recognizable as typical of the Averroist program of learning. Thus: "that the philosophers alone are the world's wise men" (154), "that no question can be argued in a rational way about which philosophers do not have the right to argue and draw conclusions" because "they have the duty of reflection on all matters in accordance with [the rules of] their several disciplines" (145), and "that the entire good of human beings consists of the intellectual virtues" (144).

The majority of the propositions showed how irreconcilable specific Averroist theses were with the foundations of the faith: "nothing can be eternal at its end that was not eternal in its beginning" (4) and "there was never a first human being nor will there ever be a last" (9); "the world is eternal inasmuch as all the species in it are eternal" (87); "if the heavens were to stop their movement, the fire in the stove would not burn because God would not exist" (156); "the intellect is not the form of the body except in the way in which the helmsman is the form of the ship, and it is not the essential perfection of the human being" (7); "it is one in number" (32) and "is eternal" (31), and even "both the active and the passive intellects are eternal" (109); "God cannot make more individual souls" (27) and "the separated soul cannot undergo changes" (113).

Further propositions defended a universal determinism (21), an intellectualism in ethics (130), creation through intermediaries (38), the denial that God knows future contingents (42, 56), that the active First Cause can produce a multitude of effects (44), and that God can cause anything new (48).

Other condemned theses were explicitly anti-theological, although they cannot be directly connected with Averroist lines of thought. Thus: "that God is not one and triune, because the Trinity is not compatible with his simplicity" (1); "that God cannot beget something like himself" (2); "that God cannot bestow perpetuity on something corruptible" (25); "that all theological discourses are based on fables" (152); "that the Christian law hinders learning" (175), "that it, like the other [religions], is full of fables and falsehoods" (174); and "that theology brings no increase in knowledge" (153). In addition there are: the rejection of a bodily resurrection (18), the denial of the value of prayer (180), and an aprioristic challenge to the principle of authority (150).

Not lacking, indeed, were theses that smacked of an authentic Aristotelianism or at least of some classical philosophical origin, but they were always phrased as denials of theological truth: "that God does not know things other than himself" (3); "that God cannot make more worlds" (34); the identification of beatitude with virtue (157) and the claim that beatitude is reached in the present life and not in another (176); "that one cannot believe in anything not self-evident or deducible from what is self-evident" (37); the doctrines of the eternal repetition of cosmic movement (6) and of the power of the stars over the human will (162); and the identification of beatitude with the leisure to philosophize (40).

In some extreme instances Neoplatonism and Averroism were mixed together, to the point of affecting even the interpretation of some Augustinian teachings, notably on the nature of time: "that all the separated beings are coeternal with the first principle" (5) and "that time and the ages do not exist in reality but only in the intellect" (200). Not omitted, finally, were some statements contrary to philosophical reason itself: "that there are several first movers" (66), or the assertion that essence and existence are identical in all separated substances (79).

B. THE THOUGHT SYSTEM OF THE ARISTOTELEAN ARTISTS

If the condemnation had any concrete effects, the most obvious was that Siger's academic career was irremediably broken off. After his flight from Paris there is no detailed information about him until he turns up in Orvieto at the pontifical court; he may have gone there to appeal the accusation of heresy, or perhaps he was forced to stay there under restraint. We learn that he was killed there, during the pontificate of Martin IV (1281–85), stabbed by an insane cleric who was probably his secretary.

It is, in fact, not difficult to discover direct wordings or echoes of the condemned theses in Siger's writings, in reports of his university lectures, and in some short monographs (among these, in addition to his *The Intellectual Soul*, I may mention a *Question on the Eternity of the World* and a *Question on the Necessity and Contingency of Causes*). There emerges from these pages a real philosophical system in which we may discern the building of a program for an integral retrieval of the method and divisions of Aristotle's thought, but it is a system deliberately structured without ever subordinating its results to a verification of their compatibility with the contents of revelation.

God is at the apex of Siger's system as the first cause and source of being, and it is possible to demonstrate his existence from different lines of *a posteriori* argumentation that seem to have been borrowed from the teaching of Thomas. But the oneness of the cause is guaranteed by the oneness of its immediate effect, which is a purely intelligible, necessary, and eternal principle. The latter is at the head of a complex hierarchy of lower intelligences that function as intermediaries in bringing to bear the productive efficacy of the first cause. The first cause acts immediately only on its first effect, and only mediately does it cause each intelligence to move the one next beneath it, along with the heavenly sphere that is subjected to it, down to the final sphere, the heaven of the moon, which presides over movements of generation and corruption in the corporeal world. Each intelligence, being immaterial, is unique in its species and is individuated by its own essence. God alone is pure actuality, while all other beings are composed of potency and act.

Everything that happens in the created universe is a necessary effect and part of an eternal mechanical cycle of events that is repeated *ad infinitum*. Yet this universal process is also marked by contingency, which is due to the natural inability of matter to receive in an effective way the necessary forms coming from the higher spheres. So, too, the human will is free due to the weakness of the capacities for judgment that are proper to the use of reason and on which the will depends directly and exclusively. The soul is the form of the body, and all its properties are geared to its being the body's moving and lifegiving principle. The soul's supreme degree of activity is identifiable with the highest level of action of the vegetative-sensible power; it is named "cogitative" and has a relation to the intellectual soul, which is the last of the separated intelligences and includes both the active and the passive intellects.

As noted earlier, this last doctrine of Siger undergoes a degree of development. In his *Questions* on Aristotle's *On the Soul* he maintains that the personal soul is radically mortal. Then, after accepting the philosophical validity of Thomas' criticisms, he gradually moves, by way of his *The Intellectual Soul* and a later commentary on the *On Causes*, to ever more moderate positions, until he finally allows that the intellectual function is part of the personal soul and guarantees the individuality of understanding. However, he still rejects the idea that the intellectual function is the form of the body and is combined with corporeity.

A like number of the propositions in Tempier's list can be found in the works of another Parisian master of arts, Boethius of Dacia, who is expressly linked with Siger in the headings of some contemporary manuscripts of his works. Little is known of his life except that he was Danish ("of Dacia") and that, perhaps after 1277, he entered the Order of Preachers. As a master of grammar and author of a treatise on *The Ways of Signifying* he was, along with some other Danes such as Martin and John of Dacia, an important representative of the "modist" movement, the so-called "speculative grammarians." These scholars studied the relationships of the laws of metaphysics (*modes of being*) and those of logic (*modes of understanding*) to the semantic possibilities of grammatical discourse (possibilities governed precisely by the *modes of signifying*).

And yet in some of Boethius' philosophical writings, such as *The Supreme Good or the Life of the Philosopher*, *Dreams*, and, above all, *The Eternity of the World*, it is possible to find important similarities to some of the propositions in the condemnation. In particular these include, on the one hand, propositions on the eternity of the world and of the human species and, on the other, propositions on divination (which Boethius thought was legitimized by medical and astronomical ideas developed by learned Arabs), on the possibility of attaining to beatitude during earthly life through the practice of the ethical virtues, and on the identification of beatitude with an authentic philosophical life and with the cognitive union of the intellect with God, something already possible in the present life.

c. "Double Truth" and the Epistemological Distinctions of the Arts Faculty

Nowhere, however, in the writings of Siger and Boethius is there an explicit defense of what Tempier's preface suggests is the principal accusation against the "straying" Artists: namely, their claim that different and contradictory truths can coexist. The Averroists did claim the right to work with reason alone and without ever subjecting its results to any requirements outside the demands of science itself. But they never said that they regarded the conclusions thus reached, when contrary to the data of the faith, as alternatives for the latter. In other words, they did not regard their conclusions as embodying a philosophical truth different from that of theology, but only as having the same right as their theological competitors to be announced, communicated, and accepted by others.

In commenting on the third book of *On the Soul* in the light of Averroes' teaching, Siger says that he does not consider himself to be in opposition to the Christian tradition; he even gives assurance that he wants to rely on revealed truth as the ultimate standard for judging his studies. He himself denounces and opposes the scourge of disagreement among the philosophers and relies on the superior quality of Aristotelean reasoning as a cure for it. At the same time, however, he acknowledges that it is not easy to determine what Aristotle's real opinion was in regard to the universal intellect. Therefore, "faced with such uncertainty," he urges as a fundamental principle the rule of "conforming to the faith, which is superior to and transcends human reason."

Similarly, at the beginning of his *Question* on the eternity of the world he says that he intends to deal in "the manner of the Philosopher" with the matters being debated in the Faculty of Arts. But then, at the end of his treatise, he points out that neither the arguments for the eternity of the world nor those rejecting it can be decisive; in any case, however, every believer is obliged to accept by faith that the world had a beginning.

Again, at the beginning of his *On the Intellectual Soul* he says that he intends to consider the problems of psychology "to the extent that they involve the Philosopher." He explains that this assertion amounts to saying that he intends to pursue understanding as far as "human reason" and experience can take him, because the object of such study is not unlimited truth, but the understanding reached by philosophers, "once we have decided to proceed according to philosophical method." According to the truth grasped by faith, "which cannot deceive," it is in fact certain that intellectual souls are as many as there are human beings, even though "some philosophers have held the contrary view" because they have proceeded according to the method of philosophy. Here again he repeats in his conclusion that "when reason is in doubt it is always necessary to stick with faith," which is always superior to reason.

These guiding principles of Siger are methodologically justified and made even more specific by Boethius of Dacia. At the beginning of his *The Eternity of the World* he sets down an interesting parallel between the "heretical" error of one who introduces reason into matters that can only be objects of faith and the "philosophical" error of one who refuses to accept valid demonstrations in matters that can be investigated by reason. He says, furthermore, that he intends to build on this foundation and to "harmonize" the teaching of Aristotle and the other philosophers on the origin of the world with revelation:

> In fact, their teaching does not in any respect contradict the Christian faith, as is claimed by those who simply do not correctly understand that teaching. The teaching of the philosophers is based on the demonstrations and rationally certain arguments that can be formulated in regard to matters that are the object of their studies. On the other hand, faith is, in most cases, based on miracles and not on demonstrative arguments. Everything that can be accepted as the conclusions of arguments is not faith, but science.

The harmony the Averroists sought between faith and reason was thus different from the harmony understood by Albert and Thomas, who subordinated philosophy to the demands of religion in order to use the tools of the former to the advantage of theological science. The Averroists, on the contrary, allowed that there could be harmony among different forms and sources of knowledge, provided a clear distinction was made between fields of study and objects known.

This position of the Latin Averroists was based directly on the epistemological doctrine of the *Posterior Analytics*. According to Aristotle the specific task of each human science is to bring out the universal and eternal necessity of the rational conclusions it is able to reach. But it is evident that the conclusions of each science must depend exclusively on the nature of the object proper to it, since it is this nature that determines the method and demonstrative procedures of the science and differentiates them from those of the other sciences. To claim, then, that possible conclusions contrary to one another but belonging to two different kinds of science are each of them true in its specific area is not the same as allowing the contradictory coexistence of many truths. The reason is that in order for different statements to contradict one another they must necessarily be located within the field of one and the same discipline.

Averroism, therefore, did not claim to accept a "double truth" or the simultaneous coexistence of two or more contradictory truths; rather, it recognized that there are different orders of truth. Consequently the order of faith, which is based on revelation and concerns the efficacy of supernatural causes that reason cannot search out, can never contradict the order of natural philosophy (physics) or metaphysics. The development and conclusion of Boethius' treatise bring out this distinction in an uncompromising and unambiguous manner:

> Christians are therefore speaking the truth when they say that the world and movement had a beginning and that there was indeed a first human being, as well as when they claim that human beings will return to life, that all human beings will exist again in their original numbers, and that corruptible things will become incorruptible. Admittedly, these possibilities can be allowed only thanks to a single cause whose power is greater than that of natural causes. But the philosopher of nature is also speaking the truth when he says that all this is not possible on the basis of natural causes and principles. In fact, the philosopher of nature neither affirms nor denies anything at all unless he is basing his claims on natural principles and causes, just as a grammarian neither affirms nor denies anything unless he is basing his claims on grammatical principles and causes.
>
> Consequently, if the philosopher of nature, looking solely to the efficacy of natural causes, says on that basis that the world could not have had a beginning, while the Christian faith, looking to a cause superior to nature, says that the world could have had a beginning, the two do not contradict each other in any way.
>
> Therefore two points are clear: one is that the philosopher of nature does not contradict the Christian faith regarding the eternity of the world; the second is that no arguments available to nature can prove that the world and movement did have a beginning. In fact, the faith says many things that cannot be demonstrated by reason . . . and anyone who does not believe them is a heretic, whereas anyone trying to know them by rational means is a simpleton. . . .
>
> It is clear, then, that there is no contradiction between the Christian faith and philosophy regarding the problem of the eternity of the world.

Boethius thus turns back on his adversaries the accusation of either stupidity or ungodliness. No one has the right to "speak ill" of philosophers, but must allow them simply to practice their own trade. In fact, everyone ought even to make an effort to understand their teaching, since they are the true sages of this world and since it is not possible to find in their words any arguments that are in any respect contradictory to the truth of the faith. Indeed, one of the fundamentals of philosophical thought is precisely a prohibition against admitting that truth can take contradictory forms; even God cannot will that what is true be not true or that two contradictory truths can exist together. It is the task of scientists to show the validity, in each particular field, of the truths concerning it, since it is only right that science should help human beings to know the world and show them how the necessary laws of nature operate.

On the other hand, it is a lie to say that a Christian cannot be a philosopher because the law of Christ has invalidated the principles of philosophy. The faithful should allow that natural causes be studied and accurately understood for what they are, precisely because the truths of the faith transcend natural necessity, for otherwise they would be the object not of belief but of everyday knowledge. But it is evident that "faith is not a science."

4. The Debate between the Franciscans and the Dominicans

Even in the writings of some of the most trustworthy representatives of the scholastic theological synthesis there can be found questions on which the opposition between philosophical reasoning and the Christian faith remains unresolvable. Albert the Great, for example, in his commentary on Aristotle's *On Generation and Corruption* adopts a neutral attitude on the question of the eternity of natural movement and says that "when philosophers discuss the order of natural causes, it is not their duty to take God's miracles into consideration." We mentioned earlier the position of Thomas Aquinas (in the fourteenth question of Part I of the *Summa*) on the impossibility of demonstrating either the eternity of the world or its temporal beginning; the truth of creation is "professed solely by faith," just as is the trinitarian mystery.

These statements by theologians on the insuperable limitations encountered in the quest for the "understanding of faith" could not fail to strike the more traditionalist followers of Augustine as the sign of a dangerous parallelism with the claim of philosophical autonomy by the Latin Averroists. John Peckham (d. 1292), a theologian and regent for the Franciscans in Paris from 1269 to 1271 before moving on to Oxford, challenged the correctness of that position in his inaugural lecture as a master; he did so in the presence of Thomas himself, who answered the criticisms in his *The Eternity of the World*. But these divergent views emerged again in a more radical way when, following the censure of 1277, the disagreement between theologians and philosophers seemed to focus on the very legitimacy of attempts to compare the arguments of philosophical speculation and the assertions of faith, attempts made even by some masters of theology, especially among the Dominicans.

In the tangled skein of objectionable philosophical opinions listed by Tempier it was not in fact difficult to see ideas or claims that could be found in the writings of well-known and authoritative masters of theology. And even though none of the condemned propositions was attributed directly to Thomas it was not difficult to see in the wording of some of them implicit criticisms of specific propositions uttered by the now-deceased Aquinas. Above all, "the philosophical argument showing the movement of the heavens to be eternal is not deceitful" (91); then, "God cannot multiply individuals within a species without using matter" (96) and "individuals in the same species differ from one another only through the introduction of matter"; "nothing can be known of God except that he is and is existence itself" (215); and, finally, the unyielding assertion of the primacy of the intellect over the will, which "necessarily follows what reason accepts and cannot but follow its dictates" (163).

In the days following the issuance of his decree Tempier intervened again to censure some positions of Giles of Rome that could clearly be connected with Thomistic metaphysics. Many contemporaries assure us that the bishop was thinking even of starting a posthumous investigation into Aquinas himself and that only under pressure from influential individuals (among them perhaps John of Vercelli, General of the Dominicans) was this undertaking transferred to Rome, where it was pigeonholed during the *sede vacante* period after the death of John XXI. Honorius IV in 1285 finally sent it back for discussion by the masters of theology (not by the bishop); the discussion ended with a finding that there was no case.

Nevertheless, on March 18, 1277, ten days after Tempier's decree, Robert Kilwardby (d. 1279), archbishop of Canterbury, in agreement with the masters of theology at Oxford, promulgated a decree censuring thirty theses as "false and abhorrent to the Catholic faith." In this case most of the theses could obviously be traced back to the teaching of Thomas. Kilwardby's action was the more momentous since he was himself a Dominican, a master of theology at Oxford, and author of a famous *Rise of the Sciences* (a complete and original division of the philosophical sciences) and of a *Question on the Nature of Theology* that was obviously indebted to the traditionalist Augustinianism of Fishacre.

Other distinguished Dominican masters, and not only those active at centers other than Paris, likewise maintained their independence of the speculative tendencies most in vogue in the Order and played down the importance not only of Thomas but of Albert as well. One such was the earlier mentioned Peter of Tarentaise (d. 1276), who was archbishop of Lyons at the time of the council there and, after being elected pope, reigned for only a few months of 1276 as Innocent V. In his university writings he went along with the main gnoseological, psychological, metaphysical, and theological views of Bonaventure. Another was Romanus Orsini of Rome (d. 1273), who in 1272 became one of Thomas' successors in the chair at Paris and who likewise maintained doctrines typical of the Franciscans.

John Peckham, elected archbishop of Canterbury at the death of Kilwardby in 1279, twice endorsed the anti-Thomist censure, first in 1284 and again in 1286, with his focus chiefly on the doctrine of the unicity of the substantial form. Since this thesis would cancel out the identity of the living body and the corpse it was accused of leading to a serious differentiation in the body of Christ before and after the Passion and before and after the resurrection. Peckham produced many writings that show, in the area of the arts, his familiarity with the scientific and experimental interests typical of Oxford Franciscanism and, in the area of theology, his dependence on the Anselmian model (still dominant in England) and the Bonaventuran (recently imported from France).

Peckham was convinced of the urgent need to halt the advance of Aristoteleanism by restoring a theological wisdom inspired by Augustine and strengthened in the areas of logic, ontology, and psychology by the speculative foundations that had by now been tested and approved by Franciscan thought. This restoration meant a metaphysics focused on the identification of God with the Supreme Good, a gnoseology based on illumination and on the identification of the agent intellect with God, the "giver of forms," and an ethics based on a will seen as capable of acting freely in face of the cognitive data provided by the intellect.

The university training of the two English archbishops is confirmation of the close connection between the censures issued by ecclesiastical authorities and the doctrinal discussions going on among the masters of theology. Hostilities soon moved over, therefore, into the area of more strictly theoretical discussion. They were begun by William de la Mare (d. 1289), another English Franciscan who had also been a regent first in Paris and then at Oxford and was linked by friendship and cultural interests to Roger Bacon.

In 1279 William published a handbook titled *Correctory* (or *Set of Emendations) for Brother Thomas* (*Correctorium fratri Thomae*) to aid in an expurgated reading of Thomas' thought. The work consisted of a list of 118 theses extracted from the latter's works and accompanied by an indication of the danger of each and an immediate refutation. Thus indictments were once again leveled at, among other teachings, the theses on the indemonstrability of creation in time, the impossibility of God creating a matter without form and having an idea of matter, the denial that divine omnipotence could create other worlds, the unknowableness of individuals, the possibility of individuation solely through matter, the unicity of the substantial form, the rejection of hylomorphic composition in the angels and the unity of the individual in each species of angel, the dependence of the will on the intellect, and the primacy of the intellect in the beatific vision.

The pupils and colleagues of Thomas immediately reacted by rebaptizing the "correctory" as the "corruptory" (*corruptorium*). They also circulated an abundant series of *Correctoria corruptorii*, these being referred to, in order to distinguish them, by the first word of their text. The first of these writers was Richard Knapwell (d. 1289), author of the *Correctorium Corruptorii Quare*, in which he cited William's text while annotating and refuting it point by point. His defense of Thomas focused in particular on the doctrine of the unicity of the substantial form, but he also emphasized the indemonstrability of the articles of faith in general and of creation in time in particular.

Another English Dominican, probably Robert of Oxford (or of Colletorto), supported Knapwell with his own *Correctorium Corruptorii Sciendum*, which was characterized by the introduction of supplementary logical distinctions that were either set alongside those of Thomas or superimposed on his. An echo came from Paris in the *Correctorium Corruptorii Circa* of John Quidort (also known as John of Paris or John the Deaf, d. 1306). This work remained incomplete, as did the later *Correctorium Corruptorii Quaestione*, the work of an English Dominican, perhaps William of Macclesfield (d. 1303).

The series of direct replies to the *Corruptorium* ended around 1299 with the publication of the *Defense of the Truth* by Rambert dei Primadizzi (or of Bologna). Rambert broadened the scope of the controversy by introducing into his defense of Thomas criticisms by other adversaries, especially Henry of Ghent and Giles of Rome. He also tried to change the direction of the controversy by telling the Franciscans, in reference to the demonstrability of creation in time, of his conviction that a vain pride in the power of reason was as sinful as the arrogance of those who claimed to be the beneficiaries of some indefinable special illumination from on high.

As the controversies over theory continued to intersect, the governments of the two Mendicant Orders officially intervened to define their respective strategies for defending the reliability of their own most respected representatives. Thus in 1282 the general chapter of the Strasbourg Franciscans demanded that all the Friars Minor read the *Correctorium* of William de la Mare as an indispensable help in gaining an "expurgated" knowledge of the *Summa of Theology*. In 1286 the Dominican chapter issued "strict" orders from Paris that all the Friars Preachers commit themselves to promoting and defending the doctrines of the "venerable master" Thomas Aquinas, this under threat of suspension from teaching.

Thus doctrinal discussion became increasingly an ideological confrontation between opposing factions in defense of two theological systems that were evidently incompatible. For the Dominicans the thought of Aquinas was a citadel to be defended against the intemperate attacks of critics they regarded as being stubborn because they were incompetent. The Franciscans, for their part, tended to take up a defensive position based on the sapiential structure erected by Bonaventure; on this foundation the Friars Minor struggled to defend their authentic theology, the only one capable of also saving the truths of the philosophers by making them serve the contemplative ascent of the soul.

As in all prolonged wars, both camps also felt the need to strengthen the structure of their own system at possible weak points on which the adversaries were leveling their critical weapons with some success. As a result some of the more rigid positions were gradually softened in one or other way due to sensible qualifications made by some of the champions more deeply engaged in the battle. This process avoided doctrinal rigidities but at the same time prepared the way for a necessary expansion of the respective cultural horizons. It was this approach that then justified, on both sides, the use of the concept of "school" in order to signify not only a schematic restatement of fixed opinions as a sign of recognized membership in a particular intellectual party, but also the relatively adaptable and constructive development and justification of the parts making up each side's doctrinal whole.

It is in this specific sense that we may correctly speak in particular of the Thomist school or tendency as a way of describing the forms, not always or in every respect homogeneous and immutable, in which the Friars Preachers gradually solidified their unique allegiance to their patrimony of "sounder and more common" teaching (the formula was henceforth used in the official documents of the Dominican Order).

Thomas' first disciples had already realized that in the vast collection of his writings one could run into variations, corrections, and changes of opinion. Faced with the need, in particular, of harmonizing some more obvious disagreements between the *Commentary on the Sentences* and the *Summa of Theology*, his followers developed the usually anonymous literature of *Concordances* and the so-called *Melius dixit* or *Aliter dixit* ("he put it better" or "he put it differently"), that is, lists of articles in which Thomas changed his opinion on particular points but without altering the substance of the system. Subsequently even some of the Thomists of the early generations began to express occasional doubts and introduce some qualifications. Bernard of Trillia or de la Treille (d. 1292), who was regarded as one of Aquinas' most faithful followers, voiced some hesitancies regarding the real distinction between essence and existence and accepted it as simply "a probable view."

Giles of Lessines, a Belgian (d. after 1304), in his *The Unicity of the Form*, and John of Paris, in his *Treatise on the Unicity of the Form*, united in opposition to Robert Kilwardby in defense of the substantial oneness of the soul. Yet, perhaps led on by the ideas of Giles of Rome, the same John in a treatise on *The Unity of Essence and Existence* came out for a strongly realistic view of the ontological distinction, to the point of allowing that God can create an existence without an essence.

In his own *Commentary on the Sentences* John also corrected Thomist teaching on the beatific vision by denying that it could be understood as a direct vision of the "simple and unveiled" essence of God. He accepted that the agent intellect was not part of the soul's essence but was infused into it by God, the supreme Agent Intellect. When it came to teaching on the nature of theological science he maintained that Thomas' subalternation of theology to the knowledge had by God and the blessed could not have the same meaning and validity as when the idea of subalternation was applied by the philosophers to the hierarchical relationships among the other sciences. The reason was that in Thomas' application the idea had a quite special meaning that Aristotle could not have envisaged since he had no knowledge of Christian revelation.

Later, Oxford master Thomas of Sutton (d. 1315/1320), a convinced but not passionate Thomist, took up this same point in his *Difficult Questions* and stated that it was pointless for Thomas' adversaries to tire themselves out proving that theology cannot be a subalternated science, because in fact it is not. Thomas says only that it is a science inferior to that of God inasmuch as "it derives its principles from that higher science and takes them for granted," in the sense that those who believe in revelation know imperfectly what God knows perfectly.

A similar tendency to qualify particular positions can also be seen, though less obviously, among the Thomists of Italy, among whom the memory of the master's teaching in Rome and Naples was especially vivid. Reginald of Piperno (d. 1290) and Annibaldo degli Annibaldeschi (d. 1272), Thomas' successor in the chair of Paris in 1261, faithfully reflected his teaching. But Remigio dei Girolami (d. 1319), a Florentine and Reader at the Dominican convent of Santa Maria Novella, made careful choices of those aspects of Thomas' thought that, in his view, deserved to be defended with greater commitment and inflexibility.

Thus, especially in his *The Subject of Theology*, he insisted on the idea that the subject of theological science is "God absolutely." His explanation: this means that theology aims at understanding God in his very essence, independently of any relationship with anything else. At the same time, however, he added that while the theological knowledge of the angels and the blessed and the knowledge possible to human beings during their earthly life is identical with that which God has of himself, they vary because of the "different cognitive capacities" of the knowing subjects. This view represented a partial departure from the realism of Aristotelean gnoseology because it introduced differentiation into the conditions for approaching a known object depending on the capacity or readiness of the knowing subject.

It is thus possible to identify, in the wide world of Thomists, the emergence of independent positions that were meant to strengthen the accepted synthesis. But the seascape painted by the Franciscan followers of Bonaventure looks even more varied and changeable, as if these followers had suffered the consequences of their own polemical fury. In the beginning, quite faithful readings of the saint's teaching were made by such men as Gilbert of Tournai (d. 1284) and Eustachius of Arras (d. 1291). But at an early date Walter of Bruges (d. 1307), regent in Paris where he occupied the chair that had been Bonaventure's, made a first attempt to harmonize Augustinianism with Aristotelean ideas drawn mostly from Thomas' *Summa* in his commentary on the *Sentences*, composed before 1270, and then in a series of *Disputed Questions*. For example, he allowed abstraction for the knowledge of natural entities, while preferring the doctrine of illumination ("along with Augustine and Plato") for the knowledge of spiritual realities. He also tended to accept the theory of subalternation and the conception of theology as a speculative and not a practical science.

Peter of Falco, regent in Paris after 1277, declared his loyalty to Bonaventure, whose main theses he accepted in a syncretistic perspective, but he adopted a nominalistic outlook in offering balanced solutions to some of the most debated subjects. For example, in discussing the source of individuation he considers it appropriate to distinguish between, on the one hand, the logical order, where the Thomists are said to be correct in asserting that in the composite entity matter is determined ("signed") while the form is universal and, on the other hand, the order of reality in which only individual entities exist and therefore only forms that are, as such, individual and susceptible of growth and completion.

Perhaps the most interesting Franciscan author of this period was Matthew of Acquasparta (d. 1302), a master at Paris and in Rome and then General of the Order, and author of many series of *Questions* and *Quodlibeta*. Having been elected a cardinal, he was a supporter of papal primacy even when, shortly before his death, the conflict began between Boniface VIII and Philip the Handsome of France. In this choice we see at work his conception of creation as a vast cosmic theocracy in which everything depends on and is directly caused by the divine omnipotence; here he was vigorously opposing Greco-Arabic teachings that attempt to make the divinity subject to anthropomorphic laws derived by reason from the study of nature.

This same basic conception also lies behind his defense of ethical voluntarism against Thomistic intellectualism. On the other hand, it is not impossible, according to Matthew, to allow reason a role in informing and guiding the will, since freedom of action is guaranteed precisely by limitations on the human ability to theorize when confronted by the utter impossibility of pinpointing the government of the world and of knowing the supreme Good as it is in itself. Matthew also undertook a new philosophical explanation of theological illuminationism; this led him, on the one hand, to accept the validity of Aristotelean abstraction as the material cause of external knowledge of the sensible world and, on the other, to consider participation in the divine light, which is the formal cause of internal knowledge, as the foundation—not as a direct object but as an instrument—of theological knowledge.

It was again an Aristotelean foundation that supported the theory of illumination in the thought of Roger Marston (d. 1303), an English Franciscan who had been a student under Peckham and William de la Mare and then became a master and rector at Cambridge and Oxford. In his view, as in that of Matthew of Acquasparta, human knowledge results from a combination of human abstraction and a supernatural intervention of divine light. In other words, it is the product of a collaboration of the universal agent intellect, which is God, and the individual's agent intellect within the soul (the latter is an "agent intellect" only improperly and through likeness with God). But Roger thinks it expedient to state that the natural activity of the soul can at best develop, from the data of the senses, a mere beginning of intelligible knowledge and that the active intervention of the divine light is necessary for imprinting on the mind (which is here entirely passive) a true and proper, certain, and objective "species."

A clearer departure from the doctrinal synthesis of his colleagues is to be seen in Richard of Middleton (d. 1308), who was rector in Paris between 1284 and 1287. He paid careful attention to the ongoing debates and did not remain deaf to the criticisms of Dominicans and seculars who were charging the Franciscans with underestimating the contribution of philosophy to theology. He then came up with the idea—a bold one at the time and quite effective in opposing the "double truth" thesis attributed to the Averroists—of an uninterrupted historical continuity between the truth of the philosophers and that of Christians. The studies of the former (he said) were often a means God used in revealing himself to human beings; their work should therefore be accepted as an essential introduction to that of the theologians.

On this basis Richard was able to retrieve a series of philosophical theses he recognized as useful in theology. Prominent among these were Aristotelean gnoseology (once it was freed from illuminationism and any other influence from outside the soul), the *a posteriori* demonstrability of the existence of God, and the Thomist conception of substantial form. He presupposed, in particular, a hierarchic gradation rather than a distinction between metaphysics, which gives a glimpse of God amid the shadows of the human condition, and theology, which crowns the efforts of human cognitive activity and reveals God fully. He can then go on to accept with the Thomists that theology is a subalternated science, but only on the basis of an imperfect parallelism with the natural sciences, because the presuppositions of theology, being of divine origin, already implicitly contain their conclusions. But he was also able to accept, with the Franciscan masters, that theology is both speculative and practical, since after making the truth fully known to human beings it orders them to seek it as the ultimate end of their every desire and action.

The ensemble of doctrinal elements that made up the Franciscan speculative synthesis had already lost its unity and vigor in the work of William of Ware (d. after 1305), who taught at Oxford in the 1290s and there earned the title of "Profound Doctor" (*Doctor Profundus*). Of special interest is his explicit clarification of a distinction that had been becoming ever more refined in preceding writers and was destined to undergo important developments in later years: that between "theology in itself," which is the knowledge God has of himself and in which the angels and the blessed participate through grace, and "theology by attribution" (*theologia per accidens*, or, in other authors, "theology suited to us" or "our theology"), which is granted to human beings in their condition as "journeyers" (*viatores*), that is, during their earthly life ("on the journey," *in via*).

In William's view philosophy is knowledge of an inferior order, meant simply to provide conceptual tools developed in the natural light of reason without any assistance or contribution that is of supernatural origin. Every philosophical idea is a mental artifact, the construction of a "mental word," and results from a process of abstraction set in motion by the senses. In contrast, supernatural light is operative only in theological knowledge, which for this very reason is, during the present mortal life, a science *per accidens*, that is, not natural, since it makes it possible to apprehend God not as a "mental word" but as a genuine reality that is knowable as such thanks to the concurrence of faith and illumination.

It is worth noting that the multiplication of such doctrinal variations undoubtedly showed a tendency toward reconciliation with opposed positions and seems at the end to have weakened especially the Augustinian-Bonaventuran doctrinal system. This system was eaten away on the gnoseological level by a cumulative rethinking of the doctrine of illumination. Perhaps for this very reason, moreover, it was inevitably launched on an attempt to overcome the crisis by means of a resolute rethinking and renewal of its own theoretical and epistemological foundations. In contrast, the monumental strength of Thomas' work allowed the Dominican authorities to emphasize officially the solidity and continuity of the Order's speculative tradition, despite or even because of the expression of various nuances.

In confirmation of this view, the approval of the decree *The Foundation of the Catholic Faith* among the canons of the Ecumenical Council of Vienne seemed to many Dominican masters to be but a first and decisive step toward the attainment of further goals by which they intended to confirm the supremacy of the Thomist school in the ensuing decades. These included the canonization of Thomas, which was solemnly promulgated by Pope John XXII at Avignon in 1323, and then, in February of 1325, the solemn retraction by Stephen Bourret, bishop of Paris, of his involvement in the condemnation of March 1277.

5. The Controversy over the Absolute Poverty of the Spirituals and Peter John Olivi

As a matter of fact the anthropological formula of Vienne, according to which it is heretical to deny that the soul is "of itself and essentially" the form of the human body, did not, at least in its original wording, express a direct approval of Thomist teaching, since it makes no explicit reference to the controverted subject of the unicity of this substantial form. The council's purpose in this decree was simply to place out of bounds an excessively troubled area of disagreement among Christian scholars. The direct target of its sanction was the views on psychology that Peter John Olivi (d. 1298) had been defending during the last thirty years of the thirteenth century. In the opinion of many there lay hidden in his writings a corrosively poisonous thinking that, starting with the subject of poverty and the "truly evangelical life," had given rise to other ideological ruptures within the Faculty of Theology.

Beginning in the second half of the century, the controversy over absolute poverty had already had drastic repercussions first at the University of Paris and then within the Franciscan Order. This state of affairs was due to the rediscovery of the prophetic perspective in Joachim of Fiore's theology of history, a perspective that seemed to reflect and endow with eschatological power the reforming ideals of Francis of Assisi. After the rejection of Joachim's trinitarian teaching by the Lateran Council of 1215 there was a rebirth of interest in the writings of the Italian abbot. The interest was not only in their theologico-dogmatic contents but also and above all in the prophetic spiritualism that pervaded them, for it seemed to fit in well with the energetic rekindling, both within and outside of ecclesiastical structures, of ideal plans for the reform of religious institutions and the moral renewal of Christendom.

Because of its special place in between the world of laypeople and the world of university wisdom, the Franciscan Order was destined to take a leading part in the satisfaction of contemporary longings for renewal and in Joachimite prophetism. It was no accident, therefore, that in the area covered by the Franciscans, probably in southern France, there began to circulate not only the authentic writings of Joachim but also apocryphal texts. Among the latter was a commentary on Jeremiah in which it was said that the imminent reign of the Spirit was to be manifested by the appearance of genuine spiritual individuals charged with preparing the way for it; these were easily identifiable with the members of the Mendicant Orders.

Meanwhile, the formation in southern France and Italy of a minority of Franciscan apologists for a literal observance of the exhortations to poverty in the founder's *Rule* and *Testament* gave rise to the movement of the so-called "Spirituals" or "poor friars," thus named to distinguish them from the majority of the friars, who took the name "Conventuals." Sustained first by the support of reformist preacher Hugh of Digne (d. 1254) and then gaining strength during the generalate of John of Parma (d. 1279), which began in 1247, the Spirituals had soon urged the thinkers and university masters of the Order to develop doctrinal foundations on which to base a theological evaluation of Joachim's prophetic assertions. This evaluation would be supported by mystical calculations and interpretations of the signs of the times whose purpose was to announce the imminent end. As a result, after an initial impulse fostered by English masters, especially Adam of Marsh (d. 1259), founder of the Franciscan house of studies at Oxford, and then even by Grosseteste, who had lent his authority to the planned renewal, some of the Franciscan masters in Paris, Odo Rigaldi in particular, had offered sympathy and theoretical support to the Spirituals.

As mentioned earlier, an Italian friar, Gerard of Borgo San Donnino (d. 1276), a student in Paris, had drawn the attention of the university world to his insertion of Franciscanism into a theology of history inspired by Joachim. The response of the secular masters of Paris had led to the investigation and condemnation of Gerard by a papal commission formed at Anagni by Alexander IV. John of Parma was accused of tolerating the excesses of the Spirituals; he too was investigated and forced to resign from the generalate in 1257. Bonaventure, his successor, had strained to find a conciliatory middle position between the danger of heterodoxy and the reformist vocation the Order could not abandon. He found it by describing the prophetic tones of Joachim's message as mere rhetorical ornaments and locating them within the more traditional and moderate Augustinian theology of history. After the Seraphic Doctor's death and thanks to his authoritative intervention the Spirituals would be able to find a place, even institutionally, among the ranks of the Franciscan Order as a group distinct from the Conventuals.

It was at this point in the complex series of events that the theological contribution of Peter John Olivi came into play. The whole affair was, in fact, to undergo further developments after Celestine V, the "angelic" pope of the Spirituals, renounced the papal throne in 1294, and Boniface VIII was elected.

Peter came from southern France, where he was born around 1248; in 1270 he was a trained bachelor of theology in Paris, but the criticisms raised by some of his theses prevented him from becoming a master. He worked as a Reader at the general house of studies in Montpellier, and it was during this period that he composed a good many of his writings, which led to further suspicions and denunciations by many of his colleagues. On instructions of the General Chapter held in Strasbourg in 1282, a commission of Franciscan theologians of Paris (among them Richard of Middleton) was charged with judging the orthodoxy of Peter's teachings; it concluded its inquiry by listing as erroneous a long series of extracts from his works. The Franciscan authorities summoned him to Avignon to retract his errors; he agreed to profess all the articles of faith to which attention was called in the commission's documents but refused to retract his speculative positions, maintaining that the "private opinions" of scholars were a free expression of thought and that the pope alone had authority to settle questions in such areas.

The very strong reaction of the Order was temporarily abated in 1287 with the election of Matthew of Acquasparta as superior general. Matthew believed in the sincerity of Peter's orthodoxy and appointed him Reader at the house of studies in Florence, where he had the thirty-year-old Ubertino of Casale as an auditor and where he came in contact with the Italian Spirituals. On returning to Montpellier in 1289 he was once again caught up in controversy. He defended his views on poverty before the General Chapter of Paris in 1292 and then withdrew, with many followers, to Narbonne. There he devoted himself to the composition of his *Reading of the Apocalypse*, while maintaining a prudent silence during the early years of the pontificate of Boniface VIII. Peter's death in 1298 did not lessen suspicions of him or prevent inquisitorial investigations into his teaching, which Ubertino of Casale, the new leader of the Spirituals, defended and continued. In 1294–95 the latter composed a substantial work of christological and prophetic theology entitled *The Tree of the Crucified Life*.

Peter Olivi set down his own theological thought in a remarkable series of exegetical and scholastico-theological works, but the attention of his contemporaries was focused chiefly on his *Reading* of the book of Revelation, which summarizes in a systematic way the key elements of his thinking. In many respects his thought is set within the framework of Franciscan speculation, some elements of which it takes over while subjecting others to a critical revision. On the whole, however, Peter's reflections create a personal and original picture that is influenced to an important degree by his lively sense of the role played by theological thought in the history of human redemption. The result is a radically evangelical conception of religious wisdom rooted in the categorical necessity of the mystery of Christ, whom Peter accepts as the unconditional beginning, the sustaining center, the goal, and therefore the final standard of validity for every approach of the mind to truth.

This truth cannot be searched out by a cold, disinterested science but demands a complete involvement of all the actions, desires, and thoughts of the human being. If, then, reason is really to contribute to the attainment of this truth it must shift away from abstract and intellectualized classification of ideas and into an active, operative, existential realm. In the latter, Francis of Assisi's prophetic message of reform can be translated into an operative, concrete knowledge of whatever in historical reality can promote the coming of the true reign of Christ. Olivi thus proposes to base on revelation not a theology *of* history but rather a theology *in* history, a concrete knowledge that in human time must become increasingly perfect until it reaches its completion at the end of time (thanks to the contribution of devout Christian scholars, which likewise becomes increasingly prophetic).

In this perspective Peter is able to justify the propaideutic and supportive role he allows to pagan philosophy. The latter always contains some spark of truth, provided that it is seen as a means and never as an end or goal of intellectual activity, or, in other words, as a pedagogical preparation for the truth of Christ. "We must read philosophy as its masters and not as its servants and be its judges as well as its followers," in order to keep philosophy from appropriating theological knowledge and turning it into just another philosophy of the world (the cited words are from his *On Reading the Books of the Philosophers*).

It is easy to understand how Olivi could see the perverted model of such an abusive and mistaken philosophy in the corrupt combination of Aristoteleanism and the Gospel that too many contemporary theologians were offering. According to him these men had attempted to turn the irreversible authenticity of human existence into an abstract metaphysical, gnoseological, and, worse still, ethico-practical theory. The most infuriating and paradoxical result of this operation was to be seen in the *Summa* of Thomas Aquinas, who claims to pass off a natural, deductive theology as a means of converting men and women from sin and leading them to the fruits of Christ's redemptive work. But many Franciscan theologians had done no better. In a desperate attempt to imitate the theoretical program of the Aristoteleans, even while not yielding to the pull of their abstract reasoning, these theologians tried in vain to turn Augustine and Dionysius, the greatest defenders of true Christian wisdom, into representatives of a philosophy that was indeed different but was still of a schematic and conceptual kind.

According to Olivi, only if philosophy frees itself of any claim to know the unknowable can it recover its real usefulness for a de-intellectualized and authentically christological theology. To this end it is necessary to lead reason to a correct understanding of human existence. This means, above all else, freeing it from intellectualist errors by means of an appropriate destructive criticism and constructing a coherent theory of how human beings are self-determined (using legitimate natural means) toward their true supernatural goals. This relativization of philosophy (and of a systematic, deductive theology), which can be seen in large measure in his *Questions* on the second book of the *Sentences*, is one of the most interesting aspects of Olivi's contribution to the history of Christian speculation; it also foreshadows many of the critical and innovative developments in Franciscan thought during the new century.

The relativizing and dismantling of the pagan-scholastic philosophical synthesis was accomplished in the three key areas of that philosophy: ontology-metaphysics, gnoseology-psychology, and ethics.

Peter first shows the uselessness and ineffectiveness of several philosophical claims: the distinction between essence and existence, the metaphysical layering of genera and species, the table of categories, and the abstract conception of matter as something subsisting without a form. Furthermore, a proper metaphysics also readily rejects the "seminal reasons" that are meant to explain the actions of matter, as well as all the other causal chains that are ineffectually introduced to explain the movement of bodies. Everything has its source in the ontological and existential richness of concrete individuality, vitalized as this is by an interior impulse to movement that flows from the very way in which God has ordered its nature and introduced it into the flow of time at creation.

In the area of gnoseology, the reduction of reality to singular, unique entities justifies the rejection of the complicated theory of illumination, which introduces a phenomenological distancing of the mind from effective knowledge of reality. It also justifies the abandonment of the absurd anthropomorphic identification of God with a separated agent intellect. Even Aristotelean abstraction should be accepted only to the extent that it enables the mind to represent to itself the existential foundation of reality. This means that true knowledge must not be satisfied with abstract concepts but must focus on what these concepts represent and signify.

Finally, the ethical control of activity must free itself from an abstract intellectualism that reduces the irrepressible human aspiration for happiness to an ineffective theory of abstract virtuous behavior. It must also free itself from every form of passivity of the will in relation to knowledge, for it is the individual, unconditioned will that produces the individual's vital energy; it is the "root of freedom" and a reflection of the utter freedom with which God determines both himself and the universe.

Having thus rediscovered the simplest constitutive elements of a being endowed with real life in historical time, philosophy goes on to show theology the reality of a dynamic, living universe that is subject solely to the pure creative causality of God and is ordered to the fulfillment of his eschatological plan. Since revelation guarantees humanity the knowledge of this plan, a true theology will take concrete form by becoming in every respect a school for the understanding of Sacred Scripture. This understanding will improve and complete the partial understanding of truth that can be acquired by means of philosophy.

Explicitly reminding his reader of Francis' exhortation to read the Gospel message with simplicity, "without any gloss," Peter says that biblical exegesis must give the very first place to the literal sense, which controls and guides the other senses as important expansions (or, in Olivi's terminology, *postillae*) of our understanding of the mission of Christ, who is the "hinge" on which history turns. In this way Olivi takes the artificially eschatological direction given to the theology of history by the more radical Joachimites and gives it a more authentically and exclusively christological orientation. That is, Christ in his person recapitulates the truth of universal history, from Genesis, which tells of the creation of the universe in the Word and through the Word, to Revelation, which foretells the final grafting of redemption onto the truly evangelical life of the members of the church.

At the end of a history marked theologically by successive phases in the process of human redemption and of the universal struggle against the Antichrist, the hope for the victory of truth could be reliably entrusted to Francis' "evangelical way of life." Francis was the neo-messianic prophet of an authentic renewal both of Christian life lived in poverty and of theology in the form of a spiritual understanding that arises from a pure, ecstatic contemplation of the mystery of Christ. This understanding is an immediate knowledge of the truth that is promised to individual believers at the end of history and in the state of beatitude, as a reward for their complete trust in revelation during this earthly life or, in other words, in an authentically historico-temporal existence that matches the way in which revelation has been communicated.

In Olivi's thought, then, the very salvation of human beings is inseparably connected with the free and unique ontological simplicity of their real individuality: "Truth exists fully only in individual reality." All this explains why the inquisitorial anger of his theological opponents focused primarily on his anthropology, which allowed that the soul has its own spiritual matter and that its function as form is carried out by the various hierarchized parts of the cognitive soul (vegetative, sensitive, and intellectual) and by the will. But it must be kept in mind that all these elements constitutive of the real life of the individual human being are distinguishable only when approached theoretically and metaphysically, and not in the human existential reality.

In fact, there is a close connection between Olivi's prophetical conception of Christianity and the idea that the intellectual soul cannot be understood as the substantial form of the body, for if it were, it would be unable to understand and would not be free or separate and immortal. His position on the soul explains why the council of Vienne not only systematically investigated and condemned his theses but also thought it timely to set down (though not with explicit reference to his opinions) the obligation of every believer to acknowledge that the individual soul is, "of itself and essentially," the form of the body.

6. The Peace of Theology according to Dante Alighieri

Everyone knows that Dante's fictional journey out of this world in the *Commedia* took place in the spring of 1300. In that year Boniface VIII decreed a grandiose celebration of the first Jubilee, when (as Peter of Belleperche, a French lawyer, said, in words similar to those used by other eyewitnesses) "the pope made the entire world go on pilgrimage to Rome." The celebration was intended as a symbolic reminder of the spiritual unity of the Christian world at a time when, as never before, all the ideals of civil and religious harmony, but especially any suggestion of philosophical and theological unanimity, seemed endangered by irremediable ruptures and disagreements. Then, in 1302, the Bull *Unam sanctam* stated in radical form the idea of the unqualified unity of truth. It did so with an almost obsessive emphasis (clear in the very wording of the Latin text) on the unity and unicity of spiritual authority, which absorbs every other authority into itself just as the unity of truth, which is the divine *Logos*, recapitulates in itself all partial truths.

In April 1303, only four months before the insult to Boniface at Anagni and the tragic end of his pontificate, the centrality of Rome, the city of cities, was still the controlling idea in the church's policy of unification. This can be seen in the text of the Bull establishing the "City's House of Studies" (*studium urbis*), that is, the Roman university. This school was open to clerics and the laity and was intended (as was the Curia's house of theological studies, in existence since 1245) to provide a sufficient training to "so many individuals coming to Rome from so many parts of the world," as the document puts it. All these texts were intended in principle to gain the acknowledgment, not only political but also intellectual and theological, of the papal fullness of authority. It is not possible to read them without seeing in the repeated references to the necessary unity of truth an emphatic and not very well concealed exhortation to rise above the new scholarly disagreements that the arrogant invasion of the voices of the pagan philosophers and their followers had introduced into Christendom.

Lay observers, too, could see from outside the furious, and useless, verbal attacks going on in the universities and the repercussions these were having on the church. To such individuals the depressing spectacle of such implacable disagreements could not fail to appear as at least contradictory to the very nature of philosophy, which ought to set human beings on the way to the truth, and, above all, of theology, which ought to assure them of its definitive and eternal possession. Thus, in the sublime reconciliation scene in the *Paradiso* when Dante, now present in the heaven of the Sun, tells of the eschatological restoration of a final harmony among the very theologians who in the present life had criticized and contradicted one another, he is not pointing to a model to be contemplated nostalgically or to be thought of as attainable only in the future life. Rather, he was giving a picture of how here on earth the science of theology should already ensure the possession of divine truth and guarantee harmony among all believers.

He had already believed for some time in this model of science. He had described it clearly in the second treatise of his *Convivio* (*Banquet*). Here he establishes the hierarchy of the philosophical disciplines in a correspondence with the system of celestial spheres (the liberal arts are related to the heavens of the moon, the planets, and the sun; physics and metaphysics to the heavens of the fixed stars; and ethics to the *Primum Mobile*). He then likens theology, or "knowledge of God," to the calm of the final heaven, the Empyrean. His reason: the divine knowledge, which theology communicates, is a single, definitive, and unshakable knowledge that cannot be changed by the opinions of interpreters or misleading arguments.

> Because of its peacefulness the empyrean heaven is like the divine knowledge, which is filled with utter peace and does not brook any quarrels over opinions or any sophistic arguments, because of the unsurpassed certainty of its subject, which is God. He [Christ] speaks of this to his disciples: "My peace I give you, my peace I leave to you" (John 14:17); he does this by giving and leaving to them his teaching, which is the knowledge of which I speak. Of it Solomon says: "There are sixty queens and eighty concubines, and young handmaids without number; one

is my dove and my perfect one" (Song 6:7-8). He describes all the other sciences as queens and paramours and handmaids; this one he calls dove because it is unstained by quarreling, and this one he calls perfect because it makes one see perfectly the truth in which the soul finds its quiet.

As its very name shows, theology is a science whose subject is God. As such, theology itself is the peace that springs from the truth about God and that Christ has left through revelation as an inheritance for his disciples. Both as a science and as peace, theology rises above all the lesser sciences and forms of knowledge, which it coordinates and unifies. In the Song of Songs Solomon describes these prophetically in their ancillary role in relation to the higher science, the only one that is uniform and harmonious, free of any possible disagreement, divergent opinion, or debate ("unstained by quarreling"). It is such because it is the only one whose true purpose is to bring our souls to "see the truth" and to make their desires cease and find rest in that vision.

A few pages earlier, in the same treatise of the *Convivio*, as he begins his description of the sciences, Dante engages in autobiography as he tells of his personal "conversion" to philosophy and the search for truth. He had been born in Florence in 1265. He was twenty-five when, to escape the despair caused by the death of his beloved Beatrice, he sought refuge in the reading of the *Consolation* of Boethius and Cicero's *On Friendship*. Here he discovered (by his own "mental powers") that "philosophy, which was the queen of these writers, these sciences, and these books, was something supreme."

Drawn by an intellectual love of this "noble lady" ("the Love that speaks reason to my mind"), he decided to go and seek her "where she truly showed herself, that is, in the schools of the religious men and in the debates of the philosophers." Between 1290 and 1295, then, he attended the study centers opened by the Mendicants in Florence: certainly that of the Dominicans at Santa Maria Novella, where he probably heard the lectures of Remigius dei Girolami, and perhaps that of the Franciscans at Santa Croce, through which Peter Olivi and Ubertino da Casale passed during those years. These were approximately the years during which he composed the *Vita nova*, which signaled a definitive passage from being a *dolce stil nuovo* poet of courtly love to being a lover of truth. Dante worked on the *Convivio* (but stopped at the fourth of the fifteen planned treatises) during the years following his condemnation, in 1302, to perpetual exile from Florence. This work provided a first systematic exposition of his mature ethical and ideological world.

The philosophy of which Dante speaks in the *Convivio* seems, as seen through his eyes, to move in two different directions. On the one hand, when thinking of his youthful delight in "the most beautiful and most virtuous daughter of the Emperor of the universe, her whom Pythagoras named Philosophy" (in the conclusion of the second treatise), he seems to be embracing a conception of the Augustinian type: one, that is, in which philosophy comprises the entire ladder of knowledge, from the liberal arts to scientific learning, to Aristotle's first philosophy, and on, finally, to theology, which stands above all the others. On the other hand, especially beginning with the third treatise he tends rather to allow philosophy a more restricted field of study, in practice coextensive with rational, natural knowledge, which is inferior to theology. Nevertheless, he assigns philosophy as such the task of "aiding," that is, bringing out, the credibility of the faith and strengthening it with its arguments.

Philosophy is in fact based on created reason, which is naturally inferior to the divine *Logos*, and it is to be distinguished from the truth reached by faith, which is based on the miracles worked by Christ or in his name. But since human beings misuse reason and doubt the reality of such miracles, philosophy shows them the great and irrefutable power of reason, which is itself miraculous, and convinces them of the reasonableness and possibility of what faith tells us. In Dante's view this clarificatory role justifies the teaching of theology in the schools, where it can use philosophy to strengthen faith. This is a very worthy role and intended by God, but its proper use is ensured only when the field of investigation and jurisdiction of the philosophical disciplines is strictly defined and delimited in relation to the science of the faith.

This delimitation, which ensures the right of philosophy and the other lesser sciences to roam autonomously within their own spheres, also guarantees that, given the limitations of natural knowledge, they can never have more than an ancillary role in relation to theology. In contrast, theology provides the only knowledge whose field of investigation is the absolute certainties of the faith. For this reason it is the only discipline that can and must be in a position to protect the human mind from bias and from opposing opinions. If it succeeds in this task it will be truly and genuinely "filled with peace."

Another section of the third treatise clearly states the point that this task is to be accomplished by taking as a model the perfect state of beatifying knowledge. Here the question is asked how everlasting beatitude, understood as a definitive and unalterable knowledge of the truth, is possible if creaturely knowledge can never attain to a full and exhaustive knowledge of the divine essence and can therefore never satisfy the mind's desire to know. Dante answers by explaining that the fulfillment of the mind's natural desire will be ensured by the gratification of the limited capacity for understanding that differs from subject to subject and is adapted to the actual nature of each. He adds that the desire to know more, being unnatural, cannot have a place in a perfect knowledge:

> This is the reason why the saints do not envy one another, but each attains to the goal of his or her desire, a desire proportionate to the goodness of his or her nature. Therefore, since it is not possible for our nature to know some things about God and some other realities, we do not have a natural desire to know them.

The saints, that is, the blessed, "do not envy one another," because they enjoy a knowledge of truth that can be considered complete in terms of the capacity of each. In the third canto of the *Paradiso* Dante would later repeat this idea in the words spoken by Piccarda dei Donati to explain how there is never any envy among the blessed despite their dissimilar places in the hierarchy of Paradise and their dissimilar participations in eternal beatitude. Every blessed soul, she says, is fully content with its state because this is fully proportionate to its capacities, whereas if it were to desire more than what it enjoys, the desire would "be at variance" with the divine will, something impossible for the blessed.

In this explanation Dante clearly adheres to the view of Giles of Rome on the beatific vision. The latter, distancing himself to some extent from Thomism, accepts a differentiated range of perfect knowledge of theological truth: from the absolutely complete knowledge that God alone possesses to that of the angels and blessed, which is always exhaustive but is measured by the limited capacities of each subject, down to the theology or knowledge of God attainable during earthly life. Once again Dante's thought clearly reflects the distinction between "theology in itself" and "our theology." According to this distinction the theological knowledge attainable by human beings "on their journey" is indeed dependent on the limited capacity of the knower, but it must necessarily move toward being univocal and concordant with that of others because it is based on one and the same revealed truth.

The period after 1302 also saw the composition, in Latin, of the *De vulgari eloquentia* (though work on this, too, was interrupted in 1304–05). Here again can be seen, though transposed to the sphere of language and communication, Dante's profound longing for the unification of human knowledge, which is made possible by, among other things, the circulation of ideas through language. In the past, human beings were able to seek this unification through their common possession of a single language that was understandable by all. But because of the sin of pride connected with the building of the tower of Babel, God punished the human race through the division and imperfection of languages and the resultant multiplication of knowledges.

In narrating this biblical incident in the first book of the work Dante displays an especially felicitous original insight when he says that after this punishment the same language continued to be spoken only by those who, while divided into distinct groups, followed the same trade. Moreover, the sacred language of Adam, the language of the original unified communication of truth, continued to be spoken only by those who had dissociated themselves from the arrogant work of building the tower and had scorned that ambitious project.

This emphasis on the division and distinction of the disciplinary fields, here said to have been a result of sin but also a sign of the imperfection of human works, is strikingly new. Later in this same short work Dante opines that the language of Adam, which only a few privileged individuals continued to speak, was Hebrew, the language in which revelation was written. If we take this fact into account, it seems once again that the distinct systems of the various particular and imperfect forms of knowledge, now useless for achieving a common and harmonious whole, stand in contrast to the unity and sapiential continuity proper to theology, which is distinct from each of those forms of knowledge and towers over all of them.

Scholars disagree on the point during the period from 1308 to 1317 at which *On Monarchy* was composed. In this well-known political treatise in three books and in Latin, Dante argues, with all the rigor characteristic of a scholastic demonstration, that the concentration of all earthly power in the hands of the emperor is justified both rationally and theologically and reflects a specific intention of divine Providence. The goal of human society is to lead men and women to happiness, and happiness for human beings consists in the activation of their intellectual powers, as Averroes' commentary on *On the Soul* (explicitly cited here) teaches. It is therefore the emperor's task to exercise a higher authority that can ensure order and justice and guarantee all human beings the possibility of reaching a complete understanding of truth.

The assertion of this philosophical theory of earthly happiness is not at variance with the Christian expectation of an otherworldly beatitude, but complements it, just as the scriptural picture of the earthly, temporal paradise complements the picture of the heavenly, eternal paradise. Just as the task of humanity's spiritual guide, the papacy, is to lead to the attainment of beatitude, so the task of making earthly happiness a reality belongs to the empire. The pope has, therefore, no right to interfere in the activity of the emperor; he neither elects nor judges him. The task of both papacy and empire is to show human beings how to reach two different goals along different paths and with different means, which by and large are identifiable either with philosophical tools or with those that are spiritual and theological. Here again, then, it is obvious how the distinction between the scope of natural law and that of supernatural law not only bolsters the autonomy of each area and makes it possible to avoid a reciprocal meddling; it also ensures the superiority of the heavenly finality over the earthly and therefore the respect the emperor owes to the pope "because this mortal happiness is in a way ordered to immortal happiness."

It is clear that all these pages of Dante are in a way connected with the theme of relations between the philosophical and theological orders, though with the differences required by different contexts. They show a perceptible influence of Averroist epistemology, which recommended that in dealing with natural and theological demonstrations there be a separation of spheres, of methodologies, and even of the necessary scope of the conclusions reachable. It was not an accident that in the first decades of the fourteenth century *On Monarchy* was accused of crypto-Averroism. Finally, during the controversies over the neo-Averroist political theses of Marsilius of Padua and John of Jandun the work was condemned in 1328 by papal legate Bertrand del Poggetto, nephew of Pope John XXII.

And yet Dante had often explicitly distanced himself from the radical theses the Averroists defended against the truth of the faith, in particular the doctrine of the single intellect and the denial of individual immortality. This last, as Dante puts it in the second treatise of the *Convivio*, "is the stupidest, wickedest, and most damnable of all dreadful errors." No less clear and recurrent in his thinking is his condemnation, in harmony with repeated assertions of Albert the Great (but also with explicit statements of Siger of Brabant and Boethius of Dacia), of natural reason when it presumptuously claims necessary cognitive results in areas outside its competence. The strength of his conviction is shown in the *Commedia* by the tragic end of Ulysses' last voyage in canto 26 of the *Inferno*. It is shown again, in canto 19, by the eternal damnation of those popes and simoniacal clerics who inverted the right order established by God by maintaining that the spiritual power could influence, and have a right to correct, the exercise of jurisdiction dealing with secular matters.

According to the most recent proposals for dating the composition of the *Commedia*, this took from 1309, for the first draft of the *Inferno*, to 1318 for the *Paradiso* (the poet died at Ravenna in 1321). It was this period that saw the fullest development of Dante's conception of the progressive human advance toward the truth—first philosophical, then theological—and toward the celestial goal of creaturely union with the divine. In light of the preceding analysis of his texts we can grasp Dante's real intention in his celebration, in the fourth heaven of the *Paradiso*, of harmony among the theologians (the "harmonious saints" of canto 13). His point is that on earth this harmony ought to be sought as a common goal of scholars in the constant trend of their theological science toward uniformity and the agreement of opinions that marks those who know the truth. This task remains, even though the fulfillment of this scholarly aspiration can come only in heaven, when all the different schools and currents of thought will definitively give way to a single vision.

It is now clear, however, that the juxtaposition (not the contradiction) of many truths, each distinct from the others and each regarded as necessary and irrefutable in its specific context, is typical of the spheres of inquiry proper to philosophy and the natural sciences. In the first "glorious wheel" of the heaven of the Sun (in canto 10) Dante makes this point in a noteworthy manner by introducing "the everlasting light of Siger / who, while lecturing on Straw Street, / reduced resentful truths to syllogisms." The immortal soul of Siger of Brabant is accepted into the circle of saintly theologians because by his teaching he bore witness to the autonomy of the research proper to each discipline within the sphere proper to it, while respecting the superiority of the knowledge gained by faith and showing how the different and possibly opposing conclusions of the various sciences do not contradict one another but are simply distinct. During his lectures on philosophy in the Parisian street where the Faculty of Arts came into being, Siger used the syllogistic method to lead the discourses of the different disciplines to different necessary conclusions, each of them valid within its specific disciplinary sphere. The truths were "resentful" of one another because they were not all measurable by the same standard. They were also "resentful" because none of them was the vehicle of a complete knowledge, such as that enjoyed by the "saints [who] do not envy one another" (as we saw in the *Convivio*).

In the thirteenth canto Thomas Aquinas, holding the hand of the very Siger whom he had so opposed during his lifetime, confirms Dante's theory of truth to which the rest of the cantos on the heaven of the Sun are devoted. Dante had asked Thomas (in canto 10) how he could speak of Solomon, king and prophet (who is one of the blessed in the first "wheel"), as the wisest of mortal beings, since this seems to contradict the common theological view that this title belongs rather to Adam or, in any case, to Jesus Christ. Thomas now answers that Solomon was the wisest only relatively and not absolutely, just as any fullness of truth among mortals differs according to the discipline in question. "Take what I say with that distinction": my words, says Thomas, are to be understood in light of the distinction among the various spheres of knowledge available to created reason ("with . . . distinction made between cases," that is, among the different kinds of study). Only on the basis of this distinction can Thomas' words stand and not contradict other truths.

So then, between the natural science of Siger and the theological peace of the blessed, and distinct from both, stands earthly theology or the knowledge of truth that is based on faith and constantly progresses thanks to the support of philosophical arguments. This is the knowledge typical of human beings during their time as pilgrims. Dante's reputation as a theologian was openly fostered by many of the early commentators on his work, down to Boccaccio who says in his *Genealogies of the Pagan Gods*: "Who is ever so unwitting that though seeing our Dante often use an admirable demonstrative prowess in solving the most tangled problems of sacred theology, he does not perceive that he," and this precisely as a poet, "was not only a philosopher but also an outstanding theologian?"

At the beginning of the fourteenth century the title "theologian" was still equivalent to "master of theology." Speaking in the first person, Dante says that he can bestow this title on himself at the end of his ascent among the blessed, as a result of the examination to which St. Peter subjects him on the nature of the three theological virtues of faith, hope, and charity (cantos 24-26 of the *Paradiso*). The description of the examinee's behavior contains realistic references to the training of a bachelor, who, in tackling the question posed by the master, needs to use the tools of reason and supply a "proof" (that is, an example based on authority) but not the "decision" (the final solution, which is left to the master alone).

Especially interesting is Dante's answer to the question about faith that is raised by the very recourse to the highest authority on this subject, that of Paul (Heb 11:1): "Faith is the substance / of things hoped for / and the argument of those not seen, / and this seems to me to be its essence." Peter asks him to explain why faith is first a substance and then an argument. Dante explains first that faith alone enables human beings during their earthly lives to grasp the "existence" of the "profound realities" that are manifested to the blessed; it is therefore accurate to say that faith brings a substantial knowledge of these realities. Next Dante explains the role and procedure of speculative theology and adds that each statement of the faith is an "argument" inasmuch as one may argue deductively from the faith as from a first principle.

Peter approves this explanation and comments that if everything learned from earthly teachers were so well understood there would be no room for discussions and confusing sophistries. Then, after this successful conclusion of the examination, as after a theological commencement, the bachelor is transformed into a theologian. And at the beginning of the next canto he himself celebrates his own advancement, his ability now to explain in his verses the most complex and daring themes of the theology of the schools. He proclaims his own crowning: after receiving the crown of a poet, he now receives that of a theologian, an event that takes place symbolically at the font where he had been baptized, that is, on the solid foundation of the true faith. "With a different voice and with a differently colored hair / I shall return as a poet, and at the font / of my baptism I shall take the crown."

Given this recognition of his new competence, the heavenly pilgrim can then begin his own ascent toward the final phase of the journey that leads the human soul from "our theology" to beatitude. In the final canto of the poem, with its ultimate supreme theophany, this beatitude is anticipated through grace in one still living.

II. Reformers, Innovators, and Dissenters: New Paths in the Systematization of Theology

1. Roger Bacon

We have observed how the decades bridging the two centuries saw the development of crisscrossing debates that brought out the peculiarities of and differences among the main scientific, philosophical, and theological systems produced at the universities. But during this same period other writers were active who distanced themselves not only from particular views prevalent on the cultural stage of the Latin West, but also and above all from the speculative foundations on which those views were based. These men attempted to follow unexplored paths and develop new methodologies for the intellectual pursuit of truth.

A first witness to the search for new prospects on which to base and restore health to theological reflection that had grown dull in the controversies of the schools was a man who belonged, chronologically, entirely to the thirteenth century. This was Roger Bacon, an English Franciscan, born in 1213, who entered the Order at a mature age. He had studied and taught in the Arts Faculty of Paris and had already produced writings of a mainly didactic and scientific kind (commentaries, in the form of questions, on the natural works of Aristotle, and treatises on the trivium). After converting to Franciscanism he enthusiastically joined the movement of the Spirituals, to whose prophetic perspectives he added the announcement of a complete reform of Christian learning in all its parts: scientific, philosophical, and theological. He appointed himself the prophet and promoter of this reform, which was to become, in his intention, the means willed by Providence for leading the whole of Christendom to ethical and spiritual perfection and to the position of universal leader of the world through the conversion of all unbelievers.

Bacon was notified by the authorities of the Order that he was suspected of colluding with the extreme Joachimites, but then for a short period was heartened by the support of Pope Clement IV, who urged him to compose his *Principal Writing* to give substance to his project. But he managed to produce only incomplete sections, which were in practice successive drafts of a program for the unification of the various human sciences under the control and management of theology. These were titled, respectively, *Major Work*, *Lesser Work*, and *Third Work*. During the following years he composed a *Compendium of the Study of Philosophy* and numerous treatises on particular scientific themes in mathematics, physics, optics, and medicine, which were meant to find their place in the unified *Major Work*, now described as *Principal Work*. He became again the object of suspicion within the Order because of his sympathy for astrology, which was an object of the decrees of 1277. But in 1290, two years before his death in 1292, he wrote his *Compendium of the Study of Theology* in which he set forth, one last time, the ideals of his reform.

The events of Bacon's life make clear how disappointed and disgusted he was by the theological literature of the day and by the rigid and factious kind of theological systematizing that characterized it. A simple comparison between what Christian theological knowledge ought to be and what it actually was inspired him to draw up a famous list of the seven capital sins of scholastic theology. When read in terms of the opposite virtues, the critique makes clear the new model of learning he was seeking in his desire for the reform of theology and the restoration of a complete theological science.

The first sin, which is the most serious and the source of the others, is the invasion of theological treatises by the philosophical method peculiar to the "artists"; this reduces the approach to vital problems such as the knowableness of the divine and the redemption of humanity to a meager analysis based on the rules of the trivium. At the same time it imposes on theology an unjustified expansion of interest in and discussions about subjects more suitable for the exercise of natural reason, such as being, matter, and the human composite.

The second sin is ignorance of those real sciences that would be useful in explaining the Scriptures. University fashion had required that everyone attend courses in logic and grammar, metaphysics and psychology, and had sacrificed studies that are much more important and truly essential for the salvation of both the soul and the body. Such are, for example, the study of the Hebrew and Greek languages, of rhetoric, mathematics, and physics, of alchemy, and, above all, the pursuit of a real knowledge of nature based on experience.

The third sin is ignorance in the sense of one-sided and limited knowledge, such as is to be seen in the boastful presumptuousness of the masters of the schools and the exaggerated admiration of those around them. This last reaches extremes of stupidity and "cult of persons" in some exaggerated cases of factionalism; two such cases are, in Bacon's scandalized judgment, the attitude of the Franciscans toward Alexander of Hales and, above all, that of the Dominicans toward Albert the Great.

The fourth sin is that lecturers have replaced the divine Scriptures with the books of the *Sentences*; in practice, lecturing on the Scriptures has been limited to the teaching activity of the bachelors and no one any longer has an adequate knowledge of the Bible. The fifth sin is the corruption of the sacred text, which no one has the philological skills required for correcting. The sixth sin is that, due to ignorance both of biblical languages and of the real properties of the realities of which the Bible speaks, no one is able to produce a valid exegesis, with a proper distinction between the literal and spiritual senses. The seventh sin, finally, is the lack of an authentic, effective, and persuasive eloquence, which has been shamefully replaced by the verbosity of university sermons overflowing with logical divisions and terminological distinctions.

Added to the ills of theology are philosophical errors, often made worse by distortions and mistakes arising from the incompetence or dishonesty of the commentators and translators, both Arabic and Latin. To begin with, it is a mistake to have based speculative knowledge on the process of abstraction. The latter can, indeed, be a useful instrument in the development of scientific knowledge, but only if one bears in mind that abstraction involves a functional distancing of the mind from the immediacy of the individual truth, communicated through the senses, of any known object. Another philosophical error is the unjustified assumption that there is a universal matter or universal form, or rather that there are universals at all. For created being always shows itself, in its every manifestation, as the center of a unique, unrepeatable, and atomistic efficacious activity.

In Bacon's view this criticism of the twofold learning, theological and philosophical, of which his contemporaries boasted manifested the ultimate effects of Adam's original sin of pride, for the root of that sin was the bold assumption that human beings could know the truth with the same absolute wisdom with which God knows it. That fundamental error gave rise in turn to the three principal and general "stumbling blocks on the path of wisdom" or obstacles to the human acquisition of truth. These are: the false principle of appeal to "authorities," which serves only to hide one's own ignorance; the comfortable role played by "tradition," which relieves the individual of the responsibility to engage in personal research; and the cowardly acceptance of "common opinion," that is, any idea concocted by a majority of individuals but accepted as though it were proved true by the experience of all.

In summary, every element in this "destructive part" of Bacon's program leads to a plea for a revision of the epistemological perspective at work in the

whole of human knowledge. This new approach will eliminate the presumptuousness and abstractness of the perspective attributed (erroneously in Bacon's
view) to Aristotle by so many Arabic and Latin interpreters. This perspective
was based, according to Bacon, on a futile structure of insubstantial systems of
conceptual deductions lacking any correspondence to reality. The authentic
Aristotelean epistemology was the one brought out and defended by Grosseteste,
according to whose teaching true knowledge is always and only experimental
knowledge, based on direct observation of and an immediate application of
reason to the data of experience. Only this kind of knowledge really ensures the
immediate effectiveness of the mental representation and the continuous possibility of verifying or falsifying what it tells us; these are essential requirements
for being correctly informed about the manner of being of the realities in question and for exercising an effective control over them.

Experimental knowledge is the primary form of knowledge, and its methodological foundations must be applied to all the other lesser sciences if the
latter are to be reliable. Experimental knowledge possesses, in fact, three fundamental prerogatives that ensure its superiority over a deductive and abstract
methodology. It is intuitive and therefore passes immediately to its conclusions,
moving from experience to necessary affirmations (or "illustrious conclusions"),
the reliability of which arises from the possibility of always submitting them to
direct verification. Then, due to that capacity, it is able to determine and establish
the first principles (or "excellent truths") in force in any other kind and degree
of a discipline. Finally, since experimental knowledge contains within itself the
foundation of its own verifiability, it is completely resistant to any interference
and judgment by any other science or form of knowledge.

This reversal of epistemological perspective evidently links Bacon to the
scientifico-experimental tradition of the Oxford Franciscans. Among the principal champions of this tradition, in addition to the revered Grosseteste, Bacon
mentions another of his own teachers, Peter of Maricourt, author of a *Letter on
the Lodestone* and a perfect exemplar of a philosopher and "master of experiments." He was capable at once of thorough empirical observation and its direct
translation into technical skill.

There is a well-known passage in Bacon's *Letter on Still Unknown Works of
Human Ingenuity* in which he writes in a manner worthy of Leonardo da Vinci
that, thanks to the scientific approach he has described, human beings will be able
to provide themselves with highly useful tools for mastering nature. Some examples: wagons that run along without horses to pull them, ships that plow the
seas without rowers or sails, machines for lifting weights, machines for descending
into the depths of abysses, and so on. Indeed, to Bacon's mind this practical usefulness of the effects of knowledge is the clearest and surest sign of its reliability
and, at the same time, the only purpose that justifies the efforts needed to acquire
it. For if the knowledge is true, that is, based on the principles of experimental
science, it contributes to the improvement of humanity's living conditions, not

only in the present life by making it healthier and wealthier, but also and above all by leading human society, "the republic of believers," to the ultimate goal to which all naturally tend: namely, the attainment of eternal salvation.

It is evident that the effective accomplishment of this soteriological task of knowledge depends on the possibility that human beings can repair the breach caused by Adam's pride and successfully and really participate in the divine knowledge. In Bacon's thinking, all this means seeking a comprehensive relocation of human intellectual activity within the boundaries set by the experimental method, which is "the gate and key to all the sciences." Such is the overall meaning of the reform that is set forth in the *Major Work* and is aimed at providing the human race with a concrete and definitive "wisdom" that includes all the particular forms of scientific knowledge available to the created mind.

In Aristotelean terms this ability of the most general science to embrace the particular sciences is called the "subordination" or "subalternation" of the lower forms of knowledge to the higher. But it is clear that Bacon has inverted these relationships as compared with the dominant theories of science in his day, since the discipline that supports all the others is not, in his view, the most abstract, with the most universal object, but rather the most direct and concrete. The latter, due to its authentically experimental nature, is able to discover the properties of things and make these known to the other sciences as something new and outside their competencies; in all of them this basic science acts as a universal regulatory authority. The basic "experimental science," then, is both a field of knowledge and a method for all the other forms of knowledge; it is present in the procedures of the latter in order to govern them formally at the very moment in which it produces them and separates them from itself.

No one will be greatly surprised, then, to find that the finishing touch in Bacon's presentation of his fundamental science is its direct identification with mathematics, the most general of the sciences. It puts the intellect in direct contact with the intrinsic manner of being of things, bringing this to light by placing them in reciprocal relationships. Founded on mathematics and grafted onto it are the subsequent developments of the disciplines of knowledge with their graduated qualitative fixing of the fundamentally quantitative nature of the being of things.

The first of these disciplines is optics or perspective, which, as Grosseteste had taught, has for its object the nature and transmission of light and thus studies the most universal and structuring prerequisite of the physical world. Next come astronomy and "good" magic (that is, distinct from the magico-demoniacal, deterministic, and superstitious arts); Bacon defends these for their ability to plumb the nature of reality beyond its immediate visible manifestation. They also help human beings to understand the hidden secrets of nature's possibilities and read the signs of the times, thus preparing themselves for the coming of the Antichrist. Finally, at the top of this ladder of philosophical disciplines there is ethics, which makes its own the very goal of human life, which is happiness.

But, according to Bacon, it is precisely in its loftiest area of study, namely moral science, that human reason savors the awareness of its limitations and its inability to link humanity once more with the fullness of divine knowledge. Thus the final result of the restoration of natural science is to have learned once and for all the lesson of the impossibility, ever since Adam's sin, of understanding and attaining true happiness apart from God. The human thirst for knowledge is hereby directly linked to that which, in the present human condition, is the only source capable of definitively satisfying that thirst: the revelation in which God has made himself the object of a new knowledge he makes available to the human race. The cognitive ascent of experimental knowledge thus finds in Christian theology its natural point of arrival that justifies the entire journey made, for Christian theology as such brings teaching that is definitively satisfying not only for believers but for the whole human race.

But theology is not simply the highest discipline in Bacon's hierarchy of the sciences. Since its certainties are guaranteed by divine truthfulness, theology goes on to extend its jurisdiction over that entire hierarchic structure and identifies itself with it in all its complexity. The knowledge God has of truth is obviously the fruit of the most intuitive and direct experimental grasp of his own mode of being and that of all things, natural and supernatural. By way of revelation theology is rooted in that divine knowledge and is therefore the truest and most complete form of experimental knowledge possible for human beings.

This last passage merits further discussion. If someone, Bacon says, has heard that a magnet attracts iron, and wants to gain understanding of this phenomenon through an experiment that will show its reality, he must first of all have faith in the testimony that brought the phenomenon within his view. Faith is therefore a form of knowledge that substitutes for experimental knowledge when the latter is impossible, but it also prepares for experimental knowledge because it enables the knower to anticipate the truth at issue and reproduce the conditions that make its acquisition possible. Thus Bacon, too, by way of Grosseteste, harks back to the theological model of Anselm of Aosta, who was the first to think of faith as a very lofty and direct experience of the truth, an experience that substitutes for sensible experience and makes up for the latter's deficiencies. In fact, as Grosseteste realized, faith brings a full cognitive illumination through which God introduces directly into the soul of the believer an assent—immediate and intuitive, that is, experimental in the strict sense—to the highest and most incomprehensible supernatural truths.

Theology, which is both the point of arrival and the point of departure of the entire Baconian reform, is the fullest and most perfect form of experimental science. And indeed it shares the three prerogatives of the latter: it is genuinely intuitive and immediately connects its premises with its conclusions; it passes judgment on the truthfulness of the other particular sciences; and it is utterly superior and autonomous in relation to them. Again the distinction between speculative knowledge and practical knowledge is transcended in theology, because all the sciences, speculative and practical, are subalternated to it. But finally theology, in its purest essence, is an authentically mathematical knowledge, because it is the non-abstractive but immediate and intuitive systematic knowledge of the order God has established as the existential system that governs all of reality "by measure and number and weight" (Wis 11:21).

It is therefore correct to give theology the name "wisdom," which allows one to grasp both its theological nature (inasmuch as it is revealed) and its mathematical nature (inasmuch as it is precise and completely informative about its object). The name "wisdom" also refers more clearly to theology's nature as comprehensive of all knowledge.

Humanity's journey toward wisdom has been long and tortuous throughout the course of history and has been marked by an alternation of, on the one hand, the conquests made by human reason and, on the other, unmerited revelatory communications from God. After Adam's sin the wisdom our first parents presumed they could acquire by their own efforts was in fact communicated by God, in a prophetic but perfect form, solely to the patriarchs, whose task it was to begin the journey of humanity back from dispersal to religious unity. Those men lived such long lives because they had to examine this knowledge and translate it into scientific terms with the aid of prolonged experience and a constant exercise of reason.

Prompted by suggestions from Hermeticism, Bacon then postulated that initiates secretly passed on this truth, which was, however, gradually obscured and corrupted by the sins of mortals; beginning with Moses its preservation was entrusted to the books of Scripture. On the other hand, after a lengthy intellectual deterioration of the human race wisdom began again to emerge publicly, but in an irremediably impoverished and corrupted form, in the teaching of the philosophers. That group included Nimrod (the first of the atheistic philosophers, whose most recent disciples were the Parisian "Artists" of the thirteenth century), followed by Zoroaster, Prometheus, Atlas, and Hermes, all of whom neglected this wisdom and forgot its divine origin. God's illuminating inspiration revealed it anew to Solomon; the Greek philosophers derived it from him but again perverted and corrupted it. These philosophers included Thales, Pythagoras, Socrates, and Plato, and their successors, among whom Aristotle stood out because of his abilities. His thought was more recently taken over by the Arabs, down to Avicenna who restored his teaching and to Michael Scotus who made it possible finally for the Latins to exalt it in their turn.

Only due to the final and definitive revelation, that of Christianity, was humanity able once again to participate in the perfect wisdom only prefigured by those that preceded. In order for this wisdom to be satisfactorily understood, communicated to all, and honored by purity of life it had to be purified from new, recent debasement through the errors and one-sidedness of philosophy. Yet whatever of good human reason has been able to acquire down the centuries will be placed in the service of this wisdom in order to help human beings toward a final participation in happiness.

If it be true that God's wisdom, the key to the cosmic order, is contained in Sacred Scripture, then everything that humanity can possibly know is contained therein. Therefore the new reformed theology of Bacon must begin with a correct understanding of the truth in the Scriptures. Reviving an ancient Stoic image, Bacon likens the exegesis of the scriptural text to the palm of an open hand while the wisdom that is born of the exegesis and developed from it clasps the revealed data in a complete and organized understanding as in a fist. Because the lesser sciences must offer their services, philology, the philosophical sciences, and canon law will provide tools that fill out theological knowledge, being useful for clarifying and giving rational form to the experience of faith guaranteed by sacred reading. Absolutely indispensable, however, will be those skills in particular, the lack of which was mentioned earlier in describing the three defects of contemporary theology: the understanding of the historical and juridical context of the narrative, the scope of the discipline, the specific kind of narrative found in the different sacred books, and, above all else, knowledge of the Hebrew and Greek languages.

When theological wisdom is thus developed on the basis of scriptural exegesis the imperfections of both theoretical and practical philosophy are eliminated by divine illumination. This illumination communicates all the information useful to human beings in dealing with, on the one hand, the being of the world and of God himself and, on the other, new principles of moral law. This cognitive completion takes seven steps that are marked by a symmetry that is the reverse of that shown in the seven sins of scholastic theology. The steps lead from Bacon's experimentalism to mystical asceticism (a process not without some interesting parallels in Bonaventure's "journey").

The stages: from an illumination received according to the procedures of science alone to an illumination in keeping with the virtues, which by enlightening the soul grant it access to further truths which it was previously unable to grasp. Then to an illumination in keeping with the gifts of the Holy Spirit, then one in keeping with the beatitudes, then with the spiritual senses, then with the spiritual fruits (peace in particular). Finally, on the seventh and last level there is an illumination enabling the attainment of the states of ecstatic knowledge (or the raptures).

And if it be true that a young and as yet uninstructed friar can be superior ascetically to so many skilled theologians, this is simply a further proof of the useless abstractionism that infects the university teaching of the time. Cognitive superiority finds its best expression not in lectures or sermons, nor even in outbursts of fervor in the spreading of pauperism (from which Bacon kept his proper distance), but only in authentic eschatological prophetism. It is also an effect not of the state of cognitive perfection proper to the wise but of the very simplicity of the truth that is expressed and communicated by it.

2. Raymond Lull

Raymond Lull, a Spanish writer whose work had no direct connection with the academic profession, produced yet another plan for a new systematization of Christian knowledge that would be an alternative to the inflated and discordant theoretical projects of the university world. Lull was born in 1232 on Majorca, which had been liberated from Islamic control only three years earlier; he died in 1316, perhaps in Tunis. His life was a long one and constantly driven by the desire to complete his own speculative religious program, the goal of which was the peaceful imposition of Christianity on all the other religious confessions.

In the genesis of the prophetico-sapiential ideal, which, as in the case of Bacon, inspired Lull's planned reform of the full range of human knowledge, a decisive factor was his birth into a frontier Christianity that had for centuries been caught up in a radical historical clash with the culture and religious spirit of Islam. In fact, his search for a new kind of theological discipline was in keeping with his intention of finding in the infidels' use of reason the conditions for their conversion and acceptance of the true Christian revelation. In this project he would bring to completion the interreligious dialogue planned in the school of Anselm of Aosta and developed by Peter Abelard several centuries before Arabic civilization revealed its own rich scientific and speculative patrimony to the West. Now that the Christian world had learned from the philosophy of the Muslims and had improved its own argumentational skills, precisely by deriving new tools and new contents from that philosophy, the time was ripe for completing Lull's plan by using effective persuasion to urge the Muslims to recognize the rational foundations and superiority of Christian revelation over all others.

Such an inspired sense of a personal mission as scholar and preacher could not but be motivated by the certainty that it was responding to a specific divine mandate. Lull regarded himself as the depository of this mandate. He was convinced that his duty was to persuade learned individuals, governors, pastors, and peoples of the value of the science he had worked out as a means of a universal conversion to truth and goodness. His hearers were to be first all the members of the Christian community and subsequently the entire human race. In autobiographical passages of his works he speaks of the radical nature of a vocation originating in a vision of Christ crucified that drove him, a man already thirty years old, to devote himself wholly to a way of life inspired by the true faith. This meant abandoning a comfortable aristocratic life, his wife and two children, and, above all, a past as a courtly poet, one who sang of an adulterous love for an idealized lady. In his first important theological work, the *Book of Contemplation*, which he wrote in Catalan, he gives a passionate account of the mystical inspiration that underlies the planning of his new commitment.

During a religious retreat on Mount Randa in Majorca, Lull had another mystical vision "that enabled him to see in an instant the order and form needed for writing books in response to the errors of the unbelievers." In his autobiography, *A Contemporary Life*, he attributes to that vision the initial insight into a new logical discipline that applies to all fields of knowledge. From that point on, this intuition became the basis of and supporting justification of his entire speculative project. This he called the "Great Art" that reveals the real structure of the created world and enters deeply into the truths of the faith in order to show the rational necessities underlying those truths.

These visionary experiences do not, however, suggest a fanciful mind or an irrational spirit of prophecy. On the contrary: according to Lull's own story they appear to be informative pointers for the development of those intellectual faculties that are in charge of the theoretical working out of projects. This is because they make the individual who is given them the recipient of a true and proper illumination, rich in cognitive content and understood in light of the Augustinian-Avicennean gnoseology adopted by the Franciscan university masters.

This gnoseological postulate is the foundation of Lull's methodological insights and justified his disciples' praise of him as "Inspired Doctor" and "Enlightened Doctor"; it is also fundamental for a full understanding of the very invention of the "Great Art." For Lull, true knowledge always results from a circular movement of truth, a movement partly coming from below, from the human rational powers, and partly from above, from the unifying effects of the divine illumination. This circular movement of truth within the human soul urges the acceptance of a unified and unremitting stream of life within the act of knowledge. It also calls on the learned to decode and formalize the operations of this cognitive stream of life that energizes and sustains all possible human perceptions of truth, from the work of the senses up to the illumination. The discovery, deciphering, and doctrinal development of the art result, therefore, from an unalterable necessity of the intellect as such, which calls "imperiously" (Lull's word) for the theoretical elaboration of a general science of all the movements of human thought.

Logic, gnoseology, metaphysics, and theology thus come together in this plan for establishing the Art as a general science that contains in itself and coordinates all the particular elements of the lesser sciences. In this perspective we see the justification of Lull's stubborn, almost obsessive condemnation of Averroism, which he regarded as responsible for the fragmentation of human knowledge into inflexible and noncommunicating compartments. Conversely, his entire intellectual activity over the course of a lifelong technical maturation was inspired by the desire to give concrete form, doctrinal support, and the possibility of communication and diffusion to a unified and self-contained wisdom, in accordance with the approach conceived after the vision on Mount Randa.

The composition known as the "Great or General Art" was the subject of continual revisions and formal alterations. It went through several phases and attempts that were reflected in a large number of works either in Catalan or in Latin (written in Latin or translated into it) and in very varied literary genres. The latter included strictly philosophical, theological, and scientific works, others of an encyclopedic, pedagogical, or polemical kind, and still others that were literary, hortatory, and poetical. But taken as whole this complex mass of documents reflects, even if with obvious differences of tone, color, and intensity, the same unwavering search for a single, accurate instrument with which to defend the faith. This instrument is thought of as a formal body of knowledge of an axiomatic-deductive kind and essentially rational in nature, a fact confirmed by the really very limited number of scriptural citations.

Foundational for the Art is the search for fundamental and self-evident principles common to all the sciences and all the forms of human knowledge. These principles have to be so absolute that they cannot fail to be true, so that in the final analysis they will be identifiable with the most arcane attributes of God. On this basis symbologies, consisting mostly of letters or other graphic symbols (these constitute the "alphabet" of the Art) and established according to general rules make it possible to discover connections and compatibilities or incompatibilities among the conclusions from the principles.

A complicated variety of schemas, grills, columns, and concentric and revolving diagrams, at the center of which God is always placed, helps readers, by means of various combinations and correspondences, to follow the outward movement of the divine attributes from the center to the circumference, down to the description of the creaturely properties defined by those attributes and differentiated into a variegated multiplicity of particular effects. The mental processes that come into play during this creative descent of reality can then be applied, according to the combinations allowed by the "tables," to specific problems in the various areas of scientific investigation. The basic conceptual schema, or "key," must therefore be capable of an inexhaustible number of applications across the entire panorama of human knowledge.

These combinatory instruments, so complicated in application and use but utterly simple in the general idea from which they spring, reveal with stirring effectiveness the deepest harmony within reality. This is in fact the direct effect of replacing the abstract and formal logic of Aristotle and Boethius with a chain of ideas and items of knowledge that is actuated by the combinations possible among the corresponding symbols in the various tables. The representational effectiveness of such combinations can be grasped by any educated mind, independently of the language, convictions, and subjective attitudes that may condition the mental processes of the individual. Therefore the name *Art of Finding Truth* sufficiently describes the eminently heuristic function of this logical method, the purpose of which is to discover in every true act of human knowledge one of the manifestations of an absolute truth that in itself is one but is also dynamic and varied in its manifestations.

A first phase of Lull's activity of study and writing followed upon the vision on Mount Randa (datable to 1274) and the foundation of the monastery of Miramar on Majorca (1276), which he envisaged as a center for the training of the followers who accepted the new missionary ideal. During that period he worked out the first version of his plan in his *Concise Art of Finding Truth*, in which the dominant schema is quaternary. He then went to Montpellier and Paris to study the arts (as a married man he was unable to follow lectures on theology). On consecutive occasions he tried in vain to convert the pope and the king of France to his enterprise.

The eighties saw the composition of his *Blanquerna* or *Book of Evast and Blanquerna, His Son*, a philosophical romance that introduces the uses of the Art into an ambitious plan for the reform of both civil and ecclesiastical society, thereby leading to the rational, linguistic, and religious unification of human-kind. He then composed his *Felix* or *Book of Wonders* in which he describes the ascent to God through contemplation of the world's marvels. Within the *Felix* is the *Book of the Lover and the Beloved*, one of Lull's most inspired poetico-mystical compositions. In it the author uses the language and situations of courtly love (while transposing them in a theological key) in order to celebrate allegori-cally the love that the mind—the Lover or Friend—feels for the divine object, the Beloved. This love is seemingly mad and incomprehensible to human think-ing; it possesses the lover completely, taking control of him and quashing his earthly life, but only in order to raise him up to a new and endless life in an eternal union with the object of his desire.

In 1290, after returning to Montpellier, Lull began a second phase with the revision of his work on the *Art*. The complexity of the first version suggested to him a more simplified form of the *Art of Finding Truth* in which the quaternary system is definitively replaced by a triadic system based on the dialectic of love (lover, beloved, love) and yielding a perfect paradigm of the trinitarian mystery. The system is structured according to a list of nine divine axioms or "imperial ideas" that explain the perfections of God by arranging them in three concentric circles from which the relationships between particular beings are sorted out in a series of descending conceptual associations and distinctions.

Just as God's essence interacts eternally with itself within the unity of the persons, so everything that acts in the universe reflects this same triadic character and bears within itself and in its activity the recognizable traces of the divinity. The knowledge, both philosophical and theological, of this organization of real-ity leads individuals through a cognitive ascent involving their whole being and all their desires to a personal union with God. This union is a definitive fusion of the lover and the beloved in a love that takes the form for creatures of an unending circular movement between the act of contemplation and the act of prayer.

Lull preferred the Franciscan Order to the Dominican, and he began dealings with the former with a view to spreading the study of his system into the schools of the Minors. He did not obtain immediate results, but he did come in contact with evangelical pauperism and the longing for universal renewal; the latter began to filter into his own thinking and give an apocalyptic tonality to his desire for a universal conversion. He also came to value some fundamental speculative theses of the Franciscans because these seemed to him very profitable for his own general view of the created order as a great system of truths that were in communication among themselves and could be unified in a single cognitive act. These theses included exemplarism, universal hylomorphism, the original actuation of prime matter and the seminal reasons, the gradation and multiplicity of forms, and the primacy of the will over the intellect. He moved about continually from his base in Montpellier in search of approval and agreement until he launched his first missionary venture in Tunis, where he was in danger of being executed but was then expelled and sent to Naples.

Here he proposed a new development of his method in his *General Table*. In 1295, in a poetical lament or *Desconhort*, he mourned the apparent failure of his program, the impossibility of finding readers disposed to follow it, and the scorn even of the learned, who did not understand it. In reaction he experienced a new creative impulse that led to the composition of the *Tree of Knowledge*, an encyclopedic presentation of the Art. Here the combinatory method is concretized in the visual image of the tree of knowledge branching out into the various faculties and cognitive disciplines, from knowledge of the material elements to physics, anthropology, ethics, politics, astronomy, angelology, and the highest levels of theology. The encyclopedic approach here seems the symmetrical converse and complement to the methodological approach that in the works devoted to the Art supports the possibility of unifying the whole of scientific knowledge. In fact, underlying both approaches is the same symmetrical and hierarchized vision of a universe governed by the participation of every particular reality in the one divine principle.

After further fruitless efforts to obtain the support of Boniface VIII, Lull returned to France, where in 1303 he composed still newer, but not definitive versions of his project: the *New Logic* and the *Short Logic*. In the latter he explained his idea of demonstration through similarity (*per aequiparantiam*), which was to replace demonstration from cause to effect and from effect to cause. Finally, in 1305 he produced his final compilation of the Art, in two versions: one, *The Final* or *Great General Art*, fuller and more structured, the other, *The Short Art*, more summary and preparatory for the first.

Lull's alphabet—that is, the basic grid or key that makes it possible "to form the diagrams and combine the principles and rules in order to search for truth"— is here attached to new symbols, running from the letter B to the letter K. To these, as to variable algebras, correspond six groups of terms that express as many manifestations of truth and can always be combined into three triads.

The first of these groups contains the absolute principles or axioms that describe the being of God according to features known to every educated mind and every religion (goodness, greatness, eternity; power, wisdom, will; virtue, truth, glory). Then there are the six relational principles, which describe the divine being in its relationship with itself and with things (difference, agreement, contrariety; beginning, middle, end; greater, equal, lesser). Next come the questions about essence and its circumstances or accidents, which lead to the key problems that contain all possible questions about reality (whether, what, of what; why, how much, of what kind; when, where, how). Then come all the subjects that can be treated on the basis of the possible combinations contained in the Art, and therefore the corresponding disciplinary divisions (God, angel, heaven; human being, imaginative, sensitive; vegetative, elemental, instrumental). Finally, there are the virtues (justice, prudence, fortitude; temperance, faith, hope; charity, patience, piety) and the contrary vices (greed, gluttony, lust; pride, sloth, envy; anger, lying, inconstancy).

Four diagrams corresponding to as many geometrical entities (line, triangle, pentagon, and circle) provide the basic structures of the syntax. Both on the conceptual level and with the support of the visual element, and by way of applications, multiplications, removals, and mixtures of these content-forms, this syntax allows the user to develop and determine the possible combinations of the data introduced into the system. Thus the ascent from sense experience to conceptual and philosophical knowledge can always be further purified to the point of transcending itself and reaching a level of purely intuitive mental connections. That level will correspond to the mystical level on which the divine names no longer represent the modes of God's being in relation to things, but represent solely, and effectively, God himself.

A new journey to Africa in 1307 and an umpteenth attempt to evangelize the Muslims, along with the composition of *A Debate Between Raymond and Hamar, a Saracen*, brought Lull once again a step away from martyrdom. The year 1308 saw the beginning of the final phase of his activity, a period in which he devoted himself to calling the attention of the ecclesiastical world and that of the masters to the importance of his project.

At Pisa in 1308 he finished his *Great Art* and then composed his *Art of God*, in which he summarized all his earlier formulations in order to show his cosmic system to be the great victory of the perfection of being over nonbeing. In Montpellier he wrote his *Book on Winning Back the Holy Land* in order to promote a crusade as the last remaining means of imposing the truth of Christianity on the Muslims; he presented this book to Clement V at Avignon in 1309, but to no avail. In Paris, he had some success when he submitted the *Short Art* for examination by the masters and bachelors of the Faculties of Arts and of Medicine: from the chancellor he obtained a letter of introduction allowing him to take part in the council of Vienne, which was in its preparatory phase. He was indeed convinced that he could persuade the ecumenical meeting to send the echo of his project throughout Christendom. But during this stay in Paris he devoted himself first and foremost to the composition of a large number of polemical works for the struggle against the Averroists.

Among the documents Lull prepared for his hearing at the council were his autobiography (the earlier mentioned *A Contemporary Life*), the *Debate Between a Cleric and Fanciful Raymond* (in which he presents himself as a great, confident utopist or, in other words, a "fanciful" dreamer), and the *Petition of Raymond to the General Council*, in which he places before the council fathers his most urgent requests. These were: the opening of schools for the eastern languages, an alliance of all the Orders of Knights in order to combine their forces in recovering the Holy Land, and a formal condemnation of Averroism. The council heeded his requests only insofar as they fitted in with general and more commonly shared hopes: it arranged for the teaching of the biblical languages in the faculties of theology; it suppressed the Order of the Templars; and, in order to avoid too much debate about the approval of the doctrine on substantial form, it avoided any reference to the Averroists.

Disappointed once again, as so many times previously, Lull went to Messina after the council ended in 1313; there, in a kind of autobiography, *The City of the World*, he lamented his failure to win a hearing at the council. He then went once more to Tunis, where he dedicated his *Art of Counsel* to the sultan, the climate being one of greater readiness for a dialogue about the past. According to some scholars he returned to Majorca; according to others, and more probably, he died in Africa in 1316.

By the time of his death groups of disciples and supporters of his project had already formed in France at Paris and Montpellier and in Spain at Valencia. The ever-closer connection of these groups with the reformist aspirations of the Spiritual Franciscans led to attacks on them and disagreements with them, until inquisitor Nicholas Eymeric (author of a *Dialogue in Answer to Lull*) became suspicious of them and in 1376 obtained a papal bull posthumously condemning Lull's teachings. In 1390 John Gerson, chancellor of the University of Paris, forbade the teaching of Lull's ideas in the Faculty of Theology. Yet Lull's *Art* continued to spread in the fourteenth and fifteenth centuries, while its symbolic components and its aspiration to produce a complete cosmological vision were several times revised. Finally it enjoyed a new success with the rise of the magical and alchemical outlook of the Renaissance and, in particular, thanks to the interest Giordano Bruno took in its mnemonic and combinatory effectiveness.

3. The School of Cologne and Theodoric of Freiberg

The heritage of Albert the Great's teaching in Cologne and the memory of his educational importance left their mark on the work of some Dominican writers who were active in the German area during the years when the debate over Thomism was most intense (from the condemnation of 1277 to the council of Vienne). The great man's influence could be seen in the emergence of an unmistakable tendency to doctrinal autonomy in regard to the speculative positions dominant within the Order. Initially this independence in relation to those "following the common teaching," that is, the followers of Thomas, found expression in homage to the authority of Albert. The latter's followers emphasized the originality of his thought, its internal consistency, and its agreement with the speculative tradition of the Fathers, especially Augustine and Pseudo-Dionysius.

In a second stage the independence of these thinkers led to the formation of an alternative system of thought. In explicit opposition to Thomist Aristotelianism, this alternative system was marked above all by an emphasis on the more

manifestly Platonic elements in Albert's speculation. It was nourished by a renewed reading of *On Causes* and Proclus, but also by further influences from
Avicenna, Pseudo-Dionysius, and even Eriugena (this last probably mediated
by the monastic literature of the twelfth century).

The first of the thinkers in this new line was Hugh Ripelin (d. 1268), a theologian contemporary with Albert but perhaps younger than he; Hugh was prior
first in Zurich and then in Strasbourg, his native city. He composed a successful
Compendium of Theological Truth that was for a long time attributed to Albert
himself. In this work Hugh takes a systematic approach that was still tied to the
traditional model of Lombard and Hugh of St. Victor since this framework was
regarded as essential for a summary exposition of all the knowledge needed by
a spiritual director. But into this framework the author introduces a cognitive
theological progression similar to that of Bonaventure in his *Breviloquium*, the
outline of which he also uses in organizing his material.

The result is an original combination of doctrinal systematizing and mystical
ascent made possible by a continuous pairing of positive and negative theology.
The author's goal is the final achievement of a further kind of theological knowledge that is at once substantive and apophatic. This is a knowledge that "goes
beyond" and makes it possible to have an experiential but non-sensorial perception of the divine; this perception, as such, would have to anticipate the conditions for the cognitive consummation in glorious blessedness. This unusual
approach explains the success the *Compendium* enjoyed among the German
mystics and representatives of the *devotio moderna* down to Cusa, despite and
even because of the technical form of its doctrinal machinery.

Ulrich Engelbrecht (d. 1277), likewise of Strasbourg, was a second theologian to anticipate the speculative renewal peculiar to the nonconformist
Dominicans of the German province. He was a student under Albert at Cologne
beginning in 1248; he then became provincial prior and died at the age of fifty
in Paris, whither he had gone to become a master of theology. He is remembered
above all for a spacious and penetrating *Summa on the Supreme Good*. The
framework of the book reflects the Pseudo-Dionysian schema of the descent of
creatures from God and their eschatological return to him. The author starts
with the doctrine of the Supreme Good and the identification of the properties
or names of God and goes on to deal with the dialectic of the Trinity and the
distinction of the personal operations. He then describes creation as the activity
of the Father, redemption as the work of the Son, and the distribution of grace
and the virtues as the gift of the Spirit. His intention was to end with the description of eternal beatitude, but he completed only six of the eight books planned.

His work was thus a quite important attempt to recover the traditional perspective of Augustinian and Pseudo-Dionysian Platonism within a systematic
treatise intended as a tool for young Dominicans in their theological studies. In
its quality Ulrich's work was not inferior to those used in the universities but
was organized in a more effective systematic way than the commentaries on the
Sentences.

One of the most interesting aspects of Ulrich's *Summa* is its methodology, the theory of which the author explains in the first book. He brings together ideas from the *Rules* of Alan of Lille and other products of twelfth-century axiomatic theology but takes as his primary basis the systematic model provided by the *Rudiments* of Proclus. He proposes to organize theological knowledge by starting with definitions, rules, and principles and then drawing from these, in a strictly deductive manner, conclusions corresponding to the explanations of the contents of the faith. Thus the entire ensuing structure of the science of God is subordinated to four fundamental axioms that precede the articles of faith and by which, indeed, these very articles are themselves confirmed. The first axiom is that God is the supreme truth and source of every other truth. The second is that whatever is guaranteed by God's testimony is true and must be believed. The third holds that those must be believed who by clear signs prove that they speak on behalf of God. The fourth is that to the extent that they obey the two preceding requirements, the Scriptures are true.

By means of these four postulates the individual events of sacred history can be proved and accepted as having a universally valid paradigmatic value and therefore as being exemplars that can lead on to the knowledge of the highest truth of all: the immutable essence of God. A noteworthy parallel with the procedures of Hugh of Ripelin can be seen in the three sets of methodological rules which make possible this movement toward God and in the warning that any cognitive progress in this direction must be subordinated to at least one of the following: predication through negation (or following the apophatic way), predication through causality (the causality proper to all the divine names that can be deduced from Scripture), and predication by way of eminence (this is proper to mystical theology and consists in transcending the limitations of the first two ways).

But the master who best represents the innovative character of this first phase of theological speculation by the Rhenish Dominicans is a younger man, Theodoric of Freiberg (earlier known as Vriberg). Theodoric was educated at the Saint-Jacques study center and then returned to teach theology in Paris, alternating this with periods of teaching in Germany and carrying out tasks within the Order during the years of the great doctrinal debate after 1277. He died in a year not further ascertainable between 1306 and 1320, leaving behind a sizable body of work that shows interest in logic, physics, psychology and gnoseology, metaphysics and theology. Writings that come halfway between philosophy and theology and by their very titles recall the speculative interests of Albert the Great include a fragment on *The Subject of Theology*, then *The Intellect and the Intelligible*, *The Knowledge of Separated Beings and Especially of Separated Souls*, and *Spiritual Substances and Resurrected Bodies*.

Theodoric constantly proclaims his own originality in contrast to the general acceptance of the Thomistic model, which even in Germany during these years was followed by the majority of Dominican scholars, who accepted "common opinion." Exercising this autonomy, he planned to develop a cognitive model that admittedly used Aristotelean thought as a source of ideas and speculative tools but would also be free from the limitations that this thought imposed on human reason. Theodoric thought to reach this goal by combining a psychological approach of an Augustinian kind with ideas from Averroism and, above all, with a Platonic metaphysics drawn directly from Proclus; he used not only the latter's *Rudiments of Theology* but also other short works and commentaries of his that William of Moerbeke translated during the seventies.

Theodoric's first philosophical work, *The Origin of Predicamental Realities*, which can be dated to around the middle of the eighties, displays an innovative approach to the formation of knowledge. Geoffrey of Fontaines honored the work by citing it in a *Quodlibet*, but it brought Theodoric severe criticisms and sanctions from the Dominican authorities of the German province. Not until he was a master in Paris around 1296–97 was it possible for him to return to the subject and defend his work against its opponents.

In fact, from the pages of the short work there emerges a gnoseological doctrine that has considerable consequences on the ontological level and boldly departs from the "common" way of understanding knowledge. The latter view of knowledge is that it is a relationship between a reality thought of as extra-subjective and a thought that conforms itself to the reality by producing a corresponding concept. Going more deeply into the matter than Giles of Rome had, Theodoric openly reverses the relationship between the extra-mental reality and the intellect. It is not true (he says) that the object by its mode of being acts upon the passive human mind; the contrary is true: that is, that the intellect itself is responsible for determining the mode in which the thing is known. The masters of logic gave this "mode" the name "predicamental reality," which was equivalent to the totality of universal (and therefore mental) determinations that characterize natural realities. Theodoric asks what degree of reality these concepts have: it is certainly greater than that of more abstract concepts (such as those of purely negative terms or of logical and mathematical entities).

The determination of the category to which the real being belongs thus depends on the intellect that knows it and from which things derive their essential and real structure. But to cause such a structure really means to cause the things themselves, which "are" insofar as "they possess a certain mode of being." Carried to the extreme, Theodoric's gnoseology becomes a courageous repositioning of the real order (the order or realm of being) within the interior of the knowing subject (the order or realm of thought). The scientific objectification of the natural entity, that is, its quiddity, understood as an existence possessing determinations of the intellectual order, can only depend on the intellect, which is here understood as the constitutive principle of the reality of things, a reality it constructs, in accordance with specific regulations imposed by its rational norms, as "first-intention" or real things, whereas things insofar as they are natural and factual external entities lack any intelligibility whatsoever.

This projection of the internal rational order in the form of an objective rationality that denotes the mode of existence of things makes the human intellect in some manner the cooperator with God in the effecting of a cosmic order. On the other hand, this order as such cannot be predicated either of the object's mode of being or of the subject's way of operating, but is as it were a third real element that results from the convergence of both.

The complete reversal of the criteria of Aristotelean gnoseology that dominated in the contemporary cultural setting also introduced a new perspective in the area of ontology; to use a modern term, this perspective might be described as "phenomenological." More simply put: even if Theodoric offers his ideas as the correct interpretation of Aristotle's thought, they represent in fact an obvious return to the Platonizing approach to relations between subject and object, an approach that, beginning with Boethius, was productive and widespread in the early medieval period. In this view of the matter, knowledge was the result of an active work of enhancement and organization of cognitive data by the different faculties of the soul. The return, with its renewed and solid analysis of the productive activity of the knowing subject, was fostered by the fruitful convergence of Areopagitism, Augustinianism, Proclian Neoplatonism, and Avicennian metaphysics that existed in the Rhenish world as it followed the teaching of Albert the Great.

The teaching set down in *The Origin of Predicamental Realities* left important traces in Theodoric's later works. Thus in various works on natural philosophy he is guided by his own conception of the object of scientific knowledge and indeed scatters remarks throughout on the correct way of understanding that conception. He never actually denies the real existence of things or the power of sense impressions to convey particular images to the soul, but this first level of knowledge has for its sole purpose to occasion the production of real, universal intentions by the individual agent intellect. The agent intellect is what Augustine, in a passage of his *The Immortality of the Soul*, calls "the most hidden depth of the mind," and that is the final emanation of the heavenly intelligences.

This point is very important because it makes it possible to show the fundamentally theological justification of this teaching on knowledge and being. The depth of the soul is in fact the place where, according to Augustine, God first reveals himself to the soul by causing it to know its own truth and the truth of the things God puts in order by knowing them and knows them by bringing them into existence. The human active intellect is therefore capable of knowing the truth of predicamental realities to the extent to which it is able to turn inward upon itself and, through the mediation of the intermediate intelligences, to penetrate to the depth of the soul. There it grasps God as the prime model both of subjective rationality, in the image of which it was created, and of the objective rationality at work in the organization of reality.

The created universe thus shows itself as an orderly system of cause and effect relations, which can, however, be perceived as such solely by the act of intellectual knowledge. Along with Albert the Great, Theodoric is able to retrieve the Neoplatonic distribution of being as a system of secondary causes that descend from God and ascend again to him according to a twofold process of outflow and return. He does so in a Christianized concordist synthesis of ideas and conceptions drawn from Augustine, Proclus, Pseudo-Dionysius, and Avicenna, but also from Aristotelean physics and metaphysics. Thus God creates the universe from nothing, but the act of creating is to be understood as bringing things into being without any antecedent conditions for the activity of the first cause. Nor, therefore, may "nothing" be understood as a condition for the free divine action.

This means that God could have brought something into existence even without proceeding "from nothing." This in turn allows Theodoric to regard as acceptable a descent of second intelligences from the divine intellect by emanation. These uncreated, simple intelligences are therefore not the angels, which (according to Scripture) were created from nothing and to which therefore a nature composed of matter and form may be attributed. The intelligences are eternal substances, always in act, individuatable not by matter but by a direct divine determination of their specific substances (this makes it possible to postulate multiple intelligences in the same species). The universal agent intellect, the last of the intelligences, is likewise a substance in act that determines itself by its reflection in the individual intelligences that act in conjunction with the corporeity of individual human beings. Precisely here, in the descending reflection in the soul of the action of the second causes, we have the explanation of how the soul, being created in the image of the perfect divine intelligence, can find within itself the knowableness and even the very reality of things.

Theological knowledge, too, fits into this Platonizing gnoseological schema. Harking back to the distinction between providence over nature and providence over wills that Augustine makes in *The Literal Meaning of Genesis*, Theodoric distinguishes two forms of theology. There is natural theology, which has Proclus for its model and advances in knowledge of physical things until it connects all of them with their divine source without referring their life and activity to celestial goals. There is also authentic theology, that of the saints, that is, the Fathers of the Church; this considers the order of the universe insofar as it is governed by God through a providence over wills in which God legislates for human wills and judges them and therefore directs the life and activity of the cosmos to its real heavenly goals.

This second theology is the authentically Christian theology, a science based on faith. It deals with many matters, that is, the various subjects the masters of theology claim for their science: God, things divine, creation, Christ, the Mystical Body, and the sacraments. But this science has only one form, namely the guiding principle that gives it its unity and links it to the divine thought. This principle is itself the real subject of theological knowledge, the subject that sums up within itself all other subjects. Both natural theology and the theology of the saints are therefore fully explicable by a phenomenological approach: the former completes the reconstruction of the cosmic order by leading the intellect to recognition of the divine cause, while the latter leads it to a participation in that higher source of truth that is the knowledge with which God knows himself.

But there is something more. In a treatise on *The Beatific Vision*, Theodoric shows that he understands beatitude, in which with the aid of divine grace the theology of the saints reaches its supernatural perfection, to be a cognitive participation of the created intellect in the divine essence; this is the supreme effect of providence over wills. In other words, beatitude is a final and direct union of the individual agent intellect with the divine intellect without any mediation by secondary intelligences; here God becomes directly the form of human knowledge.

Once it is accepted that to know is to participate in the very reality of things and to make them truly and objectively to be, Theodoric's understanding of beatitude also implies that for the created intellect, which here reaches the highest degree of its cognitive capacity, to *know* the divine essence is also to participate profoundly in it and to really *be* God. This opens up in Theodoric's thinking a glimpse (which Eckhart will point out and develop) of the possibility that theological knowledge may contain a mystical desire for the final fusion of the very reality of the human subject with the transcendent reality of the divine object.

4. John Duns Scotus

John Duns Scotus (d. 1308) has an especially important place among the writers who, during the years before the Council of Vienne, struck out on new paths that diverged from the common ways and the embedded doctrinal trends of their times. Scotus, the "Subtle Doctor" to his many followers, possessed a revisionist spirit and the inventiveness of genius as he worked within the university world of Paris. To his credit, he laid the foundations of a new system of thought that was destined to produce a school and to become in following centuries a fixed point of reference for a broad speculative current, one increasingly more capable of winning agreement among the Minors.

John was a native of Duns in the county of Berwick in Scotland (therefore "Scotus," a name also given to those who hailed from *Scotia minor*, a region of Northern Ireland that derived its name from the Christian Scottish settlers who landed on a section of its coast in the seventh century). The Franciscan Order sent him to Paris to study theology after he had received his academic formation in Oxford and other locations in England and Scotland. From 1296 to 1300 he taught at Cambridge, and then at Oxford until 1302. He returned to Paris as a Sententiary Bachelor; after being suspended from teaching for two years because of his refusal to accept Boniface VIII's condemnation of masters of theology, imposed by Philip the Fair, he taught theology in 1305 and 1306, but then transferred to Cologne, where he died in 1308.

His works were all connected with his teaching at the universities: commentaries on works of logic and on Aristotle's *On the Soul* and *Metaphysics*, *Disputed Questions* and *Quodlibetal Questions*, the treatise *The First Principle* (or *The First Principle of All Things*), and the *Theoremata*. Then, fundamental for his theological teaching, there were the several editions of his commentary on the *Sentences*; the gigantic *Oxford Work* (*Opus Oxoniense*), a true summa of theological thought, also cited as *Ordinatio*; finally the *First Reading* (*Lectura prima*) and the more summary *Notes on the Parisian Lectures*.

Beginning with the Prologue of the *Ordinatio*, Scotus focused his attention on what he saw as the central issue in the entire university debate of recent decades on the legitimacy of the synthesis of reason and faith. For him the issue was the breach between, on the one hand, natural science, which follows a rigorous method but cannot make unconditional statements about the ultimate reality of the objects known, and, on the other, a knowledge of supernatural origin that is faultless and true but is attainable only by renouncing the formal rigor and the prerogatives of necessity and representational effectiveness proper to science. Then, in the place traditionally assigned to discussion of the scientific nature of theology, namely, the commentary on the Prologue of the *Sentences*, he concentrated on the effect this situation had on the very possibility of theological thought. The distinctions he thought it necessary to introduce here meant a complete rethinking of the conditions of human thought generally.

A. THEOLOGY IN ITSELF AND THEOLOGY IN US

If theology is to be true knowledge, it must possess an unlimited capacity for thinking about its object. Well, all theological truths are virtually present in God; therefore God, considered in himself and as such, that is, as an essence ("deity as deity"), must be the primary object of theological knowledge. But the essence of God is perfect inasmuch as it cannot be grasped by any limited cognition, being infinite. Therefore only an intellect capable of knowing the infinite divine essence can be a satisfactorily theological intellect. But no created intellect can measure up to something to which it is not completely conformed. Neither the angels nor the blessed nor human beings who are still pilgrims or "in the pilgrim state" are capable of participating directly in the knowledge God evidently has of truths concerning the infinite essence. The divine essence, precisely as divine, can be grasped solely by the divine intellect.

The first necessary distinction—also made, in more or less the same terms, by other theologians during this period—is between *theology in itself*, that is, the knowledge the object of theology, namely, God, is capable of eliciting in an intellect proportioned to it, and *theology in us*, our theology, the knowledge of that same object that our intellect is qualified to receive. It is clear that God alone is fit to be both the subject and the object of theological knowledge in itself. In contrast, the created intellect cannot have a plain knowledge of a nature that is infinite in act.

Our theology, therefore, looks to God as the one who corresponds to the concept that can best signify to us, in our condition as finite knowers, the perfection of the object of theology in itself. This is the idea of infinite being, that is, the concept of being as seen in its maximum purity and simplicity and in the modality of infinity, which is necessarily the modality proper to God. There is thus only one concept that points to being in the highest degree of intensity and to which may be traced back all the other concepts that in any way express the attributes of God. Moreover, this concept is fully accessible to natural reason once it includes everything the human mind can conceive when trying to represent the divine to itself. In order truly to identify infinite being with what is assumed to be the object of God's theology it must be regarded as containing every perfection, inasmuch as it includes everything that can be referred to the divinity without implying any imperfection.

On this basis the human intelligence assumes that it can regard this object of our theology as identical with the object of theology in itself, and therefore as real and containing necessary truths. It also claims to be able thenceforth to operate with epistemological correctness, that is, to move forward with progressive acquisitions of further knowledge that follow strict rules of logic and demonstration.

But this claim of the identity of the objects of theology in itself and theology in us must cope with the different modes of the presence of this object to the subject: the presence is clear, essential, and intuitive in God, but abstractive, negative, and indirect in the human intellect. The fundamental aspiration of human theology can therefore be legitimate and justified only on condition that all its claims to know the infinite object coincide with the maximum possible thinkableness of that object as such. But the human intellect, proceeding by analogy and using only the tools of philosophy, could never exhaust the thinkableness of being because every object known in a finite world always points to something more complete and less imperfect. And yet, for the believer, the greatest possible extension of the thinkableness of the infinite being has become a reality in Sacred Scripture, which reports all the possible perfect relationships between creation and the Creator. In this trustworthy text human beings are informed about their own thinkableness; as a result, they improve their capacity for recognizing the nature that corresponds to the concept of infinite being.

In Scotus' view, then, the possessor of "our theology" is in exactly the same condition in which Anselm found himself at the beginning of the *Proslogion*. That is, he *knows* from revelation what the perfections of the infinite being must be, but he does not know them intuitively. He is therefore in a position to know them only as the object of a knowledge that must henceforth be demonstrative and the result of argumentation; thus it replaces the revelatory communication that gave rise to it and acts differently from that communication, without ever contradicting it. Our theology is therefore not faith, even though for this knowledge to exist it must be fed by faith.

B. THEOLOGY AND PHILOSOPHY

At this point a second distinction must be made: between theology (not only divine, but human as well) and philosophy. Between philosophy and theology, that is, between metaphysics and theology in us, there can be seen, even in their historical manifestations, the same division between an adequate knowledge and an inadequate knowledge. In this case the division becomes the source of a seemingly unresolvable controversy.

The common opinion of the masters of the schools looked on these two fields of knowledge as sciences directed to the same object but under different cognitive conditions or formalities. The case is similar to what happens when physics and astronomy each demonstrate the sphericity of the earth with different arguments peculiar to their own fields of study (empirical and mathematical arguments respectively).

Metaphysics claims to know being as a fixed object, the truth of which is maintained by the truth of the first principles of logic and by necessary relations between causes and effects. Metaphysics locates this object within a natural order it regards as perfect and self-enclosed, not contradictable by any internal variable. Theology, on the contrary, starts with the idea of being as directed to an end, but it assumes the impossibility of grasping this end by means of knowledge that is given by nature itself; such knowledge could never claim any end within its grasp to be an ultimate end suitable for the whole of creation and the fulfillment of all its potentialities (an end internal to creation would be finite and refer the mind to further ends). This situation demands of theologians that they be open to the indispensable acquisition of a further knowledge of truth that transcends the natural truth of metaphysics, since, once the infinite being is postulated as perfect, theologians see nature to be in some way fallen and imperfect.

Our theology, therefore, presupposes revelation not only as an addition of information about the thinkableness of the prerogatives of an infinite being but also as a source of knowledge capable of making up for the inadequacy of our natural abilities for seeking truth. The reasons that lead philosophers to reject the validity of a revealed knowledge do not require acceptance in theology. In fact, only by breaking through the limited natural parameters of metaphysics can theologians open their minds to information of a higher order that comes in the form of an unmerited gift from that same divine subject who alone is capable of knowing himself perfectly as object. Revelation acts, therefore, as a universal illumination of human thinking about the object of theology that activates the passive potency of the intellect by supplying stimulating information of a supernatural kind. Scotus gives this passive potency the name "obediential potency," that is, a potency capable of becoming what God wills or shall will it to become.

c. The Scientific Status of Theology

In order also to explain the extent and nature of our theological knowledge at the epistemological level, it is necessary to specify that the ideas coming from revelation are always "complex truths"; in other words, from the viewpoint of logic they always take the form of combinations, i.e., propositions that combine conceptual terms (for example, "God is triune"). The human intellect can admittedly know separately the individual terms making up the proposition (including "God" as infinite being), but it will never be able to have a natural knowledge of their meaning when joined in propositions. It is, therefore, the propositions, and not the concepts, of the Bible that are responsible for giving humanity knowledge that is supernatural in origin.

Theology in us comes down, then, to an instrumental analysis of the content of every proposition formulated in revelation, an analysis aided by logical categories. But then the knowledge that revelation introduces into theological learning is, as compared with natural knowledge, a "further" knowledge even simply from the viewpoint of logic, since it allows the created intellect to grasp connotations of the object that would be naturally possible for it only if it could have an unmistakable experience of that object. This situation not only does not mean a lessening of power for human knowledge but, on the contrary, elevates that knowledge to maximum perfection since it enables the mind to know even independently of the phantasms that come from sense perception and are the cause producing natural abstractive acts of knowledge.

Relying on the idea of the human passive intellect as an "obediential potency," Scotus goes on to regard the described increases of knowledge as inexhaustible and as engaging the creaturely subject, through the acquisition of the truth about God, in a process of increasing perfection. Given the infinity of the object of knowledge, this process can have no limit except what God wills. Scotus is then able also to explain the concept of beatitude as a perfect vision of the divine: the theology of the blessed will be the most perfect theology possible on the creaturely level, even though it will be different from theology in itself because the intellects of the blessed, even when reaching their highest capacity for knowledge, will always remain finite and unable to grasp the divine infinity in its essence.

Given these explanations, we understand that theology brings a knowledge of the divine essence that is completely different from the knowledge metaphysics can attain. The latter is always tied into the order of what is naturally knowable and is therefore capable, at best, of reaching a very broad and abstract grasp of infinite being, lacking the personal characteristics and important attributes of infinite being in its particularity. God is the general subject of both metaphysics and theology. But God insofar as he reveals himself is the specific subject solely of theology in us, which therefore cannot do without revelation just as the human mind cannot do without this theology as an inquiry into revelation. God as perfect being and knowable through illumination is the subject of the theology of the angels and the blessed; God as infinite existing essence is, as such, the subject of theology in itself, in which God alone can delight.

When, then, Scotus raises the question of the scientific status of theology he evidently has in mind the outstanding contemporary treatments of the subject but also the debate arising from the condemnations of 1277. First of all, he excludes the idea that theology in itself can be regarded as a science. The reason is that theology in itself excludes any increase in knowledge (any passage from not knowing to knowing) and therefore any procedure of a discursive and syllogistic kind, which is one of the fundamental conditions required by Aristotelean epistemology. As for the theology of the blessed, one may agree with Augustine that their knowledge cannot be considered discursive (since their every thought must include everything knowable of which they are capable). Yet Scotus maintains that we may speak here of theology in a full sense, insofar as the subject will always be able to distinguish between the nature of the divine object as such and its properties.

A more complex answer is required by another difficulty, this one having to do with the possibility of giving the name of science to the theological knowledge both of the blessed and of pilgrims on earth, that is, of "our theology" in all its forms. Once Aristotle rejects the idea that science can include knowledge of what is contingent, how can theology include contingent and historical (that is, not logically necessary) elements involving God's relationships *ad extra* with creatures, such, for example, as the Incarnation of Christ and its impact on sacred history? Since revelation gives us these ideas as essential to theological truth, the difficulty must be overcome by modifying the Aristotelean concept of science.

If we adhere to the standards of the *Posterior Analytics* and understand science as a knowledge of what is necessary, one characterized by certainty and evidence and proceeding deductively, it is perhaps not possible and certainly not necessary to consider theology as a science in that full sense. But the word "science" can also signify a true knowledge as distinct from opinion (an acceptance of the term allowed by Aristotle himself in the *Nicomachean Ethics*). If so, then the knowledge of contingents in theology must obviously be accepted as an integral element in its capacity for affirming the truth in a particular way. Theology can therefore be called a science. Better still, it can be called wisdom in the Augustinian sense by reason of the perfect way in which it leads the human intellect, in the present life and later in beatitude, to participate in the certainty and nobility of the object known.

In conclusion, we see confirmed once again the difference in levels between the scientific knowledge proper to the natural order with all its limitations and imperfections and the complete acquisition of truth about supernatural reality that is made possible by the unmerited access of the intellect to revelation. It is not possible to be an Aristotelean in theology; indeed, there is not even any reason for being one. In this same light we understand the complete disappearance of the theory of subalternation, but also of the claim of metaphysics and even the philosophical sciences to be tools in the service of theological wisdom. The reason is that no truth not originating in revelation can be able to orient and influence the truths of theology. The converse is also unqualifiedly the case: the truths of theology have no power to give rise to, and subordinate to themselves, true statements belonging to other realms of science, since different rules and principles are in force there.

Finally, according to Scotus the complete otherness of theology emerges from its practical and soteriological nature, which is evident alongside its cognitive nature and is more important than the latter. Given that praxis is an act of the will that essentially follows a judgment of the intellect, right action is necessarily conformed to right reason and there is no substantial difference between the cognitive and practical functions of the intellect except that the second is set in motion by the will. But then, considering that our theology is knowledge of the ultimate ends to which human life is moving and therefore of the Supreme Good and of beatitude, which consists in participating in that Good, it follows that there is no real difference between the theoretical and practical meanings of its propositions, for at the very moment in which theology expresses the truth of the Good it orients the will toward that Good by directing its actions toward the attainment and enjoyment of that end.

In short, due to the limitations implicit in its operations, metaphysics must stop when it reaches a pure, disinterested contemplation of its theological object. Our theology goes further and guides pilgriming humanity in its special relationships with the infinite divine essence. Once again, from this point of view human theology proves to be more sapiential than scientific inasmuch as it results for human beings in redemptive salvation and the acquisition of eternal life.

D. METAPHYSICS AND ONTOLOGY: THE UNIVOCITY OF BEING

The effect of considering theology in us as a knowledge superior to faith but less than vision, that is, as located between faith and the beatific vision, is to restore to philosophy a validity and autonomy of its own. Though unable to give answers regarding the supernatural ends of history, philosophy does have a complete right to decide on the scope of the natural knowableness of being, and this judgment is reserved to it alone.

Once metaphysics has been freed of any kind of subalternation to a higher and unrelated knowledge and once any dependence on revelation, direct or indirect (by way of theology), has been excluded, what does it become and what is its object? Scotus asks himself this question in the first of his *Questions on Metaphysics*. In answering, he distinguishes the opinion of Averroes (the object of metaphysics is God as first cause of the universe and the separated intelligences as second causes) from that of Avicenna (metaphysics has as its object being as being and whatever belongs to it as being). These are evidently two conflicting conceptions of the first science. In the former view metaphysics is reduced to reflection on the visible universe, which is caused by God, and therefore comes within the scope of physics. In the second view metaphysics has an autonomous field of inquiry different from that of the inferior sciences, just as it has now acquired autonomy in relation to a higher science.

Scotus unhesitatingly chooses the Avicennean solution ("Avicenna was correct, the Commentator wrong") because it ensures a distinct and special scientific status for metaphysics. For if in fact the theology of pilgriming humanity has

442   The Theological Workshop of the Late Middle Ages

for its object the infinite being insofar as knowledge of this comes through a revealed communication of its properties, then there remains the possibility of a science that meditates on the same infinite being, being as being, without being subordinated to other cognitive factors and without being supported by any kind of information external to purely rational inquiry. Thus metaphysics will also be able to speak of the infinite being as God, but without therefore conveying the preambles of faith and without having to be subjected to examination by the rule of faith, which is something outside its field of competence and its investigative scope. It will therefore be able to say about God everything that reason can determine as being proper to the "first principle of all things," the first, perfect, and infinite being, and to speak of him not only as first mover or first cause but as in himself the perfection of being.

Metaphysics can aspire to have such a "first" as its proper object because this first is the first object of the intellect. Scotus thus rejects at the outset the Thomist thesis that the direct object of intellection is the intelligible essence of material things, an essence known through abstraction and precluding any possibility of understanding scientifically the reality of individual and corporeal entities. But he also regards as patently false the Augustinian thesis based on illumination, according to which the intellect, through participation in that light, knows the essence of God and conforms itself to its truth. His reason is that the divine essence is known by the human intellect only through universal and mediated ideas.

Scotus' intention, in contrast, is to claim for metaphysics the prerogative of knowing an object that is always and immediately known to it in every act of intellection. But everything that is intelligible and an object of intellectual acts includes in itself the idea of being (in the form of genera and species) or at least contains it virtually (in the case of the affections). Therefore being is completely coextensive with reason: everything that reason knows is being, and reason can know everything that is; therefore no manifestation of being can elude it. This analysis necessarily brings the realization that being, the object of metaphysics, is univocal.

In saying this, Scotus cuts every last link with Thomist metaphysics, which appeals to the principle of analogy for the very possibility of predicating attributes common to creaturely and divine being. Scotus claims, in fact, that analogical discourse is possible only if the thinker has a sufficient and direct knowledge of the analogate. Therefore one can say that medicine is "healthy" by analogy because one has a sufficient grasp of what is meant by a patient's "health." But since the being of God transcends that of creatures, the latter cannot be the analogate, or else one introduces analogical imperfections into God. The analogate must therefore be God himself, of whom we do not have sufficient knowledge to begin with. Furthermore, analogy does not allow for syllogistic arguments since these imply an appropriateness in the middle term but in a nonunivocal and therefore equivocal sense. But this would introduce four terms into the syllogism, thus destroying the correctness of any deduction involving the being of God and that of creatures. Therefore metaphysics cannot know its proper object through analogy.

Metaphysics understands being in all its univocity as a unified concept that "suffices," that is, is able to maintain both the affirmation and the negation of its own meaning, and is therefore capable of serving as a syllogistic middle term without introducing equivocation into the argument. This univocity manifests itself in the same way at the level of reality (physical entities) and at the level of logic (logical entities), because it is the property of being itself prior to any determination (any metaphysical entity). In fact, being can only be conceived as that which "extends to everything that is" without any positive limitation of its own meaning. Univocal being is therefore the first concept of the intellect and precedes any determination whatsoever that assumes it as existing, and thus any differentiation whatsoever of its own ways of being actuated. It includes therefore both finite being and infinite being.

E. GOD AS INFINITE BEING

If univocal being includes the most general properties of both finite and infinite being, this has consequences for the metaphysical exploration of the attributes of God, an exploration that will begin with the attribute of infinity even before reasoning to the property of existence. The process must not start *a posteriori* with reflection on the properties of finite being in order then to move beyond these on the basis of an unsystematizable analogical ascent. Rather, it must directly (*a priori*) focus on infinite being as such. It is not possible, after all, to think being by starting with something that is not being, such as the modalities with which the sensible concrete presents itself to us in experience. It is possible to think being only by starting with its own modalities as being.

This intellectual operation, which Scotus propounds in numerous passages, from the *Ordinatio* to the *Notes on the Parisian Lectures* to *The First Principle*, amounts to a demonstration of the existence of God that consists of successive logical steps determined by the very conditions for the conceivability of the infinite being. The existence of God is not an obvious, self-evident truth, as is claimed by those scholastic masters who wish to demonstrate it by wrongly citing Augustine, John Damascene, or Anselm, for if God's existence were self-evident it could not be demonstrated. Instead, the existence of God is an idea that follows upon conceiving him as infinite; therefore it is demonstrable. First of all, therefore, it is necessary to prove that the concept of an infinite being is thinkable and to assess its meaning, then to examine to what extent the possibility of its existence is clear to reason, and finally to understand the necessity of its existence as evident to reason. This threefold line of argument completes the full rehabilitation of metaphysics as distinct from theology and capable of a thorough knowledge of its own object.

The conceivability of infinite being, which is equivalent to the perception that it is not contradictory, implies the identity in that being of all the possible positive predications that flow from its infinity. For example, it is immutable because mutability is proper to finite realities. It is eternal, immense, ubiquitous, invisible, and ineffable. So too it is one, true, and good, it is necessary and it is possible, it is in act and in potency, because it is all these in a way that transcends the modes of being of what is finite. For Scotus, then, the transcendentals re-appear in the complete transcendence of infinite being, which is in fact univocal precisely because it is transcendent. All the perfections are also found in finite creatures, but in God they are infinite and identified with his infinite essence. Not only, therefore, is infinity not inconsistent with the intelligibility of being; it even makes it possible to accept as true that the infinite being is the most completely intelligible being.

This perfect intelligibility supports the second phase of the mental operation that deals with the infinite being: namely, the inquiry into the possibility of its existence. To think the first being means to think of it as pure efficient cause, ultimate end, and supreme perfection. These three are distinct steps in a single process that begins with the relative thinkableness of finite being and discovers that this must be subordinated to the absolute thinkableness of the infinite being. Every finite being is, as such, producible and therefore has a cause. But it is better to think of a first cause than to go back endlessly from cause to cause, since, given any finite object, an endless causal process would not necessarily lead to the existence of that object, despite the fact that it is thinkable only as producible. Therefore a first cause is possible. In a similar way, the existence of particular ends persuasively suggests their dependence on a common ultimate end. No less persuasively, the existence of graded perfections turns the mind to perfection in the supreme degree.

Each of these three firsts is the limit that thought itself places on an infinite regression that would be useless as well as contradictory; thought thereby opens itself to the possibility of infinite being as cause, end, and perfection.

The third phase of the argument deals with the question: Does this infinite being exist necessarily? According to Scotus the attempt to prove (as the Thomists do) that the infinite being is the first efficient cause or the unmoved mover, or to rise up in some other way from effects to their producer, would be, from the viewpoint of logic, to turn back to the imperfection and instability of finite being. And it would be to do so just when we have discovered and realized that the infinite being is thinkable as embracing in itself the sum total of intelligible and desirable beings. It would mean joining Averroes and turning back to the physical world while abandoning the metaphysical dimension with all its riches. Moreover, the existent deity that could be demonstrated in this way would be little more than a natural finishing touch on the finite universe. To make God the cause only of this world would limit his omnipotence to causation and movement in a merely finite degree, whereas the infinite being is an infinite causative and operative power from which might come endless compossible effects that cannot be imagined on the basis of our experience.

Scotus suggests that in arguing to the necessity of the infinite being the thinker should proceed instead by way of eminence. That is: if we just think of the infinite truth of the intelligible entities our intellects discover as we advance in knowledge, we realize that if these are true it is because all of them are thinkable and are in fact thought by an infinite, perfect intellect. If we just think of the infinite truth of the ends that our wills gradually discover and that correct our intentions we realize that all these ends lead to an ultimate end that sums them up and is infinite. Finally, if we just think of the infinite truth of the perfections ascertainable in finite being we will realize that there is a perfection that transcends all of them and contains them all and than which no perfection can be more perfect, for otherwise it would not contain all perfections.

Then, inevitably, in this argument about the infinity that springs from the thinkableness of the infinite being there comes to the fore Anselm's "single argument." To this Scotus adds a formal complement (a "coloration" or "tint," as he puts it) when he explains that "that than which no greater can be thought" exists, provided it can be thought "without contradiction." Why? Because the infinite being is truly infinite if it shows itself to be thinkable as truly infinite, and this thinkableness consists precisely in its non-contradictoriness. Finite reality always allows that there is something superior to it; the idea of the infinite is not contradictory; therefore the finite always points to something infinite.

This is the simplest explanation of the object in which the intellect finds its greatest satisfaction, because it is perfect and is possible and therefore exists. In fact, Scotus uses Anselm's argument to prove not the existence but the infinity of God; but it is obvious that since this "first" is thinkable as supremely infinite and, as such, is the point of arrival of the intellect's cognitive aspirations, it would not in fact be thinkable as such if it did not possess actual being (or *esse existentiae*), because it cannot receive anything (including existence) from another cause.

F. DIVINE VOLUNTARISM AND ITS CONSEQUENCES:
THE REALITY AND KNOWABILITY OF FINITE BEING

Once infinite being is accepted, the univocity of being leads us back to the existence of finite being as a result of the very simple distinction between what is infinite and what is not. Finite being is not something demonstrable: unlike infinite being, it is a fact and, as such, is obvious and not deducible. It exists only because the infinite cause of all the numberless possible contingents makes it exist. This exclusive explanation of its being is the simple reason that it exists, and exists "thus and now" in its immediacy and unrepeatability.

Once this very simple observation has been made, we see the silent collapse and reduction to dusty debris of all the abstract hierarchies of secondary causes that Aristoteleanism had introduced to explain the actual nature of finite beings and that had already been called into question in the tangle of debates around the condemnation of 1277. If the divine cause is infinite, it must be infinitely free; therefore only divine omnipotence, understood as the actuation of the infinite and absolutely unconditioned will of the first being, causes things to make the transition from their thinkableness in the divine intellect, where, being intelligibles, they are possibles, to their historical, spatio-temporal reality, where they are possibles actuated by an infinite and perfect and therefore utterly free will. The ideas guide but do not limit the divine will, which chooses the order and good of the universe by making them exist as such precisely because God chooses them.

God has established two sets of laws for the universe. The first set is the natural laws he has created and fixed as ways of carrying out his own free will in the created order (this is his *potentia ordinata* or ordering power). In contrast, the second set reflects his will itself in an absolute and direct way (*potentia absoluta* or unrestricted power). As ordering, the divine power is the causal principle of the particular set of specifications that makes up the world of possibles that God chooses should exist as such. As absolute and conditioned only by itself, that is, only by the principle of noncontradiction, the divine power is the causal principle of every event whatsoever, even if not natural to or alternative to the created order, which the free divine choice makes to be compossible with that order.

From these two sets of laws there follows a conception of reality in its entirety as dependent on the divine will alone, either as principle of necessary order or as principle of every possible that does not contradict that order. Every determination of being, whether infinite or finite, from the most detailed and unyielding to the most complex, depends on the fact that God wills it.

The radical voluntarism that in this new ontological perspective characterizes all possible relations between God and the created universe has some important consequences for the entire system of reality. The first, which pertains to the metaphysical level, is that the only possible determinant of finite being in its reality is its finite being itself, which is willed to be such by the Creator. There is no other determinant: not an existential element added to existence; not a principle of individuation that is superimposed on preexisting universal traits; not an indeterminate whatness of the creature prior to its created and determinate being. There is simply its very existence, modified in a certain particular way, which makes every particular thing (*haec res*) to be as it is: simply its "thisness" (*haecceitas*), that is, its individual differentiating reality, which is intrinsically knowable in its singularity by the created intellect, not as something corresponding to the eternal divine idea that produced it but as the object of an intuitive perception of its singularity with all of its openness to contingency, just as it presents itself to the senses, which then pass it on to the reasoning mind.

A second consequence is gnoseological and epistemological: namely, the now-evident and indispensable distinction between, and different value given to, knowledge mediated through abstraction and the development of universal concepts on the one hand, and immediate and direct knowledge through intuition and in direct contact with individual realities on the other. The intuitive knowledge of created reality, though obviously imperfect, is nonetheless sufficient for recognizing the present existence of the singular thing when the knower stands before it and grasps it precisely as existing. Such knowledge is decidedly superior in its truthfulness to the results of abstractive knowledge. In the latter, the intellect attempts to lay hold of a "quiddity" or "common nature" of the finite thing by making it present in the form of an image or "appearance" (*species*) and adopting an attitude of artificial indifference to the existence or nonexistence of the thing and to its presence to or absence from the knowing subject.

If, then, the greatest clarity is that gained by intuition of the contingent, Scotus is in a position to broadcast a completely new and non-Aristotelean conception of the natural sciences. Natural science is now of an experimental kind, directed toward a probabilistic but conscious and possible consideration of phenomena that turns away from abstract efforts to build up an objective structure of connections among realities. Consequently, the object of this kind of science will not be causal connections among things, but their relationships of compossibility that are expressed in complex propositions, the clarity of which is based on simple intuition.

In this new conception of the contingent character of physical science the material entity has a natural predisposition to receive a form, not a single form but all possible forms, these being capable in turn of including within themselves lower forms that combine with matter to produce the intuitable and experimental immediacy of the singular thing. As entities that constitute the real existence of the individual, the various forms can be subjected to "measurement" based on their growth in or lessening of effectiveness (*intensio* or *remissio formarum*) within the composite. The constitutive elements of the composite are distinguishable inasmuch as they answer to different definitions and carry out different functions, but they are not really distinct from one another because their realities form a unique, indivisible thing.

According to Scotus' terminology, then, among the constitutive elements of every thing there is no real distinction or even a purely rational distinction (a distinction made by an act of the intellect without any objective reality). There is only a "formal distinction."

G. THE FORMAL DISTINCTION AND ITS THEOLOGICAL CONSEQUENCES: THE ETERNAL PREDESTINATION OF CHRIST

Among the disciples and followers of Scotus this doctrine of the formal distinction was destined to play a fundamental role in the study of the natural sciences. Scotus himself also used it in theology, with some interesting developments and improvements.

Our intellect cannot possibly represent and comprehend the infinite being, but meanwhile it finds some help by making a formal distinction among the divine perfections, which, though a single reality, answer to different formal definitions. But it is not only trinitarian theology that profits by the formal distinction, through the application made of it to the notion of person and to the divine relationships within the deity. The divine operations that deal with creatures can likewise be clarified and distinguished by means of the formal distinction.

Thus no alteration or lessening of the divine unity is introduced by the fact that the Word relates himself formally in a special way to creation or by the fact that the Incarnation of Christ is conceived as predestined from eternity, before any other reality subject to predestination. (Here again Scotus is carrying to an extreme a speculative idea of Anselm and Bonaventure.) The predestination of Christ is not only not rendered necessary by human sin; rather, even creation itself is a consequence of that predestination, since the world was created for the purpose of receiving the Word, who is distinguished from the other divine persons precisely inasmuch as he is characterized, unlike the Father and the Spirit, by embodying the perfect relationship of divine love for creatures. Redemption is therefore an additional task of the Incarnate Word, who descends to earth in order *also* to correct the deviant course of human history that has been caused by Adam's sin.

This conception also has as an integral element the eternal preservation of Mary from original sin. She was predestined to be the mother of Christ and therefore received this special privilege in order that reconciliation might be the work of a mediator who had no element of enmity against the Father. The privilege of the Immaculate Conception meant therefore a heightening of the dignity that marked the coming of Christ. (The Immaculate Conception was the subject of a question publicly discussed by Scotus in Paris and was destined to become a theme especially dear to not a few of his followers in later centuries.) The privilege is therefore highly probable; consequently, given the absoluteness of the divine voluntarism that directs the entire history of creation, it could not fail to have been chosen by God as a means of celebrating the excellence of the act uniting the human and the divine.

h. The Human Will and Its Freedom

A final and no less interesting consequence of Scotus' theological voluntarism can be seen in the emphatic psychological and ethical voluntarism that marks his ideas on anthropology. According to Scotus the human will, whose goal is union with God, the Supreme Good, acts with authentic freedom on the basis of cognitive information coming from the intellect. He distinguishes between an act of nature, which is necessitated and conditioned, and an act of the will, which is free. He thinks that a voluntary act is an autonomous rational movement of a power capable of choosing among different and even opposed objects (and even of not choosing at all), but without any necessary dependence on the intellect. The reason is that in its movement toward the infinite good through particular goods it is not obliged to respect a gradation imposed by the intellect, which recognizes a greater or lesser dignity among these particular goods. Every particular reality subsists, in fact, due to its full existential dignity; the intellect, meanwhile, is not able to know the quiddity of the infinite being (or good), and consequently is not able to compare finite goods with it so as to list them without question as more or less good. The will is therefore free to determine its own act of choosing on the intermediate levels of its movement toward the ultimate end.

On the moral level, as in the order of nature, there are two sets of laws parallel to the two ways of God's efficacious action in the created universe. There is the natural law, which reflects God's ordering power, and there is the supreme divine law corresponding to the unlimited efficacy of God's absolute power. Just as revelation guides the intellect in the passage from natural scientific knowledge to the theological understanding of truth, so too it guides the will's movement toward perfection. It leads the will from respect for the natural law, which lays the foundations of practical reason (the first rule being always to do good and avoid evil), to respect for divine law, which aids human beings by supplying higher standards (the decalogue and the commandments of love for God and neighbor) that will guide it in the choice of particular goods. Revelation alone can in fact pass beyond the intellect's ability to distinguish among choices and show these choices to be more or less consistent with the Supreme Good.

5. The Beginnings of the "Scotist Way"

The immediate success of Scotus' thought among many masters of the next generation, especially in the Franciscan Order, justified the quick adoption of the historiographical idea of a "Scotist School." But perhaps it is more in keeping with reality, at least in the early years, to speak more generally of a "Scotist Way," that is, a speculative trend under the influence and clarity of the teachings of the "Subtle Doctor."

In comparison with the emphatic differentiation of the other dominant doctrinal "obediences" of that age, chief among them the Thomist, the first followers of Scotus were characterized for the most part by a high degree of speculative autonomy and a tendency to pick and choose among his fundamental opinions. They did, however, show a united front, especially in energetically defending the master's positions against the challenges that suddenly rained down on his system from several sides. Not a few critics belonging to different groups challenged his basic choices and his distancing of himself, often in polemical terms, from the speculative foundations that determined the "common" thinking of contemporary masters, even amid the differences of schools and trends. In fact, Scotus' criticism of the speculative tradition, that is, the refutational element in his thinking, was precisely the aspect his first disciples devoted themselves to maintaining and publicizing in response to the more established trends in the philosophical and theological teaching of that time.

In particular, younger minds obviously found attractive the possibility offered by the Subtle Doctor of abandoning the rigid schematisms of classical logic and metaphysics in favor of a new, radically experimental scientific attitude. Not a few of the ideas emerging from the master's works seemed to open the way to new and interesting developments through new perspectives and new methodologies in the field of science, but also in philosophy and theology.

Some of these ideas were: the doctrine of God's absolute power, which brought with it, among other things, the admission that God has the power to create a plurality of worlds and to give the supreme heaven a nonrotational movement, with the consequent acceptance of infinite space and the possible existence of the vacuum; the plurality and measurability of forms; the essential role of intuitive evidence as the source of recognition of the actual existence of a datum; the distinction between philosophical thought and theological thought as each representing a different formality, and the conception of theology as a practical science; the emphasis on theological fideism and the rejection of natural theology as the hinge or link between metaphysical study and revealed truth.

The Scotist masters continued independently along these lines, though with different nuances and individual choices and sometimes connecting these with a basic Franciscan Augustinianism (in the process often exercising an excessively adaptable eclecticism). These masters gradually allowed themselves to be characterized first by a speculative outlook and then, later, by a real current of thought in which the Minors could find the elements of an intellectual identity that was more solid and fruitful than was permitted them by traditional doctrines.

In the first and fundamental area, that of defending the master's teachings again the immediate criticisms of contemporaries, we may single out several individuals among the first Scotists. One was Anthony Andrea (d. ca. 1320), a careful commentator and summarizer of Scotus' writings; he was a native of Saragossa and was active at Oxford, but also at Bologna, where he helped spread knowledge of the master's work among the Franciscans of Italy. Others were two Englishmen, William of Alnwick (d. 1333), who edited the writings of Scotus, and Henry of Harclay (d. 1317), a secular master of theology and chancellor at Oxford. Both men, however, began to show some desire to qualify, if not correct, some central theses of Scotism, in particular those on the ontological status of the ideas in God (Scotus held this to be merely intentional) and on "thisness" (*haecceitas*) as the principle of individuation.

In Paris the master's heritage seems to have been taken over chiefly by John of Bassoles (d. ca. 1347), who brought to a conclusion the Scotist revision of the scientific status of theology, to the point of asserting that is impossible for theology to be a science "at least as much as it is impossible for a human being to be an ass." He thus denied that it is permissible to introduce apodictic demonstrations into theological discourse and became one of the first to allow into theology the possibility of only probable arguments.

The revision of some doctrinal aspects of Scotism was continued by Francis of Pignano (or of the March) (d. 1344), who was active at the Avignon papal court as a radical defender of Franciscan pauperism. In commenting on the *Sentences* he held that the act of faith could be thought to generate an interior evidence springing from the motives of credibility and could therefore be converted, thanks to an intervention of the will in support of the assent of the intellect, into an intellectual certainty to be made the basis for theological speculation.

Another reviser, Francis of Meyronnes (d. 1328), deserves to be remembered for his thorough investigation into the subject (especially important for the construction of satisfactory physical theories) of the variations in intensity (*remissio* and *intensio*) of qualities; these variations were not readily compatible with the Aristotelean conception of form. This Francis also defended the Scotist doctrine of intuitive knowledge as signifying a direct presence of the object known to the knowing subject; he was here opposing the revision proposed, in different ways, by Ockham and Aureoli.

Finally, among the first explorers of the Scotist way who showed originality in their teaching perhaps the most representative was an Italian, John of Ripatransone (or of Ripa) (d. after 1368), a master of theology in Paris during the pontificate of John XXII. In the extensive Prologue of his commentary on the *Sentences* he turns the problem of theological method into a discussion of the measurability of the cognitive capacity of creatures in their earthly state and in the state of beatitude. In this discussion the author does not hesitate to apply variation in the intensity of forms as a tool in studying the vision of God. Accepting *a priori* the certainty of an unbridgeable distance between God and creation, he interprets theological knowledge as the progressive movement of the intelligent creature toward an intuitive knowledge of the divine essence. This goal will be reached, however, only in beatitude, in a final identification of knower and known that at last transcends all the mediations involved in abstract knowledge. This last is rather the condition Paul describes as proper to earthly theology ("through a mirror, in a riddle") in 1 Corinthians 13:12.

After making some complicated gnoseological and metaphysical distinctions, John describes the possibility of "quantifying" theological knowledge as the result of charity increased to the maximum (that is, "infinite" in act, in the Scotist sense) both of its breadth, that is, its extensive and intensive variation, and of its "information," that is, a capacity that takes the form of cognitively communicating being. At the end of this progressive, balanced, and measurable intensification of theological knowledge the intellect will acquire the ability to grasp, but always according to its creaturely possibilities, the transcendence of the idea that corresponds to the divine immensity. This will happen as the result of a vital change: a state of mystical union with God. Here John seems to be combining into a single concept the Averroist desire for the absorption of the individual intellect into the one agent intellect on the one hand and the promise of eschatological deification found in the Dionysian-Eriugenean tradition, on the other.

Chapter 7

The Autumn of Medieval Theology

I. Theological Debate in the Age of John XXII

When the Avignon popes, first Clement V (1305–14), then, and especially, John XXII (1316–34), transferred the curial study center there from Rome, their purpose was to establish at the court in Provence a new center of literary, scientific, and philosophical culture. This was meant to become, under their direct supervision, the beating heart of a renewed Christian wisdom and was thereby to wrest intellectual primacy away from the urban universities (especially from Paris).

John XXII, who had a strong interest in theology, personally spurred theological debate by raising questions and supporting doctrines. In particular he backed a questionable thesis on the conditions affecting the beatific vision of the blessed before their resurrection (in his view this differed from the vision they would have after the end of time). It is obvious that this tendentious and authoritarian control the pope presumed he could exercise over opinions, both theological and scientifico-philosophical, was incompatible with the *de facto* autonomy the university masters had long enjoyed with the support of a strong juridical tradition. Especially in the second decade of the century this state of affairs contributed greatly to creating a climate of suspicion and inquisitorial investigation. In this atmosphere papal opposition to the doctrinal positions of the theologians was interwoven with a political repressiveness connected with serious developments in the lengthy struggle for supremacy between the pope and Emperor Louis the Bavarian.

Thus the same pontificate that saw the canonization of Thomas Aquinas in 1323 was also marked by heated manifestations of dissent and resultant persecutions of the more radical dissenters. In 1317 the pope issued a condemnation, several times repeated in the following years, of the movement of the Franciscan Spirituals, whom he rebuked for a lack of discipline and a refusal to be absorbed into the ecclesiastical structure. In 1322 Ubertino of Casale was put on trial. In 1323 the Bull *Cum inter nonnullos* and in 1324 the Bull *Quia quorundam* censured the Franciscan views on the poverty of Christ.

In 1324 William of Ockham was denounced and investigated. In 1327 masters of arts Marsilius of Padua and John of Jandun were condemned for politico-ecclesiastical doctrines inspired by Averroism and opposed to the theory of the plenitude of papal power. The two men left Paris and took refuge with Louis the Bavarian, following him on his expedition into Italy where he worked to restore his imperial authority. Inquisitor Bertrand of Poggetto followed up that censure with another, already mentioned, of Dante's *Monarchy*. In 1328 the main supporters of absolute poverty fled from Avignon: Michael of Cesena, General of the Franciscans, Bonagratia of Bergamo, and Scotist Francis of Pignano, who were joined by William of Ockham. These men went to Pisa and Louis the Bavarian, who assured them of his support against the pope. In 1329 Michael was condemned and seventeen statements from the writings of Eckhart were censured.

And yet this din and roar was only an external symptom of the intellectual unrest of a period marked by ever-louder voices of dissent from the "common opinions," that is, from the prevailing views that the representatives of the Orders and the universities continued laboriously to present as the source of a now-utopian ideological harmony. Nor was the disagreement any longer over the formulation of new systems and the opening up of new speculative horizons. The very theological synthesis of reason and faith was now gradually subjected to criticisms that seemed to be prejudicially denying its effectiveness and tearing down the general principles on which it had hitherto been based.

Deeper reflection on the immediacy of physical and psychic phenomena, on the functioning of knowledge, and on the possibilities of logical regulation of the act of thinking was opening up unforeseen possibilities for the development of a philosophical thinking that would be helpful to theological reflection as well. But the soil from which these new ideas on organizing Christian doctrine were emerging was no longer that of solid systematization but of the now-victorious distinction among fields of study and, within these, the breakdown of excessively rigid systems of rational reference.

1. Durandus of Saint-Pourçain

In light of the vigorous clash of ideologies that characterized these decades, it is striking to see the commitment of some of the most authoritative Dominican masters to maintaining a doctrinal unity based on the Thomist synthesis. They acted as they did despite the clear timeliness of making corrections necessitated by the outcome of the lengthy debate at the end of the thirteenth century. Exemplary, from this point of view, was Hervaeus Nédellec (or Hervaeus Natalis, d. 1323), a master at Paris in 1307, then provincial prior of France, and finally

General from 1318 on. He was a fierce defender of Thomist orthodoxy, and yet he himself had doubts about some of Thomas' fundamental theses, such as the real distinction between essence and existence, matter as the principle of individuation, and theology as a science in the strict sense.

One of the adversaries of Thomism within the Order, those whom Hervaeus attacked so passionately, was James of Metz, who lectured on the *Sentences* at Paris between 1295 and 1302 and showed an excessive attraction to Augustinianism. But premier among them was Durandus of Saint-Pourçain (d. 1334), a master of theology in Paris from 1312 on and a lecturer at Avignon beginning in 1317. In that same year a commission of influential Dominican theologians published a list of propositions suspect of heresy because of their "deviations," but this was only the first of a series of attacks by more committed Dominicans, who refused any truce as the years went on.

Once Durandus had become bishop of Meaux and a member of the commission charged with investigating Ockham, he began courageously to repeat his own views. In 1333 he met in person with John XXII on the question of the beatific vision and incurred the censure of a pontifical commission. He maintained that in everything not an article of faith it was better to base one's opinions on reason rather than on authority. All this shows the independent spirit with which he claimed the right freely to express his own views on particular subjects, in opposition to any and every teacher.

Thinking as he did, Durandus regarded himself as free to sweep away a whole series of conceptual structures Thomas had introduced in order to explain the order of reality (individuation through matter, the action of the agent intellect as the source of abstract knowledge, the mediatory role of images or species in knowledge). His critique did not, however, result from a systematic critico-methodological examination (as would later be the case with Ockham) but from the fact that he regarded these mental schemata as insufficient and as incompatible with his fundamental doctrinal option, namely, the ontologically foundational character of teaching on relations.

He takes as his starting point the absolute perfection of the trinitarian mystery, which reason explains specifically as a form of relations within the perfect being. Then, making a general application of the Augustinian principle of the "traces of the Trinity," he deduces that the entire realm of being should be understood in light of the category of relation as a universal criterion that recapitulates all the other categories. Every being is always a mode of relation: *in itself* it presents itself as substance; *in another* it is an accident (quality or quantity, which absorb all the other categories); and *in relation to another* it is simply relation, which includes causal relations.

This distinction is real and not simply mental. Indeed, reality is always made up of relations because every being represents the actuation of an intrinsic demand, within the being itself, that it act by entering into relation with others. Relation is thus the universal mode of being, and it is not possible to find in being any alternatives to relation. This does not mean that relation is the sole and whole reality of being (this would mean doing away with the ontological weight of being): the being *is* and always has a relational connection, but not *this* connection.

According to Durandus the whole of philosophico-theological speculation can only be a celebration of the spontaneously active production of connections between beings. The world is a community of active individualities that are not individuated by something external (such as matter or existence), but subsist autonomously in their concrete reciprocal interrelations. From this situation the theory of knowledge likewise takes a specific direction: knowing is an act of cognitive relating in which the subject is never a passive recipient, even at the level of the senses and imagination, but is always active in relating itself to the object known. Durandus thus bypasses the Aristotelean theory of knowledge and adopts a gnoseological approach of the Platonico-Augustinian type: knowledge is not a conforming of intellect to reality but is always a direct, individual act of the subject that consists in producing within itself an identity (that is, a relation of identity) between the being of the object and its being as known.

Finally, this criticism of abstractive knowledge in favor of the greater effectiveness of the empirico-intuitive element of knowledge is reflected in Durandus' conception of theological knowledge. In his view this knowledge simply cannot be regarded as a science because it cannot have (as even the more moderate Thomists claim) a speculative character and a deductive method. Human beings on their earthly journey cannot have any knowledge of God, either abstractive or intuitive; this is true even if one claims to make it dependent on the knowledge the blessed have, because the latter is obviously to be understood as a point of arrival and not as a starting premise of human theological study.

The only earthly way, then, of drawing near to divine realities is that made possible by the religious self-relating of human beings to God as he reveals himself; in other words, the only way is faith. Faith is meritorious, therefore, precisely as an act of acknowledgment of the incomprehensible and unknowable. Thus it has a purely psychological value as a direct personal experience of what is communicated through revelation, and no abstractive-deductive knowledge based on this experience can ensure any growth or improvement.

2. Meister Eckhart

But disagreement with the "common way" of the Preachers was even more deeply entrenched in the German area and especially in the sphere of influence of the Cologne study center. Here the focus was on the authority of Albert the Great and on the new Platonizing trend into which, some decades earlier, Theodoric of Freiberg had introduced a different way of explaining the relationship between knowing subject and known object. A generation later, the task of drawing the ultimate consequences of Theodoric's approach was taken up by the great Dominican thinker and mystic Eckhart of Hochheim, universally known as Meister (Master) Eckhart (d. 1328). His goal was the attainment of a complete identity, in both knowledge and love, between the human subject and the divine essence.

Eckhart's theological thought had a perceptible influence on both philosophy and religious devotion in the Rhenish and Flemish cultural world, from the major representatives of the *Devotio Moderna* to Nicholas of Cusa and the first post-Lutheran mystico-theological developments. Eckhart's thinking developed in a rather restless region convulsed not only by political tensions but also by the vigorous spread of forms of lay devotion that often were difficult to bring under the control of the ecclesiastical authorities. At the end of the thirteenth and beginning of the fourteenth century these kinds of piety led to the formation of various communities more or less connected with the movement of the Beguines and Beghards. (The names are perhaps derived from Saxon *beggen*, "to pray," or perhaps from the nickname "Le Bègue," = "The Stammerer," of Lambert of Liège, whom these groups regarded as their founder.)

Repression by ecclesiastical authorities of these small, mainly female, lay communities, known as beguinages, was due to the difficulty of clearly distinguishing them from quite different heretical groups of an esoteric and gnostic kind. One such was the Brothers of the Free Spirit, who spread laxism, fanaticism, and anticlericalism throughout Europe. Thus in 1310, at Paris, Margaret Porete was condemned for the excessive erotico-mystical passion of her *Mirror of Simple Souls* and was sent to the stake. Without sufficiently distinguishing between the various movements, the Council of Vienne took measures against a variety of communities that were suspect of heresy. But it was especially during the pontificate of John XXII that the tendency to suppress all religious movements showing a critical and libertarian attitude toward the ecclesiastical structure was translated into a resolute application of steps to control and censure many communities scattered throughout the Netherlands and the Rhineland.

Eckhart had no direct connection with these movements, but many Beguines certainly welcomed and meditated on a good number of his writings, especially the *Sermons*. These they used to nourish their desires for mystical states, finding in them a solid and high-level speculative thought that might justify the linking of the Gospel call to a deep interior experience of mystical contact with God.

Eckhart's development as a student and teacher of theology took him to both Cologne and Paris, where he was licensed as a master in 1302. Then, in a move exceptional for a foreigner (Thomas Aquinas provided the only precedent), he held the chair of theology at Saint-Jacques from 1311 to 1313. For about a decade he resided in Strasbourg, where the memory of the Platonizing reading of Albert's works by Hugh Ripelin and Ulrich Engelbrecht was still alive. Here he was charged with the doctrinal training given at centers of Dominican female religious in the Rhineland; as a result he came in contact with circles of Beguines, against whom, during these very years, the bishop of Strasbourg was engaged in an inquisitorial trial that culminated in the publication of a first list of their doctrinal errors.

Inevitably, despite Eckhart's successes as an acclaimed preacher and theologian at the Dominican house of studies in Cologne, an investigation of his teachings was also begun; it was promoted by ideological dissidents within the Order. Henry II of Virnebourg, archbishop of Cologne, thus opened the first trial for heresy in which the accused was a master of Paris. He ended it with the condemnation of two lists of propositions taken from Eckhart's writings. The latter appealed to the Pope, insisting on his fidelity to the teachings of the church. When he went to Avignon he submitted to the judgment of a commission of experts whose work ended only after his death. Their condemnation for heresy extended only to the verbal tenor of some of his statements; it was confirmed by John XXII in the Bull *In agro dominico* in the spring of 1329.

It was as a highly skilled theologian that Eckhart sought for a mystical outcome of the intellectual ascent to God. On the basis of solid speculation he introduced this search into the Platonizing orientation of the Dominicans of the Rhenish area. His works, which are praiseworthy even from the literary point of view, were written, some in Latin that adheres closely to the theological and theoretical language of official teaching, and some in German; these latter are concerned more with the practico-theological aspect of interior spirituality and the experience of faith. The Latin works can be assigned to three categories in accordance with the author's plan for a "Three-part Work" (*Opus tripartitum*) that was, however, never completed. These were: commentaries on Scripture (*Expositions* but also individual *Sermons*), treatises that take an axiomatic approach in the form of *Propositions* (that is, treatises organized into theorems in accordance with the methodological type recently revived in Ulrich of Strasbourg's *On the Supreme Good*), and *Questions*. The German writings include some treatises on mysticism and, above all, a great many *Sermons*.

As the very literary genres employed make clear, Eckhart's speculative interests were exclusively theological. Especially in his mature years these interests were energized by the quest for ways of teaching doctrine that were appropriate for the intellectual and religious formation of Dominican students, particularly of the nuns placed under his tutelage.

The mystical concern that marks all his work was never separated from the solid epistemological foundations that constantly undergird the ways in which he seeks God and from which all merely lyrical and affective yearnings are absent. At the same time, a principled adoption of the rules of Pseudo-Dionysian negative theology continually guards him against the temptations to rational satisfaction that can arise from an overly analytic systematization of intellectual reflection on the divine mysteries. The God whom Eckhart seeks is a God who is known only by negation—that is, who can be grasped only when one presupposes the impossibility of subjecting him to a cognitive process that would in any case show only what he absolutely is not. In taking this starting point Eckhart was supported not only by Pseudo-Dionysius, but also by Augustine, Origen, Boethius, Proclus, the *On Causes*, and Maimonides, and, among contemporaries, Albert the Great, who commented on Dionysius, and Ulrich of Strasbourg, from whom he derived the triad of negation, causality, and eminence as criteria for selecting theological terminology and correctly applying it.

Drawing radical conclusions from these criteria, Eckhart maintains that every term predicable of God always has a solely negative semantic value. Even the term "One," which according to the Neoplatonists is the preeminent theological term, says about God only that he cannot be different and multipliable. When thus placed beyond any possible limitation, God can be defined as an infinite and absolute "region of unlikeness" (turning on its head the formula Augustine used to describe sinful humanity's state of alienation from God). To say this is to place God beyond anything involving similarity and commonality with created things: this includes even being itself. As is already clear in the (Latin) *Parisian Questions* Eckhart composed during the years in which he was obtaining his license to teach, when he says that God is not thinkable as something that *is*, he does not mean to deny God's ontological reality but only to locate it beyond the range of knowableness by creatures, as that which is absolutely nameless. Nonbeing is therefore predicated of God in a negative, causal, and eminent sense.

In the German sermons the preacher carries this unnameableness of God so far as to invite the hearers to love God as something that is in fact not lovable because he cannot be mediated through any image or representation and, again, because "he is a One something that is not-God (*nitgot*), not-Spirit (*nit-geist*), not-person (*nit-persone*), not-image (*nitbilde*)" and that he is One inasmuch as he is "untouched by any duality."

In one of the German sermons Eckhart undertakes the complex construction of an allegory by superimposing, one upon another, various interpretations of the verse that ends the account of Paul's conversion: "But Saul got up from the ground and, though his eyes were open, he saw nothing" (Acts 9:8). This means that when human beings see God they can only call him "nothing"; it means that they see God and nothing other than God, and again, that in all things they see only God; and that when Saul saw, he saw all things as a nothing. All these meanings seek to express the one certainty on which they all converge: that the vision of God has for its object something that *is not*, because it is not created, is not in creation, and is Nothing in the sense of a "nothing of anything whatsoever" (*nihites niht* in the German sermons) in comparison with creation. For while everything that is is also partially *nothing*, "what God *is*, he is completely."

But then, thanks to the words of Scripture, which has many meanings because it introduces the intellect to a truth that cannot be grasped as a unity, negation can be turned into a corresponding affirmation. Again thanks to Scripture, God can become for human reason a Being, since he is the being that is beyond every being. In the "General Prologue" of the planned *Tripartite Work* Eckhart states as follows the *Proposition* that was meant as the first of the axiomatic statements from which the entire development of theology was to be deduced: *God is To Be*, which is immediately convertible to *To Be Is God*. It can be said that God is Being, provided that this is equivalent for the human intellect to saying that God is Nothing, the Beginning that is not Begun, the Foundation that is not supported, the Word that is not spoken.

This pedagogical and instrumental retrieval of affirmative or positive theology is justified by revelation; in turn, the perspective opened by this retrieval justifies the possibility of a rational exegesis of Scripture. Moreover, it is at this level that the entire teaching of the great masters of scholastic theology (the "modern" teachers) and, in particular, of Thomas can and ought to be accepted. The intellectualism that characterizes human theology is always the result of the studies of God undertaken by natural reason, which is essential for explaining the meaning of Scripture. Eckhart could not but join in the common acceptance of Scripture as an essential tool for understanding the faith and then correctly practicing it. Thus theological reason can teach human beings to see a manifestation of God in everything that can be affirmed and, conversely, to see the presence of every affirmable perfection in the supreme truth that is God.

However, this acceptance of the affirmative and speculative theology of the "moderns" could have no value if the mind were not constantly illumined by a corrective awareness of the fundamental apophatic rule, which a true theologian must always have before him. The main difference, then, between the affirmative theology of Eckhart and that of Thomas is to be found in the fact that for Thomas predications about God are based on the substantial divine reality. In contrast, for Eckhart human theological language is always and only conditional due to the imperfection of the human intellect because, as Theodoric of Freiberg realized, the knowing subject always reproduces the nature of the object within itself according to its capacity.

Durandus was correct, then, in saying that theology is always a relational discourse. But, as the Fathers taught, the relation here does not introduce any variation or multiplication into the correlate as, on the contrary, it necessarily does into that which is related (that is, into the human subject, which speaks of God only by differentiating God from itself). The relation here is therefore one that, like all the other predications made by Scripture and theologians in order to say something about God, refers always and only to the essence or, better, the divine super-essence. This is true even of theological relational predication that tries to introduce into God relation itself as something belonging to his substance (namely, the trinitarian mystery). In fact, here above all we see how relation can be predicated of God in accordance with a truth that is always minimized by apophatism and therefore without introducing any multiplicity or diversity into God.

The assertion of the trinitarian mystery, as enunciated in revelation, amounts to the predication of the purest transcendental qualities of Being as Being (in relation to itself) and as Nothing (in relation to creation). These qualities are: One, which expresses absolute simplicity, non-composition, the lack of division in this perfect nature; True, as the uncreated perfect reality in which all things are true that exist in a composite and divided manner; Good, toward which imperfect things tend in order to enter into its perfection by participating in it. The exposition of the various names of God is essential in order to win the assent of our intellect, because the dogma of the Trinity is more of a mystery than is any other attribution of definable truth to God. Indeed, it is the primary and most effective of the expressive means used in revelation to assert the absolute truth of the divine being.

God is, then, a Trinity in which distinct realities unite and in which the generator is the generated. The unity of the Trinity is rooted in the same central meditation on Being that is quickened by the reading of the words with which God defines himself. In his *Exposition* of the book of Exodus, Eckhart is the first Christian theologian to catch the subtle nuance in the discourse in which God twice says that he is "who he is" (Exod 3:14: "God said to Moses, 'I am who I am.' And he said: 'This is what you shall say to the children of Israel: He who is has sent me to you'"). To utter the statement twice is to turn it back on itself, both asserting and reasserting, and to reveal while hiding. In this way the semantic effectiveness of the words is pushed in the direction of that "purity of affirmation" that consists in the exclusion of every negation in order that the affirmation may beget only affirmation. There is, as it were, a turning back of the affirmation of being on itself, "a boiling up or self-generation, as if the being were on fire within itself," as if it were a bush that burns without being consumed.

The image of "boiling up" (anticipated by Theodoric of Freiberg in his *The Intellect and the Intelligible*) is, in Eckhart's view, one of the most effective expressions of Being. It expresses not a differentiation or limitation, a stopping short, as it were, in the presence of another, but a continuous self-production in act without any limit and without any negation. This is a view that is rare, perhaps unique, in classical western thought, of pure being as pure self-movement, in contrast to the otherness described by the static being of what is finite.

The Prologue of John, which is theologically the supreme passage in the gospels, describes as "life" this being that is never itself (John 1:4); "life" signifies the Father's outpouring of his Being in the generating of the Son within a dynamic living identity that is the Holy Spirit. Theologians have devised another term to describe the same thing: thinking, the act of intellection in which the Father thinks himself in the Son. Why this term? Because the thinking of the Absolute as the Being who thinks himself is the purest action of this Being at the very moment in which it exists in the purest and most unalterable way: that is, because it is reflecting on itself.

As Eckhart says in the first of the *Parisian Questions*, in God knowing is the foundation of being; that is why the evangelist does not say, "In the beginning was the Being," but, "In the beginning was the Word," that is, the knowing divine Intellect, which exists because it knows. The Word can therefore be expressed by means of the philosophical tools developed by Christian theology: it is the manifestation within God of this pure Intellect. The reason: the heart of the revelation in Exodus is a *verb*: "I am"; therefore "The Word *was* God" (John 1:1), because "God is what the Word was."

But the description of God as "thinking" does not give a basis for a mental representation of the Trinity, which is of its nature not representable. That verb is, however, the highest possible expression of the Trinity that human beings can comprehend. *Think* (*intelligere*) is in fact a word that describes not only the act of being divine, but also the purest act by which human beings draw near to God ("God is grasped only by the intellect"), as all the great teachers from Anselm to Albert have taught. It is for this reason that the theological understanding of the generation of the Word as the act of thinking in which the Father conceives creation is made possible by a comparison with the cognitive act of the human intellect. Because the human being is an intellect, there is, despite the incalculable distance between God and human beings, at least a generic kind of commonality, and the human person can be said to belong to the same genus as God (*genus deitatis*).

But in order that human beings with their intellects may be able to receive this being-Intellect of God it was necessary that the latter go out of itself, that the dynamism, the "boiling up" of its Being lead it to move out of itself in another Being in a "boiling up" outside of itself. This allegory brings out the mystery of the Incarnation. The Word was "in the beginning," in the source, which in German is expressed by *grunt* (modern *Grund* = "ground"), the depth of the divinity. "There, in the beginning, in the *Grund*, the Son is begotten and from there the Holy Spirit proceeds." The true *Grund* is the deity prior to Being, the ineffable, inexplicable abyss that is denied even as it is affirmed: the *Abgründlichkeit* or lack of bottom. From there God flows out to give being and life to others —that is, creatures—but, not content with this supreme gift, he continues his outflowing and goes out of himself again as the Word who becomes flesh, as the Intellect that goes out of itself in order to make itself known in its very knowing and to restore the true being of understanding to creatures that have forgotten it in the loss entailed in their separation from God.

The human intellect, too, this most elevated place of encounter with truth, that is, with God—that which the philosophers think of as higher reason or the agent intellect—is in a sense the *Grund*, the depth of the soul, the Augustinian "abyss of the mind," which Theodoric of Freiberg understood to be an abyss of interiority into which the human self immerses itself in order to find once again the divine self. Here is found the "peak of the soul" (*wipfelin der sêle*), its "head" (*houbet*), the "spark" (*vünkelin*) that illumines and burns with the light of love, the acropolis, the little fortified citadel (*bürgelin*) of the soul.

All these images will flow into the German mystical literature of subsequent decades and centuries, where they will nourish the metaphorical understanding of the interior ascent to God. As human beings rediscover in their own intellects the impossible depths of their indescribable but real kinship with God they melt into an obscure union (a "oneness of the spirit") in which it is no longer simply human beings trying to know God, but henceforth it is God, in the intellect, "who knows himself in himself," as the German sermon *Quasi stella matutina* says. The intellect is "the temple of God"; God dwells in it, and where God dwells, God is, because he knows himself.

Such are the most daring heights of the Eckhartian theology that leads to the ultimate mystical result (these were also the heights most feared by those who did not or could not understand them). It is in the human soul, at last turned wholly to God thanks to God, who took flesh in order to make himself known—it is there, in the *Grund* of creaturely knowledge, that God himself knows himself. The God who took flesh in order to make himself known knows himself as united to the human being in an identity that does not involve any confusion of persons, but does fuse the act of human understanding with that of God and thus leads to the meeting of being with nonbeing, grace with sin, love with the beloved.

Then—and this is the supreme image of the theological result of understanding—in the human soul in which he has taken flesh by making himself known, the divine Word again generates himself as God. The rediscovery of the true divine image by the human creature takes place when the latter, through grace and in grace, shares in the divine life in its fullness. And, because the fullness of divine life consists in the generation of the Word, the human soul participates in that divine life, mystically but really, when, in the *Grund* of its being and understanding, in its human depth, "the Father begets his Son in an eternal begetting." The Word enters the soul of the believer, chooses it as his "dwelling" and makes himself a "dwelling" for it, relives his own mysteries in it, from his eternal generation to his incarnation in history; in short, he becomes a human being in the soul of the believer in order to make it divine.

Here contraries cancel each other out: the generator is the generated, the subject is the object, the knower is the known, the creature is even the creator and the creator the creature. The human ascent to God is the completion of the path on which God seeks himself outside of himself in order to know himself.

Those who see the danger of pantheism in these promises have not understood the dynamic distinction between the divine Being and the created being, which also explains their union to the theologizing intellect. In the *Defense* Eckhart composed in order to defend himself before the tribunal at Avignon he cites Boethius: "In dealing with things divine one must proceed by using the intellect and not allow oneself to be drawn toward images," anthropomorphic and realistic representations that divide being from being and never convey the efficacious immediacy of the intellect as such, the "naked" intellect that unites. Only this intellect understands how the union of the creature's intellect with God in the Word-Intellect is not an ontological fusion but a real gnoseological union. In the nullification of the world, that is, in the realization of the "nothing" of creatures, the union-participation that theologians call "deification" is the real and definitive bringing of the human intellect into the knowledge God has of himself.

3. Peter Aureoli

Peter Aureoli (or Aurelio, d. 1322) was a Franciscan from Aquitaine; he was nicknamed the "Eloquent Doctor" (*Doctor Facundus*). In several respects he was not a scholar who passively submitted to papal authority, just as he did not fall into line with any of the prevailing positions of his age. He kept his distance from all trends and was critical of all the great masters of the recent past, from Henry of Ghent to Alexander of Hales, from Thomas to Bonaventure, from Scotus to Durandus.

He did, however, have a constructive meeting of minds with papal authority, beginning around 1311 in Paris, when, still fresh from theological studies during which he followed the lectures of Duns Scotus, he took a position on the struggle within the Order between Spirituals and Conventuals. He wrote a *Treatise on Poverty and the Poor Man's Use of Things*, in which he offered conciliatory solutions that anticipated the compromise position on the ideal of poverty that was sanctioned by Clement V in the constitution *Exivi de paradiso* at the Council of Vienne. Later, after Peter had spent some years lecturing at Bologna and Toulouse, John XXII asked the chancellor of the Paris university to grant him a license to teach theology, even though he was in only his second year of bachelor studies. Those were the years in which he put the final touches on his extensive *Book on the Sentences*. In 1321 the same pope consecrated him bishop of Aix-en-Provence, a year before his death, which took place, it seems, at the court in Avignon.

In fact, this harmony with papal authority reflects his basic thinking, which led him, even in the crucial problem of relations between theology and philosophy, to adopt a moderate and conciliatory position, though one not without an element of constructive probabilism. His *Treatise on Principles* (or *on Philosophical Principles*), written between 1312 and 1313 during his time in Bologna, begins with an unequivocal statement. Among the teachings of the philosophers, and especially of Aristotle, there are many valuable truths to be gathered and preserved; in fact, the deeper their studies penetrate the more we see how they are in agreement "with the truth of the faith." But this assumption represents an aspiration, not a condition. The Faith and the authority of the pope are always superior to the thinking of the philosophers, and when the latter err, ecclesiastical authority must correct them.

In their basic inspiration these assertions are in agreement with the doctrinal bases of the pontifical theocracy Boniface VIII set down in his bull *Unam sanctam* in 1302, when Peter Aureoli was just beginning his studies in Paris. According to Boniface every error in this world can and ought to be judged solely by the church, which gives concrete expression to the truth of the Faith. The church acts as a single and unified mystical body whose head and leader is Christ and that is, with Christ, subject only to God. For Peter the church's infallibility in matters of faith is a principle regulating any and every inferior form of knowledge, precisely because of the limits native to the human intellect.

The protection given by this preliminary rule of theology allows Peter to regard himself as authorized to adopt unusual philosophical views whenever reason suggests their helpfulness: to adopt, that is, views alien to the common thinking of the masters of his time. He does so every time he thinks he should intervene to explain what seems to him to be the authentic teaching of the basic philosophical sources, namely, Aristotle and Augustine. He does this, for example, when he thinks the two sources agree in maintaining universal hylomorphism and the impossibility of matter existing without a form. He greatly opposes the admission that the soul is the substantial form of the body because he fears it may lead to a denial of personal immortality and a defective way of understanding intellectual activity.

Yet once this proposition was approved by the council it was no longer a philosophical proposition but a truth of the Faith and had to be held even if reason could not manage to understand it, as was the case also with the divine Trinity. One can understand something without being compelled to believe that it is true, just as one can believe in the truth of something one cannot understand.

The Averroists' distinction between faith and reason does not oppose two truths, because only the first is always and unqualifiedly true. This clarification of the balance between faith and reason, which is the fundamental premise of all of Aureoli's thinking, is, however, not simply a general orientation in his case. It has, instead, a solid theoretical basis in his conception of truth and knowledge, an area in which he takes a truly original position that was misunderstood and was harshly criticized by the majority of his contemporaries.

If philosophy is to claim to reach truth, it must first explain what philosophical truth is. Duns Scotus deserved credit for raising this problem in a fundamental and unavoidable way by connecting every judgment on the subject with the central question of evidence as the definitive requirement for judging the reliability of knowledge. And here he introduced the distinction between intuitive knowledge and abstractive knowledge, while pointing out that only the first is based on real evidence. Almost all the authors of this period accepted the distinction, but with nuances that led to different assessments of the degree of certainty enjoyed by intuitive knowledge.

To Scotus' mind intuitive knowledge was always and exclusively knowledge of a real object the subject grasps as present and existing. To many, however, this rule seemed overly rigid. In addition, questions were raised that called for a different explanation. Is it perhaps not possible to have an intuitive knowledge of something that does not exist? This amounted to asking whether and to what extent knowledge based on evidence can be false. Is it perhaps not possible to have abstractive knowledge that is true, the kind that arises from the simplest mathematical and logical rules? This amounted to asking whether and to what extent abstractive knowledge based on a proposition *can* be evident, or whether a non-evident knowledge *can* be true.

Thus formulated, such questions introduced a variable, namely possibility, into the definition of evidence. To what extent can knowledge be considered evident while prescinding from its correspondence to the reality of the thing known? The question has to do not with the reality of what is known but with the mode of knowing. Moreover, giving a radical depth to possibility as a variable, there was, even in Scotus, the longstanding logical impact of divine omnipotence as a theological criterion. (Ever since the time of Peter Damian the fact of divine omnipotence had been regarded as a decisive means of deciding the validity of the logical definition of human thought.) God *can* effectively cause something nonexistent to be known as really present and therefore as an object of intuitive knowledge. Thus the gnoseological distinction between intuitive knowledge and abstractive knowledge is interwoven with the theological distinction between God's absolute power and his ordering power.

The acceptance of an infinite divine power that is free (as absolute power), without creating a contradiction, to change even the most rigid laws it (as ordering power) has imposed on the universe from the beginning of creation radicalizes the problem of establishing a sure and evident foundation for knowledge by introducing the maximum extension of the concept of possibility as a hypothesis that must be taken into account. Peter Aureoli was among the first to push to the extreme this problem affecting the certainty of knowledge, as he sought to construct a satisfactory teaching on knowledge and also to define the nature of theological knowledge. Not by chance, then, the place he chose for giving his own answer to these questions was the very one that called for defining and utilizing theological knowledge: namely, his commentary on the *Sentences*.

In this new perspective Peter takes up the old problem of the reality of universals. He will have nothing to do with the Thomist teaching on mental species as representations of the analogies existing among objects (a position recently emphasized once more by Hervaeus) or with Scotus' effort to base the truth of thought on the constitutive characteristics of the intrinsic essences of things. To Peter's mind both of these solutions are unjustified, for it is not possible to admit the existence of a universal reality corresponding to the concept, and this is the real basis of the Aristotelean appeal to experience, which had been adopted by the empirical tradition of the Oxford Franciscans.

But Aureoli's Aristotle is always blithely paired with Augustine. Thus the possibility of experiencing external things is perceptible only interiorly, where the intellect distinguishes concepts by referring them to the experienced data and then structures knowledge according to various degrees of intensity, from particular to universal. These are a product of the soul's cognitive action, not modes of being of external reality. Evidence can therefore be found only at the boundary connecting the soul's interiority with external realities: that is, only in the intention with which I consider the object, looking at it sometimes in its immediacy ("this rose") and sometimes in its general characteristics ("rose as such"), which are accepted as if they are a single object that can stand for all the particular entities to which they can be applied ("the complete rose"). In knowledge, therefore, the "evident" is an object as it appears to the mind's intentional activity, that is, to the cognitive attention of the subject: "that which has only an apparent and intentional being."

Aureoli thus formulates his own teaching on apparent or intentional being and offers it as a solution to the problems inherent in all the doctrines on knowledge proposed by his contemporaries. The subject cannot be regarded as completely passive in knowing (as Geoffrey of Fontaines would have it), for otherwise it could not produce the knowledge of universals. But neither is its activity to be identified with the reproduction of an image, a "mirroring form" (as the Thomists claim), for this would uselessly duplicate the reality and hinder an effective knowledge of it. Nor, finally, is knowledge a straightforward relationship of subject to object (as Durandus proposes), for knowledge is something distinct from both.

As for the distinction between intuitive and abstract knowledges, they are distinguished on the basis not of the way in which the object is present (as Scotus requires) but of the way in which the subject ascertains it ("according to the way of knowing"). There is an intuition when the object is existent and present: not, however, simply because it is really existent and present before the subject, but rather because it appears to the subject who intuits it as if it were existent and present. In contrast, there is abstract knowledge when the object is known as not present and not existent.

In the Preface of his *Commentary*, Aureoli explains what "apparent being" is, relying on a formula that will be sharply criticized by all his reviewers: in intuition the thing appears as present and existent independently of its factual existence, that is, whether or not it actually exists:

> One and the same is the appearance in which the thing appears as present and actual and existing in the real world, whether in fact it does exist or does not exist. In the other form of knowledge, whether the thing exists or does not exist, it does not appear as present and actual and existent in the real world, but as in the imagined form of something absent.

Peter has two arguments, one empirical, the other instrumental, to show the possibility of a thing being known intuitively as present even though it is not present. The first is the observation that there are experiences of the nonexistent, such as hallucinations, nightmares, and optical illusions. The second is based on the maximum extension of possibility that is ensured by God's absolute power: God can always cause an intuition even in the absence of its object. The first argument would evoke the more important criticisms, inasmuch as it involves a confusion of intuitive knowledge with deceptive knowledge, thereby introducing the possibility of error into the very heart of what ought to be the most direct and certain form of knowledge. This critique was the basis for the accusation of skepticism leveled at Aureoli both by William of Ockham and by the Franciscan masters of Oxford. Although the latter took contrasting speculative positions, they too supported the basing of scientific knowledge on the reality of the object; such were Walter of Chatton (an opponent of Ockhamism, d. 1343) and Adam Wodham (a student and defender of Ockham, d. 1358).

In contrast, the second argument, from the absolute power of God, seemed more convincing to the critics who rejected the doctrine of "apparent being," to the point of being accepted by them as a valid hypothesis. In fact, it does provide a better perspective for fully understanding Aureoli's thesis on the possibility of a knowledge that is completely independent of the existence of the known object.

In Aureoli's view the "appearance" on which knowledge is based is not the subjective act of grasping the real presence of the object known, but is the true and proper mode of being of the thing when it becomes an object of knowledge. There is, therefore, no third element between subject and object such as the Thomist species, despite the accusation of the Oxford realists that Aureoli has uselessly introduced a contrivance between reality and knowledge. Peter says: "Every act of knowing is that due to which things appear and are constituted in their being as present." In other words, the apparent or intentional entity is a true and proper objective entity the thing takes on when it is compared with (that is, situated in relation to) the act of knowing. The real existence of the thing is necessary in order that intuitive knowledge may be true, not in order that it be possible. The possibility of intuition requires only the appearance of something as present and existent; when this condition is satisfied, there can be abstractive knowledge as the appearance of something as non-present and nonexistent.

The best implementation of this doctrine comes, according to Aureoli, when one moves on to consider the nature of theological knowledge. The principle in accordance with which understanding of the truth of the thing known can and even ought to be distinct from the necessity of admitting that it is true in the real world is that it could be true simply because God in his absolute power makes it such. This provides the best explanation of how it is possible for human beings to understand before believing and to believe without understanding.

In the realm of theology God is in fact known as an intentional truth, that is, a truth that appears to the intellect thanks to the contribution of revelation. The latter sets before the human subject, as something existent and present, everything the subject needs to know about God's essence. The fundamental consequence of all this is that theological knowledge is not a science, as the theologians of the schools claim, because its truthfulness does not depend on its object being describable as real on the basis of knowledge of it. Theology is not a science of the faith but, in the authentic spirit of Anselm's legacy, an understanding of the faith.

From this follows the rejection of any mediation by epistemological principles, whether Aristotelean or of any other kind, in the process of theological knowledge. Thomist subalternation is excluded because the articles of the faith are not a starting point but the final point of arrival of theology, which has for its task to establish them as conclusions. Also excluded is the idea that theology is knowledge infused from on high through illumination, because it takes contingent truths into account and produces in the believer an attitude that is not cognitive but one of simple faith.

On the other hand, there is no reason for not accepting that theology proceeds by argumentation. The reason is that the study of Sacred Scripture produces in the soul a theological way of thinking (*habitus theologicus*) that is purely one of belief and not of knowledge but that finds expression in a discourse that links together the various propositions expressing the concrete contents of this belief. Provided that we are talking of belief and not of knowledge, all of theology can even be regarded as a huge, complex argumentation. As a biblical master in Paris, Peter composed a *Compendium of the Literal Sense of the Totality of the Divine Sacred Scripture*. Here each sacred book is presented as a complex syllogism with its own specific conclusion, and the entire Bible as a great overarching syllogism in which supernatural and natural truths are interwoven deductively.

The theological way of thinking is thus activated in a discourse that has for its purpose the understanding of the faith; very eloquent examples of such thinking and discourse can be found in the works of the Fathers (first and foremost Augustine's *Trinity*). There is, therefore, no learning that has to be discovered, since it has already existed for centuries. This knowledge is obviously something additional by comparison with faith, but it is not reducible to a simple course of metaphysical investigation that prescinds from faith. Rather, it is a manifestative discourse on what is believed; its begins with premises that are believed, pursues a better explanation and clarification of these, and concludes with definitions of the truths in which one believes. It need not convince the intellect to believe by enunciating necessary motives, but has for its purpose a better understanding of what can be believed or not believed. Thus it fully confirms the sapiential nature of theology and, consequently, its character as a practical knowledge inasmuch as it promotes the acquisition of something that can also be acquired in another way (as, for example, medicine is practical because it promotes health, although health is of a better kind when acquired naturally). God can be reached more perfectly by faith, hope, and charity, but theology can help the soul to better direct its acts of faith, hope, and charity toward what is revealed.

A concrete example of this functional activity of theology can be seen in the position Aureoli took in favor of the Immaculate Conception of Mary; he had already defended this in 1314 at a public disputation in Paris and had then argued against the Dominican theologians of Toulouse in his *Counterstatement against the Deniers of the Sinlessness of the Mother of God*. The reasons for maintaining the innocence of Mary and her freedom from sin are based on the principle (which in the final analysis is very Anselmian) that God in his absolute omnipotence could not have failed to choose in advance the best way of accomplishing his goals, even if this meant transgressing the rules established by his ordering power.

Another example comes from Peter's theses on justification: by his ordering power God has established an exact symmetry between sin and punishment and between merit and reward, but by his absolute power he can change even these laws. If he were to think it just, he could reward the guilty, save Emperor Trajan through the prayers of Gregory the Great, and condemn St. Peter along with all the other saints. Human beings, therefore, should not deceive themselves into thinking that they can merit grace by their own powers; all should trust in God's unconditional love, which is the sole compelling cause of the divine choices and to which the only response is a corresponding and wholly disinterested act of love.

4. William of Ockham

Adam Wodham, a fellow religious of William of Ockham, wrote a Preface for his edition of the latter's *Summa of Logic* (as mentioned earlier, Adam heard Ockham's lectures at the Franciscan house of studies in London). In this Preface he stresses the usefulness of the *Summa* for the improvement and reform of learning, a usefulness all should recognize; he also sees the abandonment of the study of logic as the chief cause of the uncertainties and doubts that threaten the roots of Christian wisdom and hinder the understanding of divine revelation itself. It is necessary to revive and definitively reestablish the principles of the logical method of learning, since this is an essential tool for distinguishing truth from error, as has been unanimously taught by the greatest of the philosophers and the prince of theologians, Aristotle and Augustine respectively. Only then is it possible to relearn accurate argumentation by freeing the mind from the fetters of the sophistic illusions in which it is now ensnared and entangled.

In William's own introduction to the *Summa* he echoes the words of his young collaborator and disciple when he says that logic is "the most fruitful tool among all the arts," because without it "no body of knowledge can be known perfectly."

This is an ancient idea, widespread in the Christian world since the time of Augustine: namely, that the art of debate (known in the past as dialectic or, as the "modern" masters would have it, logic) is the true "wellspring of knowledge" (as Martianus Capella had called it long ago). This is because by formalizing the norms of thought and of the discourse that expresses thought, it ensures the identification of truth through knowledge.

But for Ockham this recall of the indispensable formal regulation of the epistemological conditions of knowledge takes on a special meaning. This is because he bases his own "correct" reinterpretation of Aristotelean logic on a rigorously concrete and individual consideration of everything that corresponds to the meaning of logical concepts and therefore to the whole truth of the scientific disciplines. This rule—that reality is one, singular, and simple—is the nervous system running through and supporting his entire plan for completing the restoration, already begun by Duns Scotus, of an authentically Christian wisdom. Working under the aegis of the fundamental principle of divine omnipotence, this wisdom is free of abstract essentialism and the necessitarianism of Greco-Arabic metaphysics.

The new logic starts with the antecedent recognition of the absolute freedom of the creative cause, a freedom that guarantees the immutability of truth, which is such only because and as long as God wills it. It will then be oriented to recognizing truth only in that which exists because it has been brought into existence by the divine will. It will therefore recognize truth only in what is singular, absolutely simple in its unrepeatable reality, and immediately knowable in its ever-new and ever-contingent mode of being.

These innovative presuppositions are uniformly present throughout Ockham's entire body of work and inspire his various teachings and his logical solutions to the problems raised by scientific, metaphysical, and theological speculation. They are the basis on which he undertakes his own radical and all-embracing reform of human learning, at the summit of which he will necessarily place a renewed consideration of the cognitive status proper to theological discourse.

A. THE "VENERABLE INCEPTOR"

William was born around 1280 at Ockham in Surrey. The title *Venerabilis Inceptor* ("Venerable Beginner"), given to him by his contemporaries, alludes to the fact that he never obtained a master's license. After he had finished his early studies and obtained his bachelor's degree at Oxford his legitimate desire to become a master was put on hold, perhaps due to early conflicts with the chancellor, John Lutterell, a secular Thomist who was worried by the applause William's innovative ideas received from a growing number of students. In 1321 he was sent to the Franciscan house of studies in London, where he lectured on philosophy and theology until 1324. At that point, in response to a formal denunciation by Lutterell, he was summoned to Avignon to defend himself against accusations of heresy.

At this period Ockham had already composed a first draft of his own interpretation of Aristotelean logic; it took the form of analytical comments on the *Organon*, collected under the title *Golden Explanation*. He had also commented on Aristotle's *Physics* and composed seven *Quodlibeta* in which he had already synthesized the speculative foundations of his own thinking. In addition he had composed the first book of his commentary on the *Sentences*; this book, which he himself wrote, is usually titled the *Ordinatio* in order to distinguish it from the subsequent books, which were composed from notes taken by his hearers and are known, in their entirety, as the *Reportatio*.

It was on these texts that John Lutterell had based his criticisms in his *Short Book in Answer to the Teaching of William of Ockham*. Here he focused on the serious theological consequences that, in his view, followed from neglect of Thomas' valuable tools for the interpretation of dogma, especially in the matter of eucharistic transubstantiation and moral theology. While a commission, which included Lutterell himself and, as mentioned earlier, Durandus of Saint-Pourçain, was investigating the orthodoxy of fifty-six propositions drawn from his writings, William worked on his own defense by completing the *Summa of Logic* and composing treatises on the Eucharist and the divine foreknowledge. In these works he turned back on his opponents the accusation of making a defective use of the rules of logic when they subordinated these in a prejudicial way to the directives of metaphysics; theirs, and not his, was "bad logic," bad because erroneous.

The meeting at Avignon with Michael Cesena and the principal representatives of the thinking of the Spirituals was decisive for William's rapid and resolute conversion to the cause of apostolic poverty. (The strong opposition of the Spirituals to the pope during these years brought to naught the pacification of the Franciscan world that had been proposed by Peter Aureoli and fostered at Vienne.) The same critical attitude that led him to apply scientific reason to demolishing the totalitarianism of universals in logic and metaphysics now drove him to oppose John XXII. He became a pitiless critic, on the ideological plane, of the pope's theocratic universalism and his unjustified assumption that unity would result from his fullness of authority, an authority artificially placed at the top of a nonexistent hierarchy of cosmic perfections.

In 1328, at almost the same time as the judgment of the inquisitorial commission that condemned as heretical seven of the propositions in the indictment, Ockham fled the papal city along with the friars most involved in resistance to the pope and joined Louis the Bavarian at Pica, later following him to Munich. In this last city Ockham spent about twenty years, until his death around 1347, working on an extensive theologico-political treatment of poverty and the opposition between papal and imperial power. He thus carried out the program that, according to the chronicles, he had announced in his first words to the emperor: "Defend me with your sword, and I will defend you with my words."

B. THE THEORY OF TRUTH: INTUITIVE KNOWLEDGE AND ABSTRACT KNOWLEDGE, SIMPLE TERM AND COMPLEX PROPOSITION

Beginning with the first question in the Prologue of the *Ordinatio*, Ockham engages in a subtle analysis of the conditions for cognitive evidence in order thereby to answer the question whether it is possible for the human subject to come in contact with reality through a cognitive act. In agreement with Duns Scotus, Ockham cannot but acknowledge that, as between intuitive knowledge and abstractive knowledge, only the former has the right to claim to be an immediate apprehension of a concrete existent and therefore a preliminary to any further acquisition of truth by the subject. Nevertheless, as even Peter Aureoli remarked, Scotus is mistaken in regarding as intuitive only the direct perception of the external presence of the object, a perception arising from the contact of the senses with particular corporeal realities. In fact, the subject is able to intuit, that is, immediately recognize as realities, its own interior acts, both intellectual operations and the unmediated movements of the soul such as pleasure and pain.

Furthermore, in this realm of interior intuition, because of the evidence with which they are endowed, a primacy belongs to the first principles that logicians place at the apex of their discipline. These are formulated in propositions that very directly strike the mind as true and thus concern not only the existence of things (as in "A is A") but also the impossibility of their existence ("A is different from non-A," and "in addition to A and non-A no third exists"). But from first principles and by way of strict deductive connections there also emerge universal and necessary propositions that are the direct object of knowledge and are themselves evident. Thus intuitive evidence extends to a rather wide range of true perceptions, from that of the concrete and individual external contingent entity to that of fundamental logical necessities.

Next comes an important reformulation of the very concepts of intuition and abstraction. For Ockham, "intuitive" describes every simple apprehension that enables us to know how things really are or, in other words, "by means of which we can know whether the thing exists or does not exist." Such an apprehension therefore enables the subject to formulate true judgments on existence or nonexistence. "Abstractive" knowledge, on the other hand, is any knowledge that in grasping the object "prescinds [abstracts] from its existence or nonexistence and from all the other conditions that contingently inhere in the thing or can be predicated of it."

Abstractive knowledge does not, therefore, arise from something other than what produces intuitive knowledge. According to Scotus' thesis, rejected by Ockham, such an "other" would be an efficacious "species" or "common nature" that the interior senses pass on to the intellect; but if these common species were real, they would in fact have to be known intuitively and would not produce an abstraction. Conversely, abstractive knowledge is simply caused by intuitive knowledge, even if this involves action at a distance, that is, is produced when the intuitive knowledge is no longer immediately present and operative. Consequently, the distinction between intuitive knowledge and abstractive knowledge does not depend on a difference in objects known, because "in both forms of knowledge the same object is always and in every respect the same"; the distinction depends on the modality of the knowledge, the different ways in which the subject grasps the object.

To the extent that they represent simple mental situations, both intuitive knowledge and abstractive knowledge always originate in something concrete that is reflected in the meaning of a term. Logical terms, considered as non-complex (that is, still not joined in propositions and eventually in demonstrations), are the foundations of all logic and every act of human knowledge, the bricks that make it possible to construct the entire architecture of a science. But as long as intuitive knowledge (and, consequently, abstractive knowledge as well) is concerned only with terms, its potentiality for being true refers exclusively to the simple meaning of the object, that is, to its status as substance or quality, but not yet to its reality. A simple (noncomplex) term is unable by itself to show the existence of the thing it signifies; it signifies only what the thing is independently of its real existence or nonexistence (a human being is a "human being," a rose is a "rose," a centaur is a "centaur," even if they do not exist).

In contrast, a judgment about truth and an assent of the intellect to the existence or nonexistence of the thing known belong on the level of complex knowledge (that is, of conjoined terms). Such judgments are propositions that attempt to establish a connection between subject and predicate ("this human being exists," "this rose is red," "this centaur does not exist"). Of the simple term we have only an apprehension or understanding; a proposition requires not only understanding but also assent. It is therefore on the level of propositions or the logic of the complex that philosophers focus their attention when they intend to verify the evidence for knowledge. Only when dealing with propositions can we ask about the truthfulness of a statement that speaks of a reality as existent or nonexistent.

It is, therefore, easy to acknowledge that propositional knowledge, the terms of which are clearly understood, is true only when it is confirmed by the intuitive recognition of its conformity to external reality. All necessary particular propositions, that is, those intuition presents as directly evident, are true. Also true, among universal propositions, are those that derive directly from the truth of first principles, the evidence of which, as we said, is intuitively perceived; to put it differently, necessary universal propositions (such as those of mathematics) are true. True, in addition, are contingent propositions concerned with the immediate mode of being of individual things or their qualities, the evidence for which is intuitively perceptible; in other words, contingent singular propositions are true. On the other hand, never true, because not evident, are the contingent and non-necessary universal propositions produced by an abstractive knowledge that is not supported by the intuitive recognition of evidence for such propositions.

C. THE DOCTRINE OF SUPPOSITION AND NOMINALISM

The human possibility of producing scientific discourse, that is, one that corresponds to reality, is at this point subordinated to an evaluation of the signifying capacity of terms within propositions that claim to be true. In other words, it is subordinated to an evaluation of their capacity to express an objective reality within propositions and along with the propositions they form.

Aristotle's teaching, as formulated in the first chapter of his *On Interpretation*, explained the role of terms in propositions by assigning them a subjective function and a predicative function. The logicians of the thirteenth century in their systematic presentations of their discipline, the best known of which was the *Summulae logicales* of Peter Hispanus, thought it necessary to add further specifications to Aristotle's teaching on the properties of terms, that is, the ways in which a term can be used in discourse. Thus they developed the theory of "supposition," which follows up the changing values a word acquires depending on its position within a proposition and in relation to the other terms.

It must be noted, first of all, that this doctrine has to do solely with terms capable of expressing, by themselves, a complete meaning (such as "man," "white," etc.). In technical language such terms are said to be "categorematic" and are distinct from terms incapable of standing by themselves (such as "every," "no" [with a noun], "only," etc.) but useful in linking other elements of the discourse and therefore called "syncategorematic." Since a categorematic term can be predicated of many things, past, present, and future, it is necessary to specify, when it is used in a proposition, the reality for which it performs its function of signifying—that is, of being put in the place of something in order to point to it (*supponere pro*). For example, one and the same term can be used in reference to quite different things: I may say "the cow walks," or "the cow is an animal," or "cow is a word." Various types of supposition are distinguished, depending on these different uses, although the articulation and presentation of the types may vary from one to another of the more important handbooks of scholastic logic.

William of Ockham, too, proposes a classification of suppositions that is original and strictly in the service of his own conception of knowledge. After excluding the various forms of supposition improperly so called (when a term is used for metaphorical or other secondary purposes), he proposes to accept three forms of supposition in the proper sense: material, simple, and personal.

There is a material supposition whenever a term is used to signify its own material self, whether vocal or graphic or verbal (for example, "camel is a word" or "camel is made up of two syllables"); in these cases the term stands for itself as a sign and not for a thing signified by it.

There is a personal supposition when a term stands for that which it is called upon to signify by reason of an elementary act of imposition of meaning. The thing it has been introduced into the language to signify may be something extra-mental, but it may also be a product of the mind and refer both to singular entities and to universals ("Socrates runs"; "the horse gallops"; but also "species is a universal").

But there is a third possibility, the "simple supposition" (as, for example, "cow is a species"). Here the term does not stand for its natural and primary meaning but seeks to express something common to the things that come under its personal meaning, but different from what these things are.

Thus, correcting a tendency common to the thirteenth-century manuals of logic, Ockham does not see a simple supposition in every universal use of a term, because when a term is used as a universal and signifies the collection of individuals conforming to the term's natural meaning, it represents, in his view, a personal supposition. In contrast, a simple supposition is one that establishes a correspondence between a term and a logical property, an intention of the mind that presents itself as something common to the things signified but is not these things. For example, when on the basis of a personal supposition the term "human being" is used to signify something universal, such as "a human being is an animal," the intention is to say that all the individuals signifiable by the term "human being" are animals. When, however, the same term is used with a simple supposition, as in "man is a species," it stands for the way in which the mind represents to itself that which ought to correspond to "being a human being."

It follows that when in a proposition a term is based on a personal supposition, something real corresponds to it. But when it is based on a simple supposition, to it corresponds something that is never a thing but always a pure product of thought: it has no metaphysical reality and no evident correspondence with an extra-mental reality. (Nothing need be said about material supposition, since this expressly does not refer to anything subsisting in the world of things.)

The importance of the theory of supposition in the search for evidence in scientific discourse is now clear. The passage from a simple supposition to a personal supposition represents for Ockham a descent in the true and proper sense (a "descent to things inferior"): from the purely mental universe of the pure concepts used by the mind to the concrete realities, signifiable by logical terms, of the particular things that make up the world. The universal as such exists only in the mind and therefore has no reality, but when it is used with a personal supposition to indicate something outside the mind it signifies the reality of all the concrete individuals, really existing as singulars, that are covered by the meaning of the term used.

An analysis of the human ability to speak of truth confirms, therefore, the fact that no product of the mind exists outside the mind. The only things existing in the real world are God's works or creatures in their independent, distinct, and non-repeatable singularity. The universal known as such is only an act by which the mind moves toward the object as it signifies it; it is an intention that directs the knower to the likeness between two or more things. Despite every attempt hitherto made by classical and medieval philosophy to demonstrate the objective character of universals, the fact is that universals never have a corresponding existing extra-mental reality. This conclusion applies to everything in the entire realm of categorical predication: that is, substances, qualities, relations, and everything that in any way expresses a connotation or qualification beyond what intuitive knowledge grasps as existing. The only thing evident to the intellect is the singular object that is intuitively understood as connected with the predicate of existence; to it alone can assent in the proper sense be given by the recognition of its extra-mental reality.

This conception of truth has traditionally and generically been described as Ockhamist nominalism. It is certain that it illumines the entire range of the "Venerable Inceptor's" speculative thought and that it has the same importance in all its varied areas of application, from gnoseology to metaphysics, physics, and theology. It is not unimportant that Ockham introduced his analysis of the doctrine of supposition both into the second part of the *Summa on Logic*, where he studies propositions, and (with all the variants and imperfections that accompany a first version) into the heart of his commentary on the *Sentences*, that is, the place where he sets forth his own theory of truth.

D. THE PRIMACY OF THE INDIVIDUAL AND "OCKHAM'S RAZORS"

In Ockham nominalism is not, as it had been in Roscellinus, simply a negative answer to the question about the reality of logical entities. His rejection of the reality of universals becomes an unqualified rejection of any kind of universality in the real order. That is, there is nothing in the created world that can be the object of an acknowledgment of a general being in which more than one entity can participate and that is eternal and immutable due to an autonomous capacity for existence. Such a being does not exist among things sensible and visible or among things suprasensible and intelligible, not even in a purely potential state (such as the primordial formless matter of which the philosophers speak). In order to name this outlook, which is not only a logical theory but an overall approach to philosophical and theological speculation, it seems best to call it the absolute primacy of the individual.

According to Ockham the logical analysis of the way in which thought works is no longer the prism through which the mental reconstruction of the metaphysical order of the universe is refracted and composed. It is rather the practical tool that captures the real being of the individual and reflects the ways in which the individual concretely exists and achieves its realization. In practice, logic is the means of knowing God's work as such. Attempts may be made to confine the irreducible truth of the created world within the net of an abstract schematism that claims to assimilate divine omnipotence anthropomorphically to human thought. But any such attempt is necessarily brought to naught by the reduction of the judgmental power of any tool of logic to the level of effectiveness of a terminism pure and simple, that is, capable of expressing exclusively the reality of singulars.

There are only singular things with their individual and contingent properties; these constitute a world that is open to many possibilities and is only one of the countless worlds divine omnipotence could have brought and can bring into existence. All the speculative problems philosophy sets itself to solve must be reduced to the immediate consideration of the singular meaning of the terms that make possible the formulation of the problems and that, at the same time, lay down the conditions for the truth of the propositions in which the problems are expressed and by means of which they are tackled.

This logic leads Ockham to an innovative conception of being that becomes in his hands a sharp and very effective tool. He uses it to refute the manifold conceptual structures, both scientific and metaphysical, that people believe, or believed in the past, to be reliable for knowing reality and thereby approaching the God who created it. For this reason the quite numerous formulas expressing this methodical conceptual reductionism that occur in Ockham's writings or in those of his followers (who liked to repeat them as decisive judgments before dealing with any kind of speculative question) have traditionally been called "Ockham's razors," since they call for the elimination of everything superfluous.

Basically there is question here of two principles that constantly guide him in his reform of human thought and that therefore control both his metaphysics and his theology. The first is that the divine omnipotence is completely unconditioned; the second, inversely symmetrical with the first, is the principle of thriftiness or parsimony. These are in fact two criteria, but they derive from a single presupposition, that of God's complete freedom from the conditions the human mind presumes to impose on it. Since God can do everything and since he is the Supreme Good, "there is no point in taking what can happen in the simplest way and assigning it several causes operating under several conditions." The Latin is, as always, more direct and effective: *frustra fit per plura quod potest fieri per pauciora.*

There are also the countless other formulas that are equivalent and say the same thing, despite the apparent mixing at the formal level of logical, metaphysical, and theological criteria. Thus "God can do anything that does not involve a contradiction"; "When a proposition is being checked by reference to the things it signifies, if two things are enough to show its truth there is no point in positing a third"; "No plurality is to be called for without necessity"; "No plurality should be assumed unless definitely required by reason or experience or the authority of Him who alone cannot be deceived or deceive." And so on, until all these were reduced to the more famous adages that were for a long time repeated in the schools; the best known of these is "Entities are not to be multiplied without necessity."

E. THE NEW CONCEPTION OF SCIENCE

We need now only indicate the concrete application of these instrumental principles and show the new structure of scientific knowledge they regulate. Obviously, science can no longer be conceived as the result of a conformity between thing and intellect; it can now be, always and only, the formulation of a discourse about the truth of propositions. A truth is a true proposition; a falsehood is a false proposition. Furthermore, the truth and falsity of a proposition depend solely on its connection with the mode of being of the thing: for example, "Socrates is running" is a true proposition only as long as "Socrates running" and "Socrates existing" can be predicated of the same thing or reality. Science is born of the assent to the truth of a proposition or set of propositions. Moreover, since a proposition is made up of terms and since, if the proposition deals with reality, the terms are categorematic and refer to singular individuals, the proposition of which one has scientific knowledge concerns only singulars and their actual mode of being.

The question arises: given these restrictions, what is left of Aristotelean epistemology, which is based on universality and on the necessity of deductive connections between concepts as reflections of real connections among things? Ockham does not, however, aim at a radical change in Aristoteleanism, but rather in the way that system was interpreted by his contemporaries. In fact, in order to preserve the requirement that led Aristotle to deny the possibility of a science of particulars Ockham agrees that science does not deal with particular things as mutable, but with the intentions of the mind that are suppositions for corruptible things or, in other words, with universals that serve as suppositions for singular entities.

However, the doctrine of supposition makes clear that there is absolutely no possibility of attributing reality to universals as such. These remain mere products of the mind, intentions of the mind the truth of which is reducible solely to things themselves, among which the mind seeks to find something in common. As a result, it will be necessary to make a distinction among sciences. Thus there are sciences of the real (such as physics) resulting from terms that "suppose" for concrete and individual extra-mental realities (personal suppositions). In contrast, there are mental sciences (such as logic itself) that result from terms that "suppose" for concepts and other intentions of the mind (simple suppositions) and are therefore true only in the mind. Logic is a science of mental objects or, better, of the propositions that can be formed about mental objects. Physics is a science of real entities, but since a science must be marked by necessity and proceed by deduction it is a science not of natural, corruptible, and contingent objects but only of the propositions that can be formed about them.

F. THEOLOGY AS WISDOM

There is, however, a third realm of knowledge that yields truths that are certain: the realm of faith. Even if this realm has validity only for believers, it nonetheless requires an openness to necessary demonstrations, that is, to a rigorous application of the principles of Aristotelean epistemology as revised by Ockham. This requirement surfaces, in fact, beginning with the first pages of the Prologue of the *Ordinatio*. Is it possible to develop a science of God that respects the same rules and uses the same tools as those of the sciences that ensure knowledge of the created world? Is there anything predicable of both God and creatures?

Ockham immediately excludes the idea (held by Scotus, but not by him alone) that a hypothetical "theology in itself" can be regarded as a science of reality. The reason: it is unthinkable that any attempt can be made to establish within ourselves evidence for and certainty about a field of knowledge that can have no counterpart in our cognitive abilities as these exist during our earthly life. Everything we might say about the modalities, contents, and forms of a "theology in itself" would reduce such a theology to a "theology in us." Faith teaches that the theological vision of the blessed will be a direct intuition of the divine, not mediated by revelation or any other cognitive screen. But theologians who are still pilgrims are unable to say anything about that vision, the conditions for it, its forms, or its real object, except that it is "possible." Also excluded thereby is the claim, of the Thomists but of others as well, that human theological science can be subalternated to that of God himself and of the blessed.

Since it cannot depend for information on the certainties of a higher knowledge, the truth of "our theology," the only theology possible for us, must depend exclusively on the knowledge provided by revelation. Thus the question whether our theology can be regarded as a science comes down to the question whether revelation can provide an evident knowledge. Now scientific knowledge is knowledge of evident propositions, but the only evident propositions are necessary propositions related to first principles or deducible from these, or else contingent propositions the terms of which are intuitively known as evident. It is clear, however, that the truths communicated by revelation are not evident either in themselves or from experience, that is, on the basis of intuitive knowledge, whether mediate or immediate. Otherwise they should be, or least should be able to be, recognized as such by nonbelievers. Furthermore, given the principle of economy or parsimony it is impossible for God to propose to human beings as an object of faith that which could be known to them as evident in some other way.

Theological truths, then, are never evident on the cognitive level and cannot become the sources of deductive arguments of a syllogistic kind. In conclusion: the theology of humanity in its pilgrim state cannot now or ever be a science, but remains a knowledge based on what is believable.

There are, however (we are still speaking of believers), pieces of knowledge of a theological kind that can be recognized as necessary. In addition to knowledge about God that is based exclusively on revelation there are other possible ways of understanding God's nature that come into play only after the acknowledgment through faith of his existence. These arise from the intuitive and necessary perception (based on the truth of the first principles of logic) of what God ought to be if it be true that he exists. These other ways do not prove that God exists, but they do tell believers what God is if they believe in his existence. All deal with the essential divine properties (for example, "God is good," "God is wise"), which are knowable on the basis of evidence intrinsic to the correspond-ing logical terms (that which is signified by the term "God" cannot but be "good" and "wise"). These are theological predications because they come after the act of faith, even though they are not learned from revelation. They are true not because they spring from a direct knowledge of the divine essence (which is impossible), but because, due to the fact that they are "suppositions" for God, they utter something sayable about God to the extent that they are related to what reason can know about God.

This increase in knowledge beyond what revelation provides shows clearly that theological knowledge is composite in nature and results from the conver-gence of many ways of acquiring the truth about God. Some of these ways are necessary and essential, others are contingent; some involve scientific demon-stration, others do not; some are of the theoretical order, others are of the practi-cal order, that is, concerned with the direction of the moral life. The subject of this knowledge is likewise not always univocal: given the conditions affecting "theology in us," it is necessary to distinguish between the subject as that for which theological discourse "supposes," namely, God himself, and the subject as that which provides the suppositions for God, namely, a term or concept that says something about God. This distinction would make it possible to harmonize, to some extent, the varied opinions put forth by various theologians past and present.

All this amounts to saying that theology, which is not a science, is yet some-thing more than a science inasmuch as it is a complex, true knowledge of a sapiential kind. But while the truth of this wisdom can be increased by numerous and diverse contributions, it is nonetheless profoundly unified because all of it is recapitulated in the supreme fact about every theological truth: that it always points to the absolute simplicity of God.

This conclusion is the very heart of Ockham's theology and is closely con-nected with the principle of economy that governs the entire range of his think-ing. In the absolute perfection of God, truth can only be absolutely simple and without distinction; therefore every theological predication acquires its maximum truthfulness when it states a property of the divine essence without referring to anything else, precisely because it is distinct from everything else that is signifi-able. For this reason every name of God is simply another name for the name that is uniquely his own: that is, God. This name expresses, with the highest possible degree of intuitiveness, that which it signifies, even though this reality is not present to the intellect. The plurality of God's attributes expresses only his unique and undifferentiated essence, and the divine essence expresses only the undifferentiatedness of its perfections, even while reflecting the complexity of the suppositional tools human beings use in thinking God's maximum and unique perfection. This perfection is not in God or of God; it *is* God.

Here we see emerging with certainty the most evident of theological truths: that God cannot be known by human beings. This is indeed the truth that best expresses the essence of God. The theology of humanity on its pilgrimage is thus brought back in the end to its beginning and source: Sacred Scripture. Scripture alone shows how to speak truly of God and to give the term "God" a suppositional capacity that can be explained in a discourse about its meaning.

G. THE FREEDOM OF FAITH

All the particular articulations and applications of Ockham's theological thought to the various spheres of knowledge arise out of its scriptural basis. This basis begins with the very assertion of the omnipotence of God, which is taken for granted as both the initial and the final criterion for the evaluation of every further truth knowable by human beings. It then continues with the assertion of the free divine will, which both creates and conserves the created world. Finally, still on the basis of faith and divine omnipotence, it includes a radical affirmation of human freedom, which is willed by God at creation and is restored to that condition by the redemption wrought by Christ.

This last point leads into a new and extensive area of Ockham's thinking, one that deals with the ethical, ecclesiastical, and political world; this is the subject of countless reflections throughout the second period of his life. The radical voluntarism of his theology and its important consequences in the areas of physics and metaphysics are matched by an equally incisive moral voluntarism. Here he again carries to their extreme consequences the (already revolutionary) views of Scotus by placing at the center of the universe human beings who are indivisible atoms moved by an unconditioned and unconditionable will. This will is free to direct all its actions and existential decisions toward its goals; these in turn can be presented for its free assent solely by a faith, equally free and unconditioned, in the authentic message of hope that God has freely revealed.

In Ockham's thought the freedom of faith is the source of his desire to liberate and purify the church from earthly subordinations and religion from any contamination by limited goods that are and ought to be alien to it. The radical character of Franciscan poverty is legitimized by the unrestricted freedom—which human beings redeemed by Christ ought to have—to carry out the commandments in the ways indicated by the gospel texts.

Moreover, the literal sense of Christ's basic political preceptive statement—namely that his kingdom belongs not to this world but to another—provides, first and foremost, the justification, both theological and ethical, for the authority of the emperor, who is deputed to rule the present world while respecting the dictates of God's law. It is in reminding earthly rulers of this law that the real primatial authority of the pope is both exercised as it should be and, at the same time, limited—not, however, by being reduced, but by being exalted. This papal authority is properly understood not as a power to govern but as a power to serve, because its purpose is to lead the entire human race toward the blessedness that has been promised along with redemption.

This picture of the ideal rebirth of the historical church shows clearly, once again, the effects of the principle of economy, which tears down every false and falsifying structure that human beings impose on the order of authentic truth by their contrivances and abstractions. The order of the universe depends not on the human mind, but on the divine will.

II. The Consolation of Theology

1. The Remedies of Theology in Francesco Petrarch

> **AUGUSTINE.** Even though there are countless things around you that continually remind you of death . . . you will find very few people who really think that they must inevitably die.
>
> **FRANCESCO.** Few, then, know the definition of the human being, even though it has been repeated so often in all the schools that it ought by now to have not only wearied the ears of people but also to have even eaten away the very columns of the buildings?
>
> **AUGUSTINE.** This empty and unending babbling of the logicians fills the mouth with similar technical definitions and boasts of offering them as food for ceaseless quarrelsome disagreement. Yet the majority of these people are ignorant of the very thing of which they speak. Thus if you ask someone in that herd for the definition not only of the human being but of anything whatsoever, their answer will be prompt and direct. But if you then try to look more deeply you will meet only with silence. Or if in accordance with their customary scholastic discourses they disgorge abundant floods of rash words, the moral behavior of such speakers will show that they truly have no real understanding of what they are able to define. Then you may spontaneously cry out against this type of people who are so contemptibly superficial and so full of fruitless curiosity: "You wretches, why do you thus weary yourselves to no purpose and exercise your talents on useless hairsplitting trickery? Why do you forget the real world, grow old amid words, and spend your time putting together children's games, you with your white hair and furrowed brows? O, if at least your foolishness harmed only yourselves and did not so often defile even the very noblest intellects of so many youths!"
>
> **FRANCESCO.** I acknowledge it: no rebukes of such monsters produced by studies can ever be too strong. . . .
>
> **AUGUSTINE.** You will never find a single shepherd who is so foolish as not to know that the human being is an animal and, indeed, the prince of all the animals. In fact, no one, when asked, will deny that the human being is an animal and rational and mortal.
>
> **FRANCESCO.** This is, then, a definition known to all.
>
> **AUGUSTINE.** No! To very few.
>
> **FRANCESCO.** What do you mean?

AUGUSTINE. That you will find only occasional persons who are so much in control of their own rational nature that they can turn this definition into a rule governing their whole lives; that thanks to it they can master all their appetites, use it as a bridle to curb all the movements of their souls, and understand that it alone distinguishes them from the bestiality of the brute animals and that they deserve the very name "human being" only if they live in accordance with reason. Only occasionally will you find persons who, in addition, are so conscious of their own mortality that they have it constantly in mind and are able to regulate their lives accordingly and to scorn all temporal things, so as to long always for that life in which, having been led by reason to transcend themselves, they truly cease to be mortal. Only then will you be able to say that someone has a true and useful knowledge of the definition of the human being.

These incisive words are uttered at the heart of the *Secretum* by the shade of Augustine, who asks Petrarch how a well-prepared teacher would deal with an attentive pupil. In them Petrarch develops a point made in the first book of Boethius' *Consolation of Philosophy*, where Philosophy asks the suffering philosopher whether he is able to look beyond the superficial sound of the words in the classical definition promulgated by the learned: "rational and mortal animal," and remember what it really means to be a "human being."

Original, however, and typically Petrarchan is the abusive rhetoric accompanying the exhortation to look behind the empty technical formulas shaped and memorized by the masters of the schools and to rediscover the tragic character of the human existential dimension. Similar expressions occur a number of times in Petrarch's other writings, as in I, 7 of the *Familiares* (private or personal letters), which was published under the title "Attack on the Old Dialecticians": "As is their wont, they venture always and only to debate, as if it is in debate that they find their supreme pleasure, so that their primary purpose is arguing as such rather than discovering the truth." *To discover the truth*: since the time of Cicero this had been the phrase describing the true task of the philosopher.

According to the most widely accepted interpretation, the dialecticians guilty of this excessive, empty formalism would be chiefly the nominalist followers of Ockham who thronged the universities of Oxford and Paris around the middle of the fourteenth century (the *Secretum* was composed between 1347 and 1352). It is likely, however, that these repeated diatribes also had a broader aim and were not to be taken as simply a criticism of the epistemological reduction of truth to propositions. The many repeated attacks on the dialecticians that in practice run through all the written works of Petrarch, at least in the form of passing references, are interwoven with passages that with somber accents deplore the general decadence of human thought, including philosophy, theology, and religion itself.

These attacks are scattered throughout Petrarch's various writings, from the *Remedies for Good and Bad Fortune* to *The Solitary Life*, from the *Books of*

Memorable Things to the countless instances in the collections of letters. They are but successive moments in a prolonged and broad-ranging indictment of the professional schoolmen. In their lecture halls—in "that nauseating world of Paris and Oxford that has already destroyed countless minds" (*Letters of Old Age* XII, 2)—those men dwell at length on the subtlety of "the most minute distinctions" and have turned the rules of logic from the means to the end of their studies, forgetting the real task of those who pursue the truth.

Petrarch was born at Arezzo in 1304 and died at Arquà in the Euganean Hills in 1374, a century after the deaths of Thomas and Bonaventure. As a traveler between Italy and France he reached his intellectual maturity during the decades that saw the emergence of different and opposed systems of thought in the European university world. Some of these represented the growth and consolidation, but also the self-isolation, of groups venerating the great authorities of the more recent past. In others new intellectual trends took shape and spread: for example, the "Scotist way" and the revolutionary positions taken by the Ockhamists, positions described as the "ways of the moderns."

This major intellectual development, though quite lively and certainly not static even within those structured ways of proceeding, had a defect that was evident to the outside observer. This was a deep and seemingly irreparable split between a much-prized *sang-froid* in the making of formal definitions and the neglected doctrinal contents that should in fact have played an essential role in theological studies, if nowhere else, in leading the human individual toward higher goals. Moreover, every new teacher, from Lull to Scotus to Ockham, always claimed to be advancing the recovery of the speculative unity of the Christian world. Yet all their attempts at renewal showed themselves by their mutual opposition to be not only failures but even heralds of further confusions and distractions from the serious problems that philosophical meditation should be tackling and solving.

There are not a few evidences of the decadence of university institutions around the middle of the century. At Paris and Oxford there was a notable decrease in the number of registered students and in the number of university manuscripts in circulation. In 1346 Clement VI, pope at Avignon, wrote a letter denouncing the very deplorable practice of masters of theology who abandoned the scriptural text and the writings of the Fathers in order to bog down in philosophical and scientific subtleties. The letter drew an angry reply from Cistercian master Peter of Ceffons, who took up the defense of the "modern" masters and justified, in language almost too unbiased, the formative value of exercises in logic, even when these were an end in themselves.

As a result the scholars continued to question and contradict one another in their disagreements on determinism, the beatific vision, or the possibility that God could know future contingents or change even predestination itself. Meanwhile the religious outlook of ordinary people and the pastoral care exercised by the church were moving ever further away from the interests of the professional theologians. The people showed an increasing interest in more direct and engross-ing devotions, and even in scholastic centers many wished that the authorities would intervene as censors and initiate a doctrinal and moral reform that would narrow the gap between theological speculation and authentic interior faith.

Francesco Petrarch was crowned with the poet's laurel wreath on the Cam-pidoglio in Rome in 1341 and was invited to receive the same honors in Paris with the approval of the chancellor and many well-known scholars of the uni-versity. Petrarch tells us of all this in his *Discourse on his Crowning*, an address composed for the occasion. He had a very detailed idea of the ills afflicting theological scholarship in his day. Nor did he hesitate to see as their primary cause the widespread acceptance of the speculative attitude of the Averroists who emphasized the separation among the various disciplines and so contributed to reducing human learning to a mere academic exercise without any influence in the moral sphere.

He gave voice to his own disagreement by writing his *Denunciations of a Physician* in four books (1351–55), directed at a French physician, a materialist and follower of Averroes. This man spouted syllogisms and claimed to be a philosopher while accusing of ignorance anyone who did not display an ability, such as he had, to debate and formulate rigorous but empty demonstrations. Petrarch made the same criticisms later on, but with even greater indignation and a more direct personal involvement, in a work written between 1367 and 1370 and titled *On His Own Ignorance and That of the Many*. This most compact and effective of his polemical writings was a response to four young Venetian Aristoteleans who had described him as "a good man but utterly ignorant." He told them that true wisdom is never found in a show of knowledge that is ac-companied by contempt for or a lack of interest in the fundamental questions about life, interiority, time, death, and eternity.

After the lively debates at the end of the thirteenth century about the ways in which philosophy and theology were corrupting one another, Averroism reap-peared during the first decades of the new century among the masters of the arts and of medicine. It took the form of an unquestioned speculative position that was rooted in an acceptance of the Aristotelean epistemological approach. The latter permitted untrammeled developments in the natural sciences without subjecting them to heteronomous limitations of a religious kind or in any case foreign to autonomous scientific investigation. Conspicuous among the principal representatives of this trend were Peter of Abano, a Paduan (d. ca. 1315–16), and John of Jandun, a Frenchman (who died at Pisa in 1328 while in the entou-rage of Louis the Bavarian). John was a companion in exile of Marsilius of Padua and collaborated with him in the composition of his basic political work, *The Defender of Peace*. Petrarch directed his criticisms not so much at the Aver-roist trend as such as at its characteristic mental and methodological outlook.

The anonymous physician accused Petrarch of ignorance of the liberal arts on which philosophy was based and, with it, the possibility of knowing nature and its laws. But it was precisely in this claim of the Averroists to cloak themselves in the mantle of a disinterested scientific curiosity that Petrarch saw the root of the wickedness and blasphemy of those who went so far as to "heap contempt on Christ with the tricks of logic." What distinguished Petrarch from these deniers of the truth was certainly not ignorance of the scientific disciplines, but a rejection of the fruitless and superabundant use of logic that permeated and supported all their discourses. In fact, precisely because he did have a good knowledge of the liberal arts he knew the correct use that should be made of them, as taught by the ancient masters from Cicero to Augustine: "It is praise-worthy to learn them, it is foolish to grow old with them alone; they are a means, not an end, except for those who have no goal in mind but wander about use-lessly, now here, now there, because their lives have no real harbor in which to take refuge."

These present-day masters think they have reached supreme happiness when during a sleepless night they have racked their brains to construct even a single frail syllogism by means of which they can only "conclude nothing from noth-ing." And it is on this futile structure of arguments that they base their very denial of knowing what they boast of teaching. Because even the greatest philosophers, the Platos and the Aristotles, were unable to inquire into the loftiest truths without contradicting one another, these men conclude that whatever human study is unable to grasp does not exist. Like the fool in the Psalm they assert: "God does not exist; it is useless to spend much time looking above!" They are content to keep rolling around in the mire of their empty so-called science, nursing their syllogisms and other plays on words as though these were babies. In fact, there is no spectacle more contemptible than an old man who amuses himself with childish things and chases after trifles while giving no thought to his own death, which is now just around the corner.

True philosophers, having once emerged from intellectual childhood, are no longer concerned with syllogisms, but speak of human beings. As the ancients had already realized and as Christians, beyond all others, ought to know, phi-losophy is a "thinking about death" that teaches human beings how to prepare for the inevitable end result of their every action. And if this is true wisdom, then the philosopher is an authentic lover of God.

At this unnervingly direct reminder centuries of thinking about truth seem to crumble into dust, and out of the rubble the stern but lovable figure of Augustine arises as the only true guide for humanity. Petrarch's *The Solitary Life* was composed at Valchiusa in the spring of 1346, and his *Religious Tranquillity* was written nonstop in the next year after a visit to his brother, who had withdrawn to monastic life in the charterhouse at Montrieux. (This last work, like the majority of his writings, was later revised during the following years.)

In these works Petrarch had already explained to himself and his readers that in order to discover the interior and certain guiding power of faith it was absolutely necessary to distance oneself, first physically and then mentally, from the demands of the external world and from commonplace and fickle successes won on the stage of temporal renown. In *Religious Tranquillity* he makes his own what he read in many of his patristic sources and links philosophers with pagans, Jews, unbelievers, and heretics as enemies of the faith and, as such, enemies, all of them, of the truth. The Jews confused true wisdom with false and were unable to recognize it in Christ. So, too, Muslims and philosophers (and therefore the Averroists) have fought against this true wisdom and set over against it their unjustified claims to knowledge, claims that are arrogant and inconsistent and are supported by "windy" and captious sophistries.

True philosophy is quite different in kind, as we are told in the second book of *The Solitary Life*, and quite different, too, are those who truly deserve to be called philosophers, that is, real lovers of wisdom gained through a practical and laborious personal experience. They are not like "the professors" of our time who have indeed earned this name in which they wrap themselves, for "in the professorial chair they play the philosopher, whereas in their actions they prove themselves to be fools." The recurring theme of this work of Petrarch is that true philosophy must be pursued in solitude and recollection; only then can the restless soul turn "with great intensity" to things that can bring it genuine repose: namely God, its own inner self (which is found in study and contemplation), and the inner selves of others who are more in sympathy with us. Because solitude disposes the soul to withdraw into itself in study and the search for truth and in the silence of interior peace it is a condition for beginning the authentic study of theology, which is the "supreme duty of the true philosopher."

In this subordination of the retrieval of an authentic theology to the solitary life and the leisure of religious persons we see, above and beyond a revival of the elitist classical ideal of the scholar and of Augustinian meditative interiority, the profoundly Platonic model of an ascetical movement from the scatteredness of multiplicity toward the reunification of truth. The bodily departure from the cities is only a first step leading to the self-distancing of souls from their bodies as they precede the latter into heaven, "something the philosophers of this world cannot even hope for." The emergence of true philosophy is thus the result of a complete conversion that begins with the detachment of the intellect from the bodily senses and is completed in the opening of "those interior eyes that perceive things invisible" and are able to recognize the divine presence everywhere in creation. But for Petrarch the removal from earthly wretchedness also means transcending the anthropomorphic boundaries of human reason, in whose chains and limitations those who claim to teach wisdom find their delight.

How are the justice and mercy of God, the creator's punishment of sin and his love, to be reconciled? It is not difficult to recognize in the very raising of such problems the intrusion of a type of earthly reasoning into matters divine. That is, the scholars think that to a cause of motion there must correspond a precise effect and that this effect is possible only if the body that is to receive it is disposed (or "ordered," as they say in the schools) for the action of the cause. Such considerations can indeed sometimes be useful either because they exercise the mind by improving the use of the tools of logic or, in another area, because they urge souls, out of fear of divine punishment, to repent of the sins they have committed.

But the same considerations can also turn into a pessimistic assessment of human limitation and helplessness and a consequent lack of trust in God's goodness, to the point of a complete and utterly perilous loss of hope: to despair, "the worst evil of all." Thus an echo of contemporary theological debates seems to have left its mark on *Religious Leisure* when Petrarch suggests that the answer to this radical human evil is to be found in the unconditional application of the most solid basis of truth, that is, the principle of unconditioned divine omnipotence. The only response to the subtle temptations of theological reasoning is to seek shelter in God's omnipotence. The mercy of God *can* go beyond and minimize the extent of human wretchedness without being logically opposed to his justice, and the goodness of God ("than which nothing more marvelous can be thought," to paraphrase Anselm's argument) will always overcome human wretchedness and the limitations of human sin. A converted theology thus takes back the helm of the soul amid the storms of the world and hands it over to hope, without which shipwreck is certain.

Another argument (once again in *The Solitary Life*) can give a new impulse to the conversion of human knowledge toward its only authentic object. Some philosophers have advised mentally conjuring up the presence of a witness who watches all our actions and keeps us from committing errors or performing actions of which we may be ashamed. But Christians do not need this "philosophical advice" because they know they have always with them the presence of Christ, an all-knowing and infallible witness who cannot be deceived. More perfectly than any other human witness and even than our guardian angel, Christ knows not only our actions but even our thoughts and therefore the intentions that direct our behavior.

Christian ethics is thus more radical than any other kind of law, since it is able even to evaluate intentions as the standard of moral judgment. With his conception of the "infallible and constant witness" whose presence the soul can grasp only when it is no longer distracted by earthly concerns, Petrarch completes the conversion and overturn of the speculative parameters of human thought that Augustine had begun in his youthful *Dialogues*. The possession of the unconditioned truth guaranteed by revelation assures the faithful of the correct theoretical alignment of their studies of the world, human beings, and God. So too the presence (not simulated and fictive but real) of the omnipresent divine witness-judge guarantees the correct practical direction of their ethical decisions.

The heart, therefore, of Petrarch's plan to restore an authentic Augustinian spirituality has two elements: trust in divine omnipotence, which is able to overcome even the inability of human beings to raise themselves up to the true and the good, and the completion of the conversion of philosophy into full theological knowledge. The *Secretum* is the composition in which this longing for the reform of true knowledge is brought to the fore in a very effective and direct way; this occurs during a lengthy and impassioned meditation on human destiny and the meaning of human life on earth.

At the beginning of the work, with its obvious reminder of the opening of Boethius' *Consolation*, Petrarch tells of how during one of his frequent, confused meditations "on how we come into this life and how we shall leave it," Truth itself suddenly appeared to him in a vision. It was personified "by a woman of indeterminate age and radiance, whose image human beings are not able to understand satisfactorily." "Eager to see her," the poet confesses, "I fixed my gaze on her, but the human gaze is unable to endure her heavenly light." Only by means of short and cautious glances and by gradually answering the little questions the woman asks him is he able to become progressively wiser and little by little to develop his own abilities to the point of being able to fix his gaze in a direct, though never exhaustive, way on this face that had at its first appearance confused and bewildered him.

The overall course of the ensuing debate on pedagogy between Francesco and the shade of Augustine, whom Truth has chosen as its representative and spokesman, is therefore that of a structured rational inquiry aimed at making sufficiently clear to the human mind a truth of the suprahuman order. In imitation of many late antique and medieval dialogues, this inquiry takes the form of an easily followed alternation of questions and answers, objections and solutions, in a literary style that is refined and elegant, but always shows a substantial respect for the most basic logical structures. The fundamental line of argument that underlies Augustine's exhortation to Petrarch is deliberately syllogistic (that is, it displays a logical sequence); it is formally accurate and correct, with the conclusion necessarily following from the truth of the premises.

The two premises formulated by Augustine and accepted as true by Francesco consist in the admission that those who suffer a serious illness want to recover their health and those who passionately desire something make every possible effort to obtain it. The conclusion, which Augustine draws correctly but Francesco does not immediately understand, is that those who suffer from their own unhappiness are already in some way happy. Then, in passage after passage, the entire dialogue explains the meaning of this conclusion: namely that the consciousness of present unhappiness, which prods human beings not to be content with partial goods that cannot bring happiness, is translated immediately into a search for the happiness promised by Christian redemption. Moreover, as soon as the soul undertakes this quest there is stirred up within it so strong a hope of immortality and blessedness that the hope already turns into an unchallengeable certainty.

True wisdom takes the form of the Socratic meditation on or preparation for death, and can be practiced only within a true and heartfelt love of God. The *Secretum* ends, therefore, when sinful human beings, whose attention has been dissipated among the distractions of earthly life, allow themselves to be restored to the only condition in which truth can be found: a definitive presence to themselves that allows them to gather together "the scattered fragments of their souls" in an unwavering consciousness of their nothingness before God. This point of arrival serves, however, as the beginning of a new program for the acquisition of authentic theological knowledge. This process will be complete when there is a total, sincere, and impassioned dedication of every action of one's remaining life to an unbroken quest of moral truth. This quest is such that, in a real confirmation of what has been formally demonstrated, those whose actions are inspired by an authentic desire for the true good will realize that they already have a real enjoyment of that good.

The image of the new human being that springs from this reform and from the new ethical direction given to theological knowledge is symmetrically contrasted with the weakness of the "puny person" (*homuncio*, "little man") whom Augustine addressed at the beginning of the dialogue and urged to recall his mortal condition. The resumption of the words "wretched" or "little man" or "unhappy fellow," though these are attested in such classical sources as Cicero and Seneca, seems to be primarily a reminder of the invitation at the beginning of Anselm's *Proslogion* to seek the truth within ourselves. Passing over the empty theological reasonings of his contemporaries, Petrarch harks back to the Christian Platonism of interiority typical of the early monastic Middle Ages.

But this action was not, to his mind, simply a return to the old. Rather, from the earlier mentioned *Discourse on His Crowning* down to his *On His Own Ignorance and That of the Many* he devotes a great many pages to the justification of his role as reformer of philosophical and theological thought. He assigns to the poet the professional duty of using the veil of figurative inventions and a pleasing language that is easily understood but inspired and permeated as it were by a higher divine energy. The poet will thereby express, in a way superior to all the speculative treatises, that profound knowledge of truth that must be attained in order to give true meaning and proper orientation to earthly life.

The idea of "the poet's theology" was not a new one. It had already emerged in the twelfth century in Bernard Silvestris and Alan of Lille and had recently been fleshed out by Dante Alighieri. The theory of it had been provided by Albertinus Mussato (d. 1329) of Padua in his seventh metrical *Letter*, in which he celebrated the capacity of poetry to express, as though it were "another philosophy," the loftiest mysteries, which human language cannot directly describe. Petrarch closely links this theology with the Platonic principle of the multiplicity of the forms and methodologies that enable the human soul to draw near to the truth.

In his *Discourse on His Crowning* (the Latin name, *Collatio*, evokes the genre of university sermons on special occasions, as in Bonaventure) the writer's main purpose is to point out and validate the lofty philosophical and theological dignity of his own poetic works. He ventures to say there that "the only difference between the task of the poet and that of the historian and the philosopher (whether moral or natural) is the difference between a cloudy sky and a clear sky. In both cases the light shining on the object is the same, but the object appears different depending on different conditions and on the ability of the observer to see it." In truly inspired poetry, which is rarer even than true philosophy, truth is more enticing but also more difficult to understand; this very difficulty, however, renders it all the more pleasing when one does succeed in understanding it.

Being a poet and "not wanting to be anything but a poet" means, then, for Petrarch, being a complete and devoted disciple of the truth, and this in the new dimension he has given to wisdom, which for him is both true philosophy and true theology. The only happiness human beings can reach in this life is wholly contained in this wisdom that urges them on to the loftiest goal although they know they will reach it only in the future life. Therefore the happy life, which it is now clear is the same as a philosophical, poetic, holy, and prophetic life, proves to be in the last analysis nothing other than a constant and never satisfied seeking after the truth, the higher good, the fulfillment of the authentic aspirations of human life.

The last years of Petrarch's life provide an astonishing example of the ability to express truth through poetry: the completion of the *Triumphs*, which he had been revising through long years of thought and meditation on human life. A profound moral and theological inspiration supports the intertwined tercets. The theological power of the poetry is shown in the final translation of the story of the earthly love of Laura into a complex conceptual structure with universal validity. This structure underpins the allegorical ascensional journey of the soul from contemplation of the passions and present sufferings to a mystical dwelling on what is changeless.

The *Triumph of Death* asserts that a final disillusionment will swallow up everything that human beings in their stupidity chase after in their anxiety to secure for themselves the passing and foolish satisfactions of this world ("Wretched are they who place their hope in transient things"). The *Triumph of Time* then takes away even the final false earthly hope, that of being able to survive one's death through the accomplishment of a work that will last for centuries, for such works, too, are destined to be obliterated as by a new, second death ("Every transient thing Time cuts off"). Only with the coming of the *Triumph of Eternity*, as poetry moves beyond even the apophatic steps in which discursive theology culminates, does it glimpse, through a divine and unmerited inspiration, the opening of "a new world that is changeless and everlasting," a world in which everything now present disappears and the entire universe is renewed and becomes "more beautiful and more joyous."

Poetry, and poetry alone, can describe this eternity that no philosopher-theologian has ever been able to define and portray. Time, which is continual change, stops. Its three parts—past, present, and future—seem to be one, and "that one to be motionless." Human thought, lifted up and drawn by God's grace, penetrates everything, just as light passes through glass. And in the absence of change, the change that is the cause of defects, everything appears to be nothing but the Supreme Good. Thus in the supreme theological reunification of all reality poetry alone experiences eternal blessedness for an indescribable instant, and then comes back to describe it, as best it can, to the mind.

2. Between East and West:
Barlaam of Calabria and Theological Probabilism

It was in 1341 that Petrarch was crowned with the poet's laurel on the Campidoglio. In that same year, at Constantinople, Barlaam the Calabrian (d. 1350), a Basilian monk, was condemned by a synod held in Santa Sophia for his criticisms of the fervent mystical spirituality of the monks of Mount Athos, the so-called "Hesychasts," whose leader was theologian Gregory Palamas (d. 1359). Barlaam was unwilling to yield to the demands of the synod and so, after the condemnation, he left the Byzantine empire and returned to Italy, his place of origin.

He had been born into a Greek family in Seminara, near Reggio Calabria, around 1290. It was, however, at Constantinople that he had won fame, popularity, and the favor of the emperor while teaching Aristotelean logic, Platonic philosophy, and Dionysian theology in the imperial school and at the monastery of the Holy Savior, of which he had become abbot. In 1339 he had already undertaken a mission to Avignon at the bidding of Emperor Andronicus III, his task being to work with Benedict XII for the convocation of an ecumenical council that would deal with the union of the churches and a military alliance against the Turks.

The negotiations produced no concrete result, but they did provide Barlaam with an opportunity to develop good personal relations with the papal court. As a result, after his definitive return to the West and after a short stay in Naples, where he met Giovanni Boccaccio (who remembered him as "small in stature but very great in knowledge"), he returned to Avignon. There Benedict XII made him welcome and appointed him Reader of Greek at the court. He was thus able to meet and become friends with Francesco Petrarch, whom he taught the rudiments of his own Greek language, although the lessons were cut short after a few months when Barlaam converted to Catholicism and became bishop of Gerace.

Barlaam's personal experiences bridged two cultural worlds and two different theological civilizations, and he was an attentive observer of both. This allowed him to keep a certain distance in his assessment of merits and defects, especially in the most radical expressions of human reflection on the faith from the most intense mysticism to the fruitless scholastic preoccupation with method. He was thus led, earlier than other western witnesses, including Petrarch, to formulate a rough but realistic and analytical diagnosis of the illness affecting contemporary theological thought. In particular, although his polemical views attracted no followers, he attacked the claim to transform the soul's assent to the truths of faith into a solid, proven certainty. This certainty was supposedly based on interior evidence, as the hesychast monks of the East claimed, or on a rigorous epistemological foundation for theology such as the university masters of the West aspired to establish.

In any case Barlaam's criticism was a revelatory sign of the times: it was an impassioned exhortation to all the theologians of Christendom to rid their thinking of the excesses that undermined spiritual unity. They must surrender the embittered dialectical formalism whose sole purpose was to challenge adversaries, as well as their factionalism and their doctrinal disagreements.

One and the same incident was the starting point for the distinct development of Barlaam's two personal attacks, one on the overemphasized spiritualism of Greek monastic religious life, the other on the subtleties pursued by the Latin scholastic mentality. In 1334 Pope John XXII sent two Dominican theologians, Francis of Camerino, bishop of Vosprum, and Richard of England, bishop of Cherson, to Constantinople to try to lay the foundations for a theological agreement between the two churches, especially on the doctrine of the Trinity. The two papal legates, both of them Thomists, explained the doctrine of the *Filioque* to the Byzantine theologians with accompanying solid logical arguments. Andronicus III asked Barlaam to reply by setting forth the doctrine of the procession of the Holy Spirit as interpreted by the Greeks.

Barlaam was convinced of the need to avoid rigid theoretical positions on so sensitive a subject, and he carried out his commission by attempting a mediating solution. This left untouched the eastern refusal to introduce the *Filioque* into liturgical formularies. It did, however, make it possible to rise above an opposition he regarded as justified solely by human stubbornness: that is, the claim of both contending parties to have authentic possession of a truth the immensity of which in fact transcends the abilities of created reason to define and prove it.

To support his reading of the problem Barlaam quickly composed a treatise titled *The Procession of the Holy Spirit: A Reply to the Latins*. In this work, despite its title, he carefully avoided emphasizing the theoretical differences between the two sides, with their refutations and anathemas against each other's teaching. Expressing surprise that no one had previously made this one elementary point, he noted especially the fact that during the centuries-long disagreement between the two churches all the arguments brought to bear by both the Latins and the Greeks in favor of their respective positions were always said to be based on strict, seemingly solid and irrefutable syllogistic proofs. This, however, was obviously impossible, given that the truth cannot contradict itself. It was evident, therefore, to anyone ready at least to listen to an adversary's arguments, that all the syllogisms used in this debate and, more generally, all the syllogisms invoked in solving problems of a theological kind were not and never could be apodictic. They could always and only be dialectical, and for this reason were always insufficient for convincing an adversary.

This distinction was obviously based on the theory of syllogisms that Aristotle had proposed at the beginning of his *Topics*; indeed, it had already been used in the West by the Averroists when they distinguished philosophical demonstration from theological demonstration based on faith. According to Aristotle the truth of the premises of an apodictic syllogism must be evident, that is, directly perceptible as such by the mind; this quality alone made the conclusion likewise evident. Dialectical demonstrations, on the other hand, can start with arguments that are only probable; for this reason the conclusion too, even if consistent with the premises, may not be true.

Barlaam now remarked, with specific reference to the more recent scholastic methodologies popular in the West, that theological reasoning can only be dialectical. The reason is that it always includes assertions, whether premises or conclusions, whose objective content is never directly perceptible by the human mind, either by intuition or by abstractive knowledge, but the truth of which all must accept by faith. In fact, the truth of such assertions necessarily precedes any other truth accessible to the mind; it can therefore never be reached as the conclusion of a demonstration, which must always result in something new and not already included in the premises.

It will therefore be a salutary first step, says Barlaam, to renounce the use of such dialectical syllogisms or to recognize that they are always and solely probable, can only help to direct the mind, and are therefore instrumental. The second salutary step will be to acknowledge that the only correct procedure in theology, the only one that will make it possible to reach agreement between divergent positions, is recourse to the teachings of the Fathers of the Church, whose exclusive and truthful sources of knowledge were revelation and illumination. And since no explicit and decisive patristic teaching on the procession of the Spirit can be found, the only thing to do is to locate the divergent trinitarian teachings of the Latins and Greeks among the particular theological opinions that no one ought to claim are absolutely true, but only probable.

The direct target of Barlaam's criticism was the Thomist demonstrative method explicitly used by the two legates. But it was equally obvious to his Greek listeners and readers that he was no less decidedly distancing himself from the exaggeratedly rigid and polemical ways of reasoning that were habitual in many traditionalist Byzantine theologians. For this reason the publication of Barlaam's treatise elicited censure from Gregory Palamas, a person of great authority in Constantinopolitan theological circles. Gregory accused Barlaam of hypocritically denying, for the sake of an agreement with the Latins, the real solidity of the trinitarian arguments on which the Greeks based their authentic orthodoxy.

The harshness of Gregory's attack and the bitterness of the controversy that followed are to be explained in light of the evolution of Byzantine theological thought during the thirteenth century and the first half of the fourteenth. The eastern empire had indeed experienced a gradual political decline aggravated first by the Crusaders' conquest in 1204 and the Latin control that lasted until 1261 and then by increasing pressure from the Turks on the northeastern frontier. At the same time, however, the empire experienced a period of great cultural, artistic, literary, and even theological vitality. But the close connection between religious thought and the dominant political interests that constantly left its mark on theological thought at Byzantium had favored the dominance in this area of a conservative and traditionalist attitude, one promoted especially by monks.

The only opportunities for deeper thinking on various subjects were provided by the intermittent attempts at reconciliation with the Roman church. But in an atmosphere of growing aversion from the Latin world that was intensified by recent political events these attempts ended mostly in structured refutations of the adversaries' errors. Thus they undermined all the proposals for mediation and union that were advanced even by some of the most discerning speculative minds of the thirteenth century. One of these was Nicephorus Blemmydes (d. 1271), who maintained the possibility of an agreement on substituting "through the Son" for "from the Son," which in his view was authorized by the Fathers. Another was Patriarch John XI Beccus (d. 1297), who because he refused to repudiate his views on union with the West was condemned and died in prison during a period of increased ideological obstinacy in the imperial party.

It was in this atmosphere with its antispeculative and antiunionist leanings that the hesychast movement was born and developed in the monastic world. Hesychasm exalted traditionalist spirituality while giving it a decisive mystical direction. The center from which the movement spread, beginning in the first half of the fourteenth century, was the monastic communities of Mount Athos on the peninsula of Chalcidice. The movement was characterized by a desire to attain to *hesychia*, the "interior peace" that arises in the soul from direct contemplation of the divine. This contemplation resulted in turn from a complicated discipline of body and mind that consisted in an intense practice of repetitive prayer in combination with a methodical mental control of the vital functions and especially of breathing.

The theory and practice of contemplation were here connected, of course, with a reduction of the knowledge of faith to the terms of a traditionalist and rigid orthodoxy, which provided solid food for interior meditations on truth. Gregory Palamas, who was born in Constantinople of an aristocratic family in 1296, withdrew to monastic life on the Holy Mountain around 1316 and became one of the most active and authoritative representatives of the movement.

Confronted with Barlaam's probabilist outlook, which led him to a global denial of any apodictic elements in our knowledge of God, the theologian on Mount Athos chiefly feared the loss of one of the cornerstones of hesychasm: namely, confidence in the operational efficacy of the special, unmerited illumination that was ensured by the Incarnation. This was known as the "Light of

Tabor" (i.e., Mount Tabor, where the transfiguration of Christ occurred) and it enabled the perfect monk to have an experience of the truth that was direct and necessary (that is, apodictic). The Calabrian monk answered by protesting that he had not been understood and by advancing explicit doubts about the theological training of his accuser. In reply to the accusation of agnosticism he in turn denounced as heretical the claim of Palamas and his monks that they effected a mixture of corporeity and spirituality, a notion that led them to the absurd assertion of a material link between soul and body by way of the umbilical cord. Barlaam therefore accused hesychasm of "omphalopsychism," a devastating coinage of his own (= "having one's soul in one's navel").

As often happened in Byzantium, the controversy over hesychasm was entwined in many ways with complicated political problems. Initially events favored the Athonite monks when a council of 1341 ruled that the "Light of Tabor" must be acknowledged to be a real uncreated manifestation of the divinity. But the dispute did not end with the rejection of Barlaam and his departure for Italy. In fact, it worsened when it became involved with the civil war that erupted over the successor of Andronicus III, during which Palamas was in his turn arrested and excommunicated for his teachings. Finally, with the advent of John V Paleologus, the hesychasts succeeded in controlling the situation again and winning a second victory at Constantinople in 1351 with the official approval of Palamas' trinitarian views.

As for Barlaam, it is not very clear what cultural influence his criticism of the theology of the schools had on Italian and French scholars during the years after his return to the West. It is worth observing, however, that both in his opposition to the papal legates and in his dispute with Palamas he reacted negatively against any exaggeratedly realistic and, in his view, anthropomorphic attempt to guarantee the human mind a direct and inalienable understanding of transcendent truth. In this reaction we can see clearly the influence of the negative theology—purely Platonic and Pseudo-Dionysian in its approach—that inspired his thinking.

As a result, in response both to the dialectical intellectualism of the western theologians and the claimed illumination (which he regarded as materialistic) of the hesychast monks, this Calabrian monk drew upon his patristic sources for the idea that the perception of the highest intelligible truths is reserved to a higher faculty of the soul. This faculty is distinct from bodily sensation and from the abstractive knowledge gained by reason. It is a source of immediate, intuitive knowledge in which human beings can participate in only a limited and imperfect way during the present life. The Platonists have correctly given the name *nous* to this higher faculty.

Barlaam's parallel critiques of speculative theology and visionary mysticism yielded some interesting sets of themes that were destined to recur insistently, under various forms, in western theological debate in the second half of the fourteenth century; they would later be taken up again and pursued during the age of humanism. These included the superiority and elusiveness of divine truth in relation to all forms of creaturely perception, the impossibility of basing understanding of this truth on the natural processes of human knowledge, the resultant rejection in theology of rigidity in argumentation, which was the cause of contradictions between contrasting visions of the same reality, a degree of moderate probabilism in dealing with any rational assertions about the mysteries of faith, a possible openness to interreligious agreement, given the awareness of human cognitive weakness, and then, but not last in importance, the essentially instrumental and practical approach that should be given the privileged place in theological study.

3. The Influence of Ockhamism and University Trends in the Middle Decades of the Fourteenth Century

Thus while outside the soil of the universities Francesco Petrarch was sowing the seeds of the future renaissance of theological thought, Barlaam the Calabrian was engaged in his isolated cultural experiment, which was indeed exemplary but had no effective sequel in either the Greek world or the Latin. Meanwhile, however, during those same years the rapid spread of Ockhamist thought was introducing a new way of thinking into the scholastic centers of the West, and doing so with public success and while eliciting lively reactions from all observers. Beginning in the thirties of the fourteenth century, this new thinking was to foster a notable transformation, in both substance and form, in the study of science, philosophy, and theology.

The influence of William of Ockham's thought on the university world had been immediate and, in many respects, overwhelming. In the first works that show a more or less clear-cut adoption of the Venerable Inceptor's doctrinal views by disciples, friends, and admirers their interest was stirred by what, as we mentioned earlier, was immediately described as "the way of the moderns." Their attention seems to have been caught above all by the incisiveness of his methodology. This was true in particular of the two key principles at work in Ockham's critique of reason: the principle of economy and the principle of the divine omnipotence, which were widely applied, even if with far from uniform results, in every area of research. At the same time it is a fact that a widespread and, on many sides, repeated insistence on effective evidence led to a methodical reduction in the area of distinctions and abstractive procedures and to a great profusion of concepts dealing with the knowledge of reality.

The spread of Ockhamism pushed to their ultimate consequences the results of the controversies that after 1277 fed the debate within the Faculty of Theology, mainly over the excesses of systematization and theological rationalism. As a critico-speculative outlook that aimed above all at a simplification of theoretical abstractionism, Ockhamism encouraged and nourished in various ways the dissatisfaction and reaction of the "moderns" against the schematisms and cultural immobilism that in their view characterized all the teachings of the "realistic" and systematic thinkers of past generations. This meant chiefly Thomas and Scotus but also Albert, Bonaventure, Giles of Rome, and Henry of Ghent.

For this reason, wherever critical attitudes inspired by the Venerable Inceptor took root they did not lead necessarily to the formation of a school or a unified current of thought. Not infrequently, however, they did lead to a (more or less moderate) skepticism and a lowering of the claims of theological reasoning. This trend created an unusual association of individuals active in the faculties of Arts or Theology but coming from quite different formative backgrounds: from the Franciscans to the Dominicans, from the Hermits of St. Augustine to the seculars.

A. ADAM WODHAM AND JOHN OF RODINGTON

The trend just described began to appear in the work of Adam Wodham (d. 1358), a direct disciple of Ockham, the editor of the latter's *Summa of Logic*, for which he wrote a preface, and in his own right a master of theology at Oxford around 1340. He was convinced of the fundamental role of intuitive knowledge as the sole source of evidence, both external or sensible and interior or intellectual, but he thought it necessary to correct Ockham's teaching on propositions. For if the object of an assent were simply a proposition (a *complexum*), then the criticism of the realists, such as the earlier mentioned Walter of Chatton (d. 1343), would be valid, namely that this thesis detracts from the objectivity of knowledge and its continuity with the mode of existence of external realities. Therefore, says Adam (who here again distances himself from Ockham), Scotus is correct in calling for the presence of the object as an essential requirement of intuition.

This does not, however, mean a fall back into realism. In order to avoid reintroducing into the theory of knowledge the unjustified presupposition of the objective metaphysical structure of things Adam offers a middle-way solution and assigns the role of object of knowledge to a kind of "state of things," a situation, a "that is the way things are" that is signified by a proposition but is not directly reducible either to a proposition or to a thing. It is neither a sign nor a thing nor an "apparent existent" (a third reality between subject and object, as Aureoli suggested). It is, instead, a pure "something" (*esse quid*) intermediate between signs and things; it does not have its existence either in signs or in things, but in between them, in the very act of "seeing."

This same conception, which seems to revive Abelard's reading of the problem of universals, returns in various writers of this period as a possible middle way between Scotism and radical nominalism. One such writer was William Crathorn, a Dominican who lectured on the *Sentences* in 1330–32. It is found later but, it seems, without direct influence from Adam, in Gregory of Rimini and other Augustinians, who popularized it under the name of *complexe signifi-cabile* ("proposition that can carry meaning"). Adam held that his interpretation of propositional logic was the only basis for the successful rehabilitation of logic in its entirety; this, as we saw in his preface to Ockham's *Summa*, he regarded as essential for the restoration to health of every area of human knowledge.

Theology, too, had its place in this approach, but with the proviso that an adequate perception of the "state of things" of the divine object was obviously beyond human powers; only in the beatific vision would the finite intellect have a satisfactory knowledge of it. The development during earthly life of a theological knowledge that is "ours," though legitimate and meritorious on the part of the human intellect and using the same methodology employed in acquiring knowledge of finite things, is therefore always limited and imperfect. For this reason Adam further emphasized Ockham's distrust of the supposed demonstrability of theological matters far beyond our powers of intuition, such as the very existence and oneness of God. All the rational proofs devised by theologians for demonstrating the existence of the God of faith necessarily retain a high degree of probability. The reason: it is always possible for some "impudent, obstinate fellow" (*protervus*), a denier of the truth of Christian revelation, to formulate rigorously argumentative propositions that lead to opposite conclusions.

Wodham's commentary on the *Sentences* was in circulation until the sixteenth century in the form of an abridgment made around 1374 by Henry Totting of Oyta, a Viennese master. As in his own writings, the editor emphasized this probabilist approach to theological knowledge by expanding the number of "neutral problems," the solutions of which cannot be strictly demonstrated; he included even the origin of the world and the spiritual nature of the soul.

The point about the *protervus* had already appeared in some passages of Scotus and was destined to play a large role in late medieval and modern theological discussion. It was developed by John of Rodington (d. 1348), a Franciscan at Oxford, in his commentary on the *Sentences*. He combines it with an explicit retrieval of the Augustinian doctrine of illumination and the theological origin of every certain human knowledge, since the latter is derived always and solely from the "eternal light" radiated by the divine ideas. Only knowledge thus coming "from a special illumination by God" is certain. In contrast, every idea that is purely natural in origin is of an inferior rank and, even if possessing a greater or lesser argumentative power, is always marked by a degree of probability and lack of evidence. As a result the *protervus* is always able to be obstinate and to harden his doubts. It follows that every attempt to develop a natural (or *a posteriori*) theological knowledge inevitably fails when confronted with this radical methodological objection. The *protervus* does not see why it is not permissible to accept an infinite regress in the automatic working of finite causality; therefore he rejects the demonstration of God's existence. It is likewise not demonstrable that God does not simply think himself but also has a knowledge of creatures, that he is infinite in act, that he is one, omnipotent, and creates from nothing.

Nothing can overcome the doubt of the *protervus* but true theology, which is distinct from philosophical thinking and from any other finite science and is located on a different and higher level, being based on faith and illumination; on that level doubt no longer has any power because there is no reason for formulating it. In thus harking back to the gnoseology of the Oxford Franciscans but also to the authoritative model provided by Bonaventure, John rediscovers, on the one hand, the theophanic origin of all certain intellectual knowledge and, on the other, the probabilist nature of theological reasoning, something that in the final analysis had been characteristic of all western Latin theology from Augustine onward.

B. ROBERT HOLKOT

The return, in the completely Augustinian manner, to the celebration of the truth of knowledge based on faith as opposed to the probability of natural knowledge is also to be seen in the Oxford theologian Robert Holkot (d. 1349), a Dominican but an independent one. He was a representative of the spirited group of scholars, scientists, mathematicians, logicians, and theologians who, in the decade from the mid-thirties to the mid-forties, gathered around Richard of Bury (d. 1345), a cultured and learned bibliophile who was also chancellor of Edward III. Robert taught theology at Oxford until 1334 and then perhaps at Cambridge; in addition to a commentary on the *Sentences* he has left three interesting *Quodlibeta* and some biblical commentaries, in particular on the wisdom books.

Like John of Rodington, Holkot was convinced of the utter impossibility of using the tools of natural reason to reach a proven certainty about dogmatic truths and, in particular, the existence of God, his attributes, and the Trinity. He was not averse to the use of secular learning in theology, but he refused to allow that it could there have more than a "decorative" and enhancing function. For example, outside of theology logic has a specific value of its own, which can be acknowledged, provided it is always applied with respect for its principles. One of the foundations of Aristotelean logic is the real distinction: that is, the recognition, based on the principle of noncontradiction, that two logical truths differ when they correspond completely and in every way to different realities. Useless, therefore, is every attempt to develop alternative rational logics and claim that they are more suitable for dealing with the divine mysteries. That is what the Scotists do when they rely on a claimed but unjustified "formal distinction" to explain the trinitarian relations in God.

As a matter of fact, our knowledge of God is never clear or evident. We cannot pass a proper judgment on the truths enunciated in the Bible (truths that logic helps us to understand) because the reality corresponding to these truths eludes us. For example, we can and ought to understand what is meant by "God is simple" and "God is triune," but we must not think we can express a judgment on the compatibility of these two judgments.

From all this it is clear that Holkot takes over from the Ockhamists the theory of the proposition as the object of knowledge, but in his first *Quodlibet* he derives from the theory an important theological distinction. Only those propositions are evident—that is, make known to us the reality of what they signify—in which the predicate is included in the concept of the subject (for example, "human beings are mortal"). Therefore, since all the terms used in our propositions are products of sense knowledge, we can never use Aristotelean logic to formulate any evident proposition about God. Furthermore, following along this line, we will never be able to formulate any evident proposition about separated substances.

In face of this criticism the entire Arabo-Aristotelean system of heavenly and incorporeal intelligences collapses. On the opposite side, it seems clear that the only possible evidence for theological truths is that provided by the teachings of the faith. Holkot thus introduces the need of theologians to accept a "different logic" in place of the Aristotelean-Scholastic kind, but this different logic is not artificially made up by the human mind. It is the logic internal to faith and equidistant from the free meritorious assent of the will and the cognitive claims of the intellect. This logic of faith is, however, always a rational logic, but "different from natural logic" and valid only to the extent that it is able to establish the principles governing the harmony among the revealed truths.

An obvious example of how this logic operates, as well as one of the foundations on which it operates, can only be the norm provided by divine omnipotence. This makes it possible to assess the truth of all the dogmatic statements of Scripture and tradition without setting any limits on either the efficient causality or the free will of the divine source. Exploiting this norm to the fullest, the theologian will reach the point of asserting that God is the sole author of everything that happens, including the free will of human beings whom God has made to be free and whom he wills with their free choices, even those that are sinful. This is not to say that God is responsible for these, but that he makes them exist and makes them exist as such, that is, as sinful, in dependence on his decision to make real the acts of the free human will.

c. Thomas Bradwardine

The same radical adherence to the presupposition of omnipotence and of the absolute freedom of the divine will inspired the work of other theologians in Richard of Bury's circle. Their outlook was strengthened by the rebirth of interest in the works of Augustine's maturity that dealt with the Pelagian controversy, the theses on justification by grace, and predestination. One of these writers was Richard FitzRalph (d. 1360), who was chancellor of Oxford University in 1334. He possessed a deep and sincerely religious spirit and was opposed to the privileges granted to the Mendicants. He composed a now-lost commentary on Augustine's *Trinity* in which, relying on the principle of the "rule of grace," that is, the omnipotent power of grace in all creation, he composed a fideist critique of the major speculative trends of his time.

The best example of the emphasis on omnipotence was Thomas Bradwardine, theologian and man of letters, lover of the classics and expert mathematical scholar, and leading spirit of the "arithmeticians" (*calculatores*) of Merton College. Like Holkot, he died a victim of the Black Plague that devastated Europe in 1349, a few months after he had been appointed archbishop of Canterbury. After lecturing on the *Sentences* at Oxford in 1333, he used the materials of his own commentary in composing a work that is of special interest for the history of theological speculation. In this work, *The Cause of God* (or *Summa on the Cause of God against Pelagius and on the Power of Causes*), he was inspired by his scientific studies and the idea of mathematical knowledge as a formal model for all the other sciences to attempt a theological system structured by axioms and deductions. He thus revived the old ideal of Alan of Lille and Nicholas of Amiens and set forth a thinking about God that was structured according to a precise geometric order.

The speculative foundation on which the entire demonstrative development in *The Cause of God* unfolds is an indemonstrable idea, and necessarily so, since the idea is a theological one. This foundation of truth obtainable by the minds of believers is maintained by Bradwardine on the basis of results emerging from a profound meditation on a verse of Paul (Rom 9:16) that becomes for him the first hermeneutical key to every further unfolding of the truth: "It depends not on human will or exertion, but on God who shows mercy (*non volentis neque currentis sed miserentis est Dei*)." Taking as his starting point this primordial access to the unrestricted divine activity in every created reality, Bradwardine (called by many the "Profound Doctor") undertakes a completely coherent theologico-demonstrative synthesis. Its deductive procedure is the very tool that enables him to construct arguments about God without falling into the temptation of anthropomorphism, that is, without introducing any temporal and contingent variables into the nature of God.

The divine perfection, which is the initial postulate set down at the beginning of the treatise, is a logical possibility that does not imply any contradiction. But human salvation, too, is only a logical possibility under the conditions of the present life. There is no other way of making the second real except to make it depend completely and in every respect on the first, or, in other words, to make the redemption of humanity dependent on the perfect, unconditioned, and omnipotent will of God. This first proposition leads to a second: the denial of the possibility of an infinite regress in beings, for that would involve a lessening of the perfect infinity of God.

The linking of further consequences is rapid and direct. Nothing finite subsists in God in a way that sets conditions for him; on the contrary, it is God who sets conditions for every finite succession. Time, space, what is necessary in various ways and what is contingent, indeed everything that happens exists necessarily only insofar as it is deducible from the fullness and freedom of the first cause. God is not subject to the necessity caused by the past, since his will makes the past as contingent as the future is. He is not subject to spatial limitation and is therefore infinitely present everywhere: in the world and in the infinite spatial void. The latter, because of the divine ubiquity, is necessarily imaginable as preceding creation and as external to it, even though it remains a mathematical concept corresponding to a reality that is not corporeal or representable in a physical way.

On the basis of this highly organized demonstration of the conditions and consequences of the free divine necessity Bradwardine goes on, in the second of the three books of *The Cause of God*, to attack the casuistic and conditional morality of contemporary theologians. Such a morality seemed to him to be a revival of the Pelagian error. In its place he constructs a human ethic based on the absolute primacy of divine grace, the impossibility of gaining redemption through works, and the presupposition that any human act is rendered effective by divine power alone. On this basis he works out a set of ethico-theological norms for human beings. The human will is necessarily free and autonomous because it is willed to be such by God, who gives all human beings the power to choose their own destiny. But while necessarily free in relation to all natural conditioning forces, that is, to all secondary causes, human beings are necessarily obliged to act according to the conditioning factors that God himself, the sole first cause, imposes on their freedom. The reason for this is that human freedom may not limit the true freedom of God, which is absolute.

Thus conceived, human freedom (the relations of which to the divine will are explained in the third book) is a kind of "spontaneous necessity" according to which "human beings are free in relation to all things under God and are servants of God alone, but servants who are free and not coerced." This means that all human beings are predestined in their every action but, whatever the action, they are redeemed if they do it in accordance with the divine will, because God permits them to do it, but they are damned if they do it against the divine will. Thus while the perfect act of Christ's will was to accept the sacrifice of himself, he could also have been obliged to undergo it without accepting it. This is the meaning of predestination "antecedent to foreseen merits," that is, a predestination that determines the destiny of human beings independently of the foreknowledge of their merits and demerits.

D. GREGORY OF RIMINI

As in Holkot, so in Bradwardine, a logic of faith seems to be at work, a logic different from that which allows us to establish definitions and develop lines of argument that are valid only in the natural order. The compatibility of human free will with divine predestination is therefore a datum the mind knows without understanding it.

Something similar is to be found in the thinking of the principal representative, during these years, of the Augustinianism of the Augustinian Hermits who were active at the University of Paris. This was Gregory of Rimini (d. 1358), an Italian who had lectured on the *Sentences* in 1343–44 and has left a record of his lectures on the first two books.

In the second, in which he too attacks the modern forms of Pelagianism, he insists passionately on the wretched state of human beings and their inability to perform any meritorious act, even if this be, in their intention, aimed at the good. In fact, in Gregory's view even actual sin is something inevitable and not the result of a deliberate rebellion of human beings against the divine law. Indeed, the source of the Pelagian error is precisely the claim that each individual is the arbiter of his or her own destiny. Sinful human nature is of itself marked by an absolute insufficiency and therefore an inability to make any good use of natural things, including its own freedom. Behind this pessimistic conception of human nature is clearly the towering presence of the late Augustine, of whose works Gregory had a critical and penetrating knowledge.

His followers called him the "Authentic Doctor"; he was an Augustinian Observant and was elected General of the Order in the final year of his life.

With his eye on the theological system of Giles of Rome, Gregory endeavored to update the unsystematic thought of Augustine by introducing it, in the form of speculatively grounded theses, into contemporary theological and philosophical discussion. As he did so, however, he was not unaware of possible agreements between Augustinian pessimism and the logic of the terminists. The latter influenced him especially in his conception of the scientific character of theological knowledge (a subject discussed, as always, in the questions of the Prologue to the *Sentences*).

The question of the status of theological knowledge depends, in general, on the definition of scientific knowledge, that is, on the nature of the object of knowledge. As mentioned above, Gregory took over, but without explicit references to Wodham and Crathorn, the idea that the object of scientific knowledge is the totality signified by a proposition. This, though it is neither a thing nor an essence, is something that exists inasmuch as the proposition locates it in a sphere intermediate between the sphere of real objects and that of statements. To this something, which is a state of things that is indicated by the proposition, Gregory gives the name *complexe significabile*. This "something" or state of things has a unique (*sui generis*) existence that allows us to regard it as endowed with a special cognitive evidence and to see in it the direct object of scientific knowledge.

Theology purports to be, in fact, a "theological discourse" that is methodically rational and deductive and is organized around the word of God. It consists, therefore, of propositions like those stating the articles of faith or theological conclusions; there must, therefore, be a corresponding *complexe significabile* (for example, the proposition "God is omnipotent" must correspond to the reality that "God is indeed omnipotent"). But such an object is not intrinsically evident since it is not verifiable and can claim only the right to be accepted as probable. Theological knowledge, however, cannot be based on probable propositions but only on evidence, and the only evidence for such statements comes from faith, in the act of assent by which believers confer on them an actually knowable meaning or, in other words, the act of assent in which they acknowledge them as actual reality. This means, in essence, that knowledge of theological statements is possible for both believers and unbelievers, but understanding of them is reserved for believers.

Faith thus produces in the intellect a particular "habit" or skill, the habit of believing (similar to the "habit of theology" of Peter Aureoli), to which corresponds a notional knowledge that is deeper and more extensive than that produced by the simple acquisition of a statement. Combined with a correct understanding of the foundations of the Christian reform of human knowledge as accomplished by Augustine and brought to completion by Anselm, this means that according to Gregory theology is indeed a science, both theoretical and practical (inasmuch as its leads to eternal salvation). But theology is such only for believers, whose faith produces in the intellect a sufficient understanding of theology's real ability to describe a state of things, that is, the total meaning of the statements of Christian doctrine.

Other Italian Augustinians took over the doctrine of the *complexe significabile* and its impact on the scientific status of theological knowledge. Some of these deserve mention. One was Bonsembiante Badoer (d. 1369), a friend of Petrarch, who at his death wrote his brother, Bonaventura Badoer, a lengthy and touching letter of consolation. In his commentary on the *Sentences* Bonsembiante describes the *complexe significabile* simply as "some kind of entity." Another to be mentioned is Ugolino Malabranca of Orvieto (d. 1373), who adds to the idea of the *complexe* a strong Augustinian implication by emphasizing the efficacy of the pure uncreated light of God that enlightens and assists the created intellect in acquiring truth. From this Ugolino draws the conclusion that what is undeserving of being regarded as a science is not theology but, if anything, philosophy. This is because it claims to develop philosophical and even theological proofs without the aid of divine illumination and therefore without a sufficient understanding of the corresponding signified reality. Consequently, while philosophy must inevitably be nothing more than a "mixture of falsehoods," theology alone is a science inasmuch as it really has as its object true *complexe significabilia*, which are not propositions but truths signified in a propositional way.

E. JOHN OF MIRECOURT AND NICHOLAS OF AUTRECOURT

The revival of themes and methodologies peculiar to Augustinianism, combined with the critical outlook of nominalism, seems thus to characterize a varied series of programs put forward around the middle of the fourteenth century. All of them aimed at a new development of theological learning based on a differentiation of the epistemological criteria governing theological knowledge from those used in the other areas of scientific study. But such efforts at transforming the frameworks dominant in theological studies were never painless. Debates and controversies easily arose as soon as thinkers began to realize that behind these efforts were the results of a destructive criticism of the most solid and taken-for-granted theologico-religious certainties.

A series of censures, issued especially in Paris, endeavored once again to check the innovative thrust of these criticisms leveled at traditional teaching on knowledge and the resultant imposition of theological theses that were openly probabilist in tenor. Once again concerns within the Faculty of Theology certainly lurked behind these controversies and the connected condemnations. But, in addition, this Parisian rejection of speculative novelties introduced by Oxford thinkers must have been influenced by political tensions between France and England, including the beginning of the Hundred Years War and especially after the defeat of the French cavalry at Crécy (1346) and the fall of Calais (1347).

One man who certainly had close connections with the theological culture of the English world was John of Mirecourt, a Cistercian who lectured on the *Sentences* in 1344–45 at the College of St. Bernard in Paris, which many English monks attended. In 1347 a commission of theologians established by the chancellor, Robert de'Bardi, a Florentine and close friend of Petrarch, condemned a large number of theses extracted from John's *Lectures*; these theses, while having a degree of originality, were clearly inspired by Ockhamist principles.

In his teaching John radically limits every possibility of evidence to intuition based on experience. He does, however, distinguish two degrees of intuitive evidence. The first, which is interior certainty, is based on the absolutely intuitive character of the principle of noncontradiction and is anchored in the impossibility of doubting one's own existence. The latter John infers from the words of Augustine in *Trinity* X, 10, 14: "All minds know themselves and are certain of this knowledge. . . . Even one who doubts lives. . . . If he doubts, he understands that he is doubting . . . if he doubts, he thinks; if he doubts, he knows that he does not know."

The second degree is certainty about an external object; this too is intuitive and unmediated, but in a way less absolute than interior certainty. The person gives assent to this certainty habitually, without fear of error, and presupposing that God guarantees the continuity of the natural order. But this presupposition also points to the opposite: that it is always possible for knowledge of the external world to be erroneous because God can change the entire spatio-temporal universe, wipe out the past, and make not to have existed that which apparently did exist. Interior evidence is therefore beyond doubting, while exterior evidence is only empirical; it is indeed indispensable for developing the physical sciences, but it guarantees only a high degree of probability. This holds for the entire knowableness of the external world.

For John, then, natural theology, too—"our" theology based on the use of reason and external evidence—is only empirical and probable. The same limitation applies to human morality, which is never absolute because any human act whatsoever, even if free and contingent, depends on the divine will. Thus God wills even the sins of human beings in the sense that he makes sinful actions exist, and exist precisely as sinful. In the final analysis everything that exists does so because God wills it and wills it to be as it is. Every certainty, then, that seeks to be more than probable can only be theological. That is: if we are to accept that the world is what we know it to be, it is because faith encourages us to believe that God is immutable and truthful, that he rewards good with good and punishes evil, that he does not subject us to deceptions or illusions when he makes us know the external world, and that whatever he does will only be for a good purpose. Human knowledge, which is limited to probability by its own natural conditions, can become certain only by relying on faith.

Bachelor and then-master Peter of Ceffons, a Cistercian, lectured on the *Sentences* in 1348–49 and composed one of the versions of *The Devil's Letter to the Clergy*, a provocative and widely circulated text in favor of theological reductionism. He took up the defense of John of Mirecourt after the latter's condemnation, but in his apologetic attempt he brought out, perhaps even more explicitly than John's *Lectures* had, the boldness of some ideas springing from this master's thought. In claiming the right of free speculation in theology Peter notes that sometimes the pagan philosophers had suggested arguments more useful and obvious than those to be drawn from Scripture. He accepted, as a working tool, the hypothesis that God can deceive human beings, even though deception is not part of God's habitual ways. He emphasized the probable character of scientific knowledge, to the point of admitting a multiplicity of worlds in addition to our own visible and perceptible one. Those who wanted to maintain the singleness of the cosmos on the basis of the principle of economy he accused of being like moles who judge unnecessary the reality they are unable to see.

During the same year in which John of Mirecourt was censured, a secular master, Nicholas of Autrecourt (d. 1350), was investigated and condemned at the end of a lengthy trial for which evidence had been collected ten years earlier at Avignon under Benedict XII and that ended under Clement VI. Nicholas was stripped of his rank as master and, in the presence of the teaching body and students of the university, was obliged to burn his nine *Letters* attacking Bernard of Arezzo, a Franciscan, as well as his treatise *Exigit ordo executionis* (title taken from the *incipit*).

The reasons for the condemnation need some explanation. In their judgment the Avignon commission and later the Parisian judges seemed to be accusing Nicholas of having introduced into metaphysics a probabilist phenomenalism that in its tendency was destructive of every certainty. But in the first two of the nine letters (the only ones that have come down to us), Nicholas protested that he was the true defender of the faith and accused Bernard of Arezzo of really being the one who derived from Ockhamist principles a skeptical rejection of any and every kind of evidence. According to his testimony Bernard maintained, first, that the effectiveness with which intuitive knowledge leads to a judgment of existence is entirely independent of the existence of the thing and, second, that because of his omnipotence God can cause us to intuit even a nonexistent thing, so that intuition does not necessarily imply the existence of its object.

According to Nicholas this extreme extension of the efficacy of intuitive knowledge leads to the destruction of all certainty. In response to Bernard's theses it was necessary to hold hard, as did John of Mirecourt, to the irrefutable evidence at least of the five external senses and the no-less-irresistible evidence of interior self-consciousness and the principle of noncontradiction, which is closely connected with it. In his treatise *Exigit ordo executionis*, to these evidences proper to simple knowledge Nicholas adds those operative on the level of complex knowledge, namely, those attaching to self-evident first principles and the conclusions flowing from them.

Nicholas is thus deeply convinced that knowledge is true only when it brings before the mind in a clear, distinct, and exhaustive way something that really exists and that appears as it does precisely because it exists. However, the radical nature of his defense of the reality of known objects leads him to extreme conclusions on the opposite side, that of the very possibility of evident knowledge. For, starting from the assertion that knowledge is true and evident whenever it depends on a manifestation of the things known, he ends with a refusal to accept as true and evident any knowledge that does not satisfy these conditions. In his view the description as true and evident and free of errors applies only to immediate intuition, whether internal or external, when this is so strong as to entail the assent of the mind. On the other hand, error depends on the no-longer-evident judgments with which the intellect meddles in the data of intuition and their immediate consequences.

But this means that by limiting true knowledge solely to certainty about direct acts of knowing, internal and external, Nicholas excludes the truthfulness of any rational construction beyond that immediate kind of knowing. He does ensure the soul a solid contact with singular realities, but at the same time he undermines everything that the systematic metaphysical speculation of the Greek, Arabic, and Christian philosophers has built up as a necessary support for the orderly organization of reality beyond what direct empirical data supply. In order to defend the existence of the real, Nicholas has in practice irreparably destroyed the very possibility of knowing the modes and conditions of that existence. These, then, are the reasons why his censors held him guilty of denying not only the knowableness but the very existence of everything that cannot be intuitively evident.

The first count in the indictment was that he had denied the possibility of inference as an intellectual operation that extends truth on the basis of evident data. For by limiting evidence solely to direct intuitive knowledge Nicholas was obliged to admit that from the certain knowledge of a particular thing it is not possible to derive any other certain knowledge applicable to other things. From this there followed—and this was the second count—a critical refusal to acknowledge the truthfulness of any cause-effect relationship: that is, it is not possible to pass from the existence of a particular thing to the existence of another particular thing that must be the cause of the first. Rather, on the basis of the principle of noncontradiction it is possible and necessary only to admit that one fact follows on another and that the repetition of this succession produces in us an expectation of causality, which is, however, only probable and never necessary.

The third reason why Nicholas undermined the speculative structure raised by traditional metaphysics was that even the concept of substance cannot be claimed as evident, if it be true that the term "substance" means the unified substratum, never visible in itself and only probably there, but providing a link between the obvious accidental data experience shows as belonging to a hypothetical shared principle. In addition, under the blows inflicted by the same gnoseological criticism the concept of end, which is inversely symmetrical with the concept of efficient cause, likewise collapses, for in this view the subordination of one thing to another as to its end is simply a result of our subjective appreciation of their greater or lesser nobility and dignity and is not based on any evidence.

The real universe that emerges from this unqualified metaphysical reductionism is nonetheless more individualized and free than the universe as conceived by Scotus and later by Ockham. Nicholas consciously returns to the simplified views of pre-Aristotelean naturalism and bypasses all the "difficulties" and "unintelligible discourses" of university debates. He conceives of the reality of things as consisting of a set of atoms, whose free movements of association and dissociation are enough to justify and explain all physical phenomena. He harks back (as Peter Damian did) to Paul's motto "Knowledge puffs up" (1 Cor 8:1) and regards himself as authorized to issue a radical criticism of the efforts of the human sciences to be systematic. An exception is seemingly made only for mathematics, because all of its teachings can be directly traced back to the immediately external character of truths closely connected with the principle of noncontradiction.

But it was especially in the sphere of theology that the disintegration of any and every speculative system showed most clearly. This it was that so greatly unsettled the traditional realism of his critics. They were being told here of the insufficiency of inference; the critique of the concepts of cause and end, which meant the uselessness of any *a posteriori* demonstration of God's existence; the impossibility of defining the reality of invisible substance, which raised serious doubts about the existence and immortality of the individual soul; the providential order of the universe as identified with the free movement of atoms, which was beyond the reach of the mental schemata developed by our intellects.

Nicholas was indeed aware of the negative implications of his views and the danger of subordinating theological knowledge to an irremediably relativistic probabilism. But he assured his judges of his own certainty that the superiority of the truths of the faith rendered them invulnerable to any metaphysical doubts and any deficiencies in the operation of reason. All his assertions belonged (he said) to the realm of methodology and had no absolute value, whereas faith guaranteed the truth even of what is not evident to the intellect. Philosophy is therefore free to deal with other areas, those that are practical, moral, and existential; here, without any disagreement with revelation, it can exercise its own empirical method and gather its fruits.

But to his judges this appeal to religious truth at the end of a systematic destruction of traditional learning was simply "the self-justification of a cunning fox." Yet even in this final fideistic summary of his thought Nicholas, like others, seems to be a witness to an increasingly widespread and indeed accentuated tendency among many thinkers of the age to restore the devotional and existential authenticity of theological thought by distinguishing it definitively and decisively from the mindset of scientific rationality.

F. JOHN BURIDAN

In 1340, at the urging of the pope, the Faculty of Arts had issued new statutes disapproving of the lack of control over the free exercise of university activity even by students and bachelors. In particular they forbade the teaching of Ockham's thought, which seemed suspect and concerning which the university authorities had not yet made any pronouncement. The document bore the respected signature, among others, of the then-rector, John Buridan (d. after 1358), one of the most skilled logicians and learned men of the time. At the same time, in his teaching of logic and physics Buridan was extensively influenced by the method and epistemology of the Venerable Inceptor. This is an indication that the official distancing of the Artists from Ockhamism had to do with nominalism not so much in its logical and methodological formulation as in its extension to other areas of study.

Buridan was critical of the excessively reductionist applications of Ockhamist epistemology and was opposed in particular to the most radical theses of Nicholas of Autrecourt. His concern was to safeguard the legitimacy of physical science and the possibility of solidly grounding it. For this reason he was greatly puzzled by the way in which many masters risked the dissolution of all human scientific knowledge because of their tendency to overemphasize the separation between logic and reality by denying the ability of words to signify the things they supposedly signified. He acknowledged the right of the modalist grammarians to concern themselves solely with the rules for connecting the words of a language. In his view, however, logic must never lose sight of the relationship between the linguistic order and the mental order, since the ultimate duty of the logician is to establish a correspondence between words and the intentions that direct thought to objective reality.

Like Ockham, Buridan was convinced of the need to curtail the objectivist claims of Aristotelean logic, but he maintained that this reduction should not be absolute. Rather, it should be limited to reconnecting the abstract categories of thought to individual and concrete realities, to their properties and relationships, and to the laws necessary and sufficient for explaining the consistency of mental language, of which verbal language is a reflection. There were those who, like Nicholas of Autrecourt, drew from Ockhamist reductionism conclusions that removed the ability of human beings to get their bearings in the world of phenomena. In contrast to these, the Paris master, who was always concerned to safeguard the requirements of natural science, proposed a moderate reform of the Venerable Inceptor's epistemology. He would maintain the evidential character of knowledge not only in intuition but also in all the forms of demonstration in which the effectiveness of the intellect in knowing external reality appeared solid and justified at least as much as empirical knowledge, with its immediacy.

Buridan also introduced corrections into Ockham's views on supposition. He eliminated simple supposition by identifying it with material supposition. He thus again accepts a constant direct correspondence in meaning between universal concepts (which are reduced to personal suppositions) and something real. This reality must, however, belong necessarily to the natural order, that is, correspond to something individual that is part of a collectivity. He therefore made a distinction within the capability of concepts to be names. On the one hand there are first intention names (which signify something real and outside the mind, whether these be names of individuals or names common to a plurality of individuals). On the other hand there are second intention names (which correspond to everything he has subsumed under material supposition, that is, purely intellectual products that state in a universal form something that does not exist as such in real individuals).

On this basis Buridan offers his own reform of epistemology: Science embraces everything that is based on first intention truths or on second intention truths that can be traced back to first intention truths. The truthfulness of science is thus reduced to the capacity the terms in propositions have of referring to realities that can be concrete objects of science.

Given these premises, Buridan claims the right to use this reformed logical method in building an authentic science of nature. Due to the power given it by experience, this science is able to move beyond the limits set in the *Posterior Analytics* toward graded degrees of evidence for what is probable; all of this favors an approach to scientific knowledge that is empirical in its tendency.

Nothing forbids establishing the existence of one thing on the basis of the existence of another, if the truth of the latter implies the truth of the former. Nothing forbids taking the syllogism as a means of bringing out a scientific, that is, evident, truth, since syllogisms suffice for bringing new evident truths out of already known evident truths through a chain of operations that goes back to the self-evidence of first principles. Contrary to the prohibitions of the Aristoteleans, nothing prevents a scientific knowledge even of the particular and the contingent, provided logic enables the appropriate language to express these realities adequately by means of terms capable of "supposing" for the condition of particularity and contingency (that is, the state of potential falsifiability). Nothing forbids defining and attempting to know even what cannot be directly experienced (such as a void or the cause of a projectile's movement as it moves away from its active cause), if logic is able to show in a coherent way the probability of such mental operations, that is, an evidence that is lesser but reliable until a better proof is found.

As everyone knows, in the last-named area Buridan linked his reputation as a student of physics to a primitive but convincing explanation of the theory of impetus. According to his explanation the mover imparts to the projectile a kind of motive power that remains in it until it has exhausted its ability to resist the obstacles that put a brake on the movement.

This new logico-metaphysical approach, which is based on the self-sufficiency and evidence of singular entities, is indeed offered by Buridan as an alternative both to Peripatetic-Arabic realism and necessitarianism and to the skeptical and antiscientific reductionism of Autrecourt. But it is also not lacking in important consequences when applied to theological study. Buridan's reform of logic allows him in fact to regard as unacceptable in the real world the meaning that corresponds to the image of an infinite regress. He is therefore able to rehabilitate the metaphysical demonstrations of the existence of God and to offer them as helping human beings in their pilgrim state to form a concept of the divine essence that can "suppose" for God when used in explaining the contents of the faith.

But if this position may seem partially to rehabilitate Aristotle, Buridan immediately criticizes the Philosopher for being unable or unwilling to take account of our mind's ability to see an adequate meaning in the idea of an actualized pure logical possibility and to translate it into the concept of infinite intensity. To traditional philosophers this idea seemed contradictory, but it is in fact the only possible effective mental representation of the real nature of God, since this can be conceived of only as a perfect and absolute freedom from any finite limitation.

In Buridan's view, then, human beings, though unable ever to enjoy an intuitive knowledge of God, can form an evident concept of him and, on the basis of this, develop by deduction a solid demonstrative knowledge for consistent conclusions in which God can function as an adequate subject. This openness to theology goes so far as to assert the existence of a first transcendent and actual Being who is the cause of the entire created order. But, courageous though this opening is and aimed at uses still unenvisioned by medieval scholars, Buridan deliberately limits it to the realm of a natural science based solely on reason and the exercise of logic. This thinker, who was twice rector of the Faculty of

Arts, never wanted to climb the ladder to the study of theology, just as his knowledge of the divine automatically imposes limits on reason and does not presume to deal with dogmatic truths. In his view, in all the problems of the faith to which metaphysics cannot give answers the philosopher must give way to the exponents of the Bible, the "divine theologians" who teach the philosophers "how these things can come about."

G. WALTER BURLEY AND JOHN WYCLIFFE

In line with Buridan's teaching, other leading figures in the Parisian renewal of logic and natural science who were active in the second half of the fourteenth century unambiguously emphasized the autonomy of scientific learning. At the same time, however, they stressed the frailty of human reasoning and its obligation to let itself by guided by the faith as a source of simple (that is, scientifically "economic") solutions to problems for which the unaided mind could not find satisfactory solutions. Two such individuals were Nicholas of Oresme (d. 1382), who was a master on the Faculty of Theology in Paris, and Marsilius of Inghen (d. 1396), who during the years of the Schism left Paris in order to help, again as a theologian, in launching the University of Heidelberg in Germany.

But among Buridan's contemporaries there were also professors of logic, one being the English Franciscan Walter Burley (or Burleigh), who likewise belonged to the circle of Richard of Bury. This group had pushed their disagreement with the metaphysical contingentism of Aureoli and Ockham to the point of proposing to resolve the problems of logic and its relations to the sciences by formulating a new, unbiased realism of a Platonic type. This was explicitly based on the acceptance of a real subsistence of universals "outside the mind." According to Burley the metaphysical reality of finite sublunary entities does not consist simply in their individual substantiality. It is due also to their being composed of a multiplicity of universal categorical entities that subsist around and together with the individual substance. The latter is distinct from them and functions as a center that links them together.

Burley's logical realism seems to be closely connected with Bradwardine's theological realism inasmuch as both distanced themselves from the probabilist contingentism of the nominalists. The former did so by his adoption of Platonic realism in its logico-metaphysical aspect, and the latter by his application of Euclidean geometry to the intrinsic necessity of the truths of the faith in their theological aspect.

These two requirements, logical and theological, having been fused together into an explicit speculative unity entailing important consequences in both fields, emerge again in the second half of the century in the quite revolutionary thought of theologian and reformer John Wycliffe (d. 1384). During his studies at Oxford, Wycliffe was influenced on the one hand by the Scotist formalism of Walter of Chatton and on the other by Burley's realism and the theological determinism of Bradwardine and FitzRalph. By the time he became a bachelor in theology in 1369 he already had to his credit a good many treatises on logic, physics, and metaphysics; these give evidence of a radical acceptance of a realism of essences that has an obvious Neoplatonic ancestry. In addition, a doctrine profoundly influenced by divine exemplarism inspired his theological and theologico-political writings, which began to appear at the beginning of the seventies in parallel with his public activity as a preacher.

During the last years of the Avignon period and the early years of the Western Schism Wycliffe was in fact an indefatigable apostle of a moral reform of the church. He was actively committed to a return of the Christian community to its original evangelical vocation, the abolition of churchmen's privileges and wealth, and the independence of the civil state from papal authority. This reform-ing mission had its theoretical justification in the fundamentals of his theological thought. Thus when he preached the idea of the church as "the whole body of the predestined" he was simply applying his conception of the absolute primacy of the universals as divine ideas. Part of this latter group from all eternity were the individual destinies of each substance, including human persons and their volitional acts, all of them eternally subject to the absolutely omnipotent divine rule that ensures the objective truth of all created things. His destructive criticism of all forms of theological intellectualism, from his disavowal of arguments in favor of ecclesiastical authority to his reduction of the number of the sacraments, was indeed obviously influenced also by the Ockhamist elimination of useless abstractions. But this rejection of everything superfluous was likewise connected to his unconditional assertion that reality is determined by the eternal divine exemplars.

These doctrinal positions make clear the deep continuity that exists, accord-ing to Wycliffe, between logico-philosophical science and theology. Knowledge of the universals makes it possible to draw near to the truth of God: for example, by guiding the mind in the assertion of a metaphysical optimism that requires seeing the world as the best possible product of an intelligent and providential divine will, in the description of relations between God and creatures, and in finding a deep structural homogeneity between the faculties of the human soul and the three persons in God. And because God wills his ideas, and in them all the individual entities that participate in them, theological knowledge of reality has obvious necessary consequences in the practical order.

The strong emphasis in his metaphysics on individuals as necessary realities that cannot be robbed of their individual participation in the eternal ideal prin-ciples also supports Wycliffe in his conception of the true church. In his eyes the true church is a spiritual community of predestined individuals, each of them made necessary by God and free of any other earthly limitation and therefore not subject to any external hierarchy and not subordinated to institutions his-torically invented by human beings in order that they might govern according to their selfish interests.

The Lollard movement attempted to give Wycliffe's reformist aspirations a concrete form in dramatic episodes of popular rebellion in the name of economic and social equality and a reduction of the church's privileges. It elicited lively reactions from the ecclesiastical authorities as well as a series of repressive steps by the monarchy and the institutions of the university. Wycliffe was tried in 1382 by two provincial councils held in London and a third held in Oxford by William Courtenay, archbishop of Canterbury, and many of his theses were declared heretical. The preacher was removed from teaching and withdrew to Lutterworth, but died unexpectedly two years later. But the movement that held to his teachings continued to cause turmoil in the English social world during the following years. In 1415, at the Council of Constance, Wycliffe's censure was confirmed. On the same occasion John Hus, the reformer from Prague, was condemned and executed for leading the rebellion of the Bohemian people against the Catholic hierarchy in the name of theological principles quite close to those that had guided Wycliffe's thinking.

4. Mysticism and Religious Individualism in the Rhenish and Flemish Areas

In Paris, but also in the other main centers of study throughout western Christendom, the professional theologians had become increasingly absorbed in subtle discussions and intense controversies about the method followed in their studies. Meanwhile, the products of their thinking and even their speculative interests seemed increasingly remote from the interior experience and religious life of the faithful. Francesco Petrarch's strong attacks were perhaps the noblest expression of a heartfelt and widespread feeling of distrust of and an undisguised lack of interest in the university world and its theological and scientific thought. This situation was very obvious especially at the lower and less educated levels of both the lay population and the ecclesiastical hierarchy.

One of the most symptomatic results of this situation was the emergence of isolated but frequent episodes of heightened mystical spirituality that could be observed, especially among the ordinary people, as early as the end of the thirteenth century. For the most part these instances of an intense and absorbing individual religious involvement were alien to theological learning of an educated kind but quickly became widespread among the people. This was due precisely to the immediacy and ready communicability of intensely felt interior experiences that could be told to others and affect them greatly, and all this without need for higher education. Numerous instances of visions by women were associated, especially in Italy, with the spirituality of the tertiaries of the Mendicant Orders and accompanied by a reputation for holiness that quite often migrated beyond regional boundaries.

The individuals were often illiterate women who lacked education but did acquire a solid background of knowledge of the Bible. They would report the content of their visions to a confessor who also served as a secretary, gave it a literary form, and consented to making it known. Among the best known of these women we may mention Angela of Foligno (d. 1309), Clare of Montefalco (d. 1308), and the most celebrated of the fourteenth century, Catherine of Siena (d. 1380), a Dominican tertiary.

Northern Europe likewise saw similar instances of a primarily feminine spirituality that was saturated with biblical wisdom and gave rise a flourishing devotional literature in both Latin and the vernacular. The women in question belonged to the beguinages and were influenced in an especially deep way by the mystical thought of Meister Eckhart. The memory of the Meister was kept alive during these years by the spiritual writings of a group of lesser masters and preachers who had adopted his teaching. Deserving of mention here are two brothers, John and Gerard Korngin of Sterngasse, Dominicans both. Gerard was also the author of *Meadow of Souls, or a Cure for the Sluggish Soul*, a successful psychologico-spiritual meditation that described the struggle of the soul, aided by the gifts of the Holy Spirit, against the vices and for the virtues. The work's lyrical style imitates the *Psychomachia* of Prudentius, but the author also makes prudent use of more recent scholastic sources.

These thinkers formed a direct link between the official culture of the Mendicant Orders and the spread of a strong current of devotional spirituality of a more popular and lay kind that took the name *Devotio moderna* (*Modern Devotion*). The thinkers had, therefore, to be careful in their preaching and texts (often written in the vernacular) to use a high level of theological rhetoric for the obvious purpose of keeping their spiritual meditations on a consistently orthodox plane. They had to avoid the danger of contamination by extremist movements of protest that were spreading dangerous anticlerical and libertarian attitudes (one such during the fourteenth century was the previously mentioned Free Spirit movement).

Closely linked to the house of studies in Cologne during these same years was the teaching of Berthold of Moosburg (d. 1361). He was a Dominican master who, following in the steps of Theodoric of Freiberg and Eckhart, helped to strengthen the speculative Neoplatonic foundation of spiritual mysticism in the circles we have been describing. His principal work was a learned *Explanation* of Proclus' *Rudiments of Theology*; characteristic of the book was his careful examination of the speculative affinity between the thinking of the late antique Neoplatonic philosopher and the theological structure of the cosmology and psychology of Pseudo-Dionysius.

Berthold had a clear grasp of the necessary distinction between the ways of natural metaphysics and the higher results of Christian theology, which are guaranteed by the mediation of the Word. On this foundation he developed a coherent description, obviously philosophical in kind, of the ascent of the soul toward the Supreme Good. This ascent was destined to end, after a complex journey of intellectual growth, in the theological acquisition of the beatific vision and therewith in a complete union with the divine Intellect. This goal, however, could be reached only through a free gift of grace that is entirely exceptional and reserved to a very few of the elect.

Other important representatives of this learned theology with its strong mystical leanings were more directly concerned with the spread and control of a more spontaneous spirituality that had a strong emotional attraction for the communities, primarily of women, connected with the birth of the *Devotio moderna*.

John Tauler (d. 1361) was a Dominican who was closely linked to Eckhart in people's minds and was active in the Rhenish area around Strasbourg and then at Basel in Switzerland. His eighty sermons are rich in citations of the Fathers and the Cistercian and Victorine spiritual writers of the twelfth century. Dominant in these sermons is the Eckhartian exhortation to enkindle a love-charity for Christ in the innermost, unfathomable depths of one's interior and so to prepare it for the indescribable final experience of the divine. This experience takes the form of a true and proper interior generation of the Word in the depth (the *Grund* or spark or source) of the soul, something possible only by divine grace. The final attainment of an unmediated perception of God present in his essence in this innermost depth of the soul is the source of supernatural happiness (this depth is described, along obvious Platonico-Christian lines, as the ultimate root of the human union on earth with that originating truth out of which the human person came forth at creation).

According to Tauler the only preparation for the achievement of this goal is a lengthy exercise of detachment from earthly goods and concerns and an unqualified devout practice of recollection that is aided by meditation on human weakness and a training for death. Preparation for mystical experience, which receives nothing from external, empty, and illusory knowledge, must be fostered by the practice of the virtues, a conversion to an interior life, a passionate imitation of the example of Christ, and a clinging to the sufferings of his Passion. All this means a lengthy journey of love illumined by the magnificent allegories of the Song of Songs, which exalt the soul and bring it into the presence of the divine bridegroom. It is worth noting that Tauler, anticipating Christian humanism, is convinced that penitential practices are not appropriate on that journey; they are not necessary and even become an obstacle to prayer and meditation. These are fostered rather by a state of bodily relaxation, which is useful for concentration and an openness to the inner life.

Henry Suso (or Seuse; d. 1366) was likewise a Dominican and a native of Constance. He had heard Eckhart lecture in Cologne and later was himself a Reader; he became prior first in Constance and then in Ulm. Around 1326 he composed his *Little Book of the Truth* for the purpose of defending the Meister's teachings, especially against the accusation that these promoted extreme positions such as those of Free Spirit movement. As a result, in 1330 at the General Chapter in Maastricht Suso was accused of accepting the errors of Eckhart that had been condemned a year earlier; he was suspended from teaching. From that point on he devoted himself to the spiritual welfare and formation of the religious women of the Order. In tones resembling those of an indignant Petrarch he voiced his own uneasiness in regard to the theological debates of the schools, which he likened to a game in which the aim of the participants was simply to keep throwing the ball back against the opponent without paying any attention to the latter's real views. But since the subject about which the disputants were quarreling was the Scriptures, they were in fact playing games with the Christian faith itself.

During these years he composed his *Little Book of Eternal Wisdom* and, in Latin, his successful *Horologium Sapientiae*; these turn the metaphysical and dialectical structure of Eckhart's thought into a song about divine Wisdom's love of the believer, her "beloved" servant. The latter is urged to return her affection with the help of intuitive and seductive explanations of the mysteries of the faith, especially the Passion, for in this mystery suffering renders so evident the likeness between God and the human person as to permit the start of a unitive asceticism that culminates in mystical union. Notable here is Suso's effort to transpose into simple and psychologically effective language that which he wants to preserve of systematic scholastic theology; as a result, the latter is effectively communicated without losing its speculative solidity.

The bypassing of scholastic intellectualism in favor of a practico-contemplative meditation that opens the doors to mystical experience is more obvious in the writings of John Ruysbroeck of Brabant (d. 1381; Ruysbroeck was the place of his birth). In 1343 he founded a congregation of Canons Regular at Groenendaal near Brussels. He deliberately gave no time to the world or the methodologies of the university or its focus on speculative systems. He did, however, leave behind a rich and original set of works, written chiefly in Middle Dutch but soon translated and circulated in German and Latin, that made a noteworthy contribution to a theological and poetic exaltation of the themes most widespread in the practice of the *Devotio moderna*.

His chief work, *The Adornment of the Spiritual Marriage*, and another written in his later years, *The Twelve Beguines*, show in the best possible way the transformation of theoretical discourse into the passionate development of a way to practico-contemplative mysticism. These texts repeat the nuptial allegories, the exhortation to virtue and detachment from the world, and the call to meditation on the life and mysteries of Christ, but they enrich all these with further images and intuitive insights into supernatural truth. All this has as its goal the "restoration to oneness" of the human soul. This concept, obviously Neoplatonic in origin, is here transformed and given great anagogical power by a direct and seductive language that makes its content more easily accessible to a religious mind that lacks philosophical training.

In the following decades many followers of Ruysbroeck, notable among them Gerard Groote (d. 1384) and John of Schoonhaven (d. 1432), took up the task of continuing to strengthen and spread the master's teaching. They had to defend it chiefly against not a few opponents who criticized the emphasis on spiritual individualism, which they interpreted as a call to move away from the ecclesiastical magisterium and from communal religious practices.

5. Toward a Rebirth of Theology

The Western Schism (1377–1449) caused a tragic and for a long time irreparable division between two papal allegiances and two contrasting religious outlooks. It inflicted the most serious wound imaginable on the very heart of a religious thought that had been born, ten or more centuries before, of a paradigmatic principle: the unity of the faith and the indivisibility of truth.

Undermined by the stubborn hostility between opposed views and the emergence of a widespread though moderate skepticism of a pragmatic kind, scholastic theology had for some time been displaying the signs of serious deterioration. Petrarch's cry of alarm and the spread of the *Devotio moderna* were parallel witnesses to the need to open up new paths of theological knowledge and liberate it from the exclusive lecture halls of the schools. The latter had taken possession of theology only to make it soporific and contaminate it with the subtleties of philosophy. Now the need was to rekindle and feed the fire of a more authentic and interiorized religious thinking about the meaning of earthly human life and about its relationship to Christ and his church.

Yet the university world itself was aware of the fundamental rightness of these criticisms and calls for renewal. Amid the tragic historical events at the end of the fourteenth century and the beginning of the fifteenth it could not help asking whether it could find within itself the motivations and resources for changing the directions, procedures, and purposes of theology. The theologians of the schools knew that a productive reform of their discipline had to be first among the tasks they were called upon to execute. They also saw clearly that the success of this operation had long depended on the revision, if not the abandonment, of overly rigid rational formalisms and the rediscovery of the real foundation of Christian knowledge. This foundation was the pure substance of the faith, from which all their thinking had to derive its vitality and reason for existing.

Only apparently, and then for the advantages it provided, do we find some masters, who were sincerely committed to restoring the original dignity of theological studies, taking an approach to this program that can be described as a renunciatory revisionism. That is, their approach seemed to borrow from late scholastic probabilism the ability to weaken rather than strengthen the speculative solidity of their discipline.

We see this in the thinking of Peter Philargus of Candia (Crete) (d. 1410), a Franciscan who was a bachelor at Oxford and a master in Paris between 1378 and 1381 and then became archbishop of Milan. He played a personal role in the failed attempts to settle the Schism when he was elected pope by the Council of Pisa in 1409 and took the name of Alexander V. He anticipated some aspects of Italian humanism when he did not hide his sincere affinity for Plato, his "fellow countryman."

He had no intention, however, of subjecting the doctrines that most attracted him, especially exemplarism as rethought in an Augustinian perspective, to the criticisms and different speculative views of Aristotle. Disagreements among neighbors occur frequently, he remarked, but this does not mean that we cannot derive useful ideas from listening now to the one, now to the other. He took the same attitude to the opposition between the Scotists and the Ockhamists: due to their starting points and methods, they differ in their approach to a reality, that of metaphysics and theology, the truth of which the human mind can never exhaust. This does not mean that such very divergent systems of thought can both claim to be regarded as legitimate in their entirety. One and the same doctrine (for example, the univocity of the Scotists), however, can be useful and convincing in metaphysics, but less useful in other areas of knowledge.

"I do not regard the one as truer than the other, but it is right to explain several ways of approaching a problem, for the convenience of those who want to eat now bread, now cheese." His words display irony and simplicity, but not simplification or speculative fatigue. Peter of Candia knew how to make distinctions ("the one man is speaking of logic, the other of metaphysics"), and his ability to judge shows that his attitude to speculation (which, with necessary adaptations, recalls that of John of Salisbury) was in its basic inspiration not skeptical but constructive and conciliatory.

In contrast, Peter d'Ailly (d. 1420) was, more than anyone else, a representative of the nominalism of the "moderns" when he asserted that the philosophy of Aristotle belonged more to the realm of opinion than to that of science. But his downgrading of the cognitive claims of reason both in philosophy and in natural theology turned into a radical and enthusiastic fideism in the area of Christian theology. This fideism fed a disdain for the machinery of the schools and the subtleties of their disputations.

Peter received his licentiate in theology at Paris in 1380; he was appointed chancellor there in 1389 and then bishop of Cambrai in 1397. Together with John Gerson, his successor as chancellor, he was one of the most active promoters of the Council of Constance, which was meant to seek a conciliarist solution of the Schism; both men sought this solution with all the authority of the university they represented. In the area of ecclesiastical politics as in that of theological study their proposed method came down to combining the absolute certainties of the faith with valid abilities of reason. In its enlightened simplicity their position was simply a return to the authentic teaching of Augustine.

Faith does not spring from knowledge, but also not from the will alone; it arises from the cooperation of both. To them, moreover, a third essential element must be added, namely probability, which allows the synthesis of the two. Knowledge, faith, and opinion are distinct but complementary, and all three are essential components of theological knowledge that is geared to the salvation of believers. Knowledge is the highest component and opinion the lowest, but this ranking can be reversed because opinion can help faith to accept truths on which knowledge does not dare to pronounce. The protracted and useless debates of the theologians often arise from a failure to distinguish among these three levels and from the claim that opinion has the status of knowledge, or vice versa, to the obvious detriment of faith.

Recognition of the probable and therefore nonevident nature of many theological truths, especially among those not essential for redemption, makes it possible to surmount misunderstandings without reining in, and instead even nourishing and developing the investigative powers of reason. Why? Because the goal of the activity of reason, even though never fully attained in the present life, is to make the probable become evident and true. But these are only the premises of an authentic theology. Above and beyond this combination of real knowledge and probable knowledge, believers can only trust in the higher stability of revelation for all the theological truths that are indispensable for their personal salvation.

For Peter d'Ailly, therefore, theology true and proper is not a science but a firm acceptance that is never touched by doubt. It is knowledge, but one founded on faith, and faith's absolute and irrefutable superiority enables theology to enter into dialogue with the other forms of knowledge, both theoretical and practical, that human beings can acquire. From these theology can derive useful improvements in its method and no longer be left to the mercies of empty, fruitless dialectics.

The necessary return to the theological supremacy of the Bible and more particularly to the literal sense, which does not allow subjective and disputable interpretations, is therefore the primary and fundamental mark of a theology that is seeking a rebirth. At the beginning of the fourteenth century a key factor in this return was the work of Franciscan exegete Nicholas of Lyra (d. 1329), whose *Postilla* (a continuous commentary on the Old and New Testaments) successfully led, even outside the universities, to a reading of Scripture that closely followed the text and the events narrated. His historical exegesis certainly did not exclude the consideration of particulars as examples, which Thomas Aquinas had proposed as essential for making theological knowledge useful. But in including this Nicholas did not dilute the fundamental importance of an understanding of the literal sense as the key that gives access to further levels of exegesis and doctrine. The identification of theology and Sacred Scripture has perhaps never been so strongly and incisively made as here.

In a short treatise *On the Literal Meaning of Sacred Scripture*, written at Paris in 1412, John Gerson (d. 1429) expressly appeals to Nicholas as he himself likewise accepts what he regards as the only foundation of authentic theological wisdom. The most serious sin human beings commit, the "sin against the Holy Spirit" (Mark 3:29), which is spreading and causing heresies and divisions throughout Europe ("not only in England, Scotland, Prague, and Germany but even, to our pain and shame, in France") is the rejection of an evident and acknowledged truth. And the worst form of this rejection is the rejection of the evident literal meaning of Scripture, which is the unquestionable and inescapable foundation of every theological truth.

Those who do not respect the literal sense do not recognize the limitations of the human intellect, but believe that only what they understand can be true. It is this error that gives rise to disobedience to the church and to the social and civil order, as well as to the use of sophisms and deceptive arguments in justifying errors in matters of faith and rejections of dogma. The division of heretics into sects thus parallels the intellectual deviousness and audacity of those who would use the philosophy of Plato or Aristotle in order to undermine the simplicity of the faith.

This conviction guided Gerson in his effort to settle the Schism and to effect the moral and intellectual healing of France. It also served as his guide in a series of implacable attacks against representatives of some popular trends (ranging from the Lullists to John of Ripa and from Ruysbroeck to Wycliffe). These he condemns indiscriminately as having been sickened by an excessive realist formalism. They have therefore become representatives of the determination to subject God's omnipotence and free will to conceptual limits, logical distinctions, the presumptuous claims of human free will, and Platonic intermediaries, all invented by the human mind.

Above all, the same conviction sustained him in the difficult task of leadership as chancellor of the University of Paris. In that lofty office he set himself to reform theology and restore it to its ancient and true task as moral and spiritual guide of humanity, as he wrote in 1400 in a well-known letter to Peter d'Ailly. This restoration could come about only if the masters of theology were to cease "playing games" and "indulging in fancies," that is, getting bogged down in child's play and inventions that are laughed at and scorned by the masters of the other faculties, who regard the masters of theology as unintelligible madmen. Such masters are "theologizers" but not "theologians," as Gerson puts it in another programmatic work, his *Lectures against the Empty Curiosity of Students*, which he delivered to masters and students in Paris in November 1402.

The issue was not simply the improvement of particular aspects of theological teaching. What was needed was a complete change in the attitude scholars displayed in their disagreements. They suffered from two fundamental vices: useless curiosity, which had been the deadly sickness of ancient philosophy, and the desire to be unique, which led them to search for odd and unusual doctrines and caused them to neglect matters really essential. In the university faculties the two vices had merged to form one: curiosity in search of uniqueness or, in other words, an intolerance of anything acquired and now settled, and this for the pure pleasure of applying their critical skills to the study of unusual and unexamined teachings. This contagious sickness urged scholastic thinkers of whatever order and degree to devote all their energies chiefly to attacking other masters by contradicting them and refusing to "make a personal contribution to the search for a possible harmonization of different teachings."

The model to be studied in beginning the cure of these vices could only be the one provided by the Fathers of the Church and the religious tradition of the West. That tradition had learned to base the superiority of theology on the propaideutic activity of all the other forms of learning and knowledge. Following this model necessarily required a sincere and heartfelt interior asceticism that consisted of achieving a correct interaction of the cognitive and affective faculties of the soul. The tripartite hierarchic ordering of these two sets of faculties, to be learned from the monastic sources of the twelfth century and from Bonaventure's *Journey*, leads to the final cognitive and loving contemplation of truth. Gerson devoted one of his most important works, *Mystical Theology*, to the attainment of this supreme goal.

Mystical theology is distinct from the bookish theology of the schools, but is presented by Gerson as the end result and justification of that theology. In Gerson's thinking, mystical theology is the authentic interior experience of the Pseudo-Dionysian "hidden God" and results from a systematic and complex interior practice of intellectual activities and the moral virtues.

This authentic crown set upon knowledge will certainly not emerge from an uncontrollable upsurge of religious feeling such as that which, in Gerson's view, is the dangerous mark of the extreme forms of the *Devotio moderna*. But neither can it be the fruit of the natural intellectual powers of the speculative theologian. In the Prologue of his work Gerson urges such a theologian to remember that he is but a "little man" (*homuncio*) whose ability to understand and nourish devotion is but a gift granted to him solely for the profit of others, including lowly women and illiterates, that they may be enlightened and become fervent while he himself "like a lighted wax candle melts down into his own ashes."

Mysticism is learned, then, not in the school of reason but in that of love ("school of the affections"). It comes about in the convergence of divine grace with human effort and practice. It takes the form not of a lesson learned but of a constructive union of lover and beloved in a theological discourse that cannot be assertive or a quest for knowledge but only, like the result of any human movement toward God, a prayerful discourse. All this is expressed with outstanding clarity in the forty-fourth "Consideration" of the first part of the work.

> In the present life the perfection or happiness of the rational soul is to be found rather in perfect prayer or in mystical theology than in intellectual contemplation. Indeed, contemplation considered in its essential reality, apart from love or any affections that flow from it, is still restless, curious, unthankful, and presumptuous. . . . It is therefore permissible to conclude that, other things being equal, the school in which one learns to pray is more praiseworthy than the school in which one learns one's letters, just as the school of religion that gives rise to the affections is superior to the instructional school that leads to understanding.

After the end of the Council of Constance, Gerson was forced to flee France in order to escape persecution by John the Fearless, Duke of Burgundy and Regent of France, who was acting on behalf of the English crown. Gerson took refuge in Austria, first at the abbey of Melk and then in Vienna. In 1419, having experienced in his own person the ancient tragedy of Boethius' exile, he wrote *The Consolation of Theology*, a short work in dialogue form. This work symbolically ends the history of medieval theological thought, which had begun with the search for a philosophical consolation.

Theology personified intervenes directly in the conclusion of the dialogue in order to show how her power to console is superior to and more effective than that of Philosophy, whose arrogant presumptuousness leads to the rambling of speakers and contradictions among the learned. Human life is a theater of uncertainties and sufferings that are fed by the desire for power and by beating others down.

But if everyone judges Christians to be obsolete, they are nonetheless the only truly happy people because they offer their lives for the salvation of the world. Those who want a true knowledge of Theology must start from that radical premise, and in consoling themselves they will console and renew Theology itself, which nowadays is insulted by all and split apart, scorned, or misused. Thus Theology will in its turn console and comfort Philosophy as the latter realizes the inevitably incomplete results of its studies.

Like prayer, theology cannot precede faith but ought to follow upon it. Authentic theological knowledge is gained when the effort to understand takes for granted and investigates the truth about God, which is the object of belief and which faith makes available to it. For this reason theology, like prayer, is an unfolding of the faith. Again as with prayer, it is by thinking theologically that human beings draw nearer to God in the measure of their potentialities.

> Up to this point I have been speaking of Theology. Now let us briefly summarize the gist of her and our discourse and make our own the profitable and indeed necessary consolation it offers us in all our trials. Let us raise our eyes to heaven and yearn for it with our whole heart, thinking: God is the Father of mercies and all consolation; we must hope in his mercy; it is our duty to bend to his will; from him comes the virtue of patience; in him is peace of conscience. Let us take all that we have discussed intellectually during these days and use it to inflame our affections.

Biblical Index

Index of Names and Terms

School of Chartres, 201–16
School of Cologne, 429–35
School of Laon, 166, 191, 215
School of Poitiers. *See* Gilbert of Poitiers
School of Rheims, 167
School of St. Victor, 182–87
Scipio, Publius Cornelius (the African), 14, 203, 206
Sedulius Scotus, 69, 73
Seneca, Lucius Annaeus, 5, 13, 56, 187, 206, 491
Shlomo Ibn Gebirol. *See* Avicebron
Siger of Brabant, 386, 387, 389, 390, 391, 392, 413, 414
Sylvester I, pope, 113
Sylvester II, pope. *See* Gerbert of Aurillac
Simeon, the New Theologian, 123, 125
Simon of Tournai, 200, 247, 294
Simplicius, Neoplatonist, 256
Smaragdus of St. Mihiel, 69
Socrates, 5, 30, 32, 33, 158, 187, 197, 349, 350, 421
Solomon, king of Israel, 19, 44, 408, 409, 414, 421
Stephen II, pope, 55
Stephen of Canterbury. *See* Langton, Stephen
Stephen of St. Geneviève, 188
Stephen of Vénizy, 310
Stilicho, Flavius, 243
Stoics, and Stoicism, 5, 30, 49, 235, 422
Sufi, Islamic mystics, and Sufism, 264, 269
Suidas, 123
Suso, Henry, 518, 519

Tarasius, patriarch of Constantinople, 52, 99
Tauler, John, 518
Tempier, Stephen, 386, 387, 390, 391, 394, 395
Templars, religious order of chivalry, 429
Terence Afro, Publius, 56, 111
Theutberga, queen, wife of Lothar II, 73
Thalassius of Libya, 51
Thales of Miletus, 421
Themistius, 280, 306, 367

Theobald of Canterbury, 234
Theodolinda, Lombard queen, 29
Theodore of Studios, 99, 122
Theodoric of Chartres, 208–12, 213, 214, 215, 234, 235
Theodoric of Freiberg (or of Vriberg), 429–35, 456, 460, 461, 517
Theodoric, king of the Ostrogoths, 7, 26, 28, 29, 35
Theodulf of Orleans, 57, 64
Theon of Alexandria, 49
Theophrastus, 49
Thomas Aquinas, and Thomism, 23, 134, 253, 281, 289, 293, 312, 318, 333, 342–71, 372, 374, 375, 376, 380, 381, 382, 383, 384, 385, 386, 387, 389, 390, 392, 394, 395, 396, 397, 398, 399, 401, 402, 405, 414, 453, 455, 457, 460, 464, 472, 485, 499, 522
Thomas of Canterbury (Thomas Becket), 234
Thomas of Ireland, 281
Thomas of Sutton, 398
Totting of Oyta, Henry, 500
Trajan, Ulpius, Roman emperor, 470

Ubertino of Casale, 404, 409, 454
Ugolino of Orvieto (Ugolino Malabranca), 506
Ulrich Engelbrecht of Strasbourg, 430, 431, 457, 458, 459
Ulysses, mythic hero, 413
Umayyads, dynasty of caliphs, 269
Urban II, pope, 129
Urban IV, pope, 345, 353

Varro, Marcus Terentius, 46, 18, 209
Victor of Aquitaine, 114
Vincent of Lerins, 9
Virgilius Grammaticus, 15, 44–47
Virgilius Maro, Publius, 5, 12, 56, 83, 110, 203, 235, 243
Volmar of Triefenstein, 219

Walafrid Strabo, 72
Waldensians, 241
Walter of Bruges, 399